MONTAGNAIS

MICMAC

MALECITE

OJIBWA

ALGONKIAN

ABNAKI

MENOMINI

SAUK

KICKAPOO

FOX

WINNEBAGO

OTTAWA

POTAWATOMI

HURON

NEUTRAL

IROQUOIS

MAHICAN

PENNACOOK

MASSACHUSET

MOHEGAN

METOAC

ERIE

CONESTOGA

DELAWARE

ANTEE

IOWA

MIAMI

MOSOPELEA

NANTICOKE

MONACAN

POWHATAN

TO

ILLINOIS

MISSOURI

A

OSAGE

SHAWNEE

CHEROKEE

PAMLICO

TUSCARORA

CATAWBA

QUAPAW

CHICKASAW

YUCHI

CREEK

CUSABO

CADDO

49

TUNICA

CHOCTAW

50

HITCHITI

YAMASEE

NATCHEZ

48

MOBILE

APALACHEE

ATAKAPA

BILOXI

TIMUCUA

ARANKAWA

CHITIMACHA

ACOLAPISSA

CALUSA

This Land Was Theirs

...so long as the waters shall flow
and the sun shall shine...

Also by **Wendell H. Oswalt**

Mission of Change in Alaska

Napaskiak: An Alaskan Eskimo Community

Alaskan Eskimos

Understanding Our Culture

Other Peoples, Other Customs

Habitat and Technology

An Anthropological Analysis of Food-Getting Technology

This Land Was Theirs

A Study of North American Indians

third edition

Wendell H. Oswalt

University of California, Los Angeles

John Wiley & Sons

New York · Santa Barbara · Chichester · Brisbane · Toronto

Text Design: Nicholas A. Bernini, Blaise Zito Associate Inc.
Cover & Chapter Opening Art: Joseph Zito

Library of Congress Cataloging in Publication Data:

Oswalt, Wendell H
    This land was theirs.

    Bibliography: p.
    Includes index.
    1. Indians of North America.   I. Title.
E77.08   1978   970'.004'97   77-14986
ISBN 0-471-02342-6

Printed in the United States of America

10 9 8 7 6 5 4 3

to
Edward H. Spicer

Acknowledgments

I am grateful to Dagmar Givant, Melburn D. Thruman, Arnold R. Pilling, and Sharlotte N. Williams for calling my attention to errors in the second edition of this book. I likewise appreciate the help of Roger W. Allington and Frederica de Laguna in obtaining information about the Tlingit. Lowell J. Bean and Gerald A. Smith aided me with Cahuilla sources, and Eskimo information was kindly provided by Jorgen Meldgaard. John W. Stafford was kind enough to read and comment on a draft of the historic section about the Crow, and James W. VanStone was especially helpful in my search for photographs. During the summer of 1976 I flew across the Canadian arctic collecting information with George Higgins as my pilot. I applaud his flying skills and appreciated his good company. Again, and as usual, I owe a great deal to Helen Taylor Oswalt for her editorial assistance.

Los Angeles,
California

WENDELL H. OSWALT

Los Angeles,
California

W. H. OSWALT

Contents

x

Contents

Illustrations

Plates

XV

xvi

Plates

This Land Was Theirs

Queries about Indians

How Are We Influenced by Indian Cultures?

We tend to forget that we are most indebted to American Indians for our country because this land was theirs. Our thoughts about native North American influences on our lives more commonly are of material goods borrowed from them, such as birch bark canoes, moccasins, parkas, snowshoes, and toboggans. The shortness of this list reflects the vast differences between the life-styles of aboriginal and modern Americans. Our industrial technology is so foreign to Indian culture that they could not be expected to have contributed a great deal to it. We have lost any intimate association with the land, a quality that typified American Indian life.

Our feelings of collective guilt about our treatment of Indians gnaws increasingly on our conscience, and currently Indians are fashionable. Motion-picture stars rally to the cause of a tribe, Indians are the subjects of depressing television documentaries, and they are increasingly portrayed as heroes in other celluloid dramas. An Indian folk singer recounts old and new injustices, and we listen. Indian folklore and philosophy have emerged as increasingly appealing topics for book-length presentations. Legislators less often speak of Indian assimilation into the American "melting pot," and VISTA workers on reservations have emerged as outspoken critics of Federal administrators. Alaskan Eskimos flex their political muscles as the "ice block" in the statehouse, Canadian Eskimos seek to establish their own province in the arctic, and the Iroquois want their wampum back from museums. Who would have paid attention a few short years ago?

The place of American Indians in our cultural heritage may be minimized but never denied. Yet it is doubtful that the thoughts of most people linger on Indians for very long. We take them for granted, which is a clear indication that they are an intimate part of our lives. We learn about their ways in grade school and something of their history in high school. We may visit Indian reservations and read novels about Indians. In these ways Indians most often intrude on our thinking. Another dimension of their presence is worthy of at least a moment's reflection. Indians are our challenge because our responses to them represent a homegrown experiment in tolerance, understanding, and compassion.

In historical perspective one enormously important borrowing by white Americans occurred along the eastern seaboard during colonial times. Precariously established early European settlers acquired the knowledge and technology associated with corn (maize) from local Indians. They were taught by Indians how to cultivate and store corn and how to prepare it as food. This Indian technology may not seem significant today, but at that time it was immensely important to European survival, and corn has emerged as one of the most important crops in the modern world.

If we were to cite the discoveries and inventions of Indians in all of the Americas, the earlier list would be much longer because American Indian cultures were most elaborate in Central and South America. To the list would be added beans, chili peppers, chocolate, cocaine, peanuts, potatoes, quinine, sweet potatoes, tobacco, and tomatoes, as well as a few material items such as hammocks, pipes, and the rubber syringe. Again the list is not long, but some of the plants and rubber products are of immense economic importance in the modern world. It may be asked whether in worldwide comparisons North American Indian culture was not comparatively unelaborate, and the answer is yes. This is not from any lack of intelligence among Indians but rather from their environmental setting and its potential for development. The New World was devoid of animals such as the cow, horse, and pig, which could be domesticated, and neither were there grains such as barley and wheat. More important, in the New World the animals and plants with potential as domesticates were not concentrated in one restricted geographical area. A contrary situation existed in the Old World, where the basis for most of Old World civilization emerged in the Near East about 8000 B.C. New World developments, however, are not to be cast aside as failures. One must recognize that in aboriginal Mexico and Peru complex societies emerged with large populations and elaborate life-styles; in these regions the environmental potential for indigenous cultural developments was far greater than in settings to the North.

American English words and phrases based on a background of Indian

2
Queries about Indians

contacts persist. Examples such as Indian summer, happy hunting ground, wild Indian, Indian giver, and burying the hatchet are known widely. When place-names are added, the list becomes staggering; included are not only lakes and rivers but also states and cities. Indian trails were important not only for their names but also as roadbeds for future highways.

Indians played an important role in shaping the belief system of one of the few large and important religions originating in the United States, the Church of Jesus Christ of Latter-Day Saints, or Mormons. The Book of Mormon relates that Indians originated from a Jewish population that entered the New World before Christian times. According to Mormon beliefs, Indians descended from the Lamanites; although these were thought to be a degenerate people, the Mormons have been inordinately kind in their dealings with Indians. As noted by A. Irving Hallowell (1958, 461) the inclusion of population theory in a religious dogma "could hardly have occurred anywhere but in early 19th-century America." It might be added that the nondoctrinal part of the Book of Mormon most likely originated from an unpublished novel by Solomon Spaulding.

In early American literature no subject had greater appeal than the Indians, but their literary image has been far from uniform. The Indian entered into American literature through speeches recorded during treaty deliberations. The oratorical skills of Indians were appreciated, and the texts were printed for general circulation in the eighteenth century. Because Indians were close at hand in the eastern states and were an obstruction when whites coveted more land, they soon were looked on as foes. As the frontier expanded westward in the first half of the nineteenth century, the image of the Indian reverted to that of a nonantagonist, in fact to a romantic figure. Drawing on accounts about Indians, James Fenimore Cooper wrote his great novels and conceived the character of Leatherstocking, a white Indian without literary equal. Henry Wadsworth Longfellow's *Hiawatha* too is a literary monument of this era. One of the most popular nineteenth-century American plays was *Metamora*, and playwrights have continued to build plots around Indians. Included in the first American opera, *Tammany*, performed in 1794, was a Cherokee melody, and the Indian exists in such American folk songs as Charles Cadman's "From the Land of Sky Blue Waters" and "Red Wing" by Thurland Chattaway and Kerry Mills. Other Indian contributions to the arts are now a part of American history; these include the Wild West show, the Indian medicine show, the cigar store Indian, and the romantic Indian as a subject for painters.

Along the western frontier Indians assumed the cast formerly seen in the East among white Americans who sought land. The Indian impeded "progress" and was a form of vermin to be exterminated. After Indians had been defeated in skirmishes and wars and remnant Indian populations were confined to reservations, these people again could be viewed romantically; even before the West was colonized, the Indian was a figure in nearly half of the 320 dime

3

How Are We Influenced by Indian Culture?

novels originating in the 1860s. The Indian theme never died but was recast with the introduction of motion pictures and radio. Needless to say, American television owes a great debt to the Indian, nor is he forgotten in contemporary novels.

Who Is an Indian?

In the sixteenth century as ever-increasing numbers of European maritime explorers ventured to the Americas, there was no difficulty in establishing who was an Indian. The racial, linguistic, and cultural differences separating Europeans and Indians were apparent to all observers. Indians belonged to the Mongoloid racial stock in obvious contrast with the Caucasian racial background of the intruders. Indians spoke languages that differed widely from one tribe to another, but none could be understood by the explorers. Indians dressed in an unaccustomed manner, and their bodily adornments were unusual, if not bizarre, to a traveler from England, France, or Spain. Then, too, the main crops that Indians raised, maize and beans, were not cultivated in Europe. Thus the people of the New World stood in striking contrast to Europeans and their ways.

The problem of classifying a person as an Indian became more complex with the arrival of European adventurers, fishermen, missionaries, settlers, traders, and trappers. Three conditions resulting from these contacts were important. First, white men mated with Indian women to produce persons of mixed blood; second, Indians sometimes captured whites and made them "Indians"; and third, some Indians lost their identity by assimilation into white society. To identify an Indian with clarity after the period of early historic contact we must deal with two primary factors—racial and sociocultural. Socially it can be imagined that whites who were assimilated into an Indian tribe would be considered "Indians," in spite of their race. Likewise Indians who disassociated themselves from other Indians came to be judged as "whites." For individuals of mixed Indian and white ancestry, the distinctions are clear when they consistently followed one life-style or the other. Such persons may, however, behave as Indian in one context and white in another, Indian or white exclusively throughout their lives, or Indian at one time in life and white at another. The identification of an Indian has become a matter of definition and is most reasonably considered in a legal sense.

Before considering Indian identity further, one point requires clarification. Euro-Americans class Aleuts and Eskimos as separate from Indians because of their dissimilar physical appearance and cultures. In racial terms Aleuts and Eskimos are the most Mongoloid of indigenous New World peoples, and their economic adjustments stand apart from those of other aboriginal Americans. However, the cultural differences separating some Indian tribes from each other are greater than those that separate Aleuts and

Eskimos from many Indians. Thus Aleuts, Eskimos, and Indians all may reasonably be called Indians.

In the history of United States Indian law there has not been a uniform definition of an Indian. In general, however, if a person is considered an Indian by other individuals in the community, he or she is legally an Indian. The degree of Indian blood in an individual may be important, but under most circumstances this is secondary to sociocultural standing in the community in which he or she lives. Examples will illustrate why there is so much confusion. If an individual is on the roll of a Federally recognized Indian group, then he or she is an Indian; the degree of Indian blood is of no real consequence, although usually he or she has at least some Indian blood. In *Federal Indian Law* it is stated that a person may, on some reservations, be considered an Indian even if records show that fifteen of sixteen immediate ancestors were not Indian. However, the real need for defining an Indian is with reference to a piece of legislation at a particular time. A person who is on the roll of a tribe and lives on a reservation clearly is an Indian; if that person moves from a reservation but remains on the roll, he or she continues to be an Indian. If he or she receives a clear title to allotted reservation land, he or she may or may not subsequently remain an Indian, depending on the circumstances. Indian status also is lost by voluntary disassociation from other Indians and by identifying with some other social segment of society.

In the United States all Indians did not become citizens until 1924 when the Citizenship Act was passed by Congress. Previously about 250,000 Indians had become citizens by other means; the act made citizens of about 125,000 persons. As early as 1817 individuals were granted citizenship under treaty arrangements if they met certain provisions, such as the acceptance of title to individual lands in contrast to living on tribal lands. For many years the prevailing opinion of the Federal Government was that Indians who followed tribal customs and were not under the control of the state or territory in which they lived could not be citizens. Becoming a citizen was given a different basis with the passage of the Dawes Act in 1887. This act was designed to break up reservation lands into individual and family holdings. After a man received a clear title to land, he became a citizen, or if he adopted civilized ways and lived apart from any tribe, he also became a citizen. Because he was an Indian he might still retain a special status and receive treaty or other benefits. Thus he was a citizen with special privileges not granted to other citizens. In 1888 a law was passed making Indian women citizens if they married citizens, the assumption being that these women were following the path of civilization. As noncitizens Indians were not inducted into the armed services during World War I. However, those who volunteered were made citizens by Congressional action. By 1938 seven states still refused to allow Indians to vote, and only in 1948 were voting rights granted to Indians in Arizona and New Mexico. Opposition to Indian suffrage was based on their special relationship to the Federal Government.

One provision in the Canadian Indian Act of 1876 was that any Indian who had a university education or its equivalent thereby became a citizen. In other instances an individual, or the band by majority vote, initiated enfranchisement proceedings; this method required a probationary period before becoming effective. When a man with a wife and minor unmarried children became enfranchised, his family was granted the same legal status. These provisions were not generally applied to the Indians of British Columbia, Manitoba, or the Northwest Territories. For the next fifty years Canadian Indian policy fluctuated between voluntary and forced enfranchisement. Finally, as a result of the Indian Act of 1951, Canadian Indians became subject to the same general laws that applied to other Canadians. They could vote in national elections and could consume intoxicants legally for the first time.

Eskimo-white relations in Greenland stand in contrast with the policies of Canada and the United States toward aboriginal peoples. The modern history of Greenland began in 1721 when the Norwegian Lutheran missionary Hans Egede left Denmark to found a mission and trade settlement near Godthaab, the modern capital of Greenland. The trading enterprise was not successful initially, but the mission slowly prospered. For the first fifty years Danish traders and missionaries dictated in an autocratic manner to the Eskimos along the western coast of Greenland. When it became apparent that the vast island could not be self-supporting, it was closed to outsiders. The Noble Savage concept of Jean-Jacques Rousseau made a great impact on influential politicians at the Danish royal court, and the king was persuaded not to destroy Greenland's Eskimo culture. In *Instructions* issued in 1782 concerning trade, the welfare of Eskimos had priority over the trade itself. Relations with whites were rigidly controlled, and the introduction of potentially harmful items, such as alcoholic beverages, was prohibited. Furthermore, the Royal Greenland Trade was made responsible for the welfare of the poor, and it set prices for all goods bought and sold. Thus Eskimos were sheltered from the outside world and the ills of civilization. As Diamond Jenness (1967, 32) remarked, Denmark set out "to create in her arctic colony a Garden of Eden." By 1840 all profits from the trade were used for the welfare of the Eskimos, an almost unheard-of policy for a colonial government.

Political life in Greenland was controlled by missionaries and Danish administrators until a reform movement in 1908 resulted in the formation of Municipal Councils. Only Greenlanders could serve to maintain public order, settle civil disputes, administer relief funds, and elect representatives to the higher advisory council that reported to the local Danish administrators. A major change introduced in 1925 resulted in Danes becoming eligible for selection to the councils. The following year the social welfare program was expanded broadly to provide funds for all persons over fifty-five years of age who could not care for themselves and their families. Eskimo always had been the official language; Danish was a second language, the one of instruction in the schools, which remained under church control. While Denmark was oc-

6

cupied by the Germans during World War II, Greenland was administered by the Danish representatives to the colony, and its economic ties were with Canada and the United States. During this era Greenlanders first learned to cope with the world at large. Subsequently the most far-reaching change was that an elected Greenland Provincial Council was created in 1950 as the governing body for most of Greenland, and the island was incorporated as a province of Denmark.

Where did Indians Originate?

Determining the region of the world from which American Indians originated is intriguing and has had lasting romantic appeal. Probing the origins of anything is a legitimate concern of humanists, laymen, or scientists, and persons in all these categories have long puzzled over the original home of Indians in the Americas. Surprisingly each of the major theories advanced to explain the derivation and spread of Indians involves something that is lost to modern times. The Lost Tribes of Israel, the lost continents of Atlantis and Lemuria (Mu) and the sunken land bridge across Bering Strait—each stands as a candidate for consideration. They share the common characteristic that supporting data must be indirect because fully conclusive evidence remains elusive.

Speculation about Atlantis predates the discovery of the Americas. Once aboriginal Americans were known to Europeans, Atlantis seemed a logical stepping-stone for early migrants from the Old to the New World. Plato reported that Atlantis was a vast island beyond Gibraltar and had a complex civilization before being destroyed by a cataclysm. The idea lingered among the Romans and was accepted by some persons in medieval Europe, but before the Atlantic Ocean was explored, no one could be certain whether or not the island existed. Christopher Columbus appears to have sailed toward its presumed position, and some thought that the land he discovered was Atlantis. The thesis that native Americans were derived from Atlantis crystallized in sixteenth-century Spain and first emerged with clarity in the writings of Francisco Lopez de Gomara, which appeared in 1552. He proposed, for example, that "atl," which was the word for water among Indians in one sector of Mexico, was a lingering remembrance of their homeland called Atlantis. By the 1880s the island's disappearance still was attributed to a major cataclysm that had occurred after the people destined to become American Indians had left its shores, and the theory was advocated by some more staunchly than ever. Each author who supported the theory of this lost island was struck by the cultural similarities between American Indians, usually those in Mexico, and some early Old World civilization, usually Egyptian.

A second lost continent theory involves the prehistoric presence of a great Pacific island called Lemuria or Mu. This thesis has found considerable support among some laymen. Its proponent was James Churchward, and his last

7

book on the subject appeared in 1931. He reportedly traveled in India and met a priest who saw him attempting to decipher some old inscriptions. The priest befriended Churchward and spent two years teaching him what was said to be the original language of people. Later Churchward was shown some secret inscribed tablets that recorded the original creation story, with Lemuria detailed as the place of human origins. The mystical nature of this theme, the failure of anyone else to be aware of this original language, and an inability to produce the original or similar inscriptions seriously weaken the entire argument.

Rivaling these lost continent theories is another that contends that Indians are descendants of the Lost Tribes of Israel. Samuel F. Haven long ago summarized the evidence. Ten tribes of Israelites, defeated by the Assyrians, were removed to the northeastern sector of the Assyrian empire. Here they became lost by wandering into Asia, and they ventured on to a point nearest the Americas, where they crossed the waters to another land. This was the New World, and evidence to support the Hebrew ancestry of the Indians was to be found in certain of their customs, words, and idioms. The theory long has been popular and continues to find particularly active support among members of the Church of Jesus Christ of Latter-Day Saints.

A host of other conjectures have been advanced to explain the origins of American Indians. Some speculators have singled out seafaring peoples such as the Carthaginians or Phoenicians as responsible for the original occupation. Others felt that the Tartars, sometimes viewed as remnants of the Lost Tribes of Israel, were the earliest occupants of the Americas; they were relatively near the New World in geographical terms and were a far-ranging people. The Chinese, Ethiopians, Scandinavians, Polynesians, and Welsh similarly have attracted speculative attention. Cotton Mather in colonial America advanced one of the most unique explanations for Indian origins. He wrote that "probably the *Devil* decoyed those miserable salvages hither, in hopes that the gospel of the Lord Jesus Christ would never come here to destroy or disturb his absolute empire over them" (Drake, 1837, 9).

In 1570 the Jesuit missionary Father Joseph de Acosta went to Peru, and about 1580 he began to write his *Historia natural y moral de las Indias*. The book appeared in its first Spanish edition in 1590, three years after he returned to Spain. Acosta reasoned that since Adam was the original ancestor of humanity and since Indians were people, then they must have come from the Old World, which Adam's descendants had peopled. He rejected the ideas of Atlantis or Hebrew origins for Indians, and he did not think there could have been a second ark or that angels accounted for aboriginal New World peoples. He reasoned that the New World and the Old World were connected, or separated by a narrow strait, because certain land mammals were the same in the respective hemispheres. He felt that people and animals alike had traveled along the same route. The human entry was visualized as having taken place slowly and as having been caused by overpopulation, famines, or the loss of former living areas. Thus, Acosta was the first to advance a land bridge theory and to offer

Queries about Indians

an explanation of why peoples entered the New World. He also theorized that the original occupants were hunters who later developed a more complex way of life. Therefore any comparisons between New and Old World civilizations could not be very meaningful.

Modern anthropologists support the general thesis of Indian origins first advanced by Acosta. People did not evolve in the New World but migrated to it. The animals most closely related to humans all are found in the Old World, and no remains that represent early stages of human development have been reported in the Americas. In the Old World, and especially in Africa, bones that are clear markers along mankind's evolutionary trail have been found repeatedly. In the same context, the earliest human remains in the New World date about 20,000 B.C. and belonged to individuals who were essentially modern in physical appearance. From the fossil record we must conclude that people entered the Western Hemisphere in the relatively recent past.

Geological evidence indicates that former continents did not exist in either the Atlantic or Pacific oceans. Thus, the lost continents of Atlantis and Mu could not have served as stepping stones to the New World. Neither does it seem likely that the first people entered the Western Hemisphere by traveling from one known island to another, across either the Atlantic or Pacific oceans. If this were the case we would expect to find their archaeological remains on at least one of the possible islands involved. However, no sites ever have been reported from Iceland, Greenland, the Aleutian Islands, or the islands of Polynesia that would suggest they served as way stations for the first entrants to the New World. Furthermore, at the time people presumably first entered the Americas, they did not possess boats capable of crossing sizable bodies of open water.

In all likelihood the first people to arrive in the New World entered over a land bridge in the Bering Strait area. They probably lingered in Alaska for a considerable length of time and eventually followed western mountains southward into Canada, ventured on into the western United States and Mexico, and finally continued southward into South America. The economic lives of the earliest migrants must have been based on hunting methods adapted to subarctic conditions. The Bering Strait entryway appears to have served as a cultural filter through which only hunters could pass. Their way of life must have been unelaborate, and most of the later complexities in their cultures must have developed in the Americas. In much later times, but long before the arrival of Columbus, new groups of people from the Old World continued to enter the Americas along the Bering Strait route and possibly via a number of other passages.

How Long Have Indians Been in the New World?

The accepted theory of American Indian origins suggests the northeastern sector of Siberia as the most probable point of departure. The next question is:

How long have they lived in the Western Hemisphere? Before turning to the current evidence we may briefly consider the subject in historical perspective.

In 1590, Acosta felt that Indians had inhabited the Americas about 2000 years or even less, and at the time this was a reasonable supposition. Theologians then presumed that the world and people were created by God in the very recent past. It generally was agreed that humanity had been created about 4000 B.C., a figure established by calculating the generations represented in biblical genealogies. The date, which a revisionist specified as 9:00 a.m., October 23, 4004 B.C., was not called into serious question until the science of geology began to emerge. By 1830 it came to be realized, especially by the English geologist Charles Lyell, that the earth was changing very slowly in physical terms and therefore it must be very old. Before long a French civil servant, Boucher de Perthes, established from archaeological studies that people once lived among animals now extinct. Boucher's conclusions were a direct challenge to the idea that God in his wisdom had created a perfect world and that all the creatures that existed originally still lived. In the 1840s the thoughts of Charles Darwin were crystallizing and soon would produce the evolution revolution. Not until the knowledge gained by investigators in the first half of the nineteenth century had been sorted, ordered, and broadly accepted could a reasonable synthesis of American Indian prehistory be advanced.

During the 1860s it was thought that people in Europe had made stone tools and hunted now-extinct animals as long as 240,000 years ago. It was expected that finds similar to those in Europe would be made in the New World. As a result of searches for these early remains, tools found in gravels near Trenton, New Jersey, were attributed to the Paleolithic, and a human skull from a California gold mine was considered of Pliocene age. This dating was not to endure, and by the turn of the present century a reaction had developed against assuming a great antiquity for New World humans. Aleš Hrdlička, a physical anthropologist and archaeologist, spearheaded the attack. From a detailed study of all the reportedly ancient finds he concluded that people had been here only in postglacial times, about 11,000 years ago at the earliest. Although Hrdlička was dogmatic and overemphasized the conclusions that could be drawn from the morphology of human bones, he also pointed up the poor field methodology that had led to much of the confusion.

The antiquity of people in the New World remained largely speculative until 1926 when paleontologists in northern New Mexico uncovered the bones of bison considered as long extinct. In the dirt from the excavation were found two pieces of a flint projectile point, and then another point fragment was recovered embedded in clay near the rib of an animal. It seemed that here was clear evidence of early Americans hunting ancient animals during the Pleistocene, but archaeologists were reluctant to accept the validity of the association. Nevertheless J. D. Figgins, the director of the Colorado Museum of Natural History, from which the field party emanated, ordered a continuation of

10

Queries about Indians

the excavations the following year. After four broken flint points were found near bison bones but free from the matrix, a fifth was observed in place. Work was stopped, and leading anthropological institutions were telegraphed to send representatives to the site. Those who responded accepted the validity of the association. The projectile points were named Folsom after the discovery site, and the bison came to be known as *Bison antiquus figginsi.*

At first the Folsom points and the remains of extinct bison were thought to date from the Pleistocene, but it now is known that these flints and bones date around 8000 B.C. It also has emerged that the Folsom point makers were specialized bison hunters who lived on the Great Plains for a comparatively brief period. We know too that earlier, around 10,000 B.C., Americans hunted mammoths using spearpoints now termed Clovis. The distinctive Clovis and Folsom points may have served as knives and projectile points. Very little is known about these hunters apart from their stone artifacts, which are unrelated to specific developments in any other area of the world. This general stage of American prehistory often has been termed Paleo-Indian, and a most intriguing question is whether any artifacts in the New World have greater antiquity.

A tantalizing find in this respect was made near Lewisville in northeastern Texas. Charred organic remains in hearths were dated by the radiocarbon method as being from plants living about 35,000 B.C. Unfortunately someone "planted" a Clovis point in the deposit hoping that it would be found and considered a valid association. The Clovis point was recovered, but eventually the hoax was revealed. Because of it, the site is tainted to many, perhaps most, commentators. Nonetheless the evidence is worth considering. Some twenty feet beneath the surface the remains of twenty-one hearths were uncovered at varying levels. One hearth was an irregular circle about eight feet across and included the dated plant remains as well as the bones of birds, deer, horses, prairie dogs, rats, snails, terrapin, and wolves; a short distance away a flint scraper was found. Near a group of four other hearths was a crude quartzite chopper, and a quartzite hammerstone was recovered on a nearby erosion surface. These three stone tools, the hearths, and the scattered bones, some of which were burnt, seem to be a valid triumvirate. The site appears to have been the camp of early Indian hunters.

Another intriguing site is on Santa Rosa Island off the coast of southern California. In the late Pleistocene, when the sea level was much lower than now, there probably was only a narrow channel of water separating this island from the mainland, whereas today Santa Rosa Island is forty-five miles offshore. On the island about 27,000 B.C. there lived a species of dwarf mammoth; the skeletons of some have been found disarticulated, with vertebrae and skulls often missing, an indication that they might have been butchered. Skulls were recovered that had been smashed, apparently to remove the brains, and some bones had been burned. Added to these finds was a piece of chipped stone recovered among the bones. Finally, large abalone shells were found in the locality, possibly carried there by humans.

Some archaeologists, perhaps even a majority, would not accept the Lewisville or Santa Rosa remains as clear evidence of people in the New World around 30,000 B.C. and somewhat earlier. However, a symposium organized by Richard Shutler and devoted to early humans in North America indicates a growing body of evidence that people have been in the New World for at least 35,000 years.

Many books have been written about Indian prehistory in the New World. A reader especially interested in North American developments might first consult the volume by Jesse D. Jennings. For an overview of archaeological finds in the Americas, a book by Betty Meggers and another by William T. Sanders and Joseph Marino are worthwhile points of departure. The prehistory of the Americas in the context of worldwide archaeology is best presented in a work by Chester S. Chard.

What Later Influences Came Across the Seas?

Pre-Columbian voyages to the New World have almost boundless popular appeal. For people to have set sail in small boats, headed they knew not where, is spine-tingling. The romance of the idea has led commentators to visualize a wide variety of voyages originating from diverse sectors of the Old World. Even after setting imagination aside, the realities of what may have been are in themselves most inviting.

The only pre-Columbian voyages beyond reasonable dispute must be cited first, and these involved Viking, or more properly Norse, explorers. Iceland was settled in the ninth century by Scandinavians, and within a hundred years Greenland was discovered. After becoming involved in a series of homicides, Eric the Red was exiled from Iceland for three years. He spent the time, A.D. 982–985, exploring southwestern Greenland, and on his return he organized a colonizing expedition. It left for southwest Greenland in 986, and additional settlers arrived later. The Greenland colony was occupied by the Norse until about 1540 and had a maximum population of about 5000 persons. Given the turbulent weather in the north Atlantic Ocean, many ships heading toward Greenland were lost or blown off course. One vessel strayed to the coast of North America but did not land. About the year 1000 the son of Eric the Red, Leif Ericson, purposely sailed for continental North America. In the centuries to follow a number of planned trips were made to northeastern North America from Greenland, especially to obtain building timber. The Norse appear to have settled briefly in northern Newfoundland at L'Anse aux Meadows, which was discovered and partially excavated by Helge Ingstad. Radiocarbon dates indicate that the site was occupied about A.D. 1000. The presence of a few Norse artifacts and wrought iron at the site leaves little doubt that these were Norse remains. However, no evidence exists to suggest that these Europeans had any influence on the cultures of aboriginal Americans.

If voyagers from the Old World, apart from the Norse, did arrive in the New World during pre-Columbian times, we might expect to find artifacts that they brought with them. Conversely, if travelers ventured in the opposite direction, we would expect to recover objects in the Eastern Hemisphere that were made in the Americas. In spite of the thousands of excavations in which millions of artifacts have been recovered, not one such artifact has been found in clearly valid context. Admittedly these objects may exist in unexplored sites, and if any are found, our thinking must be revised or even reversed. The fact remains that currently there is no reason to think, on the basis of the specific artifact forms discovered, that any pre-Columbian voyagers other than the Norse reached the New World.

If there were Old and New World contacts of a substantial nature, we would expect to find evidence in linguistic ties. Relationships between languages cannot be based on a small number of words with the same form and meaning because such parallels may be accounted for by chance alone. To demonstrate historical connections between languages, there must be clear phonemic and grammatical similarities as well as numerous parallels among words. Is there any evidence of this nature to link pre-Columbian peoples of the two hemispheres? The answer is yes, but it occurs only in the Bering Strait area. The Eskimo-Aleut language family, which spans the American arctic, and the Chukchi-Kamchatkan family of northeastern Siberia are related closely and belong to the American Arctic-Paleosiberian linguistic phylum. Thus the New and Old Worlds are joined in linguistic terms but not in the manner that speculators might assume.

To find Old World artifacts in prehistoric New World sites may be expecting a great deal, if only because few objects might survive long ocean voyages. Similarly, the speakers of Old World languages could have arrived, but their languages may have passed out of existence when the original migrants died. This raises the question of whether there were *influences* from the Old World reaching the Americas. In order to consider the question it first is necessary to make one critical observation. Innumerable examples exist of the people in one part of the world inventing artifacts similar to those independently conceived and produced by a distant people. Thus we must be cautious when deducing that a form was invented independently in different parts of the world or that it had a single place of origin and spread from there. Furthermore, if coherent groups of Old and New World artifacts are similar, the evidence is of greater potential significance than are similarities between isolated artifact types or design motifs.

A persistent but cautious advocate of transpacific contacts has been Gordon F. Ekholm. He suggests that wheeled toys from Mexico and Asia might have common origins and wonders too whether pottery-making in the Americas is not from an Old World source. The iron pyrite mirrors of Meso-

13

What Later Influences Came Across the Seas?

america and the copper axes used as currency in Mexico during the Aztec period suggest the bronze mirrors and ax money in China. The Olmec people of Mesoamerica exhibited the earliest complex culture in this region, and in its first known stages it is already quite sophisticated but without any local basis. The great Olmec stress on the tiger motif in art recalls a similar stress in the early bronze age Shang dynasty of China in the latter part of the second millennium B.C. Around the time of Christ the cylindrical, tripod pottery vessels found in parts of Mexico recall similar shapes in pottery and bronze from the Han period in China. Furthermore, in certain Maya sites of the Late Classic and Postclassic periods are some forms suggestive of Hindu-Buddhist developments in India and Southeast Asia; included are lotus panels, phallic sculptures, tiger thrones, and the "tree of life" motif.

Perhaps of greater importance is the occurrence of certain Asian-like artifact types in sites along coastal Ecuador, dating about 200 B.C. As Emilio Estrada and Betty J. Meggers have noted, this cluster is largely restricted to Ecuador. Included are pottery models of houses with saddle-shaped roofs and columns, figurines with one leg folded above the other, and the coolie yoke. They suggest that a seagoing vessel from Asia arrived and the migrants successfully introduced these and other novelties.

The evidence for pre-Columbian Old–New World culture contacts based on linguistics and artifacts is conclusive only with reference to language ties across Bering Strait and Norse artifacts in northeastern North America. Hints and suggestions that bonds reached tenuously across the Pacific Ocean exist but are not as yet convincing. Another approach to the problem centers on evidence of another nature: domestic plants and animals transported by pre-Columbian peoples to the New World. In a symposium organized by Carroll L. Riley, he and his associates considered cultigens. I can do no better than quote their summary remarks (Riley, et al., 1971, 452–453). "The consensus of botanical evidence given in this symposium seems to be that *there is no hard and fast evidence for any pre-Columbian human introduction of any single plant or animal* across the ocean from the Old World to the New World, or vice-versa. This is emphatically *not* to say that it could not have occurred." Thus, the case rests on a largely negative note.

How Have Indian Cultures Been Studied?

No matter where Europeans settled in North America, it soon became apparent that Indians had arrived at an earlier time and that a great deal of diversity existed among them. In physical appearance the members of some groups differed greatly from those found elsewhere, and even within a community there might be considerable variation. Then too some Indians were primarily fishermen as others farmed and still others hunted. They spoke highly diverse languages and organized themselves in ways ranging from

Queries about Indians

small, mobile, autonomous communities to large, stable confederations. To understand this diversity necessitates defining some of the concepts that have proven useful in ordering information about Indians.

Any reasonably systematic account about the lives of a people is called an ethnography. Their manufactures, language, social and political organization, art, knowledge and myths, all are ethnographic dimensions. An ethnography is overwhelmingly descriptive and pertains to a brief period of time. In more exacting terms, an *ethnography* is a descriptive framework for behavioral information about a population for a particular point in time. The peoples considered by ethnographers usually have been aboriginal or are from an aboriginal base, and the time coverage is a typical calendar year. Ethnographic data are collected as systematically as possible and are checked for internal consistency; for these reasons, most accounts by explorers, travelers, or journalists do not qualify. There are two general categories of ethnographies: baseline studies made about life at the time of historic contact and others made for later points in time. A *baseline ethnography* describes a people before they had any significant degree of contact with representatives of literate or civilized societies. Thus the data represent conditions before the people studied were influenced or disrupted by Europeans, Euro-Americans, or the members of other clearly foreign groups. In a strict sense, a baseline ethnography should be compiled before European trade goods or diseases of European origins prevailed. Yet capable observers seldom were present to record a broad range of information about an Indian population, in a systematic manner, before their customs were altered by agents of Western civilization. The first comprehensive ethnography of an Indian tribe, or of any aboriginal people for that matter, that made a significant impact on anthropology was written in 1851. The author was Lewis H. Morgan, and his study was of the Iroquois Indians in New York state. Thus, ethnography as a distinct intellectual pursuit is comparatively recent in origin.

Trained investigators did not begin making thorough studies of American Indians until the turn of the present century. Usually they attempted to collect verbal information about Indian life at the time of historic contact, or at least for a period as far back in time as an informant could recall. An ethnographer talked with Indians about the past, observed current customs, and consulted written sources. By using these data a *reconstructed baseline ethnography* was assembled. The primary difficulty in such an enterprise was obtaining reliable information about the early historic period. Most ethnographies written by anthropologists about American Indians are reconstructions made long after the first historic contacts of the groups studied. A major difficulty was to validate informants' statements, especially when documentary sources had not been studied thoroughly, a typical failing of early ethnographers. The time factor often could not be held constant for the early historic period, and as a result many descriptions were actually composites of customs at various times.

As the lives of Indians changed following prolonged firsthand contact with exotic complex societies, the Indians were said to be undergoing the process of acculturation; the end product was either stabilized pluralism or assimilation into the dominant society. Thus we may consider *acculturative ethnographies* as the second type of study. They present a description of life relating to a brief span of historic time and may be assembled from documents or by observations and interviews. An ethnographic approach of broader temporal scope is the study of a people throughout their history to plot changes in their lifeway; this form is called *ethnohistory*. The sources consulted are standard ethnographies, the Indians themselves if possible, and diverse writings ranging from early to late in their history. *Ethnoarchaeology* is the use of archaeological techniques to acquire ethnographic data about a particular population. The time range represented by the artifacts recovered is of no consequence in a study of this type; the major consideration is that the artifacts must be identified with a particular people. If broad or narrow generalizations are drawn from diverse ethnographies, the study is termed *ethnology*, which is the comparative study of ethnographic data.

Thus far the units for study have been termed "peoples" or "populations," but a clearer distinction is desirable. Different groups of Indians usually are termed "tribes," yet no general agreement for the criteria of a tribe accommodates all North American Indians. The difficulties in deriving a concept that encompasses the diversity of social norms and cultural forms may be illustrated by a rather typical definition. Alfred L. Kroeber (1925, 474) stated that a true tribe "has a name, a dialect, and a territory." Yet among the nearly fifty major Indian groups in California, only the Yokuts of the San Joaquin valley had all three characteristics. Most California Indians did not have a distinct tribal name; they identified themselves only as members of a particular community. Efforts to define a tribe on the basis of political cohesiveness are equally unrewarding. As John R. Swanton (1953, 1–2) has pointed out, the reported variability seems to defy the use of a single label. The Creek confederation was comprised of dominant and subordinate tribes; the term Powhatan embraced about thirty tribes or subtribes united by conquest; the term Ojibwa (Chippewa) included small groups of people who had little if any sense of political unity, but each Pueblo village governed its own affairs and was in a sense a small tribe.

Kroeber (1955, 303–314) attempted to bring some order to the terminological maze. He wrote, "What are generally denominated tribes really are small nationalities, possessing essentially uniform speech and customs and therefore an accompanying sense of likeness and likemindedness, which in turn tended to prevent serious dissensions or internal conflicts." Within such nationalities were smaller sovereign states, usually termed "bands" or "villages," that were in fact economically self-sufficient and had a recognized territory and political independence. Kroeber reasoned that a "tribe" was rather like a German state before the consolidation in 1871; each state functioned in-

Queries about Indians

dependently although they shared a common language, culture, and ideology. In the United States these units were more properly nations in the seventeenth and eighteenth centuries. Actually the concept "tribe" or nation most often was a product of white contact; government officials grouped bands or villages so they could more conveniently negotiate treaties, arrange resettlements, and so on. Aboriginal decision making most often was at the band or village level, although some people were consolidated into larger political aggregates. For the chapters to follow, the difficulties in defining a tribe are not overwhelmingly important, but the reader should be aware that a tribe is not consistently a "tribe." Those interested in pursuing the topic further are referred to a volume on the subject edited by June Helm (1968).

Formulation of an adequate definition of a tribe has not been the only persistent problem. Another is that historic contact with Indians differed widely in time from one region to another. Many tribes in the eastern United States were destroyed by disease and homicide or displaced from their lands before others to the north and west had ever heard of white people or knew of the diseases that they carried. Historic contact began about A.D. 1000 in northern Newfoundland, while in the Southwest it was 1540 and was 1885 in one sector of central Alaska. Thus no single decade or even century represents the "contact" period. This means that there is a *sliding historical baseline* for the beginnings of Indian history on a regional basis. Swanton (1953, 3–6) suggested that if A.D. 1650 is taken as a base date, it is possible to establish the indigenous Indian boundaries for the southern and eastern United States as well as for eastern Canada. In the northwestern sector of the continent there appear to have been no major relocations of peoples between 1650 and the time of their actual historic contact, making it possible to tentatively include them under this date as well. For the balance of the continent north of Mexico, the date of 1650 is less satisfactory. An adjustment backward in time to around A.D. 1540 might be more accurate to accommodate the peoples of the Southwest. The plains area would require several dates over a considerable time span. The most important conclusion is that the boundaries and positioning of many tribes on standard ethnographic maps, including those in this volume, are not entirely accurate for any single time period. Instead they attempt to represent the area of any particular tribe at the moment in history when it was surveyed and located on a map.

What Do We Know of Indian Languages?

An estimated 1,200,000 Indians lived north of Mexico when first contacted, and they spoke about 300 different languages. In some sectors, such as among Eskimos along the arctic rim, the same language was spoken over a great lineal expanse. In other regions, as in northwestern Canada, a large block of different but closely related languages prevailed. Elsewhere highly distinct

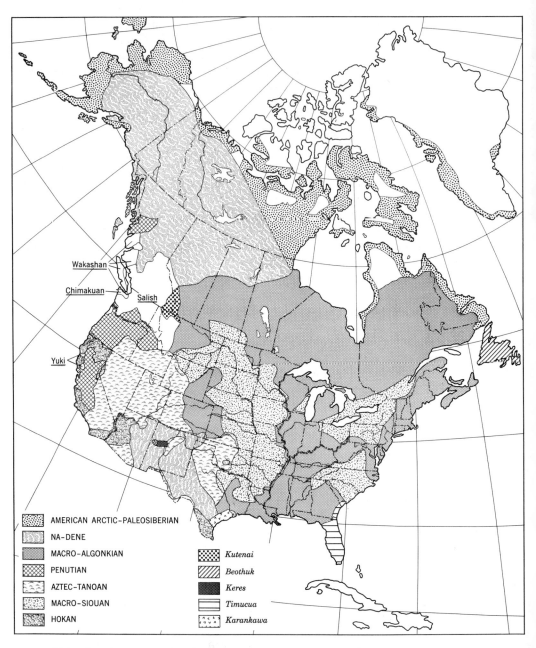

Major linguistic groups for aboriginal North America north of Mexico. The widespread phyla are designated in capital letters; the phyla for which there is a single representative language are in italics, and the families for which there are no established phyla are underlined (After Voegelin and Voegelin, 1966: Curtesy of the American Ethnological Society).

18

languages might exist in a limited area. In California, for example, far greater linguistic diversity existed than is found in all of modern Europe.

European settlers could ignore Indian customs if they wished since they lived in separate communities, but they could not ignore Indian languages if they hoped to communicate with them. Since typical colonists felt superior to Indians, they seldom attempted to learn an Indian language; most often Indians or persons of mixed blood became bilingual. Yet for missionaries intent on converting Indians to Christianity it was essential to learn the languages of peoples among whom they worked. The first landmark in American Indian linguistics was the publication in 1663 of a Bible translated into Massachuset, an Algonkian language, by the missionary John Eliot; in 1666 he published an Algonkian grammar.

The first prominent student of Indian linguistics was Thomas Jefferson. He was concerned that these languages were disappearing rapidly, and before he became president in 1801 he had collected considerable linguistic information. Jefferson (1801, 149) reasoned that preserving linguistic data from Indians in the Americas would make it possible to trace the relationships among these peoples. The first comparative linguist of stature in the United States was Peter S. Du Ponceau. French by birth, he served in the Revolutionary War and later practiced law in Philadelphia. Among the notable conclusions drawn by Du Ponceau in his study of languages was that a relationship existed between the Chukchi of Siberia and Eskimos in arctic America. However, no Asian language was identified as spoken in North America, and he suggested tentatively that no south Pacific area languages were spoken along coastal America.

The next linguist of note is Albert Gallatin, the first person to analyze and classify diverse Indian languages of North America. This Swiss-born language teacher became a businessman, later the Secretary of the Treasury, and finally a minister to France and then to England. In 1836 Gallatin published a classification of languages in North America north of Mexico and east of the Rocky Mountains. He also supported Du Ponceau's conclusion about the essential homogeneity of American Indian languages compared with those found elsewhere in the world. When John W. Powell published his definitive study of American Indian linguistic families in 1891, he credited Gallatin as the person who previously had contributed the most to the subject. The essence of Powell's classification has withstood the test of time, but he deserves credit primarily for assembling sources rather than for making a highly original contribution. A map was prepared on which fifty-eight language families were identified; it was revised slightly in 1907 and has been reproduced on innumerable occasions. The classification that prevails at present is based on the studies by Gallatin and Powell. Compiled by C. F. and F. M. Voegelin, it appears in simplified form on page 18.

In conclusion, it should be noted that of the approximately 300 aboriginal languages spoken during the early historical period, about half are now ex-

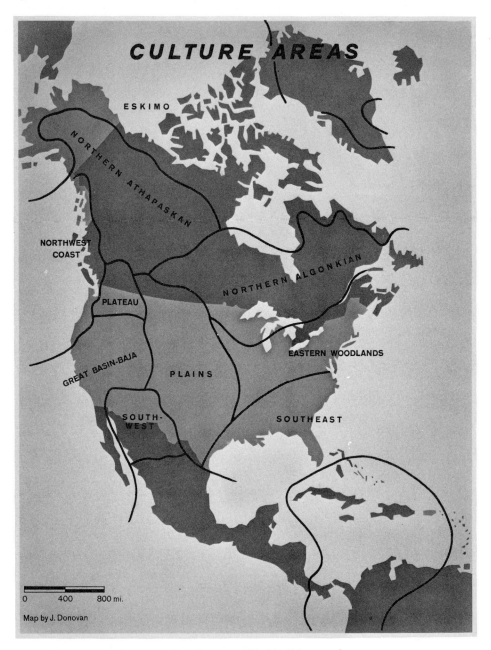

CULTURE AREAS

ESKIMO

NORTHERN ATHAPASKAN

NORTHWEST COAST

PLATEAU

NORTHERN ALGONKIAN

GREAT BASIN-BAJA

PLAINS

EASTERN WOODLANDS

SOUTH-WEST

SOUTHEAST

0   400   800 mi.

Map by J. Donovan

(From *Other Peoples, Other Customs:* World Ethnography and Its History by Wendell H. Oswalt. Copyright © 1972 by Holt, Rinehart and Winston, Inc. Reprinted by permission of Holt, Rinehart and Winston, Inc.)

20

tinct. Wallace L. Chafe estimates that about half of the surviving languages are not spoken by children of the tribes involved, and it seems unlikely that these languages will endure beyond the present century. The languages that seem likely to last longest are Cree, Chippewa, Eskimo, and Navajo; Chafe doubts, however, that they will be spoken 150 years from now.

What Are Culture Areas?

Linguists first established relationships among tribes on a sound basis by identifying families of related languages. After the Powell linguistic map was available, the 300 tribes were grouped into fifty-eight meaningful units, and tribal diversity was reduced to an almost manageable whole. At the World's Columbian Exposition at Chicago in 1893, the Indian collections appear to have been arranged by Otis T. Mason according to the linguistic groups on the Powell map. By 1896 Mason had formulated a means for grouping ethnographic information based on environments or culture areas. The idea of describing Indians in terms of geographical clusters was relatively well-accepted at this time, but Mason was the first to detail the characteristics of each area. A *culture area* is a geographical sector of the world whose occupants exhibit more similarities with each other than with peoples in other such areas. Culture areas were in theory determined on the basis of baseline ethnographies and by taking the sliding historical baseline into consideration. The concept was applied to American Indians most systematically by Clark Wissler, and it has served as the organizational basis for most continent-wide discussions of Indians. The system has the advantage of fitting all tribes into a relatively small number of groups. Its major disadvantages are that it refers to a single point in time and tends to stress material culture. We find too that one area may include peoples with different ways of life and that tribes along boundaries may share the characteristics of two areas. Finally, no two classifiers agree on the same number of areas and their boundaries, which partially reflects the impressionistic basis for the evaluations. Since the culture area approach provides a useful ethnographic overview, a table listing the characteristics of the ten areas identified is included, and it is accompanied by a map of the culture areas.

Culture Area	Languages	Subsistence	Descent
Eskimo	Eskimo-Aleut	sea mammals caribou fish	bilateral
Northern Athapaskan	Na-Dene	caribou salmon in west whitefish in east	bilateral matrilineal
Northern Algonkian	Algonkian	caribou moose fish	bilateral patrilineal
Great Basin-Baja	highly varied	acorns pine nuts mesquite beans game	bilateral
Plateau	Salish	salmon hunting collecting	bilateral
Plains	Macro-Siouan	bison in west hunting & maize in east	bilateral patrilineal
Northwest Coast	Na-Dene in north Salishan in middle Wakashan in south	salmon land mammals sea mammals	matrilineal, in north patrilineal, in south

Political Organization	Religion	Housing	Manufactures & Other
charismatic leaders bands	shamans good & evil spirits ceremonies in west	wood, stone, sod in east & west snowhouse in central area	tailored clothing elaborate harpoons umiaks, kayaks, dog sleds sinew-backed bow feuds over women infanticide
charismatic leaders bands	shamans Nakani	double lean-to rectangular log-frame	semi-tailored clothing spruce root & birch bark baskets toboggans & snowshoes bark canoe deadfalls & snares cannibalism during famines
charismatic leaders bands	shamans shaking tent divination	conical tent	semi-tailored clothing toboggans, snowshoes bark canoes deadfalls & snares hunting dogs
bands	elaborate female puberty ceremo- nies shamans diverse super- naturals	impermanent brush, bark, grass	developed basketry seed grinding stones sinew-backed bow nets for land mammals
villages	shamans diverse spirits	semisubterranean winter reed- or mat- covered sum- mer	basketry important bark fiber clothing
bands band alliances military societies warfare important	vision quest guardian spirits emerging ceremo- nialism	skin tepee	developed bone & skin working dog-drawn travois game surrounds hide shields
village	potlatch elaborate cere- monial round complex masks	rectangular, plank multifamily	elaborate wood-working dugout canoes social classes, slaves

What Are Culture Areas?

Culture Area	Languages	Subsistence	Descent
Eastern Woodlands	Macro-Algonkian Macro-Siouan	maize, beans, squash hunting fishing	matrilineal patrilineal
Southwest	Hokan Aztec-Tanoan	maize, beans, squash hunting	matrilineal bilateral
Southeast	Macro-Algonkian Macro-Siouan	maize, beans, cane hunting, fishing	matrilineal

References

Chafe, Wallace L. "A Challenge for Linguistics Today," in *The Philadelphia Anthropological Society*, Jacob W. Gruber, ed., 125–131. New York. 1967.

Chard, Chester S. *Man in Prehistory*. New York. 1975.

Churchward, James. *The Lost Continent of Mu*. New York. 1931.

Crook, Wilson W., and R. K. Harris. "A Pleistocene Campsite near Lewisville, Texas," *American Antiquity*, v. 23, 233–246. 1958.

Drake, Samuel G. *Biography and History of the Indians of North America*. Boston. 1837.

Driver, Harold E., and William C. Massey. "Comparative Studies of North American Indians," *Transactions of the American Philosophical Society*, n.s., v. 47, pt. 2. 1957.

Ekholm, Gordon F. "Transpacific Contacts," in *Prehistoric Man in the New World*, Jesse D. Jennings and Edward Norbeck, eds., 489–510. Chicago. 1964.

Political Organization	Religion	Housing	Manufactures & Other
tribes confederations	developed cere- monial round harvest stress secret societies dogs eaten cere- monially	dome-shaped wigwam multifamily palisades	hide clothing bark canoe
village	elaborate cere- monial round kiva masked dancers	pueblo-type	developed pottery & bas- ketry cotton garments fermented beverages domestic turkey irrigated farmland
tribes confederations warfare important	complex cere- monies sun worship priests	rectangular multifamily fortified	feathers over netting for clothing house-like storage facilities "black drink" emetic

Estrada, Emilio, and Betty J. Meggers. "A Complex of Traits of Probable Transpacific Origin on the Coast of Ecuador," *American Anthropologist*, n.s., v. 63, 913–939. 1961.

Federal Indian Law. U.S. Department of the Interior. 1958.

Gallatin, Albert. "A Synopsis of the Indians within the United States east of the Rocky Mountains and in the British and Russian Possessions in North America," *American Antiquarian Society Transactions and Collections*, v. 2, 1–422. 1836.

Hagan, William T. *American Indians*. Chicago. 1961.

Hallowell, A. Irving. "The Impact of the American Indian on American Cul- ture," *American Anthropologist*, v. 59, 201–217. 1957.

Hallowell, A. Irving. "The Backwash of the Frontier: The Impact of the In- dian on American Culture," *Annual Report of the Smithsonian Institution, 1957-58*, 447–472. 1958.

Hallowell, A. Irving. "American Indians, White and Black: The Phenomenon of Transculturalization," *Current Anthropology*, v. 4, 519–531. 1963.

Haven, Samuel F. "Archaeology of the United States," *Smithsonian Contribu- tions to Knowledge*, v. 8, 1–159. 1856.

References

Helm, June. *Essays on the Problem of Tribe*. American Ethnological Society. Seattle. 1968.

Holmes, William H. "The World's Fair Congress of Anthropology," *American Anthropologist*, v. 6, 423–434. 1893.

Huddleston, Lee E. *Origins of the American Indians*. Austin. 1967.

Hutton, James. *Theory of the Earth, with Proofs and Illustrations*. London. 1899 (original ed. 1795).

Jefferson, Thomas. *Notes on the State of Virginia*. New York. 1801.

Jenness, Diamond. *Eskimo Administration: IV. Greenland*. Arctic Institute of North America Technical Paper No. 19. 1967.

Jennings, Jesse D. *Prehistory of North America*. New York. 1974.

Krieger, Alex D. "Early Man in the New World," in *Prehistoric Man in the New World*, Jesse D. Jennings and Edward Norbeck, eds., 23–81. Chicago. 1964.

Kroeber, Alfred L. "Handbook of the Indians of California," *Bureau of American Ethnology Bulletin 78*. Washington, D.C. 1925.

Kroeber, Alfred L. "Nature of the Land-Holding Group," *Ethnohistory*, v. 2, 303–314. 1955.

Lyell, Charles. *Principles of Geology*, v. 1. London. 1830.

Mason, Otis T. "Influence of Environment upon Human Industries or Arts," *Annual Report of the Board of Regents of the Smithsonian Institution, 1895*, 639–665. Washington, D.C. 1896.

Mason, Ronald J. "The Paleo-Indian Tradition in Eastern North America," *Current Anthropology*, v. 3, 227–246. 1962.

Meggers, Betty J. *Prehistoric America*. Chicago. 1972.

Oswalt, Wendell H. *Other Peoples, Other Customs*. New York. 1972.

Powell, John W. "Indian Linguistic Families North of Mexico," *Seventh Annual Report of the Bureau of Ethnology, 1885-'86*. 1–142. 1891.

Riley, Carroll L., J. Charles Kelley, Campbell W. Pennington, and Robert L. Rands, eds. *Men across the Sea*. Austin. 1971.

Sanders, William T., and Joseph Marino. *New World Prehistory*. Englewood Cliffs. 1970.

Shutler, Richard, ed. "Papers from a Symposium on Early Man in North America, New Developments: 1960–1970," *Arctic Anthropology*, v. 7, no. 2, 1–91. 1971.

Swanton, John R. *The Indian Tribes of North America*. Smithsonian Institution, Bureau of American Ethnology, Bulletin 145. 1953.

Voegelin, C. F. and F. M. *Map of North American Indian Languages*. American Ethnological Society. 1966.

Wauchope, Robert. *Lost Tribes & Sunken Continents*. Chicago. 1962.

Wilmsen, Edwin N. "An Outline of Early Man Studies in the United States," *American Antiquity*, v. 31, 172–192. 1965.

Wissler, Clark. *The American Indian*. New York. 1938.

Wissler, Clark. "The American Indian and the American Philosophical Society," *Proceedings of the American Philosophical Society*, v. 86, 189–204. 1942.

Wormington, H. H. *Ancient Man in North America*. The Denver Museum of Natural History. Denver. 1957.

The Chipewyan: Subarctic Hunters

Environment

Chipewyan country is a vast expanse of tundra extending as much as 500 miles from east to west and nearly 900 miles from north to south. The climate is continental with long, cold winters and short, hot summers. Everywhere there are interlaced networks of waterways, foaming as well as hesitant streams and rivers, great lakes, and countless smaller lakes. Barren rocks show obvious signs of glacial wear on their smoothed or striated surfaces. Results of glacial action are especially evident in the north where rolling masses of bedrock give way to boulder-strewn valleys with adjacent lines of eskers. Lichens alone grow on highlands, but valleys are covered with dwarf birch, mosses, lichens, and willows. This region is known to the Chipewyan as the Barren Grounds, a fitting term now incorporated in geographical writings. Along river bottoms on the southern Barrens stands of spruce appear as outriders of their species; this is the taiga, where the tundra and northern forest meet. Still farther south the spruce are dense, and aspen, birch, and juniper stands are fringed by marshy bogs and upland tundras. The forested area was foreign to the aboriginal Chipewyan, but it became important to them in historic times.

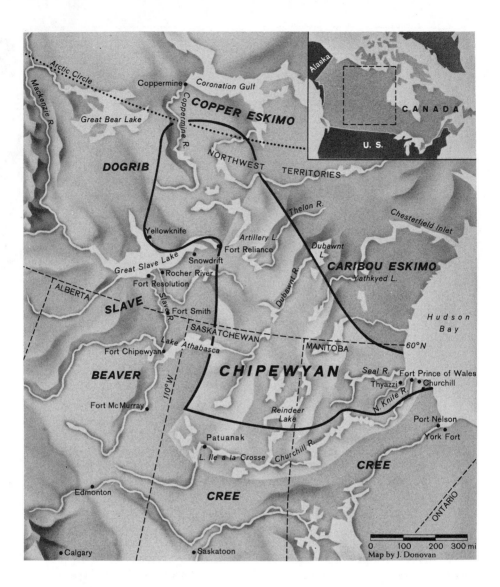

30

People and Population

Chipewyan is a Cree word meaning "pointed skins," a reference to the dangling point at the front and back of the poncho-like garment of men. These people called themselves "Dene," meaning "humans," and were unified on the basis of language and life-style. Most, but not all, individuals were related by blood or marriage to other persons who called themselves Chipewyan, and this formed the primary basis for their identity. The major subgroups were territorial and were based on the exploitation of regional caribou herds. By the time of contact with Europeans the Chipewyan numbered about 4500 and had one of the lowest population densities among North American Indians.

Reasons for This Selection

The Chipewyan were chosen to represent the subarctic for cultural, ecological, historical, and social reasons. They are one of the numerous Northern Athapaskan tribes that controlled interior Alaska and northwestern Canada. Most subarctic peoples depended on caribou and fish for food, and the Chipewyan were reasonably typical in this respect, although caribou were far more important in their diet. We know more about them than most other Northern Athapaskans, largely because of historical chance. They were reasonably well described by Europeans soon after historic contact, and in 1960 a thorough study was made of a modern community. Furthermore recent ethnohistorical studies and additional field researches have been made among these people. We do not have information of comparable scope for any other Northern Athapaskan tribe. The sociocultural reasons for describing the Chipewyan are equally significant because their lifeway was one of the simplest reported for North American Indians. They illustrate a family-based social type with feelings of solidarity primarily at the band level. The Chipewyan also provide an opportunity to analyze the impact of the fur trade, which changed them from caribou hunters to beaver and marten trappers. Finally they occupied much the same environment as the Caribou Eskimos, to be discussed in Chapter 3, and thus illustrate cultural differences between two peoples dependent on caribou for their livelihood.

Language

The Chipewyan language belongs to the Na-Dene linguistic phylum and the Athapaskan family. The Na-Dene lived from near Bering Strait to the western shore of Hudson Bay and were scattered southward to the Mexican border. Small groups of Athapaskans had settled in the Pacific northwest of the United States, and others, including the Apache and Navajo, were in the

American southwest. The Na-Dene were primarily inland peoples and were relatively recent migrants to the New World. The major dispersal of the Athapaskan family took place during the Christian era, and it appears on the basis of lexicostatistics that they consisted of one closely related group of Indians in northwestern Canada around A.D. 700. Some of these people spread south to form the Pacific group, and another cluster went on to the southwest. These internal splits were not completed until about 1800. Diversification in the Northern Athapaskans took place between 900 and 1400, with the Chipewyan completing their divergence at the later date. The extremely close cultural and linguistic bonds between the Chipewyan and Yellowknife lead modern ethnologists to consider them as a single people, an interpretation accepted in this book.

Prehistory

The span of human occupancy in Chipewyan country is poorly known, and it is possible only to offer a tentative statement based on scattered finds. The earliest diagnostic remains in this general area are large chipped-stone points (termed Agate Basin, Alberta, and Angostura) that are nearly indistinguishable from similar finds made in Alberta, South Dakota, and Wyoming. On the Barrens these forms appear to have been used about 6000 B.C. At sites along the Thelon River, dating shortly after 3000 B.C., the finds (termed "Archaic") reflect an Indian type of hunting economy. Further evidence exists, especially after about 200 B.C., that this general tool complex eventually was adopted by the Chipewyan from their Indian predecessors. In sum it appears that Northern Athapaskan Indians have lived on the Barren Grounds for at least 2000 years and that the Barrens had been occupied since 6000 B.C., or even earlier, by other caribou-hunting Indians.

History

According to nearly all standard sources the Chipewyan lived in the northern forests at the beginning of their history and were driven into the Barren Grounds by the Cree after the latter had received firearms. However, ethnohistorical studies by Beryl C. Gillespie show this was not the case. Instead the Chipewyan lived in the taiga and tundra during early historic times and began to exploit interior forests only under stimulus of fur traders. The Chipewyan received their earliest historic notice in connection with the Hudson's Bay Company efforts to expand the fur trade. Company administrators at York Fort, founded in 1684 along southern Hudson Bay, were anxious to have the Chipewyan trade at the post, but these Indians were afraid to come to the area because it was occupied by their enemies, the Cree. In 1715 William Stewart visited Chipewyan camps accompanied by a Chipewyan

The Chipewyan: Subarctic Hunters

woman who induced her people to settle their differences with the Cree and to trade at York Fort. Through the efforts of Stewart the country to the south of Great Slave Lake soon was open for trade. The next move of the Hudson's Bay Company was to establish a trading center on one margin of Chipewyan country. The former whaling station of Churchill along the western shore of Hudson Bay was selected, and a post was built in 1717. The great stone fort named Fort Prince of Wales was erected nearby between 1732 and 1771.

Still the heart of the Chipewyan area had not been brought under realistic control. As a few "Far Indians" began trading at Churchill, some knowledge of the great area to the north and west was accumulating. Moses Norton, governor at Fort Prince of Wales, was anxious to open trade relations in the more remote area and to determine the location of a reported copper deposit. The Chipewyan, however, were making tremendous profits as middlemen in the trade with more distant tribes, and as a result they were reluctant to guide Hudson's Bay Company explorers. In 1768 Norton visited England to consult with Company officials, and he convinced them that a search for the copper deposits in the northwest would be an important enterprise. When approval for a land expedition was finally given, the name of Samuel Hearne became intimately associated with the Chipewyan, copper, and explorations in northwestern Canada.

Samuel Hearne was born in London in 1745, and after naval service in the Seven Years' War he joined the Hudson's Bay Company. In 1766 he became a seaman on a small vessel engaged in trading and whaling along the western shore of Hudson Bay and continued this work until 1768, when his fortunes came under the influence of Moses Norton. Hearne was assigned to make the trip into Chipewyan country, and after abortive attempts in 1769 and 1770, he launched a more rewarding third try. The ultimate success of this venture hinged on the Chipewyan guide, Matonabbee, who had his own opinions about how to travel. The key to his plan was to take women along to relieve the men of the many burdensome chores, and Matonabbee had six wives at that time. The trip to the Coppermine River and Coronation Gulf was completed successfully by mid-1772 and is one of the most noteworthy feats of individual exploration anywhere at any time. Hearne's maps were not accurate, and for this he has received periodic criticism, but far more important, his book is a classic in exploration literature and the first balanced account of the Chipewyan. The manuscript was accepted by the publisher in October 1792, and its author died the following month.

The map prepared by Hearne and his knowledge of the country facilitated further expansion to the northwest. The first trader to settle in the midst of Chipewyan territory was Peter Pond, who established himself near Athabasca Lake in 1778. The organization of the North West Company in 1783 introduced an era of fierce competition with the Hudson's Bay Company, and not until their amalgamation in 1821 did trading conditions become stabilized. The history of Chipewyan country centered about the quest for mineral wealth, the expanding fur trade, and disappointing searches for a water passage to the Pacific Ocean. Later the search for souls was begun. In 1846 Roman Catholic missionaries founded a permanent mission at Lake Ile a la Crosse, and the Anglicans located at Churchill in 1912. Even today it is fur and souls that attract most outsiders to Chipewyan country.

Aboriginal Life

ORIGIN MYTH   Most people have at least a passing concern about their beginnings and seek some rationale for their existence. In the absence of a strictly historical perspective, they usually explain their presence in legendary or supernatural terms. Most often a creation myth accounted for their genesis.

The Chipewyan regarded the primordial world as centering about a woman who lived in a cave and subsisted on berries. In time a dog-like creature followed her into the cave and lived with her. She thought that she dreamed this animal turned into a handsome young man who had sexual intercourse with her, but it was no dream, and the woman became pregnant. At this juncture a giant man approached; he was so tall that his head reached nearly to the clouds. With a stick he outlined the bodies of water and caused them to fill. The giant tore the dog-like being to shreds and threw its internal organs into the water, creating various fish. The flesh was tossed on the land in bits and became land animals, and the skin was torn and thrown into the sky to become birds. The giant told the woman that her offspring would be able to kill as many of these creatures as they required and she need not worry about the animals' abundance, since it was his command for them to multiply. The giant returned from whence he came and was never seen again. In this way order in the world emerged, and the abundance of game was assured. This tale justified the indiscriminate killing of game and gave rise to a supernatural association with dogs, since the woman's human offspring were descended from a creature related to the dog. The creation myth was not only taught to children but also guided thoughts about the adult world.

CLOTHING   Garments were made from the skins of caribou killed in the early fall when the hides were strong and the hair dense but not long. Eight to ten skins were required to outfit an individual for winter. The upper garment of a man consisted of a loose-fitting, sleeved poncho with the hair side out and the skins cut to a point in front and back. He sometimes wore a fur boa when the temperature was low, and his ears might be protected by a fur band or cap. His ankle-length leggings were of dehaired skins, and moccasins were sewn on at the bottom. In severe weather a caribou skin cape was draped over the shoulders. The garb of a woman included a sleeved dress that reached her knees or her ankles; to hold a long dress up from the ground a belt girdled the waist. Vanity was not unknown to Chipewyan women. According to Hearne, on one extremely cold February day, a woman held her dress high with a belt so she could "shew a clean heel and good leg," and managed to freeze her but-

34

tocks and thighs so badly that huge blisters developed. It was a joke to all except the sufferer. The leggings of women reached from below the knee to the ankle and may not have had attached moccasins. The women also wore capes, and both sexes used mittens of double thickness. They could slip their hands out of the mittens without the chance of losing them because each was attached to a leather harness that hung about the neck.

SETTLEMENTS Habitations ranged from isolated family dwellings to clusters of as many as seventy units, but aggregates of more than a few families usually were of brief duration. The size of a community was above all else a function of the time of year and the local availability of food. People lived in a subarctic variety of the tepee best known from the American plains. A Chipewyan tent was framed with poles set in a circle and bound together near the top. The cone was covered with as many as seventy caribou skins sewn together, and it measured over twenty feet across at the base. An opening at the apex of the cone permitted smoke from the central fireplace to filter upward. If spruce boughs were available, they were placed around the fire and covered with caribou skins; on these people relaxed, worked, and slept.

In and around the tents one would expect to find most of their manufactures. A well-supplied camp included tripods of poles from which hung caribou skin bags filled with meat. Among the possessions of women were cooking and storage containers of birchbark or skin. A basket of folded and sewn bark was commonly used for cooking by filling it with water, preheated stones, and raw meat. The women probably had skin bags in which they kept sewing awls and thread of caribou sinew. The men's tool kits included antler wedges for splitting planks from logs; a crooked knife with a copper blade and antler handle, the most important form of knife; a curved, wooden-handled knife with a beaver incisor for a blade, another highly useful tool for cutting small sections of wood; and a hand drill with a copper bit and an antler handle, the only drill form known. Awls were of copper, and a copper ax head was hafted on a wooden or antler handle. These uses of native copper, and its use in ice-pick points, arrowpoints, spearheads, and spoons, reflect a reliance on this metal. The copper tools were made by pounding a raw lump of the metal into shape. These people never heated or smelted copper but processed it in the same manner as stone.

CONVEYANCES The little that is known about aboriginal Chipewyan boats suggests that they had only small skin-covered canoes with wooden frames. These vessels probably served primarily for ferrying people across rivers and for hunting caribou as they crossed lakes. The toboggan for winter transport was up to fourteen feet long and about fourteen inches wide. It was made from thin juniper planks that were steamed and bent upward at the front. The planks were joined to crosspieces, probably with thongs. Chipewyan women, not dogs, pulled toboggans. If wood was unavailable, toboggans could be made by using sewn caribou leg skins as a substitute. The

Plate 2–1 A man carrying a small birch bark canoe in early historic times. (From Hearne, 1796)

cariole, which is a more complex toboggan with sides and a back, was a European invention.

Snowshoes were essential for travel over deep snow. They were made by lacing babiche (thin, dehaired caribou skin strips) through holes in birchwood frames. These snowshoes had slightly turned-up tips and were asymmetrical in outline; the outer edge flared, but the inner edge was relatively straight. Men prepared the frames, and women laced the babiche into place with eyed snowshoe needles. When traveling on snowshoes, the men jogged along at a pace that was faster than a walk, and they traveled in this manner for hours at a time.

HOUSEHOLD ACTIVITIES   In camp women prepared meals and cared for children, as would their counterparts throughout most of the world. To these obligations was added one of their most important activities, the task of processing skins, particularly those of caribou. After a caribou had been killed by a man his wife retrieved it, skinned it, and removed bits of flesh and fat with a bone scraper. If the hair was to be removed, the woman set a wooden beam obliquely in the ground, draped the skin over it with the hair side up, and removed the hair with a scraper. A dehaired skin often was smoke-cured by hanging it over a pole framework under which decayed wood smoldered. A skin to be used with the hair intact was scraped, softened in water, wrung out and dried, and a paste of partly decayed caribou brains was rubbed on the inner surface. Later the skin was dried once again and finally scraped with a copper-bladed end scraper. The skin probably was rubbed by hand to make it pliable and relatively soft. This process of skin preparation is detailed because it was an important complex of technological knowledge among a people who relied on skins not only for clothing but for bedding, dwelling covers, containers, and ropes. It should be added that American Indians did not tan skins in the technical sense of the word.

The preparation of food was a major reason for a household's existence. Favorite edibles were primarily caribou products: the head and fat from the back, a fetus either raw or cooked, and grubs from under the caribou's skin. Steaks and chops were not considered luxuries. Food, which most often meant

The Chipewyan: Subarctic Hunters

caribou meat, or fish if these animals were not to be found, could be eaten raw or cooked. In addition to being boiled in a birchbark container, flesh was roasted over an open fire. The Chipewyan diet rarely included plant products, although a moss soup is reported and moss could season meat soup. Meals at camp were prepared by women, but men ate first. The women received only what the men had not consumed, which might at times amount to nothing. One other food was pemmican, which usually is thought of as characteristic of the Plains Indians. Pemmican, from a Cree word meaning "manufactured grease," was made from lean meat that had been cut into strips and dried by the sun or near a fire. The dry meat was pounded into a powder, mixed with fat, and stuffed into caribou intestines; this highly concentrated food was a favorite of travelers.

SUBSISTENCE ACTIVITIES   When caribou could not be found, summer camps were located near lakes or rivers, and fish became the staple. The principal fishing device was a gill net, which was made from strips of babiche and strung with wood floats and stone sinkers. These nets were set across narrow streams, at eddies in rivers, or at spots in lakes favored by lake trout, northern pike (jackfish), and whitefish. Gill nets had the general appearance of modern tennis nets. The dimensions of the openings, or mesh, depended on the size of the species of fish for which a net was set. When these fish attempted to swim through the netting, their heads were held fast by vertical netting strands that caught in their gills.

The Chipewyan felt that each net had its own personality; one net could not be joined to another because jealousy between them would prevent fish from being caught. Other precautions included attaching charms to the corners of a net; without them it was believed that no fish would be taken. Charms often were attached to antler, bone, or wooden fishhooks, and the first fish caught with a new net or hook was boiled, the articulated bones removed intact, and burned. Other fishing implements included dip nets used for fish confined by weirs, which were brush fences across shallow stretches of water. Barbed fish arrows were shot from bows, and leisters (fish spears) were used from canoes.

Fish were an important food in times of stress, but the Barren Ground caribou was the staff of life. The word for meat was derived from that for caribou, and some Chipewyan said that they preyed on caribou herds in the manner of wolves. In the early spring bands of hunters prepared to range over the Barrens to intercept caribou. At a birch grove on the northern forest edge a party would cut tent poles and make canoes for crossing deep or swift water. As many as 200 persons might assemble, including women taken along primarily as bearers. A strong woman carried about 140 pounds of camping equipment, an impressive burden considering the nature of the terrain. While traveling, the men hunted on both sides of the trail taken by the women and young girls as they pulled the heavily loaded toboggans along the most direct route. Dogs, laden with parcels of tent skins, containers, and poles, accompanied the women.

In the fall six hundred persons might gather at well-known caribou crossings and camp in a single locality. Families seeing each other for the first time in months or years followed an established etiquette at their reunion. At first they sat apart from each other and said nothing. Then an older person of one party recounted all of their personal traumas since the last meeting, and women of the other group wailed on hearing of the misfortunes. The fate of the second party next was recounted and responded to. Men then greeted one another, and women exchanged presents as well as good news. When caribou appeared, their number might be truly fantastic. Sometimes so many were killed that only the skins, long bones, fat, and tongues were taken, and the carcasses were left to rot. As the caribou moved the Indians followed, drying as much meat as they could conveniently carry.

When caribou rutted in October, a hunter sometimes attached lengths of caribou antler to his belt so that they rattled as he walked. A bull caribou in the vicinity thought he heard two other bulls fighting over a female and boldly approached, expecting to lead off the female. A bull could be killed more readily this way than by the usual method of stalking against the wind. At these times hunters used the self bow, a one-piece wooden shaft strung with babiche. Caribou-killing arrows had unbarbed bone or stone points and were vaned with feathers. An alternative and preferable fall hunting method was to drive large herds of caribou into water and kill them from canoes with spears.

In the eastern sector winter and early spring camps were established on promontories along the forest edge, in a locality frequented by caribou and near lakes containing fish. People moved only once or twice during the winter from an ideally situated camp, one accessible to lakes or wide rivers along which caribou normally passed. Here funnel-shaped caribou surrounds were built. Converging lines of brushy poles were erected, with poles at about twenty-yard intervals. When caribou approached the wider end of a funnel, they were unaware of the poles, which sometimes spanned three miles. As animals entered the surround, the women, boys, and some men appeared from behind to herd them. The caribou were driven into a trap, which was a large enclosure of branches at the end of the funnel, with snares set at narrow exits. After the entrance was blocked with trees, snared caribou were speared, and arrows were shot at loose animals.

When the snow was soft and deep, caribou sometimes were tracked on snowshoes. This meant following a single animal until it was exhausted from floundering in the snow. In the winter, the men might set gill nets beneath the ice of lakes or jig for fish through a hole in the ice with a hook. In the western area of Chipewyan country fishing was more important than among the eastern bands.

Other significant, but secondary, means for taking game included the use of deadfalls for bear, marten, squirrels, and wolverine. Nets were used for tak-

The Chipewyan: Subarctic Hunters

ing beaver in summer, but in winter, after their lodges had been broken open, the animals were taken from retreats beneath the ice along stream or lake edges. Babiche snares were set to entangle hares or ptarmigan. Even though these Indians reached Hudson Bay at Churchill, they did not hunt the sea mammals abundant there at certain seasons.

Additional details of Chipewyan hunting and fishing activities could be presented, but it already is obvious that caribou, and fish to a lesser extent, were the primary staples. Relying as they did on very few species, food was sometimes scarce and people starved. Famine probably was more common among Northern Athapaskans than among any other block of American Indians. At these times the people ate berries, mosses, or other plant products and later consumed items of clothing; under extreme conditions they turned to cannibalism.

SOCIAL DIMENSIONS   These people were described in less than glowing terms by Europeans, no doubt because the Chipewyan firmly believed that they were more intelligent than whites and assumed a haughty attitude toward the outsiders. The men are described by Europeans as being patient and persevering but morose and covetous. Still they were peaceful insofar as this meant not shedding the blood of another Chipewyan male. When angry with one another, they wrestled, pulled their opponent's hair or ears, or twisted his neck. In a scale of honesty for the eastern tribes of the Northern Athapaskans, the Chipewyan were ranked as superior to all others; they abhorred a thief. However, whites were not considered quite human, and to take their property was not really theft.

No description of these people could be complete without commenting on the status of women as recorded by Hearne. According to him females were subordinated in every way, were treated cruelly, and were held in gross contempt by the men. Female infants were occasionally permitted to die, a practice viewed by adult women as kindly. In fact, they are said to have wished their mothers had done it for them. Women were beaten frequently, and although it was an odious crime to kill a Chipewyan man, it was no crime for a man to beat his wife to death. We probably will never know whether this was typical behavior toward women, but we may suspect that Hearne exaggerated or that his description was based on the actions of Matonabbee and men associated with him. Matonabbee unquestionably was a very powerful and self-centered person. The treatment of women as recorded by Hearne seems inordinately severe and out of character for Indians north of Mexico. Furthermore a similar pattern did not prevail among the Chipewyan in more recent historic times.

As was typical for many foragers (collectors, fishermen, and hunters) around the world, the constraints on individual behavior were defined largely on the basis of age and sex. Each household was self-sufficient and could exist in isolation until a member sought a spouse. Group responsibilities or community cohesion hardly existed, and individuals had a great deal of flexibility in their behavior. A man, however, was responsible for his family, and every woman was dominated by her husband. Environmental resources were open to exploitation by everyone on an equal basis; family hunting or trapping territories did not exist.

POLITICAL ORGANIZATION   Aggregates of people structured in a formal manner and functioning as cohesive units did not exist. Instead, as studies by James G. E. Smith and others indicate, local groups were amorphous and highly flexible. In ecological terms it is important to note that regional bands were defined largely on the basis of the separate herds of caribou exploited, and a regional group was divided further into localized bands of one hundred or more people who hunted together. Seasonally, when great numbers of caribou were available, several localized bands might assemble for a hunt. However, when caribou did not follow their normal migration routes, people divided into smaller hunting groups. Conditions influencing the movements of caribou included fires, weather variations such as sudden thaws or blizzards, and, in all likelihood, cyclical variations in their number. The most important observation about the nature of a band is its flexibility in number as a function of local food resources.

Diverse families sometimes united under the aegis of a charismatic leader. Such a man was above all else an outstanding provider with an inordinate ability to take game and fish. Hearne's guide, Matonabbee, is an example. He supported himself, six wives, seven biological children, and two adopted children. Once a man's reputation as a leader was established, a father of marriageable daughters sought him as a son-in-law. This was to the personal advantage of the father-in-law because the pattern of marriage residence was for a husband to join his wife's natal household (matrilocal residence). Subsequent wives could be sisters of the first, but other women could also be chosen. Such a man had to be physically strong since he was obligated to validate his claim to a wife, especially a younger wife, by wrestling if challenged by another man. Less successful hunters, relatives, and nonrelatives cast their lot with him for greater security. An important characteristic of this form of leadership was that it was very transient. A man could keep his wives and other followers only as long as his powers of persuasion, hunting skills, and physical strength endured. As he began to fail physically, he sometimes could retain his position of authority by craft and intrigue, but this was only a temporary respite before he slipped into obscurity.

SUPERNATURALISM   External threats came from the neighboring Cree and Eskimos. The hostility stemmed in part from the belief that the shamans of these people sent evil by supernatural means to cause illness. The Chipewyan believed that death or disease occurred from natural causes only among the aged. Thus, in theory, each physical disorder of a younger person resulted

The Chipewyan: Subarctic Hunters

from the hostile activities of a foreign shaman. Chipewyan shamans attempted to negate the effects of such evil by acting through personal spirits that they controlled. When someone fell sick, a shaman sang and danced to summon his supernatural aids or "shadows," who were animal, bird, or imaginative familiars. He then sucked and tried to blow the intrusive disease substance from the patient. For serious cases a shaman treated an ill person in a special small, square tent built with no opening at the top. Death and disease led to frequent hostilities with any non-Athapaskan neighbors, and sporadic forays were made into the lands of their tormentors. In one reported raid on Eskimos the attackers carried wooden shields on which they had painted designs representing their individual guardian spirits. After the encounter the raiders observed numerous taboos to placate the spirits of those they had killed. A raid of this nature united the participants against a common enemy but did not require elaborate organization. Raids were bizarre melees for individual prestige, plunder, potential glory, and tribal security.

DESCENT, KINSHIP, AND MARRIAGE   These people calculated their ancestry through both female and male relatives (bilateral descent); the descent group (kindred) was like that which prevails in the United States today. When a man married, he attached himself to the household of his parents-in-law, and his ideal mate was his father's sister's daughter (patrilateral cross-cousin). In *recent* times at least some Chipewyan called a father's sister's daughters and mother's brother's daughters (cross-cousins) by the term for "sweetheart," a convention that gives strength to the assumption of cross-cousin marriage. As the anthropologist Fred Eggan has pointed out, a man relied on his son-in-law for support, and the son-in-law in turn would be aided by his wife's brother's son. It appears that in the aboriginal system of kinship terminology the cousin terms were of the Iroquois type. Father's brother's children and mother's sister's children were termed the same as siblings, but different terms were employed for a father's sister's children and mother's brother's children. This terminology would be compatible with cross-cousin marriage. For the generation above Ego the kinship terms for father and father's brother are alike, and mother's brother is distinct. Mother, mother's sister, and father's sister are all termed differently. Thus the terminology on the first ascending generational level was bifurcate collateral for females and bifurcate merging for males. This terminology indicates that probably siblings and parallel cousins of the same sex (who were terminological siblings), particularly if they were males, extended mutual aid to one another and regarded their cross-cousins as possible mates. With the further presence of wife exchange, we find an integrated network of blood relatives on Ego's generational level. On the parent's generation the same social distance separated aunts and uncles from one another as from parents. The inference is that these individuals were not as important socially or economically as near relatives of one's own generation.

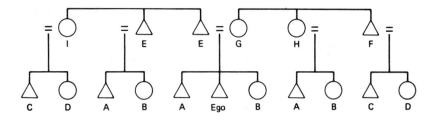

ENTERTAINMENT   Games and other forms of amusement were few, and the only dancing was a step borrowed from the Dogrib Indians. A popular pastime was the widespread hand game, a guessing game in which two opponents sat opposite each other with ten to twenty counters beside them. One man had an object in one hand and, behind a skin, shifted it. His opponent then guessed the hand that contained the gaming piece. A correct guess gave the winner one counter, and the game was won when one man had all of the counters.

LIFE CYCLE   Tracing the pattern of hypothetical lives from birth to death provides invaluable insight into the forms and norms that produced and sustained the sociocultural system identified as Chipewyan. No ethnography is reasonably complete unless such a sketch is included. While information about aboriginal Chipewyan life histories is not balanced or complete, it does lend itself to presentation in brief.

The Chipewyan, as other North American Indians, realized that conception resulted from sexual intercourse. As the time of delivery approached, a small tent or brush-covered structure was erected for the pregnant woman away from the main camp. Here she bore her offspring and remained apart from normal camp routine for about a month. Her isolation was enforced whether the group was traveling or at a relatively permanent camp. The mother was cared for by other women, but she had no contact with men. The father did not see his infant until the period of isolation ended. Similar isolation was the norm for a menstruating woman and for a girl at her menarche. The blood associated with women at these times was considered antithetical to fish and game, and men avoided contacts with females in these conditions. Apparently the women were successful in keeping the true nature of the menstrual cycle a secret from men. When a woman sought to avoid her husband, which might be several times in one month, she simply crawled out of the tent beneath a side, to indicate that she was beginning to menstruate, and went to the menstrual hut.

During the first year of life an infant was carried on its mother's back next to her skin; the baby was held in place by a belt that passed from the middle of the mother's back over her breasts. In this secondary "womb" a baby wore only a moss-padded diaper. A female infant was named after a form or charac-

The Chipewyan: Subarctic Hunters

teristic of a marten, such as Marten's Heart, Summer Marten, or White Marten. The names for males were taken from the seasons, a place, or an animal. Unfortunately, little is known about the social environment of children. Males clearly occupied a favored position compared with their sisters, but children in general were treated as adults. Conversations in the presence of children were free and frank.

Childhood betrothals prevailed, and parents were careful to prevent a girl from participating in sexual intercourse before she married. Matches were made by parents or other relatives, and a girl had no choice. The usual marriage was between a pubescent girl and a man who was at least twice her age. Since there was no marriage ceremony, the man simply attached himself to his wife's household. A marriage assumed stability only after an infant was born. Offspring seldom were born during the early years of marriage, and from this it may be presumed that the young brides were passing through adolescent sterility, which tended to delay conception. A nuclear family (a man, his wife, and children) was neither a stable nor long-lasting unit. The possibility of death by accident, disease, or starvation always existed, and life expectancy was probably less than thirty years for the average person. These factors, plus a growing dislike for a spouse, could rupture a household. Furthermore wrestling to retain one's wife whenever challenged did not lead to familial stability. Skill in wrestling was developed during youth, and the rule was that the man first thrown to the ground was the loser. An opponent could be downed most readily by grabbing his hair—thus it was cut short—or by seizing his ears—so they were greased. The woman being fought over had no voice in these matters but was expected to follow the winner dutifully. Sometimes, however, a newly won wife had to be taken by force. In one instance a group of Chipewyan chanced upon an enterprising Dogrib woman who had lived alone for seven months while attempting to find her way back home after escaping from captivity. The Indians who found her considered her a fair and desirable prize; she was won and lost in some six wrestling matches during a single evening. Chipewyan men also were not averse to a group rape of women belonging to their own tribe but not known to them previously.

A wrestling match for a wife did not always end well. In one case the husband killed a potential rival. He and his wife then were forced to live in isolation, and whenever other Chipewyan happened on the couple, they would take everything they owned except their clothing. Women deserted their husbands, but because of the physical isolation of most camps this was a dangerous undertaking. The woman might be caught and beaten by her husband or seized by another man before she found safety with a man she desired. Men guarded their wives jealously, not allowing them out of their sight if the opportunity for adultery existed. Wives generally were faithful to their husbands, even though a particular wife sometimes shared her husband with as many as seven co-wives. The exchange of wives for a night perhaps helped temper any urge to seize a woman for sexual purposes alone. Wife exchanges were made by men and had implications that were more economic than sexual. The bonds thereafter established between men provided continuing friendship and mutual aid. If one of the men died, his partner at least temporarily assumed the responsibility of caring for the widow and her children.

As a person aged and was less capable of supporting himself, he became an unwanted burden. Old people had the poorest of tattered clothing, and their food was undesirable. Abandonment usually occurred when a camp was to be moved. A shelter was built for them, and the travelers would say, "They were dead; they appeared alive, but they were dead," and leave them to starve alone. A person dying in isolation was not buried subsequently, and even the corpse of one who died in camp was simply placed on the ground. In either case, the bodies were eaten by animals. Property of the deceased was destroyed, and the immediate relatives also destroyed their own property. A widow cut her hair short as a sign of her bereavement, and some of her shorn hair might be placed beside the deceased. She wailed about camp, stripped of her clothing and other possessions, to be aided and soothed by relatives and friends but not to remarry for a year.

The supernatural world of the Chipewyan included animistic spirits that hovered about constantly. Some were more potent than others. Because the spirits of wolves and wolverine were dangerous, these animals usually were not hunted or killed. The bear, too, was dangerous; when one was killed, its skin might be burned and the large bones scattered in the four directions. A woman could not touch or step over a bearskin; thus one placed before a door was a means of keeping women from entering a tent. The spirits of a shaman were powerful, and even the spirit of an ordinary person was sometimes feared. Only a vague notion existed of a future life, which was like that on earth but free from cares, according to one observer. Not all accounts agree, however. One states that the soul of the deceased crosses a river, and if the individual has been good on earth he reaches an island on which life is free from worry. If he was evil, he struggles up to the neck in the river forever.

Early Historic Changes

RECENT STUDIES   A few years ago Chipewyan history was unknown except in terms of obvious sources such as the work by Samuel Hearne. Recent ethnohistorical studies, however, make it necessary to correct and revise accounts about the Chipewyan, in terms of both baseline and acculturative ethnographies. The thoughtful analyses of historical sources by Beryl C. Gillespie, David M. Smith, and James G. E. Smith demonstrate that the data do not simply yield ethnographic bits and pieces but reveal configurations of patterned change. Works by these authors provide a dramatic illustration of what may be learned from existing but previously ignored or underutilized sources.

The Chipewyan: Subarctic Hunters

CONFLICTING ATTRACTIONS   James G. E. Smith (1976, 14) aptly characterized the course of Chipewyan life from contact to the present in his statement that "one may view the history of the Chipewyan from the early 18th century to the present as one of conflicting attractions to the caribou of the taiga-tundra ecotone on the one hand and to the fur trade and the fur bearers of the full boreal forest on the other." Smith states that in early historic times the Chipewyan occupied a major portion of the Barren Grounds and the adjacent taiga. Some bands began moving south and west into the northern forests during the late 1700s, but the shift to exploitation of spruce forests was made slowly and even reluctantly by many groups. European trade goods were desired, and the only way they could be obtained was by participating in the fur trade. Hudson's Bay Company officials settled Cree and Chipewyan differences, and by 1721 the Chipewyan were encouraged to trap furbearers in the northern forest; the species sought, beaver and marten, were rare on the Barrens. The Chipewyan were able to trap marten without serious disruption to their caribou-based economy. However, trapping beaver meant a commitment to life in the forests where beaver were most abundant and required an accompanying shift from their predominantly caribou diet.

Among the technological changes made to participate effectively in the fur trade was a shift from walking and the use of a small, one-man canoe to larger canoes capable of carrying at least two persons, pelts, and supplies. When the Chipewyan first traded at Churchill, they arrived on foot. By the 1700s they were building small birch bark canoes that were partially decked and were ribbed with spruce. This type of canoe, propelled with a single-bladed paddle, was carried by summer travelers for hunting and for ferrying people and possessions across lakes and rivers. By the 1790s much larger canoes provided effective mobility along waterways while carrying substantial loads.

EPIDEMICS   Early in their history the Chipewyan appear to have lost much of their vitality because of exposure to new diseases. A destructive smallpox epidemic struck in 1781–1782, and Hearne, referring to a portion of the total population, estimated that only 10 percent of the people survived. In 1819 there was another smallpox epidemic that "carried away whole bands" (Simpson, 1938, 81). Thus they were a remnant people early in their history. Weakened by disease they were less able to support themselves and more subject to famines. Another momentous change took place as a direct result of the fur trade. When they began to trap intensively, they spent less time hunting caribou and lived within a more tenuous economic system. They desired trade goods and trapped to obtain them but thereby deprived themselves of the opportunity to acquire their basic foods. Thus, if they did not take large numbers of fish and caribou at certain seasons, they faced starvation. Famines made devastating inroads into the vitality of the society; although famines were not new, they now occurred more often. At Fort Resolution in 1833

Plate 2-2 A 1913 photograph of Chief Squirrel. (Courtesy of the National Museums of Canada Neg. No. 26070)

some "forty of the choicest hunters" died in a famine (Back, 1836, 209), and between 1879 and 1881 "many died in hunger and misery."

LEADERSHIP In aboriginal times the charismatic leader was respected because of his unique abilities, and a number of such individuals, among whom Matonabbee was an outstanding example, are reported. This leadership did not embody the qualities of power and authority however. With the advent of the fur trade a different form of leadership developed. Traders preferred dealing with a group representative, not with individuals, and this led to the emergence of trading chiefs. Traders strengthened a trading chief's standing by deferring to him and presenting him with clothing, medals, and a formal reception on his arrival at a post. By the late 1880s it is noted that the "chief" distributed the meat of caribou and moose to whomever he chose, ir-

The Chipewyan: Subarctic Hunters

Plate 2–3 Dwellings and a canoe in 1913. (Courtesy of the National Museums of Canada Neg. No. 26068)

respective of the wishes of the man who killed the game, although the hunter personally kept the skins or pelts of animals. If this was the norm, we must conclude that a chief possessed authority and some form of power. By 1908 chiefs represented groups in dealings with officials of the Federal Indian Affairs Branch, but, as we would expect, they were not very effective.

CHANGING STATUS OF DOGS It is insightful to consider the changing status of dogs. It will be recalled that a dog-like creature was thought to have fathered these people, and the dog, along with bears, wolves, and wolverine, had strong supernatural associations. In the 1820s the people were convinced by a powerful man that they should not use such closely related animals to do their work, and consequently they destroyed all of their dogs. It was for this reason that during the early period of contact the people had very few dogs or none at all. Apparently dogs were not widely used as beasts of burden, nor did they pull toboggans, until some time in the mid-1800s. Yet Hearne mentioned that in his time dogs hauled birch poles as hunters moved into the Barrens. Certain taboos still surrounded dogs in the early 1930s. For example, dogs were not shot, and to feed a dog a moose head or bear intestines brought ill fortune.

BELIEFS The unformalized supernatural system of the aboriginal population absorbed Cree concepts, and by the early 1800s they had borrowed the concept of manitou. An evil manitou was blamed for sickness, disease, or bad luck. Some Chipewyan, by 1908, had learned many of the Cree folktales, including the trickster-hero complex.

Dependence on caribou and fish continued, but the prohibitions surrounding the treatment of these species were far from balanced. It was noted that in aboriginal times precautions were necessary in setting fishnets or using fishhooks, yet early references to taboos surrounding caribou hunting are rare. The implication is that this animal could be taken adequately by existing means so that any ritual appeals were unnecessary. By the early 1940s taboos surrounding caribou were recorded for the Chipewyan living along the eastern sector of Great Slave Lake. For example, if a woman's skirt were to pass over a hunting knife, there was fear that the caribou would not migrate in that direction during that year. Again a woman must pierce the caribou's eyeball before she butchered the carcass to prevent the spirit of the deceased animal from reporting its fate to others. The implication might be that these taboos emerged as caribou hunting became less dependable.

Modern Life

The first detailed study of modern Chipewyan life was made by James W. VanStone at the community of Snowdrift along Great Slave Lake. VanStone's fieldwork from 1960 to 1962 provides the bulk of information about the recent past. These findings about Snowdrift are updated with field data collected by Wendell H. Oswalt in 1976. From these studies it is possible to plot continuity with the past and to note recent changes that are giving a different cast to Snowdrift Chipewyan life.

SNOWDRIFT HISTORY　　The settlement, beyond the margins of aboriginal Chipewyan territory, is in a forest setting along one of the many indentations on the southeastern shore of Great Slave Lake. The local people traditionally had traded at Fort Resolution, founded in 1786, but after the Hudson's Bay Company built a post at Snowdrift in 1925, families in the region began trading there to avoid the long trip to distant stores. Yet it was not until 1954 that most people began to settle at Snowdrift. A permanent village emerged in response to pressure by the Federal Indian Affairs Branch agent at Yellowknife. In 1960 the community consisted of twenty-six houses, most of them built of logs. In addition there were frame buildings belonging to the Hudson's Bay Company, a Roman Catholic church, other buildings belonging to Federal agencies, and cabins owned by white sport-fishing and mining entrepreneurs who did not live there permanently.

The commitment to settled village life was a radical change with far-reaching implications. The people previously lived at scattered seasonal fishing, hunting, and trapping sites. The move to Snowdrift, in response to gov-

The Chipewyan: Subarctic Hunters

ernmental pressure and the presence of the store, radically changed the nature of social contacts, and subsistence activities were negatively affected. Many people now were clustered together, exploiting the same resources, and it became increasingly difficult to maintain their previous standard of living. Furthermore they were under the control of Federal agents, whereas previously these ties were tenuous or absent. In studying this process of change it is essential to recognize that Federal intervention was largely responsible for the new conditions.

CLOTHING   Most garments were quite unlike aboriginal forms although a few men wore hooded and sleeved caribou skin ponchos rather than manufactured parkas. From the Hudson's Bay Company store men bought long underwear, shirts, trousers, and sweaters. Women purchased briefs, cotton stockings, dresses, petticoats, shoes, skirts, and sweaters. The most important locally made items of aboriginal derivation were moccasins for men and skin slippers worn by women during the summer. Young girls wore clothing like that of the women, with the addition of slacks and colorful lightweight jackets. Young girls often curled their hair, and young women as well as girls wore lipstick. The young women used commercial perfumes and set off their appearance with brooches, earrings, and finger rings. The young men were particularly fond of wide leather belts with large buckles and short, ornamented, black leather jackets. The implication of the modern clothing styles is at once obvious. Most items were obtained from the store, and it was necessary to have something that the outside world valued for their purchase.

THE SETTLEMENT   Family dwellings had an air of permanence unknown in the recent past. About 1912 the first ridged commercial canvas tent was bought locally, and soon this style replaced the conical tent of old. After 1950 most families began to construct more substantial dwellings. The Indian agent obtained Federal support for the construction or renovation of the cabins at Snowdrift. The Indians at first were reluctant to participate in the program since they were hesitant to commit themselves permanently to the village. Most of the dwellings were one-room log cabins with board floors. The furnishings included homemade beds, chairs, a table, and shelves. Light was supplied by kerosene lamps, and heat was furnished by wood-burning sheet-iron stoves. A household inventory included trunks or bags for extra clothing and bedding, a battery-powered radio, a hand-operated sewing machine, and utensils. In nearby log storage sheds were frozen or dried fish, dog harnesses, outboard motor parts, traps, snowshoes, fishnets, and rifles. By 1976 nearly all families lived in substantial frame houses. Electric lights and stoves were powered with electricity from a central power plant. The houses had oil furnaces, and oil delivery as well as garbage service was provided. The solid dwellings, services provided, and proliferation of material goods made families increasingly sedentary and committed to Snowdrift.

Plate 2–4 The community of Snowdrift in 1976. (Photograph by the author)

CONVEYANCES   In 1960 each established family owned a large, square-ended, commercially manufactured canoe, an outboard motor, and a small canvas-covered canoe. Although a form of toboggan existed, it was purchased from the Hudson's Bay Company store and was more correctly a cariole, for it had a rear panel and canvas sides. Dogs, not women, pulled the cariole. Each family owned about five dogs, which were chained near the homes. The use of dog teams and outboard motors as sources of power unquestionably had greatly increased the families' mobility. By 1976 the "iron dog" or snowmobile typically was used for winter travel. This meant a further dependence on cash to buy a snowmobile and keep it in operation, and there was an accompanying decrease in the need to provide dogs with food. Likewise the canvas canoes were being replaced by aluminum boats, which required a substantial cash outlay.

SUBSISTENCE ACTIVITIES   Traditional economic life had centered about caribou and fish, and these foci persisted with the addition of trapping furbearers. Even by 1960 most men did not hesitate to abandon their traplines if caribou appeared in the vicinity. The lure of the hunt remained very strong, and as recently as 1930 hunting was more important to these Chipewyan than trapping. A trapper was obliged to hunt for food while on a trapline and took primarily hares, ptarmigan, or spruce hens. Likewise he fished through the ice with a gill net for dog food. A trapline was reached after one to three days of

The Chipewyan: Subarctic Hunters

dog team travel, and commercial steel traps or wire snares were set for lynx, marten, mink, white fox, and wolverine. Cross, red, or silver fox were not sought since their market value was very low. Trapping was difficult and was surrounded by many uncertainties. Enough food had to be obtained for one-self and the dog team; wolverine sometimes ate the animals caught in sets or might spring a line of sets and remove the bait; a Canada jay, ermine, or other creature might spring a trap, and in addition, the working conditions on a trapline were difficult. A canvas trapping tent was small and impossible to heat adequately, and the men found it difficult to work alone for weeks on end. The increasing tendency was to range from the village for only short periods during November and December when the pelts of most fur animals were in their prime.

Trapping was linked to the Hudson's Bay Company, for only at this store could a man exchange his furs for trade items. The account by Hearne of an Indian's relationship with traders was in many ways similar to the observa-tions by VanStone. The Indians attempted to outwit the trader and resorted to diverse subterfuges to obtain credit. In Indian eyes the only good traders were those concerned with Indian welfare. In spite of their opposing goals, the Indians and the Hudson's Bay Company were economically integrated. The price of pelts was not very high; in 1959–1960 the average take per trapper was worth about $320. Since white fox prices were relatively high, they were trapped conscientiously in the winter. The most important furbearer trapped in the spring was beaver, and there was a Federal limit to an individual's take. In theory no man could take more than five animals, and each pelt was tagged before being exchanged at the store. Energetic trappers, however, bought unused tags issued to others and increased their take in this manner. When an Indian agent proposed the registration of traplines, the people opposed the suggestion because they felt it would further restrict their mobility. In the recent past a man was accompanied by his entire family on a trapline, but often this was no longer possible because school-aged children were obligated to attend classes. The income from trapping was not sufficient to meet subsis-tence needs, and by 1976 the yield from trapping made no significant con-tribution to the welfare of the community as a whole. Thus the one major con-tribution of these people to the worldwide economic system had ended and had not been replaced by an alternative.

In the early 1960s dependence on caribou remained great, and the late summer hunt was of prime importance. A household head felt that he required about one hundred caribou per year, yet harvests of this magnitude were no longer realized. The people traveled by large canoes to the Fort Reli-ance area for caribou, and if there were no animals available, they portaged east to the vicinity of Artillery Lake. Burdened by their families, large amounts of equipment, and big canoes, they were unable to reach the best hunting grounds. As a result they were not likely to kill many animals. The meat obtained was smoked and brought back to the village to be stored in the

Plate 2-5 A Snowdrift man checking a gill net set beneath lake ice in 1960. (Courtesy of James W. VanStone)

Indian Affairs Branch cold-storage unit. In 1960 nearly half of the households were unrepresented in the fall caribou hunt, although some families shared in the take of others because they had provided a hunting party with equipment.

In the late fall nylon or cotton gill nets were set in the lake or along nearby rivers; they were fitted with stone sinkers, wooden floats, and large anchor stones at each end as in aboriginal times. Lake trout and whitefish were caught most frequently, and these fish were hung out for partial drying and then were stored as winter food for dogs and people.

In recent years most men preferred wage labor jobs to hunting, fishing, and trapping. Few such positions existed, however, and most were of a temporary nature. Construction jobs were few after the community physical plant was completed; work on commercial fishing vessels was unpredictable and physically demanding. Firefighting was sporadic and important but seasonal and recently was abandoned in this region. Serving as guides for tourist fishermen had yet to reach its full potential. Thus making a living by wage labor was even more uncertain than following subsistence pursuits of old.

Aboriginal foods were increasingly replaced by purchased edibles. People

The Chipewyan: Subarctic Hunters

preferred fish and meat with each meal, but since these often were unavailable, bannock had become an important staple. Bannock, the standard fare of poor Eskimos and Indians throughout Alaska and Canada, is made of white flour and baking powder mixed with water into a paste and spread in a greased skillet to be fried. Often this was the only food at a meal; bannock and tea are the bread and water of depressed subarctic living. The dominant method of cooking was by boiling; after a food was well cooked, it was allowed to cool and then eaten. When families were able, they purchased prepared foods from the store. The imported items most desired were flour, sugar, tea, coffee, crackers, peanut butter, canned meats and fruits, evaporated milk, and seasonings.

DESCENT, KINSHIP, AND MARRIAGE   The people of Snowdrift traced their descent along both the female and male lines (bilateral descent), as they had in early historic times. Cousin terminology, however, was of the Eskimo type (similar to the current classification of cousins in the United States). At the same time preferential cousin marriage no longer existed; in fact people did not recall it as an aboriginal practice. The one hundred years of contact with Roman Catholic missionaries who spoke against cousin marriage probably had produced the change, yet premarital fornication between cousins prevailed.

When a person married, he was most likely to select a mate within the community (village endogamy), and immediately after marriage the couple lived with the in-laws who were best able to receive them (temporary bilocal residence). As soon as possible the couple built a separate dwelling and lived alone (neolocal residence). In 1961 most households were nuclear or nuclear core families, the latter being comprised of a nuclear family to which were added a near relative or two of the husband or wife. Plural marriages no longer existed, and capable providers did not attract followers who lived with them. The overall impression is that the nuclear family was still the most important social unit, although it was not as autonomous as before.

SOCIAL DIMENSIONS   With subsistence activities and material culture changing so much from aboriginal times, we would expect and do find equally significant differences in other aspects of living. The old attitudes toward women and their harsh treatment as described by Hearne are not reported. Although VanStone was not explicit on the subject, he conveyed the impression that domestic harmony existed. Certain activities, such as food preparation and childraising, remained female obligations, but men performed these tasks when the need arose. Women could profit monetarily from their own labors. A woman who processed a moose or caribou hide or sewed skin garments for someone outside her family was paid directly and retained the profits. The favorable position of women at Snowdrift may have resulted from the fact that they were a distinct minority; since it therefore was difficult to

Plate 2–6 Snowdrift woman sitting in front of a smokehouse in 1976. (Photograph by the author)

obtain a wife, she was treated with care.

Social bonds beyond those based on kinship were new and of expanding importance. Village life produced feelings of unity, and people thought of themselves as economically, morally, and physically superior to persons in adjacent settlements. Other evidence for emerging village cohesion was the widespread sharing of locally available foods. By the time a successful moose hunter beached his boat he had given away most of the meat, and the same applied to a catch of fish. Food was shared in aboriginal times, but apparently

54

The Chipewyan: Subarctic Hunters

not in as pervasive or egalitarian a manner. Furthermore, an intensive pattern of reciprocal borrowing had developed, and this included major as well as minor items of material culture. These attitudes and their behavioral manifestations clearly were beginning to integrate the community on a social and economic basis.

POLITICAL LIFE   The Snowdrift Chipewyan were included in Treaty Number 11, which was signed by the Indians in 1921 and provided them with direct monetary and other benefits. The Indians gave up their aboriginal rights to the land but at the same time were protected in their exploitation of local resources. In exchange, they received tangible benefits such as formal education, health services, and material goods. Each year a band member received a cash payment of $5; the band chief received $25, and counselors, $15 each, and in recent years the Indian Affairs Branch had provided fishnets, ammunition, and items such as roofing and doors for house construction. Furthermore, families in need, as defined by the Indian agent, received a "ration" from the Indian Affairs Branch through the Hudson's Bay Company store. A national program of old-age assistance provided for the welfare of persons sixty-five years of age or older. Even more important was the "baby bonus," which was a national program. The Family Allowance, as it was called, was paid to each family every month; $6 was received for each child under ten and $8 for those ten through sixteen. The program was designed to improve child care, and it probably served this end at Snowdrift.

One result of living in a stable community was intensified contact with the Indian agent. Stationed at Yellowknife, he visited Snowdrift and called meetings on matters of villagewide concern. Attendance usually was poor, and it was difficult to conduct a general meeting because each Indian was inclined to raise issues of personal interest, usually specific requests for aid. Thus the process of democratic group action failed. Unity, when it was manifest, consisted of a stand against a proposal rather than any positive approach. The Indians preferred to deal with the agent on a private, almost secret basis, concerning specific requests. They felt that an agent was in a position to grant favors, and for him not to do so was regarded as pure stubbornness.

Visits to the village by the Royal Canadian Mounted Police (R.C.M.P.) in the 1960s were more a show of power than the result of actual need. Crimes as defined in the Canadian legal system were rare, and the most common cause for arrest was the manufacture of home brew. Since everyone was secretive when making home brew and avoided being seen intoxicated when the police were present, few arrests were made. The Indians felt that it was wrong to appeal to Canadian legal authorities for the settlement of personal disputes, and they rarely did so, although they might threaten such action.

In 1960 the bands were reorganized to make allowance for the physical movements of people from one band to another. Under the reorganization Snowdrift Indians had their own chief and two counselors. The Indians had a

Plate 2–7 Snowdrift house and tepee in 1976. (Photograph by the author)

clear formulation of what they considered to be ideal behavior for a chief. In theory, he did not interfere in the affairs of villagers, but he adopted a stern attitude toward Euro-Canadians in general and toward the Indian agent in particular. Whites, by contrast, expected a chief to be cooperative; if he was not, they bypassed him and acted through the trader or teacher. This pattern of the whites for accomplishing their purposes undermined Indian authority and contradicted the purpose of having a chief, counselors, and recognized Indian authorities.

For years the Canadian government encouraged the development of local political power at the band level. However, in 1969 Federal administrative obligations shifted largely to the government of the Northwest Territories, and it fostered the democratic process through local settlement councils that are in direct competition with the band. Furthermore a regional native rights organization has become increasingly militant in fostering Indian interests. These competing institutions have above all else intensified local factionalism and divided the community in terms of effective political action.

RELIGION AND SUPERNATURALISM Everyone was a participating but nominal Roman Catholic. The priest serving the village was stationed at Fort Resolution and visited the settlement frequently throughout the year. He sometimes stayed two months at a time, and he always was present during the Christmas and Easter seasons. Church dogma and belief were understood poorly by the people, but participation in formal ceremonies was high. In general, the Church was regarded as something beyond the context of daily living. The Indians felt that the Church was wealthy and that people should be

The Chipewyan: Subarctic Hunters

paid for any labor performed on its behalf. Thus the feeling of belonging to a church and strengthening its purposes was not understood by the members. Interestingly enough, it was in the supernatural sphere that Indians admitted openly that they were different from whites. The concept of a "bush man" prevailed here as it did among other Northern Athapaskans. This creature was a man who wore manufactured shoes and appeared at a distance during the summer. He kidnapped children, but apparently he did not harm adults as long as they remained beyond his reach. The Indians believed that certain supernatural beings could harm them but did not affect whites. There also were beliefs about trapping practices, but these were of unknown dimensions.

The curing of physical illness had passed out of the hands of a shaman, who no longer existed, into the domain of the Indian and Northern Health Services and a lay dispenser, usually the Hudson's Bay Company manager. If a case was considered serious, the nurse at Yellowknife was contacted, and she decided what course of action was to be followed. This nurse, sometimes accompanied by a medical doctor, visited the village at intervals. These Indians were concerned about their health but did not use patent medicines or turn freely to Euro-Canadians for aid. They seemed to enjoy talking about their aches and pains, but they sought treatment only when they were quite ill.

ENTERTAINMENT   Square dancing was a popular pastime, and the steps probably had been learned from commercial fishermen who often stopped for a few days of relaxation during the summer. Men played guitars or violins and learned dance music by listening to village phonographs or broadcasts from the Yellowknife radio station. The square dances were called expertly by village men, and participation at dances was good. Less formal entertainment included nightly card games, which were extremely popular, particularly blackjack and gin rummy. Men and women often played together, and the stakes ranged from small change and ammunition to $3 hands in gin rummy games if men were affluent. While adults were playing cards, children sometimes gambled by pitching coins to a line. The hand game of old was known but seldom played; card games were considered more exciting.

The consumption of alcohol was as much a ritual as a form of entertainment, and prescribed drinking patterns rarely were ignored. The only alcoholic beverage regularly consumed was home brew, produced from yeast, raisins, sugar, and water. It was made secretly by two or three men and allowed to age for about twenty-four hours. It was thought better if it aged longer, but anticipation negated the possibility. The brew was drunk in the home of one of the makers or in the brush during the summer, and the object was to become intoxicated. A cup was dipped into the three-gallon pail, the beverage drunk, and the cup passed to the next participant. Normally some brew was stored in bottles, to be consumed after the brew pail had been drained. When participants became reasonably intoxicated, they visited one house after another, regardless of the time, and drank as they chatted with

Plate 2–8 A summer card game at Snowdrift in ca. 1960. (Courtesy of James W. VanStone)

their reluctant hosts. Sometimes they offered to share their brew, but this was not consistent. The conversations of intoxicated men were about village life, and they became more outgoing during drinking sprees than at any other time of their adult lives. By 1976 home brew was far less popular than in the recent past. It had largely been replaced by intoxicants imported from the Yellowknife liquor store.

PERSONALITY CHANGES   In a study of folktales Ronald Cohen and VanStone explored the nature of Chipewyan self-sufficiency and dependency. They analyzed early twentieth-century tales recorded among these people and compared them with original stories written by Chipewyan children in 1961; a sample of Grimm's fairy tales served as control material. As a basis of analysis the authors assumed that "taken broadly, self-sufficiency and dependency refer to a basic and universal quality of all human social experience, namely, action by ego which affects his environment, i.e., self-assertiveness or self-sufficiency, and action directed towards ego over which he has no control, i.e., dependency." Different social systems would be expected to exhibit both qualities in varying proportions. An analysis of Grimm's fairy tales reflected the Protestant ethic and exhibited a high degree of self-sufficiency. The folktales of the Chipewyan exhibited about equal proportions of self-sufficiency and dependency, suggesting that these people established a balance in their relationship with the environment. An increase in dependency, reflected in the

The Chipewyan: Subarctic Hunters

Plate 2–9 Girls at Snowdrift in 1976. (Photograph by the author)

children's stories, suggested two alternative but not mutually exclusive explanations. Either Federal welfare programs had made the Chipewyan less capable and less desirous of caring for themselves or the contact situation had caused them to feel that their efforts to affect the environment were more likely to fail than to succeed.

Overview

In the early 1960s VanStone characterized these people as moving toward the stagnation of deculturation. They had lost most of their old design for living and were unable to replace it with a Euro-Canadian model. This pattern was especially evident in the economic sphere since trapping only partially replaced the subsistence-based life-style and the existing combination did not provide a satisfactory standard of living. This led VanStone to use such terms as "poor white" and "lower class." The depressed standard of living at Snowdrift indicated that these people were at the fringe of modern developments in the north. They not only lacked technical skills and formal education, but they had not made the changes in their values that would lead to an improved living standard. Therefore the more rewarding local jobs went to white Canadians. These Indians might, as Jacob Fried has suggested, become an increasingly depressed economic class in Canadian society.

The effects of changes begun in the late 1950s have become increasingly clear. By the mid-1970s the government had created a comfortable physical environment at Snowdrift when judged by Euro-Canadian standards. The houses were well built, heated with oil, and supplied with electricity. Water was delivered and sewage picked up. Nursing Station personnel provided local health care, and a community hall had been built. Yet people had comparatively little confidence in their own abilities and little purpose to guide their lives. One reason was that they felt they lacked an effective voice in decisions about their future. Regional officials of the Government of the Northwest Territories at Fort Smith controlled their destiny. The people were accustomed to responding to proposals rather than initiating them. With a commitment to settled village life their previous hunting and trapping economy had nearly disappeared. They had a sense of community identity when dealing with outsiders, but their primary loyalties were to family groups.

Each of the three dominant extended families was represented on the Settlement Council charged with running local affairs, but they only acted in crisis situations. A major stumbling block was that most council members did not really understand what was expected of them in relation to governmental agencies. When "day trippers," government officials who chartered aircraft for less than a day, visited Snowdrift to explain their programs firsthand, the people listened, but they did not really comprehend. To admit that they did not understand was thought degrading; thus they agreed without an appreciation of the matter before them.

The Chipewyan of Snowdrift are acutely aware of their economic dilemma, especially after a major source of cash, firefighting, was discontinued. The council in its most concerted effort attempted to have the local area opened for commercial fishing in 1976. They were attempting to break their dependency relationship with the government by initiating a development program of their own, to which government officials were sympathetic. They did not achieve their goal, but they planned to keep trying. This effort brought people together as never before, which is encouraging. For the 260 villagers in 1976 starvation and poverty had disappeared, and the community was now a comfortable if not commodious place to live. Yet in the absence of a sound local economic base, life on this northern frontier has lost much of its purpose.

Additional Readings

In this chapter the information provided by Birket-Smith, Hearne, and VanStone was emphasized in describing the Chipewyan. The reader interested in additional details about early historic Chipewyan material culture and ecological adjustments should consult the work by Birket-Smith, which covers these topics with respect to the eastern bands. Yet it is increasingly clear that there were, and are, many regional variations in Chipewyan culture and society. For comparison with conditions at Snowdrift an article by David M. Smith deals with the Chipewyan at Fort Resolution in ecological terms, and a monograph by this author considers historic changes in religious beliefs at the same settlement. The economic round of the Chipewyan at Patuanak in northern Saskatchewan is developed fully in an article by Robert Jarvenpa. An appreciation of the problems raised by generalizing about Chipewyan kinship is

The Chipewyan: Subarctic Hunters

set forth by Henry S. Sharp in his article cited in the references.

For additional ethnographic sources dealing with the Chipewyan and all the other peoples considered in the chapters to follow, the interested reader should consult the ethnographic bibliography by George P. Murdock and Timothy J. O'Leary.

The reader interested in learning more about diverse Northern Athapaskan tribes must consult the definitive study by VanStone, *Athapaskan Adaptations*.

References

Back, George. *Narrative of the Arctic Land Expedition*. London. 1836.

*Birket-Smith, Kaj. *Contributions to Chipewyan Ethnology*. Report of the Fifth Thule Expedition, v. 6, no. 3. 1930. The bulk of the information in this volume applies only to the Churchill area Chipewyan as they were in 1923 and as the past was reconstructed with the aid of informants. The descriptive emphasis is on material culture; other aspects of culture and society are incompletely described. In spite of its shortcomings this study is second only to Hearne's work in importance.

Blanchet, Guy H. "Emporium of the North," *Beaver*, Outfit 276, 32–35. 1946.

Bryce, George. *The Remarkable History of the Hudson's Bay Company*. Toronto. 1904.

Campbell, Marjorie W. *The North West Company*. Toronto. 1957.

Cohen, Ronald, and James W. VanStone. "Dependency and Self-Sufficiency in Chipewyan Stories," *National Museum of Canada, Bulletin 194*, 29–55. 1963.

Curtis, E. S. *The North American Indian*. v. 18. Norwood. 1928.

Eggan, Fred, ed. *Social Anthropology of North American Tribes*. Chicago. 1937.

Fidler, Peter. "Journal of a Journey with the Chepawyans or Northern Indians, to the Slave Lake, & to the East & West of the Slave River, in 1791 & 2," *Publications of the Champlain Society*, v. 21, 493–555. 1934.

Franklin, John. *Narrative of a Journey to the Shores of the Polar Sea*. London. 1823.

Fried, Jacob. "Settlement Types and Community Organization in Northern Canada," *Arctic*, v. 16, 93–100. 1963.

Giddings, James L., Jr. "A Flint Site in Northernmost Manitoba," *American Antiquity*, v. 21, 255–268. 1956.

Gillespie, Beryl C. "Yellowknives: Quo Iverunt?," *Proceedings of the 1970 Annual Spring Meeting of the American Ethnological Society*, Robert F. Spencer, ed., 61–71. 1970.

Gillespie, Beryl C. "Changes in Territory and Technology of the Chipewyan," *Arctic Anthropology*, v. 13, 6–11. 1976.

Harp, Elmer, Jr. *The Archaeology of the Lower and Middle Thelon, Northwest Territories*. Arctic Institute of North America Technical Paper no. 8. 1961.

*Hearne, Samuel. *A Journey from Prince of Wale's Fort in Hudson's Bay to the Northern Ocean*. London. 1795: Dublin. 1796. (Two more recent, noteworthy editions of this work have appeared. The earlier was edited by Joseph B. Tyrell and published by The Champlain Society in 1911, and the second was edited by Richard Glover and published by the Macmillan Company of Canada in 1958.) Hearne's book is the standard source on the Chipewyan as they lived soon after historic contact. It is indispensable reading for any serious attempt to understand the culture of these Indians.

Hoijer, Harry. "The Chronology of the Athapaskan Languages," *International Journal of American Linguistics*, v. 22, 219–232. 1956.

*Irving, W. N. "The Barren Grounds," *Science, History and Hudson Bay*, C. S. Beals, ed., v. 1, 26–54. 1968. This relatively brief but thorough survey of Barren Grounds archaeology provides the best introduction to the subject.

Jarvenpa, Robert. "Spatial and Ecological Factors in the Annual Economic Cycle of the English River Band of Chipewyan," *Arctic Anthropology*, v. 13, 43–69. 1976.

*Jenness, Diamond. *The Indians of Canada*. National Museum of Canada, Bulletin no. 65. 1963. A reading of the chapter on the peoples of the Mackenzie and Yukon river basins provides a view of the Chipewyan in their relationship to other Canadian Athapaskans.

*Jenness, Diamond, ed. "The Chipewyan Indians: An Account by an Early Explorer," *Anthropologica*, v. 3, 15–33. 1956. This article contains abstracts of the Chipewyan information from a previously unpublished manuscript probably written by John Macdonell in the early 1800s. The descriptions are very good and provide a supplement to Hearne.

King, Richard. *Narrative of a Journey to the Shores of the Arctic Ocean*. 2 v. London. 1836.

Lowie, Robert H. "The Chipewyans of Canada," *Southern Workman*, v. 38, 278–283. 1909.

The Chipewyan: Subarctic Hunters

Lowie, Robert H. "An Ethnological Trip to Lake Athabasca," *American Museum Journal*, v. 9, 10–15. 1909.

Lowie, Robert H. *Robert H. Lowie, Ethnologist, A Personal Record*. Berkeley and Los Angeles. 1959.

*MacNeish, June H. "Leadership Among the Northeastern Athabascans," *Anthropologica*, v. 2, 131–163. 1956. Historical sources are evaluated and the Chipewyan discussed along with other Canadian Athapaskans. The major contribution of this paper is a classification of leadership patterns in aboriginal and historic times.

MacNeish, June H. "Kin Terms of Arctic Drainage Dene: Hare, Slavey, Chipewyan," *American Anthropologist*, v. 62, 279–295. 1960.

Mason, John A. "Notes on the Indians of the Great Slave Lake Area," *Yale University Publications in Anthropology*, no. 34. 1946.

Munsterhjelm, Erik. *The Wind and the Caribou*. London. 1953.

Murdock, George P., and Timothy J. O'Leary. *Ethnographic Bibliography of North America*. 5 v. New Haven. 1975.

Penard, Jean M. "Land Ownership and Chieftaincy among the Chippewayan and Caribou-Eaters," *Primitive Man*, v. 2, 20–24. 1929.

Petitot, Emile. "On the Athabasca District of the Northwest," *Canadian Record of Science*, v. 1, 27–53. 1884.

Rich, Edwin E. *Hudson's Bay Company, 1670–1870*. 3 v. Toronto. 1960.

Richardson, Richard. *Arctic Searching Expedition*. New York. 1854.

Robinson, J. "Among the Caribou-Eaters," *Beaver*, Outfit 275, 38–41. 1944.

Robson, Joseph. *An Account of Six Years Residence in Hudson's Bay*. London. 1752.

Ross, Bernard. "Notes on the Tinneh or Chepewyan Indians of British and Russian America: The Eastern Tinneh," *Smithsonian Institution Annual Report, 1866*. 304–311. 1867.

Russell, Frank. *Explorations in the Far North*. University of Iowa. 1898.

Seton, Ernest T. *The Arctic Prairies*. New York. 1911.

Sharp, Henry S. "Introducing the Sororate to a Northern Saskatchewan Chipewyan Village," *Ethnology*, v. 14, 71–82. 1975.

Simpson, George. "Journal of Occurrences in the Athabasca Department, 1820 and 1821," *Publications of the Champlain Society. Hudson's Bay Company Series*, 1. 1938.

Smith, David M. "INKONZE: Magico-Religious Beliefs of Contact-Tradition Chipewyan Trading at Fort Resolution, NWT, Canada," *Mercury Series, Ethnology Division Paper*, no. 6. National Museum of Man, Ottawa. 1973.

Smith, David M. "Cultural and Ecological Change: The Chipewyan of Fort Resolution," *Arctic Anthropology*, v. 13, 35–42. 1976.

Smith, James G. E. "The Chipewyan Hunting Group in a Village Context," *Western Canadian Journal of Anthropology*, v. 1, 60–66. 1970.

Smith, James G. E. "Introduction: The Historical and Cultural Position of the Chipewyan," *Arctic Anthropology*, v. 13, 1–5. 1976.

Smith, James G. E. "Local Band Organization of the Caribou Eater Chipewyan," *Arctic Anthropology*, v. 13, 12–24. 1976.

Tache, Alexander A. *Sketch of the North-West of America*. Montreal. 1870.

Tyrrell, Joseph B., ed. "David Thompson's Narrative," *Publications of the Champlain Society*, v. 12. 1916.

VanStone, James W. *The Economy of a Frontier Community*. Northern Coordination and Research Centre, Department of Northern Affairs and National Resources. 1961.

*VanStone, James W. "Changing Patterns of Indian Trapping in the Canadian Subarctic," *Arctic*, v. 16, 159–174. 1963.

*VanStone, James W. "The Changing Culture of the Snowdrift Chipewyan," *National Museum of Canada Bulletin* no. 209. 1965. This report and the preceding one contain most of the reliable information on the modern Chipewyan. Although the data are limited in scope to the community of Snowdrift, the generalizations most probably have wider applicability for other Chipewyan populations.

VanStone, James W. *Athapaskan Adaptations*. Chicago. 1974.

The Caribou Eskimos: Hunters on the Tundra

3

Environment, People, and Population

The most remarkable quality of Eskimos was their adaptability to diverse arctic and subarctic settings. Typically they hunted sea mammals along treeless coasts, and far less often they lived as riverine fishermen or inland caribou hunters. The Caribou Eskimos of the Barren Grounds in central Canada had nearly abandoned the seacoast and the exploitation of aquatic resources to concentrate on a single edible species, the caribou. As an inland tundra-dwelling people, they feared the scrawny spruce forests to the south and shunned the waters of Hudson Bay as another dangerous unknown. Their primary homeland until very recently was a rock-strewn interior region where lichens grew in the open country and dwarf birch were established in sheltered localities. They may have numbered 1000 at the turn of the present century, but by the early 1920s they totaled about 500 persons. Collectively these Eskimos referred to themselves as "Inuit," which translates as "real people." They were termed the Caribou Eskimos by the first anthropologists to work among them, and more recently they have been called by the somewhat inaccurate but pleasing name "People of the Deer" by Farley Mowat. The names that link these people of the Barrens with caribou and deer are anthropological and pop-

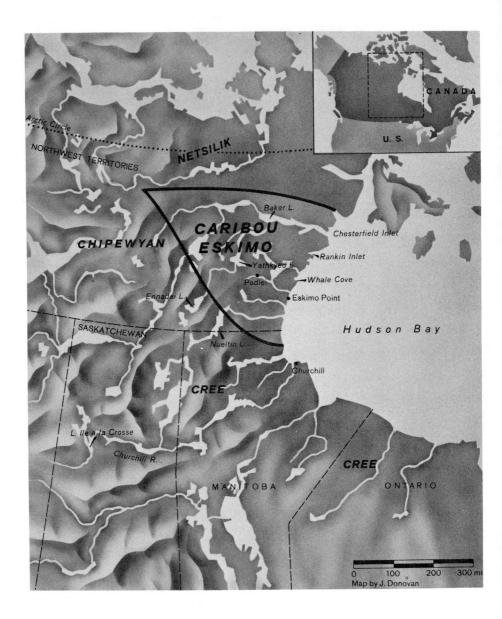

68

ular artifices, but each is appropriate since these people were above all else specialized inland hunters of caribou.

Reasons for This Selection

Humanistic and scientific reasons led to including the Caribou Eskimos. In a cultural context they have figured prominently in theories of Eskimo cultural origins and have been characterized as among the most "primitive" Eskimos. In environmental terms no inhabited sector of arctic America had more limited economic potential, and thus the Caribou Eskimos stand as a fine example of a people's adjustments for survival. In 1922–1923 an outstanding Danish anthropologist, Kaj Birket-Smith, compiled a baseline account of these people as they became enmeshed in a trapping and trading economy. Some twenty years later they attracted widespread attention through the efforts of Farley Mowat, a prominent Canadian writer who lived among them and wrote a touching plea to the outside world about their privation and the need for drastic changes in their administration. Mowat's writings were supplemented with poignant photographs by Richard Harrington, and whites awakened to the plight of these people. In 1955 the Dutch anthropologist Geert van den Steenhoven visited the Caribou Eskimos and authored a notable account about their customary law. These works, supplemented with more recent descriptions, make it possible to plot old and new patterns in Caribou Eskimo life.

The following sketch about these people invites comparison with the account of the Chipewyan in the previous chapter since both people were inland, subarctic caribou hunters. Comparisons between their respective adaptive strategies illustrate the contrasts and similarities between aboriginal peoples with different cultural and social backgrounds who lived in similar environments and exploited the same species. The fact that both people were strongly influenced by the fur trade provides an additional basis for comparisons.

Language

Eskimoan languages belong to the American Arctic-Paleosiberian linguistic phylum, which includes Eskimos in northern North America and a small area of eastern Siberia, as well as other peoples in northeastern Siberia. Thus there are clear linguistic ties between the Old and New Worlds in the vicinity of Bering Strait. This particular phylum includes two language families: the Chukchi-Kamchatkan in Siberia and the Eskimo-Aleut in the American north. The latter extended from the Aleutian Islands to Greenland and Labrador and included three major subdivisions or subfamilies whose languages are not mutually intelligible: Alaskan Eskimo, Aleut, and Central-Greenland Eskimo.

The Caribou Eskimos belong to the Central-Greenland subfamily; their dialect was very similar to that spoken by Eskimos along adjacent coastal areas, which suggests that the coastal and inland Eskimo populations of central Canada were a single people in the not-too-distant past.

Prehistory

Birket-Smith advanced the hypothesis that the Caribou Eskimos represented an archaic inland strain of Eskimo culture that existed widely before most Eskimos became intensive coastal sea mammal hunters. When Elmer Harp began excavating sites in Caribou Eskimo country in the 1950s, no one knew for certain whether or not Birket-Smith was correct in his interpretations. Harp determined that the Caribou Eskimos did not represent an old form of Eskimo culture, and the primary reason for drawing this conclusion was that none of their sites had great antiquity. It appears that coastal Eskimos in central Canada who stressed whale hunting were forced to abandon their primary livelihood about A.D 1400 as the earth's crust uplifted, making the seas shallower and uninhabitable for large whales. It was then that some Eskimos became divorced from the sea, developed an economy based on caribou hunting, and emerged as the Caribou Eskimos. The shift was not extremely difficult because even as coastal whalers they knew how to hunt caribou, and there were no doubt large if not vast herds on the Barren Grounds. The decision to move inland permanently was not a choice of convenience but one of necessity. Not all coastal Eskimos could remain at sealing grounds, and those with more of an inland hunting orientation settled in the Barrens. Caribou Eskimo culture emerged as one of material poverty and regression toward greater simplicity. As Harp noted, and as I too have observed, abandoned Caribou Eskimo camp sites contain few artifacts; there was little for them to leave behind except immense piles of broken caribou bones.

History

For hundreds of years history in the making nibbled away at the fringes of the Barren Grounds, with any intrusions by outsiders only temporary. The exploration of Hudson Bay and the founding of trading centers along its western shore first brought Caribou Eskimos into contact with explorers and agents of the Hudson's Bay Company. The early exploration and settlement of the Churchill River mouth has been outlined in discussing European penetration of the Chipewyan country. Little of pertinence may be added regarding any special relationships with the Caribou Eskimos. We know that they visited Fort Prince of Wales and that trading vessels contacted some groups along the coast, but such intercourse did not directly affect most Caribou Eskimos. The

The Caribou Eskimos: Hunters on the Tundra

great adventures of Samuel Hearne were the first extended travels into the Barrens, but he met no Caribou Eskimos. Subsequent explorers along northwestern Hudson Bay contributed little information about these people. The first reasonably adequate accounts date from 1878–1880 when Frederick Schwatka and his party crossed the northern Barrens. After this time travelers to the area were more numerous, but any contributions to our knowledge of the Caribou Eskimos are comparatively minor until 1922. It is with gratitude and relief that we turn to Birket-Smith and then to Knud Rasmussen of the Fifth Thule Expedition for our baseline study of these people.

Aboriginal Life

APPEARANCE AND CLOTHING   These people smelled of rancid fat and wood smoke because they never bathed, and the exposed areas of their bodies were dark from weathering and from the smoke of their fires. Some men cut their hair so that it was short all around, some let theirs hang as long bangs around their heads, and others parted their long hair in the middle, holding each segment in place with a browband. Whichever form was adopted, the crown often was tonsured. Women had exposed skin that was darker and grimier than a man's because women squatted before the smoky cooking fires. The faces of many women were tattooed with line and dot designs made either by threading a needle with a soot-covered human hair and sewing designs in the skin or by pricking the skin and rubbing the wounds with soot. A popular hair style for women was a middle part with the segments braided, rolled over each ear, and bound in place with strips of skin.

Of all their material needs, caribou skin clothing was extremely important, especially since sub-zero temperatures were common most of the year and their essentially unheated winter dwellings were built of snow. The hooded inner parka of a man had the hair turned inside and was split up each side to form front and back flaps. It was trimmed along the cuffs and hood with strips of short-haired skin and with a fringe along the bottom. The outer winter parka was loose-fitting, with slit sides. In severe weather men wore belts around their waists to keep cold air from circulating beneath their parkas. Winter garb of men included inner trousers with the hair facing the body and outer trousers with the hair facing the opposite direction. Men also wore skin stockings with sewn-in feet, skin boots, and mittens that had the hair inside.

The clothing of women took the same general form as that for men; the principal difference was in the proportions of the garments. The parkas for women were baggier to accommodate an infant inside. These garments had long hoods, broad shoulders, a short rounded flap in front, and a wide back panel that extended to the ankles. The trousers for women reached from the waist to below the knees, and they wore only a single pair, with the hair side out. Women's winter traveling boots bagged grossly above the knees and cov-

Plate 3-1 An Eskimo Point woman in 1959, carrying a child in the pouch at the back of her parka. (Photograph by the author)

ered the lower part of the trousers. One item of clothing with no counterpart for men was a cloak of caribou skin unmodified except for processing. The people were not careful about keeping their skin garments in good repair, but they did attempt to keep them as dry as possible. This was difficult to do, especially in an unheated snowhouse. Parkas were made so that they fitted loosely to cut down the amount of moisture from perspiration. Additionally, the snow was removed from a garment with a wooden snowbeater in the shape of a knife.

Both men and women used small skin bags to hold small items since their garments were pocketless. A skin bag was suspended from a cord passed around the neck and over one shoulder. Infants were carried in the backs of their mothers' inner parkas, not in the hoods, and a belt from the small of a woman's back to over her breasts held the infant in place. The only clothing worn by a baby was a caribou skin bonnet. From the time children were able to crawl until they were about six years old, they wore hoodless combination suits that had a split up the back. Children also wore boots, mittens, a bonnet, and a scarf of caribou skin strips.

SETTLEMENTS   Caribou Eskimos, like all other Eskimos, were extremely sociable. They enjoyed the company of not only relatives and friends but almost anyone except Indians. They liked to talk about their clothing, hunting, or what was stored in their meat caches. Whenever possible, meaning when food was available, families concentrated, if not next door to one another at least within a few miles. Families clustered most often in the fall at locations along rivers where caribou preferred to cross on their migration southward. If numerous animals were killed and the meat was cached nearby, a camp assumed a degree of permanence. At the same time it was not unusual for a family to strike out on its own in search of better hunting grounds. The settlement pattern was one of unstable concentrations of people in aggregates that never were very large. If a family thought that they would not kill any more caribou during a particular fall and if their meat caches were low, they moved to lakes known to contain fish.

When Eskimos are called to mind, most persons envision a fur-clad people living in dome-shaped houses of snow blocks. It is certainly accurate that Eskimos wear fur garments, but most Eskimos have never lived in snowhouses. The snowhouse was limited in use to much of central Canada and northwestern Greenland. The Caribou Eskimos were among those who made winter homes of snow blocks. In building a snowhouse it first was necessary to locate snow of the proper texture, and until this was possible the people lived in skin tents, which afforded little protection from the cold and winds of late fall. Before the end of October the preferred type of snow, firm but not densely packed, usually was available, and it was cut into blocks with a snow knife. These knives probably were made from antler and edged with ice for sharpness. The blocks were about thirty inches long, twenty inches high, and eight inches thick; preferably they were cut by one man and fitted into place by another. The blocks were cut from the floor area, within a circle thirteen or more feet in diameter. After the first row of blocks was in place, the blocks were cut to slope inward. The succeeding blocks also were trimmed and pushed firmly into place. When the last block was fitted into the dome top, the builder, who was encased in the house, cut an opening that became the entryway. The gaps in ill-fitted blocks were chinked with snow, and finally, the women piled loose snow outside against the lower part of the wall with wooden shovels. Over the entrance a block of clear ice replaced a block of snow and served as the window. Next an entrance passage was built with its floor at a level somewhat lower than the house floor to hold out the colder air. Storage rooms were built off the tunnel, and blocks of snow were piled outside the tunnel entrance as a windbreak. A small room to use for cooking was added to the side of the house.

At the back of a snowhouse was a snow platform covered with a mat of willows and caribou skins. Additional caribou skin covers were rolled up against the rear platform during the day. It was here that a family slept, ate, lounged, and, in short, lived. A man stretched out on the platform with his back against the rolled skins; women customarily sat with their legs tucked beneath them and children were everywhere.

When the spring thaw made a snowhouse unlivable, the family erected a tent. The conical caribou skin tent (tepee), with the hair side out, was built around a frame of about eight poles some thirteen feet in length; a flap of caribou skin served as the door. The family slept and lounged at the rear of a tent on caribou skins. To the left of the entrance was a stone-lined fireplace. A tent was occupied by one family or less often by small, related families. Once the

73
Aboriginal Life

Plate 3–2 People living in a skin tent near Padlei in 1959.
(Photograph by the author)

winter's snows had left and it was possible to camp on high ground, families moved their tents to ridges where the mosquitoes were less bothersome and where they could watch for caribou and Indians.

HOUSEHOLD ACTIVITIES   The kitchen compartment of a snowhouse had a conical roof with an opening at the top to create a draft for the fire. Women cooked on flat stones, using as fuel twigs from small plants and dry moss but never oil. A fire was lighted by striking pieces of iron pyrite together or else was kindled with a strap drill. Before being boiled, meat and fish were cut into chunks with a woman's knife or *ulu*, a half-moon slate-bladed knife hafted in a wooden handle. When fuel was scarce in the winter, fresh fish and meat might be eaten raw. Popular food included raw caribou kidneys, liver, marrow, and fat from the back of an animal taken in the fall. Most parts of a caribou were considered edible; the eyes were eaten raw, as were the contents of the stomach and the fly larvae in the skin; the hoofs were boiled, as were the brains and intestines. Excrement was not eaten deliberately, but if it found its way into the cooking pot it was not avoided. Meat was served on oblong wooden trays, where it cooled, and men ate before women. A man took a piece of meat in hand, stuffed as much as possible into his mouth, and cut off the surplus with a knife. Marrow was extracted with a long bone probe after

The Caribou Eskimos: Hunters on the Tundra

cracking one bone against another. A musk-ox horn ladle full of soup was passed from one person to the next to sip. Water was stored in skin pails and ladled out with a dipper. In the spring water was sipped through a bird-bone tube to prevent one's lips from cracking in the dry air. After a meal was completed, each person wiped his fingers on a bird skin.

In a snowhouse a woman's constant responsibility was tending the lamp, which was made from a flat stone or a piece of soapstone hollowed into a saucer shape. The fuel, most often caribou fat, burned at the end of a cone-shaped moss wick. It is significant that even when seal oil was available it was not used as fuel and that these Eskimos did not cook over lamps, using them solely to provide heat. Although a snowhouse was not purposefully heated, it was relatively warm. The interior temperature rose to and remained at about twenty-five degrees Fahrenheit in spite of temperatures of from twenty to fifty degrees below zero outside. The insulation provided by the snow, the absence of a direct opening to the outside, the body heat of the occupants, and heat from the lamp warmed the dwelling.

Women possessed a well developed body of knowledge and accompanying skills for processing skins. After a caribou had been killed and skinned, the hide was dried and stored for future use. When it was time to prepare a hide further, the woman slept with the skin side next to her body for a night to soften it. She then scraped the inner surface with a caribou scapula to remove the subcutaneous fibers and fat, and after draping the skin over her thigh, she

Plate 3–3 A woman near Padlei cooking in a brush and caribou skin shelter in 1959. (Photograph by the author)

went over it vigorously with a piece of sandstone. The skin was wrung by hand after being moistened and was scraped again the following day. A skin to be dehaired before making a kayak cover or summer boots was softened first by placing it on the house platform to be sat and slept on. The next step was to soak it in water for a few days, after which the hair could be scraped off easily. Skins were sewn with an eyed needle made of caribou bone and thread consisting of sinew from the back of a caribou.

CONVEYANCES   Survival on the Barrens depended to a large degree on being mobile during the long winter to hunt and to retrieve cached supplies of meat. Caribou Eskimos ranged widely by using dogs to pull their sleds, which looked like ladders more than anything else. The spruce runners were as much as thirty feet long and were set parallel about seventeen inches apart. Nearly a quarter of the distance from the front, the first of some twenty crosspieces was lashed with thongs through holes drilled in the runners beneath. In front of the first crosspiece was a rawhide line, and onto it the traces to individual dogs were attached. Most families had about three dogs, for it was difficult to feed more. Dogs were fed once a day or less often during the winter; they were left to roam unfed in the summer, at which time they hunted small animals and ate human feces to survive. In all likelihood some dogs had a strain of wolf blood, and while they were not vicious neither were they friendly. The Eskimo attitude toward dogs was one of detached interest. A man whipped a dog that did not pull his share of a load, but he would not kill a dog or utilize its skin in any manner. Individual dogs were named, often with names of persons. Each team had its lead dog, chosen for its knowledge, as well as a "boss" dog who dominated the other members of the team but was not necessarily the lead dog. When not in use, a sled was placed on pillars of snow blocks above the reach of the perennially hungry dogs.

In the spring the last winter camp was abandoned, and the family's possessions were carried across the tundra to a summer camp. They did not make the large, open skin boats (*umiaks*) so common among most Eskimos, due probably to the nature of the drainage systems and the fast water. All of the people and dogs, except for infants, the aged, and puppies, carried something. Dogs either dragged tent poles or carried two small packs of caribou skin, one on either side of their backs. The men and women were loaded with bundles of equipment carried on their backs. During the summer families were generally dispersed, but whenever game was plentiful in one locality, they camped near one another. When the weather was warm and pleasant, the women cooked and scraped skins outside, protected by a windbreak of brush. If hunting had been productive, men lounged about the tent, but when meat was in short supply, they ranged far from camp to hunt alone. If a man was unable to return home the same day, he slept in the open, drawing his arms inside his parka for warmth.

The Caribou Eskimos: Hunters on the Tundra

SUBSISTENCE ACTIVITIES   Caribou obviously were the focus of the economic lives of these people, and without caribou their precarious existence would have been impossible. Thus by describing the ways in which caribou molded their lives, we begin to understand the essence of their culture. It was said by knowledgeable elders that there once was a time when caribou did not exist, but then a man cut a great hole in the earth because he wished for caribou. From this opening caribou emerged until the earth was nearly covered with them, and the man closed the hole. This origin of caribou enabled people to live on the Barrens. Since caribou were creatures of the earth, from out of the earth, they existed independently of direct human or supernatural control.

A settlement consisting of four or five snowhouses was the winter-long residence if the families had caches of caribou meat in the vicinity. Yet the men did not rely solely on their meat reserves, but hunted caribou throughout the winter since small scattered herds often remained on the Barrens. For a winter hunting excursion a man used a short form of the ladder sled, on which he placed his bow and quivered arrows. The bow was fashioned from a shaft of wood, and along the length of the front, strips of sinew held in place with half-hitches served to strengthen the bow, which was strung with a sinew cord. The wooden arrow shafts were tipped with barbless antler points and vaned with feathers. The effective range of an arrow was up to about sixty-five feet, which meant that a hunter stalked an animal or waited until it wandered extremely near; either technique was difficult since caribou normally were wary during the winter months.

When winter meat supplies were low and caribou could not be located, the only option was to fish through the ice. Winter settlements were established with this alternative in mind. Ice fishing did not appeal to these Eskimos, for the rewards were few and the effort tedious. Winter fishing meant cutting an oblong hole in the ice with an ice pick at a spot where fish were likely to congregate along a river or more often in a lake. A lure fashioned from a fish skin so that it inflated as it faced the flow of water was raised and lowered on a line by the fisherman, who stood poised above with a fish spear (leister). A fish attempting to take the lure was impaled on the leister. A second fishing method involved using a barbless hook on a bone shank that was attached to a sinew line paid out from an antler reel. Fishing for whitefish and lake trout could be rewarding or very unprofitable. Without caribou meat, however, the choice was to fish or to starve.

Life was in greatest jeopardy during the spring when starvation was most expected. Before the caribou began to arrive on their spring migration, people hunted ptarmigan to tide them over this very lean period. These birds might be stunned with stones or more often shot with blunted arrows.

The people anxiously awaited the first sighting of caribou moving northward on a migration route that was eight hundred miles long. Even when caribou were only a short distance away the hunters did not rush to the kill but waited until animals wandered near. To a people who encountered privations so often, it mattered little if one suffered hunger for a few more days. In the late spring when the herds came within easy reach they were hunted but not with persistence. After numerous animals had been killed, the people became unrestrained gluttons until the supply of meat was exhausted. Only then did they once again worry about the problem of food.

In the summer, migratory waterfowl as well as fish provided a change in the normal diet of caribou meat. Molting waterfowl were pursued by kayak and killed by hand when they were exhausted. They also were taken with bird spears, which had two barbed prongs attached to the end of a wooden shaft; these spears were hurled with the aid of throwing-boards. In the summer arctic char ascended certain rivers to spawn, and as fall approached they returned to the sea. In river shallows stone weirs were built to trap these fish in basins, where they were taken with leisters. Fishweirs belonged to their makers, but they could be used by anyone. Fish also were taken in shallow waters with gorge sets. A short piece of caribou leg bone was sharpened at each end to form the gorge, and a piece of fish skin was attached over it. The baited gorge was tied to a line with a float attached and placed in the water. A fish seized and swallowed the skin-covered gorge, which toggled in its stomach to hold the fish fast.

Fall was the time of year that hunters most anticipated. Caribou were fat, their skins prime, and they moved in vast herds. It was the success or failure of the fall hunt that predicted whether the members of a camp would thrive, barely survive, or starve during the winter to come. The families moved to a locality where caribou were likely to pass, such as where a lake narrowed. A man trusted his judgment and experience to help him determine the right time and place to intercept the migrating animals. One method of fall caribou hunting involved the use of converging lines of stone cairns. The cairns technically were owned by their builders but might be used by anyone. The women and children slipped behind a herd, driving it by shouting toward the cairns, which were hidden by a ridge. Passing over the crest of the ridge and seeing the cairns, the caribou assumed that they were people and nervously kept within the boundaries, thereby converging on the spot where the hunters were hiding with their bows and arrows. Cairns also were used to guide caribou into a lake or river where hunters waited in their kayaks. Once the animals were in the water the hunters approached rapidly, using double-bladed paddles, and dispatched great numbers, even thousands, with spears. In the late fall when a thin layer of ice had formed on lakes, caribou were driven onto the ice, where they broke through and were killed easily.

When caribou mated in October, mature bulls jealously guarded the females in their company and attempted to keep other males away by force. At this time a hunter sometimes held a set of caribou antlers over his head and imitated the grunting of a bull. A bull caribou protecting his females would approach the disguised man much nearer than normal and could be shot with an arrow. After a reasonably heavy snowfall covered the ground, a solitary

The Caribou Eskimos: Hunters on the Tundra

Plate 3–4 An old man near Padlei in 1959. Caribou meat is cooking in the foreground and is being sun dried in the background. (Photograph by the author)

snow cairn was used to attract curious caribou. On the path to the cairn a pitfall was dug in the snow, and any animal walking up the slope to investigate the cairn fell into the pit and was trapped. This method was successful only when caribou were so numerous that they were not too cautious. With all of these fall hunting techniques more animals usually were killed than could serve immediate needs, and a hunter cached his surpluses. Boulders were cleared from a spot, and a layer of old bones was placed on the ground to form a rack for air to circulate beneath. The meat was laid on top of the bones, and boulders were placed over the pile to prevent foxes from eating the meat. Scattered about the camp of a successful hunter were many such caches, topped with a caribou's head.

The only other large land mammal hunted was the musk-ox, but it did not range widely over the Barrens and does not appear to have been very plentiful. When a herd was discovered, the usual pattern was to release dogs to bring the musk-oxen to bay. These shaggy monsters formed a defensive circle with their heads facing outward. In this position they were killed readily with spears or arrows. An entire herd could be taken since any live animal stood guard over its fallen companions.

SOCIAL DIMENSIONS   The fondness of Eskimos for the company of relatives, friends, neighbors, and nearly anyone else who was not a threat is legendary. Their genuine and infectious warmth led families to camp together whenever food was abundant, but large camps could not be maintained very long. Therefore, social life was organized around the nuclear family. In this as in all human societies the division of labor was based on sex and age. The duties of women and men were distinct, but neither was unwilling to aid the other. The work of men required hard physical effort, but it was interspersed with periods of comparative leisure; the working pattern of women was one of sustained but less strenuous activity. Men built snowhouses; women caulked the holes and shoveled snow around the base. Women usually pitched the tents; men hunted. Both men and women dressed skins. Both sexes fished, but men did so more often. Women were responsible for raising the children, sewing, and cooking, whereas men drove the dog teams and manufactured artifacts. Since the family's welfare was largely in the hands of the male as the hunter and provider, his decisions guided family life, but a woman had a significant voice in family affairs.

Social control was not a major concern, but on occasion it was necessary to take some action against a nonconformist. The difficulty in dealing with abnormal behavior was that social expectations were vague and no individual had any effective control over others. Certain guidelines, while not precisely conceived by the people, did regulate community activities. There were rules for the division of game, and each man was expected to hunt unless he was physically ill or aged. Also, no one could settle at a camp without the consent of established residents. Obviously the distribution of food was a matter of primary concern. When starvation threatened, all food belonged equally to the community members, and another person's meat caches could be opened with impunity. A lazy man who did not provide food for his family soon was deserted by his wife and children. Such an individual did not starve because someone always would feed him, but he was considered a worthless person. If as sometimes happened an individual was a good hunter but refused to share his take with others, he was considered antisocial. Mild ridicule probably would be followed by a derisive song, and if that did not have the desired effect, he would be ostracized as socially undesirable.

The social conventions arising from custom granted the individual a great deal of freedom; he literally was responsible to no man in the ordinary course of life. Political action in its usual sense did not exist since no adult was vested with authority or power to control others; conformity was induced by subtle means that did not require force. Songs of derision were important in bringing problems into the open and reducing tensions. After any bountiful evening meal, someone was likely to sing. A drum was found for accompaniment, and the course of the evening was set. Songs were sung by men, and women formed the chorus. A man usually sang and danced at the same time; he moved his feet very little but swayed back and forward from the waist as the drum was struck in a series of single beats. The songs frequently were about hunting caribou or musk-oxen; they might be remembrances of great hunts in the past. Some songs exposed the behavior of others to public scrutiny; these were biting and very much to the point. Usually the victim took the criticism in stride, although fist fights did sometimes result. Such songs included as their subject matter a man hiding food from his wife; illicit sexual relations; a man leaving his family to starve; and a man losing an argument to his wife. In each instance the actions of the offender were not punished except by exposure to ridicule.

Although derisive songs sufficed in most instances to cope with problem behavior, songs were not enough when a murder had been committed. In theory, each murder required blood revenge against the offender or his immediate family, but after it had been exacted no further retaliation was sanctioned, which avoided blood feuds. Under unusual conditions it was possible for murders to go unavenged. An instance of this nature was recorded by Knud Rasmussen. A man planned to marry a girl, but her family arranged her marriage to another man since they did not care for her suitor. The rejected individual went to the igloo of the girl he hoped to marry and killed her father, mother, two brothers, and their wives; afterwards he took the girl as his wife. The man who committed this mass murder was no ordinary individual. Rasmussen (1930, 33) met him when he was older and wrote that the man was "wise, independent, intelligent and exercised great authority over his fellow-villagers." Thus, the response to murder was tempered by the individual's personality and the circumstances. Geert van den Steenhoven (1962, 104), who investigated traditional Caribou Eskimo law in the 1950s, recorded that a highly respected man said that "In case of dispute, I rather would run away than fight." In order to rid themselves of "one for whom we do not care" they would move camp suddenly without notifying the offender, simply to avoid his distasteful behavior in the future.

The only other antisocial behavior worthy of comment was theft, but it was not a source of great anxiety. In a society such as this, where possessions were few and each person's belongings were known to everyone, thefts could not go undetected. A man owned his weapons, clothing, kayak, and tools, while a woman owned her lamp, clothing, cooking pot, and household items; both a man and woman might own dogs. If someone borrowed an item and it broke or was unreturnable for some other reason, the owner would not object; by releasing the artifact in the first place, he demonstrated that he had no absolute need for it. However, if something was taken without permission, this was theft, and the owner probably would ask for it back. A person who stole repeatedly was looked on simply as a strange person.

SUPERNATURALISM   The affairs of people and animals alike were guided by one particular spirit, *Pinga*, "The One up in the Sky" who was especially concerned with man's relationship with caribou. Pinga was offended when men were careless or wasteful in handling caribou that they had killed; therefore, it was necessary to cover all evidence that a kill had taken place. It was essential, too, for the killer of a caribou to leave a piece of meat and fat beneath a nearby stone to appease the animal's soul. Dogs were prohibited from eating the muzzle of a caribou or chewing its bones or antler. No matter how attentive a man was to these and the other rules pertaining to caribou, he had no hope of controlling their migrations, because these were guided by the caribou themselves.

The only part-time specialists were shamans, who acquired their power through the effective control of spirits and were able to heal people of diseases and perform acts of magic. Rasmussen's account of one shaman's training is an enlightening document. This individual chose to gain his power by enduring hunger and suffering from cold, although he could have elected to be "drowned" or "killed" to become a wise man. This man, the same person who committed the mass murder related earlier, was instructed by his father-in-law, not the man he killed but the father of another wife. The instructor took the novice to an isolated spot and built a tiny snowhouse for him. After the novice shaman sat alone in the unheated igloo for five days, he was brought a little warm water. Fifteen days later he was again given warm water, and finally after ten more days he was permitted to eat. All during his isolation he concentrated on his desire to become a shaman so that Pinga would "own" him. A helping spirit appeared to him after about thirty days, and he slowly regained his strength. Only after a year was he permitted to sleep with his wife and eat normally. To diagnose a case or see into the future he wandered about the countryside for two or three days, eating little and seldom resting. Each morning he returned to camp and reported his progress, only to leave again in search of answers. He was aided not only by Pinga but by *Hila* as well. The latter was in many ways confused with Pinga, whose special charge was caribou; Hila was everything feared, as the cold when the sun was gone or the storms that brought enforced inactivity with the possibility of starvation.

A shaman wore a special belt to which he attached amulets received from diverse individuals, and a special wooden shaft was a part of his equipment. The shaft was tied to his belt and served as an entry path for spirit aids from the ground. The shaft also was used for divining; questions were asked and the answers judged by presumed differences in the shaft's weight. It was believed that all disease was of supernatural origin but at the same time there were a few secular cures for injuries. For example, fat from a wolf and burnt moss from a lamp were applied to frostbite, broken limbs were splinted, and wounds were bandaged with animal membrane. In most instances of sickness a shaman held a séance to establish what taboos a patient must observe to ensure recovery.

DESCENT, KINSHIP, AND MARRIAGE   The system for designating near relatives consisted of distinct terms for nearly every close category of kin.

The Caribou Eskimos: Hunters on the Tundra

For individuals on the generational level above Ego there were different words for father, mother, maternal aunts and uncles, as well as paternal aunts and uncles (bifurcate collateral terms). On Ego's generational level there were distinctive words for older brothers, younger ones, older sisters, and younger ones. Maternal cousins were termed differently from paternal cousins, but there was no differentiation by sex for cousins; the cousin terms do not fit into any common type. Many Eskimos have "Eskimo" cousin terms, which are of the type found in the United States today, but the Caribou Eskimos are an exception, as are most Alaskan Eskimos. The terms alone suggest a highly fragmented set of role expectations from kin. Close relatives were conceived separately except for the terminological grouping of cousins. Likewise the terms for wife and temporary wife were different; nearly a quarter of the men had two wives. Relatives were traced along both the male and female lines (bilateral descent), which provided a widespread network of kinship obligations.

A newly wedded couple most often attached themselves to the household of the husband (temporary patrilocal residence), but this arrangement was flexible. As soon as a couple was able, they set up their own separate household (neolocal residence). It was not at all unusual for the partners to separate and remarry someone else. When there were children in a family, they accompanied the mother; however, the presence of children tended to keep a couple together. Apparently a man married his brother's wife (levirate) if his brother died. A man left his wife in the care of his brother if she could not accompany him when he traveled. Men also exchanged wives for short or long periods, which led to binding friendships between the men involved. However, a woman was not free to make such an arrangement since this would be an infringement on her husband's rights.

ENTERTAINMENT   During leisure time the most common diversion was to lounge and chat, but games were played in the evenings or on nonworking days. The day after a shaman had held a séance no one hunted, but adults played a ring and pin game. A thong was suspended from the ceiling with a strip of antler tied to it, and the lower part of the thong was weighted with a stone. A hole was drilled through a midpoint of the antler, and the object of the game was for the assembled men and women to penetrate the hole with any pointed object thrust at the moving antler. Since one's hand was likely to be pierced by the probes of others, a mitten was worn for protection. A stake was put up, and the winner offered the next prize. The stake was sometimes an item of little value, but it could also be very valuable. Caribou Eskimos were avid gamblers, playing different games for stakes. A form of roulette was played with a soup ladle. The ladle was spun in the center of a circle of players, and the winner was the individual whom the handle faced when it stopped spinning. They had a hand game, in which one's hands were placed behind his back and a stone shifted from one palm to another; the object was to guess which hand concealed the stone when they were both placed in front again. The intensity with which a man gambled sometimes resulted in the loss of many possessions, even one's sled, dogs, or wife. Pastimes engaged in for pleasure alone included making cat's cradles, playing ball games, and testing one's strength by pulling an opponent.

LIFE CYCLE   Particular conventions surrounded pregnancy and birth to ensure a safe delivery and a healthy offspring. For example, as the time of delivery approached, a woman untied her hair as a means of facilitating the birth. An offspring was born in the family residence, and the mother was aided by experienced women. One held her hands as the second applied downward pressure to hasten the delivery. The infant was wiped with bird skins, and the umbilical cord was severed with a piece of quartz. The afterbirth was hidden to prevent dogs from eating it. For the next month the mother was restricted to the dwelling and could not sleep with her husband. In addition she cooked and ate from containers that were separate from those of other family members. Following her confinement she threw away all the skins and clothing that had touched her body. Infanticide rarely was practiced, probably because the infant mortality rate was high.

Names were not associated with a particular sex. Before an offspring was born, it was named after a recently deceased individual. As soon after an infant's birth as possible, it began to acquire amulets. These usually were bird or animal skins or insects that had been caught unharmed. The particular species that served a person in this manner could not be killed by him. These skins or insects were sewn into skin bags attached to the inner parka.

Children were neither physically nor verbally punished until they were about seven years old and began to understand adult values. If a child misbehaved, he was threatened with the hare as a "bogey man," and if this ruse failed, the parents simply allowed the child to have his own way. Children played games that were imitations of adult pursuits, using small sleds, kayaks, and snow knives. They also had toys designed for entertainment alone. A buzz was made from a piece of sinew looped through two holes in a circular piece of skin. An oblong piece of wood with notched edges was attached to a sinew cord and made a whistling sound as it was twirled; this was a bullroarer, which to some other peoples was a sacred object. Girls owned dolls dressed in skin clothing to resemble men or women. They might entertain each other by flipping their fingernails against their teeth, to produce a variety of different tones. They enjoyed swinging around until they became dizzy, and they also danced the "cossack" step for fun.

At the onset of a girl's menarche she changed to an adult style parka and was subject to the food taboos for a menstruating woman. Boys passed into adolescence without formal recognition of the physiological change. When a boy actively hunted caribou, he was on the path to manhood. The first caribou he killed was butchered inside a dwelling, which normally was forbidden, and the meat was eaten by all except women and children. Marriage, which was without ceremony, took place as soon as the man was able to support a

84

The Caribou Eskimos: Hunters on the Tundra

Plate 3–5 A man and his wife repairing a kayak near Padlei in 1959 as their son looks on. (Photograph by the author)

wife. Although there were no clearly established prohibitions against marrying a near relative, it seems unlikely that couples were more closely related than second cousins. Infant betrothals were the rule, and persons with the same name were prohibited from marrying. It was customary for a man to present his father-in-law with material goods as compensation for the loss of a daughter.

The physical hardships, starvations, and discomforts of life limited the productive years of an adult, and as a result few persons attained old age. When an individual was old or became infirm, he or she remained as active as possible but realized that death was not far off. Caribou Eskimos did not as a rule kill old people (senilicide). Individuals sometimes were abandoned to die alone, but this was not the common practice encountered among some other Eskimos. It was more customary for an old or ill person to commit suicide by hanging, often aided by a dutiful relative. More taboos surrounded handling the dead than any other facet of social life. When someone died, the survivors behaved in a precise manner to avoid further deaths in the settlement. Although men continued to hunt caribou, no one could drive a sled, and many food taboos were observed. The body of a person who died during the day was removed from the snowhouse or tent as soon as possible. If the death was at night, a man's body remained at the back of the dwelling for three days and a woman's body for five days. Mourning women loosened their hair, and the survivors wailed when a corpse was in the house. To insure that the soul of the deceased would not harm the living during this period, each person slept with a knife beneath his head. During these three or five days, the household possessions were placed outside to air. Only old women and young girls handled the body, and they wore mittens when they flexed the corpse and shrouded it in a skin. The body was removed through an opening made at the back of a snowhouse or tent and was taken to the place of burial by near relatives, who plugged their nostrils with caribou hair. Some graves were ringed with stones, and other bodies were covered with a pile of stones. A long pole was set obliquely in the ground at one end of a grave. Grave goods were included in the burial, but some property of the deceased was divided among the survivors. Numerous food and behavioral prohibitions were observed by surviving housemates, but these usually were of brief duration, except that bone and wood could not be cut with a knife for a year. Souls of the dead traveled off to Pinga, who returned them to earth as another person or in animal form.

COASTAL ADAPTATIONS   Thus far mention of the few Caribou Eskimos who visited the coast as a part of their economic activities has been avoided to eliminate confusion, but it should be noted that some of these people utilized maritime resources. By the early 1920s only two families remained at the coast throughout the year, and the members of one particular band visited the coast each summer to hunt seals and walrus. It should be emphasized, however, that seal blubber rarely was burned in lamps and seal meat was considered fit for dogs more than for people. Furthermore, kayak covers were made of dehaired caribou skin but not of the superior sealskin. Thus it appears that the coastal side of their economic life was relatively unimportant.

Early Historic Changes

FUR TRADE   History came late to these Eskimos of the Barrens, and the life-style just described prevailed into the 1920s. After this time their future became quite uncertain. It was no longer simply a matter of successfully intercepting caribou herds to obtain the necessities of life. The procurement of exotic clothing, matches, steel-bladed tools and ornaments seen at trading posts became an increasingly important goal. The market for caribou skins was insignificant compared with that for white fox pelts. The white fox pelt was the only item of economic importance to persons beyond the Barrens. With these furs the people could obtain goods that traders brought into their country. Exotic manufactures long had been known; perhaps the first iron was obtained from the vessel and structures left by Jens Munch when he wintered at the mouth of the Churchill River in 1619–1620. With the establishment of the English at Fort Prince of Wales in the early 1700s trading sloops were sent north-

The Caribou Eskimos: Hunters on the Tundra

ward along the coast, and some Caribou Eskimos began to obtain important goods. These trips were highly irregular, but by the end of the century some of the more southerly bands traded at Fort Prince of Wales. Then the trading sloops began to frequent the western shore of Hudson Bay more often, and in the late 1800s commercial whalers often wintered there. In the 1920s there were Hudson's Bay Company stores at Chesterfield Inlet, Baker Lake, Eskimo Point, and elsewhere; by this time the pattern for the future had become ominously apparent.

The commitment of fashionable European and American women to fur coats, coupled with the presence of white fox on the Barrens and the Eskimos' desire for trade goods, joined two disparate sociocultural systems. The only means that the people had to obtain material items was by trapping fox. Their decision to do so caused a chain reaction in their culture. In order to encourage fox trapping the traders furnished men with traps, other equipment, and food on credit against their potential catch. One of the first purchases by a hunter was a rifle and ammunition, for in theory a man with a gun could hunt caribou much more efficiently. At this point the picture seemed bright. An individual could even obtain merchandise from a store, trade it to more distant peoples who did not have access to European goods, and thereby reap a great profit. However, the Eskimos had no foresight concerning the future, and the Hudson's Bay Company was more concerned with immediate profits than with what was happening to the people.

RIFLES AND STARVATION   As strange as it might seem, the rifle worked to the detriment of the Caribou Eskimos. Shooting caribou with guns at their traditional crossing places apparently led to shifts in migration patterns, and the herds could no longer be intercepted as of old. Indians in the south also had rifles, and they killed many caribou at their wintering grounds. Caribou were increasingly scarce, but fox usually were abundant. Taking fox was difficult because a man was obligated to feed his family and at the same time range from a base camp to tend his traps. To do this he required food from a store, and although credit was obtainable, adequate amounts were given only to the best trappers. Some years fox were abundant, and when the prices for pelts were high, the people could obtain great quantities of material goods and food from traders. A trapper took his catch to a trader and was given trade goods immediately; he did not handle money nor was he encouraged to have credit on his side of the account. A trader always attempted to keep a trapper in debt. Thus Eskimos bought canned meats and other imported foods at astoundingly high prices, and a few men even purchased such items as harmoniums. Trapping successes drastically reduced the physical mobility of a family since they acquired more goods than they could move. Even more unfair, or more incomprehensible from the Eskimo's view, fox prices fluctuated widely from year to year. However, a trader always bought pelts since the company could store skins against the time that the world market price would rise; traders made every effort to keep the Eskimos trapping. Gambling with fox, caribou, and rifles under these conditions was fatal for the Caribou Eskimos. In years when caribou could not be intercepted and fox prices were low, a man might be unable to obtain enough food from the trader, and his family would go hungry or even starve. Even when the price of fox pelts was high, if caribou could not be located and killed for food during the trapping season, a family's survival hung in doubt. It often is said, and probably is true, that men have been found who starved to death with hundreds and even thousands of dollars' worth of fox pelts in their possession.

In 1919 one-fifth of the Caribou Eskimos died of starvation.

The most important weapons and facilities for hunting and trapping were the rifle and steel trap, respectively. Novel means for taking game included the famous blood knife. A sharp steel knife was covered with a coating of blood and set in the snow with the blade upward. A wolf smelled out the blood and licked the blade to obtain it, cutting his tongue in the process and eventually bleeding to death. One change in the hunting pattern of old was the Canadian government's prohibition on taking musk-oxen. Since musk-oxen were never very important, this restriction was not critical. Traders introduced gill nets, which greatly increased the fish catch, but since there was a prohibition against eating fish that had died in a net, some of the value of the innovation was negated. Commercially manufactured canoes made it possible to carry heavy loads by water, but the weight of the vessels and the large number of rapids in the rivers tended to minimize their importance. Whaleboats were advantageous for coastal travel, but the people did not become confident sailors along Hudson Bay.

By the early 1920s canvas tents with ridgepoles began to make their appearance, and the ubiquitous primus stove was used for cooking. New dietary items included bannock made from flour and baking powder; this was the staple when nothing else was available. Tea had become a very popular beverage, and the people drank it in great quantities. The Caribou Eskimos became inveterate smokers from a very tender age. They mixed tobacco with dried and cut whortleberry leaves and smoked the combination in a monitor type pipe. The bowl was made from soapstone mounted above an opened cartridge that had been fitted into a wooden bowl.

MISSIONARIES   Traders were the first influence from the world beyond the Barrens, and they were followed by missionaries. The most active group in this sector of Canada was the Oblate order of the Roman Catholic Church. They had a mission among the Chipewyan in 1846 along Lake Ile a la Crosse, and Father Alphonse Gasté visited the Caribou Eskimos in 1868. In 1912 the Hudson's Bay Company and the Oblates established themselves at Chesterfield Inlet among the more northerly segment of the Caribou Eskimos. It was to the distinct advantage of the priests to found stations at trading posts since Eskimos visited the stores and the missionaries could contact them there.

The first mass held by the Oblates at Chesterfield Inlet was regarded by the Eskimos as a striking example of sorcery, but the missionaries were unaware of their impression on the people. Missionaries were regarded as shamans capable of killing Eskimos who offended them, and thus it was necessary to tolerate their presence. It became apparent to the priests that to convey any meaningful understanding of their purpose they must learn the language of the people. By 1915 Father Turquetil preached a sermon in Eskimo, but the people remained unconvinced of his sincerity, especially since the trader, who probably was both Scottish and protestant, told them he did not believe in the teachings of the priest. Furthermore the trader maintained that the priests were insane and had come to preach their madness to the Eskimos. This description of the Hudson's Bay Company trader was written by an Oblate priest in a history of their northern mission. While it may come as a surprise, there is no reason to question its validity. This exemplifies the type of problem faced by the missionaries in dealing not only with the people whom they hoped to convert but with other whites. It is no wonder that the first Eskimos were not baptized until 1917.

CONTRASTING BELIEF SYSTEMS   Some of the differences between the supernatural systems of the aboriginal Caribou Eskimos and the Roman Catholic missionaries are worth consideration. The gulf between Western and Eskimo culture was indeed wide. Many complex core ideas about Christianity had no counterparts in the experience of Eskimos. This was a formidable obstruction, for even though the priests spoke Eskimo, new means of expression had to be created for new concepts. The priests were full-time specialists in dealing with the supernatural, which was unheard-of among Eskimos, and they did things no rational being would do. They handled the dead without fear and were sympathetic and helpful to people whom the Eskimos regarded as of little social worth. The success of the missionaries was due largely to their deep devotion to their duty and to the Eskimos' final realization that these truly were good men.

The Caribou Eskimos were still inland hunters and trappers when they were visited by the young Canadian writer Farley Mowat and the gifted photographer Richard Harrington. In 1935, at the age of fifteen, Mowat had traveled to the edge of the Barrens and after World War II he was determined to return to the interior. He flew to Nueltin Lake and visited an Eskimo camp briefly in the spring of 1947, and he spent the next summer in the same locality. Mowat wrote a series of articles about these Eskimos, and in 1952 he published a book titled *People of the Deer*. It includes descriptions of the country and the caribou, but most of all it is about the Caribou Eskimo band called the Ahearmiut (Ihalmiut) who lived to the north and west of Nueltin Lake. The book describes the decline of the people as a result of disastrous famines. Mowat vividly conveyed the plight of the Caribou Eskimos. He hoped to convince Canadian and American readers that these people were being destroyed by starvation through bungling governmental policies and greedy traders. He could see that the same process was taking place elsewhere in the Canadian arctic, and he hoped to avert repetition of the tragedy.

In the winter of 1950 Richard Harrington traveled to Padlei and visited the surrounding Eskimo camps. The inland area was one of desolation where starvation loomed. At the Padlei post a fox pelt was worth $3.75, caribou were rare in the vicinity and had been scarce on their fall migration, while fish could not provide a sustaining diet. The thirty Eskimos around the post were receiving Destitute Rations of flour or rolled oats. This was a poor substitute for caribou meat, and yet it kept the people from starving. Their dogs, however, had starved, and without the mobility provided by a dog team, fox could not be trapped in numbers nor could caribou be hunted efficiently. The pictures that Harrington took were printed, along with his stories of the starvation, and the ensuing attention directed to the Barrens and its people brought from the outside world a temporary relief.

Modern Life

ESKIMO POINT HISTORY   Developments at the community of Eskimo Point along Hudson Bay encapsulate much of what has happened among the Caribou Eskimos in the recent past. For many years the Hudson's Bay Company sent trading vessels to the vicinity of Eskimo Point, and a store was built nearby in 1923. A year later a Roman Catholic mission was founded by the Oblate priest, Lionel Ducharme, who had served earlier at the Chesterfield Inlet mission. In 1926 an Anglican Church mission was established by Reverend Donald B. Marsh, and in 1928 the entire settlement was relocated to the present site. A Royal Canadian Mounted Police post built at Eskimo Point in 1936 completed the Canadian representation.

Through the early 1950s Caribou Eskimos visited Eskimo Point to trade, but none were year-round residents. Apparently the food stresses of the late 1940s and early 1950s first led some families to use the settlement as a central base from which to hunt and fish. In the late 1950s numerous interior people starved, and others were murdered as people struggled to remain alive in these times of trauma. Survivors were drawn to Eskimo Point, where they knew that they would be fed by traders, missionaries, and government representatives. By 1959 about 165 Caribou Eskimos lived at Eskimo Point along with thirty Canadians and an equal number of Eskimos from more northerly settlements. While the Caribou Eskimo population fluctuated somewhat depending on the accessibility of caribou, as a group these people were clearly and quickly abandoning their traditional lifeway. Eskimo Point, with its missionaries, police, and trader, emerged as a Federal administrative center. Local representatives of the Department of Northern Affairs and National Resources, subsequently designated the Department of Indian Affairs and Northern Development, were politically the most powerful group.

The remainder of this chapter stresses developments since the late 1950s, especially at Eskimo Point. The primary sources are the anthropological studies by James W. VanStone and Wendell H. Oswalt in 1959 and Valene L. Smith in 1969 plus a number of insightful reports prepared for the Federal Government. The purpose of the following text is to document the sweeping changes that have taken place among the Caribou Eskimos in the last generation.

CLOTHING   Canadian style clothing, as represented in the Hudson's Bay Company store inventory, prevailed by 1959. For men there were trousers, shirts, socks, sweaters, and jackets. Younger women and girls bought slacks, blouses, and sweaters, but older women preferred dresses of cotton print. Colorful shawls were worn by the women, and kerchiefs were popular. Light canvas was sewn to make parka covers, and duffel was made into footwear. Skin boots, shoes, and shoepacs were worn as well. Caribou skins were so scarce that it was difficult for families to make and maintain a set of garments for each hunter. By the late 1960s most garments were imported although parkas of skin and cloth continued to be made. In recent years caribou skins have become more plentiful, and a revival of aboriginal clothing styles has been attempted in formal sewing classes for children and adults. This is but one effort to perpetuate select aspects of Eskimo culture.

THE SETTLEMENT   In the late 1950s the physical plant was organized around Euro-Canadian institutions: the Anglican and Roman Catholic churches, Hudson's Bay Company store, Royal Canadian Mounted Police post, and Federal school. Most of the Eskimos lived in tents during the summer and snowhouses for the remainder of the year. The general pattern was for Christian Eskimos to cluster near the mission with which they were identified and for non-Christians to occupy property not controlled by a mission. The special constables of the R. C. M. P. lived in frame dwellings provided by the government, and the school janitor occupied a government-owned log house. Additionally in the late 1950s three Eskimo families lived throughout the year in jerry-built rectangular dwellings of wood, cardboard, and canvas. Four frame houses owned by Caribou Eskimos dated from a period of high fox prices; these rarely were occupied by their owners but served primarily as caches for equipment. The members of the households were nuclear families, although they might include one or more relatives of a husband or wife.

By 1961 about 240 Eskimos lived at Eskimo Point, and it became apparent that they were permanent residents. Since snowhouses were maladapted to life in large, stable communities, and since tents were cold, wet dwellings in late spring and fall, plans were made to introduce substantial, year-round dwellings. In 1963 the Federal Government began building the first houses for

Plate 3–6 A year-round Caribou Eskimo dwelling at Eskimo Point in 1959. (Photograph by the author)

the people; additional buildings constructed included a community hall, curling rink, bathing and laundry facilities, a water and garbage collection system, community power plant, adult education center, library, and a large airstrip. By 1975 nearly 900 Eskimos lived at Eskimo Point, and the buildings contrasted radically with those of the 1950s. Canadian institutional models dominated, and the people were "Caribou" Eskimos in name only.

CONVEYANCES   Formerly a man's mobility as a hunter and trapper depended largely on his ability to maintain a dog team. Neither caribou hunting nor fox trapping dominates their economic lives currently, and the snowmobile has replaced dog traction. Motorscooters and even a few automobiles have been introduced. Large canoes powered by outboard motors play an important part in summer travel, fishing, and sea mammal hunting.

SUBSISTENCE ACTIVITIES   Caribou hunting has ceased to be an important economic activity except during those years when caribou appear near the settlement. Stable economic alternatives to hunting must be found if the lives of most residents are to be imbued with meaning. Experimental whale hunting yielded such a slight return that it was discontinued. Mink ranching or reindeer herding are possible, but the potential for economic success through such enterprises, based on experience elsewhere in the far north, seems tenuous. Since white fox were plentiful along the coast and Caribou

The Caribou Eskimos: Hunters on the Tundra

Eskimos were superior trappers, it might appear that trapping could provide much-needed cash, but the steady decline in popularity of long-haired pelts has had an adverse effect on the market for fox pelts. In 1956 a skin brought about $11, which was less than the investment required for a trapper. Within a few years polar bear pelts were valued at as much as $450, but the government set a limit of four per year to be taken locally. Hunting skill did not guarantee this catch since the licenses were obtained by lottery. Sealskins were worth as much as fox pelts or more, but they could be obtained only during a brief period and by only the few men who were skilled enough to hunt safely among the ice floes. Fish were not plentiful, nets were expensive, and these people lacked a commitment to fishing.

Smith observed, "As the 1970's begin, the economic picture is not rosy, but neither is it alarming." Welfare payments had begun to decline, largely as a result of the creation of an Arts and Crafts Center that enabled individuals to earn cash. The program was initiated in 1965, and a large building served as a workshop, although individuals were encouraged to work at home. The most successful efforts have been in stone sculpturing, which previously had become a well-established craft enterprise in the Canadian arctic. The Caribou Eskimos had no aboriginal craft tradition of this nature, yet about seventy persons were soon able to earn about $75 each per month. Thirty others produced stone sculptures to supplement their earnings from other sources. In order to promote the growth of the craft, the governmental representative purchased each item produced regardless of its quality.

In essence intermittent hunting and fishing, service jobs, and welfare became the principal sources of income, and it appears that make-work and social welfare programs will dominate in the immediate future.

SOCIAL DIMENSIONS   Social life has continued to center in nuclear family households, which typically include a couple with two or three children. Most of the residents of Eskimo Point belonged to the Padleimiut band, but a distinction existed between those whose ties to the coast were old and others who had migrated from the interior only recently. The interior people were considered inferior by their more-established neighbors, but the differences between them were not of great significance. Another segment of the population consisted of coastal families who had long been associated with whites (Kabloona). They were termed "Kabloonarmiut" by other Eskimos and identified more with whites than with the remainder of the Padleimiut. The social interaction between Eskimos as a whole and the thirty adult whites tended to be formal but sincerely friendly; they did not visit in each other's homes, however. Whites referred to Eskimos by their Eskimo names, which included no surname; Eskimos spoke of whites by their family names.

The local bathhouse and laundromat became favorite places for people to meet and visit, and the community hall, where motion pictures were shown, was popular. Another focal point was the curling rink, curling being a favorite

Plate 3–7 A view of Eskimo Point in 1969. (Courtesy of Valene Smith)

sport in the Canadian arctic. These people appeared to feel increasingly identified with their community. Nothing reflected community spirit so much as the construction of an adequate airstrip. A government employee during his off hours prepared a rough airstrip with a bulldozer, but the large rocks and stones that remained on the field were dangerous for aircraft. "Stone-picking bees" were organized, and participation was intense. This cooperation eventually led to the completion of a 4000-foot runway with an apron and an airstrip that was serviceable throughout the year.

RELIGION   The factionalism that separates the largely Protestant English from the Catholic French in southern Canada also is found in the Canadian north. At Eskimo Point families belonging to the same Christian church, whether Roman Catholic or Anglican, tended to live near one another, with Roman Catholic integration apparently a bit stronger. The cohesiveness along religious lines was reinforced in the social halls maintained by the missions; these attracted members during their leisure. The Roman Catholic social hall was better equipped, better lighted, and more attractive than the one of the Anglicans, and Roman Catholic services were held daily. The Anglicans held services for their members only on Sunday. It is not surprising that the Roman Catholics developed stronger feelings of identity among their membership. The fact that there was no resident Anglican missionary between 1946 and 1957 led some families to abandon the Anglican Church. Religion as a focal point for social life was such that Roman Catholic and Anglican Eskimos tended not to marry each other, and until the Federal school began to

The Caribou Eskimos: Hunters on the Tundra

function in 1959, each of the missions maintained its own parochial school. The non-Christian Eskimos seemed to fall into one of two groups. Either they were not interested in Christianity and were successful materialists, or else they were unsuccessful providers of the type known as "tea and tobacco natives," meaning that their attitude toward religion was to consider either church as their own if they could gain materially from the identification.

One of the most dynamic religious leaders among the Caribou Eskimos, Reverend Armand Tagoona, is of Eskimo and German ancestry. He became a lay catechist at Baker Lake in the Anglican Church and later was ordained a minister and stationed at Eskimo Point. However he soon left the Anglican Church and organized his own congregation to be free of white domination. He has since built a church at Baker Lake and attracted a substantial following of Eskimos in central Canada. Tagoona is an extremely capable preacher who combines Christian beliefs with Eskimo philosophy and pragmatism. The day of white missionary power has passed in the north, and Tagoona represents a dynamic new voice for religion.

VALUES   Smith found that their heritage as hunters was deeply ingrained in the value system of the Caribou Eskimos, even after years at Eskimo Point. An able provider whose family prospered because of his hunting prowess had self-esteem and prestige. The mobility and freedom of a hunter contrasted strikingly with the sedentary life of a part-time wage earner. The attitudes of women about life at Eskimo Point appeared different from those of men. Women enjoyed sendentary village life with its relative economic secu-

Plate 3–8 Baker Lake community during the winter of 1976.
(Courtesy of Cheryl Kabloona)

rity, comfortable physical accommodations, and the intense social contacts, which contrasted with living in an isolated hunting camp. They had more leisure time, and some women were beginning to emerge as energetic leaders. An interesting and possibly not unimportant effort was initiated by males to perpetuate their roles as hunters and trappers. They organized a school for boys to learn hunting and survival skills. The program included field trips led by adults and was to be expanded with the formation of partnerships between experienced hunters and youths. It was favorably received by Federal authorities as well as by the Eskimos in general. Obviously the idea of going back into the Barrens as caribou hunters still lingered as a hope, if not for fathers, possibly for their sons. Although dog teams were being phased out of existence, skin clothing had become old-fashioned, and the construction of snowhouses was a dying skill, the new way of life offered only an uncertain hope.

POLITICAL LIFE   The charismatic leader of aboriginal times, "the one who is thinking," has passed out of existence. Such an individual was an outstanding hunter who through his skill and insight was able to locate and kill vast numbers of caribou. He usually had more than one wife, and less successful families gravitated to his camp. He was a man of influence to whom everyone paid attention because experience had proved him to be wise. In this new setting caribou hunting skill was not nearly as important; hunting failed to keep the people from starving and good hunters could not solve the problems of the day. The Hudson's Bay Company trader more than anyone else controlled the economic future of a family. The trader judged a man's worth to be his abilities as a trapper, and on this basis he extended credit for food and equipment. A trader was powerful and usually handled his clientele in an authoritarian manner. A trader's success, in the eyes of the company, was measured in terms of the inventory of furs that he assembled, not in terms of his kindness to Eskimos or concern for the future of these people. As the trader was a leader, so were the police, for they controlled Family Allotment and Destitute Ration funds. The police could and did at times intimidate the people. The same applied to the missionaries but not to as great an extent as to the trader and police. Thus, all economic matters, except for bringing in the fox pelts, were in the hands of white Canadians.

In 1959 important decisions in a local political context effectively passed from the trader, missionaries, and police to the teacher of the new Federal school, who became the Northern Service Officer and the governmental authority. With this major shift in administrative structure, the teacher wielded more power than anyone else, and his decisions were binding. In an effort to develop local leadership an Eskimo Point Community Council, Residents' Association, and Eskimo Housing Council were organized. These bodies were developed in order to foster local participation in governmental institutions. A more far-reaching effort by the government to cultivate political autonomy was embodied in the Hamlet Ordinance enacted by the legislature of the

The Caribou Eskimos: Hunters on the Tundra

Plate 3–9 People from Baker Lake at a spring fish camp in 1974. (Courtesy of Cheryl Kabloona)

Northwest Territories in 1969. It provided for the establishment of local elected councils to govern small communities such as Eskimo Point, and this experience was designed to prepare the people for a transfer to provincial status.

Overview

In terms of long-range Eskimo well-being in the Canadian north, the greatest prospect for their economic security appears to be the exploitation of natural resources. An Eskimo proposal is before the Federal Government to create a new administrative unit in the Canadian north that eventually would gain provincial status. Eskimo activists seek political control over the lands they traditionally have occupied. Since there have never been reserves (reservations) set aside for them, they feel that some settlement with the Canadian government over land is appropriate. Independent commentators feel that there is great potential for the extraction of mineral wealth and natural gas within the foreseeable future, and Eskimos seek to gain regional control before extraction begins. When it is realized that about 17,000 Eskimos and 4000 whites live in the area involved, it is quite clear that Eskimos are numerically dominant. Furthermore it appears that the land may yield hundreds of millions of dollars in wealth. Thus it is not inconceivable that within another generation Canadian Eskimos may have one of the world's highest per capita incomes. With this prospect the future of the surviving Caribou Eskimos is not nearly as bleak as it was a generation ago.

Comparisons with the Chipewyan

The Chipewyan and Caribou Eskimos each exploited the Barrens and stressed caribou hunting over fishing, but as Indians and Eskimos respectively, they had contrasting cultural backgrounds. Then too indications are that the Chipewyan and their immediate ancestors were long-term residents in the region, while the Caribou Eskimos arrived there in the recent past. Thus we are provided with a fine opportunity to note contrasts in life-styles derived from essentially the same economic base. Although the ethnographic information for these tribes is not strictly parallel, it is apparent that small family groups dominated in both societies and that there was very little political organization or formal religious activity. The reader is invited to make more detailed comparisons and to suggest possible evolutionary, functional, or historical explanations for the differences and similarities in these sociocultural systems.

A final comment is appropriate about the differences between Chipewyan and Caribou Eskimo relationships with the Federal Government. In 1921 the Chipewyan accepted a treaty with the Federal Government that clearly defined the obligations of both parties; in essence the Indians gave up title to their land, but were granted perpetual use of it, in exchange for stated goods and services. The Caribou Eskimos by contrast never signed a treaty and have only recently received aid from the Federal Government on a largely informal basis. Thus the Caribou Eskimos, and most others in the Canadian arctic, have no strictly legal status but are now seeking political accord. This prospect in turn has led the Chipewyan and other Northern Athapaskan Indians in Canada to attempt to renegotiate their agreements with the Federal Government for a more favorable settlement.

Additional Readings

The reader interested in additional details about Caribou Eskimo technological adaptations in early historic times should consult the study by Birket-Smith. Very little recent information has been published about the Caribou Eskimos although a number of studies are being written. Perhaps the most pertinent article is one by Ernest S. Burch dealing with the characteristics of caribou and their exploitation by aboriginal peoples. The Caribou Eskimos, other Eskimos, and the Chipewyan are placed in comparative perspective with additional circumpolar peoples in a book by Nelson H. H. Graburn and B. Stephen Strong that is well worth consulting. For an analysis of the recent impact of snowmobiles in the Canadian arctic an article by Lorne Smith is worthwhile reading. The relationship between whites and Eskimos in the Canadian arctic is set forth in a monograph by F. G. Vallee and in an article by Ditte Koster.

In 1962 Elman R. Service published a book titled *Primitive Social Organization* in which he developed an evolutionary approach to the structure of societies at different levels of complexity. This important work has led to a number of reevaluations of band society structure. For a commentary on the Service thesis for Eskimo bands an article by Lee Guemple should be consulted. A discussion of Chipewyan bands, with the work of Service as a point of departure, is found in an article by James G. E. Smith (1976) referenced at the end of Chapter 2.

The best comparative discussion of aboriginal Eskimo life is *The Eskimos* by Edward M. Weyer (New Haven, 1932; reprinted, Hamden, Conn., 1962). The best general work about Eskimos in aboriginal and more recent times is *The Eskimos* by Kaj Birket-Smith (London, 1936; London, 1959; New York, 1971). The book edited by Victor F. Valentine and Frank G. Vallee titled *Eskimo of the Canadian Arctic* (Toronto, 1968) includes superior articles about traditional and modern Eskimo life.

References

Baird, P. D. "Expeditions to the Canadian Arctic," *Beaver*, Outfit 279, March, 44–46; Outfit 280, June, 41–47; September, 44–48, 1949.

*Birket-Smith, Kaj. *The Caribou Eskimos*. Report of the Fifth Thule Expedition, v. 5, pts. 1, 2. 1929. This work constitutes the standard ethnography for the Caribou Eskimos and is the basic source. The author was among these people in 1922–23 at the time that they were just coming into intensive contact with Europeans.

Brack, D. M., and D. McIntosh. *Keewatin Mainland, Area Economic Survey and Regional Appraisal*. Northern Affairs and National Resources, 1963.

Burch, Ernest S. "The Caribou/Wild Reindeer as a Human Resource," *American Antiquity*, v. 37, 339–368. 1972.

Eskimo Point, Northwest Territories. n.d. Eskimo Point Residents' Association.

Gasté, Alphonse. "A Pioneer of the Eskimo Missions," *Eskimo*, v. 56, 8–14, 1960 and v. 57, 3–17. 1960.

Graburn, Nelson H. H., and B. Stephen Strong. *Circumpolar Peoples: An Anthropological Perspective*. Pacific Palisades, California.

Guemple, Lee. "Eskimo Band Organization and the 'D P Camp' Hypothesis," *Arctic Anthropology*, v. 9, 80–112. 1972.

Harp, Elmer, Jr. *The Archaeology of the Lower and Middle Thelon, Northwest Territories.* Arctic Institute of North America Technical Paper no. 8. 1961.

Harrington, Richard. *The Face of the Arctic.* New York. 1952.

Hirsch, David I. "Glottochronology and Eskimo and Eskimo-Aleut Prehistory," *American Anthropologist*, v.56, 825–838. 1954.

Koster, Ditte. "The Emerging Confrontation Between Inuit and Kabloona in the Northwest Territories," *Western Canadian Journal of Anthropology*, v. 4, no. 2, 1–15. 1974.

Lotz, James R., Northern Research Officer, Northern Affairs and National Resources. Personal communication, May 13, 1963.

Morice, Adrian. *Thawing Out the Eskimo.* Boston. 1943.

Mowat, Farley. *People of the Deer.* London. 1954.

Mowat, Farley. *The Desperate People.* London. 1960.

Pruitt, William O., Jr. "Behavior of the Barren-Ground Caribou." *Biological Papers of the University of Alaska*, no. 3. 1960.

*Rasmussen, Knud. *Intellectual Culture of the Caribou Eskimos.* Report of the Fifth Thule Expedition, v. 7, no. 2. 1930. No other anthropologist understood Eskimos as well as Knud Rasmussen. His conversations with Caribou Eskimos and observations about their way of life add an essential dimension to a reconstruction of the culture and society of these people. However, when the information provided by Rasmussen contradicts that of Birket-Smith, the latter source has been used since Birket-Smith spent more time with these Eskimos than did Rasmussen.

Smith, Lorne. "The Mechanical Dog Team: A Study of the Ski-doo in the Canadian Arctic." *Arctic Anthropology*, v. 9, 1–9. 1972.

Smith, Valene L. Eskimos and Caribou: The Padlimiuts of Hudson Bay. Manuscript.

Vallee, F. G. *Kabloona and Eskimo in the Central Keewatin.* Northern Affairs and National Resources. 1962.

*Van den Steenhoven, Geert. *Leadership and Law Among the Eskimos of the Keewatin District, Northwest Territories.* Rijswijk. 1962. In 1955 and 1957 the author collected information in the field on Eskimo social life with particular emphasis on political organization. The case studies are very revealing, and there is considerable information provided on the culture of the people.

*VanStone, James W., and Wendell H. Oswalt. *The Caribou Eskimos of Eskimo Point*. Northern Affairs and National Resources. 1960. The 1959 field study of these authors focused on the modern cultural and social scene with particular emphasis on the deteriorating economic position of the people.

The Kuskowagamiut: Riverine Eskimos

4

Reasons for This Selection

Eskimos most often are regarded as a happy people who wear skin clothing, hunt seals, live in snowhouses, munch on raw meat, and freely share their wives. This characterization is unfair to Eskimos as a whole because the customs of many groups were quite different from the prevailing stereotype. At the time of historic contact nearly half of all the Eskimos lived in southwestern Alaska where salmon, not seals, were the most important food. They never lived in snowhouses, seldom ate raw meat, and more important, had far more complicated customs than those usually associated with Eskimos. In part these people are described to show that more diversity exists in Eskimo culture than generally is recognized; the Kuskokwim Eskimos contrast strikingly with the Caribou Eskimos. The latter were specialized caribou hunters whose quarry was not very predictable in its movement and could be taken only by hunters with considerable mobility. The Kuskowagamiut, on the other hand, depended on salmon for food; not only were these fish predictable in their movements, but also great numbers of them literally swam next to Eskimo settlements. Thus we have a clear contrast in subsistence base between these two groups of Eskimos and may anticipate cultural differences of considerable magnitude.

103

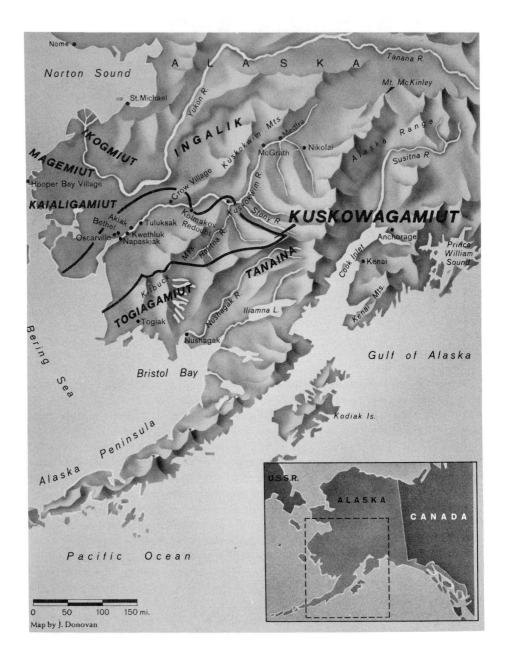

104

People, Population, Language

In the manner of Alaskan Eskimos in general, those living along the Kuskokwim River in the southwestern sector had recognized boundaries and a tribal name, the Kuskowagamiut, but their dialect was shared by other Eskimos in the region. No one is certain of their aboriginal population total, but an early Russian explorer estimated their number at 7000, which seems reasonable. The Kuskowagamiut and all other Alaskan Eskimos southward from the vicinity of Nome spoke a language called Yupik, which was divided into four dialects (Nunivak, Pacific, Mainland, and Siberian). Kuskokwim Eskimos belonged to the Mainland or Yuk dialect. The early historic Yupik population total may have been about 26,000, including 2000 in Siberia. In Alaska north of Nome and extending across Canada to Greenland, the Eskimos were Inupik speakers with relatively minor dialectic differences, and they may have numbered about 30,000. In linguistic terms Inupik and Yupik belong to the Eskimo-Aleut language family and the American Arctic-Paleosiberian linguistic phylum.

Culture Areas and Eskimos

As suggested in Chapter 1, the culture area concept often masks, or ignores, significant localized and regional differences among the people in a single culture area. This failing of the classification is well illustrated by the differences among Eskimo bands or "tribes." They all subsisted on fish and game, had few if any political leaders, and depended on shamans to intercede with supernaturals. Yet beyond shared characteristics such as these many significant contrasts prevailed. For example, diverse kinds of settlements existed in early historic times, and food-getting activities varied widely. In one sector of east Greenland the Eskimos occupied communal houses built of wood, stone, and turf, and there was a single house per settlement. Here the people subsisted primarily by hunting seals from kayaks. Eskimos in central Canada lived on the sea ice in snowhouses most of the year and hunted seals at their breathing holes in the ice. They moved about frequently as small family groups and had no permanent settlements. Eskimos along the northern coast of Alaska maintained permanent villages and built houses of wood and turf; a number of small families lived in each house. They hunted great whales, seals, and walrus; whale hunting in particular required cooperation and coordination of effort. Additional differences in food-getting patterns prevailing among Eskimos are conveyed in this and the preceding chapter. The contrasts in dependability, abundance, and distribution of food resources led to divergences in social life, leadership, and religious behavior from the basic patterns that they shared. Thus what was "typical" of some Eskimos was unheard of among others. The Eskimos described in this book, the Caribou Eskimos and Kuskowagamiut, represent two extremes of adaptation within the same culture area.

Prehistory

The linguistic divisions cited above offer clues to Eskimo prehistory. The relative homogeneity of Inupik from northern Alaska to Greenland suggests that these Eskimos share a common cultural background. The dialect differences within Yupik indicate far greater internal linguistic diversity, implying that the time depth of Yupik speakers in the specified region was greater. We know that Aleut and Eskimo are distantly related to the Paleosiberian languages of eastern Asia and that Aleut as a subfamily probably has greater time depth than either Inupik or Yupik. A reasonable presumption is that distant ancestors of modern Aleuts and Eskimos ventured into Alaska from northeastern Asia. By about 3000 B.C., maritime sea mammal hunting economies had been developed by Eskimos in Alaska. From excavations along the Kobuk River in northern Alaska it appears that Eskimos repeatedly surged inland during prehistoric times, only to be replaced by Indians. The same sequence may have occurred along the Kuskokwim River, but no archaeological evidence is available to support or deny it.

Early History

The first direct contacts between Kuskokwim Eskimos and outsiders were with fur traders. In 1818 Russians founded Alexander Redoubt (modern Nushagak), their first settlement along a Bering Sea drainage. From here the Russian-American Company hoped to expand its trade in beaver and river otter farther north. Eskimos from inland areas north of the redoubt or fort brought many pelts to the Nushagak station. During the summer of 1830, Ivan F. Vasilev, an ensign in the Pilot's Corps, led a small party up a Nushagak River tributary, over a divide to the Holitna River, down the Kuskokwim to its mouth, and back to Alexander Redoubt. Because Vasilev reported favorably on the fur resources of the Kuskokwim, the company built Kolmakov Redoubt as a year-round post along the central Kuskokwim in 1841. The redoubt was operated by the Russians until 1866 when they withdrew in anticipation of the purchase of Alaska by the United States.

Aboriginal Life

ORIGIN MYTH   No known traditions account for Eskimo movements to the Kuskokwim River system, but one myth does explain the origins of the

106
The Kuskowagamiut: Riverine Eskimos

people, the land, and its configurations. The tale reports that in primeval times the only creature in existence was Raven. He flew about in darkness without a place to land until He grew so weary that He created land in order to rest. He became discontented because His creations could not be seen, and so he went off to find the sun. As he returned to earth with it, some light was detached and formed the Milky Way; the holes burned in the sky by the sun became stars. Once Raven saw the bleakness of His creation He made mountains and valleys, caused plants to grow, and made all the rivers flow into the sea. In order to share the world with others He created animals, birds, and fish. Raven's effort to make people of stone failed, and so He created them from mud. Spirits were created to govern all living things, and if people were to prosper, they could not offend these spirits.

APPEARANCE AND CLOTHING   These people are relatively short in stature, with long trunks but short legs. The men are lean and muscular, but women may be plump. Eskimos, the most mongoloid of New World aboriginal populations, have extremely high cheekbones, distinct epicanthic folds, and shovel-shaped incisor teeth, all reflections of a clear racial affinity with Asian populations. The people are dark-skinned only on their faces and hands where they color deeply from weathering. Many men have rather heavy beards, but in aboriginal times whiskers were removed with tweezers. They wore their hair either long over the shoulders or tonsured with bangs over the face. Women did not cut their hair and might gather it together at the back. They often strung small glass beads on a sinew and inserted it through a hole in the nasal septum. The beads were obtained in trade from Siberia before direct contact was made with the Russians. Women usually had pierced ears from which earrings or strings of beads were hung. Likewise their faces were tattooed from the lower lip to the chin, and they wore one or more labrets, or lip plugs, beneath the lower lip. Men wore a medial labret or lateral ones beneath the lower lip, but they were not tattooed.

The winter garment most typical for both sexes was a loose-fitting sleeved parka reaching the calves or ankles; it was made from ground squirrel skins with the claws and tails often attached. The parkas of women were hooded, frequently trimmed with caribou hair and fur strips, and split up the sides; a man's parka was hoodless and had no slits in the sides. A man protected his neck from the cold with a bearskin collar sewn onto the neck opening of his parka, and he wore a head cover of skin or fur. Men apparently wore short caribou skin undertrousers in addition to their skin trousers that reached just below the knees. Socks of caribou skin or woven grass were worn inside knee-length caribou skin boots with sealskin soles. Women preferred sealskin boots that reached the hips. Both men and women wore caribou skin mittens. Garments intended for summer use included rain parkas made from sewn strips of intestine or from fish skins. These parkas were hooded and probably reached below the knees. During rainy weather people also wore fish-skin boots of varied lengths and fish-skin socks.

Plate 4–1 An 1880 illustration of men in long squirrel skin parkas. The parka of the man on the left is adorned with pieces of cloth and squirrel tails. The other man has his parka bottom held up with a belt about his waist, which was the pattern when walking. (From Petroff, 1884)

SETTLEMENTS   These people lived along the central and lower Kuskokwim River, which is broad and gently flowing in the area that they occupied. The lower river and estuary land is low and laced with diverging waterways, lakes, and ponds. In unprotected areas a tundra vegetation flourishes, but in depressions sheltered from the wind dense willow thickets, rare stands of birch trees, and dwarfed spruce manage to grow. Animal species of economic importance were caribou, muskrat, mink, hare, and an occasional river otter.

108

The Kuskowagamiut: Riverine Eskimos

Farther upstream the tundra is less common, and spruce growths become denser. As the central sector is reached, higher hills are encountered, and soon hills and low mountains front the river. Animals along the central river include black bear in addition to the species known from the lower river. Migratory waterfowl pass through the country in the spring and again in the fall, while spruce hens and ptarmigan live in the region throughout the year. Salmon contributed the most to economic welfare, and the most important species were dog (chum), king (chinook), red (sockeye), and silver (coho). In the main river, lakes, and sloughs, blackfish, burbot, northern pike, and whitefish abound at certain seasons. The only other fish of importance are smelt, which ascend the lower river to spawn in the early spring and were taken in dip nets.

Settlements, whether large or small, were built where there was ready access to food resources, especially salmon. Adult women, their daughters, and young sons occupied the houses. These dwellings looked like mounds of dirt because they were built partially beneath the ground and were covered with sod. The main room was built in a rectangular excavation extending about fifteen feet in the longer direction. An upright post was placed about six feet away from each corner, and beams were set on top of these posts to join them. A row of wall logs extended from the outer edges of the excavation to the tops of the beams on each side, and the low roof was made with split logs. An opening was left in the center for a skylight, and the removable wood

Plate 4–2 A settlement photographed in 1884, with houses and caches in the background. In the foreground is a sled for portaging kayaks, with kayaks resting on supports behind it. (Courtesy of the Moravian Archives, Bethlehem, Pa.)

frame fitted there was covered with sewn fish skins or animal intestines. Except for the skylight opening the entire structure was covered with dry grass and then with sod. Beneath the skylight was a fireplace where meals were cooked, and smoke from the wood fire drifted out through the opening. A house generally included a wood-framed anteroom and a passage that led to the main room; the passage prevented cold air from entering the living area. Around the walls of the main room were low benches covered with grass, grass matting, and animal skins for sleeping; a floor area of dirt surrounded the fireplace.

To a non-Eskimo the odor inside a house would have been its most striking feature. The smells of stale urine, skin clothing that was never cleaned, and dried salmon made a pungent combination. The interior was relatively dark because of the accumulated soot on the walls and ceiling, but some light penetrated the translucent window. This covering was set aside during warm days for still more light from outside. Artificial light came from the fireplace or from bowl-shaped clay lamps. The lamps were placed on stands in front of the rear bench or at the edge of a side bench. Oil, preferably seal oil, burned on a wick of moss. The central floor space was filled with cups, food trays, wooden water buckets, and pottery cooking vessels. Common household items included a woman's sewing equipment in a neatly folded leather container, her semilunar slate-bladed knife or ulu, wooden cutting boards, chipped and ground stone scrapers for processing skins, and awls.

The men's house or *kashgee* was the home of most adult males and older boys. The largest building in a village, this structure served as a bathhouse, ceremonial chamber, and workshop. A large kashgee might measure as much as thirty feet on a side. The walls were made of planks and split logs set vertically, and the roof was cribbed. Access was through a tunnel either at ground level or beneath it, and some men's houses had both varieties of entrance. The floor of a kashgee was covered with planks except for an area some four feet square at the center. Here was a fire pit which could be planked over when not in use, and above the fire pit was a skylight. Kashgee furnishings included two or three tiers of benches around the walls and at least two large bowl-shaped oil-burning lamps to provide artificial light.

Inside a kashgee were all of the tools and equipment used by the men. Conspicuously absent were cooking vessels and eating containers, for these were brought in by females at mealtime and removed after the men and boys had eaten. The most important woodworking tools included the ubiquitous crooked knife, wedges, mauls for driving wedges, slate-bladed adzes, whetstones, and engraving tools. Near each man's assigned position on a bench were his sinew-backed bow and arrows, spears, and other weapons. Hanging from the ceiling on exhibit until a later ceremony were the bladders of animals and the stuffed skins of birds and small animals.

Scattered about a settlement were pits in which stored salmon heads became headcheese and other pits for preserving silver salmon caught so late in

110
The Kuskowagamiut: Riverine Eskimos

Plate 4-3 Women photographed in front of a cache in 1907. Smelt are drying on the pole. (Courtesy of the University Museum, Philadelphia)

the season that they could not be dried. Salmon taken earlier were sun dried and placed in caches erected on four posts. Above an overhanging wooden platform was the rectangular wooden structure with a gabled plank roof and an oval entrance facing the front. Inside a cache were stored dried or frozen fish, herbs, and equipment such as snowshoes and nets. Sleds often were stored on the cache platform beyond the reach of hungry dogs who would eat the lashings.

CONVEYANCES From late spring until late fall these people traveled almost exclusively by water, using rivers and sloughs as well as lakes. In the lower river area each man owned a kayak made by covering a driftwood frame with dehaired sealskins. An extended family unit owned a large, open skin boat or umiak. Along the central river both forms were used in addition to a small type of canoe covered with birch bark and decked a short distance fore and aft. The only other vessel was an improvised umiak made by hunters after animals had been killed. The fresh skins stretched over a rude wooden frame served to carry meat and men from a distant hunting camp to a settlement.

The usual winter conveyance was a wooden sled. The bed was built up on stanchions mortised and bound to the bed and runners with babiche (thin, dehaired caribou skin strips). Sleds with low flat beds were used to carry umiaks over the snow to spring camps. A small but similar type of sled was carried on the aft section of a kayak or canoe and served to portage the vessel from one lake or slough to the next. Finally snowshoes were essential for traveling overland when the snow was deep and not crusted, conditions that prevailed in timbered areas. Here snowshoes were long with light birch frames webbed with babiche; elsewhere snowshoes were crude and often improvised.

The lower river families went to their fall camps by umiak before the lakes and flowing waters froze or else waited until after freeze-up and traveled by dog sled. Three or four dogs were harnessed to a sled by attaching individual towlines to stanchions at the sides, a highly inefficient hitching method. In all likelihood, a man pushed at the rear of a sled as women and children pulled in front. Not until about twenty years after the arrival of the Russians were dogs harnessed tandem at the front of a sled as in eastern Siberia.

HOUSEHOLD ACTIVITIES   In a strict sense household life focused narrowly on females since the only males present were young boys. A man lived with his wife and all their unmarried children only at tundra camps and at summer fish camps maintained away from a village. Ideally, daughters remained with their mothers after they had married and raised the next generation of children in the same house. Only when the number of females overcrowded a dwelling or when a house became uninhabitable did they move. A line of females lived in lifelong intimacy, whereas males were more closely associated with others of their own sex. The normal obligations of women in these close-knit domestic units included the preparation and processing of food, caring for children, manufacturing and repairing clothing, picking berries and a few other plant products, and collecting firewood. Men were expected to provide their wives with fish, fowl, and land mammals, but their duty did not extend beyond bringing such items to the settlement. Once a harvest was at hand, a man's wife had total responsibility for and control over its preparation and distribution.

DESCENT, KINSHIP, AND MARRIAGE   Aboriginal Kuskowagamiut marriage and residence patterns are reconstructed from comparatively recent sources and may not be entirely correct. These people appear to have attempted to arrange marriages within a community (village endogamy). Since households were comprised of female lines, this meant that a man became associated with his wife's natal unit (matrilocal residence) whether he had been raised in her settlement or elsewhere. Some men, especially shamans, had more than one wife (polygyny), and if so the women seem to have been sisters (sororal polygyny). Relatives were traced along both the father's and mother's line (bilateral or nonunilineal descent) to a given degree of collaterality; this meant that each person, except for brothers and sisters, was a member of a different bilateral kin group (personal kindred). A mother's sister's children and father's brother's children (parallel cousins) were called by the same terms as brother and sister (siblings), but mother's brother's children and father's sister's children (cross-cousins) were termed "cousin." On the parental generation the word for mother was different from that for mother's sister, but the latter

112
The Kuskowagamiut: Riverine Eskimos

term was the same as for father's sister; the same patterning applied to father, father's brother, and mother's brother (lineal avuncular terms). We would expect that since parallel cousins were termed brother and sister their parents would be called "mother" and "father," but such was not the case. Thus, we would be led to conclude that this terminology was in the process of change at the time it was described.

SUBSISTENCE ACTIVITIES   After the winter's ice had broken up on the main river and the accompanying high water had subsided, the people moved from their hunting camps on the tundra to riverbank settlements in anticipation of the first runs of fish. Gill nets strung with wooden floats and antler sinkers were readied for use. The netting was made from the inner bark of willows or more preferably from rawhide thongs, and a net probably was about thirty feet long and six feet deep. Nets were set in river eddies and tended daily from a canoe or kayak. Whenever possible a man set his net in the same eddy that he had used the previous year; otherwise he lost his claim to it. Since the river channel shifted frequently, no eddy had real permanence. The first species caught was most likely the sheefish, and the few taken were boiled for immediate eating.

A fisherman was most anxious to take king salmon in his set net. After a number had been caught, he took up the net and tied it to all the additional king salmon netting he might have. The net, in a wooden container to prevent tangling, was placed in his kayak, and he paddled nearby to a straight stretch of river with no obstructions above the depth of the net. He threw out a large wooden float attached to a line leading to the net that he paid into the water. One end of the net was tied to the kayak, and the fisherman paddled so that the net drifted at right angles to the current. When he saw a float bob violently, he knew a fish had struck the net, and he detached the net rope from his vessel, tied a large wooden float to the end, and threw it overboard. Paddling to the spot where the fish had thrashed, he gently lifted the net from the water and either clubbed the salmon to death or stuck a bone bodkin into the base of its head. The fish was killed as efficiently as possible, for if it thrashed violently a section of the net was likely to be destroyed. The dead fish was taken aboard and the net straightened to drift evenly with the current. After a drift of about two miles the net was hauled in and the process repeated if the take had been small. This fishing technique, called drift netting, was possibly the most important means for taking salmon. King salmon were caught in this manner, and with smaller-meshed gill nets dog, red, and silver salmon were harvested.

When a man finished drift netting for the day, he returned to his base, put the fish in a wooden bin, and covered them with a grass mat to keep flies away. His wife or daughter processed the fish for immediate consumption or for storage. Salmon soon to be used were cut into chunks and boiled in water or were partly dried and later boiled, but most fish were gutted and dried for winter. The heads might be dried for dog food or buried to make headcheese; the roe was eaten after being mashed or mixed with oil or was dried to serve as preferred food for travelers; the guts were buried or dried as food for dogs. The body of a fish to be dried was cut and hung over a drying rack made from poles, and during wet weather the fish were covered with grass matting to prevent them from molding. Beneath the rack a small fire of alder wood was sometimes built to prevent flies from laying their eggs on the fish and to smoke-cure the salmon. After the fish had dried, they were bundled and stored in caches. Any fish not prepared for drying were placed whole in the ground. Here they decayed slowly and became "stink fish," as later whites termed them. When asked how he could tolerate the smell, the standard reply of an Eskimo was, "We don't eat the smell."

Late nineteenth century reports indicate that families fished for salmon only until they felt that they had enough to last them the winter. If a man took a large number of king salmon, he was desultory about fishing for later, smaller species. Salmon always ascended the river to spawn in the small adjacent streams, but high water made it difficult to net them in certain years. However starvation from failure of the salmon run apparently did not occur.

Some, or perhaps even most, families did not remain at their village to fish for salmon but scattered to nearby fish camps along the banks of the river or sloughs. Families camping along stretches of the central river where shallow water ran over a gravel bottom might build weirs across the channel. At intervals in a weir funnel-shaped fish traps of spruce splints were set facing downstream. In these traps salmon, whitefish, and northern pike were taken. More ambitious individuals maintained similar traps in the narrow streams leading from lakes into sloughs and rivers. At the end of the salmon fishing season families moved back from their camps, taking with them their winter supply of dried fish.

During early winter the men sledded to tundra camps, where they set fish traps in small streams leading from the lakes. Their primary purpose was to take the small blackfish that left the lakes via these streams during the fall. Blackfish were caught in great quantities and stored frozen in woven grass bags. Later in the winter they served as food for both people and dogs. Another fall activity of the men was to snare hares, marmot, and squirrels; mink and river otter were caught in fish traps or in smaller traps of the same design. Ptarmigan snares were set in clusters around willow thickets, and if beaver were nearby, they were captured in nets set beneath the ice. Whenever possible men hunted caribou with bows and arrows in the late fall when the animals were fat, their skins prime, and their meat at its best, but caribou were not abundant. By midwinter people gathered at their riverbank settlements where caches usually were well stocked with food, and as the weather grew colder they depended almost entirely on stored edibles. This was the ceremonial season, and when supplies were plentiful, few cares disturbed the tranquillity of winter.

114

The Kuskowagamiut: Riverine Eskimos

With the approach of spring, villagers grew restless and were anxious to return to their tundra camps. They went by dog team before the trails became free of snow and before the sloughs and rivers were covered with melt water. Here, as the last snow disappeared, they harvested ptarmigan and migratory waterfowl with arrows or snares. Women collected berries, especially the highbush cranberries clinging to the dried bushes from the year before, and men refurbished blackfish traps that they set in small streams leading to lakes. Gill nets were set in larger sloughs for northern pike and whitefish; the surplus fish were dried for later use. Men traveled by kayak once there was open water, hunting and snaring fur animals. When they judged that their take was sufficient or when they simply wearied of the tundra camps, they returned to their riverbank communities. They did so, however, only when reasonably certain that the river ice had broken up and the flood waters had subsided.

SOCIAL DIMENSIONS   Men dominated subsistence activities and lived apart from women, thereby giving rise to social networks focused in the kashgee or men's house. Each male who lived there occupied a specific spot: old men on the bench at the front above the entrance, young men on the opposite bench, middle-aged men on the outer benches, and young boys on the floor. Early in the morning before anyone was up, a wand was placed across the exit, indicating that no one was to leave, and old men began to talk to an audience that appeared to be sleeping. In monologues or dialogues they lectured about life from childhood to maturity. They spoke of traditional customs and of new rules as responses to changing conditions. Discussions might be of behavior in public or on trips and of actions necessary in case of accidents or other emergencies. After the presentations were over, those men who planned to travel a considerable distance that day dressed and left the kashgee as others split wood for a sweat bath. Preparations for a bath included removing the planks that covered the fire pit, setting aside the skylight cover, and building a great fire. After the wood had burned to a bed of coals, the gut window was fitted back in place, and men stripped to bathe. In the intense heat their ears might blister before they began to perspire. As the room became hotter, men wailed loudly for the dead who were missing a fine bath. When the heat subsided, they washed in urine, and in the winter a man might sit in the snow to cool off.

After hunting or fishing during the day, men returned to the settlement and went directly to the men's house. A close female relative unloaded the catch and put away the equipment of each man, and after the men had bathed again, women brought in the evening meal and dried the men's clothing. In the early evening men told of what had happened to them during the day, and the old men commented on what was said. As everyone settled down to sleep, an old man began telling a traditional story. The audience at first responded with "e-yee" to encourage the storyteller, but before he had finished, most men and boys were asleep.

POLITICAL LIFE   With villagers living together for at least half of each year, we might expect a degree of political integration, but group decisions that affected the entire community seem to have been rare. This condition is partially a reflection of subsistence activities being individual, not community, endeavors. A man most likely supervised the hunting and fishing activities of his sons, and an older brother, in the absence of a father, guided the economic life of a younger brother. It is probable, too, that older men informally resolved routine problems, such as disputes over property or hunting and fishing rights. Possibly a wider range of opinion was sought concerning differences with persons in other settlements or the formalities of arranging ceremonies. If any one individual had a prominent voice in the decision making, it probably was the shaman because of his supernatural affiliations. The nonconformity of any individual would lead first to gossip and then to mild ridicule, which was usually sufficient to bring deviant behavior into line with community expectations. If a father was annoyed at the behavior of a son, he expressed his dissatisfaction to a close friend during a sweat bath, and this person would make known the father's feelings to the son. Ridicule songs appear to have been sung as a more forceful and face-to-face means of pointing up individual failings.

The nearest approach to a secular leader was a highly successful hunter and fisherman who could feed orphans and widows, provide oil for the kashgee lamps, and furnish food for feasts. Such an individual took an active role in all village activities and thereby earned the most worthy title of "a man indeed!"

The most serious rupture of social harmony was the murder of a person by an outsider, but such an occurrence appears to have been rare. If it happened, an influential relative of the deceased assembled the men from his and adjacent communities, entertained them, presented each with a gift, and requested their aid in exacting blood revenge. Balance prevailed after someone in the family of the murderer was killed, and there were no additional murders. Sometimes revenge flared out of hand, and a family feud erupted. This would cease only with the flight or murder of one faction. Formalized war did not exist.

RELIGION   When defined as dogma, rules, a ceremonial round, and ritual leadership, religion played a critical role in Kuskokwim Eskimo life. As so often is the case, some aspects of their religious life were more secular than sacred and were integrated with economics and entertainment. Ceremonies and "feasts" followed a well-developed calendrical cycle, whereas shamanistic activities, the other ritual events, took place primarily at critical and unscheduled times.

Shamans were reported to be far more powerful among the Kuskokwim Eskimos than among most others. They often were members of particular male lines, and although women might become shamans, they normally were

116

The Kuskowagamiut: Riverine Eskimos

Plate 4–4 Mask representing a spirit that lives in the ground and leaves no hole when it emerges. This spirit sometimes dislikes men and will jump through them without leaving a mark but killing them in the process. (Photograph courtesy of The Museum of the American Indian, Heye Foundation)

considered less powerful than males. A young male with a predilection to shamanism was apprenticed to a successful practitioner and did not perform independently until he reached adulthood. During his training he acquired supernatural aids, learned to drum and sing, and practiced performing tricks. Shamanistic sessions were held to diagnose, predict, and cure by supernatural means as well as to demonstrate a shaman's power. It also was a shaman's duty to make certain that people observed the necessary behavioral norms, and he became a secular practitioner in performing certain cures that did not require supernatural aids. Other persons, especially the old, also might function as secular curers. When a settlement included more than one shaman, people turned to the one regarded as most capable in times of greatest crises.

When someone's illness had no obvious cause, a shaman's help was sought. If the patient did not improve or died, the shaman might be accused of witchcraft, in which case he could be murdered. A curing session involved apprentices who drummed and sang the shaman's songs while he summoned his spiritual helper. Once his body was host to this force he behaved strangely, reflecting the motions and sounds of the helping spirit, which often was an animal. The disease substance was driven from the person's body by sucking or brushing it away. It sometimes happened, too, that as a shaman was possessed by a spirit he learned that a villager had caused the illness by breaking a taboo; after the offender confessed, harmony was restored to the universe. A shaman performed at traditional ceremonies as an actor and trickster, showing off his skills before an audience. His sleight of hand and vanishing acts impressed those who did not perceive the trickery. Shamans also interpreted unusual events. An eclipse of the moon was expected to usher in illness and death, an earthquake was an ominous sign, and comets foretold starvation.

Witchcraft was the worst form of antisocial behavior. The malevolence of a witch living in a distant village could be counteracted by a powerful local shaman. If the witch lived in one's own settlement, this was much more dangerous. Examples of witches using their powers within their own community are rare, but one instance was recorded. In this case an old woman reportedly killed several of her own children. The accuser, who was her husband, clubbed her to death and then severed all of her joints. Afterwards her remains were covered with oil and burned.

The ceremonial round is known incompletely but in enough detail to realize that it was well developed. Ceremonies commonly spanned four days, and people from one or more adjacent villages were guests. The villagers prepared for the celebration by storing large quantities of food, composing songs, and manufacturing dance masks, along with practicing their roles until they were perfected. The general supervision, at least along the lower river, was in the hands of a dance leader who as host made certain that the activities were carried out in a traditional manner. This office tended to pass from father to son. The most important ceremonial event was the Great Ceremony for the Dead, performed every four to ten years, depending on the number of deaths and the time required to assemble the assets for holding the event. On alternate years reciprocating villages held a Sending a Messenger Ceremony as the climax to yearly ceremonials.

The Great Ceremony for the Dead was designed to free the souls of the dead so that they could rest forever in a world in the sky. The Sending a Messenger Ceremony was in honor of the recently deceased and included the institutionalized giving of gifts. The person or persons hosting the celebration were relatives of the deceased and had accumulated food and property in large quantities. Messengers were sent to the guest community with a mnemonic stick on which symbols were carved or appended. An announcement was made formally, and the signs on the stick were to convey the details of the invitation. When the guests arrived, they were greeted ceremonially, and during the evenings of the festivities dances and songs were performed to commemorate the dead and his merits. If the deceased was not a noble person about whom any good could be recounted, the praises of his ancestors were sung. The climax of the ceremony came a few days later when gifts were distributed to the guests in honor of the deceased; there was no obligation to make a return gift.

The Bladder Ceremony that was so important at adjacent coastal Eskimo communities also was held by these riverine people. The bladders of all important animals killed were saved because it was thought that an animal's soul was in its bladder. The first birds and small animals killed by boys also were preserved after the meat and intestines were removed. The skins and bladders were hung in the kashgee during the time of the festivities. Included were sporting events, songs, storytelling, gift exchanges, and feasting. On the tenth and final day everyone assembled in the men's house for a feast, and bits of food were thrown on one wall for the dead. The purpose of the ceremony was to renew the game killed, and at the end the bladders probably were submerged in a hole in the river ice. The focus of the event on bladders was not entirely appropriate for Kuskokwim Eskimos since they depended so heavily on salmon, which were not specifically honored. This is an example of a ceremony maintained even though some aspects of its original form were no longer fully pertinent.

LIFE CYCLE   A woman gave birth at home, aided by her mother or another female relative. She delivered in a squatting position, and downward pressure was applied to her abdomen if the process was delayed. The birth of a female was a joyous occasion only if the woman desired a daughter. If there were daughters already in the family, or if it was a lean time of the year, female infanticide was likely to be practiced. Infanticide was not restricted to the newborn but might take place at any time during the first two or three years of life. The attitude was that since part of the soul of a deceased individual returned to the body of the next one born, this was no real destruction of life. A baby was named after the person who had died most recently in the local area, and the relatives of the deceased behaved toward the namesake as they had toward the deceased. Parents were known by the name of their firstborn, a custom termed teknonymy. Thus if the firstborn was named Kamoucha, the mother was called Kamoucha's mother. Names obviously were not sex linked, and they were changed if their bearers were plagued with misfortune. Growing up in a household dominated by older females, infants and small children were pampered and catered to; this treatment was based as much on supernatural beliefs as on natural affection. Since an infant had the soul of a recently deceased individual, he mirrored the feelings of the deceased and was appeased in order not to offend the watching spirits. This association decreased in importance as the individual matured and acquired a distinctive personality of his own.

A maturing girl soon was integrated into the household routine of the older females. Her toys usually were facsimiles of the artifacts used by her mother, and by the time she was nine years old she was a reasonably capable housekeeper. Indications are that the bonds between a maternal grandmother and granddaughter were extremely close. The granddaughter's activities and world view appear to have been molded largely by this older woman, who occupied the rear platform in a large household. Recognition of the grandmother's importance stems from a study of stories told by contemporary Eskimo girls. These stories, or storyknife tales as they are known, were illustrated with stylized representations of people, boats, houses, and other forms. The drawings were made on a mud or snow surface with an oblong-bladed implement known as a storyknife. Storyknife tales were a vital part of

Plate 4–5 An Eskimo family photographed in 1884. (Courtesy of the Moravian Archives, Bethlehem, Pa.)

the women's world, and their content suggests that grandmothers originated them and taught them to their granddaughters. There is no evidence of males either telling or listening to storyknife tales. The stories told by a grandmother entertained and also instructed. The main characters most often were a grandmother and her granddaughter; repeated episodes in stories were that one should offer food to visitors, that nonrational behavior is expectable from males, and that a granddaughter who disobeys her grandmother brings harm to the grandmother.

By the time boys were ten years old they had left their natal homes and moved into the kashgee. Here they came under the supervision of the older males in their families and under the indirect control of all the older kashgee residents. The boys were no longer regarded as children; more and more was expected of them, even though their activities were supervised casually. Steps toward adulthood were achieved by an adolescent as he increased his hunting skills. The first birds and small animals killed by each boy were skinned and stuffed to be displayed from strings in the kashgee during the Bladder Ceremony, at which the boys danced in places of honor and were feasted. At the

The Kuskowagamiut: Riverine Eskimos

completion of the rituals the skins were secreted away to a safe location. After a male had killed one of each species of animal, he was considered marriageable. Ceremonial recognition was given a girl when she picked the first of each species of berries, but a more important event was the ceremonial acknowledgment of her menarche. At this time she probably was restricted to one corner of the dwelling, wore old clothing, and observed food as well as behavioral taboos. Possibly at about this time a girl had sexual intercourse with a male shaman; this was essential for a maiden before she could be admitted to kashgee ceremonies.

A female was nubile at about the age of fourteen, but a male was likely to be at least four years older and sometimes as much as twenty years older than his bride. The marriage itself was without ceremony and was arranged by the

Plate 4–6 An 1884 photograph of a woman with beads suspended from a hole in her nasal septum and a labret beneath her lower lip. (Courtesy of the Moravian Archives, Bethlehem, Pa.)

Plate 4–7 Grave goods above burials photographed in 1907.
(Courtesy of the University Museum, Philadelphia)

families of the couple or by an older man directly with the girl's family.
Thereafter the man slept with the girl in her mother's house; she was responsible for preparing his meals, caring for his clothing, and processing the subsistence items he obtained. In the event either of the couple became dissatisfied with the other they ceased cooperating and cohabiting. A marriage might also be terminated with a wrestling match. Any man was free to challenge another to wrestle, and the man thrown to the ground was obligated to give up his wife. Usually men wrestled only for young women without children. No stigma was attached to divorce, and most individuals had at least two partners during their lifetimes. A marriage tended to stabilize after the woman bore a child, particularly if it was a male.

As adults, the activities of a man and his wife were complementary, and even though marriages may have been brittle, an adult did not willfully remain unmarried for long. In the early years of marriage the partners might remain cool toward one another, but as time passed they were more likely to become congenial partners. The personality of an adult Eskimo manifested a phlegmatic realism, and an even-tempered, jovial person was the ideal. Verbal aggression or physical dominance was abhorred, and to be withdrawn or caustic was symptomatic of the sick or diseased. Aged people were not killed but often came to be respected for their knowledge. Some old men were great storytellers and passed the traditions of their fathers on to the men and boys of the next generation. Old women held forth from the rear platforms of their dwellings with advice and criticism, both of which were offered freely.

A dead person's body was flexed with the knees bound up to the chest. The women wailed, and the men killed the dogs of the deceased. His clothing

The Kuskowagamiut: Riverine Eskimos

and other property, except those items that were kept as mementos, were destroyed or deposited on the grave. The body was removed through a hole made in the wall of the kashgee or dwelling; after the opening was closed, the spirit of the deceased could not find its way back into the structure. The small plank coffin was placed above the ground on four short poles in the cemetery, usually located on a hill or rise near the settlement. At the head of the coffin a board might be placed between two poles; on it were pegged wooden carvings of human faces. Sometimes, too, the coffin of a man was painted with animal figures representing the species he had taken during his lifetime.

Early Historic Changes

RUSSIAN INFLUENCES   Between the beginning of local contacts with Russians in the 1830s and their withdrawal in 1866, two Russian institutions had an important influence on the lives of local Eskimos. These were the Russian-American Company and the Russian Orthodox Greek Catholic Church. The trading organization was by far the more immediately important, but Orthodox Church influence was more enduring. The Russians were searching for new sources of furs, and by the 1820s they had turned to the region north of the Alaska Peninsula. Of the earliest traders we know comparatively little except that two men, Fedor Kolmakov and Semen Lukin, were most instrumental in opening the inland fur trade. Kolmakov was of aboriginal Siberian and Russian ancestry, while Lukin appears to have been of Eskimo or mixed Russian and Eskimo ancestry. Both men traveled widely, exploring the Kuskokwim River drainage and adjacent areas in their quest for furs, especially beaver pelts. Since beaver were concentrated along the central and upper reaches of the river, the lower river held little attraction to them in this early stage of penetration. In 1853, however, trade in white fox pelts began, an indication that the Russians had initiated trading ties with Eskimos along the lower river, since white fox could be obtained only from areas near the coast.

TRADING CENTER   The most permanent inland Russian trading center was at Kolmakov Redoubt along the central river. A stockade surrounded the main settlement, two small cannons were the primary means of defense, and there was a blockhouse with gun ports. The station also included a bathhouse, chapel, living quarters, store, and outbuildings. Lukin was the first manager, and he maintained this position throughout most of the Russian era. He was a religious man authorized by the Orthodox Church to baptize converts, and even before a chapel was constructed he led weekly church services in the store. He was well-regarded by the local Eskimos, and while there were intermittent rumors of pending attacks on the settlement, none ever materialized.

Kolmakov Redoubt was not a bastion in the north. It usually was staffed with about a dozen employees of Russian, Eskimo, or mixed blood, and no military garrison was stationed there. The post never really thrived because the worldwide demand for beaver pelts was in a decline when the redoubt was founded. Because this was the most remote Russian trading center, the trade goods available usually were small, highly portable, and not readily destructible. Items such as tea, beads, knives, metal containers, needles, and copper ornaments were stocked; even so the post often was without these imported goods and then dealt only in local products such as oil and dried fish. The overall impression is that the Russians adapted to Eskimo ways and made very few radical changes in the traditional patterns.

RUSSIAN MISSIONARIES   The first Orthodox missionary to visit the Kuskokwim was A. Petelin, who arrived from the Nushagak station in the 1840s. We have no knowledge of an Orthodox missionary being stationed along the river until the arrival of Hieromonk Illarion in 1861. He visited Kolmakov Redoubt intermittently until his departure from the area in 1866. By the end of the Russian era many if not most of the Kuskokwim Eskimos along the central river considered themselves to be Christians. They had been baptized and given Russian names, but the core of Christian dogma was certainly poorly understood.

STEAM BATH   Yet another Russian introduction must be mentioned briefly, and this is the Russian steam bath. A bathhouse was constructed by Lukin at Kolmakov Redoubt. The Eskimos trading into these posts were familiar already with bathing in intense heat, but the Russian bath was somewhat different from the sweat bath in the kashgee. It was taken in a small structure, and stones were heated above a stove or in an open fire. When water was poured over the rocks, bathers sat back and enjoyed the hot air moistened by the steam. Initial Eskimo reaction probably was unfavorable, but as time passed the Russian bath was to assume more importance.

EARLY EPIDEMIC   During the initial period of contact with the Russians, Kuskokwim Eskimos seldom were hostile; in fact, they appear to have welcomed the Russians for the trade goods which they brought. However, this harmony was tested severely in 1838–1839. During these years as many as half of the riverine Eskimos perished in a local smallpox epidemic. The survivors thought that the Russians deliberately plagued them with the disease, and some Eskimos from the Kuskokwim massacred the Russians at a post on the Yukon River. The epidemic destroyed the fabric of aboriginal social life, and the distrust engendered probably never completely passed during the Russian period.

AMERICAN TRADERS   For nearly twenty years following the purchase of Alaska by the United States the only interest in the Kuskokwim was of a commercial nature. The Russian-American Company, which had held a mo-

The Kuskowagamiut: Riverine Eskimos

nopoly on the Alaskan trade since 1799, was bought out by Hutchinson, Kohl & Company, soon to become the Alaska Commercial Company. Kolmakov Redoubt continued as a trading center, but the main post was located nearer the mouth of the river at a village that came to be called Bethel. Neither the Russian nor the early American trading along the Kuskokwim developed into a major commercial enterprise. The stores were not a great source of profit, and consequently their inventories were quite limited. The change from the Russian to the American period brought no abrupt break in trading patterns; in fact, two of the three traders during the early American period were Russian or of Russian-Eskimo extraction.

MORAVIAN MISSIONARIES A series of events occurring in Bethlehem, Pennsylvania, in 1883, were to have the next significant influence on Kuskokwim Eskimos. During this year the Presbyterian missionary and Federal agent for education in Alaska, Sheldon Jackson, spoke to an audience of Moravians at the Moravian College and Theological Seminary in Bethlehem. He convinced church officials that they should take an active interest in the Eskimos of Alaska. Inasmuch as the Moravians had long maintained missions to Eskimos in Greenland and Labrador, it is not surprising that they responded favorably to this request. In 1884 an experienced Moravian mis-

Plate 4–8 An Eskimo trader and his family at Bethel in 1884.
(Courtesy of the Moravian Archives, Bethlehem, Pa.)

sionary from Canada, Henry Hartmann, accompanied by a seminary student, William H. Weinland, set off to find a site for a new mission in Alaska. After traveling as far upriver as Kolmakov Redoubt, they concluded that a small lower river village was best suited for their purpose. The following year Weinland graduated from the seminary, and he, along with another graduate, John H. Kilbuck, and their brides, set off to found a mission center at Bethel. Since that time the line of Moravian missionaries at Bethel has been unbroken. Bethel emerged as the most important town along the Kuskokwim after it was discovered in 1908 that a deep channel reached from the estuary as far as the settlement. In terms of regional administration, education, and health services, Bethel has been the focal point through which innovations were introduced.

ECONOMIC INNOVATIONS   The feverish search for gold in northwestern North America around the turn of the century brought profound changes to many areas but not to the Kuskokwim, where major deposits were never found. One introduction of prospectors, the fish wheel, was of lasting importance, however. This device is a log raft with a large opening at the center over which is mounted a horizontal axle hung with large baskets and paddles. The river current propels the paddles and baskets, which rotate in the direction of the current. Fish swimming upstream within reach of the baskets are lifted into them from the water and then slide down a chute into a box at the side of the raft. The fish wheel is an extremely effective method for taking fish since it operates in the absence of a fisherman, but it can be used successfully only above tidewater where the water is opaque and flowing rather fast near the bank.

Through Moravian efforts a small number of reindeer were brought to the lower Kuskokwim in 1901. The successful introduction of reindeer herding among Alaskan Eskimos in 1892 was another of Sheldon Jackson's accomplishments. The Kuskokwim herds increased until about 40,000 head were grazed along the river system in the 1930s. Then in the early 1940s the herds decreased rapidly, and by the end of the decade they were no longer in existence. Thus the early hope of creating a new basis for the economy ended in failure.

RECENT EPIDEMICS   Before turning to more recent happenings, two events with long-range effects should be discussed briefly. The first was a severe epidemic that took place in 1900–1901. During these years influenza, accompanied by whooping cough, measles, and pneumonia, devastated the riverine population. A medical doctor in the area at the time estimated that half the population, including all of the babies, perished. Some villages were deserted completely, and the people were seriously demoralized. Continuity with the past was interrupted or perhaps even broken in most settlements. The cultural and social effects must have been great, particularly since this was the gold rush period in which many Anglo-Americans were entering or

The Kuskowagamiut: Riverine Eskimos

passing through the area. The Eskimos seem to have reacted by giving up many of their old ways and rapidly adopting American customs.

EXPANSIONS INLAND   The second change, which began after the smallpox epidemic of 1838–1839 and accelerated with the epidemic of 1900–1901, involved the movement of Eskimos much farther up the Kuskokwim. The country that they entered belonged to Athapaskan Indians, and by the early 1840s they had gone far enough inland to share a village across the river from Kolmakov Redoubt with Indians. The traditional hostility between most Indians and Eskimos apparently did not exist along the central river. By 1960 Eskimos occupied the banks of the main river as far inland as the Stony River junction, and by 1970 Eskimos had moved to the trading center of McGrath as well as the Indian villages of Nikolai and Medfra. Eskimo genealogies in the recent past suggest a pattern of Indians marrying Eskimos and adopting Eskimo ways. Thus we see the continuing adaptability of Eskimos in their deep penetration of interior Alaska.

Modern Life

NAPASKIAK HISTORY   The emphasis now shifts to one village, Napaskiak, to plot continuity with the past and historic change. In 1955–1956 I lived at Napaskiak and collected information about conditions at that time. The oldest villagers reported that the settlement had been occupied for many generations and that their ancestors previously had lived at nearby villages that are now abandoned. They have no traditions of moving into the area, and the earliest known reference to Napaskiak is on a map dating 1867. Moravian missionaries visited there repeatedly in the 1880s but were unable to make a significant number of lasting converts, and by the 1950s nearly all residents were members of the Russian Orthodox faith. Directly across the river from Napaskiak is the settlement of Oscarville, important to Napaskiak because of its trading post. An Orthodox church was built at Napaskiak in 1931, and a Bureau of Indian Affairs school opened there in 1939.

THE SETTLEMENT   Napaskiak stretches along the southeastern bank of the river, and in 1956 the twenty-seven frame and seven log houses were occupied by 141 persons. The most imposing structures were the Russian Orthodox Church and the Bureau of Indian Affairs school with its adjoining residence. Scattered around the houses were caches, fish-drying racks, privies, smokehouses, and bathhouses.

Closely related nuclear families tended to live in adjacent houses, and the dwellings of larger families usually included two or three rooms, with the second or third rooms serving primarily for sleeping and storage. Each house had an attached anteroom or storage shed that contained a jumble of objects. A

Plate 4–9 A Napaskiak scene in 1956. In the foreground are racks for drying gill nets and salmon, with a cache and houses behind. (Photograph by the author, courtesy of the University of Arizona Press)

gasoline-powered washing machine often was the largest item in the shed; stored there as well were foods soon to be eaten, winter parkas, a chamber pot, and assorted woodworking tools. The rectangular houses usually had at least one curtained window on each side, plank floors, and walls and ceiling usually covered with painted wallboard. Furnishings included a table and chairs, cast-iron woodburning stove with a clothes drying rack above, a home-made wooden cupboard, and a washstand with an enameled basin. Overhead hung a gasoline lantern that supplied the only light in most households; two families owned gasoline-powered generators to furnish their houses and those of near relatives with electricity. Each house contained trunks or suitcases piled somewhere and filled with clothing not then in use. On one wall there was always an Orthodox Church calendar around which hung prints of icons and a container of holy water. Notably no household furnishings were of aboriginal form. In most dwellings the only artifact of traditional Eskimo manufacture was a knife or ulu, now made by mounting a blade cut from an old wood-saw blade on an ivory handle.

A search for manufactures in the traditional technology produced few forms. The most obvious examples were canoes and kayaks, but the frames of both styles were lashed together with cords and covered with canvas. The large plank boat made of spruce and powered with an outboard motor had long since replaced the umiak. Raised caches retained their form of old, as did gill nets, although the netting was made from cotton, linen, or nylon twine. Hunting weapons were rifles and shotguns. A few boys used bows and arrows, but they preferred slingshots or air rifles. Most of the equipment necessary for living off the country was purchased ready-made from nearby stores, and even items of local manufacture such as plank boats, sleds, or fish traps were constructed from imported materials.

The Kuskowagamiut: Riverine Eskimos

CLOTHING   Men wore trousers, shirts, underwear, and shoes bought from a local store or a mail-order house. A few men, especially older ones, wore sealskin boots, but they were slowly passing out of style. The most popular outer winter garment was a surplus military parka, but some young men wore tight-fitting, lightweight cloth jackets even in the coldest weather. Conservative women, young or old, wore handmade cotton bloomers and petticoats. More cosmopolitan women and older girls wore ready-made underwear. Most women preferred cotton housedresses, but some wore knit sweaters and slacks. Older women wore sealskin boots, but most of the younger ones wore shoes or short rubber boots. Many women, especially those middle-aged and older, had squirrel-skin parkas adorned elaborately with calfskin trimmings, but skin parkas were being replaced by ready-made jackets. In summer, particularly when cleaning fish, a woman wore a hooded cloth parka over her dress. A male child had the same type of clothing as his father but was more likely to wear skin boots, and a girl's garments were similar to those of conservative women.

SUBSISTENCE ACTIVITIES   For each family to thrive it was essential for the male head to possess diverse skills. A man had to be a salmon fisherman, and to vary the diet, he set fish traps, nets, or hooks for other species. He needed to be a good trapper to obtain pelts that could be traded for imported foods and manufactured goods. In theory, a man worked for wages whenever possible to buy items from stores and mail-order houses. Then, too, he should be a capable carpenter and hunter. If he possessed all these skills, he could always compensate for a poor season of trapping, an inadequate harvest of fish, or poor wages by emphasizing an alternative activity. A high degree of flexibility was required since it was almost impossible to fall back on gains from the previous year. As a result, any deficiency in a man's subsistence abilities led to a rapid deterioration in his family's living standard.

In the late fall before the sloughs and lakes froze, some of the men traveled by boat and outboard motor to tundra camps, where about three men shared a single camp. The principal activities before freeze-up were to haul firewood and shoot migratory waterfowl. After the small streams leading from lakes froze, the men set traps for blackfish. They harvested these fish by the thousand and froze them in burlap sacks for dog food later in the winter. When it was safe to travel by dog team, they returned to the village with fish and meat. Most men no longer went to tundra camps; instead they set blackfish traps within about half a day's sled trip from the village. Fall trapping camps on the tundra were no longer family abodes. The people were torn in two directions. A man had to obtain furs with which to purchase imported goods and foods, but he disliked being without his family. The women and children remained in the village because children were obligated to attend school and also because most women no longer accepted the primitive living conditions at camp.

With the approach of winter men fished for burbot through the ice in front of the village with set hooks, and both men and boys spent a great deal of time cutting firewood at nearby stands of alders. With the beginning of the mink trapping season in November, men sledded to their tundra camps. Most camps were about four hours' traveling time from the village, and the particular trapping area might have been in a male line for a number of generations. One or two dozen steel traps were set for mink and were visited every few days.

The distance between a man's trapping camp and the village was related to the number of mink he took. When he ventured a long distance, he was less likely to return often to the village and was more likely to spend his time setting and checking traps. In 1956 mink pelts brought $20 to $25 from local traders, and an average catch was $300 for the season. Most of the men ceased trapping about a week before Christmas. Although it often was quite cold, the primary reason for gathering up their traps was to be at the village during Christmas festivities.

During the extended Christmas celebrations families relied on their food surpluses, and until early spring there were very few subsistence activities possible. In March ptarmigan became plentiful in the willows along sloughs, and hares became active and more easily snared. Again the blackfish began to ascend small streams and could be trapped through the ice.

As the snow began to melt, burbot hooks again were set beneath the river ice, and women jigged for northern pike through holes in the ice. As the days lengthened and snow disappeared from southern exposures, preparations were made for the spring move to tundra camps, usually the same ones as those used in the fall. If a family head had not gone to camp by boat the previous fall, a plank boat had to be hauled by dog sled to provide a means of returning to the village after breakup. By late April most families had settled in tents or small wood and sod houses at camps that bustled with activity. The first concern of the men was to kill as many ducks and geese as possible to satisfy their hunger for fresh meat. The girls and women gathered last year's berries, and the men set small-meshed gill nets in sloughs for pike and whitefish. The men and boys hunted muskrats, the rationale for going to spring camp. They traveled by canvas-covered canoe and kayak from one lake to the next, hunting along the way. In 1956, a relatively poor year for muskrats, a pelt was worth up to 85 cents, and the value of the take per man ranged from $20 to $200. When the muskrat take diminished and the ice cleared from the lakes, people returned to the village by boat, arriving just after the breakup of the Kuskokwim.

By early June large-meshed gill nets were set in the river eddies, and a few sheefish were taken. Soon the season's first king salmon were caught in set nets, and then these nets were used for drift netting salmon. The technique differed from the aboriginal pattern in the use of long commercial nets, a plank boat, and clubs for killing the fish. As in the past the catch was placed in a wooden bin; women prepared the fish for drying by using the techniques of their grandmothers. The intensity of netting species of salmon arriving later

130
The Kuskowagamiut: Riverine Eskimos

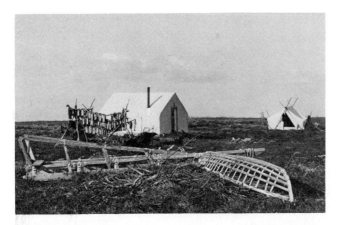

Plate 4-10 The spring camp of two Napaskiak families in 1956. A canoe frame and freight sled are in the foreground, and northern pike are drying on a rack at the side of one tent. (Photograph by the author, courtesy of the University of Arizona Press)

depended on how many king salmon were taken. The last salmon of the season, the silvers, were buried whole in oil drums to become dog food during the winter. Because of their Orthodox beliefs men did not fish on Saturday afternoon or night so that the women would not be obligated to process fish on Sunday, nor did they normally fish on Sunday.

Salmon fishing was largely village-based because the mobility afforded by plank boats and outboard motors made moving to fish camps unnecessary. Efficient boats and motors also made it possible for men to travel to the mouth of the Johnson River, some nine miles downstream, to gillnet whitefish in the fall or to travel about a hundred miles up the Kuskokwim and its tributaries to hunt moose. Family excursions also were made in the summer to gather berries, particularly salmon-berries, which were placed in small barrels and stored for winter use.

The traditional importance of salmon fishing was declining, for men considered wage labor during the summer essential. As many as twenty men earned about $100 each unloading supply vessels docked near Bethel. About the same number also were flown to the Bristol Bay salmon canneries, where they earned $300 to $600 each for the season, and a few others had summer jobs. Only one man, the general assistant at the Bureau of Indian Affairs school, had a permanent job; he earned about $3000 a year. A form of income unassociated with the immediate environment was the money received from Territorial (in 1956) and Federal agencies. Thirteen persons received monthly checks from the Alaska Department of Welfare because they were more than sixty-five years of age and without means of support. Two men received Aid to the Blind, and eight families were helped by Aid to Dependent Children.

Plate 4–11 A Napaskiak man who has just returned from drift netting for salmon in the summer of 1956. (Photograph by the author, courtesy of the University of Arizona Press)

Social Security earnings were received by two men over sixty-five and by three heirs of men who qualified. The total community income from these sources was about $18,000 a year.

Food habits reflected far greater continuity with the past than did the material inventory. Salmon continued to be the most important staple in nearly all households. The aboriginal processing techniques persisted; that is, fish were dried and smoked or might be buried whole. Smokehouses were used, a possible change from aboriginal times. The principal means for cooking salmon was still by boiling, and dried salmon continued to be stripped from the skin in pieces and dipped into seal oil before eating. However people considered that a meal of only salmon was plain fare. They ate unleavened bread for breakfast and drank coffee or tea. Coffee was preferred by most, but tea was substituted when a family's resources were low. In the 1950s every family regarded sugar, flour, salt, canned milk, tea, coffee, tobacco, and cooking oils as necessities. They also bought canned meats and fish, crackers, candy, and canned fruits, depending on their resources.

DESCENT, KINSHIP, AND MARRIAGE   As of old descent was traced equally through the male and female lines (bilateral). The kinship terminology included separate terms for father and mother, as well as uncle and aunt terms for the brothers and sisters of one's parents (lineal type). Cross-cousins were "cousins," whereas parallel cousins were grouped with siblings (Iroquois cousin terms). However, some terms for older and younger biological siblings

The Kuskowagamiut: Riverine Eskimos

Plate 4-12 A Napaskiak woman filleting salmon in 1956. The fillets were held open with small sticks to assure uniform drying. (Photograph by the author, courtesy of the University of Arizona Press)

were not normally extended to parallel cousins. The most important set of relationships seems to have been between males who were classificatory or biological siblings, as previously mentioned. By the time a girl was thirteen she usually was courted by older boys, but since marriages still were arranged by older women and parents, courtship did not lead directly to marital ties. If at all possible, parents found mates for their children in the village (community endogamy); alternatively the girl moved to another village, or, very rarely, to Bethel. A bride was expected to move into the house of her husband's family (temporary patrilocal residence) until the couple could build a house of their own (eventual neolocal residence).

SOCIAL DIMENSIONS   Only the persistence and good fortune of a male family head made it possible for a household to prosper, and the relationship between a father and his son was of key importance. A son learned subsistence-directed skills largely through informal instruction from his father. In his father's company a young man was unassuming; although he might covertly disagree with the older man, a son never overtly expressed his dissatisfaction in a face-to-face situation. The pelts that a son trapped and the wages that he earned were at the disposal of his father. The father, too, had first call on the use of the dog team or boat and outboard motor. Ideally an aged father was cared for by his son, but in all likelihood the old man received Old Age Assistance. With this cash income a father sometimes continued to dominate the economic activities of a household. The relationship between a father and daughter was cooler and more distant. Girls married and moved to their husband's household and offered a father few comforts in his old age.

The bonds between a mother and her daughter were close and overtly warm. After bearing a son, every mother hoped for a daughter to help her with household activities, and a sincere affection bound the pair. A mother sought to find a spouse for her daughter in the community to keep her near, and she vigorously defended the girl against real or imagined abuse from her husband or his family. Mothers also were the most outspoken defenders of their sons, but the same warmth was not expressed toward a son. The relationship between siblings, which extended to parallel cousins, was one of friendship and mutual aid. Married male siblings might live in the same household, draw their food from a common cache, and share equipment. An older male managed the subsistence affairs of the household in the absence of the father. Siblings of the opposite sex were not socially close during their adult lives, but they could be depended on in times of crises. The ties between cross-cousins were looser, and the degree of closeness was largely dependent on the personalities of the individuals involved. It was these persons with whom one joked and, if called on, they rendered mutual assistance.

Four or more times a week nearly all men took steam baths that lasted for hours on end. The small Russian-style bathhouse had an outer dressing room and an inner steam room; each could accommodate about a dozen persons. There were nine such bathhouses in the community, and certain men bathed together frequently. These structures had replaced the kashgee as the place where men bathed and relaxed in each other's company. Unlike the kashgees of old, however, these bathhouses also were used by women. Sometimes a woman bathed with her husband; only in rare instances would one bathe with any other man. In the home the old sexual dichotomy existed still. A woman was primarily responsible for the household's functioning, and her husband was something of an outsider. Thus a subdued but pervasive individualism dominated home life. It was reflected in the behavior of old people, both men and women, who frequently preferred to live alone in their own houses, a pattern facilitated by old age assistance funds.

The village problem considered most critical by the people and government officials alike was illness, and tuberculosis was the most dangerous disease by far. Among the 180 permanent residents in 1956, forty-five had active cases of tuberculosis, and unquestionably there were additional cases. Villagers had vague notions about the germ theory of disease but recognized that no one cure was invariably successful. Therefore, in an effort to increase their chance of recovery, they attempted diverse cures for this or any other serious illness. They tried patent medicines and the traditional pharmacopoeia, then might take steam baths, consult a shaman, drink holy water or pray in church, and finally turn to prescription medicine dispensed by the teacher and the Bethel hospital. A major program of tuberculosis control was being implemented largely through a chemotherapy program at the village level by the U. S. Public Health Service.

The most intensive contacts outside the community were with the urban settlement of Bethel. The five large stores, U. S. Public Health Service hospital, pool halls, restaurants, and theaters were among the greatest attractions in Bethel for the villagers. Here, too, they met friends and relatives from other settlements and ordered intoxicants flown in from Anchorage. Thus Bethel was the center of diverse forms of socializing. Contacts with adjacent villages were largely social or religious in nature. A family traveled to visit relatives, attend a funeral, or arrange church business. The only other local trips were taken downriver in the spring to hunt seals and upriver in the fall to hunt moose. A few men went to distant urban centers in Alaska to work briefly; more men went to Anchorage each spring to attend an encampment of their local U. S. National Guard unit. The only other contact with the outside world was a stay in a hospital at Anchorage, Seward, or in the state of Washington.

Not all exotic contacts necessitated leaving the community. One could listen to a battery radio, which was found in most houses, and learn what was happening beyond the local area. "Tundra Topics," broadcast from Fairbanks, was especially popular, for it presented news about isolated settlements. Then, too, people came to the village from urban areas in connection with some form of governmental work. The only outsider to reside in the community was the Bureau of Indian Affairs teacher, but the Bureau also sent supervisors and maintenance workers to the settlement on occasion. U. S. Public Health Service field nurses and those working with the special program for the control of tuberculosis made regular visits. Scientists were rather frequent callers; their work usually had to do with some aspect of public health. An occasional U. S. National Guard officer or enlisted man from the Bethel headquarters came on official business, and the same applied to the U. S. Deputy Marshal from Bethel. Sometimes there was even a stray tourist seen in the village.

POLITICAL LIFE   From as long ago as anyone could recall until 1950 Napaskiak had a kashgee, which served the same functions as in other aboriginal Kuskowagamiut settlements. In the kashgee, two or three older men who were respected for their wisdom constituted an informal council of elders. Their judgment was not likely to be challenged nor would the opinions of an important shaman be disregarded. In rare instances of irreconcilable differences between families, the weaker family and its allies left the settlement. In 1906 a Russian Orthodox priest visited the village, and his appointed representative became the first "chief." Apparently the head of a large extended family, he soon was replaced by his son, for he was an old man at the time of the appointment. The original duty of a chief was to arrange matters pertaining to church affairs, and this has remained one of his most important functions. In 1947 the first elected chief took office. His duties had come to include secular as well as sacred obligations and were confused in the minds of most villagers. Some said that he was head of the village, but others regarded the

Orthodox Church Brotherhood as the collective head of local affairs. The authority of any particular chief seemed to be dependent on his personality. Part of the confusion resulted from the efforts of the Bureau of Indian Affairs officials to introduce an elected council into the village. Local Indian Affairs personnel were promoting the Indian Reorganization Act, as extended to Alaska in 1936, when the first teacher arrived in 1939. The teacher attempted to induce the people to organize under the terms of the act but never was successful. The villagers did elect a council in 1945 but did not request Federal recognition. The council was partially ineffective because its members were reluctant to take any overt action against other persons. The most serious problem was intoxication. The usual course of action was to warn a heavy drinker; on rare occasions, a warrant for an arrest was sworn out with the U. S. Deputy Marshal at Bethel. Meetings also were called to collect funds for village medical needs, to establish a curfew for school children, or to request that the airline offices in Bethel refuse to accept orders for intoxicants from villagers. However, there usually was little reason for council meetings since little community cohesion existed along secular lines.

Warfare was not a part of village life except as it was imposed through the political control of the United States. Early in World War II the Alaska Territorial Guard was organized as a scouting unit for the U. S. Army at a time when an invasion of the Alaskan mainland seemed likely. In the village unit older men were appointed as officers, and the younger ones became enlisted men. Very little military discipline prevailed, but large quantities of military equipment were issued. Since men here were permitted to use the clothing and guns daily, real economic advantages were gained by belonging to the Alaska Territorial Guard. After the war ended this organization was replaced by the U. S. National Guard, and the policies changed drastically. The older men were discouraged from re-enlisting, especially if they spoke no English. Promising younger men were sent to special training schools, and regular drills became a routine part of membership. The village unit came to reflect military norms and emerged as a disruptive institution in village life, particularly since it encouraged the overt authority of young aggressive men, an unprecedented village behavior pattern. Younger men regarded the National Guard as romantic, and the yearly two-week encampment near Anchorage was a great adventure. The older men who remained in the unit did so because of the monetary rewards.

RELIGION   Christianity was introduced to the Kuskokwim in its Russian Orthodox form, and in the 1950s all of the people at Napaskiak, including a practicing shaman, considered themselves Christians. Since there had never been a resident missionary, Orthodox dogma was not well understood. Most villagers agreed that helping other people when in need was one of the most important Christian ideals. After an individual died, the soul automatically went to hell if he or she had not been baptized or if death was from suicide.

136

The Kuskowagamiut: Riverine Eskimos

Otherwise God evaluated a person's deeds, and on this basis the spirit was admitted to heaven or hell. At times the ghost of a dead person returned to the community; to decrease the likelihood of a visitation the windows were opened after death and closed after burial. An icon was hung on the door to prevent the spirit from returning through the doorway.

The ceremonial cycle duplicated the Orthodox Church calendar elsewhere in the world. Along with regular church services, special observances were held at Russian Christmas and New Year, the Epiphany, the Easter Season, and during the annual church conference. Russian Christmas was of far greater importance than any other ceremonial event, and preparations were elaborate. The choir practiced Russian Christmas songs in both Russian and Eskimo, the men hauled and chopped enough wood to heat their houses during the holiday season, wine was ordered through an airline, the ceremonial equipment was made ready, and special foods were prepared. Finally, visitors arrived from surrounding communities. The central theme of the three days of processions was to announce the birth of Christ in each household by singing Christmas songs while carrying a guiding star made of metal. Since the singers and their followers were fed at each house, most of the three nights were taken up with eating vast quantities of food. The Russian New Year was celebrated by putting lighted kerosene lanterns on the graves of the dead, as was done also at Russian Christmas. At about midnight, fireworks and guns were shot off while the Christmas trees which had decorated the houses for the season

Plate 4–13 Napaskiakers and the Russian Orthodox Bishop of Alaska in 1956. (Photograph by the author, courtesy of the University of Arizona Press)

were burned in front of the village. The climax of the event was a short service in church about the ideals of behavior for the coming year.

One reason for the ineffectiveness of the village council was that the Orthodox Church Brotherhood long had cared for the crisis needs of the community and held monthly meetings to deal with ongoing problems. The general purpose of this organization was to coordinate church activities and to provide welfare aid for members. Because all of the families participated in at least some Orthodox Church functions, with only one man claiming membership in another church, the welfare provision embraced everyone. The Brotherhood had elected officers with established duties. The specific obligations of its members were to prepare coffins and bury the dead, to arrange for the annual trip of the bishop to the area, to aid the aged, to maintain the church structure, and to perform certain ceremonial obligations. From the time of its organization in 1931 the Brotherhood provided food and funds to families without means of support until this function was assumed by the Alaska Department of Welfare and the Bureau of Indian Affairs shortly after World War II.

RECENT DEVELOPMENTS: 1970   By 1970 Napaskiak had grown considerably as a physical settlement, and yet in many respects it appeared to be much the same as in 1955. The church and National Guard armory were unchanged, but the physical plant of the Bureau of Indian Affairs school had been enlarged. Although a few houses had been torn down and rooms had been added to others, most of them looked as they had fifteen years before. New buildings included a community hall and a structure that housed a community well and water storage tank. Old bathhouses had been replaced, and behind most houses were new privies. Fifteen years earlier numerous dogs were tied behind the houses, and although this was still true in 1970, many snowmobiles also could be seen. Other physical changes were more subtle and yet important. Few canvas-covered canoes were to be seen, and most kayaks were falling to pieces from obvious disuse. The people had more plank boats and far more high-powered outboard motors than previously. Within the houses certain changes were quite notable such as the quality of the imported tables and chairs, the factory-made beds, the presence of oil-burning space heaters, and a number of expensive radios and clocks. Household inventories were far larger than before and reflected far greater capital investment.

By 1970 the population had grown to 260, and this figure includes only a handful of migrants to the village. The striking population increase is explained in part by the decline in infant mortality that has enabled more individuals to survive into adulthood. These young people, who came from large families, have begun to raise large families of their own. In addition, tuberculosis, a pervasive killer and crippler in the past, was eradicated through U. S. Public Health Services efforts. It truly is astounding that the death rate from tuberculosis, which among native Alaskans in 1950 was 653 per 100,000 (compared to 22.5 for all races in the United States), had declined to 3.7 in 1969 and was nonexistent in 1970.

138

The Kuskowagamiut: Riverine Eskimos

The dramatic population increase was accompanied by greater affluence. This resulted from two changes: an expanding economic base and more comprehensive welfare programs. The local incomes from trapping, National Guard membership, and work at Bristol Bay salmon canneries continued, but in addition the wage labor opportunities at Bethel had increased so much that numerous persons commuted there to work. Furthermore, by 1970 the Alaska Department of Fish and Game permitted commercial salmon fishing along the lower river. The partial displacement of dogs by snowmobiles meant that fewer salmon were required as dog food, and as a result men sold much of their catch to commercial buyers. Because of liberalization of welfare aid requirements and the availability of more funds, unearned income from government sources was significantly increased. Furthermore, and of real importance, the food stamp program enabled families to obtain far more adequate food supplies than ever before.

Another dramatic change centered around intoxicants; the scope and intensity of drinking had mushroomed. More money was available to buy alcoholic beverages, and they were available from a liquor store and at a bar in Bethel. In the 1950s intoxicant consumption was not a disruptive force in community life, but the same was not true in 1970. Deaths, usually by drowning, directly attributable to drunkenness were common; by village standards a number of men were alcoholics, and most younger men drank heavily. In the 1950s doors to houses had simple interior locks or just a piece of cord wrapped around a pair of nails on either side of the jamb. In 1970 each house had a substantial lock and sometimes paired, locked doors to protect family members against roaming drunks.

Subsistence fishing as well as hunting and trapping continue to play a very important part in regional economic development, yet there is an increasing commitment to wage labor and commercial salmon fishing. Christianity prevails as the religious focus, the men's houses—when they exist at all—have lost their traditional meaning, and social life has been recast in new molds. Although it is no longer possible to think realistically in terms of aboriginal culture, Kuskokwim Eskimos have a growing awareness of their cultural heritage as Eskimos. This change is most clearly seen as villagers cope with the settlement of land claims against the Federal Government. Traders, missionaries, and Bureau of Indian Affairs representatives have lost control as Eskimos gain title to their traditional lands and begin to direct their own affairs.

LAND CLAIMS   A brief review of Alaskan Eskimo land claims is appropriate. When Alaska was purchased from Russia by the United States in 1867, the treaty provided that "The uncivilized tribes will be subject to such laws and regulations as the United States may, from time to time, adopt in regard to aboriginal tribes in that country." No formal effort was made by the Federal Government to consider aboriginal land claims until 1906. At that time individuals could gain "restricted" title to 160 acre plots, but few selections were made because the grants were inappropriate in terms of their Eskimo needs.

The first effort by aboriginal Alaskans to organize for their rights as citizens was in 1912 when the Alaska Native Brotherhood was founded, but this effort, discussed in Chapter 10, was restricted largely to the Tlingit of southeastern Alaska. The Indian Reorganization Act of 1934 encouraged the establishment of reservations, but few Eskimos or Indians claimed lands under its provisions, and no large blocks of land were set aside along the Kuskokwim. The greatest threat to local Eskimo control and use of land came when Alaska became a state in 1959. The new state was granted the right to select 103 million acres of land from the public domain. In 1961 Guy Okakok, an Eskimo from Point Barrow, was instrumental in organizing Inupiat Paitot (The People's Heritage); the newspaper *Tundra Times* was founded by the Point Hope Eskimo Howard Rock in 1962, and in 1966 the Alaska Federation of Natives was organized. All of these efforts were directed primarily at achieving a settlement of native claims throughout the state. The first important victory was the imposition by Secretary of the Interior Stewart Udall of a "land freeze" on state selections. Finally after years of proposals and counterproposals, the Alaska Native Claims Settlement Act was passed by Congress and became law in 1971. The major provisions were that Alaskan Natives were to receive fee simple title to forty million acres of land and that 962.5 million dollars was to be paid to the Alaska Native Fund over a period of years as compensation for extinguished claims. The money was to come from congressional appropriations and 2 percent of the mineral revenues from certain Federal and state lands in Alaska. U. S. citizens in or from Alaska having one-fourth or more Aleut, Eskimo, or Indian blood were enrolled and became stockholders in regional corporations and usually village corporations as well. In general the regional corporations held mineral rights to village lands. Payments were from the Alaska Native Fund to regional corporations on a per capita basis; the regional corporations retained part of the money and turned the balance over to village corporations and to individuals.

The Calista (meaning "the one who works") Corporation is the regional corporation including most of the Kuskokwim River drainage, the lower Yukon River, the land extending to the Bering Sea coast between these rivers, and the adjacent islands. The original enrollment in Calista was about 13,500 persons in fifty-six villages; the largest village corporation is Bethel, with 1725 stockholders. By the end of 1974 the Calista Corporation had received nearly thirty-four million dollars from the Alaska Native Fund, of which about sixteen million was retained by the regional corporation, the balance going to village corporations and individuals. The Calista Corporation has invested in diverse business ventures, including an Anchorage hotel and office building, a trailer park in Valdez, and a planned community near Anchorage that includes a country club, an eighteen-hole golf course, and riding trails.

With the land settlement proceeding, a great deal of money being received, and a more sympathetic working relationship with the Bureau of Indian Affairs, Kuskokwim Eskimos have found a new pride in their culture. For years the B. I. A. policy strictly prohibited Eskimo children from speaking

The Kuskowagamiut: Riverine Eskimos

Eskimo in school, but now the Yupik dialect is taught in many schools. Bethel has a thriving museum, Yuktarevik (The Place of the People's Things). The Bethel Regional High School students have an ongoing publication series devoted largely to articles on ethnographic and ethnohistorical topics, some of which are excellent. The Bethel high school has classes about fishing, boat building, and the repair of outboard motors. In a Cultural Heritage Program during the spring of 1974 about 500 high school students visited nearly thirty villages for two weeks to learn more about their cultural traditions and held a fair on their return to Bethel to exhibit their newly-developed skills and handcrafted articles. The Kuskokwim Community College was formed in 1972, and classes are conducted at Bethel as well as in the villages. Topics for instruction include management of village corporations, small engine repair, land and resource management, and teacher training.

The infusion of large amounts of money controlled by Eskimos, the efforts by the Federal and State Governments to educate leaders, schools responsive to regional needs, and a pride in Eskimo culture make the future look bright, very bright for the Kuskowagamiut.

Comparisons among the Kuskowagamiut, Chipewyan, and Caribou Eskimos

Although all three peoples were hunters, fishermen, and trappers in aboriginal times, significant contrasts are reflected in their customs. The Chipewyan and Caribou Eskimos had far more in common than the Caribou and Kuskokwim Eskimos, even though the Eskimos shared a common cultural background. Note that the Kuskokwim Eskimos had relatively permanent settlements, larger aggregates of people, a well-developed ceremonial life, and more material goods than the others. These differences may in part be explained by the more reliable food resources available in southwestern Alaska. The reader may care to consider why Kuskokwim Eskimo culture was not more elaborate in aboriginal times, why leadership was not more fully developed among them, and why their traditional lifeway was not more durable in the face of Russian and American contacts. Comparisons among these peoples in terms of their responses to contacts with Euro-Americans are also worthy of consideration.

The chapters about the Chipewyan and two Eskimo groups include reasonably complete information about life at particular villages in the 1950s and 1960s. Studies of northern communities have been appealing to anthropologists because of the continuity they exhibit with aboriginal conditions. Acculturative ethnographies of comparable scope are far less frequent for peoples presented in later chapters. Thus the Chipewyan and Eskimo data provide a better opportunity to plot recent historical changes at the village level, and comparisons are invited along these dimensions.

Additional Readings

Alaskan Eskimos in the Bering Sea region are known for the complexity of their technology; the best descriptions of their material culture are in the monograph by Nelson. Unfortunately comparatively few recent studies have been made about Kuskokwim Eskimos. An ethnoarchaeological monograph by Wendell H. Oswalt and James VanStone (1967) makes it possible to gain insight into the material changes introduced to the region by the Russians and early Americans. In his book about Alaskan Eskimo education, John Collier devoted a major portion to the Kuskowagamiut; more than any others, this study analyzes the methods and results of the B. I. A. school system. An unpublished doctoral dissertation by Lynn D. Mason, although not widely available, traces the impact of exotic disease and trauma in the lives of the people in one Kuskokwim Eskimo community.

Alaskan Eskimos (San Francisco, 1967) by Wendell H. Oswalt is a comparative study of aboriginal conditions for this segment of the Eskimo population.

References

Anderson, Eva G. *Dog-Team Doctor*. Caldwell. 1940.

Arnold, Robert D., et al. *Alaska Native Land Claims*. Anchorage. 1976.

Collier, John. *Alaskan Eskimo Education*. New York. 1973.

Gordon, George B. *In the Alaskan Wilderness*. Philadelphia. 1917.

Johnson, M. Walter. "Tuberculosis in Alaska" (paper presented at the Second International Symposium on Circumpolar Health, Oulu, Finland, 1971).

Kilbuck, John H. "Something about the Innuit of the Kuskokwim River, Alaska." Manuscript in The Archives of the Moravian Church, Bethlehem, Pa.

Mason, Lynn D. "Disabled Fishermen." Ph. D. dissertation, University of California, Los Angeles. 1972.

Nelson, Edward W. *The Eskimo about Bering Strait*. Bureau of American Ethnology, 18th Annual Report, pt. 1. 1899.

*Oswalt, Wendell H. *Napaskiak: An Alaskan Eskimo Community*. Tucson. 1963a. This 1955–1956 study of one Kuskokwim Eskimo community supplies virtually all that we know of contemporary riverine Eskimo life in southwestern Alaska.

*Oswalt, Wendell H. *Mission of Change in Alaska*. San Marino. 1963b. A his-

The Kuskowagamiut: Riverine Eskimos

torical reconstruction, supplemented by the author's field notes, of Kuskokwim Eskimo life, with concentration on the period from 1884 to 1925. Additional summary information is provided on the Russian era and events subsequent to 1925.

Oswalt, Wendell H. "Traditional Storyknife Tales of Yuk Girls," *Proceedings of the American Philosophical Society*, v. 108, no. 4, 310–336. 1964.

Oswalt, Wendell H., and James W. VanStone. "The Ethnoarcheology of Crow Village, Alaska," *Smithsonian Institution, Bureau of American Ethnology*, Bulletin 199. 1967.

Petroff, Ivan. *Report on the Population, Industries, and Resources of Alaska.* United States Department of Interior, Census Office. 1884.

Schwalbe, Anna B. *Dayspring on the Kuskokwim.* Bethlehem. 1951.

Weinland Collection. The William Henry Weinland collection of manuscripts, letters, and diaries. Henry E. Huntington Library, San Marino, California.

Wrangell, Ferdinand von. *Statistical and Ethnographic Data Concerning the Russian Possessions on the Northwest Coast of America.* St. Petersburg. 1839 (in German).

*Zagoskin, Lavrentiy A. *Lieutenant Zagoskin's Travels in Russian America, 1842–1844.* Henry N. Michael, ed., Arctic Institute of North America, Anthropology of the North: Translations from Russian Sources/ No. 7. Toronto. 1967. This early historic Russian traveler's account is the primary source for aboriginal Eskimo life along the Kuskokwim River.

The Cahuilla: Gatherers in the Desert

5

Origin Myth

In the beginning, there was no earth or sky or anything or anybody; only a dense darkness in space. This darkness seemed alive. Something like lightnings seemed to pass through it and meet each other once in a while. Two substances which looked like the white of an egg came from these lightnings. They lay side by side in the stomach of the darkness, which resembled a spider web. These substances disappeared. They were then produced again, and again they disappeared. This was called the miscarriage of the darkness. The third time they appeared, they remained, hanging there in this web in the darkness. The substances began to grow and soon were two very large eggs. When they began to hatch, they broke at the top first. Two heads came out, then shoulders, hips, knees, ankles, toes; then the shell was all gone. Two boys had emerged: Mukat and Tamaioit. They were grown men from the first, and could talk right away. As they lay there, both at the same time heard a noise like a bee buzzing. It was the song of their mother Darkness (Hooper, 1920, 317).

With this great event the natural world began to emerge as an orderly system; at least this was said to be so by the Iviatim, the descendants of Mukat

145

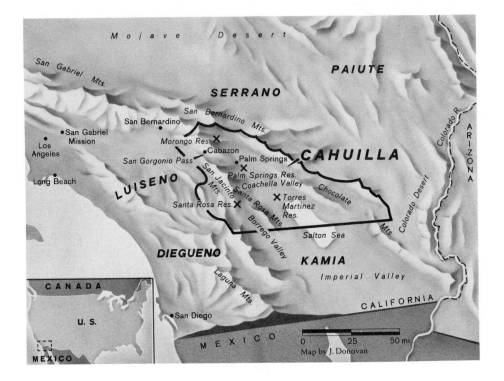

Map by J. Donovan

146

and Tamaioit, who have come to be known in the ethnographic literature as the Cahuilla (Coahuillas, Kawia), a word that may have meant "masters."

Once the twin creators existed, Mukat reached into his mouth and then into his heart to remove a cricket, another insect, a lizard, and a person. These creatures were charged with driving away the darkness, but they failed. From their hearts the creators removed tobacco, pipes, and a coal to light one pipe. Mukat and Tamaioit argued over which one was born first and which was the more intelligent. Mukat became associated with making things black, and Tamaioit made forms that were white. Together they created the earth, ocean, sun, moon, people, and some plants and animals. Finally Mukat and Tamaioit disagreed so violently that Tamaioit disappeared beneath the ground, taking with him many of his creations. It was then that mountains emerged, the earth quaked, and water from the ocean overflowed, forming streams and rivers. After this Mukat lived in a big house with people and animals who had human qualities. The moon was there as a lovely female who instructed women about marriage, child rearing, and both menstrual and pregnancy taboos. Mukat, who had created her, desired to make the moon his wife. She knew this but said nothing. Since she could not marry him because he was her father, she traveled to her present home in the sky. When she was asked to return, she said nothing; she only smiled. One day, while in a humorous mood, Mukat caused the people to speak different languages. As the sun grew hot, some of these people sought shelter and were transformed into different plants and animals. Those who had stayed with Mukat remained human. He told the people how to make bows and arrows and how to shoot at each other, which led to the first deaths. It was about this time, too, that the sun turned people different colors. Those people who were nearest the sun's rays became Negroes, those that were far away stayed white, and the Indians turned brown because they were in between.

The people became angry with Mukat after he had caused a rattlesnake to bite a friendly little man, the moon woman to leave, and people to kill one another. They decided to kill Mukat but did not know how to do it. Mukat lived in the middle of the big house and only went outside to defecate when everyone was asleep; this a white lizard discovered. One night a frog caught the feces of Mukat in his mouth, and Mukat grew ill. The shamans pretended to try to cure him, but Mukat became sicker. As he was dying, he sang songs and told the people how to conduct a mourning ceremony in memory of the dead each year. After his death, Mukat was cremated, the big house was burned, and the essence of the world was established.

Population and Language

The Cahuilla lived in the interior of southern California and numbered 3600, or possibly many more, in early historic times. By 1885 their population

147

had declined to about 800, and it remained at this level for some sixty years. In the mid-1970s about 1500 retained their identity as Cahuilla by being on the tribal roll, but most did not live on the five small reservations. In early historic times and more recently they identified themselves as members of the Desert, Mountain, or Pass groups, but a sense of tribal solidarity probably originated in response to Mexican and Anglo-American contacts.

The Aztec-Tanoan linguistic phylum, which is represented widely in the western United States and Mexico, includes Cahuilla. These Indians belong to the Uto-Aztecan language family. The emergence of the Cahuilla as a separate people is revealed through linguistic rather than archaeological researches. Unfortunately, no archaeological sites excavated and published on provide clues to their past. Linguists, however, do offer some insight into the past affinities of these people. Kenneth Hale, after analyzing the vocabularies of certain Aztec-Tanoan languages, concluded on lexicostatistical grounds that the Cahuilla became a separate linguistic group about 1000 B.C.

Reasons for This Selection

A major reason for selecting these and the other peoples described in this book is that the ethnographic and historical data about them are more comprehensive than is typical for most tribes. We have a fine Cahuilla ethnobotany by David P. Barrows, a comprehensive account compiled around the turn of the century by Alfred L. Kroeber, and a somewhat later report by Lucile Hooper. In 1959 Lowell J. Bean began reconstructing an aboriginal baseline ethnography, and he has emerged as the ranking authority on the Cahuilla.

Anthropologists have not been the only persons with a vested interest in the Cahuilla. They have attracted attention from B. I. A. employees, land speculators, lawyers, and especially municipal officials in the resort city of Palm Springs. For the most part the concern of these persons has been neither humanistic nor philanthropic but monetary. Certain reservation lands are of fantastic value, and very few Indians occupy them. The Desert Cahuilla afford an excellent opportunity to analyze the relationship between a now-prosperous Indian group and their Anglo-American neighbors. Although we tend to think that the era of grabbing Indian land is not only past but best forgotten, the Cahuilla example illustrates that Anglo-Americans have not changed their goals, simply their methods. All of this is especially interesting when it is realized that among the Cahuilla the women resolved their serious land problem. Until recently the Palm Springs Cahuilla had the only Indian council comprised of women. In a historical context, the Cahuilla have romantic appeal through the novel *Ramona*. Once fabulously popular, it depicts the life of a Cahuilla woman, and its writer, Helen Hunt Jackson, played a significant role in the lives of southern California Indians just before the turn of the century.

In the following discussion of the Cahuilla the stress is on the Desert

The Cahuilla: Gatherers in the Desert

group and the Palm Springs (Agua Caliente) subgroup. However, it was not always possible to determine from a source that a specific trait prevailed in both the general desert region and at Palm Springs. As is true of most ethnographic reconstructions, the text to follow will not apply in every detail to a single community, but it does represent a composite for the desert region.

Early History

The Cahuilla often are classed as Mission Indians, but this is not an accurate label. They were not subject to the mission environment in the manner of coastal Indians in southern California, and most Cahuilla had only indirect contact with Roman Catholic missionaries. The first Europeans to travel into Cahuilla country were Pedro Fages in 1772 and Juan Bautista de Anza in 1774, but neither made any known impact on these Indians. De Anza attempted without success to establish an overland route from Mexico to Alta California. Following the War for Independence in Mexico attention again turned to the interior of southern California. At the request of Indians in the San Bernardino area for a mission, an outpost or rancho was established among them in 1819. Jose Romero was charged with opening an overland route, and a small party set out from Tucson in 1823. From an expedition member's diary annotated recently by Bean and William M. Mason it is apparent that the Desert Cahuilla, at least those as far south and west as Palm Springs, were in rather close contact with the San Bernardino mission rancho. Some of the people in the Coachella Valley were raising maize and pumpkins, crops that they probably acquired from Colorado River area Indians, and the Cahuilla of the desert were growing watermelon, an Old World domestic plant introduced by Europeans to the New World.

Before 1834 the California missions were under the control of Franciscans, who introduced most European ideas and technology to the region. After this date some missions, including the one founded at San Gabriel in 1771, became secularized, and the missionaries lost control. In 1834, the San Bernardino rancho was sacked and burned by Indians. With secularization the rancho passed into private ownership, and marauding Indians raided the herds of livestock. A Mountain Cahuilla leader, "Captain" Juan Antonio, and his small band were recruited to end the raids, which they did with great success. In 1846 the United States acquired California, and a few years later, in 1852, the San Bernardino rancho was purchased by Mormon settlers. During the late Mexican and early American periods the raids by Mohave, Paiute, and Yuma for livestock, especially horses, contributed to the hostile attitude of whites toward most Indians in southern California. The Cahuilla were not combative by nature and apparently played an insignificant part in these raids. Since they did not intrude on the activities of whites, the Cahuilla were left very much to themselves.

In 1850 the U. S. Congress sent a special commission to California to negotiate treaties with Indians and assign lands to them. A Cahuilla treaty arranged in 1852 set aside land from San Gorgonio to Warner's ranch, an area about forty miles long and thirty miles wide. The U. S. Senate, however, refused to ratify any of the eighteen treaties with California Indians. Congressional resistance stemmed from a number of facts: the commissioners had committed the government to spend a great deal of money, white citizens of California were vigorously opposed to the treaties, and it was thought that some of these lands might contain gold.

In 1852 Edward F. Beale was appointed Superintendent of Indian Affairs in California, and he selected Benjamin D. Wilson as the subagent for the southern part of the state. Wilson, a former mayor of Los Angeles, was a landowner and merchant married to a Spanish-American. In a report that may have been written by Wilson's friend Benjamin Hays, we have contemporary comments about the Cahuilla and a good account of conditions among southern California Indians. The Wilson Report noted that the last ties with missionaries were severed in 1834 and that old ethnic groups were disrupted by 1852. Living among the Desert Cahuilla were Diegueno and Luiseno Indians; one of the Cahuilla leaders was a Yuma. The elders and many others spoke Spanish by this time. The Indians worked as underpaid laborers and domestics on the ranchos of whites and were frequently intoxicated. The report pointed out that under Spanish law the Indians had rights to their settlements and pasture lands, and in theory the State of California recognized Indian landrights. State laws were characterized as "*All* punishment. *No* reform!" The positive recommendations of the Wilson Report made no recognized impact on early American policy, probably in part because of the recent rejection of California Indian treaties by the U. S. Senate.

In late 1852 Beale recommended that lands be set aside for Indian occupation; this was the beginning of the modern reservation system in the United States. The lands would be military reservations as well as places where Indians could be instructed in farming and other skills. Soldiers were to be stationed there to maintain order, and the military would be supported from surplus Indian harvests. The first reserve opened at Tejon in 1853, and after initial success the political enemies of Beale charged that he was making a personal profit from the reservation. Although he finally was vindicated fully, the reservation system had losts its impetus and did not become important in California.

In the mid-1850s the Cahuilla reportedly numbered about 3500 males, of whom 1500 were of fighting age. These figures unquestionably included many non-Cahuilla, but in any event Indians far outnumbered the local white settlers. The Indians were discontented after the Federal Government failed to honor the treaty; they complained that they had not received farm equipment as promised and that whites were trespassing and squatting on traditional Indian lands, from which they took water and wood. In 1862 a smallpox epidemic spread from Los Angeles, and although it is not recorded how many peo-

150

ple perished, the epidemic probably was a significant factor in eroding the people and their way of life. Throughout the latter part of the nineteenth century some Cahuilla worked on the ranches of whites, the men as laborers and the women as domestics. The men also tended orchards and vineyards, cut mesquite wood, and labored at salt works. When the Southern Pacific Railroad was being built through the area in the 1870s, they were employed as laborers. They continued to collect products of the desert, and some of the better-watered localities were farmed.

Aboriginal Life

SETTLEMENTS   Cahuilla tradition states that they originally lived in the desert but were forced to flee to adjacent mountains by a great flood, a probable reference to the emergence of the inland sea that once covered much of the present lowland and subsided about 500 years ago. The San Jacinto and Santa Rosa mountains where they sought refuge consist of steep granite ridges and barren tablelands at medium elevations, but higher up are streams, open meadows, and forests of oak and pine. After the flood subsided, the Desert Cahuilla moved into the Coachella Valley, a desert environment in which cacti, mesquite, and screw beans were economically important plants. The region has very little precipitation, and summer temperatures may reach 120°F. Although it seldom rains, precipitation, when it comes, is often torrential and causes widespread erosion. Furthermore, severe duststorms may whip across

Plate 5–1 Desert Cahuilla house in 1907. (Photograph by Alfred L. Kroeber, courtesy of Lowie Museum of Anthropology, University of California, Berkeley)

the valley. Some sectors, particularly in the eastern part of the Desert Cahuilla range, are devoid of vegetation. The Pass Cahuilla occupied the country surrounding San Gorgonio Pass; here were open grassland and some oak groves as well as desert areas.

Desert Cahuilla settlements usually were clustered around hand-dug wells and water holes, but the Palm Springs people lived near streams flowing from canyons at the base of the San Jacinto Mountains. Communities were permanent as long as the water supply lasted. Their dwellings were substantial rectangular structures with forked mesquite posts at each corner; in the post crotches rested roof beams. Along the sides and on the beam tops were arranged lengths of brush held in place with horizontal poles. On some houses the brush was smeared with a coat of mud, and a layer of dirt was added to the roof. At the front of a house was a ramada or porch constructed like a house but walled only on the windward side. A settlement included a bathhouse framed with posts and poles; built in a shallow pit, it probably was covered with brush and then a layer of earth. A fire was built in the fireplace, and smoke was allowed to drift out the doorway until the people were ready to bathe. Cahuilla caches were of a distinctive form and were found in every set-

Plate 5–2 A 1907 Desert Cahuilla granary. (Photograph by Alfred L. Kroeber, courtesy of Lowie Museum of Anthropology, University of California, Berkeley)

The Cahuilla: Gatherers in the Desert

tlement. They usually were raised above the ground on a pole platform and were made by intertwining small branches; they looked very much like birds' nests some two to four feet in height and were used to store plant products. The only other structures were a brush enclosure used for certain ceremonies and a large enclosure, walled on three sides and attached to the house of a male leader. Among the Palm Springs Cahuilla in 1925, the social and ceremonial leader occupied the dance house, which was about forty feet in diameter with walls of fitted boards and a palm-thatched roof. At the back was a room where the sacred bundle was kept; in front of the structure was a fenced enclosure.

An aboriginal house would impress an observer with its relative coolness, even in the hottest weather. The inside was dark from the soot on the walls, and natural light filtered in only through the doorway. On one side of the entrance were a woman's food grinding stones. People the world over who collect seeds as food usually use a set of stones to crush the shells. The Cahuilla spread seeds on a flat or slightly concave stone called a milling stone, quern, or metate; the smaller pulverizing stone is called a hand stone or mano. On the other side of the doorway was a pottery vessel used for water and filled each morning. Toward the center of the room fire-blackened cooking pots encircled the fireplace; at the back of the house were blankets and animal skins that served as mattresses. Attached to the roof beams or in the thatch were bundles of plants or dried meat for future use. Near every house a section of log was set vertically into the ground; the top was flat except that the center was hollowed out a foot or more in depth. A smooth pole some two feet in length served as the pestle for this mortar. The combination was designed to pulverize mesquite beans, which were an important item in the diet.

Most artifacts around a settlement were made from plant fibers. Baskets, usually fashioned by coiling and often having black geometric designs woven on the sides, were the most varied cluster of forms. Among the more common styles were globular baskets used as utensils or containers for small objects and round forms for food or seed storage. Mescal fiber nets used as carrying baskets looked like small hammocks and had loops at each end for cinching cords. A woman carrying a basket passed the cord over her forehead and rested it against the front of her basket hat.

The only domestic animal, the dog, served as a pet and watchdog rather than as an aid in hunting. The dog was not an ordinary pet because it possessed certain supernatural powers. Dogs could understand human conversation but could not speak, and like people, they had souls. At the time of Mukat's death, the people had only one dog, and among the twentieth-century Desert Cahuilla, some dogs still were named after the first dog. Other dog names referred to their appearance or to some behavioral characteristic.

CLOTHING   In aboriginal times clothing seems to have been nonexistent, although it is possible that women wore short skirts of plant fiber and men wore breechclouts. A more certain item of apparel was footwear, which consisted of sandals made from mescal fiber pads. Women sometimes wore ill-fitting, flat-topped caps made of basketry. They were tattooed on the chin, and certain men, most likely leaders, had their nasal septums pierced and inserted a deer bone in the opening. Both males and females wore strings of beads in their pierced earlobes. The beads were thin curved and circular pieces of shell received in trade from the coastal regions of southern California.

SUBSISTENCE ACTIVITIES   These people identified three primary seasons: the budding of trees, hot days, and cold days. Some persons divided the year into eight more specific seasons, each associated with the development of mesquite beans. The beginning of a season arrived when a particular star appeared; this was a moment for rejoicing and a time to make preparations for an appropriate collecting activity. Star watching was especially important in the spring when food supplies might be low and edible plants were ripening.

The most important Desert Cahuilla food plant was the mesquite tree, which grew in groves from the desert floor to heights of 3500 feet in better-watered areas. Stands were particularly numerous near springs or streams and in washes. In the early summer the blossoms were picked, roasted in a pit of heated stones, formed into balls, and stored in pottery containers; later the balls were boiled in water and eaten. Mesquite beans ripened from June through August, depending on the locality. At this time, or even earlier if pods were to be artificially ripened in the sun, they were picked by entire families. Children helped by climbing the trees to dislodge pods from high branches. The pods were not gathered indiscriminately, for the beans of some trees were regarded as more palatable than those from others. The pods could be stored from one year to the next, which may have been necessary on occasion, since the trees of a particular grove were not as productive every year. The ripened pods were crushed in an upright wooden mortar with a stone or wooden pestle, and the juice was made into a beverage. The pods might be ripened artificially, picked ripe, or gathered after they had fallen from the trees. The dried pods, either complete or broken into small sections, were stored in raised caches. Further processing included grinding the pods in a mortar or on a milling stone. The meal then could be placed in pottery or basketry containers and moistened; when it had dried, the cake of meal was removed and stored in the rafters of a house. Sections of the cakes were broken off and eaten as a snack or carried by travelers as food. The meal could also be made into a gruel or soaked in water to make the mesquite juice beverage. Loose ground meal was stored in pottery or basketry containers to be made into gruel later.

The mesquite bean was the most important staple, but the people of the desert areas also ate screw beans. The screw bean or tornillo grew under the same general conditions as the mesquite and was processed in the same manner. In ethnographic studies of California Indians acorns often are specified as an important staple. This clearly was the case over much of the state, but the acorn was not as important among the Cahuilla as elsewhere. Of the six varieties available, the acorn from the Kellogs oak was preferred for its taste and consistency. As was true with mesquite beans, when the first acorns were collected, they were eaten ceremonially in the homes of male leaders. If an individual collected acorns prior to this ceremony, he was expected to become ill or die. In the groves controlled by patriclans or groups of families related through males, each family owned particular trees, and in October and November the men climbed their trees to knock ripe acorns to the ground. Women cracked the acorns between two stones, spread the kernels out to dry for several weeks, and then pulverized them with pestles in stone mortars. To remove the bitter tannic acid the meal was spread out on a loosely woven basket or in a depression made in sand. In either case grass or leaves were placed in the leaching basin to prevent the meal from washing away. Then water, either cold or warm, was poured over the meal several times; during this process the mixture was stirred. The capabilities of a woman were measured by her skill in leaching and grinding acorn meal. Finely ground meal was made into cakes and baked in hot coals, while coarse meal was made into a gruel. Acorns that were not ground at gathering time were stored in platform caches.

Mesquite and screw beans were the most important foods, but over sixty different plants played a part in the diet. Growing in well-watered localities was a species of *Chenopodium* locally called careless weed. The seeds were collected, ground, and baked in cakes. One of the most important seed-producing grasses was chia, a member of the sage family. A seed beater dislodged the seeds from the whorls onto a flat basket. They were parched and ground to be baked into cakes or mixed with water to make a nourishing drink. When the century plants or agave of the canyons produced stalks, the stalks and "cabbages" were roasted in sand pits heated with stones. To this list could be added many others, but the examples cited suggest the broad range of plants collected and the varied means of food preparation.

Contrary to expectations the overwhelming emphasis on plant foods did not mean that hunting was neglected nor that the inventory of weapons and traps was impoverished. Adult males trapped animals and also stalked, chased, and intercepted them. The principal weapon was a shaft (self) bow with a plant fiber bowstring. The arrowshafts were vaned with split feathers, and shafts simply sharpened at the point probably were for birds and small game. Arrows with cane shafts and wooden arrowpoints probably were used against large game and enemies; some arrows apparently were tipped with poisons made from rattlesnake venom and other toxic substances. Another weapon was the nonreturning boomerang, commonly called a throwing stick when reported in western North America. It was a flat, curved piece of wood thrown at birds and small game. Hunters also used calls and decoys to lure game near enough to kill with arrows. Additional facilities for taking game included nets set along trails, deadfalls, and snares. Hunting was surrounded by numerous restrictions. For example, the Desert Cahuilla regarded mountain lions and grizzly bears as shamans and avoided killing them. When a mule deer was killed, people gathered to sing all night and eat the deer the following morning. In general, a man or boy did not consume any of the animals that he killed. Rabbits, squirrels, and other small game taken by a young boy in a communal hunt usually were given to his mother's family. The kills of an adult male were given alternately to his own family and to his wife's family.

DESCENT, KINSHIP, AND MARRIAGE   All the peoples described previously traced their descent through their father's *and* mother's hereditary lines; this is the bilateral (nonunilineal) descent system familiar to us since it currently prevails in the United States. (Our descent system should not be confused with our pattern of taking our father's surname. This practice may give some added stress to the father's line, but a mother's line may be equally or more important in the lives of some individuals.) Many people around the world give special stress to the male *or* female lines. The Cahuilla emphasized one line and thus had a unilineal descent system. Since they considered the male line far more important, their descent system was patrilineal, and a married couple resided with or near the husband's family (patrilocal residence). A typical Cahuilla settlement was formed around a group of males who traced their descent to a *known* common ancestor (patrilineage). Closely related patrilineages with a *presumed* common ancestor comprised a larger unit (patriclan), which was the most important social and ceremonial group.

In the kinship terminology a male Ego distinguished among his older and younger male and female siblings and made similar distinctions between his father's brothers and mother's sisters. He employed still other terms for his father's sisters and mother's brothers; these did not take relative age into consideration. A male Ego referred to his father's older brother's and his mother's older sister's son and daughter by the same term as his older brothers and sisters. Similarly, the son and daughter of his father's younger brother and mother's younger sister were referred to by the same terms as his younger brothers and sisters. In essence parallel cousins (children of father's brother and mother's sister) were termed the same as siblings, with the same age distinction as for siblings. For cross-cousins (father's sister's and mother's brother's children) the male-female kin terms were the same but different from

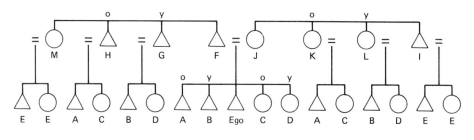

The Cahuilla: Gatherers in the Desert

those for siblings or parallel cousins. This cousin terminology is of the Iroquois type, while the terms on the first ascending generation are bifurcate collateral. The Iroquois cousin terms make particular sense since moiety exogamy existed. Thus certain near relatives, such as father's brother's children and mother's sister's children were of one's own moiety and reasonably called brother and sister. Cross cousins on the other hand were of a different moiety and termed differently, but in spite of the terminological difference one could not marry such a person.

SOCIAL DIMENSIONS In the Cahuilla origin myth Mukat and Tamaioit were associated with the wildcat and coyote respectively, and all Cahuilla identified with one or the other of these groups (moieties). Among the Desert Cahuilla the Wildcat moiety included eight clans, and the Coyote moiety consisted of ten clans. In aboriginal times the members of each clan theoretically occupied a single settlement, but in actual fact, persons from a number of clans might live in one settlement. We may presume that at one time all the members of a patriclan lived in a single village. As their number increased and they could not support themselves at the village site, the surplus, most likely members of a junior patrilineage, formed a new village or joined another clan at its settlement. A clan section or patrilineage founding a new village might eventually become so expanded that it qualified as a clan, with its own name and leader or clan "chief" called a *net*. The office of net usually passed from father to eldest son (primogeniture), and it included extremely important obligations. Nets lived in dwellings with dance houses attached and were the trustees of sacred clan bundles. A net directed subsistence activities, settled conflicts between members, represented the clan before other clans, and was responsible for the correct performance of ceremonies.

Plate 5–3 Palm Springs Cahuilla homestead, ca. 1900. (Courtesy of the Southwest Museum)

In sum, small family groups lived in a village and were related through males to a known common ancestor (patrilineage). In the same settlement were members of other patrilineages, but all the people residing in a community assumed that they had a common male ancestor (patriclan). Among the Desert group there were about eighteen clans, and their members were divided into two groups, the Wildcats or Coyotes (moieties). Moiety exogamy prevailed, which meant that a Wildcat was obligated to marry a Coyote and vice versa. Persons in opposite moieties maintained a joking relationship and friendly rivalry.

POLITICAL LIFE   Hereditary leaders did not exist above the clan level, and in instances where the activities of one clan impinged on those of another the differences were resolved by the nets in council. Decisions of a clan as a collectivity were made by the net, who ideally was a man of exceptional abilities. A net was required to know the boundaries of all clan lands, all clan traditions, and a broad range of esoteric facts important to the clan's viability; he also was expected to be a good orator and fair minded. He did not possess more material property than anyone else, but families presented him with the first fruit of any plant harvest, which was partial compensation for the time he devoted to clan activities. At the rear of the net's house was a small room where sacred objects, termed the "heart" of the clan, were kept. Eagle feathers were a vital part of each sacred bundle. Clearly the net, as conveyer of clan knowledge and guardian of the most sacred clan objects, was the paramount leader.

A second important political and religious functionary was the *paha*. His role existed only in certain localities, and his exact duties have not been reported in detail. Apparently where the office existed the paha was primarily responsible for ceremonial preparations and the maintenance of order on such occasions. In addition he was a leader of hunting parties and a spokesman and messenger for a net. Upon his death he was replaced by a son or another close male relative.

Formalized warfare or even feuds with neighboring ethnic groups were rare. To the east the desert area had no permanent occupants until the Colorado River was reached; here the aggressive Yuma lived. The Cahuilla feared the Yuma, but the intervening desert was an effective barrier to intensive contacts. The Chemehuevi, who lived to the east along the Colorado River and into the deserts of California, were friendly with the Desert Cahuilla. The southern neighbors of the Desert Cahuilla were the Yuman-speaking Kamia, but contacts with these people have not been described in any detail and are assumed to have been infrequent.

RELIGIOUS ACTIVITIES   Shamans were responsible for dealing with intermittent disaster and personal trauma, while the net and paha guided ceremonies focusing on the life cycle as well as those related to seasons. The Eagle

Killing Ceremony belongs to the latter category and was a highlight in religious life. In the mountain lands of some clans were eagle nests that were closely watched. A guard was posted to observe the nest from a vantage point, and when the eggs were laid, the clan was notified and a feast was held. When the eaglets were well-feathered, the clan net, regarded as their owner, sent men to retrieve one or more of the nestlings. A captured eaglet was caged in the net's house and fed by his family. When it attained full plumage, the neighboring clan or clans were notified and the ceremony planned. After everyone assembled, the members of a guest clan sang special songs throughout the night about the death of eagles. They were joined in song and the accompanying dances by the audience. Next the eagle was removed from its cage and rolled into the clan's ceremonial mat, and it was held by the net's nuclear family members as they danced in a circle. As dawn broke the eagle screeched and died, probably from being squeezed gradually. Its body was placed by the fire, and people wailed over its death. After the sun had risen, the eagle was skinned. The net kept the feathered skin; the body most likely was burned. The skin was rubbed soft and placed in the sacred bundle. Some feathers might be made into a ceremonial skirt, and others were set aside for adorning images in the Mourning Ceremony.

Among the Desert group the status of a shaman was not hereditary, and a number of practitioners might belong to a single clan. A shaman often had been ill frequently as a child, and the healer who treated him became aware of the child's potential as a curer, magician, and seer. As a young man the novice dreamed of a song that became a tangible manifestation of his inordinate powers. Mukat was responsible for implanting the dreams and guardian spirits identified with shamans. A novice danced before the people of his clan for three nights and afterwards was qualified to pursue his calling. In his dreams he eventually learned other songs, dances, feats of magic, and bewitching methods. In his dreams too a shaman learned of herbal cures for particular ailments, while at other times harmful or curative spells were revealed to him. When not drawing from his pharmacopoeia, he attempted to cure by sucking on the afflicted part of a patient's body. Reputedly he removed the disease object without breaking the skin. Sometimes plant products were applied externally; golderino weed was put on a snake bite, and an unspecified plant product was used on the bite of a poisonous spider. Only a few plants were used in curing, however, which contrasts with the extensive botanical knowledge and the many uses of plants as food. Certain creatures, such as the coyote, fox, hummingbird, and owl were messengers for shamans who brought warnings of impending illness. As a youth a shaman did not accept material rewards for his services, but as he grew older and established, he charged a fee.

If a shaman became malevolent in the use of his special powers, he posed a threat to the security of a community. In the latter part of the nineteenth century one old man was considered the world's most powerful shaman. When shamans exhibited their skills, he always performed last and challenged the others to kill him. None was able to do so because he was protected by spirits on all sides. Finally the old shaman was told by a man of a different clan to stop killing people. The man who gave the warning was soon struck by a "pain" which no shaman could remove, and he died. Everyone knew that the old shaman was responsible. A man from the shaman's clan and men from other clans met and decided that he must be killed. The executioner was to be the net of another clan because he was strong and brave. This man and another visited the sorcerer and were invited to spend the night. After everyone else was asleep, the net crushed the old man's skull with a stone pestle. At the head of the victim's bed were found a variety of small feathers and the skin of a gopher snake, objects used by the old man to make pains. As they were trampled into the ground, a thunder-like sound was heard. In the morning people came to view the body, and later the same morning the body and the house were burned. This is one of the rare recorded instances in which collective action was taken for the good of all the people.

ENTERTAINMENT   Of all the forms of recreation the most important was *peon*, a hand game that was played at secular gatherings and during ceremonies. A team from one village played against one from another settlement. Shamans aided their respective sides, while women sat behind the men of their team and sang at certain times during the game. One person was the mediator, and it was his duty to keep a fire burning by which the game was played, to hold the stakes, settle disputes, and take charge of the tally sticks. The game was played by eight men, four to a side, who knelt or sat cross-legged with a blanket between them. Lots were drawn to determine which side would first have the peons. A peon was a small bone tied to a string about two feet long; at the opposite end of the string was a small piece of wood. Each man on the starting team held the wood in one hand and the peon in the other and crossed his arms with his fists beneath his armpits. These men then took a blanket in their teeth to hide the manipulation of their hands. They swayed from side to side in time with the singing of the women on their side, switched the peons back and forth, and then suddenly dropped the blanket, revealing their arms still crossed and fists beneath their armpits. They continued swaying, and their opposites attempted to guess which hand held the peon. For every correct guess the second team took the peon, but with each incorrect guess the first team received one of the fifteen tallies. A particular game ended when one side had lost all four peons or had won all of the tallies. Then a new game was started and new stakes put up. Peon was played frequently throughout the night, and as one player tired he was replaced by another.

Other games included races between two groups of men. A wooden ball was kicked for several miles and then back again to the starting point. The men on each team took turns kicking the ball, and the team that finished first was the winner. Another race took place on the night of a new moon. The

The Cahuilla: Gatherers in the Desert

first boy to see the moon would call the others, and they would race to a spot where they could swim. After swimming they raced home, and by so doing they would bring good luck in the coming month. Cat's cradles were made by persons of both sexes. This skill had supernatural implications since before a person's spirit could pass into the world of other spirits, it was required to make string figures.

LIFE CYCLE   At critical times during an individual's life numerous rules were followed, and one of these periods was pregnancy. A potential mother refrained from eating any more than necessary; she drank only warm water, ate very little meat, and consumed no salt. If a pregnant woman ate fruit pecked by a bird, her infant would have sores; if she ate meat from the legs of game, a breech presentation would result; but if she was industrious when pregnant, her offspring would be energetic. These are but three of the rules to insure a safe delivery and a normal offspring. As soon as a woman gave birth and the placenta was dispelled, she lay in a specially prepared trough dug in the floor of a house. The depression was lined with hot sand, and after the woman stretched out, more hot sand was piled over her body. Here she remained for about ten days, leaving the trough only to urinate and defecate, to have the sand reheated, and to be bathed with hot water each morning. During the month following parturition the mother remained subject to food taboos, and the father could eat no foods containing salt. A nursing mother did not have sexual intercourse with her husband, for to do so was thought to spoil her milk. She was the object of teasing if she weaned her infant early.

An offspring was not named formally until several children had been born into the clan and each child's parents had accumulated food and wealth for a feast. This meant that children were between the ages of four and twelve before being named; if they were not formally named by thirteen, they would be known by nicknames throughout their lives. The naming ceremony was held in the clan dance house, with the members of the fathers' and mothers' clans invited. The participating children received traditional names of deceased ancestors selected by the clan net. The names for males tended to be of animals, birds, or insects, and those for females were most often from plants or household artifacts. The ceremony climaxed with singing and dancing as the net held each child up and shouted its name three times; afterwards the name was repeated by the audience. Sometimes a net would not state the real name for fear an "enemy" clan would learn of it and incorporate it into their songs. In this case the correct name was revealed in secret. A father also might acquire a new name at this ceremony and thereby gain additional standing. Following the naming ritual, presents such as food, baskets, a deerskin, and even ceremonial equipment were distributed to the guests. With the presentation of gifts the ceremony was concluded.

When a Desert girl approached adolescence, she was tattooed by her mother's sister as guests from the operator's clan watched. The tattoos were made with cactus thorns pricked in straight or angled lines from the lower lip to the chin, and black paint was rubbed into the wounds. At this time the earlobes of a girl were pierced. When a girl menstruated for the first time, the net summoned the clan of the girl's mother to a ceremony that began in the evening. A fire was built before the net's house to heat the ground, and afterwards a trough was dug. The girl was placed in the depression, and her body was covered with hot sand. Throughout the night the members of the girl's clan danced and sang around the pit. In the morning the girl was removed, bathed in warm water, and her head covered with a white paint. For the next three weeks she was subject to food taboos very much like those surrounding pregnancy. The girl stayed in or near the house, and she scratched her head with a special implement rather than her fingernails to prevent her hair from dropping out. Subsequent menstrual periods were surrounded by the same taboos, and in addition, a married woman was forbidden to touch her husband when she was menstruating. The good health of a couple depended on how well the woman obeyed these rules.

Some Desert Cahuilla do not appear to have initiated adolescent males, but an appropriate ceremony prevailed at Palm Springs. Boys between the ages of ten and eighteen were selected by elders for initiation and taken to a brush enclosure outside the dance house. The boys were secluded there for five days and saw only those persons who brought them special foods. During three nights the old people danced until morning. The climax came on the fourth night when the initiates were brought out and given a drink of cooked jimsonweed, or toloache as it is known in Spanish. After taking it, the boys danced briefly, but they became dizzy and were placed in a corner while the older people continued to dance. The following evening the effects of the jimsonweed had worn off, and for the next five nights the boys were taught how to dance, sing particular songs, and behave correctly as adults. This ceremony seems to have symbolized the death of initiates as children and their rebirth as knowledgeable adults. The only forms of body mutilation among males were piercing the ears and the nasal septum. The latter operation was not common and was performed only on young boys with promise as leaders. In the opening at the base of the nose pieces of deer bone were inserted.

When members of different clans assembled, especially for the tattooing of a girl or the piercing of a boy's nasal septum, songs known as "enemy songs" might be sung. Between clans, especially those that were geographically removed from one another, a rivalry of unknown origins existed. Members of competing clans composed derisive songs in which they incorporated the personal names of individuals in rival clans. These names had been bestowed by a net in secret, and the fact that they were known to the members of other clans was shameful. First one clan performed and then the other, with victory going to the side mentioning the most names of rivals and heaping the greatest abuse, or to the clan whose members were physically able to sing longer. Enemy songs were an obvious means for giving vent to aggressive behavior in a socially approved manner. The joking relationship between moiety members served the same purpose in a friendlier atmosphere.

The Desert Cahuilla marriage pattern included not only moiety exogamy but a prohibition against seeking a spouse from known relatives on either side of the family. Since genealogies were not remembered over many generations, one could marry a distant cousin in the opposite moiety. A thirteen-year-old girl was most likely to wed a male of eighteen from a nearby community. The match was arranged by parents, and after the formalities had been settled, the bride was led into the groom's house (patrilocal residence). She sat facing a corner with her back to the assembled relatives of the groom. The groom then sat next to the girl, and the couple was given food as the boy's relatives ate. When the feasting was over, the couple was considered married, and that night the newlyweds were given a single blanket with the theory that if affection did not bring them together the cold desert night would. A girl who was unhappy in the home of her in-laws might return to her mother's home, but if she did this repeatedly, the presents which had been given were returned and the marriage considered dissolved. The groom and his parents had the right to expect the bride to bear an infant within two or three years. Failure to do so might annul the marriage and again mean a return of the wedding presents. A man could, if the woman's parents agreed, receive a younger sister of his wife if the latter died (sororate). It was less common for a woman to marry her deceased husband's brother (levirate). Among these people monogamy was the prevailing form of marriage, and familial relationships appear to have been quite stable.

In the routine of adult life a woman was the outsider in the extended family household of her husband. The husband and wife were expected to be reserved in the presence of others, and the wife generally was retiring when with her in-laws or around men. Ideally, younger persons were thoughtful and unselfish in their dealings with older persons; these values were instilled in children when they were still quite young. Young boys who hunted or collected the first plant products of the season were expected to take them to the aged. The most respected adults were those men who hunted best and those women who could work most efficiently.

Death brought immediate destruction of a Cahuilla household in the distant past. It was recalled that on the morning following the death of a person, the body of the deceased and the house in which the death had occurred were burned. More recently, however, this pattern was modified. When an individual died, the members of his and other clans assembled, bringing presents. The body was washed, dressed, and taken to the clan dance house of the deceased. Here the assembled mourners sang over the body throughout the night. If a man had died, the creation narrative was sung; for a woman, a song about the moon was sung, since it was the moon who had originally instructed women. The body was burned the morning following death, and within a week the person's house and possessions were burned.

Each fall or winter a seven-day Mourning Ceremony was held for clan members who had died during the previous year. This was the most complex Cahuilla ceremony, and an essential feature was a narration of the creation myth. In it Mukat had described the proper death rituals, and they were performed for the first time at his death. The clan net, paha, and others began preparations months in advance for the yearly ceremony. Guests were persons from other clans who were related to the deceased by marriage and those individuals who had brought gifts following the death. Members of each clan arrived on a specific night so that the assembled group was not overwhelming. The first three nights shamans of the host clan or other clans performed tricks, danced, and attempted to communicate with the spirits of the dead. At one Mourning Ceremony a shaman tied a band about his head and inserted clusters of owl feathers in it. Another cluster of owl feathers was attached to a stick about eight inches in length that he held in his hand. As he sang and shuffled around the fire, he began trembling violently and then pushed the stick down his throat three times. The third time he brought up a small black object said to have been a lizard. After the "lizard" was removed from his heart, he stopped shaking. A more common performance upon such an occasion was for the shaman to place live coals in his mouth and swallow them.

Throughout the three nights to follow, different clans sang all night long. Those individuals singing the last night aided the relatives of the deceased in making images of each person who had died and for whom the ceremony was being held. The images were nearly life-sized and were constructed from reed matting and clothed with deerskins. The male images had bows and arrows and eagle-feather headdresses; the female images had baskets decorated with eagle feathers. At sunrise on the final day guests were presented with food and gifts. The host net led a procession in which he was followed by women, each carrying the image of a near relative. Then came the throng of participants and attendants. The people gathered in a circle in front of the dance house, and the images were placed in the center of the circle as the people danced, sang, and wailed. Objects of wealth were thrown over the images to show respect for the dead. These items could be retrieved but not by members of the clan hosting the ceremony. Next, the images were carried to a designated place and burned. People who had been invited to the ceremony were presented with strings of beads made of small round shell disks, and then they departed. The souls of the dead were now released, further mourning was unnecessary, and their names were no longer mentioned.

The presence of a soul in a living person was manifest when people fainted or dreamed; on those occasions their spiritual essence was thought to wander. Spirits also left the bodies of persons months before they died. A spirit's wandering might be unknown to its possessor, or the individual might become ill and a shaman be summoned to retrieve his soul. When the soul of a person was beyond recall, it went to a place created in the east by Mukat. Here stood two mountains which clapped together and then separated. Souls found their way to these mountains, and once there a deathless guardian spirit questioned and tested them. After passing the tests, which included making cat's cradles and answering questions, the soul attempted to go between the clapping mountains. Only those who had lived according to the rules of Mukat were able to pass untouched. Otherwise they were crushed by the mountains and became butterflies, bats, trees, or rocks nearby.

Historic Changes

Ethnohistorians have yet to plot the changes in Cahuilla life from early historic to modern times, and we are limited to the random observations of diverse reporters. It is known that by 1925 farmlands were owned by clans, as probably had been the case for about a hundred years, but the amount of arable land was small because water was scarce. Changes were notable at this time in dwelling forms since frame houses had replaced the aboriginal type; a frame house was not burned, however, until three members of the household had died. In the desert a clan dance house still was occupied by a net and his family, but it looked different because the roof now was pitched like a shed. By the late 1950s few aboriginal traits remained. Although acorns still were processed, they were consumed only on special social and ceremonial occasions.

Social life moved in new directions as the present century began. The rule of moiety exogamy fell into decline, and money was substituted for the gifts formerly presented to a bride's family. The girl's family received $30 around the turn of the century, but twenty-five years later a female infant was termed scornfully "a paper," meaning a marriage license which no longer

Plate 5–4 Pasqual, a Cahuilla man said to be 90 years old, ca. 1890. (Courtesy of the San Bernardino County Museum)

brought a gift. The pattern of leadership long had been impinged on by diverse outside influences. Supraclan leaders did not exist in aboriginal times, although one outstanding charismatic leader, Juan Antonio, emerged in the mid-1800s. In order to exercise effective control over the Cahuilla, whites appointed "chiefs" or "captains" through whom they dealt. It was said by informants that one such person was appointed as the Desert Cahuilla leader and was given "papers" and a horse by the Mexicans as symbols of his authority. When he died, the office passed to his son. These leaders, even as late as the 1920s, were not effective spokesmen for their groups.

Ceremonial life reflected reintegration and disintegration during the same period. The major shift was toward combining unrelated ceremonies with the Mourning Ceremony into a "fiesta" week. For example, among the Pass Cahuilla in the late 1880s, the Eagle Killing Ceremony was joined with the Mourning Ceremony; the eagle feathers were used to decorate the images, which were burned two days later. In aboriginal times the people had cremated their dead; under Spanish, Mexican, and Anglo-American influence, they began to bury the dead. Interment sometimes included placing food, clothing, and bedding with the body in the hope that these things would be useful to the spirit if it did not soon find a permanent resting place. Changes in the Mourning Ceremony included dressing the images in manufactured clothing, even hats and veils. Coins and buttons replaced shells for the eyes of the images, while the nose and ears were appliqued pieces of cloth. Coins were thrown on these images near the end of the ceremony. Indian-owned lunch counters sold food and coffee to participants and observers. By 1931 the Mourning Ceremony at Palm Springs was biennial and was held by alternating clans for the dead of the two previous years. Among the Desert Cahuilla one of the last nets died in 1958. He had directed local ceremonial life, but when he died, the ceremonial structure, his house, and all of the ceremonial equipment were burned, an end not only to his life but also to the net ceremonials.

Palm Springs Cahuilla

EARLY LAND CLAIMS   In the course of Desert Cahuilla history, especially for the Palm Springs group, a dominant theme from the late 1860s onward has been Indian rights to land. In 1869 the Superintendent of Indian Affairs for California hoped to set aside lands for Indians before whites encroached further, and he succeeded in establishing small reservations in San Diego County the following year. Then in 1875 President Ulysses S. Grant authorized the founding of the Agua Caliente (Palm Springs) and Cahuilla reservations. A Mission Indian agency began to function out of San Bernardino in 1879. For the first time slight but realistic efforts were being made to recognize the needs of Indians in southern California. In 1881 Helen Hunt Jackson

The Cahuilla: Gatherers in the Desert

Plate 5–5 The Cahuilla woman Ramona Lubo at her home, probably photographed around the turn of the century. Her life was fictionalized in the novel *Ramona* by Helen Hunt Jackson. (Courtesy of the Southwest Museum)

published a book titled *A Century of Dishonor*, a scathing indictment of the treatment of American Indians. Because of her crusading interest in Indians, she was retained to report to the Commissioner of Indian Affairs about the Indians of southern California. Her study was conducted with Abbott Kinney, and their report, in part a chronicle of wrongs against Indians and partly a series of recommendations, was submitted in 1883. This study did not make the impact on Indian policy that Jackson felt was essential, and so she decided to write a novel about the plight of these people. As a novel *Ramona* was highly successful, but it failed to bring about the reforms advocated by Jackson.

The problem of Palm Springs Indian land rights is complex, but the diverse legal maneuvers must at least be presented in brief. The modern reservation, created in 1896 under the conditions of the Mission Indian Relief Act of 1891, set aside 32,000 acres in essentially a checkerboard pattern around the town of Palm Springs in Riverside County. The Mission Indian Relief Act was based on the General Allotment or Dawes Act of 1887, and the keystone to this act was to allot reservation lands to family heads. After a period of twenty-five years an allottee could, with approval of the Secretary of the Interior, receive a fee patent title to the land, making him the legal owner and entitled to do whatever he might choose with the land. Allotments were first issued in 1923, and the land per family was limited to 160 acres. A Federal agent went to Palm Springs to assign allotments to the band members, regardless of whether or not they accepted the division of land into individual parcels. Many persons were so dissatisfied that in 1927 the agent made allotments only to Indians who requested them; nearly half of the members made

Plate 5–6 Louisa Costa Rice making baskets in 1938 at the Soboba Reservation. (Photograph by Maxine Smith, Courtesy of the San Bernardino County Museum)

requests. These allotments consisted not of 160 acres but of five acres of irrigable land, forty acres of dry land, and two-acre lots in the town of Palm Springs. None of the 1927 selections were approved by the Federal Government, and legal action was taken by the Indians in the late 1930s to force approval. Meanwhile, the Indian Reorganization Act of 1934 was passed, bringing a basic change in Indian policy. As it applied to the Palm Springs land dispute, further allotments were prohibited unless the Indian group had voted against coming under this act. The Palm Springs band voted against it, and thus allotments were still possible. Bureau of Indian Affairs officials were very much against allotments, however, and they obstructed allotted land grants at Palm Springs as elsewhere. The courts held that the Secretary of the Interior could not be forced to make allotments, which brought the litigation down to 1940. New action was taken the following year to have the allotments approved. The U.S. Supreme Court required a review of the litigation; the result was the 1946 verdict that the allotments were valid. Some allotments were approved in 1949; the ones that were unapproved involved conflicting claims, but finally selections were approved for the entire band.

One of the suits involving allotment selections resulted in a 1950 court decision that allotted lands should be of approximately equal value for each individual since this was the original intent of the law. In actuality, the allotment values, based on 1949 estimates, ranged from approximately $17,000 to $165,000, with a total value of lands allotted and pending allotment being about 7.4 million dollars. To equalize the allotments it was proposed that the

The Cahuilla: Gatherers in the Desert

Secretary of the Interior organize a tribal corporation and convey to it all of the tribal assets. This organization would be empowered to issue equalization stock redeemable from the sale of or income from the lands managed by the tribal organization. Persons who held equalized allotments would receive only membership stock until the equalization process was complete. Then all members would receive dividends equally.

The U.S. Senate bill proposed in 1957 was to provide equalization of allotments along these general lines, but the Indians objected and sent tribal representatives to Washington, D.C., to seek modifications. The Bureau of Indian Affairs representatives refused to make any changes and stated that if this legislation were not passed, the tribal reserves would be used to equalize the allotments. These reserves, the cemeteries, hot springs, and particularly the canyons, were the prime centers of tribal identity. To allot them would be to destroy the tribe as a social and political unit. The Bureau of Indian Affairs forwarded the bill to the Committee on Interior and Insular Affairs of the House of Representatives, and since the bill involved persons from his district, Dalip S. Saund was given the privilege of introducing it. Saund studied the bill and stated later, "I came to the conclusion that under no circumstances would I be a party in introducing the bill." He was instrumental in having the bill set aside until a hearing could be held in Palm Springs. During the hearing held in October 1957, it became evident that the bill was not in the best interest of the Indians nor could it be considered just. Probably the most dangerous provision was that a tribal corporation was to be established and given title to all unallotted land. It would issue equalization stock to bring each individual's allotment to the value of the most valuable allotment and would redeem the stock from income or from disposal of the land. This was in fact a liquidation corporation, and it is highly questionable that either legal or moral justification could be offered in its defense by the Bureau of Indian Affairs. At the hearing, diverse issues were aired, including the problems of the control of the proposed tribal corporation and the status of the reserve lands. The city attorney for Palm Springs favored taxing Indian lands to aid in the support of the city government. The subcommittee was outspoken in its condemnation of this stand. Another problem was whether the State of California might tax the tribal corporation if the bill were passed. Federal immunity against taxation was to be provided, but such assurances were not forthcoming from the state officials. Further evidence was given concerning the inadequacy of the leasing laws.

As a result of the 1957 hearing Congressman Saund submitted in 1959 two new bills before the Eighty-sixth Congress, and these became law. The major provisions of the equalization bill, Public Law 86-339, follow. Allotments would be made to all band members who had not received them, but no future-born members would receive allotments. Equalizations would be made on the basis of 1957–1958 appraised land values. The cemeteries, Roman Catholic church, hot springs, and certain canyons were to remain tribal re-

Plate 5–7 Shaman with a live coal from a wood fire in his mouth, photographed in 1963. (Courtesy of Lowie Museum of Anthropology, University of California, Berkeley)

serves not subject to allotment, but all other lands were to be allotted regardless of prior acreage limitations and in proportion to the highest monetary value of the prior allotments. The second bill, Public Law 86-326, provided that reservation lands could be leased for a period not exceeding ninety-nine years except for grazing land, which could be leased for not more than ten years. The 1957–1958 allotment appraisals ranged from approximately $75,000 to $630,000, in contrast with the 1949 appraisal range of $17,000 to $165,000. Obviously the land was rapidly becoming fantastically valuable. Even with the passage of the first bill, it was impossible to equalize the allotments fully. Some 80 percent of the band obtained allotments valued at not less than $335,000; the remaining 20 percent of the allotments had values in excess of $335,000. Most of the land was still in trust status by 1962 and thus was not producing income. However, changes in leasing laws made it likely that over the next ten years individuals would derive considerable profit from it. The first large leasing enterprise was the Palm Springs Spa complex at the hot springs. The Spa was completed in 1960 at a cost of $1.8 million, and an adjacent hotel, also on Indian land, was completed in 1963. In 1961 the city of Palm Springs purchased lands allotted to eight adults and twenty-two children for $2,979,000, which was shared by the allottees. Without the honesty and integrity of the "Congressman from India," Dalip S. Saund, the future which now looks so bright for these people would have been clouded and dismal.

The most notable aspect of all the Palm Springs land disputes is the leadership role assumed successfully by women. When the issues were coming to a climax in 1957, the band included only thirty-two adults and sixty-four minors. At that time there were ten adult males and twenty-two females; of the males two were in the U.S. Navy, two were over seventy years of age, and two were incapable of handling their own affairs. At this point one of two courses of action was possible: either the band could trust the Bureau of Indian Affairs and its lawyer to handle its business affairs completely, or the women could assume the role of leaders. The latter alternative was pursued. In aboriginal sociopolitical life there was no precedent for female leadership

The Cahuilla: Gatherers in the Desert

except that a woman did occasionally hold an office in trust for a son and old women sometimes were very active in clan ceremonies. The net was always a man, and in the early historic period whites appointed Indian men to act as intermediaries and later as reservation leaders. These persons seem to have been clan leaders. In the Cahuilla acculturation process a differential rate of adaptation for females and males appears to have developed. The men continued to follow a "collecting" pattern in their economic activities; they worked only sporadically as grape pickers, ranch hands, woodcutters, or railroad laborers. In their jobs they interacted most often with other Indians, not whites. Women by contrast often worked as domestics in the homes of whites and therefore became much more familiar with the new ways. Possibly this was an important reason that women could become the stable core around which the society was reorganized. In 1935 a woman became secretary to the band business committee, and by 1954 an all-woman tribal council was elected, with Vyola Olinger as chairperson. Mrs. Olinger, who was an active member of the band, was an apt choice, for she was not only intelligent and articulate but willing to work constructively with the Bureau of Indian Affairs officials. The men had by this time come to distrust virtually all proposals by the bureau. Under the tribal council of women the major land disputes were resolved. In 1961 a young male was elected to the council, and this brought an end to the era of all-female political dominance, but it was the women who had handled the vital issue.

LAND CLAIMS: 1960s   By the early 1960s a small group of determined Indians had gained a settlement, and surely the avarice of whites had become just another episode in our blemished past; justice had prevailed. Alas, it was

Plate 5–8 The Palm Springs Tribal Council in 1959. From left to right are Elizabeth Monk, Le Vern Saubel, Eileen Miguel, Doro Joyce Prieto, and Priscilla Gonzales. (Photo courtesy the *Palm Springs Desert Sun*)

not to endure. In 1967, George Ringwald, a reporter for the *Daily Enterprise* of Riverside, California, wrote a series of articles about the administration of Palm Springs Cahuilla lands and funds. He demonstrated beyond any doubt that greedy whites still were taking grossly unfair advantage of Indians. Among the individuals involved in the immoral and often illegal handling of Palm Springs Cahuilla affairs were:

Bureau of Indian Affairs personnel;

a Superior Court judge;

a municipal judge;

a former mayor of Palm Springs;

a Palm Springs real estate broker;

a host of attorneys-at law.

As a result of Ringwald's journalism the Bureau of Indian Affairs was forced to conduct an investigation into the system of court-appointed guardians and conservators. It was demonstrated, for example, that a municipal judge and one attorney had, over a seven-year period, collected $485,000 in fees. From 1956 to 1967, approximately 40 percent of the 10.8 million dollars received by eighty-four estates went to conservators, guardians, or their attorneys under the supervision of the Riverside County Superior Court. Congressional action in 1968 put an end to the conservator and guardian management of these valuable lands.

A fair-minded person would hope that Palm Springs Indian land problems have ended, but such is not the case. In 1938 when Palm Springs incorporated as a city, Indian land was included within the city boundary without any consultations with the Indians involved. Over the years the city passed zoning ordinances and in 1965 adopted a master plan that included presumed control over reservation lands in the city. The Palm Springs Indians have formed legally constituted planning commissions and have prepared zoning ordinances of their own. Theirs do not agree with those of the city planners. In 1966 the Indians won a judgment against the city with reference to zoning procedures, but because the city still had not made the required modifications by 1972, further litigation was initiated. The Indians accuse the city of preventing the development of Indian lands and thereby decreasing its value. For example, at one street intersection where white and Indian land meet, the corners belonging to whites have shopping centers and other businesses, but the Indian lands are not developed, even though financing is available, because the city will not grant the necessary permits to the Indians. Among the issues before the courts are whether Indian lands can legally be included in a city and whether city zoning ordinances represent an infringement on tribal government.

The Cahuilla: Gatherers in the Desert

Plate 5–9 The Palm Springs Spa built on land leased from the Agua Caliente Band. (Courtesy of the Agua Caliente Tribal Council)

On a per capita basis the 175 Palm Springs Cahuilla are the most wealthy group of Indians in the United States. Their total assets are valued at approximately 200 million dollars. Irrespective of their wealth—or because of it—the battles go on in their never-ending land war.

Comparisons

Although a small number of Cahuilla appear to have farmed in early historic times, they were principally foragers like the Caribou and Kuskokwim Eskimos and the Chipewyan. The Cahuilla, of course, were primarily collectors of plant products, while the others were almost exclusively hunters and fishermen. The resource base of the Cahuilla obviously was far richer and more diverse than that of the Chipewyan or Caribou Eskimos, which makes an inviting point to explore in terms of accompanying social and political adaptations. The Kuskokwim Eskimos, like the Cahuilla, had a dependable food supply, but these Eskimos did not develop social and political institutions like those of the Cahuilla. The reason, at least in part, turns on the nature of environmental differences; it might be a useful exercise to compare all of these peoples in terms of their environments, especially the diversity of species harvested, species mobility, and the seasonality of food resources, and try to explain social and political differences in projective terms. Note too that the Cahuilla, far more than any of the others, emphasized ties with the mythological past, physiological changes during adolescence, formal marital arrangements, and death. The reasons for the Cahuilla contrast invite further study, hypothesis formulation, and thoughtful speculation.

Note About Clan

The word "clan" previously was defined in this chapter as a unilineal descent group with a presumed common ancestor, and it will be used in this manner throughout the book. A clan may be traced along either the male line (patriclan) or female line (matriclan); in this book a prefix is used to introduce the rule of descent and later in the chapters if required for clarity. Originally the word "clan" was restricted to people who traced descent through females, and the word "gens" was used when these ties were traced through males. The word "gens" is no longer employed, and clan now applies to both cases.

George P. Murdock in *Social Structure* (1949, 68) proposed that clan be more rigidly defined. In his terms a genuine clan has a unilineal rule of descent uniting a core of members; residential unity, meaning that residence and descent are consistent (e.g., matrilineal descent and matrilocal residence), and social integration, especially in the acceptance of in-marrying spouses. Murdock proposed that "sib" be used to refer to a unilineal descent group through males (patrisib) or females (matrisib) if the other qualifications for a clan were not met, and there is good precedent for this usage. Following Murdock's definition the Cahuilla did not have clans since in-marrying spouses were not integrated into membership; instead they had patrisibs. The differentiation by Murdock has not been widely accepted, however, and in terms of the more standard pre-1949 definition of a clan the Cahuilla had clans.

Additional Readings

Early historic Cahuilla material culture is best presented in the monographs by Hooper and Kroeber. Again, and as usual, comparatively little has been written about recent developments among the Cahuilla, and as noted previously no one has attempted to plot their ethnohistory. Fortunately, however, studies by Bean and Katherine S. Saubel supplement and in part supplant the pioneering work of Barrows about plant utilization and should be consulted for any thorough understanding of subsistence patterns. For a com-

The Cahuilla: Gatherers in the Desert

prehensive reconstruction of aboriginal Cahuilla life *Mukat's People* by Bean is the key source.

References

Ames, Walter. "Palm Springs Indians Still Protest Land Split," *Los Angeles Times*, November 12, 1961.

Bancroft, Hubert H. *History of California.* 7 v. San Francisco. 1890.

*Barrows, David P. *The Ethno-Botany of the Coahuilla Indians of Southern California.* Chicago. 1900. Reprinted by Malki Museum Press, Banning, California. 1967. A general history of the Cahuilla precedes a description of the local geography. These sections are followed by a discussion of houses, baskets, and the utilization of plants. The botanical information in particular is quite comprehensive and serves as a standard source.

*Bean, Lowell J., and William M. Mason. *Diaries & Accounts of the Romero Expeditions in Arizona and California.* Los Angeles. 1962. The publication of these records offers a previously unknown historical dimension to the Cahuilla. Their primary value is in conveying certain details of Cahuilla acculturation by Spanish-Americans.

Bean, Lowell J., and Katherine S. Saubel. "Cahuilla Ethnobotanical Notes: The Aboriginal Uses of the Oak," *Archaeological Survey, Annual Report 1960–1961*, Department of Anthropology & Sociology, University of California, Los Angeles, 237–249. 1961.

Bean, Lowell J., "Cahuilla Ethnobotanical Notes: The Aboriginal Uses of the Mesquite and Screwbean," *Archaeological Survey, Annual Report 1962–1963*, Department of Anthropology & Sociology, University of California, Los Angeles, 55–76. 1963.

Bean, Lowell J., and Katherine S. Saubel. *Temalpakh: Cahuilla Indian Knowledge and Usage of Plants.* Malki Museum Press. Riverside. 1972.

*Bean, Lowell J. *Mukat's People.* Berkeley. 1972. This work demonstrates that insightful ethnographic reconstructions occasionally can be made long after the era of early historic contact. Bean explains the relationship of the Cahuilla to their food resources and the accompanying influences on other aspects of their lives. His study is especially perceptive on subjects such as world view and values that have been neglected by most other students of the Cahuilla.

Beattie, George W., and Helen P. Beattie. *Heritage of the Valley*. Oakland. 1951.

Bolton, Herbert E. "In the South San Joaquin Ahead of Garces," *Quarterly of the California Historical Society*, v. 10, 211–219. 1931.

Bourne, A. R. Some Major Aspects of the Historical Development of Palm Springs between 1880 and 1938. Occidental College, Master of Arts thesis.

Caughey, John W. *California*. New York. 1940. (See also Wilson, Benjamin D.)

Ellison, William H. "The Federal Indian Policy in California, 1846–1860," *Mississippi Valley Historical Review*, v. 9, 37–67. 1922–1923.

Gifford, Edward W. *California Kinship Terminologies*, University of California Publications in American Archaeology and Ethnology, v. 18. 1922.

Hale, Kenneth. "Internal Diversity in Uto-Aztecan: 1," *International Journal of American Linguistics*, v. 24, 101–107. 1958.

Hooper, Lucile. *The Cahuilla Indians*. University of California Publications in American Archaeology and Ethnology, v. 16, no. 6. 1920. Most of what is known about the aboriginal Cahuilla will be found in this ethnographic reconstruction, a similar reconstruction by Alfred L. Kroeber, or the analysis of social life and settlement patterns by William D. Strong.

Jackson, Helen H. *A Century of Dishonor*. New York. 1881 (an 1890 edition contains the Report on the Conditions and Needs of the Mission Indians of California).

James, Harry C. *The Cahuilla Indians*. Los Angeles. 1960.

*Kroeber, Alfred L. *Ethnography of the Cahuilla Indians*. University of California Publications in American Archaeology and Ethnology, v. 8, no. 2. 1908. A brief but valuable ethnography which concentrates on material culture. It supplements the reconstructions by Lucile Hooper and William D. Strong.

Land Allotments on Agua Caliente Reservation, Calif. Hearing before a Special Subcommittee of the Committee on Interior and Insular Affairs, House of Representatives, 85th Congress, 1st session. Serial No. 17. 1958.

Ringwald, George. *Riverside Press-Enterprise and Riverside Daily Press* articles, 1967.

Rush, Emmy M. "The Indians of the Coachella Valley Celebrate," *El Palacio*, v. 32, 1–19. 1932.

Saund, Dalip S. *Congressman from India*. New York. 1960.

Shinn, George H. *Shoshonean Days*. Glendale. 1941.

*Strong, William D. *Aboriginal Society in Southern California*. University of California Publications in American Archaeology and Ethnology, v. 26. 1929. The best information about aboriginal social structure, the movements of people, and settlement patterns.

Transmitting Report by Subcommittee on Indian Affairs. State of California, Senate Committee on Rules Resolution No. 8. Sacramento. 1961.

Wilson, Benjamin D. *The Indians of Southern California in 1852*. John W. Caughey, ed. San Marino. 1952.

1962 Progress Report, Agua Caliente Band of Mission Indians. Long Beach. No date.

6

The Fox: Fighters and Farmers of the Woodland Fringe

Reasons for This Selection

Most Indian populations in the east-central United States disappeared long ago, but a small group known as the Fox have survived despite a history of wanderings and sufferings. In colonial times the French set out to destroy them and were nearly successful. Later the Fox resisted the settlement of their lands by whites, and the turmoil climaxed in an Indian war. The survivors were displaced, causing their number to become depleted even further. The Fox were haughty, independent, and had an exceptional nobility of purpose. A striking instance of their resilience occurred in 1854. After being defeated and relocated by whites a generation earlier, some Fox left their reservation in Kansas and returned to an area of Iowa where they once had lived. They bought small parcels of land from whites and settled down to follow their old way of life. Although their aboriginal customs were rapidly disappearing by the turn of the twentieth century, the Fox have managed to retain both their identity and their Iowa lands to the present.

The ability of the Fox to endure in the Midwest and to retain their identity is a compelling reason for reporting their lifeway. In addition, conveying the diversity of Indian life requires that all significant economic adaptations be considered. Hunters, fishermen, and plant collectors have been presented, and

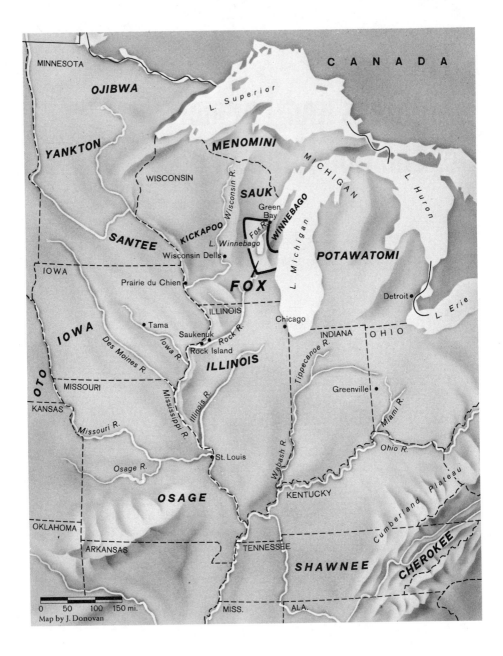

MINNESOTA

OJIBWA

CANADA

L. Superior

YANKTON

MENOMINI

WISCONSIN

MICHIGAN

L. Huron

SAUK

KICKAPOO

Wisconsin R.

Green
Bay

WINNEBAGO

SANTEE

Fox R.

L. Winnebago

L. Michigan

POTAWATOMI

Wisconsin Dells

IOWA

Prairie du Chien

FOX

Detroit

L. Erie

ILLINOIS

IOWA

Tama

Chicago

INDIANA

OHIO

Des Moines R.

Saukenuk

Rock R.

Iowa R.

Rock Island

Tippecanoe R.

OTO

ILLINOIS

MISSOURI

Mississippi R.

Illinois R.

Greenville

KANSAS

Missouri R.

Wabash R.

Miami R.

Osage R.

St. Louis

Ohio R.

OSAGE

KENTUCKY

Cumberland Plateau

OKLAHOMA

ARKANSAS

TENNESSEE

SHAWNEE

CHEROKEE

0   50   100 150 mi.

MISS.

ALA.

Map by J. Donovan

180

it is time to consider Indians who farmed. The Fox not only cultivated plants but also depended heavily on foraging activities and therefore represent another economic focus. In addition they are considered because of the Fox Project, a vehicle of change organized by Sol Tax, an anthropologist at the University of Chicago. Some anthropologists conceive their role to be that of scientific observers whose only duty is to record the ways of different peoples. This certainly is a valid intellectual stance, but other anthropologists feel obligated to lend their skills in making the adjustments smoother for peoples in the throes of change. Anthropologists with this point of view are not rare, but for them to make constructive changes is unusual. Thus the Fox Project and the results achieved were not unimportant in the decision to include the Fox in this book.

Two difficulties emerged in preparing an account of past life among the Fox. First, most pertinent information does not date from the period of early historic contact. Thus an aboriginal baseline account, one describing the Fox before their customs were altered by fur traders, cannot be presented. However the Fox are regarded as highly conservative, and except for superficial changes, we may assume that accounts about their recent past are more representative of aboriginal patterns than would be the case for many American Indians. A second difficulty in dealing with the Fox is their close association with the Sauk. It is impossible in some instances to separate the Fox and Sauk in historical contexts. Although my descriptions are confined to the Fox insofar as possible, frequent reference to the Sauk is required.

People, Population, and Language

The Fox know themselves as the Mesquakie, which translates as "Red-earth People." This name stems from the red earth of their creation as recorded in a myth. They appear to have received the name "Fox" when members of the Fox clan told a party of French that they were Fox, meaning of the Fox clan and Mesquakie tribe, but interpreted as the name of the tribe itself. The Fox and the Sauk (Sac), with whom they are closely identified, numbered about 6500 persons at the time of historic contact; possibly 2000 were Fox. In the 1950s nearly 1000 Fox lived in Oklahoma, 500 in Iowa, and 125 in Nebraska. By 1970 about 500 lived in the vicinity of Tama, Iowa. In 1976 there were 902 persons on the tribal roll, and of this number 329 were under 18 years of age.

The Fox, Sauk, and Kickapoo were neighbors and spoke closely related languages in the Algonkian (Algonquian) linguistic family, one of the nine families comprising the Macro-Algonkian phylum. Algonkian speakers occupied a vast sector of eastern Canada and a smaller area in the eastern United States. Remarkably, the other groups with whom they are affiliated linguistically include two small northern California tribes, the Yurok and Wiyot. The earliest historical records locate the Fox along the Fox River of eastern Wisconsin.

Prehistory

In the Great Lakes region the first settlers were hunters, Paleo-Indians, whose general way of life is reflected in scattered assemblages of stone tools. A distinctive form among their manufactures was the Clovis point. These mobile mastodon hunters occupied the area by about 10,000 B.C. and remained there until the climate changed and their prey became scarce. Indians identified as Aqua-Plano dominated from about 7000 to 4500 B.C., and they must have depended heavily on caribou, deer, and elk. By the end of the era two new patterns of culture had emerged: the Boreal Archaic and Old Copper. Each was adapted to a forest environment and possessed woodworking tools, such as the adz, ax, and gouge that were present in the earlier period. Stoneworking shifted from flaking to grinding, and some copper tools were annealed. The bearers of these two traditions possibly continued to stress hunting. Their most important weapon was not the bow and arrow but the spear used with the spear-thrower. The technologies of these Indians gradually increased in efficiency until about 500 B.C., when two radical innovations appeared, artificial burial mounds and pottery. The basic economy appears to have remained much the same until the era of the Hopewell culture of the Early Woodland tradition. The Hopewell people, centered in the Ohio River valley, built great earthworks on which they must have expended an inordinate amount of time and energy; their skills also included producing elaborate grave goods for the important dead. Although still dependent on hunting, they raised beans, maize, and squash. The Hopewell Indians pushed into the Great Lakes region and reached a climax in complexity around A.D. 400. During the Late Woodland period, from about A.D. 800 until historic contact, the cultures were locally variable, but a basic continuity with the past was predominant.

Excavations at the Bell site, a historical Fox village apparently destroyed in 1716, indicate that aboriginal artifact styles and trade goods often existed side-by-side and served the same general purposes. The settlement, built on a high bank, was composed of pole-framed and bark-covered houses surrounded by palisades, and the people were farmers and hunters. They used awls made from bone or iron; containers were made from turtle shells or local clays and existed along with brass kettles received in trade. Bracelets were fashioned from bone or brass wire, and clay pipes were manufactured locally or imported. Thus material goods from distinct cultural traditions competed at this early stage of Fox history.

182

The Fox: Fighters and Farmers of the Woodland Fringe

Euro-American Influences

The first direct contact between the Fox and Europeans was in 1665 as the French entered the western Great Lakes region. In 1670 a mission was founded among them by the famous Father Claude Jean Allouez, but he could convert only the ill or dying. As the French pushed west, they armed the Ojibwa (Chippewa) and the Siouan-speaking enemies of the Fox. This led to French and Fox conflict, which tipped in favor of the French after they founded Detroit in 1699 and made peace with the powerful Iroquois a year later. Because the French continued to arm their enemies, the Fox sought aid from the British and from friendly tribes. The Iroquois assured the Fox of a home among them if they were defeated by the French.

Hostilities with the French began to peak in 1728 when nearly 500 whites and 1200 allied Indians moved against the Fox. The destruction of Fox settlements was a severe blow, and by 1730 the French and their Indian allies had killed nearly 1200 Fox. The Fox survived only because surrounding Indians released their Fox prisoners and because the Sauk sheltered and protected them against the French; soon both the Fox and Sauk were forced to flee south. Peace was made with the French in 1737. Subsequently the Fox began returning to Wisconsin, but they did not feel secure until the British assumed control of the Great Lakes region and replaced the French at the Green Bay post in 1761. Before long the Ojibwa drove the Fox from Wisconsin to Illinois, where they came into increasing conflict with Americans around 1800. By then the Fox were dependent on the fur trade to obtain goods, and they often were in debt to traders. Still the relationship between the Fox and Sauk and traders, especially the British, seems to have been very good. The Fox expected certain privileges, such as being entertained when they were at the trading post, receiving gifts from the traders, and being cared for in times of stress. At the same time they relied on trusted traders to help guide tribal and village affairs. With the influx of additional white settlers to the Northwest Territory increasing pressure was applied to move all Indians from the Midwest. The position of the Fox and Sauk was not favorable since they had sided with the British during the American Revolution. In 1804 a small party of Fox and Sauk went to St. Louis and signed a treaty with the United States releasing their lands along the Mississippi River. Trade goods worth $2000 were distributed to the Indians plus an annuity of $600 to the Sauk and $400 to the Fox. The treaty authorized further settlement of Illinois lands by white settlers. Not only were the Indians at St. Louis unauthorized to negotiate, but the tribe as a whole did not know that a treaty was under consideration until after the chiefs returned from St. Louis. The Treaty of 1804 was the cause of great anger against the Americans. The Fox felt that they had been deceived and that these lands were seized illegally. This treaty was the one document to which Americans referred constantly in asserting their claims to Fox and Sauk lands. The treaty was made, the damage was done, but the bitterness always lingered in the minds of the Indians.

The most serious American difficulty in dealing with Indians stemmed from the conflicts between tribes. These not only disrupted trade but made white settlement of the country difficult. To end the fighting the major tribes in the upper Mississippi River drainage were invited in 1805 to a council held at St. Louis with Governor William Henry Harrison of the Northwest Territory. To impress the Indians with the power of the United States select Indians were taken to visit Washington, D.C. About a third of the group were Fox and Sauk. Even as some chiefs were in Washington, however, others were on the warpath against the Chickasaw and Osage. Thus this effort to bring a peaceful settlement of Indian differences failed. In 1805–1806 Fox and Sauk war parties roved along the Missouri River raiding Osage camps, and Americans also were killed. Settlers brought increased pressure on the government of the Northwest Territory to arrange a more effective settlement of Indian differences. To compound the governor's problems, additional settlers entered the Northwest Territory between 1806 and 1812. They were particularly active in clearing the land and establishing farms between the Ohio and the Mississippi rivers, precisely the region with the greatest Indian unrest.

Early Indian Leaders: Shawnee Prophet, Black Hawk, and Keokuk

By this time Indians in the Midwest were desperate, and they rallied around an Indian leader best known as the "Shawnee Prophet." He reportedly died and was reborn; while dead he visited the land of the spirits and was given a view of the future. This messiah saw contentment only for those who gave up white ways and returned to the old Indian way of life. With Greenville, Ohio, as the center of his activities he received tribal representatives from the surrounding region. The movement coalesced into an effort to rid the country of the "Long Knives" or Americans. With the Treaty of 1804 as the rallying point for their grievances against the Americans, the Fox and Sauk were ready and willing to follow this confederation organized by the Shawnee and actively fostered by the British. In the Battle of Tippecanoe Creek of 1811 the Shawnee Prophet's prestige was destroyed by Harrison's stand against the Indians. Although the battle was not decisive, it was unlikely that an Indian confederation could emerge afterwards. In early 1812 an Indian delegation that included Fox and Sauk went to Washington, D.C., and this time they were well received because the War of 1812 had erupted into open conflict. The most the Americans could hope to do was keep the Indians from joining in the conflict on the side of the British. To prevent Fox and Sauk participation the Americans decided to move these Indians to Missouri, where they would be beyond effective contact with the British. They succeeded in mov-

The Fox: Fighters and Farmers of the Woodland Fringe

Plate 6–1 Black Hawk. (After McKenney and Hall, 1934)

ing approximately 1500 members of the combined tribes to these new lands.

The fortunes of the Fox and Sauk soon were guided by two Sauk leaders, the pro-British Black Hawk and Keokuk, who emerged as pro-American. Black Hawk distinguished himself as a warrior at the age of fifteen, and by the time he was nineteen he had led a party of 200 warriors against an equal number of Osage. In this conflict nearly half the Osage were killed; Black Hawk alone killed six persons. By 1812 he was the most respected leader of the combined tribes. Early in the War of 1812 he journeyed to Green Bay, Wisconsin, with 200 warriors and was well received by the British. They convinced him that the first effort should be to secure the Great Lakes region.

While Black Hawk was away, American troops threatened to destroy the principal village of Saukenuk near the mouth of the Rock River in Illinois. The people had decided in council to flee, but an unimportant Sauk, Keokuk, asked to be heard. He was a fine orator and maintained that they should resist the Americans. His persuasive speech convinced the people, and when the American force failed to arrive, Keokuk became a hero. By his abilities as an orator and determined stand against the Americans he established himself as a rival of Black Hawk.

Black Hawk's effort to contain the Americans was moderately successful, but by the fall of 1814 the course of the War of 1812 had changed in the Northwest Territory. The Indian war was not well managed by the British, and the American forces were consolidating. The Treaty of Ghent brought an end to the conflict, but the Fox and Sauk were deeply divided. Those who had settled in Missouri had been largely neutral, and most of the others had fought the Americans. In spite of the American victory many Indians in the Northwest Territory still looked to the British for help in their struggle against the

Long Knives. Unsettled conditions among the Fox and Sauk led to sporadic raids against frontier settlements and clashes with those Indians on whose lands they encroached. To end these killings the Americans called a meeting in 1820 of Indians along the upper Mississippi. By now Keokuk had emerged as a powerful instrument of white appeasement in the central prairies. He was willing to abide by American decisions as long as they furthered his own interests, and the effective influence of Black Hawk declined.

Finally, in 1825, the Treaty of Prairie du Chein was signed by the Fox, Sauk, and Siouans. Boundaries were established, and Indians were to give up their ties with the British. Although the Fox ceded lands that subsequently were occupied by whites, the Indians did not leave, causing further conflict. Five years and another treaty later found Black Hawk still determined to resist. His followers did not have enough food for the winter of 1830–1831 because they had sold most of their equipment to obtain intoxicants. To complicate conditions further heavy snowfalls made it impossible for the Indians to hunt efficiently. By this time Black Hawk was desperate and appealed to other tribes to form a confederation to resist the whites, but to no avail. In the spring of 1831 Black Hawk and his "British Band" returned to Saukenuk, and the women began planting corn. The 300 warriors in the party maintained an uneasy peace with white settlers. To remove the Indians, militiamen were dispatched to put down what was termed an Indian uprising. Saukenuk was bombarded even though the Indians had left, and the village was destroyed. Black Hawk was forced to agree not to return to Saukenuk and to submit to Keokuk as the leader of the combined tribes. At this point it would seem that resistance against the Americans was no longer feasible, but Black Hawk's determination was renewed by a false report from one of his subordinates that other tribes and the British promised support.

In the spring of 1832 the British Band, including 2000 persons with something more than 500 warriors, crossed the Mississippi River and moved toward Rock Island. By this time the frontier was in turmoil, volunteer militiamen were called out, and troops were moved into the area to prevent Black Hawk from reoccupying his traditional country. The American military effort was hopelessly confused; at the same time, Black Hawk was unaware that he had been deceived by his lieutenant. As Black Hawk traveled up the Rock River, he came in contact with the Potawatomi. They told him they could not give his people the corn they needed, and they also warned that no British were going to aid the Indians. Under these circumstances, Black Hawk felt that he must surrender, and he sent a party of warriors back to the camp of the whites beneath a flag of truce. The whites, however, who were not under any realistic military command, misunderstood the purpose of the warriors and killed one of the three Indians carrying the flag. The other two and the Indian scouts who had followed them raced back to their encampment. Black Hawk now was forced to fight. He rallied around himself forty warriors to hold off the whites. The Indians ambushed the oncoming whites, and soon the

The Fox: Fighters and Farmers of the Woodland Fringe

militiamen were fleeing in panic. The rest of the troops were routed, and all were swept along in the retreat. These disorganized volunteers fled to relate exaggerated stories of the Indian numbers and of the defeat they had suffered. After the skirmish Black Hawk and his followers returned to the American camp, looting and mutilating the bodies of the slain whites, and then they withdrew to the headwaters of the Rock River. When a regular military contingent reached the battleground, they found that only eleven individuals had been killed by the Indians. As the Indians retreated, they massacred a group of whites on a farm and sent scalping parties into the settlements along their path. This caused settlers and the government to demand decisive action. The American forces were reinforced, and by the end of June the United States military operation included about 3600 men, had cost about $300,000, and still had not defeated the Indians.

The Americans moved on the Indians from two directions, and Black Hawk made a desperate effort to rejoin Keokuk or to find refuge in the prairies. Black Hawk reached the banks of the Wisconsin River before the Americans were near enough to attack the entire band; here the Indians were driven into the river bottom, and nearly seventy warriors were killed. In spite of earlier deaths from exposure and starvation, abandonment by their few allies, and casualties in battle, the British Band crossed the river bottom and reached the eastern bank of the Mississippi River. Black Hawk advocated retreating farther north, but the majority felt that their best chance for survival was to cross the Mississippi. Fifty moved northward with Black Hawk, and 100 escaped across the Mississippi River. Black Hawk eluded capture until he had reached the vicinity of the Wisconsin Dells; here he was made a prisoner, and the Black Hawk War was ended.

Removal

The ensuing treaty required that the Fox and Sauk forfeit about 6 million acres of land along the western bank of the Mississippi River in the state of Iowa. They agreed to remove themselves from this land onto a small reservation in Iowa. As immediate compensation for the ceded lands they received the services of a blacksmith, a gunsmith shop, and an annual allotment of tobacco and salt. They also were given winter provisions and $40,000 for paying debts to traders. Over the next thirty years they were to receive further payment of $660,000 for the cession. The treaty stipulated that Black Hawk and other chiefs were to be taken to Fort Monroe on Chesapeake Bay as prisoners to prevent further violence along the frontier. Black Hawk arrived in Washington, D.C., in late April but was a prisoner at Fort Monroe only briefly. He was released in the custody of Keokuk and was given a tour of the major cities in the eastern United States to impress him with American power. He was overwhelmed by the seventy-four gun *Delaware*, amazed by the mobs of people that surrounded him, and awed by the arsenals that the Americans maintained. According to the historian William T. Hagan, if Black Hawk had accompanied one of the earlier Indian parties to Washington, D.C., and had realized at that time the power of the Americans, the Black Hawk War probably would never have been fought.

Early Historic Life

ORIGIN MYTH   At a place that is not on earth and is so far away that no one is able to travel there, a place where it is always winter, lives Wisaka. In the remote past he lived on earth with his younger brother, but the manitous met in council and plotted to kill the brothers. They killed the younger brother, but the older one, Wisaka, survived. First they tried to kill him with fire. Then they created a great flood, but Wisaka climbed a tall tree on a mountain top, a canoe appeared at the top of the tree, and he paddled about on the water. A turtledove brought him twigs, and a muskrat brought mud from which he made a ball. He threw it into the water, and it grew into the earth as we know it.

Wisaka created all the things on earth, including people. The Fox, according to their traditions, have such great antiquity that they do not know when they first arrived on earth. They were the first people to dwell on the land made by Wisaka, and they lived by the sea. From the sea came a great fish with the head of a man. As this fish walked on the land, he became fully human, and he was followed by other fish who made the same transformation. These individuals established a community near the Fox, and every aspect of Fox life was copied by the fish-turned-to-men. These were the manitous of the world. When Wisaka formed the Fox, they were red, the same color as blood. As time passed, people grew more distant from the manitous, and the world in which they lived changed. In recent times animals and birds have begun to disappear, and the manitous who control the universe are unhappy about this new state of affairs. Sometime in the future the manitous will destroy the earth, the Fox will revert to their original red condition, and the world will begin again.

APPEARANCE AND CLOTHING   The appearance of Fox men was striking, largely because of their roached hair style. A man shaved all the hair from his head except for a palm-sized tuft at the crown. Most of the tuft was about two inches long, but at the center grew a scalp lock that never was cut and usually was braided. From this braid hung an eagle quill, and along the middle of the tuft were attached lengths of deer hair that very frequently were painted red. The typical clothing of a male included a skin cape for cold weather, a buckskin breechclout, leggings, and high-topped moccasins. Women dressed their hair by parting it in the middle and drawing it to the

The Fox: Fighters and Farmers of the Woodland Fringe

back of the neck. Most probably the women wore long buckskin dresses and short leather moccasins. Young children usually wore only a long, loose shirt, and older children followed adult clothing styles.

SETTLEMENTS   Summer villages were in lowlands along rivers and streams where the ground could be cleared and crops planted. The dwellings were oblong, bark-covered structures with pole frames up to forty feet in length and twenty feet in width. Along each interior sidewall was a raised bark- and skin-covered platform that served as seats and beds. In the open space at the center of the house were fires for cooking and heating. Clusters of lodges were occupied from April through much of September, but in the winter small family groups dispersed to follow a wandering life. The winter dwellings were oval structures framed by placing the ends of poles in the ground, bending the poles, and tying them together at the top. Over the framework were placed reeds or mats, and at the doorway hung a bearskin.

SUBSISTENCE ACTIVITIES   The economic cycle around 1820, and most likely before, was divided into two phases. In the spring and summer the Fox tilled lands adjacent to their lodges. Here the women planted and maintained the gardens while the men hunted. The principal hunting weapon was the bow and arrow; the bow was sinew-backed, and arrows were placed in a buckskin quiver. The most important game animal was deer, valued not only for its meat but for its skin and fat. Birds and small game were hunted, as was the bear, which the Fox considered a choice meat. The staples, however, were maize, beans, and squash cultivated by the women and the wild plant foods that they collected. These foods were dried and stored in cache pits, in bark baskets, or in the rafters of a bark house. In mid-September when families left their summer settlement they took a small quantity of corn and their other possessions to a winter hunting area. The scattered families lived in dome-shaped, mat-covered structures until the number of game animal kills declined in late winter. They then assembled in large camps and were not active again until they began to trap beaver in the spring. Following the beaver trapping season they traveled back to their villages, planning the trip so that they would arrive simultaneously. This was done to minimize the exposure of small groups to hostile peoples and to prevent anyone from taking provisions from another's cache.

By the time records about food habits are reasonably complete, we find that an iron kettle hung from a hook above the fire was the usual cooking utensil. When the Fox lived in Wisconsin, wild rice was an important food, but in later years they were able to obtain it only in trade. Their staple was maize, and many different dishes were prepared. Corn was boiled or processed as hominy by leaching the shells with wood ash and washing away the lye. Corn also was parched in a fire, but most often it was ground into meal and boiled as gruel. They raised beans and squash as additional staples. Squash fruit was processed for storage by cutting it into rings that were dried in the sun. Among the wild plants collected were broad-leafed arrowhead corms, either gathered from the plant rootlets or robbed from muskrat caches. These "potatoes" were boiled, sliced, and strung on cords hung from the rafters of a bark house. A potato-like growth was the groundnut, which grew along the plant roots and was as much as three inches in diameter; it was peeled, boiled, sliced, and dried to be cooked with meat in the winter. Additionally, the Fox collected sugar-maple sap, which was an important seasoning in cooking, and a few plants were used specifically for seasoning. Hickory nuts, butternuts, and walnuts were eaten, and diverse forms of wild fruit were consumed either at the time of collection or later in the winter after they had been dried.

DESCENT, KINSHIP, AND MARRIAGE   The most important kinship ties of the Fox were traced through males (patrilineal descent), and persons with a presumed but unknown common ancestor comprised a patriclan, the most important descent group. The members of any clan were obligated to seek spouses from another clan (clan exogamy). The leading clans were named Bear, Fox, Wolf, Thunder, Swan, Eagle, Sturgeon, and Bear Potato; the largest ones and possibly the oldest were the first four. The succession of paramount chiefs came from particular clans. The Fox, Thunder, and Bear clans contributed most chiefs, the leaders of war parties, and council members; the other clans normally provided only councilmen. The clans appear to have formed two groups (moieties) that rendered reciprocal services in ceremonial activities; the Bear and Wolf reciprocated with the Eagle, Fox, and Thunder clans. It must be added, however, that the exact nature of these mutual obligations is not known.

A second type of moiety division has been recorded. In this arrangement each person was assigned to one of two groups, the To'kana or Kicko, depending on birth order and the father's affiliation. A firstborn was usually assigned to the division to which his father did not belong, and the second to the group of his father's affiliation. The third belonged to the moiety of the first and so on. Assignment was irrespective of the sex of the person and had nothing to do with marital arrangements. Between the members of the moieties there was a friendly rivalry. They competed in games, and the division was important in certain festivities, hunting arrangements, and the assignment of camp police.

In the Fox kinship terminology collected in the 1930s we find that on a male Ego's generational level specific terms existed for older brother and older sister, whereas younger brothers and sisters were grouped as younger siblings. These terms were extended to father's brother's children and to mother's sister's children. There were additionally distinct and separate terms for father's sister's son and daughter as well as for mother's brother's son and daughter. The terms for father's sister's son and daughter were the same as for sister's son and daughter. This form of cousin terminology is termed Omaha. On the generational level above Ego we find that the word for father was extended to father's brother, but there was a different term for mother's brother. It was ex-

190

tended to all males in the direct line from mother's brother—for example, mother's brother's son, mother's brother's son's son. The terminology for males on the first ascending generation above Ego is bifurcate merging. The most important observation to be made about the terminology is that there was the inclination to group individuals on both sides of one's family into a small number of categories and to ignore generations. In kinship behavior there tended to be egalitarian relationships between sets of individuals. For example, between a father and his son we find the behavior tended to be as between two brothers in the ideals of modern American society. Among the Fox, the mother-son relationship was more like that between sister and brother; restraint was necessary without avoidance. Again between a father and his daughter there was the brother and sister attitude, while the mother and daughter relationship paralleled that of a father and son.

SOCIAL OVERVIEW   According to the able analysis of early historic Fox life by Natalie F. Joffe, the most important social and economic unit was the small extended family. It might include about forty individuals since a man sometimes had two to five wives, and their children sometimes brought spouses into the household. In addition, there might be household members from other tribes who had been adopted or were considered captives. Female prisoners might marry Fox men, and their offspring were regarded as Fox. A family group also might include individuals adopted to take the place of deceased persons; these individuals did not take up residence in the household but were regarded as members of it.

POLITICAL LIFE   Political control was organized around the village and the tribe, but little is recorded about the tribal level of action. The paramount chief was from a particular lineage in the Bear clan, and other clans contributed lesser chiefs. In the event that the elder son of a chief could not or would not succeed his father (primogeniture) the title and position were passed to a younger son, a brother, or a nephew of the chief. The chief organized village subsistence activities and raiding or war parties. A village chief was in office for an extended period of time, and his influence was great even though he had

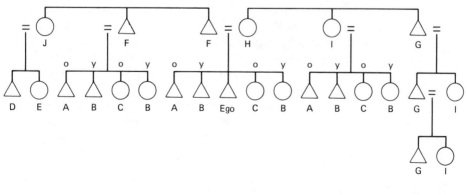

little power. He was expected to be nonaggressive, and he served as an arbitrator in collective discussions. The council, which made community-wide decisions, had a required membership from different patrilines but also included other men with outstanding qualities. The village chief listened to discussions and attempted to reconcile conflicting views. The chief and council were quite powerful, but their actions most often were guided by tradition. The Fox, as Walter B. Miller stresses, were rugged individualists who knew what was expected of them, and in normal activities they strongly resented anyone's attempt to direct their behavior. As the Jesuit missionary Father Allouez (Miller, 1955, 286) wrote long ago, "These people are self-willed beyond anything that can be imagined!"

To illustrate how the political system operated, it is instructive to follow what took place when a man killed his wife. She was of course a member of a different clan, and her male relatives summoned the murderer to appear at their main lodge. He did as he was directed and squatted on the floor while the men of the woman's clan seated themselves on the platforms. One man held an ax which would be used to smash the murderer's skull if he were to be executed. When the jury was assembled, a man at one end of the line silently nudged the person next to him; this was a vote to kill the murderer. This man nudged the one sitting on his far side and so on until one man failed to nudge his partner; this indicated that he did not approve of the death penalty. Since a unanimous verdict of guilt was required, the murderer was not doomed to die, and his relatives were permitted to offer gifts as compensation. This example demonstrates that the crime of murder was not judged on the tribal or village level, but was considered an offense against the kin group of the deceased individual. The example also illustrates that alternatives of action, death or compensation, were possible.

WARFARE   One activity at which the Fox excelled was physical combat with enemies, but this was "war" only in a loose sense of the word. Aggression against other Indians or against whites was organized by the tribe or as individual raiding parties. A national war such as those fought against the French, the Americans, or Osage met with overall approval, but even these actions rarely involved large numbers of warriors and large-scale battles. Raids organized by individuals against a particular enemy to accomplish a specific purpose were most common. Warriors ventured forth to secure hunting areas against intrusion by others, to acquire new lands on which to hunt, to avenge the death of a Fox, or to gain prestige and honor. A war leader was able to organize a raid if he had prior success and supernatural power. He supervised the strategy, but his authority was limited since any warrior could return home at any time without the loss of honor. Even though a warrior might submit to the temporary control of a war leader and follow instructions, he was obliged to bend to the war chief's modicum of authority only during the period of the raid. The important point is that the Fox war leader had more

The Fox: Fighters and Farmers of the Woodland Fringe

authority and power than any other individual at any other time, and yet his prerogatives were very few indeed. As if to emphasize the temporary nature of his position, after returning from a raid he was obliged not to enter his settlement until he had been purified ceremonially.

Within Fox society a great deal of honor was heaped upon the successful warrior. To be a great warrior was a value instilled in boys from early childhood. A male child was given portions of the eyebrow or heart of a brave but slain enemy so that he might eat them and acquire the qualities of the deceased. A boy attempted to join a war party as soon as possible so that he might boast of his exploits according to the custom for all warriors. Anyone could attempt to lead a war party; if he dreamed and his dreams were judged propitious by other warriors, they pledged themselves to join the raid. Before departure, war songs were sung, and men abstained from the company of women. Although a woman might join her husband on a war party, she would not have sexual intercourse with him during the trip. A raiding party advanced slowly, hunting along the route and caching the dried meat for the return trip. If the party numbered twenty or more persons, a sacred bundle was taken along for supernatural protection; a smaller party relied on the party leader's medicine bundle to secure supernatural aid. Some men served as scouts, and one was designated as the cook. An attack always was planned to surprise the enemy. If the party was successful, the return was led by the man who made the first kill; in defeat, each warrior returned home as best he could. If captives were secured, the aged ones often were killed on the way home. A successful raid ended with a scalp dance and feasting at the village of the warriors. A woman could gain important status and rights among men if a male relative permitted her to club the head of an enemy he had killed. For a Fox man to steal horses was honorable; however, such theft did not have the social value reported among most Indians of the plains and prairies. A warrior could and usually did take new names repeatedly if he excelled in warfare. Warfare among the Fox was not nearly as elaborate as among many Indians of the plains, but it did manifest most of the important features found farther west.

RELIGION   The most distinctive characteristics of Fox religious life were the importance of personal rapport with supernatural forces and the more secondary role of group ceremonies. Supernatural matters centered in the concept of manitou, a fickle, mysterious, and pervasive quality in nature that persons communicated with for power. Manitou was approached with humility and apprehension, and it could impart to the seeker a sense of strength. The usual way to contact a manitou was by fasting for a prolonged period, but at critical or even ordinary moments this force might be seen or heard. Its manifestation could be received through a song, an object, or a ritual. In discussing supernatural experience among the Fox, Miller stresses that religious systems are essentially projections from social experience and an extension of the manner in which people deal with each other. The central religious concept of manitou was as an abstract, impersonal, and pervasive supernatural force. Yet it was received by an individual, and a personalized manitou was drawn into the experiences of an individual. The blessing and cooperation of a manitou had no built-in permanence. It could be lost at any time, and therefore an individual receiving such power always sought to reinforce it. The varieties of manitou were endless. The force could be animal, human, organic, inorganic, material, nonmaterial, natural, or supernatural.

To gain the cooperation of a manitou an adolescent boy darkened his face with ashes and fasted alone in the forest for four days and nights, or even longer. Near the end of his isolation he dreamed of a manitou or received a vision that included instructions. The receipt of power was contingent on following rules set down by the supernatural. These usually included the avoidance of menstruating women and a periodic offering of tobacco to the manitou. In addition, other instructions might be given, such as wearing a certain item of clothing, singing a particular song, or obtaining an object that would become the basis for a medicine bundle. If a boy behaved properly in his relationship with a manitou, the association was lasting, but if the boy failed in his duties, the manitou withdrew support. If this happened, a youth fasted and isolated himself again to obtain an affiliation with another manitou. A faithful manitou not only remained with a man during his life but was with him even after death.

The most important personification of a supernatural force was the Gitche Manitou, the Great Manitou. Another was the creator and culture hero Wisaka, addressed as "my nephew." Other mythological creatures might be helpful; bears, deer, and snakes made one swift of foot. An individual's contact with these animals served as a basis for the emergence of a sacred bundle, the essence of Fox ceremonialism. The founder learned essential rituals from a supernatural, and a cult developed around each bundle. Affiliation with a sacred bundle and its ceremonies was along a clan line, but an outsider could be incorporated into a group by learning the rituals and by being invited to participate.

The most important annual ceremonies were held by clans during the spring, summer, and winter. The spring and summer rituals were held in the bark house of a clan. Here singers and drummers consistently sat on the south side of the structure. Hoof or gourd rattles were used by certain clans, and rasps were used by others. Participants performed four dances and ate three times, with the main feast following the third dance. In all the ceremonies an emphasis was placed on dogs as ceremonial food, seating position according to moiety, and the sacrifice of tobacco. A ceremonial leader committed ritual speeches to memory and punctuated his delivery of them with other episodes. Such an individual followed established tradition in his performances, and his authority was limited to these specific times.

The most important supernaturals, apart from manitous, probably were

The Fox: Fighters and Farmers of the Woodland Fringe

witches envisaged as either human males or females. Witches reportedly were often from the Bear clan, and they learned their skills from other witches. The nearness of a witch at night was indicated by flashes of light or a hissing sound made as it passed. The evil power of witches took diverse forms: part of a person's body swelled because of a witch or a death from no apparent cause was a witch's doing. If a person was bewitched, certain techniques could be used to turn the malevolent power back against the witch.

The Fox considered most phenomena as supernatural. Thus, the sun was a man, a manitou, and the grandfather of the Fox; he was not always considerate of the people. The moon, as their grandmother, had a gentle quality and could be looked upon at any time. The months were named and associated with the arrival of each new moon. The Milky Way was a river of stars, and other stars in the sky either were persons who had died and had gone to live in the sky, or else they were great manitous. The four stars forming the body of the Big Dipper were thought of as a bear; it was followed by three stars who were hunters. They killed the bear in the fall, and its blood fell to earth, turning the leaves of some trees red and fading the color of others. Then the bear came back to life, and the hunters pursued it for another year. The color red symbolized the fall of the year; it also signified hostility and was used for decoration. Black was the color for winter, for fasting, and for mourning. Green was for spring and peace; it was the special color of the chief's clan. Yellow symbolized summer.

Curers among the Mesquakie used plant products and to a far lesser extent animal substances to heal patients. As a plant was collected, it was necessary to follow certain rules. Songs were sung before removing roots, and an offering was placed in the ground where a root had been to appease Grandmother Earth because plants were the hairs on her head. The earth was the grandmother of Wisaka and the Fox as well; her name was Mother-of-all-Things-Everywhere. When plants talked to one another, their conversation was heard as the wind blowing through trees. Plants could be happy or sad; they mated in the spring and bore fruit in the fall. Wisaka was appeased so that plants would be potent cures. There were proper methods and a proper season for collecting medicinal plants, and only stipulated amounts were taken.

LIFE CYCLE   For a woman to conceive, the Fox believed that repeated copulations with one man were essential, and during pregnancy many restrictions surrounded her behavior. For example, to ensure a normal birth the woman abstained from eating nuts so that the embryo would not break through the membrane; she could not touch a corpse for fear her baby would die, and to stare at a corpse would make the baby cross-eyed. In childbearing a woman knelt and leaned forward, supported by a rawhide strap. She did not cry out no matter how severe the pain. If the delivery was long and difficult, a shaman or woman sang around the outside of the hut but usually offered no other assistance. Paturition took place in a small hut away from the family dwelling, and here the mother was cared for by an old woman for ten days after the birth. For the next twenty days she slept in the main house apart from the other occupants.

A baby was placed on a cradleboard and carried by its mother for nearly a year. As children grew older, the parents did not favor one child over the other unless a boy became an outstanding hunter. Children were told not to visit other families often, for if they did people would think that they always were in search of something good to eat. They were expected to be retiring and honest, and when someone died, to fast and be quiet. These fastings prepared boys for the fasts in later years that were an important part of becoming a man. Abstaining from food also was emphasized for girls, especially as their menarche approached; the purpose was for them to have a long and good life. These ideals may not have been followed exactly, but they did constitute the normal expectations for children. A role assumed for two years by young males of high social standing was that of a "slave" in the service of a chief. After this period the volunteer was freed from the drudgery of menial tasks such as cooking and camp chores throughout his life.

As mentioned earlier, the relationship between a father and his son was somewhat comparable to the behavior between brothers in our society. Hunting instruction began when a boy was about seven, and by the time he was twelve he was given a gun and expected to obtain small game. He was taught not only objective hunting skills but associated magical practices. When a boy killed his first game, a feast was held in his honor, a widespread practice among North American Indians. A son who disobeyed was not punished physically but was instructed by his father to fast. To fast and seek solitude was not new to the child, but it became intensified. While the boy was still young, he was expected to seek out a manitou. When he went alone into the forest on his quest, his parents mourned the loss of their son; after establishing this supernatural relationship, he would no longer be a child. To fast and paint one's face with ashes made a manitou approachable and encouraged it to grant the young man success in the hunt and in war, and give him longevity as well.

At about the same age that a boy began to receive hunting instructions, a girl was taught domestic skills by her mother. She learned to sew, to cook, and to care for the garden. About the age of twelve, she began to acquire the more complex skills necessary in making moccasins and house mats. At her first menstruation she was isolated from the settlement in a small hut where she lived for ten days with a blanket over her head. Her companion during this isolation was an old woman, who instructed the girl about adult behavior. At the end of this initial isolation the girl bathed in a stream, and her skin was pierced, especially about the back and sides, until she bled freely. The bloodletting was to ensure that the girl would not menstruate excessively. She then moved within sight of the settlement, living there for twenty days. After this

The Fox: Fighters and Farmers of the Woodland Fringe

time she took a second bath and finally was permitted in the family dwelling once again. During all subsequent menstrual periods, a woman was isolated in a hut. She was not only potentially dangerous to herself but to men and supernaturals. If she were to touch her hair, it might fall out; if she ate sweet or sour food, she might lose her teeth. She could kill a tree with her touch or cause a crop to fail if she ran through a garden. Most important manitous abhorred menstruating women, and such women were avoided by men so that they would not jeopardize their special powers.

A girl was not ready to marry until she was skilled in making fine beadwork and ribbon applique. Her behavior was supervised carefully by her mother and her mother's brother, who was a joking relative. He not only joked with her but made certain that she behaved properly since he would be shamed if she misbehaved. She was taught not to be promiscuous nor to giggle, for giggly girls were open to sexual overtures. As a boy became a young man, he was expected to be respectful toward girls and to have sexual intercourse only with the girl he planned to marry. A young man sometimes courted a girl by playing a flute near her home, which was an attempt to lure the girl outside. The melody of the flute conveyed his desire, but for a girl to accept the lure invited seduction. The parents of a courting couple preferred to have the man visit their home openly to win their daughter in marriage.

The principal means for obtaining a wife was by bride service, but less commonly a couple might elope. A suitor usually established a friendship with the girl's brother and broached the subject to him. The girl of course was from a different clan than the man, and after the girl's family declared the match acceptable, they usually required the services of the groom until the first offspring was born. Alternatively a man's family presented the girl's family with gifts in lieu of bride service by their son. This was attempted especially when the boy's parents did not want to lose him as a hunter. If gifts were accepted in place of bride service or when the service was completed, the couple was free to establish an independent household or to join either set of in-laws. An elopement occurred when a man persuaded a girl to join him on a summer hunt; on their return he presented the parents of the girl with gifts. Another less common arrangement was for a girl to be offered to a warrior by her father. This happened when a man had rendered extraordinary service to the family of the girl. For example, if a warrior prevented the scalping of a man's dead son, gave the son a warrior's interment, or rescued the son from an enemy, he might be offered the sister as a wife.

At least a few Fox remained unmarried and lived as transvestites. A dance held annually centered about and emphasized the position of such a person. The *berdache*, as he was termed by the French traders and trappers, was danced around by men who had had a sexual relationship with him. The transvestite wore the clothing of a woman, and because of his unusual role he was regarded as sacred.

The dissolution of a marriage usually resulted from sterility or from an

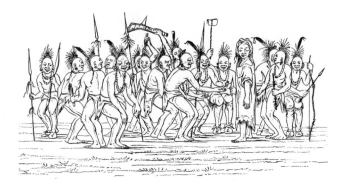

Plate 6–2 Fox and Sac dance to the berdache, after an 1836 painting by Catlin. (From Donaldson, 1886)

inability of a couple to tolerate one another. Some personality characteristics such as extreme jealousy or ill temper led to divorce. When a marriage was dissolved, any presents that had been exchanged during the marital arrangements were returned, but personal property was retained by each partner. Sometimes a husband left his wife after a few days of marriage; this was said to have occurred when the bride was not a maiden. In extreme cases of a wife's infidelity the offended husband might kill the couple; a milder alternative was for the husband to cut off his wife's ears or bite off her nose.

A conspicuous characteristic of adult life was that each individual knew what was expected of him and was resentful of being instructed in any manner. A person's behavior was dictated by tradition; he did as his father had done before him, or as he had done the year before. He communicated with the supernaturals as an individual with no other person standing between him and the manitou. He functioned in the institutions of the society without supervision, and in his personal life, again, he was his own authority. Thus, it is not surprising that individualism was the social norm, and strong resentment was exhibited by any Fox who was told to do anything.

When an adult died, there were three possible forms of interment. The body might be placed on a scaffold or in a tree; an honorable interment for a warrior was to place him in a sitting position above the body of a slain enemy. Most common perhaps was to dig a shallow pit and arrange the body in a seated position with the head above the ground and covered with rocks or a small shed. Food and water were placed with the body, but weapons were not, since spirits might use them against the living. At the foot of a grave a stake was erected after the bark was peeled from it. Among the final acts were

The Fox: Fighters and Farmers of the Woodland Fringe

sprinkling tobacco on the body and killing a dog on the site of the burial. The dog's spirit protected and guided the dead to the next world. Just before the body of a warrior was abandoned, an old warrior recounted the number of persons the deceased had killed, which meant that their souls would serve as his slaves in the land of spirits. The ritual leader distributed the property of the deceased, along with items contributed by relatives of the dead person, to his helpers.

After disposing of the body, the clan to which the deceased belonged held a mourning ceremony. A second dog was killed and its hair singed by four firebrands taken from the hearth of the deceased. The dog was cooked, and the clan's mourning songs were sung until about midnight when the participants ate the dog. The principal mourners dressed in tattered clothing and blackened their faces. They remained in this state up to four years, which was the maximum time limit before an adoption ceremony and an end to mourning. The adoption ceremony was performed by the relatives of the deceased and served to release the soul of the dead permanently. The soul had left the earth after four days but returned at intervals until the adoption rituals were completed. If this did not happen within four years, the soul became an owl. The adoption was of an unrelated friend of the deceased who was of the same sex and approximate age. This individual assumed the kinship position of the deceased but also retained his own prior kinship ties. If the deceased was a warrior killed by an enemy, the adopted warrior was obligated to kill an enemy in order to release the widow from mourning.

Each individual had two souls that served different purposes. A small soul came from a particular manitou and was equated with the individual's life; it left the body at the time of death and through subsequent adoption ceremonies was reborn three times. The larger soul, from Wisaka, had entered the neonate's body at birth and was never reborn. In the world of spirits a division was made. In one section lived persons who had been good on earth, and in the other, persons who were evil. Some of these concepts may have been inspired by Christian missionaries.

Recent Historic Changes

IOWA RESERVATION   Following the end of the Black Hawk War in 1832 the Fox and Sauk lived on such a small, inadequate reservation in Iowa that they could not possibly follow their traditional way of life very long. They hunted and planted crops until the land was depleted of game, and then they turned to the west to hunt bison. Soon this was an unprofitable subsistence base, and they spent more and more time wintering among whites. They dealt with unscrupulous traders, dishonest Indian agents, and generally hostile whites. They were plagued with disease, and the consumption of intoxicants became almost a way of life. As if these troubles were not enough, internal dissension between the Keokuk faction and another brought serious conflict. Furthermore the Fox and Sauk were thrown into close contact with their Siouan enemies, and the resultant raids led to an embittered attitude on both sides. To climax all of this, an increase in the number of local white settlers forced the Fox and Sauk to move again. Americans concerned about them attempted to introduce modern farming methods, but the Indians would have no part of the program. Neither would they permit schools to be established, and they rejected the efforts of missionaries to convert them to Christianity. Their crystallized pattern of hostility against white customs was based on 200 years of bitter experience. Again in 1842 these Indians were forced to sell all of their land in Iowa and soon were obligated to relocate at the headwaters of the Osage River in Kansas.

FROM KANSAS TO IOWA   The Fox obtained nearly 400,000 acres of land in Kansas, but it was prairie country, ill-adapted to their farming and hunting economy. They hunted bison and other game but depended largely on annuities from the government. Hunting on the prairies brought them into conflict with the Arapaho, Comanche, and Kiowa, who resented Fox and Sauk intrusion. The number of warriors among the Fox and Sauk always was small, but they were brave and had superior weapons. However by the 1860s their number was so badly depleted by diseases and losses in warfare that they could no longer resist the more populous hostile groups.

The Fox never were reconciled to their Kansas reservation, and during the winter of 1851–1852 nearly a hundred Mesquakie returned to Iowa. They bought and settled eighty acres of land in Tama County. Legal recognition of these Fox was extended by the state government in 1856, and the land was held in trust by the governor of the state. In 1858 other Fox from Kansas, defying the Federal Government, moved to Iowa. Amazing as it may seem, the Indians were welcomed by the whites. Altruism was not their motive; the ease with which the Indians could be separated from their annuity payments was what brought the friendly reception by the whites. In 1862 more Fox moved to Iowa after a disagreement about annuity payments on the Kansas reservation. Finally, when the Fox and Sauk were forced to give up their Kansas reservation and move to Oklahoma in 1869, still more Fox returned to Iowa. By about 1870 there were some 300 Fox Indians in Iowa, and they began to settle down to a new way of life in an old environment.

The Indians who struggled back to Iowa, beginning in 1851, were miserably poor. Their economy was based on hunting and trapping, gardening, begging, and selling curios. Whenever they obtained surplus money, they purchased additional lands. They remained extremely distrustful of outsiders; for example, the school built in 1876 was not attended by Indian children. Family units continued to frequent hunting and trapping areas in the winter. In the late 1880s the Fox still refused to allow their children to attend school, and the men would not learn the skills necessary to become farmers. In 1894,

The Fox: Fighters and Farmers of the Woodland Fringe

Plate 6–3 A woman with her child, ca. 1900. (Courtesy of the
State Historical Society of Iowa)

after the sale of land allotments that had been held for them in Oklahoma,
they were able to expand their holdings in Iowa to 2800 acres. Apparently at
about this time they began to rent farmlands to whites, lands that did not
belong to the core of their holdings, and they used the rent money for the
payment of taxes.

A visitor to the Fox lands in Iowa in 1897 and 1898 reported that the population was about 400, and the winter dwellings were described as oblong,
pole-framed structures with mat coverings, just as in aboriginal times. The
ground inside a house was covered with old blankets, and a fire in a central
fireplace provided warmth, light, and heat for cooking. The only items seen in

Plate 6–4 Men on horses with summer sun shade and reed-covered dwellings in the background, ca. 1904. (Courtesy of the State Historical Society of Iowa)

one such dwelling were containers and food. The standard fare seems to have been flour, lard, and maize. The flour was fried in lard to make a bannock, which was eaten with dried sweet corn. Dogs remained an important source of meat for festive occasions. A few families, particularly those of younger men, lived in frame dwellings with adjacent outbuildings. In the summer the people lived along the bottomland near the Iowa River in dwellings covered with boards and bark topped with mats. Inside, a platform extended along the length of the room on both sides. An additional structure was a hut nearby for menstruating women.

By the end of the last century most Fox had abandoned their old hair-dressing and clothing styles. A few men still kept the traditional hair style, but most men had long hair braided into a small pigtail from which silver ornaments and beadwork hung. A man's most important ornament was made from silver and protected his scalp lock. Men dressed in store-bought shirts and trousers except at home, where they wore a breechclout and blanket. Moccasins had changed from buckskin to cloth, and the skin cape was replaced by a blanket or shawl. The shirts and skirts of women were made from calico; women wore at least two shirts, which were loose at the waist and buttoned at the front. They wore two or more skirts, which hung loosely from the hips to just below the ankles for younger women and girls and reached just above the ankles for older women. Women wore short woolen leggings that reached their knees. They preferred beaded shawls, but those who could not afford shawls wore blankets. Men and women alike were partial to silver jewelry, which was considered "good medicine."

The Fox: Fighters and Farmers of the Woodland Fringe

Modern Life

SETTLEMENT AND SUBSISTENCE   By 1937 Fox lands near Tama, Iowa, consisted of one large 3800-acre parcel where the people lived, and another 520 acres that were tilled by white farmers on leases. The population of 450 supported themselves either by farming or by wage labor. If a family did not farm, its plot could be leased to another Fox. A family dwelling consisted of a frame house with usually one or two rooms, and adjacent outbuildings included a barn, corncrib, chicken coop, roofless privy, and canvas menstrual hut. During their monthly periods or at childbirth the women ate in the menstrual huts but slept in the houses. Another important structure was made of canvas or mats covering a frame of poles. It was rectangular, resembling the summer house of old, and was often attached to an arbor. On the arbor platform men sat and children played, and much of the cooking was done by women over an outdoor fire nearby.

The average family income in 1937 was about $500 per year, including money from all sources. About half of the ninety-one families farmed, and the others supported themselves by wage labor. In the farming activities, women cultivated garden plots after the land had been prepared by the men, and the men raised the field crops, which were important sources of cash income. Men who did not till the soil labored in nearby towns.

Food habits reflected a certain degree of continuity with the past, since maize was shelled and dried or made into hominy as of old, and squash was sectioned, dried, grated, and stored for future use. The people still collected local plant products and took small game. New crops included oats, alfalfa, potatoes, beets, and onions. They obtained wheat flour and most meat and dairy products from a store, and their maize was ground at a commercial mill. Innumerable dogs were kept, and young ones remained an important ceremonial food. About half of the families owned horses for hauling buggies and wagons or for plowing and riding, but it was primarily younger persons who rode horses. The material culture in the late 1930s seemed typical of rural Iowa. About half of the families owned automobiles, and most shopping was done in Tama, where some effort was made by the storekeepers to stock goods with an appeal to Indians, including shawls, silk neckerchiefs, and beads. Special items for use on festive or ceremonial occasions, such as seed beads, were purchased from mail-order houses; deerskins were obtained from other Indians.

By the mid-1950s the Fox supported themselves as skilled and unskilled laborers and artisans in communities surrounding the reservation. Most often they commuted each day, but in some instances they returned to the reservation only on weekends. The Fox had all the obligations of other United States citizens; they paid all the diverse forms of taxes and had the same rights to vote or to receive relief if they were without economic means. At that time about eight families received relief, paid for by State and Federal Governments. The Indians also received from the Federal Government some services not offered to non-Indians.

SOCIAL DIMENSIONS   In the 1930s, and apparently to the present, a typical residence unit included a man, his wife, their biological children, unmarried relatives, and perhaps children by a former marriage. These nuclear-core households were the economic and social units, although all residents might not contribute equally to the family's support and the near relatives of the couple often were transient. In general, a new household was established near the home of relatives, and there was a tendency to be more closely linked to a wife's family than to the husband's. Yet relatives on both sides of one's family (kindred) offered the typical individual a widespread network of kin, numbering between fifty and one hundred persons, distributed among about a dozen households. It is significant that although the Fox were patrilineal, the important social ties in their daily lives were with both sides of the family. Family ties were expanded through adoption, which was of the same nature as in aboriginal times, a deceased relative being replaced by an adopted individual of approximately the same age and sex. Although adult life centered about one's family, many forms of entertainment existed outside the family. Tama pool halls were frequented by men and boys; a men's baseball team and a girls' softball team were active, and during the winter gambling was an important form of diversion for men and women.

POW-WOW   One of the most pleasurable and lasting of all new Fox institutions has been the Pow-Wow held each August. From the time the Fox returned to Iowa, whites probably had been invited to attend certain of the ceremonies. In later years nonreligious attractions were added, although the religious core of the celebration remained. In 1913, as a response to white enthusiasm, the Pow-Wow was organized formally as a four-day affair, primarily intended as entertainment for whites. The committee controlling the Pow-Wow was structured as a tribal council, with representatives selected from the fifteen major family lines. In 1922 the group was reformulated as a corporate body in a legal sense, with a constitution, officers, and committee members. By 1951 committee membership had been expanded, and even though the positions were elective, the idea of representation by major family groups was preserved. By the early 1950s the rather elaborate Pow-Wow arrangements were guided largely by the committee secretary, a person familiar with whites; since such matters as publicity and the various forms of local arrangements had to be managed through whites, he served as a link between the Indian and white communities. There was no real authority to guide the event; the participants followed traditionally established norms for the celebration, which resembled a county fair but had a strong Indian emphasis. By 1951 there were twenty-four family souvenir and food concessions; the old dances and songs

The Fox: Fighters and Farmers of the Woodland Fringe

Plate 6–5 Fox Indians from Oklahoma welcomed to the Tama Pow-Wow in 1950. (Courtesy of the State Historical Society of Iowa)

were performed, and a guitar group sang cowboy songs. In good weather it was not unusual for 7000 persons to attend the event, and most families camped at the Pow-Wow grounds during the event. All normal routine ceased when the time approached, and this was the one time of year that the people all worked together as Fox.

ATTITUDES: FOX AND WHITE   The attitudes of local whites and Fox toward one another are of continuing importance since the groups frequently interact. In the 1950s whites considered the Fox lazy, which they were by white standards, and as living off Federal dole, which largely was untrue. They thought the Indians were sexually promiscuous and physically dirty. These attitudes probably were reasonable in light of observed Fox behavior; nevertheless, Indians clearly were not as lawless as the whites thought. Furthermore, the whites regarded the Fox settlement as temporary and expected them to be assimilated into the American melting pot. By contrast the Fox thought that the whites were greedy and aggressive, which they were by Indian standards, and that their behavior was artificial. The Indians also believed that they were discriminated against. Both groups agreed that the Fox had been maltreated in the past; this made the whites feel guilty and led to hostility from the Fox.

Plate 6–6 Young dancers at the Tama Pow-Wow, ca. 1959.
(Courtesy of Joan Liffring Zug)

POLITICAL LIFE   Fox political institutions understandably had changed
a great deal by the 1930s. Divisive factionalism existed and appears to have
originated in a controversy over recording individual names for a tribal roll in
1876. The members of a conservative faction refused to tell the Indian agent
their names, but the progressives did so, which led to inequities in the annuity
payments. In addition, a chief was appointed in 1881 who was not a member
of the Bear clan. No issue was made of the fact at the time, but when the chief
later led the progressives, the conservatives questioned his right to the leadership. This division continued to be important in the 1930s. Families, but not
clans, tended to act as units in the factionalism, but these differences did not

The Fox: Fighters and Farmers of the Woodland Fringe

affect ceremonial activities in which clans were important. Marriages tended to be within a faction, but when they did cut across, it was most often the woman who joined the side of her husband.

In 1916 the last chief appointed a council that functioned until 1929, when a council was elected. The elected members of the contending factions could not agree, however, and they never met. Although elections continued to be held, the council remained inactive, owing to internal differences. Then in 1937 the tribe organized under the Indian Reorganization Act, and the seven elected council members began to work together. However, the details of council operations were not recorded. In their political relationships with the State and Federal Governments, Fox lands continued to be held in trust by the Federal Government but were subject to taxation, eminent domain, and other judicial procedures that applied to any individually owned land in the state. Personal differences usually were settled verbally, although women sometimes fought and one man might strike another on the head. The most common offenses prosecuted were drunkenness and differences over property rights. These legal actions often were brought by Indians, but they did not seek intervention from whites for problems such as theft.

The status of warrior once again became important in Fox life during World War II. Of the forty-seven veterans, twenty-two became members of a local American Legion post organized in 1949. Initially, the Fox veterans had joined the Tama post, but when they were refused intoxicants, they resigned. The Federal restriction against selling intoxicants to Indians was still in force although it had been suspended when Indians were in the armed services. The Fox post was founded through the efforts of a white legionnaire from a nearby community, and the post served primarily as a means for veterans to find greater recognition in white society. The large public meetings, involving both Fox and whites, were attended well by both members and nonmember veterans. The Fox community turned to the veterans for leadership, but this was

Plate 6–7 Members of the Robert Morgan American Legion Post 701 at Tama, Iowa, ca. 1950. (Courtesy of the State Historical Society of Iowa)

not forthcoming since veterans were no better able to cope with local problems than any other segment of the population. Initially the leader preserved the Fox ideal of behavior and assumed authority only with reluctance. While the next leader was more assertive, the group would have foundered except that a white veteran assumed the organizational responsibilities. When he left, the organization passed out of existence, partially because Federal officials learned that beer was kept in the government building and withdrew permission for the Indians to meet there.

RELIGION   The concept of manitou persisted, and formal religious activities coalesced around the sacred bundles of the clans or voluntary religious associations. Christianity, the use of peyote, and the nonaboriginal Drum Society all offered limited opportunities for religious participation. The peyote cult was small in 1937, although ceremonial use of the cactus had been known since around the turn of the present century. Peyote was valued mainly for its reportedly curative properties; a person who tried other cures and then turned to peyote often continued to take it after he had recovered. The Drum Society was a religious group organized in 1932 and probably was derived from the Potawatomi. The members were from the progressive faction even though the power of the ceremony was derived from a manitou. The ritual involved the use of four drums, and the ceremonies were held four times a year. The drums were associated with particular leaders, each having specific functions.

Religion still focused on the sacred bundles, which were hereditary either in a patriclan line or across clan affiliations. Forty sacred bundle groups in eleven major categories existed, and within each category were major and minor bundle groups. It was possible to acquire membership in a sacred bundle group through an invitation, which most often was extended to an individual who was a good singer and knew the songs associated with the particular bundle group. Certain reciprocal functions linked the groups into various activities. The bundle affiliations did not regulate marriage although this was apparently an old ideal. The ceremonies were held in summer longhouses and extended from morning until sunset of a single day. Food was prepared by the hosts, and the most important dish was stewed puppies that had been ceremonially killed with clubs. The stew was served by members of another sacred bundle group, and after the meal the bones carefully were collected and burned. The dances were in sets of four, and the sacred bundle was opened and various items used in the ceremony. Both men and women participated in the summer rituals, but only men were active in the winter festivities.

Witchcraft and sorcery were still very much a part of Fox life in the 1930s. Malevolent power was obtained in a vision quest, and a sorcerer might take the form of a bear or snake. If a potential victim could shoot a gun at the spot where a witch was thought to be, the sorcerer would die within four days. One important use of sorcery was as love magic, and if properly employed, it led to the irresistible attractiveness of the user. A nonresponding

The Fox: Fighters and Farmers of the Woodland Fringe

victim would be driven to insanity and eventual suicide. The ability to cure, which came from a vision, was limited to shamans, who employed a variety of techniques. A shaman visited the patient, and if he was compensated enough he accepted the case. The curing procedure entailed singing, administering herbs, and sucking out the disease. Because a bear or snake had given supernatural power to the medicine man, a claw or bone formed the core of his medicine bundle and might be used to suck out the substance causing the illness.

In the 1950s the supernatural system continued to be organized around the traditional ceremonials. Apart from the yearly Pow-Wow, it was still clan-affiliated religious activities that most often brought people together. The clan organization, which was weak and somewhat vaguely defined, served primarily as the structure around which the traditional religious ceremonies were organized. According to Charles Callender of the Fox Project, clans probably served the same general function in the past. Community elders provided the greatest support for the old religious system, and some middle-aged persons followed their lead. Younger Fox tended to be nonreligious, but some seemed ready to adopt Christianity had they not been restrained by elders. The Drum Society members still tended to be progressive, and participants numbered about forty individuals. In the late 1940s participants in the peyote rituals included about a dozen persons. Membership in the two Christian denominations was limited to about thirty persons. The missions were the United Presbyterian and Open Bible Gospel; both were maintained and encouraged by whites, although some meaningful Fox leadership was beginning to emerge.

FOX PROJECT   As mentioned earlier Sol Tax, an anthropologist at the University of Chicago, organized this program to help guide culture change among the Fox. The work by Tax and his associates, especially Fred Gearing, is a fine testimonial to the accomplishments possible under dynamic and effective leadership. Tax had studied the Fox in 1932 and 1934, and Natalie F. Joffee made her study in 1937. With anthropological training and after a course in Fox history, a group of anthropology students from the University of Chicago embarked on the Fox Project in 1948.

As Fred Gearing has stressed, the stereotyped views held by the Fox and whites were being reinforced constantly. As long as this continued, any hope for constructive change was unrealistic. The Fox Project members, after careful preliminary studies, initiated a campaign to change these attitudes. They contacted the whites through newspaper articles, radio and television presentations, and speeches both to various white organizations and to individuals. The Fox were reached largely through conversations with individuals and during meetings. Some of the attitudes toward Indians that were considered most amenable to change follow: the Fox were temporary residents of the state; the Fox lived in poverty; the Fox were not good farmers; the Fox were improvident. The Fox Project dealt with these misconceptions in order to help the

Plate 6–8 Seated in the foreground are the Fox couple, Mr. and Mrs. Willie Johnson, surrounded by their grandchildren and great-grandchildren in 1962. (Courtesy of Joan Liffring Zug)

whites understand Indians. At the same time an effort was made to alter those Fox ideas about whites that were untrue.

The most successful of the Fox Project innovations was the college scholarship program for Indians who had completed high school. Initial discussion of the idea took place between Tax and the tribal council in 1954. When the idea moved into the planning stage, the Fox overwhelmingly approved. By 1955 the problems of sponsorship were solved, and Fox youth began to attend local colleges under the program. By the early 1970s about twenty-five Fox and Sauk Indians from this area were attending colleges or other institutions of higher learning. Under Fox Project encouragement, a community craft industry was organized to produce tile kits, decorative tiles, greeting cards, and

The Fox: Fighters and Farmers of the Woodland Fringe

jewelry in quantity as well as individual craft items. The Fox reaction to the proposal was enthusiastic, and by 1957 the Indians were actively engaged in the industry. Much of the stimulus came from the local Indian artist Charles Pushetonequa. He also was active in bringing others into the program as participants. The craft project has been successful, and the products are well received by whites.

The Fox Project personnel of the University of Chicago made studies basic to an understanding of Fox society and culture before they launched the program of change. The programs they originated or fostered had succeeded or seemed likely to be ongoing when the project was terminated in 1960. It appears that through this interest by anthropologists one American Indian group was made a little more viable. One of the basic assumptions made by Fox Project personnel was that Mesquakie culture need not be assimilated into American culture; rather, it had something to offer the modern world. Therefore, the projects initiated were designed to lend stability and durability to the sociocultural lives of the Fox as Indians.

The question is whether or not the social survival of the Fox will continue. An answer is in part provided in Steven Polgar's study of the three

Plate 6–9 Curtis Youngbear at his home in 1972. (Courtesy of John M. Zielinski)

211
Modern Life

Plate 6–10 Adrian Pushetonequa, a Fox artist, in 1972. (Courtesy of John M. Zielinski)

boys' "gangs" in 1952 and 1953. One group of boys who interacted habitually with one another was a gang as this term is used in American society, but other groups of boys were not gangs in the same context. The members of the first group had a high rate of absenteeism in school, and they were suspected of theft and property damage. The clothing they wore was "Indian" in its type; they preferred bright colored clothing and Navajo jewelry. Most of them were from nonnuclear families, and their relatives were not active in local politics. The members were cold to both white and Indian worlds and were delinquent in both worlds. The second group of boys was oriented toward white society as well as their own in a positive manner. This was especially true of its leader. These boys did not wear flashy clothing, and they were participants in the traditional clan ceremonies. They did not habitually participate in the Pow-Wow or other less traditionally oriented activities, as did the first group. It is from the second gang that Polgar expected the traditionally oriented leaders of the next generation to emerge. The third gang was much more oriented toward the attitudes held by the dominant white society. All the members had spent at least a few years away from the reservation, and they were able to compete successfully for jobs in white society. In addition, three of the eight members entered college. Six of the eight still danced in the Pow-Wow, however, and most attended the clan ceremonies. These boys had begun to find acceptance in white society and were able to move away from Fox traditions although they did not wish to sever their ties with Fox culture.

From this analysis of Mesquakie boys' gangs, it is apparent that one gang

The Fox: Fighters and Farmers of the Woodland Fringe

was composed of boys whose behavior was antisocial in the eyes of both the whites and the Fox. The members of the third gang were moving rapidly and successfully toward assimilation in the dominant white society. It was the members of the second gang who seemed to have the greatest potential for the continuity of Fox life. They appeared to be adapting to both societies successfully and exhibited a pattern of biculturation, which means straddling the sociocultural fences. If the Fox are to continue their separate ethnic identity, it is these individuals who provide the greatest hope for the future.

LAND CLAIMS   In 1969 the Federal Government partially rectified injustices of old. In that year the U.S. Indian Claims Commission awarded the Fox and Sauk of Iowa nearly a million dollars for lands ceded in 1830 for which they did not receive just compensation. Each adult received $500, with a like amount held in trust for each person under eighteen years of age. Sixty percent of the settlement money was held by the Fox Tribal Council for planning and development. Of the nearly 800 persons on the tribal roll, only about 500 lived in or near their lands in Iowa at that time. With an inadequate land base economic conditions had forced some persons to leave their homeland-by-purchase. A further settlement in 1976 ended a twenty-eight-year court battle over 17 million acres of land taken by the Federal Government for which the Fox had not been compensated. Of the 6.6 million dollar settlement each adult received nearly $6000, and this amount was held in trust for each of the 329 minors to receive when they reached the age of eighteen. About 1.3 million dollars was held in trust by the Federal Government for tribal projects. It does not appear that the cash received by the 573 adults will have any long-range impact on their lives.

Comparisons

Many contrasts separate an analysis of the Fox from the other peoples thus far presented; there is no aboriginal baseline study of the Fox, they were battered by history far more than any of the others, and we have no contemporary study of them. Yet comparisons are feasible and worthwhile along certain dimensions, especially in religious life. Note the stress on the individual supernatural experience among the Chipewyan, Eskimos, and Fox, but among the Fox it was far more pervasive. The Fox emphasized supernatural power through personal rapport with a manitou. Their ritual calendar was not well developed, although the emphasis on clan ceremonials has clear parallels with the Cahuilla and is worthy of further consideration. The egalitarian nature of Fox social structure is an important characteristic, and one might seek also to explain why a superior deity was addressed as a nephew or why a mother treated her daughter as she dealt with her sister. Is an explanation based on Fox personality type, history, economic adaptations, or perhaps a combination of these factors?

Additional Readings

As a background to modern Fox life the Fox and Sauk history by Hagan is required reading, and for accounts of more traditional aspects of Fox life the writings of Jones and Michelson are best. Chapter-length studies by Joffee and Tax provide a wealth of information about conditions in the 1930s. The best accounts of the Fox Project by a participant are the documentary history and the book *The Face of the Fox* by Gearing. For a critical review of the goals and methods employed in the Fox Project an article by Larry R. Stucki is required reading as is the follow-up evaluation by Elizabeth E. Hoyt. John M. Zielinski has published a pictorial history of the Fox in Iowa that includes up-to-date pictures and text in an attractive format for the general public.

References

Bicknell, A. D. "The Tama County Indians," *Annals of Iowa*, (3rd series) v. 4, 196–208. 1901.

Bureau of Indian Affairs. Sac & Fox of Iowa, mimeographed, n.d.

Caldwell, Joseph R. *Trend and Tradition in the Prehistory of the Eastern United States.* American Anthropological Association, memoir no. 88. 1958.

Catlin, George. *North American Indians.* v. 2, 207–217. London. 1844.

Donaldson, Thomas. "The George Catlin Indian Gallery in the U.S. National Museum," *Annual Report of the Board of Regents of the Smithsonian Institution, 1885.* pt. 2 Appendix. 1886.

English, Emory H. "A Mesquakie Chief's Burial," *Annals of Iowa*, (3rd series) v. 30, 545–550. 1951.

Gearing, Frederick O. *The Face of the Fox.* Chicago. 1970.

*Gearing, Frederick O., Robert McC. Netting, and Lisa R. Peattie. *Documentary History of the Fox Project 1948–1959.* Chicago. 1960. The Fox Project of the University of Chicago, Department of Anthropology, was designed to compile information about these Indians and to apply anthropological knowledge in the solution of Fox problems. The volume includes documents relative to the project as well as selections of various published and manuscript studies. The information provided is basic to any realistic understanding of the development of modern conditions among the Fox of Iowa.

Green, Orville J. "The Mesquaki Indians, or Sac and Fox in Iowa," *Red Man*, v. 5, 47–52, 104–109. 1912.

The Fox: Fighters and Farmers of the Woodland Fringe

*Hagan, William T. *The Sac and Fox Indians.* Norman. 1958. Hagan's definitive history of the Sauk and Fox begins with the early historic period and is carried through in detail to the reservation period in Kansas. There is very little information for the time after 1860.

Hoyt, Elizabeth E. "The Children of Tama," *Journal of American Indian Education*, v. 3, no. 1, 15–21.

"Indians Win Battle—for $6.6 Million," *Los Angeles Times*, October 17, 1976.

Jenks, Albert E. "The Wild Rice Gatherers of the Upper Lakes," *Bureau of American Ethnology, 19th Annual Report*, pt. 2, 1013–1137. 1900.

*Joffe, Natalie F. "The Fox of Iowa," in *Acculturation in Seven American Indian Tribes*, Ralph Linton, ed., 259–331. New York. 1940. The 1937 field study of the Fox near Tama, Iowa, by Joffe, when consulted in conjunction with the 1932 and 1934 field data of Sol Tax for the same people, provides an excellent view of the historical background and emerging modern conditions for the group.

Jones, William. "The Algonkin Manitou," *Journal of American Folk-Lore*, v. 18, 183–190. 1905.

Jones, William. "Notes on the Fox Indians," *Journal of American Folk-Lore*, v. 24, 209–237. 1911.

*Jones, William. *Ethnography of the Fox Indians.* Bureau of American Ethnology, Bulletin 125, Margaret Welpley Fisher, ed. 1939. Jones, who was of mixed Fox and white descent and an anthropologist, was killed in the Philippine Islands in 1909. Some of his field data on the Fox were edited and published by Truman Michelson and Franz Boas a few years after his death. About twenty years later his notes were presented to the Smithsonian Institution and were edited for publication by Margaret W. Fisher. This volume is ably annotated and is an essential source on the Fox. In it is provided a rounded view of Fox life for the period just before 1900.

McKenney, Thomas L., and James Hall. *The Indian Tribes of North America.* v. 2. Edinburgh. 1934.

Michelson, Truman. Review of: *Folk-Lore of the Musquakie Indians of North America* by Mary A. Owen in *Current Anthropological Literature*, v. 2, 233–237. 1913.

Michelson, Truman. "How Meswakie Children Should Be Brought Up," in *American Indian Life*, Elsie C. Parsons, ed., 81–86. New York. 1922.

Michelson, Truman. "The Autobiography of a Fox Indian Woman," *Bureau of American Ethnology, 40th Annual Report*, 291–349. 1925. The Fox woman recounting the story of her life supplies a wide range of ethnographic details concerning her people for what must have been late in the nineteenth century. It is only to be regretted that the autobiography is not longer and more detailed.

Michelson, Truman. "Notes on Fox Mortuary Customs and Beliefs," *Bureau of American Ethnology, 40th Annual Report*, 351–496. 1925.

Michelson, Truman. "Notes on Fox Gens Festivals," *Proceedings of the Twenty-Third International Congress of Americanists*, 545–546, New York. 1930.

Michelson, Truman. "Miss Owen's 'Folk-Lore of the Musquakie Indians,' " *American Anthropologist*, v. 38, 143–145. 1936.

Miller, Walter B. "Two Concepts of Authority," American Anthropologist, v. 57, 271–289. 1955.

Owen, Mary Alicia. *Folk-Lore of the Musquakie Indians of North America*. London. 1904. It is difficult to know how much of this volume is reliable in view of the criticisms by Truman Michelson (1913, 1936). In compiling the material on the Fox, only Owen's information on material culture was utilized. This section of the book does not come under fire from Michelson and, in fact, is almost praised.

*Polgar, Steven. "Biculturation of Mesquakie Teenage Boys," *American Anthropologist*, v. 62, 217–235. 1960. During the summers of 1952 and 1953 the field study of teen-age boys was made, and it was established that although some of the boys seemed on their way toward assimilation in white culture, others were delinquent in both Fox and white cultures, and still others were able to participate successfully in both white and Indian cultures. This is a very insightful paper and probably reflects an acculturation patterning for many Indians other than the Fox.

Quimby, George Irving. *Indian Life in the Upper Great Lakes*. Chicago. 1960.

Quimby, George Irving. *Indian Culture and European Trade Goods*. Madison. 1966.

Rideout, Henry M. *William Jones*. New York. 1912.

Smith, Huron H. *Ethnobotany of the Meskwaki Indians*. Bulletin of the Public Museum of the City of Milwaukee, v. 4, 175–326. 1928.

Stucki, Larry R. "Anthropologists and Indians: A New Look at the Fox Project," *Plains Anthropologist*, v. 12, no. 37, 300–317. 1967.

*Tax, Sol. "The Social Organization of the Fox Indians," in *Social Anthropology of North American Tribes*, Fred Eggan, ed., 243–282. Chicago. 1937. The core of this article is devoted to the Fox kinship terms and the social units, but there is additional information provided about conditions among the Tama area Fox as they lived when Tax visited them in 1932

The Fox: Fighters and Farmers of the Woodland Fringe

and 1934. The emphasis of the chapter, however, is on a reconstruction of the social system of the past.

White, Leslie, ed. *Lewis Henry Morgan, The Indian Journals,* 1859–62. Ann Arbor. 1959.

Zielinski, John M. *Mesquakie and Proud of It.* Kalona, Iowa. 1976.

7

The Pawnee:
Horsemen and Farmers
of the Prairies

Reasons for This Selection

In early historic times the Plains and Prairie border in mid-America was primarily the home of small bands of mobile hunters. When the horse was introduced, these Indians readily became equestrian hunters, thereby increasing their mobility but not changing the basis for their economic livelihood. On the Prairies other Indians who accepted the horse were farmers who lived in semi-permanent communities. Among these were the Pawnee, who raised crops near their earth lodge villages. The Pawnee typify those Indians who might have successfully combined farming and an adaptation to the horse if they had been able to deal effectively with the changing historic political environment. They rapidly declined in number as a result of disease and death at the hands of enemies. Buffeted by intruders, both Indians and whites, the Pawnee barely managed to survive as a tribe. Their plight and cultural demise was typical of the Indians who lived in this region as farmers, and for this reason they are described.

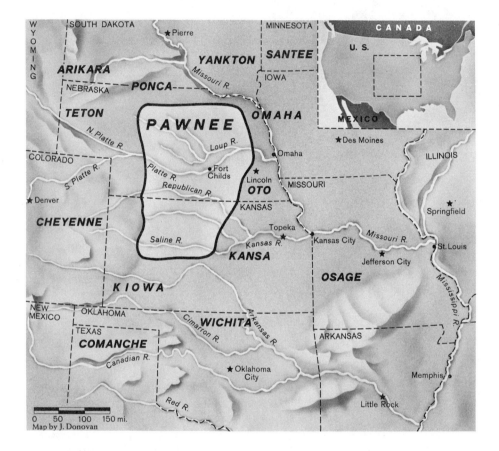

People, Population, and Language

The name Pawnee is of unknown origin and was not used by these people until after it had been in common usage by whites for some time. They knew themselves as the Skidi, Chaui, Kitkehahki, or Pitahauerat, depending on the band to which they belonged. They probably entered Kansas and Nebraska by ascending the Arkansas River and pushing northward to the Kansas River drainages. At this point they separated to occupy two different habitats. One segment settled the Plains of southwestern Nebraska, and the other established itself in eastern Nebraska. They lived in small settlements near which they raised domestic plants and hunted. The eastern groups tended to emphasize fishing whereas those to the west stressed bison hunting. In 1837, about 300 years after historic contact, the tribe totaled about 10,000. In 1840, with the first actual count, their number had dropped to about 6200, and by 1881 there were only 1250. In 1940 the population was near a low of 1000, but by 1970 the total had risen to 2000. In linguistic terms they belong to the Macro-Siouan phylum and the Caddoan family; the language Pawnee is very similar to Arikara.

Prehistory

In Nebraska, the historic core of the Pawnee homeland, the open prairie grasslands of the central region give way to alluvial valleys in the east, with well-watered streams, fertile soil, and groves of trees. According to Waldo R. Wedel, who has had an abiding interest in the archaeology of the Plains and Prairies, the first human occupancy of the central plains began around 8000 B.C., and the earliest people hunted big game, especially mammoth, using Clovis spearpoints. With the extinction of these animals the emphasis shifted to hunting large, now extinct forms of bison; the kill and camp sites of these people, who made Folsom points, were more numerous than those of the previous era. These technologies were replaced by other lithic industries, and new peoples entered the area around 5000 B.C. As the herds of large bison were exterminated, and as new influences from the Great Plains came to bear on the local cultures, different economic patterns emerged. Around 1500 B.C. small groups lived on buttes, where they had hearths and nearby storage pits. They hunted contemporary species of bison and collected vegetable foods. The inventory of stone tools was more diverse and complex than had been found previously.

Central Plains prehistory resumes again about A.D. 200 when farmers and hunters from the east with Hopewellian traditions settled along the Missouri River near Kansas City. The Hopewellian group, which originated in the Ohio River valley, brought the first domestic plants, beans and maize, but its life-style never became established on the Plains. Shortly after A.D. 1000 life on the Plains assumed new directions, and although there were regional variations, the most significant changes were as follows: squash and sunflower cultivation added to that of maize and beans; a material inventory far more extensive than in earlier periods; earth-covered houses with tunnel entrances and central fireplaces, and clusters of houses in small communities. The nature of certain artifact forms indicates that these people rather clearly maintained contact with the central Mississippi valley. The relationship of these Indians to the Pawnee is still uncertain, although the general similarities with subsequent Pawnee culture in this region are apparent.

Spanish and French Influences

In 1541 when Francisco Coronado and his party moved north and east from New Mexico, they were guided by an Indian who was to take them to Quivira, which the Spanish believed contained untold riches. The exact location of Quivira is not known, but probably it was somewhere in southern Kansas. When it was reached, Quivira offered no riches, and the Indian guide was murdered by the angry Spanish. In all probability Quivira was then the home of at least some Pawnee, and this was their earliest historic contact. Those who settled on the Republican River, the Skidi branch, probably moved there during the seventeenth century, and by 1715 they had established eight villages. Following the Sieur de La Salle expedition of 1679–1682, French traders from the Mississippi area were in contact with some Pawnee. The traders offered ever-increasing amounts of goods, including guns, to tribes in the west. To stabilize these expanding trade relations, the French dispatched a party from New Orleans in 1724. Surprisingly the enterprising French representative, Etienne V. de Bourgmont, succeeded in establishing peace among the Apache, Iowa, Oto, and Skidi Pawnee, the most important tribes contesting the region. Two years later French traders pushed into eastern Colorado, but this expansion soon was halted by Comanche raids.

Epidemic and New Arrivals

A smallpox epidemic plus hostile Indians on almost every quarter reduced the eight large Skidi villages of 1715 to a single village during the early 1800s. Through the mid-1700s the Skidi were the only Pawnee to occupy Nebraska in any number, but shortly after 1770 the Black or Southern Pawnee moved north from their location on the tributaries of the Missouri River. These new arrivals were to emerge as three tribes: the Chaui, or Grand Pawnee; the Kitkehahki or Republican Pawnee, an offshoot of the Chaui; and the most southerly branch, the Pitahauerat or Tapages, sometimes designated as the Smoky Hill Pawnee. The arrival of the new Pawnee brought conflict with the Skidi. The disagreements were largely over hunting territory, and the Skidi

The Pawnee: Horsemen and Farmers of the Prairies

could not maintain control of some key areas. The terms for peace included the stipulation that the Skidi would leave their villages, and they did so temporarily. Although they were forced to recognize the Grand Pawnee as the leaders of the combined tribe, the Skidi never became as fully subordinated as their conquerors had hoped.

American Influences

The Spanish in New Mexico were anxious to develop ties with the Pawnee area if only to prevent the spread of French and American influence. However, none of their expeditions from Santa Fe were particularly successful in realizing this goal. Countermoves by the Americans were not effective either until four Pawnee chiefs, each representing one of the tribe's branches, went to St. Louis in 1818 at the request of the Indian superintendent for the area. They signed a treaty of peace and friendship with the United States and subsequently were drawn into a new and different type of relationship. Unlike the French or Spanish, the Americans had an aggressive interest in the Pawnee, an attitude of dominance that extended far beyond trade relations. The Indians who went to St. Louis were impressed by American strength, but those at home were not convinced of the power of the Long Knives. They harassed American traders and soldiers until the Americans withheld trade goods; this induced the Pawnee to return their loot and even promise to whip the offending warriors. In 1825 the Pawnee signed another treaty with the United States, agreeing not to interfere with Americans traveling to New Mexico.

Further Epidemics and Missionaries

Pawnee difficulties during the 1830s were severe. At the time that they were battling other Indians, they were being devastated by smallpox. The epidemic of 1832 is said to have killed more than 3000 persons, including nearly everyone over thirty years of age. In 1837–1838 another smallpox epidemic struck, killing about 2000 persons. During this period the Pawnee were fighting not only local Indians but others who recently had been moved west. To prevent Pawnee annihilation, agents of the United States arranged a treaty in 1833. It granted hunting rights in western Kansas to most immigrant tribes, negating the exclusive rights of the Pawnee to a great area south of the Platte River, but offered government protection to the Pawnee in return; this was in fact a Federal attempt to make them become farmers. In 1834 two now-famous Presbyterian missionaries, John Dunbar and Samuel Allis, entered the area and wintered with the Pawnee to learn the language and begin their mission activities.

By 1838 the situation had deteriorated even further. Smallpox epidemics had destroyed the population core, raids of enemy tribes were increasingly devastating, and the Pawnee had no dependable allies. Frequently they returned from a bison hunt in the plains to find their villages and cached supplies looted and destroyed. When they received their annuity payment in 1839, they asked the Indian agent to establish a mission and to teach them American agricultural techniques. When the time came to settle in one community, however, the Pawnee would not move to the site selected by the government. In 1841 a Presbyterian missionary party of fifteen whites founded a farm and mission to induce the Pawnee to settle down around the Pawnee Mission on Loup Fork in Nance County, Nebraska. Within a few years the government added a blacksmith shop, a school, and an agency center. Some Pawnee began to settle nearby, but a terrible Sioux attack in 1843 led the people to flee south. When they returned, the missionaries Dunbar and Allis, who understood the people best, saw the tribe making slow but steady progress. They encouraged the Indians to settle down, but others of their church group advocated what George E. Hyde has termed "muscular Christianity." They beat the women and children to try to make them conform to Christian standards. An Indian boy was shot in the back for stealing corn, and a Pawnee girl was beaten nearly to death by a missionary's son. To disgrace the scene further the Indian agent, whose background was southern and slaveholding, supported the harsh treatment of the Indians and removed those government employees who worked harmoniously with them. Continuing difficulties with the Sioux led government workers and missionaries to withdraw in 1846, leaving the Pawnee without the protection promised.

Early Historic Life

ORIGIN MYTH   Long ago before the present races occupied the earth, there lived a people who were giants. They were so big and powerful that one was able to run down a bison, kill it, and carry the carcass over his shoulders. Such men did not believe in Tirawa, as the Pawnee do, but felt that all power rested in their own hands. Finally this made Tirawa so angry that he caused the water level to rise. All the land became soft, and the giants sank into the ground and died. Tirawa next created a man and a woman in the proportions of people today. From this couple the Pawnee were derived.

In their view of the universe the Skidi, and probably other Pawnee as well, thought that there were two great forces in the sky, the male to the east and the female to the west, and that life was derived from the zenith. The supernatural power at the zenith where the male and female forces combined was termed Tirawa, and even his name was sacred, to be spoken quietly. Men sought his aid, but he dealt with them through lesser supernatural beings. The first people came to earth upon the winds from the Morning Star, and from each of the seven winds one expected different qualities. The east wind swept

The Pawnee: Horsemen and Farmers of the Prairies

in with the dawn, bringing life into a person's body; the west wind brought life and direction to life; the north wind was associated with the North Star; the wind of the spirits drove ghosts from north to south; another sent game, and yet another drove the animals, while the south wind came from the star spirits.

APPEARANCE AND CLOTHING   Women wore their hair in two braids, and the style for men possibly was roached, with a scalp lock hanging from the back. Pubic and axillary hair was plucked by men and women alike because it was considered unclean; the hair was buried because to burn something was to offer it to the supernaturals. A man plucked the hairs of his beard and ordinarily painted his face and chest with red, white, and yellow pigments; black was reserved as war paint. Men's necklaces were made from bear claws, beads, or strung sections of bone. A man's clothing consisted of a breechclout of deerskin that passed between his legs and overlapped a belt in the front and back, moccasins, and tight-fitting buckskin leggings that were trimmed with long fringes sometimes adorned with human hair and beaded designs. A robe of bison or wolf skin was thrown over the shoulders. The women wore leggings from the knees to the ankles, moccasins, and a wrap-around skirt that reached below the knees. A band of skin was worn about the chest and was held in place with shoulder straps. Women also wore bison-skin robes. A young boy went naked, and a small girl wore a loose shirt.

Plate 7–1 A man named Buffalo Bull from an 1833 painting by Catlin. The head of a bison bull painted on his face and chest represents a spirit protector. (From Donaldson, 1886)

SETTLEMENTS   A visitor to a Pawnee village in the early nineteenth century found well-beaten paths converging on the settlement. For miles around scattered gardens were planted where the sod was thin and the soil could be worked with a digging stick or hoe. Women, accompanied by their small children and older daughters, cultivated these plots; when enemies were about, one or more warriors remained with the women. Horses and mules roamed nearby and were tended by small boys or an occasional man. In 1820 a Grand Pawnee and Tapages community had 180 earth lodges and 3500 inhabitants. The lodges, with attached entryways, were closely grouped in an irregular manner. Framed with logs and covered with grass and then with earth, they were up to fifty feet across. About five families or twenty persons lived in a typical dwelling. Inside an earth lodge were platform beds along the north and south walls. The area allotted to each family was curtained off from the next with mats, and behind the curtains were the family's possessions. At the open area in the center was a fireplace, and a hole in the roof above allowed the smoke to escape. At the back and center of a lodge was an altar with a bison skull on top; this was the place of honor where the head of the house presided. Hanging from the west wall of every important man's lodge was a sacred bundle, wrapped in deerskin and blackened with age. The bundles were surrounded with taboos. They were opened only on special occasions and represented an important link with the past and the supernaturals. Near each home was a log corral for horses and mules. Before each lodge was the home-owner's tripod, on which hung his painted shield and a rawhide case of war supplies. On top of many lodges were scalps on short poles. During the summer, families slept out-of-doors under arbors; one was constructed for each lodge.

On summer or winter trips to bison country women and children walked single file, each leading a horse, as the men ranged beside them on horseback or on foot. A typical day's march was about seven miles, in part because three hours were required to break or prepare a camp. Women erected the tepees, which were made of a bison skin cover fitted over a pole frame that was as much as eighteen feet across at the base. Reed mats were spread on the ground, and an opening at the top of the cover allowed the smoke to pass out from the central fire pit.

SUBSISTENCE ACTIVITIES   The dependence of western Indians on bison is well known, yet it is worthwhile to cite the many Pawnee usages. The meat from a freshly killed animal could be eaten raw, cooked, or dried for winter. Summer skins were made into tent covers, ropes, and containers. Winter skins, with the hair intact, served as blankets and robes. The sinew was fashioned into bowstrings and used as thread. Bison brains were smeared on skins to soften them and make them pliable. A hoof became a hammer, and bones were fashioned into scrapers, awls, and other tools. The bladder was used as a water container, and bison dung was the standard fuel in woodless localities. Bison skins were the major product offered by Plains Indians in exchange for trade goods in historic times.

Pawnee life was influenced profoundly by the introduction of horses about 1700. Obtained in raid and trade from tribes to the south and west, horses gave the Pawnee new mobility. Settlements now were abandoned in the summer and early winter as families searched for bison herds. In the summer of 1835 the Tapages, Grand, and Republican Pawnee traveled west in three columns of 4000 people, thousands of horses and mules, and about 7000 dogs. While on the move to and from bison country, the orderliness of the hunters contrasted with the medley of women, children, and animals moving at a walking pace as they hauled the tents and household equipment. Chiefs and warriors rode fine horses, but poor men walked so that their horses would be fresh for the hunt. Docile old horses pulled travois or carried packs; they were controlled by a strip of leather tied around the lower jaw and hand held or fastened to a saddle. Tent poles tied to either side of a saddle extended from the horse's head to the ground behind the animal. Across these poles might be tied short poles, and on this bed were placed leather containers of dried meat and bison-skin robes. On such a travois or litter an ill or wounded person might ride. Tent skins, robes, and household articles were loaded on the saddle, and on top of the pile a woman and her children might ride. Colts carried light packs, and young horses were ridden by boys. Horses without loads ran freely about the column.

A well-organized force of warriors supervised a bison hunt. These were men on whom the chiefs could rely to maintain order and plan the hunt so that the animals would not stampede prematurely. A column approaching a herd of bison was led by chiefs and shamans. Each hunter had a particular position in the riding order, and each attempted to have a special horse used

Plate 7–2 An earth lodge community in 1871. (Courtesy of the Smithsonian Institution National Anthropological Archives, neg. no. 1245-B)

only for hunting bison. When the herd was sighted, a crier relayed the deployment message to the hunters so that they could converge on a herd from different directions. Once everyone was in place, they descended on the bison at a given signal. The favorite hunting weapon was not the gun, but the bow and arrow. Each hunter rode naked, carrying only his weapons, in the same manner as he went into battle. After as many animals as possible had been killed, they were butchered and brought back to camp, where the women cut the meat into thin slabs and put it on pole frames to dry over a fire in the tent. Afterwards they pounded the dried meat on stone anvils and packed it into rawhide satchels.

At the end of the summer hunting season the people returned to their villages, where they had planted crops in the spring. This was the most pleasurable season of the year, for food was abundant, with a good harvest of corn, beans, and squash. This was the time for social as well as for religious activities. In the fall and early winter hunting parties returned to the bison country and made a special effort to obtain prime skins. In February or March they returned to their villages with the meat and skins. Some skins were exchanged with traders for imported goods, and others were processed for use. Although in a typical year the Pawnee might be away from their villages for about eight months, the villages continued to be an important home base.

Spring was the lean period when food was limited to dried meat and cached maize, beans, or squash. At this time the women began to prepare the garden plots, which seldom were over an acre in extent. The most important crop was maize, which was not only a food staple but had ritualistic and mythological significance. The cultivated areas were at the mouths of ravines where the soil was fertile and the sod cover not extremely thick. After maize was harvested, it was boiled or roasted, then cut from the cob and dried, or stored on the cob in caches. Women also cultivated beans and squash; the latter were sun-dried in strips that then were woven together for convenient storage.

The most important uncultivated vegetable food was the wild "potato," which became part of the diet in times of food scarcity. Berries, wild plums, cherries, and mushrooms were also collected. In general, these were supplements to maize and bison meat. According to one description, an evening meal during a bison hunt consisted of dried bison meat, followed by a combination of maize and beans, then ground parched maize, and corn mush; the meal ended with an ear of roasted corn. Also hunted and eaten were elk, deer, bear, otter, and raccoon; dogs were eaten on occasion.

DESCENT, KINSHIP, AND MARRIAGE   The members of a village traced their descent from a presumed common ancestress (matrilineal descent and matriclan), and they married within the community (village endogamy). A man lived with the family of his wife or was associated intimately with her residence unit (matrilocal residence). The Pawnee were not completely matri-

The Pawnee: Horsemen and Farmers of the Prairies

lineal, however, since the chieftaincy and priestly duties could and did pass down a line of males. Each settlement posessed a sacred bundle that contained objects of immense religious significance for the villagers; it was thought to have been passed down a direct male line from the original owner. The village sacred bundle was a supernatural focus for this social grouping, and village endogamy may have been practiced in order to keep the sacred bundle as a distinct village trust. Village political life was under the direction of a hereditary chief, his subordinates, and a council. Villagers were bound together through participation in joint religious ceremonies and in a joint council.

In the kinship terminology of the Skidi Pawnee a male termed his father and his father's brothers alike, whereas his mother's brother was called by a different word. The word for mother was extended to mother's sister and father's sister (bifurcate merging), and the same term was used for a father's sister's daughter. The father and father's brother term was applied to a father's sister's son. The patrilateral cross-cousin terms were different from the matrilateral cross-cousin terms; the latter were not distinguished by sex and were the same as for Ego's son and daughter. Parallel cousins on both sides of the family were termed alike but with male-female distinctions. The words for brother and sister were extended to parallel cousins, and the latter were Ego's classificatory siblings (Crow cousin terms).

SOCIAL DIMENSIONS   The Skidi Pawnee are the group best reported by ethnographers, but they were more conservative than the other three bands. As a tribe the bands rarely cooperated, and the Skidi felt closer to the Arikara than to the other bands of Pawnee. The closest lifelong ties within families were between siblings, especially brothers; by contrast, deep emotional ties did not exist between a husband and wife. A warm relationship probably existed between a man and his mother's brother's wife, since this woman, or these women as the case may have been, were sexual partners for the young man from the time he reached puberty until he married. The mother's brother was responsible for the marriage arrangements of both the sons and the daughters of his sister.

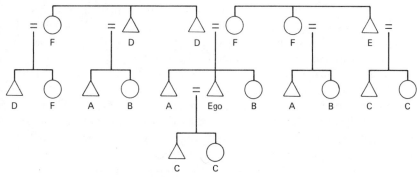

The labors of a woman are described as arduous. Besides the processing of skins, cooking, and gardening, she also was obliged to saddle and unsaddle her husband's horse, and in the tent she occupied the coldest fringe. As though to compensate for their position, women talked steadily by habit and were very sharp-tongued. By contrast the men seemed devoted to warfare and hunting; they had a great deal of leisure time during which they slept, lounged, talked, sang, feasted, and smoked.

The social position of a male was based largely on the achievements of his immediate male ancestors; thus there was a degree of rigidity in the social structure. At the same time there existed the ideal of a poor but ambitious and honorable young man achieving great success. The class system, which molded the lives of most persons, found its sanction in supernatural beliefs, with prerogatives and duties of the leaders similarly derived. One set of divinely instituted obligations directed that a segment of the population must protect the settlement from human enemies; these were the leaders and participants in war. A second group, the priests, took charge of religious obligations, and a third, the shamans, protected the village from disease and famine. These were upper class responsibilities; the lower class consisted of poor people who had little or no influence in village affairs.

POLITICAL LIFE   Each Skidi village had its hereditary chief, and a particular sacred bundle represented his authority. The bundle and the status of chief passed to his eldest son, if this individual was capable. The decision about chiefly succession was made by the chiefs' council, who accepted or rejected the logical successor. If a chief's eldest son was not capable, a younger son or another close male relative was chosen. The village chiefs selected warriors of the highest rank from the village to become nonhereditary chiefs, and thirty-one chiefs made up the chiefs' council for all the Skidi. An extremely able warrior was made a chief by being invited to join the hereditary chiefs in their lodge on four occasions. The first three invitations were refused, but the fourth was accepted and gifts presented to the chiefs. The man then became a chief for his lifetime.

The appearance of chiefs during their council meetings differed from that of ordinary men. A chief wore an eagle feather in his hair, and on his bison robe were representations of stars, the sun, or battle scenes. His leggings were fringed with hair from human scalps and with eagle feathers. His face was painted red; from ear to ear across the forehead was a blue line, and a design symbolic of the Turkey's Foot constellation decorated his forehead.

A hereditary chief promoted community welfare and was the guardian of the people, but he was not expected to be aggressive. As Gene Weltfish (1965, 6) has noted, Pawnee chiefs "were the focus of consensus, not the wielders of power." Four braves served a hereditary chief, helping to preserve civil order and prepare for religious ceremonies. They were appointed for life and carried war clubs or tomahawks as symbols of their office. Warriors were men who

The Pawnee: Horsemen and Farmers of the Prairies

had risen to positions of authority through their own efforts. From their group the nonhereditary chiefs were chosen, since warriors had by their sacrifices obtained supernatural favor. They were privileged to wear the sacred warrior's costume into battle and to paint three dots on their foreheads, symbolic of an eagle's claw marks.

Political decisions were made jointly by the hereditary and nonhereditary chiefs in council, but they apparently could be overruled by the priests. When a council met, issues were decided by consensus even if general feelings ran counter to the will of the leading chief. The deliberations of these councils probably focused most often on where and when to hunt and relations with friendly and enemy peoples. In early historic times the principal chief, who apparently took precedence over all the others, was from the Chaui subtribe.

Half or fewer of the Skidi males were not hereditary chiefs, braves, or warriors, nor were they shamans or priests. Instead they were commoners without authority in the village to which they belonged. These men owned few or perhaps no horses, their lodges were small, and often they received necessities from persons of wealth. Another group was composed of men who attached themselves to the households of important men and performed menial tasks in return for economic support. At the fringes of a settlement were the outcasts of one type or another, persons who had disregarded tribal customs.

Disagreements between individuals or families in a village seem to have been settled without outside interference. The most common dispute appears to have been between men when they gambled. Contestants fought but stopped when blood was drawn. Poor persons were those most often accused of theft, and if the culprit's identity was established, he was punished physically by the victim. In instances of a woman's adultery, the offended husband was irate because he felt his property had been taken from him, and he punished the man by beating or whipping him. Adultery apparently was not uncommon nor particularly serious, but this was not true of rape. Consent or lack of consent by the girl was not important; the girl's age was the crucial factor. A man who fornicated with a young girl was beaten badly and became an outcast. An unprovoked murder led the relatives of the deceased to seek blood revenge by killing the murderer, who was not defended by his relatives if they considered the case against him to be just. If each family involved considered its position legitimate, a feud erupted between them.

WARFARE George B. Grinnell (1961, 303) wrote, "The Pawnees were a race of warriors. War was their pleasure and their business. By war they gained credit, respect, fame. By war they acquired wealth." The emphasis on physical conflict among Indians in mid-America is legendary, and the Pawnee justly are remembered as being among the best warriors. They fought under two sets of circumstances with contrasting purposes. When they left their settlements seeking an enemy, they were in search of glory, evidenced by scalps taken and horses captured. The Pawnee fought defensively against enemies

Plate 7–3 Young Spotted Horse. (Courtesy of the Nebraska
State Historical Society, Lincoln)

who came to their settlements by night to steal horses and to take scalps, or
when a large enemy party arrived by day to scalp, kill, and loot. Either on offensive raids or in defensive stands the Pawnee warrior was a very brave man.
Still the standards of behavior in war differed greatly from the norms in
Anglo-American society. On a raid the ideal was to slip into an unsuspecting
enemy camp, kill as many persons as possible before arousing the populace,
and then escape with the best horses. These raids were most like guerrilla warfare in Western society. The question of a fair fight was not considered, since
the primary aim was to catch the enemy unaware and take full advantage of
his vulnerable condition. There was no disgrace in not attacking a well-armed
or alert camp, nor did a man lose standing by running away if he was outnumbered.

The Indians living to the south of the Pawnee knew them as the Wolves, possibly a derogatory designation but more likely based on their skill as scouts and horse thieves. A group of Pawnee setting off on a raid organized a temporary association, or Wolf Society, whose origins were traced to mythological times. The supernatural patron of warfare was the wolf, and they patterned themselves after these animals. Items from a sacred bundle or war regalia were covered with a wolfskin and taken along to provide supernatural assistance. A raiding party attempted to move across the landscape in the manner of wolves. One reason for assuming this guise was that prairie wolves were common and often entered Indian camps at night; looking like them, they attracted little attention. All but one of the raiders kept to ravines or river bottoms as they

Plate 7–4 Night Chief and The-Man-that-Left-His-Enemy-Lying-in-the-Water. (Courtesy Amon Carter Museum, Fort Worth, Texas)

neared the camp of an enemy; the lone individual was disguised as a wolf and scouted from the hilltops. The other raiders covered themselves with wolf-skins when they entered the camp of an enemy and imitated the behavior of these animals, thereby hoping not to attract attention to themselves.

A raiding party was organized by any man who could attract a following. He was most likely a successful warrior, but an aspiring youth sometimes could convince others to follow him. The leader prayed to Tirawa while meditating, smoking, or eating. The men selected by a leader to take part in his raid were called together, and the plan was announced. If they wished to accompany the group, they smoked a sacred pipe. If someone declined to participate, he passed the pipe on to the next man without smoking. The leader then secured the aid of a priest, ceremonies were performed, and the priest presented the group with a sacred bundle to take with them. Every man provided himself with as many as twenty moccasins, each stuffed with food for the trip. The food consisted of pounded, cooked corn and pemmican. A warrior also carried sewing awls and sinew to repair his footwear, a bow and arrows, and a robe. The leader carried a sacred pipe and tobacco. They set off on foot, and when they reached country occupied by hostile Indians, they became cautious. If any sign along the way was interpreted as an ill omen, they might turn back by common consent. Otherwise the organizer of the raid directed the activities of the others.

The primary purpose of a raid was to steal horses. Since an enemy kept his best horses near his tepee, often tied just outside the entrance, it required great daring to cut a number of horses loose and escape. The most likely time for a raid to succeed was late at night when one or more men could slip into a camp unnoticed. The leader was expected to be the most daring, and if he alone obtained horses, he shared them with other members of the party. He might also give a horse to the priest who had aided them with his prayers. One privilege of a successful war party was for its members to change their names, assuming new names that reflected great deeds. Repeated success in horse stealing was a rapid road to prestige and riches, to which any daring man could aspire. Great skill was required to steal horses, but it took even greater bravery to make peace with an enemy tribe because it was necessary to expose oneself to great danger by openly entering an enemy camp. Among the greatest leaders were the chiefs of peace, and according to other tribes the peace pipe originated among the Pawnee.

Battles in defense of a community were organized in a different way. An attacking party might number hundreds of warriors who suddenly would appear one morning on the hills surrounding a village. Each man in the attacking force was mounted on his best horse and wore his most majestic garments, set off with an elaborate feather headdress. The attackers did not ride pell-mell into the settlement, but waited. As soon as the party was sighted, the village men seized their weapons, their best horses, and rode out naked to meet the enemy. The women corralled the remaining horses and climbed on top of the

234

earth lodges to watch the battle. The two long lines of opposing warriors rode slowly toward each other and stopped when about 600 yards separated them. The men on each side chanted war songs and shouted insults to one another. A warrior from one of the lines would advance before his comrades to make a speech disparaging the enemy, praising his companions in arms, and boasting of his own achievements. When his oration was completed, he galloped toward one of the enemy's flanks, and when within bowshot he rode furiously before the mounted column but in such a manner that little of his body was exposed to enemy fire. He shot arrow after arrow into the line of men. Those that he passed pursued him, and if he or his horse were not struck with arrows, he rode back to his own line and his pursuers returned to their original positions. If, however, he were disabled in any way, his comrades rushed forth to save him. The horsemen were soon at close quarters, fighting with war clubs or anything else at hand. In close conflict men were injured but not usually killed. If the person who made the speech was killed and scalped, his friends withdrew without attempting to recover his body. If he was not scalped, the opponents returned to their original lines and repeated the battle plan again and again until one side withdrew. The Pawnee rarely if ever were routed when making a stand at home, for if they were, their families and the settlement would be destroyed.

If a captive was taken during battle or in a raid, his fate was decided in council. He was most likely turned over to a women's society, which was an amorphous organization functioning only under this particular set of conditions. The women were young, single girls, old maids, or widows, who performed with warbonnets of corn husks, bows made from sticks, and lances of reed stalks. They tortured a captive for four days, during which time every indignity conceivable was heaped upon him before he finally was killed.

The Pawnee fought well but too often, and their failure to make effective alliances led to their ultimate defeat.

Traditionally, anthropologists have analyzed Plains Indian warfare as an all-consuming game. Clearly an important value was placed on war, but it was far more than a game, with lives, loot, and prestige at stake. According to the thoughtful analysis of William W. Newcomb, conflicts were limited to small numbers of participants at any one time, and the outcome of a battle or raid usually was indecisive. Newcomb stressed the importance of the horse in the emergence of specialized bison hunting patterns that led to intense competition over game lands and produced armed conflicts. In addition, the displacement of eastern tribes to the West and Anglo-American expansion brought new forms of competition for land. The eastern tribes, furthermore, possessed guns, and this aided them significantly in their encroachments. Conflict was particularly fierce at the edges of the Plains, where bison were not as abundant as in the heartland. The erratic seasonal movements of the bison were difficult to follow even when they were numerous. As the herds decreased in size and increased competition developed for the surviving animals, there was bound to be intense conflict over hunting territories. In addition, there was the policy of the French, Spanish, British, and Americans of pitting one tribe against another. Thus, it would appear that the fundamental causes of Plains Indian warfare were economic, which is a far more reasonable hypothesis than the supposition that these Indians fought solely for the sake of fighting.

RELIGIOUS SYSTEM   The Pawnee religious system embraced all things in the universe. The supreme deity was Tirawa, and his earthly agents were priests, who supervised the ceremonial round and were guardians of the sacred bundles that joined the people with their gods. The Skidi word for a sacred bundle translates "wrapped up rainstorm," symbolizing the origins of the supernaturals to the west. Such a bundle also might be called "mother," a reference to the two ears of maize found in each bundle; these ears were the symbolic mother of the people. One settlement, Center Village, had associations with the Evening Star bundle, which was the greatest of the western powers, the supreme and original authority. This and six additional sacred bundles integrated the Skidi in dealing with their gods. The thirteen confederated Skidi communities joined to hold the Four Pole Ceremony, whose details are not recorded, but the rituals rather clearly reinforced the unity of the Skidi with the supernaturals.

Sacred bundles were the gifts of particular stars or were made under the supervision of a star; they symbolized village and band unity. The sacred bundle rituals passed from a priest to his successor, usually a relative. The hereditary chiefs, however, were responsible for the physical bundles and obtained their position by virtue of this association. Another feature was that a sacred bundle was not held by a priest but was kept by a woman, who knew certain facets of the bundle's rituals but could not take part in the ceremonies. Among the Pawnee as a whole the bundle societies were organized for warfare, for hunting, or for both purposes. These societies were voluntary associations (sodalities), in which members found pleasure and other rewards from the social contacts. Each society was divided into two segments, according to their seating in a lodge. Those on the north led the winter ceremonies, and members to the south guided summer rituals. Society members performed an important ritual to renew their lances annually. Old lances were set aside for the graves of great warriors, and new ones were fashioned for the ceremony. The new lances were sanctified with smoke, a feast was held, and the lances were exhibited by their bearers during a dance. In battle the lance-bearers planted their standards before the enemy and were the last to retreat. A lance stuck in the ground served as the advance rallying point for the warriors. If it appeared that a lance would be carried off by an enemy party, someone who was not a lance-bearer could carry it off, and the bearer then could withdraw.

Another cluster of sodalities, six in number among the Skidi, appears to have been more transient. These were organized by men who did not qualify as members in established societies but were ambitious enough to form their

The Pawnee: Horsemen and Farmers of the Prairies

Plate 7–5 Performer in a Skidi sacred bundle ceremony. (Courtesy, Field Museum of Natural History, Chicago)

own organizations. After having a dream or vision to sanction the founding, members were recruited and rituals established. When the group was successful in battle or during a hunt, it acquired prestige, but if it failed or when the leader's abilities waned, the members were likely to disband. The Crazy Dog Society is an example. Each member carried a ring-shaped rattle as a symbol of membership. When they danced, it was in the nude with a cord tied around the penis foreskin. Reportedly they had a "no flight" obligation in battle, for the cord then was attached to a stake in the ground; from this they could not release themselves. The Children of the Iruska was a "contrary" society. The members reversed normal expectations in their behavior. If the camp were attacked, they continued whatever they were doing before the alarm; if someone told them not to go on a raid, they went; and if a mysterious animal which normal persons feared were near the camp, they hunted it. The number of contraries was small, six or seven. They never married and were painted black, indicating that they always were ready to fight. Members were selected by the leader because they were strange, but the society apparently came to an abrupt end when most members were killed in a battle.

Priests were trained as ritual specialists after deriving their positions from a star or planet. They led the important religious ceremonies designed to ensure community success in farming, the hunt, and warfare. The prime prerequisite for becoming a priest was to have an excellent memory, and the second was to be related to a priest. As a mediator between people and Tirawa, a priest was more effective than an ordinary man because he knew more and was more expressive. The most important sacred bundles were in his charge, and he possessed the necessary esoteric knowledge for handling them. The four leading Skidi priests were associated with the four most sacred bundles. During any particular year, from the first thunder in the spring until after the fall bison hunt, just one of the four led the ceremonies and was responsible for band welfare. Although the ceremonies of the bundle societies differed in details, all of the bundles were opened at the first thunder of spring, and dried bison meat was burned as an offering to the supernaturals in the west. The two retainers in each priest's lodge aided in ceremonial activities, and his criers, old and honored men, announced when ceremonies were to be held and recited certain parts of the ritual instructions.

RELIGION: SHAMANS Shamans were the second main category of supernatural specialists. Shamanistic power was given by Tirawa when he originated certain specific human roles. The original shaman received from Tirawa a blue paint to wear during ceremonies. Shamans controlled spirits existing on earth to cure the ill, but they did not command in the manner of a traditional chief. A particular shaman's power was from an animal that in turn had acquired power from a specific star. An emerging shaman might receive power directly from his animal guardian, but more often he became an apprentice of an established practitioner. Shamans were organized into their own societies and usually performed rituals at the first thunder in the spring and again in the fall. Their activities were designed to purify as well as to renew the power associated with their sacred objects. The rituals involved the use of sacred altars, body paints, rattles, and drums; sleight of hand, and smoking tobacco as an offering.

RELIGION: CEREMONIES Each major subgroup of Pawnee held a Twenty Day Ceremony late in the summer after the harvest and bundle ceremonies were over. Among the Skidi a mythological water monster was honored. Its image was fashioned by members of all the shaman societies. The head was covered with a bison skin, and its teeth, made from willows, showed inside the open mouth. The body was a willow frame covered with mud, and it had a fish-like tail. The image of a turtle was fashioned in the fire pit, and a new fire representing the sun was built on the turtle's back. Large and small figures of men and women were hung from the ceiling. The ceremony in-

The Pawnee: Horsemen and Farmers of the Prairies

cluded public displays of power by shamans. Feats included maize maturing before the audience or a tree bearing fruit miraculously. Likewise, a bear shaman took the liver from a living man and ate it; then the man walked away unharmed. A feat performed unsuccessfully meant expulsion; its success brought permanent membership in the group. During the final days of the celebrations rituals were performed in association with the sacred bundles. Finally, the objects constructed in a lodge for this event were taken to a body of water and placed in a pile.

Preparations for the summer or early fall bison hunt were important ceremonially. The public rituals were preceded by fasting, prayers, and sacrifices by priests. The ceremony was supervised by the sacred bundle priest presiding that year, and he decided which of the sodalities would police the hunt. At a village-wide gathering, twelve bison skulls were arranged in a semicircle at the back of a lodge. Nearby stood the chiefs and shamans with bison staves, sacred bows and arrows, and other hunting equipment. Invocations were made to Tirawa for success in the hunt, the implements were placed on the ground within the line of skulls, and the prayers were continued. When the appeals to the all-powerful supernatural were completed, warriors performed the bison dance, which continued uninterrupted for three days prior to the hunt. During the hunt eight carefully selected men carried the bison staves at the head of the moving column. In the 1870s the staves were spruce poles wrapped with beaded red and blue cloths to which hawk and eagle feathers were attached.

The Pawnee looked to the heavens as the source of life and as the dwell-

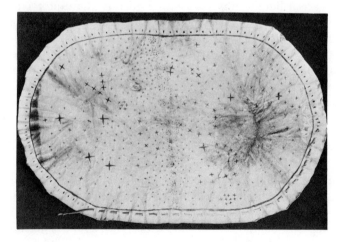

Plate 7–6 A Pawnee star and constellation map that reportedly is at least 350 years old. The Milky Way is in the center; the stars on the left side represent the summer skies and on the right, the winter skies. The magnitude of stars is represented by their comparative size. (Courtesy, Field Museum of Natural History, Chicago)

ing of the gods. In Skidi lore two great forces in the sky, the male in the east and female to the west, met at the zenith where Tirawa resided. Particular stars or planets were associated with specific events in their mythology, and priests understandably studied the heavens. An old Pawnee star map found in a sacred bundle is marked with stars of five different sizes, each drawn as a four-pointed figure. The largest three sizes were the most important; the others represented the Milky Way or served as fillers. The Milky Way was at the center of the map; the stars on one side represented the summer skies and those in opposition, the winter sky. The constellations recognized are those known to us; seasonal changes were recorded as well as the presence of double stars. The map demonstrates clearly that the Pawnee were rather sophisticated astronomers.

The Skidi sacrifice to the Morning Star is one of the most widely known American Indian ceremonials. In spite of its bizarre aspects, beauty and harmony were embodied in the symbolism. The sacrifice was possible only when Venus, or perhaps Mars, was the Morning Star and when a man dreamed that the offering should be made. The dreamer obtained from the keeper of the Morning Star bundle the warrior's garb that was part of the bundle. He set out with other men to find a victim from an enemy tribe. The captive, usually a young girl, was dedicated to the Morning Star as soon as she was seized. She was taken to the Skidi chief of the Morning Star village, and rituals that centered about her were performed for four days. The ceremonies began to climax near the end of the fourth day when songs were sung of the Morning Star's quest for the Evening Star, and as each song was completed, a tally stick from the sacred bundle was set aside. Evidently the captor represented the Evening Star, and the sticks symbolized the removal of the victim from this world into the sphere of the supernatural. On the afternoon of the fourth day a rectangular scaffold was erected. The two upright poles represented day and night; the four cross-poles forming the bottom of the frame represented the four directions, and an upper cross-pole represented the sky. The girl, who it was hoped did not know of her fate, was taken to the scaffold the next morning. She was stripped of her clothing, and if she climbed to the upper cross-pole willingly it was regarded as a good omen. Her hands were tied to the upper bar and her feet to the uppermost of the four lower bars. As soon as the Morning Star rose, two men came from the east to touch her armpits and groin with flaming torches. Four other men touched her with war clubs. Her captor shot a sacred arrow through the girl's heart, while another man hit her on the head with the war club from the Morning Star bundle. The priest for the Morning Star bundle cut open her breast with a flint knife and covered his face with her blood. The observers, men, women, and children, shot arrows into the body and then left the scene. The captor of the girl held meat beneath her body so that her blood dripped down to cover it. The blood-covered meat was burned as an offering to the deities. Finally the girl's body was cut down, and the arrows were removed by the priest. The corpse was left to be eaten by animals.

The Pawnee: Horsemen and Farmers of the Prairies

Plate 7–7 Painting of Petalesharo by John Neagle in 1821. (Courtesy of The Historical Society of Pennsylvania)

Although these sacrifices by the Skidi probably took place until 1838, the most dramatic one known occurred about twenty years earlier when the son of a chief interrupted the ritual. This young man, Petalesharo, was present as a Comanche woman was to be sacrificed. He cut her free from the scaffold, rode off with her on a horse, and later gave her a horse so that she could return to her people. Petalesharo performed his feat because his father opposed these sacrifices, and he succeeded because of his daring and high standing among the Pawnee. In 1822 Petalesharo visited Washington, D.C., and was presented with an engraved silver medal by the girls of Miss White's Seminary to commemorate his rescue of the Comanche girl. On one side of the medal is depicted the sacrificial scaffold and the surprised leaders of the ritual, and on the opposite side Petalesharo is shown leading the girl away. When Petalesharo died, the medal was buried with him. In 1884 the medal was taken from his grave, and eventually it was presented to the American Numismatic Society of New York City.

FOLK TALES   The Pawnee possessed an extremely rich and varied body of folk tales and ritual texts. An example conveys the beauty of their oral traditions. This particular tale was recited by Skidi adults during the winter

for the benefit of children, who were expected to memorize it because the account reportedly was related by the Evening Star, the first mother. Like the tales of many people, this example is filled with symbolism meaningful only to the Pawnee, and therefore interpretive comments are offered. The text was translated by James R. Murie, a Pawnee who collected a great deal of the ethnographic information published by the Pawnee authority George A. Dorsey (1906, 350).

> Listen, the girl (1) in distress walks to and fro on top of the
>   mountains.
> Listen, the girl's ears tremble, as she runs to and fro, listening.
> From the girl is truly descended a fine tribe of people.
> There are left behind grass lodges (2).
> They rub their backs upon the poles of the lodges.
> Many buffalo shall be consecrated, and shall be carried
>   one by one at the foot of the hill.
> Yonder are high hills and low, covered with waving
>   grass.
> Now listen, pay attention, they (3) give out their words in
>   their own tongue.

242

The Pawnee: Horsemen and Farmers of the Prairies

Yonder on the slopes of the willow-covered hills is a cave.
Turtle (4) shall speak and say, "We will destroy you."
Now I make holy this Comanche (5) who is brought into the
  lodge.
Meat shall be taken from the back of the buffalo (6).
The rays of the sun (7) shall enter the lodge.
Burnt-offerings of flesh and human beings shall be made.
The earth (8) then shall become a plain.
When this shall happen, people shall see the streams as bows (9).
You shall live under the heavens, and move about over the land
  as a tribe.
Then the people shall come together, and all shall live as one
  people.
The earth shall be fruitful.
The owl (10); the owl.
You shall go to the ravines (11).
The carcass of an animal that has been eaten to the bone.
The spotted rabbit (12) had his way, like a warrior, and he
  counts coup upon the enemy.
The mouths shall look round (13).
The noise of sticks (14) and voices shall move to and fro.
May the fathers wave the sticks (15)!

The girl (1) was the first person on earth; she looks and listens for other people. The grass-covered dwellings (2) reportedly were the first type used by the Pawnee, and when abandoned lodges of this type were common, the bison rubbed against the poles. The supernatural powers of animals, they (3), are found in different places. A turtle (4) created a flood to destroy four monsters, and this reference contains the implication that people will destroy one another and particularly that there will be the Morning Star sacrifice. The reference to the Comanche (5) is a further allusion to the sacrifice; the bison meat (6) is for an accompanying feast, and the sun's light (7) consecrates the victim. The earth (8) appears to be flat when shrouded with mist, but as the sun rises the mist disappears and shadows cast by the sun's rays reveal the hills and mountains. The reference to bows (9) is associated with killing animals, dedicating meat to the gods, and offering human sacrifices. Owls (10) are wise; the priests chant their night rituals like the owls. In the ravines (11) are the remains of animals, who like men, die. The Rabbit (12) is a star near the Milky Way who offered a way of life opposed to that of the Evening Star. When the people have an abundance of food, their mouths will be round (13) from singing and shouting. The sticks (14) are a reference to arrows shot at the Morning Star victim, while the sticks (15) next mentioned are associated with a blessing of children by waving pipe sticks.

LIFE CYCLE   When a woman became aware that she was pregnant, she and her husband observed certain prohibitions. The most important of these was that the man could hunt and kill only deer and only his wife could eat the meat. A wide range of additional taboos was observed to prevent any deformity of the embryo. Each embryo acquired an animal familiar, and its identity later was revealed by the actions of the individual when ill. When the woman began labor, her husband left the dwelling for four days. During this time he continued to observe taboos, and he wore his hair loose because Tirawa did so while creating. A laboring woman took medicine and was aided by an old female shaman or keeper of a sacred bundle. The woman knelt and leaned forward against a stick as she gave birth. The umbilical cord, which was cut and tied by the midwife, was kept to be buried with the mother at the time of her death. The infant was washed, wrapped in a blanket, and placed on a cradleboard. The afterbirth was placed in a tree where it would not be disturbed by birds or animals. That night the child's relatives observed the stars and the weather; if the wind did not blow and the following day was clear, they assumed the infant probably would not be ill or plagued with difficulties in life. The near relatives of the mother cared for the neonate until the umbilical cord dropped off; then the parents again braided their hair, the midwife was compensated, and the infant was returned to its mother. Were a woman to die in childbirth or the offspring to be stillborn, it was assumed that taboos had been broken. In an informal adoption an affluent family raised a child belonging legally to a poor family. It appears to have been somewhat less common to adopt a child formally. If a favorite boy or girl died, a child that resembled it might be formally adopted if the real parents approved. Infanticide was unknown, and the possibility could not be imagined. Male shamans were thought to be able to produce an abortion by using herbs, and an unwed woman might attempt to induce an abortion by applying pressure on her abdomen.

A baby was named by the midwife based on his appearance or behavior just after birth. Examples for the Skidi included Round Eyes, Fatty, and Young Bull. The names White or Black were favorites for boys, and Bright Eyes for girls. A small child might receive another name if his father sacrificed a scalp for the occasion in a formal ritual. This name usually was retained by the individual until after marriage. A third name was bestowed by a father after his son's marriage, but it might be changed to insure success in warfare or after a brave deed. Likewise a man might receive the name of an honored relative. So long as a child nursed, it was called by a word comparable to "baby," and the sex was not distinguished. This period lasted for about three years, after which the terms for male and female children were different.

Young children were under the supervision of their grandmothers, who were severe instructors. If children misbehaved, they were reproved verbally, and if they did not obey the rules of childhood behavior, they were whipped. Children were expected to learn tribal lore from the grandmothers. They were

244

reproved for not being quiet and withdrawn when among adults, for being inattentive during ceremonies, or for approaching the altar at the rear of a lodge. Older sisters, the mother and father, and the grandparents all served as authority figures for a child.

A girl's training in the essential household skills was under the direction of her grandmother. When a girl menstruated for the first time, no ritual was performed unless the girl's mother was the keeper of a sacred bundle. In this instance the girl was isolated, probably with her maternal grandmother. The girl's behavior and diet were restricted, and the same pattern was followed during subsequent menstrual periods. All menstruating women avoided contact with sacred bundles and did not attend any bundle ceremonies.

Until a boy was about twelve years of age, he helped his mother with such household tasks as hauling water. Older boys came under the supervision of their grandfathers, and to acquire archery skills was an important part of a boy's life. A favorite pastime was to shoot at an arrow shot by another boy. Older boys followed their fathers on bison hunts, and as soon as a kill was made, they helped butcher the animal. The horse they had ridden was used to transport the meat to camp. Puberty for males was not marked by ceremonial recognition, but a maturing boy was identified by a word translated as "grown" or "straight up" and became a member of a new age group, where he remained until he married. Up to this time he went naked except that he wore a robe in cold weather. After puberty he dressed as a man and was linked closely with his mother's brother's wife. When her husband was away, the boy served as a supplementary husband for a few years until acquiring a wife of his own. Young braves were exceedingly vain about the appearance of their horses and themselves. A favorite horse was groomed, painted, and its tail adorned with feathers. After a rider and steed were fully presentable, they paraded through the settlement to be admired by all. For a young man to seduce an unmarried girl was disreputable since girls were expected to be virgins when they married. Were a young couple to fornicate and be found out, the parents prevented further meetings. If, however, the girl became pregnant, a hasty wedding was arranged if the man was considered a suitable husband. If not, he might be beaten badly, and no one would defend him, for it was difficult to find another man willing to marry the girl under such circumstances.

The partners in a typical marriage had been raised in the same community (village endogamy) but were not more closely related than third cousins, if related at all. A man did not marry until after he had participated in at least one raid, had stolen horses successfully, and had killed bison on a hunt. The woman was about twenty-two years old, and the couple lived with the wife's parents following the marriage (matrilocal residence). When a man married a woman from another settlement, the couple always resided in the community of the woman, and children were affiliated consistently with the village of their mother.

Marriages usually were negotiated by a man's mother's brother and the potential bride's mother's brother. If the girl had no maternal uncle, her brothers or grandfathers made the decision. A prospective groom who strenuously objected to an arrangement left home for a year or two. A girl could attempt to influence her uncle, but she was forced to abide by his decision. The maternal uncle of the man, were he from a leading matrilineage, selected a chaste girl with a reputation for hard work. A formal wedding ceremony was performed when leading lineages were involved, but for persons of lesser standing this was not considered necessary. Marriage ceremonies were led by the priest, and formal approval was given by the girl's relatives in a ritual that included smoking and recitations of the young man's merits. Further ceremonial smoking followed, and gifts were given to the male relatives of the girl. The marriage ceremonies were considered completed when the couple ate and then slept together. After marriage males were referred to by a word meaning "man" and females as "woman." A man normally lived with his wife's family although he might in later years set up an independent household. A young husband was referred to by his in-laws as "the one that is sitting among [us]"; he in turn referred to them by a term that meant "I am in the house for your benefit." In formal terms a man called his wife "I own her," and she referred to her husband as "he owns me." Informally they called each other "spouse," or "old man" and "old woman" when they were close.

In theory, a man did not physically punish his wife because it was through two female deities, Evening Star and Moon, that he was able to obtain bison and maize. In fact, it seems that a man rarely abused his wife to the extent that her relatives intervened on her behalf. Skidi Pawnee divorce seems to have been rare, and when it occurred, the grounds were most likely to be adultery or failure of the husband to be a good provider. Barrenness of the woman was not grounds for divorce. A man could leave his bride on the wedding night if she were not a maiden. Such a woman, along with those who freely fornicated before marriage, or loose widows, lived on the fringes of a community as prostitutes. An adulterous wife was deserted, and an adulterous husband might be ordered out of the house by his female in-laws. Children of divorced parents remained with their mother. In times of domestic stress a man always was welcome in his sister's home. If a married man died, his younger brother acquired the widow as a wife (levirate). In plural marriages the wives were sisters (sororal polygyny); a man could obtain the younger sisters or sister of his wife if the wife's family was satisfied with his abilities as a provider. Secondary wives were acquired as they came of age without an accompanying ceremony. One Skidi man had eight wives from two families, apparently a record.

During their stay in a village, the members of a family bathed in a nearby stream or river each morning. They ate their first meal around noon, and when a number of families lived together, women alternated in preparing the meals. A number of food taboos were observed. Shamans and chiefs could not

The Pawnee: Horsemen and Farmers of the Prairies

eat fish; the tender meat around a bison's anus was saved for old people; and young people were not to eat the stomach of a bison cow. To break any of these taboos was to court some particular type of disaster. If men were hunting bison, persons remaining in the village were cautioned to keep the lodge clean and to make offerings of maize to the bison skull on the household altar. Likewise, menstruating women were not to approach the skull for fear of angering the bison spirit.

If someone died, the corpse always was buried within a few hours. The body of an old person or one of rank was painted by a priest with sacred red pigment. The corpse of a man was shrouded in his bison robe, and his ceremonial equipment, if he had been a member of a voluntary association, was buried with him. The nature of further observances depended on the importance of the deceased and the manner of death. For an old man, one who was no longer a hunter or warrior, and a woman after menopause, mourning lasted through the day of burial. A man who died in middle age from natural causes was not mourned at all since such a death indicated that he was a useless person. An important chief normally was mourned for months, but the period was shortened to four days if the death took place just before the sacred bundle renewal ceremonies. If a man died at the hands of an enemy, his close friends and relatives secured an enemy scalp as soon as possible after the death. They consecrated it and tied it to a long stick above the grave. When a man died, it was his brothers and sisters who truly mourned the loss. A surviving brother mutilated himself, while a sister cut her hair. It was said of a wife, however, that she would spit on her hands to pretend tears, simultaneously peering through her fingers in search of another husband. A widow was expected to mourn for a year before remarrying. After a man's death, his wife was considered the owner of their lodge and tepee in addition to her own utensils and tools; his personal property, such as robes, horses, and riding equipment, was usually inherited by his sister's sons. A widower was obligated to mourn for at least two years, and frequently he did not remarry.

The dead almost always were interred in the ground, usually on a hilltop, and over the body a low mound of earth was piled. A corpse was flexed, covered with matting, and grave goods were placed nearby. Items never included as grave goods were those thought to have originated in the sky. The most important objects of this nature seem to have been meteorites, which sometimes were part of a war bundle. They were from the stars and belonged to the sky.

Recent Historic Changes

THE RESERVATION   In the early 1850s the Pawnee did more begging and stealing from wagon train immigrants than they did raiding and killing. The Skidi attempted to hunt bison on the plains in the early 1850s, but Sioux harassment was devastating. Finally white settlement south of the Platte River made life unbearable for the Indians there, and they could no longer live north of the Platte because of the powerful Sioux. In 1857 the Pawnee accepted a small reservation on the Loup Fork, and Federal aid compensated them for the loss of their land. They received $40,000 per year for five years, and $30,000 a year thereafter. In addition they were promised active protection against the Sioux, and an agent was to help them settle down as farmers. In 1859 they moved to their new reservation. Yet the Sioux raids continued, and a good Indian agent was replaced by a greedy one. When the villages were attacked by their enemies during the summer bison hunt of 1862, they were defended with valor by the old men, the available young ones, and women. In 1864 the Sioux raids were so devastating to whites that troops were sent into the region. Although some Pawnee aided the soldiers, American leadership was so ineffective that there was no contact with the hostile Indians. In 1865 a new U.S. Army commander was appointed, and his military success was due largely to Pawnee cooperation.

QUAKER MISSIONARIES   Still, the Pawnee were rovers. They refused to remain on their reservation, and the efforts of corrupt and incompetent Indian agents contributed nothing to their welfare. In 1869 the reservation was put under the administration of Quaker missionaries in an attempt by the Indian Service to rid itself of dishonest representatives. The first Quaker missionary found that the Indians could speak no English and that none of them could read or write even though a school had been established about twenty-five years before. Horticulture carried out by the women was still the only type of farming. The Quakers set out to destroy Pawnee customs as rapidly as possible. In 1870 some of the Pawnee chiefs were induced to cultivate fields with a horse and plow; in earlier times it was unheard of for any man to work as a woman. As others followed the example of the chiefs, American farming practices were introduced. The missionaries and Indian agents were not satisfied with this progress and sought to break up the villages and place families on separate plots of farmland. The missionaries pressured Congress to sell 50,000 acres of Pawnee land to finance the resettlement program. In the summer bison hunt of 1873 some 400 Pawnee were trapped by a force of nearly 1000 Sioux, and almost 100 Pawnee were killed. During the fall of the same year grasshoppers and potato beetles destroyed their crops, while white settlers were taking timber and hay from their lands. With all of this adversity the people were demoralized, and two-thirds of them went south, intending to abandon their reservation. Although most returned the following spring, there remained among the Indians an unsettled question about whether they should move south to Indian Territory or stay in Nebraska.

REMOVAL   With government pressure, removal became a necessity, and in 1874 more of the tribe followed the first group. The land selected for their reservation was to the west of the Arkansas River and north of the Cimarron

The Pawnee: Horsemen and Farmers of the Prairies

Plate 7–9 Peta-la-sha-ra photograph taken in 1868. (Courtesy of the Nebraska State Historical Society, Lincoln)

River. By late 1875 all of the Indians had arrived on their new lands. The Quaker ideal of providing 160 acres and a house for each family was fine, but money to implement the program was not available. There could be no compromises for these Quakers, and the people were destined to live half-starved in canvas tents, with very inadequate clothing; even their horses were stolen by whites. The missionaries were delighted when the warriors were forced to trade their weapons for food! The population figures indicate that misguided Quaker idealism became genocide: in 1872, there were 2447 people in the tribe; in 1876, 2026; 1879, 1440; and finally, in 1890, 804. In an effort to force the Pawnee to become more intensive farmers, the government in 1882 cut off the rations it had provided. Some families managed to adjust, but most simply reduced their standard of living and depended on annuities and lease money provided by white cattlemen who grazed their animals on Indian lands. In 1883 the government established a concentration camp for children, euphemistically called a boarding school. Parents were prohibited from visiting their children, and the committed child remained in Federal custody for years on end. The purpose of all of this was to force the Pawnee to give up their Indian ways.

GHOST DANCE   Information about the Pawnee from the recent past is rare, but we do have the detailed study by Alexander Lesser of their participation in the Ghost Dance of 1890. This was the last major effort of the tribe to reaffirm its cultural identity as Indian. The originator of the 1890 Ghost Dance was a Paiute Indian from Nevada named Wovoka (Jack Wilson). He reportedly died during an eclipse of the sun in January, 1889, and went to heaven, where he saw all the dead Indians living in an idyllic state. God reportedly said that if Wovoka returned to earth and taught the people to perform the Ghost Dance, the dead and living would be reunited. Wovoka cautioned people not to fight with each other nor with the whites, and neither should they lie or steal. If these instructions were obeyed, there would be no more illness, old age, or death. Performing the Ghost Dance was to hasten the dawning of this new world.

Word of the Ghost Dance doctrine spread rapidly and was modified by different tribes. Wovoka often was regarded as Christ who had come to save Indians. Rumors about the Ghost Dance spread to the Pawnee, and in 1891 a Pawnee man, Frank White, participated in the ceremonies in southern Oklahoma. He returned to his people and became their leader of the Ghost Dance. During dances the participants who went into trances revealed that they saw the Messiah and the dead. The leader preached that the world was to change soon and that the whites and persons of mixed Indian and white ancestry would be blown away or destroyed by the wind. Believers, however, would see the dead return, and bison again would become plentiful. Dances were held throughout 1891, and by 1892 most Pawnee had accepted the doctrine and were participating to hasten the time when a new world would be created. Many persons were so convinced that the present world was coming to an end that they did not plant their crops. When the Indian agent expressed opposition to the dance, it was performed secretly. Finally, Frank White was arrested for leading a Ghost Dance and was held for about two weeks. During his hearing the judge sternly warned him against continuing his "insurrection."

As the Ghost Dance movement climaxed, the Federal Government was exerting every effort to induce the Pawnee to change the nature of their landholdings. With the passage of the Dawes (General Allotment) Act by Congress in 1887, reservation Indians were encouraged to select plots of land for which they eventually would receive clear titles. Unallotted reservation lands then were to be sold to whites. The Pawnee resisted the program, correctly viewing it as an attempt to destroy the tribe. In mid-1892 Federal agents told these Indians that if they accepted individual land allotments, they would pass from Federal control and could then hold their Ghost Dances as often as they wished. This argument apparently was convincing, for by the end of that year the allotment process was completed. The following year the nonallotted lands were opened to white settlers. Over the next few years the Ghost Dance was continued but in a less militant form, and the Indian agents could do little to stop it.

After the death of Frank White in 1893, or possibly somewhat earlier, the Ghost Dance became a more formalized series of four-day ceremonies. It focused Pawnee attention on being Indian, for one of the doctrines was to give

The Pawnee: Horsemen and Farmers of the Prairies

up the goods and ways of whites. This introspection led to a renewal of the importance of sacred bundles, sodalities, and aboriginal games. By 1892 the sacred bundle rituals had nearly ceased to exist, and the elaborate shamans' performances likewise had declined. A number of conditions ran counter to a bundle ceremony revival. Some bundles had been buried with the last priest of a bundle group, and when a bundle did survive, the priest in charge of it was not likely to know all of the esoteric lore surrounding it. Lesser (1933, 108) noted that in the late nineteenth century there was a "cultural forgetting" and that the functions of the ceremonies were fading, making the continuity of ritual knowledge from a priest to his apprentice less likely. Then, too, many persons were dying, and with them went their store of knowledge. The Ghost Dance, with its emphasis on individual vision experience, was a mechanism to revive the nonesoteric aspects of aboriginal life. As Lesser (1933, 117) has written, "The Ghost Dance proved not only a force for cultural revival, but with a return to the past as an inspirational source and guide, and vision sanctions as immediate drives, the doctrine was an impetus to cultural development."

PEYOTE CULT　　In historic times many Indian tribes of the Plains and Prairies accepted peyote and integrated its use into their supernatural system. Peyote, a small cactus plant grown in Mexico, has a small "button" appearing above the ground. These buttons were collected and dried for ritual use. They contain nonaddictive stimulants and sedatives that produce a narcotic effect. The first knowledge of peyote was received by the Pawnee from the Quapaw about 1890 when two young men visited the latter tribe. Somewhat later more details concerning its use were learned from Arapaho visitors. When under the influence of peyote, one man learned songs and rituals that became the basis of the Peyote Cult, and he emerged as the leader. As is common among American Indian tribes, elements of Christianity were integrated into the belief system, and in part the taking of peyote was associated in the minds of the Pawnee with the Ghost Dance.

LAND CLAIMS　　In the 1890s it appeared that the Pawnee once again could reaffirm their Indian identity, but this was not to be the case. With the allotment program, the reservation was divided into small parcels of land, and whites who purchased unallotted lands lived next door to Indians. The Indians received an $80,000 advance for the lands they had released and a continuing $30,000 a year annuity plus interest from the balance of the sale of Nebraska and Oklahoma lands. These funds were either directly or indirectly available to the approximately 160 families. Furthermore, the Pawnee leased farmlands, grazing lands, and even their houses to white cattlemen and farmers. The result was that by the turn of the century the Indians were well-to-do financially but lived without purpose. There was no positive side to their security, for they lived from day to day, spending their money as rapidly as they received it. The net result was that they became deculturated, no longer retaining their Indian ways, and adopting only the superficial aspects of the dominant white society.

Fewer than 700 Pawnee survived in 1900, but by 1970 their number had increased to nearly 2000 persons with one-quarter or more Pawnee blood. In 1962 the Pawnee received about 7 million dollars from the Federal Government through the Court of Claims for lands they had relinquished without receiving just compensation or settlement. Evidence suggests that this money has been used by the recipients to improve their economic conditions. Thus, the Federal Government once again has provided money in an effort to buy justice, but the compensation has a hollow ring.

Comparisons

The Pawnee are the first people described who traced descent through females, and we may ask why. A partial answer is that the farming activities of women were very important to the tribe's economic well-being, and this led to an emphasis on the female line. (But if this is the complete answer, why were the Fox patrilineal and yet heavily dependent on the farming of women?) With the introduction of horses the Pawnee emerged as intensive bison hunters and fought over hunting grounds. This shift to a focus on males for economic welfare had social ramifications that might well be studied.

The kinship terms used by the Pawnee bear special consideration because they deemphasize generational distinctions, a tendency already seen among

Plate 7–10 The bitterness between the Pawnee and their Sioux enemies ended in 1925 near Trenton, Nebraska. A conference was held, and representatives of both sides smoked a pipe of peace. (Courtesy of the Nebraska State Historical Society, Lincoln)

The Pawnee: Horsemen and Farmers of the Prairies

the Fox. It well may be asked, What characteristics of Pawnee life could have led to the existence of kin terms that are the same for different generations?

The social life of the people described in earlier chapters was essentially egalitarian, although certain class distinctions based on birth existed among the aboriginal Cahuilla and Fox. The Pawnee social system was far more rigid. For example, note the rich-poor distinctions and hereditary-nonhereditary chief differences. These and other social dividers may be thought of as status distinctions. *Ascribed statuses* are assigned to persons at birth, irrespective of personal abilities (e.g., male-female, young-old, or son-daughter). *Achieved statuses* are reached through competition and individual abilities (U.S. today, e.g., car salesperson, lawyer, president, or mechanic). If a status is neither clearly ascribed nor achieved, it is most likely in a state of flux. The greater the number of achieved statuses, the higher the degree of role differentiation that becomes possible in a society. Comparisons of the Pawnee with the other peoples are rewarding with respect to these dimensions and help to identify rigid versus more flexible systems.

The Pawnee had a political life far more organized on a formal basis than did any of the others described heretofore, and one might seek to explain its relatively high degree of development in economic terms. What economic differences separated the Pawnee from other peoples, and why did these differences assume such significance among the Pawnee?

Pawnee religion was so much more refined than that reported for the others that it might seem to defy meaningful comparisons. The degree of specialized knowledge required of Pawnee priests, their rituals filled with complicated symbolism, and the annual rotation of power are distinctive. Yet similarities are found among the Cahuilla in terms of ceremonial leaders, sacred bundles, and calendrical ritual sets. In any effort to explain the differences the backgrounds of the Cahuilla and Pawnee must be researched over a broader horizon. Such comparisons should include what these people set out to accomplish with rituals in their efforts to influence actual events in a real world.

Additional Readings

The Lost Universe by Gene Weltfish is the most comprehensive ethnographic reconstruction for ca. 1867 and a key source. The Pawnee history by George E. Hyde is a standard work, as are the writings of George A. Dorsey, John B. Dunbar, and James B. Murie.

References

Buckstaff, Ralph N. "Stars and Constellations of a Pawnee Sky Map," *American Anthropologist*, v. 29, 279–285. 1927.

Bureau of Indian Affairs. "Pawnee Indians," n.d. (mimeographed).

Catlin, George. *North American Indians.* 2 v. London. 1844.

Donaldson, Thomas. "The George Catlin Indian Gallery in the U.S. National Museum," *Annual Report of the Board of Regents of the Smithsonian Institution, 1885.* pt. 2 Appendix. 1886.

Dorsey, George A. "Social Organization of the Skidi Pawnee," *Fifteenth International Congress of Americanists,* 71–77. Quebec. 1907.

Dorsey, George A. "A Pawnee Ritual of Instruction." *Anthropological Papers Written in Honor of Franz Boas,* 350–353. New York. 1906.

Dorsey, George A. "The Skidi Rite of Human Sacrifice," *Fifteenth International Congress of Americanists,* 65–70. Quebec. 1907.

*Dorsey, George A., and James R. Murie. Alexander Spoehr, ed. "Notes on Skidi Pawnee Society," *Anthropological Series, Field Museum of Natural History.* v. 27, 67–119. 1940. The definitive study of Skidi social structure with notes on the life cycle of the individual as well as information on certain aspects of political organization.

*Dunbar, John B. "The Pawnee Indians," *Magazine of American History,* v. 4, 241–281, v. 5, 321–342, v. 8, 734–754. 1880–1882 (reprinted, New York, 1883). This is an integrated historical and ethnographic account of the Pawnee by a pioneer missionary.

Fletcher, Alice C. "Pawnee Star Lore," *Journal of American Folk-Lore,* v. 16, 10–15. 1903.

*Grinnell, George B. *Pawnee Hero Stories and Folk-Tales.* Lincoln. 1961 (originally published in New York in 1889). Grinnell describes diverse aspects of Pawnee ethnography, but none in detail. Emphasis is on folk-tales and stories about warfare, but it is still an essential source for a balanced account of these Indians.

Hodge, Frederick W. "Pitalesharu and his Medal," *The Masterkey,* v. 24, 111–119. 1950.

*Hyde, George E. *Pawnee Indians.* Denver. 1951. This book is the definitive history of the Pawnee but has very little to offer about events after 1900.

Irving, John T., Jr. John F. McDermott, ed. *Indian Sketches.* Norman. 1955.

Lesser, Alexander. "Levirate and Fraternal Polyandry among the Pawnees," *Man,* v. 30, 98–101. 1930.

*Lesser, Alexander. *The Pawnee Ghost Dance Hand Game.* New York. 1933. The focus of this study is on the Ghost Dance and the revival of a

254

game at the time of the Ghost Dance, but the volume also contains a summary of Pawnee history down to about 1900.

"Letters Concerning the Presbyterian Mission in the Pawnee Country, near Bellevue, Neb., 1831–1849." *Collections of the Kansas State Historical Society*, v. 14, 570–784. 1918.

Linton, Ralph. *The Thunder Ceremony of the Pawnee*. Field Museum of Natural History. Leaflet 5. 1922.

Linton, Ralph. "The Origin of the Skidi Pawnee Sacrifice to the Morning Star," *American Anthropologist*, v. 28, 457–466. 1926.

McKenney, Thomas L., and James Hall. *The Indian Tribes of North America*, v. 1. Edinburgh. 1933.

*Murie, James R. *Pawnee Indian Societies*. Anthropological Papers of the American Museum of Natural History, v. 11, pt. 7. New York. 1914. This short monograph is the most complete and readable account of sacred and secular Pawnee societies. It includes also information about other aspects of Pawnee life and is a required source of ethnographic materials.

Murray, Charles A. *Travels in North America*, v. 2. London. 1839.

Newcomb, William W., Jr. "A Re-Examination of the Causes of Plains Warfare," *American Anthropologist*, v. 52, 317–330. 1950.

Roe, Frank G. *The Indian and the Horse*. Norman. 1955.

Thurman, Melburn D. "A Case of Historical Mythology: The Skidi Pawnee Morning Star Sacrifice of 1833," *Plains Anthropologist*, v. 15, 309–311. 1970.

Thurman, Melburn D. "The Skidi Pawnee Morning Star Sacrifice of 1827," *Nebraska History*, v. 51, 269–280. 1970.

*Wedel, Waldo R. *An Introduction to Pawnee Archeology*. Bureau of American Ethnology, Bulletin 112. 1936. Not only are the details of Pawnee archaeology presented, but historical and ethnographic data are analyzed into a fine synthesis of sociocultural data.

Wedel, Waldo R. *Prehistoric Man on the Great Plains*. Norman. 1961.

*Weltfish, Gene. *The Lost Universe*. New York. 1965. The author, an ethnographer and linguist, worked among the Pawnee from 1928–1936 and collected texts systematically. Following the introductory chapters the book presents a yearly round for ca. 1867 as a series of texts from Pawnee informants. This is the definitive ethnographic reconstruction.

Wissler, Clark, and Herbert J. Spinden. "The Pawnee Human Sacrifice to the Morningstar," *American Museum Journal*, v. 16, 49–55. 1916.

The Crow: Plains Warriors and Bison Hunters

8

Reasons for This Selection

Plains Indian life long has captivated white Americans and Europeans, sometimes to the point that all other Indians are ignored. Warriors astride horses recklessly chasing herds of bison or enemies across the plains conveys a sense of daring and freedom. The Crow typify this life-style shared by other Siouans* and Algonkians such as the Blackfoot, Cheyenne, and Gros Ventre. The Crow are presented because any book about American Indians is incomplete without including a people of the northern Plains. Their lifeway, based on hunting herd animals from horseback, and their emphasis on warfare represent a major regional configuration in North American Indian culture. The Crow also illustrate the flexibility of some Indians in making ecological adaptations. About seventy-five years before their discovery the Crow began receiving domestic horses, and they molded their economy around this animal in a remarkably brief period.

---

* The diverse uses of the word "Sioux" merit a clarifying note. The Sioux Nation or The Seven Council Fires consists of three major groups: the Santee (Dakota or Eastern Sioux), Middle Sioux (Nakota), and Teton Sioux (Lakota, Teton Dakota, Western Dakota, or Western Sioux). Dakota, Nakota, and Lakota are dialectic forms for "allies" or "friends." The Middle Sioux are divided into two groups, the Yankton and Yanktonai. The most important subtribes of the Dakota are the Burnt Thighs (Brulé), No Bows (Sans Arcs), Oglala, and Two Kettles.

Map by J. Donovan

258

People, Population, and Language

These people called themselves Abarokee (Absaroka), which means "Children of a Large Beaked Bird" in Hidatsa. The reference may be to either a raven or an extinct bird. Before lasting contacts were made with the Crow, the tribe suffered a series of terrible smallpox epidemics. The early French trader François A. Larocque estimated that they occupied 300 tepees in 1805, but he reported that 2000 tepees had existed just before the first smallpox epidemic. In 1833 the Crow had 800 tepees with an estimated population of 6400. By the early 1930s their number had declined to about 1600, but in the 1970 census there were about 5000 Crow. Their language belongs to the Macro-Siouan linguistic phylum and to the Siouan family. Their closest linguistic relatives are the Hidatsa, and it is probable that in the comparatively recent past the Crow and Hidatsa were one people. Other tribes in the Siouan family include the Dakota, Iowa-Oto, and Mandan.

Early History

Diverse opinions prevail about Crow origins and their movements in prehistoric times, but none is entirely acceptable. Traditional Crow history, referring to the not-so-distant past, states that they came from a place with many lakes, which is thought by some to have been the Lake Winnipeg area in Manitoba, Canada. They settled briefly in earth lodge communities along the Missouri River as farmers and hunters who came to be called the Hidatsa. Differences between two chiefs led one of these men to separate with about 500 followers; this new group emerged as the Crow. Perhaps the split occurred in the 1700s since some Crow remained closely identified with the Hidatsa as late as the 1830s. We can assert with reasonable confidence that the Crow began moving south and west about 1700 and began living in their historic homeland about 1750. Archaeological sites clearly identified with the prehistoric Crow have not been found.

As they obtained horses soon after 1730, Crow life began to assume its historic focus. In aboriginal times they were a hunting people with dogs to bear packs and pull travois. The Crow were fully accustomed to a mobile way of life, and the horse vastly increased their movements. A host of Plains tribes raided for horses or exchanged horses for firearms and other imported manufactures. The availability of horses at the eve of white contact heralded a virtual cultural revolution. As wandering hunters the Crow had a distinct advantage over sedentary Indians who farmed at earth lodge communities and were stationary targets; the Pawnee are an example of semipermanent farmers. With horses Crow economic and combative activities expanded. They could strike a distant enemy suddenly or travel far to hunt. By the same token they were subject to raids by other equally wide-ranging equestrian hunters, and these widespread contacts facilitated the rapid spread of deadly new diseases. With horses as pack animals the Crow could transport large quantities of dried meat, accumulate more property than before, and build larger tepees. The aged were no longer a burden; they could be fed and transported easily by horses. With old people living longer the basis for cultural learning was broadened. The horse, as a unit of wealth and an object of prestige, resulted in social distinctions between those who had many horses and others with only a few animals.

Initial contacts with whites apparently were in the 1740s, and the Crow soon earned a reputation as clever thieves and shrewd traders. Early in their history they also had the distinction of disdaining alcohol, which they called "white man's fool water." The 1804–1806 expedition of Meriwether Lewis and William Clark traveled through Crow country on its return from the Pacific coast in 1806, but it is not clear whether the explorers met any of these people. In the early 1800s the heart of Crow country reportedly was in the Big Horn Mountains, where they lived as a loosely integrated tribe. About 1825 two rival chiefs, Arapooish and Long Hair, disagreed and split the people into two groups. The Mountain Crow, as the followers of Long Hair, ranged south of the Yellowstone River in southern Montana. The followers of Arapooish, the River Crow, lived farther north along the Musselshell and Judith tributaries of the Missouri River.

In the early decades of the nineteenth century fur traders and Mountain Men were attracted to Crow country in their quest for beaver, and these Indians became involved in the competing interests of trading companies, free traders, and white trappers. The impact of the fur trade was not as great as might have been expected because of the difficulty in obtaining access to the region, the presence of hostile Indians, and the declining market for beaver pelts. The first trading station in Crow country was Fort Lisa, built in 1807 at the mouth of the Big Horn River, but it and numerous other forts of the period failed. The first Fort Sarpy, for example, at the junction of the Rosebud and Yellowstone rivers, was founded in 1850. Previously the Crow had traded bison hides and beaver pelts at forts among the Arikara and Mandan along the Missouri River. With the founding of Fort Sarpy, the Crow camped in the vicinity during the fall and winter to harvest bison skins that they exchanged for trade goods. Crow at these camps were easy prey for Assiniboin, Blackfoot, and Sioux raiders. During the summer the Crow attacked their enemies to avenge their losses, but they declined in number because they faced so many hostile tribes. Fort Sarpy was abandoned and burned by the resident trader in 1855. It had proved very difficult to bring in trade goods and take out pelts along the dangerous rivers. Furthermore, persons stationed there often were the virtual prisoners of surrounding Indians.

A terrible smallpox epidemic in the early 1830s was described by the fur trader Edwin T. Denig, but by no other observer; the same disease struck in 1837 and again in 1848 but not as destructively. Yet in 1849 an influenza epi-

Plate 8–1 George Catlin (1926, v. 1, 216) wrote of this painting, "I have painted him as he sat for me, balanced on his leaping wild horse with his shield and quiver slung on his back, and his long lance decorated with the eagle's quills, trailed in his right hand." (From Ewers, 1965)

demic was said by one observer to have killed 150 persons and 600 by another reporter. In addition the Crow were outnumbered by their Blackfoot and Sioux enemies. For example, there probably were at least two and a half times as many Blackfoot as Crow.

As the United States began to assert control over the region in 1825, an agent was sent up the Missouri River to the Mandan villages where the Crow were visiting. A Treaty of Friendship was signed by Long Hair, but Arapooish refused to sign. Among the treaty conditions was Crow recognition that the United States controlled Crow country and had the right to regulate trade and intercourse. They further agreed not to harm Americans locally or to trade with aliens. By and large the Crow were faithful subjects, and the eventual protection provided by the U.S. Army probably saved them from extinction at the hands of the Sioux.

Father Pierre-Jean DeSmet was the first Christian missionary to seek out the Crow. He visited them in 1840 and in 1842, being well received on both occasions. They were friendly and admired him, but he had no impact on their life-style. After hearing the tenets of Catholicism, one man responded that only two Crow men would not go to hell for killing, stealing, and other non-Christian behavior.

In 1851 the first Treaty of Laramie was negotiated; in it land in northern Wyoming, southern Montana, and western South Dakota was set aside for the Crow. By agreeing to the conditions of this treaty the Crow and other tribes involved were granted annuities, while the Federal Government obtained the right to build forts and roads in the region. The treaty was amended in 1852, limiting the annuities to ten years, but the Crow refused to sign the revision. They gradually abandoned the Big Horn Mountains under pressure from the Sioux, because the game was disappearing and because whites were moving into the area on their way to a gold strike in western Montana. The second Treaty of Laramie in 1868 confined the Crow to a reservation south of Yellowstone River in southern Montana; they have continued to live on a small portion of this area to the present.

Early Historic Life

ORIGIN MYTH   Once there was only water, and waterfowl alone lived on it. The only supernatural was the Sun, called Old Man or Old Man Coyote. He went to the waterfowl and told a large mallard that it was not good to be alone. He told the mallard to dive and try to retrieve some earth, but it failed. Two other species of duck also failed, and finally on the fourth try a grebe was able to bring up a little mud between its webbed feet. By starting in the east and traveling west Old Man Coyote spread the mud to make the earth. A wolf appeared on earth and then a coyote, and a person at a distance became transformed into tobacco, the only then-living plant. Old Man Coyote made people from mud and then created the mountains, trees, and hills.

APPEARANCE AND CLOTHING   To the Crow a handsome man was tall, had a straight nose, and a face free from blemishes or scars. The noble appearance and bearing of men attracted favorable comment from most early travelers. Men greased their long hair and sometimes made it even longer by gluing on additional human or horse hair. One great chief, Long Hair, was inordinately concerned about the length of his hair for supernatural reasons and grew it to about ten feet in length. Men plucked their whiskers, and both sexes apparently removed axillary hair. Strings of ornaments hung from the hair on each side of a man's head, and abalone shell earrings cut into angular designs were worn. Men painted their faces red, and yellow paint highlighted their eyelids. Bear claw and bone disk necklaces and bone pendants were popular. Men in general, and young men in particular, were fastidious about their appearance. Men wore hair-trimmed leggings held up by tucking the top ends

The Crow: Plains Warriors and Bison Hunters

into a belt. Other items of male clothing included a shirt, moccasins, and a bison robe.

Crow women were not pleasingly portrayed and were often reported as wearing dirty, greasy clothing. When they mourned the loss of a relative, which was often, their hair was cut short, and their faces were spotted with clay and dried blood from self-inflicted wounds. Dresses of deer or mountain sheep skins reached from the neck to mid-calf. The most distinctive characteristic of their dresses was that the fronts and backs were decorated with rows of elk teeth; openings on each side of a woman's dress were for nursing an infant. Women wore moccasins and leggings from their thighs to their knees. Young boys went naked until they were about nine and then wore the clothing of men; girls dressed in the manner of women.

SETTLEMENTS   The Crow had no permanent villages but moved from one campsite to the next in search of game. After so many people died from smallpox, most of the tribe camped together for protection against enemies. Camps were dominated by tepees in early historic times. A tepee was framed with about twenty poles, each some twenty-five feet in length, set in the form of a cone and covered with bison skins. A tepee of this size could accommodate about forty persons. An opening was left at the top as a smoke hole, and two external poles were attached to flaps at the top of the cover to open or close the smoke hole. Before the Crow had horses to carry tepee poles and covers, it appears that their dwellings were much smaller. There was a fireplace at the center of a tepee, and along the sides toward the back were hide mattresses beneath sleeping robes; the seat of honor was at the back and cen-

Plate 8–2 Lodge, after a painting by Catlin. (From Donaldson, 1886)

ter. Other structures of importance were circular arbors with conical roofs made from boughs used as sun shades. They also made small dome-shaped sweat lodges where men bathed by pouring water over heated stones. Sweatbaths were taken only in a ritual context.

When a band moved the caravan might be miles in length. Scouts were on the lookout for enemies, and hunters scattered in search of game. Men wore their best buckskin garments and carried their weapons in case of a sudden attack. Women rode astride horses as did men, and from the saddle of a wife's horse hung her husband's shield and sword if he owned one. Small children were tied to saddles, but five-year-olds rode alone. Meat, tools, utensils, and other property were packed in skin containers tied to horses. One horse carried a tepee cover and another dragged the poles. Some horses pulled pairs of tent poles with a frame attached to carry wounded or ill persons; this conveyance, a travois, was in earlier times pulled by dogs. The most important purpose of dogs appears to have been to warn of the approach of enemies or strangers.

HORSES   Wild horses lived in the North American Plains during the Pleistocene, but they disappeared about 8000 B.C., or perhaps in more recent times, possibly hunted to extinction by Indians. The domestic horses used by Indians in North and South America all were descendants of those introduced by Europeans in historic times. The Spanish took domestic horses to Mexico in A.D. 1519, and by the end of the century large herds of domestic and feral animals ranged over northern Mexico. Thus North American Indians did not begin to use domestic horses until the early 1500s. Horses possibly began to filter into the historic Crow area by 1730, and therefore these people only had access to horses for about seventy-five years before they began to be described in reasonable detail by whites.

Crow men, women, and children always were described as excellent riders who depended on horses so much that they were poor walkers. The saddles were high in the front and back but were not used for hunts or during war. Most horses could be guided without a bridle. A rider leaned in the direction in which he wanted to turn, and a horse turned in that direction until the rider sat upright.

Around 1850 a horse was worth from $60 to $100 and was the major form of wealth as well as the standard medium of exchange. In a proper marriage a groom presented horses to the brothers of the bride. In later times ten good arrows equaled a horse in value, and a woman skilled at preparing hides for a tepee cover might receive a horse for her labor. Personal conflicts in a camp, which usually involved women, might be settled with horses. If a man eloped with the wife of another, the offended husband took all his rival's horses; in doing so he not only had the support of his clan members but the backing of most persons in the camp. The offender kept the woman, and his clansmen gave the former husband horses to compensate for his loss, although eventual

The Crow: Plains Warriors and Bison Hunters

Plate 8–3 A man on horseback. (Courtesy, Field Museum of Natural History, Chicago)

repayment was expected. The same pattern prevailed if all a man's horses were stolen.

By the mid-1800s the Crow had more horses than any other tribe east of the Rocky Mountains. A poor person owned at least twenty animals, and a middle-aged man had up to sixty. The Crow received horses in trade from the Flathead and Nez Perce, but they more often were obtained during raids. The Blackfoot also had large herds, and mutual raids for horses led to the seizure of hundreds of animals a year and many skirmishes. Raids for Crow horses by the Blackfoot and other tribes, expecially the Sioux, meant that younger men spent a great deal of time guarding their horses. When an enemy raid was expected, the best horses were tethered at the entrance of their owner's tepees so that horse thieves could be pursued quickly at any time. Once it was realized that horses had been stolen Crow warriors gave pursuit, each riding his fastest horse and leading another. They rode day and night, and when the first horse was exhausted they rode the other; when it gave out they might continue on foot. If they caught up with the thieves they first attempted to recover their horses and then to kill and scalp an enemy if it was possible to do so without the threat of losing one of their number.

SUBSISTENCE ACTIVITIES   In the 1840s part of the Crow habitat was described by Denig (1961, 139) as "perhaps the best game country in the world." He reported immense herds of bison from the Rocky Mountains to the mouth of the Yellowstone River and herds of hundreds of elk along the river as well as many black-tailed and white-tailed deer. Antelope "covered" the prairies and badlands near the mountains, while in the mountains were many bighorn sheep and grizzly bears. The truly majestic Rocky Mountains, high valleys, fast-flowing streams and rivers, meadows, hot springs, and great forests characterized this idyllic land.

The Crow economy was based on hunting large game, expecially bison, deer, elk, and antelope; in fact they did not eat fish or berries. Except for the maize that they traded from the Hidatsa for a change in diet, the most important use of plant products was as seasoning for meat dishes. Cooperative hunts were the norm, and the purpose was to kill or maim herd animals by driving them over cliffs or riverbanks. Alternatively animals were driven into a valley with a single narrow exit, and a fence was erected after the animals were confined. To guide them into a trap the Crow sometimes built rock cairns in converging lines with persons stationed between the cairns to keep animals headed toward entrapment or their death. The planning and coordination required for large-scale hunts was under the supervision of the camp police, and to further insure success hunting rituals were performed.

The bow and arrow was the primary weapon for the hunt or for war. The wood-shafted arrows were tipped with points of bone or stone. Bows were fashioned from bison or mountain sheep horn or elk antler; pieces were cut, smoothed, spliced, glued, bound together, and then backed with sinew (composite, sinew-backed bow). Arrows were carried in skin quivers that were ornamented with porcupine quills.

A woman's life was physically demanding. She supplied the household with firewood and water, cooked the food, cared for children, collected plant products, and made and repaired all the clothing, skin containers, and tepee covers. Women were also responsible for erecting and taking down tepees. A woman groomed her husband, saddled his horse, and took off his leggings and moccasins in the evening. Women usually followed men on bison hunts and skinned the animals killed. One of the most highly developed skills of women was working skins. Depending on the skin involved, and the purpose served, hides or skins were dehaired, prepared on one or both sides, smoked or not smoked. To break down the texture of a skin and make it supple a skin was spread with a preparation made from bison brains and liver. In addition to processing bison hides for tepee covers and skins for clothing, women made small skin pouches for pipes and sacred objects. The best known rawhide container, termed a parfleche, was folded, often painted with designs, and was used primarily for storing and transporting dried meat or pemmican. Although other American Indians were skilled in basketry, pottery, weaving, and elaborate wood carving, the Crow did not practice these crafts.

For men camp life was as leisurely as it was busy for women. They made tools and equipment, but these were not time-demanding activities. Some men

The Crow: Plains Warriors and Bison Hunters

were part-time specialists in making bows or arrows. The major pursuits of men, hunting and fighting, usually took place at a distance from a campsite.

DESCENT, KINSHIP, AND MARRIAGE   Descent was traced through women (matrilineal) since each person was identified with the mother's clan (matriclan). Thus an individual was a member of the same clan as his or her mother, mother's sisters and brothers, mother's mother, mother's mother's brothers and sisters, and so on. The thirteen named Crow clans reported for both the Mountain and River Crow included Thick Lodge, Sore-Lip Lodge, Tied-in-a-Knot, and Bad War Honors. Clans in turn were grouped into two, or in one case three, units (phratries) that were not named; it may be that one of the two-clan clusters was in fact a single clan. It appears that in most instances a spouse was from any other clan (clan exogamy). Yet the bonds between some paired clans seem to have been so close that members could not marry each other (phratry exogamy). The residence pattern after marriage appears to have been temporarily matrilocal, and following the birth of a child the husband was free to set up an independent household.

The Crow kinship terminology is the type designated as "Crow"; the basic form is identical with that diagramed for the Pawnee in the previous chapter. The Crow termed father and father's brother alike and used a different word for mother's brother. Likewise father's sister was termed differently from mother and mother's sister, who were termed alike (bifurcate merging). Furthermore father's sisters' daughters, and their daughters' daughters were termed as father's sister; the term really designated women of the father's clan from his generation downward. The same logic applied when father's sister's husband was termed "father" as was his son. By ignoring generational distinctions in these contexts clansmen were made equivalents. In a like manner the "mother" term was extended to her clan sisters. The most rigid behavioral taboo was for a man to talk with or have any contact with his wife's mother or her grandmothers. Likewise a woman did not interact with her daughter's husband or her daughter's daughter's husband.

SOCIAL DIMENSIONS   The worst possible insult was for one Crow to say to another, "You are without relatives," meaning that the accused had no merit. Supportive relatives protected one from slander, came to one's defense in times of conflict with others, and provided material aid in times of stress. A matriclan was the largest integrated social unit, and one's obligations to it were great. Although members of the same clan do not appear to have camped adjacent to one another, they often ate together.

The bonds within a clan were most severely tested when a person from one clan killed someone from another clan. In these rare instances all the members of the murdered person's clan were obligated to kill either the offender or one of his clansmen. However, the matrilineal focus in Crow society should not be interpreted to mean that a father did not feel strong bonds of blood with his sons. In fact, as the ethnographer Robert H. Lowie (1935, 18) recorded, when someone asked a special favor a common phrase was "By the love you bear your children, I beg you."

Nearly every man belonged to a voluntary association (sodality) that played a major part in his social life. Young male relatives of recently deceased members or persons with outstanding achievements were actively recruited. Since intense rivalry prevailed among sodalities, a man usually belonged to only one. Among the Crow the best-known of these fraternal organizations were the Lumpwoods and Foxes. There were other functioning sodalities of importance in the early nineteenth century, but by the 1860s most men were members of one of these two groups. Each such tribal-wide organization had its own distinctive styles of adornments, dances, and behavioral character-istics, but the core activities were much the same.

Formerly the Lumpwoods were called the Half-shaved Heads. They re-ceived their prevailing name when a member counted coup with a knobbed club; thus Knobbed Sticks is a more proper designation for them than Lump-woods. In the fall after the first snow Lumpwood men met and ate in the tepees of one member and then another. The membership was distinguished partially on the basis of age grades, and officers served for one year. The four pairs of officers were called elders, straight staff bearers, hooked staff bearers, and rear men. Being offered a pipe and smoking it were symbolic of selection and acceptance of an office. Men often were reluctant to become staff bearers because after a straight shaft was planted in the ground by its bearer during a battle he could not retreat from the spot unless another Lumpwood rode be-tween him and the enemy. After a hooked staff had been placed in the ground, it could not be moved, and the bearer defended it until he was killed. The bearers of these staffs counted a double coup if they struck an enemy because of the danger involved.

Sodality members extended mutual aid to fellow members in stressful times; they sometimes fought together, and they honored a member killed in battle by excessive mourning. One Lumpwood behavioral peculiarity was that when a member mourned the loss of certain relatives the other Lumpwoods had the right to make jokes about the loss to his face. This behavior would have been very insulting for anyone else, irrespective of the circumstances.

The Foxes were organized much the same as the Lumpwoods, and com-petition between the two sodalities was keen. This was most dramatically expressed in the abduction of wives. In the spring either group could initiate the proceedings, and any man was free to abduct the wife of a member in the other fraternity if he had been her lover. Sometimes a woman was kidnapped without cause, and women sometimes hid to avoid abduction. A wife might also successfully plead with a potential abductor and not be taken away. Men who suspected that their wives would be abducted often made a point of being away during these times. Yet if they were present custom dictated that they should make no effective effort to prevent their wife's capture. These women were paraded about and were received as brides by their abductors' families. A stolen wife could not return to her husband; a man caught sleeping with such a woman was tied up and smeared with feces. This period of license lasted about two weeks, and then the Lumpwoods and Foxes went on the warpath, each attempting to count coup first so that they could ridicule their opposites. After the first snows fell the rivalry abated, only to surge again the next spring.

WARFARE   The Plains Indian stereotype is that of a bloodthirsty killer for whom war was by choice a dominant cultural focus. Yet as noted in the Pawnee chapter economic factors best account for the intensity of warfare on the Plains and Prairies. We find that the Crow rarely killed whites although they often had ample opportunity and just cause, especially to kill white trappers (Mountain Men) in their midst. This situation contrasted with the animosity between white trappers and the members of surrounding tribes. Furthermore when the Crow were at peace with another people they appear never to have initiated a new conflict. Their primary reason for launching a raid was to avenge the death of a Crow killed by the members of a tribe attacked. Unlike most Plains Indians the Crow killed men, but they usually captured women and children. The children were adopted and captive women worked beside Crow wives. An adopted boy who was raised as a Crow did not hesitate to kill men from the tribe of his birth. In rational terms, by not initiating a war and by assimilating captives the Crow compensated for their relatively small number and their losses in war. They went to war for what most often was a combination of three purposes: revenge, glory, and horses.

The word translated as "chief" really meant "good, valiant," and to achieve this title a man performed four feats: led a successful raid, captured tethered horses from an enemy camp, was the first to touch (count coup) an enemy, and took a bow or gun from a live enemy. Warriors who performed each of these deeds at least once were "chiefs," but this did not mean that they were political leaders. The greatest living chief in 1910 was Bell-rock; he had led at least eleven war parties, taken at least two tethered horses, counted coup six times, and seized five guns. Such a man boasted of his achievements at public gatherings, depicted his brave deeds on a robe that he wore, and had distinctive adornments on his clothing. To take a scalp was important but was not ranked as a major achievement, and when a man listed his war honors scalps were not mentioned.

The foremost weapon of war was the bow and arrow, but it soon was replaced by the gun. Spears sometimes were used, but they apparently were not very important. For close combat a war club with a stone head bound at one end of a wooden shaft prevailed. The shields men carried had a purpose more supernatural than practical, except in defensive circumstances. These circular pieces of bison hide might have bird skins, feathers, or animal tails hanging from them. Either a shield or its leather case was painted with symbols or

Plate 8–4 This is one of the finest Crow shields, and it was famous for its power. It belonged to the chief Arapooish and is said to represent the moon. Attached to the left side of the cover are the head and body of a crane. At the top right is an eagle feather and below it is a deer's tail. (Photograph courtesy of The Museum of the American Indian, Heye Foundation)

scenes revealed to its owner in a vision. Men also went forth with ornamental sticks used to count coup. These were tied together at intervals with skin strings ornamented with quills.

Ideally each youthful male longed to achieve personal honor in battle and believed that the greatest glory was achieved by dying young in warfare. Yet every effort was made to prevent the death of a Crow in combat, and a war party was never successful if it lost a single member. The fearless in battle were persons convinced of their invincibility on supernatural grounds or else reckless by nature. Still, the positive value placed on an early death was a recurrent theme in Crow childrearing. Typically a young man eagerly sought his first opportunity to join a party of raiders. As a novice he performed menial tasks such as carrying the meat supply and hauling water. He likewise was the butt of jokes as a part of his informal initiation into the life of warriors.

An attack was organized by a "raid planner," who usually achieved his position from a dream or vision that detailed the tribe for attack and the booty to be gained. An ambitious warrior not blessed with a personal vision could turn to a shaman and, by following the shaman's instructions, succeed. Some warriors might doubt an announced leader's abilities and decline to follow him, but recruiting a war party does not appear to have been difficult, especially for previously successful war leaders. Raiders typically set off on foot with a supply of moccasins often carried by dogs. As enemy territory was approached, the scouts were especially watchful. Once an enemy camp was sighted the war leader performed sacred bundle rituals. To further insure success, each participant attached sacred objects to his body and painted himself in an appropriate manner. One or two warriors were chosen to enter the enemy camp, usually late at night, and to drive off as many horses as possible without being discovered. They made their escape by riding the remainder of the night, all the next day, and the following night before relaxing. As they approached their home camp, they shot guns into the air and paraded the captured horses. The booty belonged to the leader of the raid, but he freely gave horses to the participants. These raids often were dangerous ventures. If a horse was not captured for each raider, some warriors were forced to return on foot and risked being overtaken by the pursuing enemy. Raiders sometimes went for days without food and rode so long and hard when attempting to escape that their "buttocks were worn out."

Plate 8-5 Dancers at Crow Agency, Montana, in 1889. (Photograph by May Sawyer Flood, courtesy of The Montana Historical Society)

Early Historic Life

As warriors the Crow were daring and merciless enemies. In open battles, especially if a number of Crow were killed, they slaughtered every man and then tortured the wounded to death. Hands and feet were cut off, eyes gouged out, and intestines exposed to be pierced with sharp sticks. The brains and hearts of the dead were hurled in the faces of the living while the victors scorned their victims. It should be added that in defeat Crow warriors suffered a similar fate.

A newly taken scalp was the focus of a three-day celebration. Warriors carrying their weapons, their faces painted black, and wearing their finest clothing danced in a partial circle to the accompaniment of drums and rattles. The scalp was carried on a pole, and the warrior who had made the kill mounted a horse and was led by a chief in the midst of the dancers. At night young men walked around the camp, and at each chief's tepee they sang songs about his particular accomplishments. During the next day the scalp was tied to the bridle of a horse on which a young man rode while beating a drum and singing. When many scalps were taken in a battle, the celebration was far more elaborate and sometimes included a reenactment of the conflict.

Denig reported that a Gros Ventre girl was captured by the Crow at about the age of ten and became a great chief. As a child she preferred the activities of boys, and her adopted father encouraged this behavior. She soon was playing with bows and arrows, riding fearlessly, and as a youth she was trusted to guard horses. As an adult she always wore women's clothing, and when her adopted father was killed she became the head of his household. Later in a raid against the Blackfoot she killed and scalped one enemy and counted coup over another. She came to be known as Woman Chief after she consistently distinguished herself in other raids. Before long she sat as an equal in the council of chiefs. Woman Chief deplored the idea of doing woman's work and obtained first one woman as a "wife" and then three more. Thus she lived as an honored person for twenty years until she tested a peace with the Gros Ventre and was killed by them after they discovered her origins.

When a man was killed by an enemy, everyone in the camp mourned as the body rested in state out-of-doors. The face of the corpse was painted, he was clothed in his best garments, and was especially honored by members of his military society. They cried and sang over the body as drums were beat. They pierced their limbs and bodies with arrows or cut themselves with knives. These men also distributed the dead man's property. Relatives took the body to a tree or scaffold for interment and wept. Their period of mourning did not end until a member of the enemy tribe that had killed him was murdered. Thus it was near relatives who most encouraged warriors to avenge deaths.

POLITICAL LIFE   Control of the day-to-day social unit or band was in the hands of a man who had performed each of the four honored deeds in war

The Crow: Plains Warriors and Bison Hunters

and had demonstrated the qualities of a leader. His authority expanded further if he was generous with booty, a shaman of note, and an able narrator of tales. Thus individual achievement, open to nearly all, was the avenue to honor and prestige in a political context. Tacit agreement determined who was to be band chief, and there was no formal installation ceremony. A band chief decided when a campsite was to be abandoned, where to move, and the placement of tepees. Yet he had little control over people since he neither judged or punished in a manner often associated with chiefly powers. It appears that as long as the people who camped together enjoyed good fortune, their chief retained his office. When he failed he was replaced quietly and informally. One of his most important duties was to appoint the members of a particular military society to take charge of the spring bison hunt. At larger camps the chief appointed an outstanding man as a crier; his duty was to ride among the tepees repeatedly making announcements about matters of public interest and making the chief's opinions known about matters of current concern.

Within a camp or band of the Mountain or River Crow members of the thirteen clans formed the largest political entities. They dealt with each other as equals, and they recognized no superior authority to which they all were responsible. Feuds between clans were the greatest threat, but intermediaries attempted to settle conflicts as quickly as possible before they became emotionally charged and out of hand. Language, culture, and common social norms unified clans. Crow survival was partially contingent on cooperation among clans for common good. If a segment of a clan separated from the main body, it could muster comparatively few warriors and would be destroyed by enemies. The tranquillity of camp life in tribal tradition was upset the most when an aggressive person with a small number of related followers dominated. This especially was true of a person who was regarded as having powerful supernatural guardians. Such individuals might seize the horses or wives of others, but, as Lowie pointed out, such a man was a *de facto* but never a *de jure* leader.

The members of the military society policing a bison hunt could and did severely punish nonconformity. The worst offense was for men to hunt bison alone or in small groups because they scattered the herds and made it difficult for others to kill bison on the legitimate communal hunts. Likewise on a group hunt if a man broke and charged a herd prematurely, he might scatter the animals and ruin the opportunities of others. These nonconformists might be whipped, their weapons destroyed, and the kill seized. The warrior society in charge also had the right to prevent raiding parties from setting forth at inopportune times, and they attempted to settle differences between the people in camp peacefully, especially when a feud threatened to erupt between clans. Disagreements between members of different clans may have been reasonably common, but for one Crow to kill another was almost unknown. Any crime, except murder, could be compensated for with an exchange of property.

When the Crow split into two major bands, the River and the Mountain, it was Arapooish (Arapoosh, Sore-belly, Rotten-belly) who led the River Crow. A brief sketch of his life illustrates the qualities of leadership that he possessed. Arapooish was a retiring and even surly person who said little but spoke in an authoritarian manner. As a relatively retiring shaman he controlled powerful supernatural forces, and he apparently had many wealthy clansmen. He was fearless in battle. Time and again he successfully raided horses from enemies without any loss of Crow life. He saw to it that the Crow always were on the alert for enemies, and raiders who approached were killed. Arapooish was a confident aggressor and able tactician in the large battles that he planned. In a battle against the Cheyenne more than 1000 horses were captured, 200 Cheyenne men killed, and 270 women and children captured; the Crow lost five men. But he was a man possessed, and he courted certain death when he charged a Blackfoot fortification in 1834 shouting "One last stroke for the Crow Nation" (Denig, 1961, 183) and was killed. Arapooish came to be known as *The* Chief.

RELIGION   The individual basis for supernaturalism centered about a highly personal rapport with a guardian spirit. An unsought spirit aid might reveal itself, but far more often it was gained in a vision quest. All personal glory, power, and wealth ultimately were attributed to valid visions. Thus religion among the Crow did not form a coherent system of beliefs with accompanying dogma that impinged on the course of daily life. In Crow linguistic expression a vision or a dream of supernatural portent were the same. A youthful male sought a personal spirit aid as he began to emerge into the world of adults. If he was fully successful, he might seek no other vision later in life. Were he to do so it usually was to cure a sick child or in an extraordinary quest for vengeance.

A vision seeker sometimes, or perhaps most often, first purified himself by taking a sweatbath. Stones were heated in a fire near a small dome-shaped and skin-covered bathhouse. The stones were taken inside where water was sprinkled on them to produce steam that was an offering to the Sun. In ideal circumstances he next went to a mountaintop where he fasted, drank no water, and wailed. Lightly clad and covered only with a robe at night he slept until the Sun began to rise. The seeker then chopped off the final joint of his left forefinger, placed it on a buffalo chip, and held it up as an offering to the rising Sun with an accompanying prayer for glory and success in life. As the blood flowed he fainted and was unconscious until evening, but he could not sleep in the cold of night. Three nights passed, and on the fourth one he could not sleep until late because of the cold. With sleep came a vision.

Alternative ways prevailed for obtaining a vision. One man might have another cut slits in his chest or back through which one end of a thong was passed, the opposite end being tied to a pole. The aspirant ran around the pole until he tired; he rested, only to run again and again. He might or might not tear the thong free in his quest. Another means to the same end was to have

Plate 8–6 A man in ceremonial costume smoking a pipe. (Courtesy, Field Museum of Natural History, Chicago)

one's back pierced with two holes and a thong tied from them to a bison skull that was dragged about in the first stage of the search for power.

A supernatural visitant might assume the form of an animal such as a bear or bison, a bird, an insect, the earth, moon, or stars. A person could be blessed by association with more than one such power, and literally anything might be revered by an individual. The Sun was the supernatural to whom a direct appeal was made, but it rarely was the actual source of power received; thus it was not a god worshipped in the usual sense. The supplicant might be taught a sacred song, learn of a symbol that could be represented graphically, or be instructed to follow certain taboos. A feather, stone with a strange shape, braided rope, or weasel skin, among other forms, symbolized the receiver's power and formed the core of a sacred (medicine) bundle. A bundle and its power could be transferred to a near relative after proper instruction and even purchased by a nonrelative; thus the control of supernatural forces could pass from one generation to the next. The degree to which any particular bundle was revered depended directly on the fortunes of its possessors.

TOBACCO SOCIETY   In this as in other ceremonial societies purification in a sweatbath was a prelude to rituals, smoking tobacco always was important, incense was burned, and songs were repeated four times. Tobacco had great supernatural power and symbolized Crow tribal identity. The seeds of sacred tobacco reportedly were from the originally cultivated strain, and it was thought that the Crow would endure only as long as they continued to plant these seeds. Furthermore tobacco ceremonialism contributed directly to year-to-year prosperity because the planters had the power to influence events in the natural world, such as warding off disease and renewing the supply of game. The role of Tobacco Planter was hereditary although a person could purchase the right and be adopted into the Tobacco Society. The ritual included fasting and abstaining from water for days and then having one's arms and chest cut and burned to produce wounds that healed slowly and left deep scars. In exchange for the honor of receiving sacred tobacco seeds a Tobacco Planter gave up all his worldly goods.

Tobacco ritually was sown near the end of April at one of a number of plots where everyone had assembled. About half an acre was cleared to the accompaniment of beating drums and songs. The following day the ground was broken with hoes made from bison shoulder blades. The third day everyone collected wood, but the first person to return with a load was a woman who never had committed adultery. Such a person once was so difficult to find that they nearly abandoned this ritual. A man who had never had illicit sexual relations brought in the second load of wood, and then everyone else did the same. The wood was smoked over, spread on the garden, and burned; the plot was hoed again and leveled with willow branches. Finally the seeds were sown and covered.

The next step in the Tobacco Ceremony was to build a huge tepee that would hold up to about 300 people. The interior was decorated with cloth streamers adorned with beads and other ornaments. Here people ate and danced to the accompaniment of bells, drums, rattles, and whistles in deafening combination. A few persons cut their arms and bodies and danced to exhaustion. These ceremonies spanned three days, and when they were over the people moved camp only a short distance each day to indicate that they reluctantly were leaving their sacred tobacco plants. Everyone was anxious for rain to germinate the seeds, and a person in the Tobacco Society was placed in charge of rainmaking. He was given as much as $3000 worth of property by people as sacrifices to the rain clouds. With the gifts hanging from nearby bushes the rainmaker smoked and prayed for rain. If he was successful all the gifts were his and he gained great fame. If he failed he blamed people for not fulfilling their vows. In late August the people returned to the tobacco plot, harvested the crop, and collected seeds.

Tobacco was smoked only by men. The most important times were when making peace with other tribes, during rituals, or by shamans in curing severe illness. Even when it was smoked on less ceremonious occasions the first puffs were dedicated to the earth, heavens, spirits, and the Sun. Each man present took only four puffs and then passed the pipe on to the person on his left because this was the direction in which the sun moved. Furthermore each man had personal smoking habits. One man would not smoke if a pipe had touched grass, another would not smoke if women were present, and another must empty his pipe on bison dung. These details were dictated by individual relationships with guardian spirits.

Subgroups of the Tobacco Society emerged from time to time on the basis of individual revelations, but the chapters did not overtly compete with one another. In the latter half of the nineteenth century these included Elk, Otter, Weasel, and White Bird in addition to Tobacco. The Crow termed all of these groups in the same manner as the military sodalities discussed previously, but the Tobacco Society chapters seem to have had more clearly sacred charters. Apart from planting sacred tobacco seeds the most important ceremony was the initiation of new members, which was regarded as a form of adoption. Before initiation a novice was instructed in the rites and rituals of the group and then formally presented to it. A married couple usually was inducted together, and membership normally was for life. Another means of induction was for a man with a sick child to pledge it to membership, or himself to become a member, if the child recovered.

SUN DANCE   The Sun as a powerful if remote supernatural was the focal point of the most sacred Crow ceremony. A man pledged that he would hold a Sun Dance in return for obtaining a special vision that revealed how to avenge the killing of a relative. The commitment was so great that an elderly person might have witnessed only about six performances. The person making the pledge was called a Whistler, and he sought out a shaman who owned at least one sacred doll. These small wooden or skin-covered figures had painted features, Morning Star designs, and feathers attached to them; they also were used to bring war parties success. A doll served as the vehicle through which the Whistler obtained his vision. The shaman and Whistler were the central actors in a great ceremony that attracted all the tribe. As the preparations began the Whistler fasted and became haggard in appearance. Bison tongues were collected as special food for each noonday meal during the ceremony. A special kilt was made for the Whistler, and after many preliminaries involving incense and smoking a special lodge was built a few miles away. The Whistler, painted with cross-shaped designs symbolizing the Morning Star, blew a whistle and danced slowly toward the lodge while holding a wooden hoop with the doll figure representing the Sun attached at the center. He tied the doll to a lodge pole at eye level. At the same time other men who sought visions had their bodies daubed with white clay and slits cut in their chest or back to receive skewers tied to lines attached to lodge poles. Each man pulled against his skewer until it ripped free. The Whistler neither ate nor drank water after entering the lodge; here he gazed at the doll and danced before it as one chief and then another described his deeds of valor and acted out his moments of glory. The Whistler, who was not skewered, slept at the lodge, and a sham battle was fought the next day as the Whistler danced on. His performances might extend over days until he finally received a vision that he usually did not reveal. At this point the ceremony ended, and the Whistler sought out the enemy.

SHAMANS   Physical disabilities and death usually were attributed to supernatural causes such as breaking taboos or by ghosts. One category of practitioners depended primarily on secular knowledge. They used plant products, lanced a swollen part of the body, or applied a poultice as ordinary treatments. A particular root that was considered a cure-all was rubbed on sores, placed on an aching tooth, or chewed and swallowed to cure a cold. The botanical pharmacopoeia was extensive and most often appears to have been secular in application. Other curers, more properly shamans, had the ability to treat specific traumas because of revelations in visions. Included were cures for snake or spider bites, wounds, or disease caused by a foreign object in a patient's body. Shamans were very adept at sleight of hand; they appeared to transform bark into meat or change mud balls into beads in either public or private performances. Competitive exhibits of their skills often were dramatic contests. These were men who had the most powerful guardian spirits, and it was primarily in this respect that shamans stood apart from persons who had less potent spirit aids.

Sorcery sometimes was practiced by ordinary persons to settle grudges against other Crow by supernatural means, but it appears to have been relatively uncommon. One technique was to draw the figure of an antagonist along a riverbank near the water's edge. Incense was burned and smoke blown toward the figure. As the water washed the drawing away, the victim was expected to die. Other magical practices led to lifelong disabilities. The only sure safeguard against sorcery was for the victim to have more powerful supernaturals working in his behalf.

LIFE CYCLE   As the time for a birth approached, the husband, other men, and boys were excluded from a tepee, and the woman was aided by a male or female specialist who was well paid. The woman knelt over padding and grasped two sticks. To hasten delivery she might be given potions or her back might be rubbed with a special preparation. The particular aid used depended on the techniques that the birth specialist had learned in a vision or had obtained by purchase from someone else. A woman present at the delivery cut the umbilical cord, and part of it was encased in a container that hung from the cradleboard of a baby girl and later from the back of her dress. The

278
The Crow: Plains Warriors and Bison Hunters

new mother observed food and behavioral taboos for a brief period, but the father's activities were not restricted. Within a few days and without ceremony, a neonate's ears were pierced with a hot awl; the holes were held open with small greased sticks until earrings could be inserted. Offspring were placed in cradleboards and rocked to sleep with lullabies. The parents of a small child who cried often placed him on his back and poured water down his nose. When the child cried at a later time, they said, "Bring the water!" which usually was enough to quiet him.

A few days after a birth an infant was named, but names were neither clan or sex specific. A name most often was bestowed by a noted warrior at the request of the father. The name chosen was based on some outstanding personal achievement of the namer in warfare or on a visionary experience. Thus a woman might be named Captures-the-Medicine-Pipe or a boy His-Coups-are-Dangerous. For this service the namer often was presented a horse. As a name was given the infant was raised into the air four times, each time higher than the last. Women only changed their names when someone with a like name died, but this was not the case for men. They assumed a new name to commemorate a brave deed, or to improve their fortune. However, nicknames might be more commonly used than formal names, and they often were bestowed on the basis of unusual behavior. One woman pretended to be sleeping with a man, but after it was discovered that the "man" was in fact a hide container, she was called Lying-with-a-Dry-Hide. A man who took an old dog to carry his moccasins on the war path came to be called Old Dog as a result.

Adults placed few constraints on the behavior of children. They interrupted the conversations of adults, even at formal meetings, and typically children were both forward and self-confident. Boys were especially boundless in their freedom. Denig (1961, 154) wrote, "the greatest nuisance in creation is Crow children, boys from the ages of 9 to 14 years. These are left to do just as they please. They torment their parents and everyone else, do all kinds of mischief without either correction or reprimand." Boys swam and played water games, hurled sticks at each other with the ends covered with mud or mud and live coals. Individually or in teams they shot at targets with arrows, and the arrows were stakes for the winner. In the winter boys coasted down hills on toboggans made by covering bison rib frames with rawhide. Every youthful male ate part of a raw grizzly bear heart to bring him strength and a clear head in times of trouble. Thus he could say "I have the heart of a grizzly" in the face of adversity. When meat was plentiful in a camp, boys might cover themselves with mud so that they could not be identified and run into camp where meat was hanging to steal as much as possible before they were chased by old women. The thieves cooked the meat away from camp, and the boy who had stolen the best piece ate the choice parts first. Boys hunted small game, and after a bison hunt of the men, they might ride out to kill the calves, bringing home the meat and giving the skins to girls for tepee covers. A pair of boys sometimes became close friends, and the bond could extend into adult life when they fought together and shared the same woman, either a wife or mistress; these men referred to each other as "little father" and were closer than with any other persons.

At about the age of ten, boys and girls began imitating the camp life of adults, an activity called "calf-skin tepee." Girls from affluent families had small tepees that they set up at a distance from the camps of their parents. Boys pretended to be their husbands and took food from their families for their "wives." The boys organized themselves in the manner of men, even to the point of kidnapping girls belonging to another group. When the boys killed a coyote or wolf, they returned in triumph with a piece of the pelt as a "scalp," and the girls danced with it in imitation of women dancing with scalps obtained by warriors.

Puberty went unacknowledged for males and females alike although when a girl or woman menstruated she was prohibited from approaching sacred objects and avoided a wounded man or men preparing for a war party; most persons denied that women were isolated physically during menstruation. Girls appear often to have married before they reached puberty, and while marriage to a person in one's own clan was forbidden (clan exogamy), it also was considered in bad taste, at least in the eyes of some persons, to seek a spouse from the clan of one's father. To marry someone from a father's clan with whom no blood ties could be traced was acceptable although not desirable.

Marital arrangements varied although the parents of a girl often seem to have had some influence, if only because a daughter was so young when she married. A man might meet a girl while she was alone and propose that they elope and offer her a horse for going off with him. A couple could summarily announce that they were going to live together or a man might seek the aid of a go-between to make the arrangements. Young men seldom hunted before they married. They slept late and spent most of the day grooming themselves to show off on their horses. They courted girls with flute music and sometimes did not return home until daylight.

The most proper marriage proposal, especially for a woman of virtue, was for a man to offer horses to the girl's brother and meat to her mother; these arrangements produced the most lasting marriages. A man who had offered wealth for his bride had the right to claim her younger sister in marriage (sororal polygyny), and the girls' parents were likely to agree when the first daughter was well cared for. In the early 1800s perhaps half of the men had more than one wife, and apparently a few men had as many as twelve. They did not all live together, and some might simply have been betrothed to him. A woman could marry her deceased husband's brother (levirate), but she would not be forced into the union.

Crow sex life was free and open, especially for men, but women were far from pawns. Men and women alike might have many love affairs and made little or no effort to conceal their feelings and sexual activities; their philandering ways often were noted. When a married woman took offense at the affairs

The Crow: Plains Warriors and Bison Hunters

of her husband, she might hold him up to ridicule in songs about his behavior. Men and women alike hurled "a fine variety of beautiful epithets" at each other according to Denig (1961, 151) and other observers. A woman could leave her husband and take her children as well as her property, including horses, skins, and the tepee, with her; boys not fully dependent on their mother joined their father. Yet after a couple had separated, irrespective of the reason, they could not live together again without bringing disgrace on them both. As noted previously, during a particular time each year a Fox or Lumpwood could abduct and marry a man's wife if she previously had slept with him. If he did seize her the woman could not return to her husband. Divorce was common except for virtuous women and could be initiated by either partner. Just as a marriage was without ceremony so was a divorce. Men were expected to be unfaithful to their wives; in fact for a man to keep the same wife for many years was unmanly and a source of ridicule. Yet some men were jealous of their wives to the point of always taking a favorite wife along on a hunt, and strongly resenting it when she committed adultery.

Male transvestites, or berdaches, were reasonably common among the Crow and were not regarded as abnormal, but as a third sex. According to Denig some boys preferred the company of girls in their preadolescence and eventually were dressed as girls by their parents. They then embarked on a lifetime of female activities and might "marry" a man.

The hand game was a very popular form of entertainment, with garments and beadwork commonly bet on the outcome. To the accompaniment of beating drums and songs a pair of male or female players participated. One person held an elk tooth or bone gaming piece in one hand and gestured wildly as the piece was switched from hand to hand. If the guesser failed to identify the hand that held the piece, a tally stick was lost; the person who obtained all the tally sticks, three or ten in number, was the winner. Women also played dice games for stakes. One game involved the use of six dice that were marked on one side and plain on the opposite face. They were placed in a wooden bowl and shaken. The game was scored with tally sticks according to the combination of plain or marked dice facing up. A popular game, called shinny or stickball, was played by women in the spring. The object was for the members of two teams to drive a ball to opposite goals by using curve-ended sticks. Another widespread game played by men was hoop-throwing, and they bet on the outcome. The object was to throw a dart through a rolling hoop that might have webbing in the middle. The man whose dart entered the hoop or was nearest to it won a tally stick.

When someone died the body was painted, clothed in fine garments, and shrouded in part of a tepee cover. The spirit was told not to turn back and the body removed under a side of the tepee to prevent further deaths in the household. Interment was either in the crotch of a tree or in a scaffold above four support poles. After the body had decayed the bones sometimes were removed and placed in a crevice of rocks. Mourners from the immediate family pulled out their hair or cut it short, slashed themselves with knives, and often cut off finger joints. The practice of removing a finger joint was so common that scarcely a person had complete hands. However men usually did not mutilate their thumbs or the fingers used to draw a bow or shoot a gun. The soul of a person first lingered near the corpse and might give out an owl-like cry, but it later went to the camp of the dead. The Crow had little interest in the fate of souls; although ghosts might return to harm the living, they could also be a source of helpful visions.

The expectation in this matrilineal society was for material property to be inherited along the female line, going to brothers, sisters, and their heirs rather than to a man's sons. But a dying man's request to pass his property to nonclan members was honored. A man could bequeath horses to his wife or sacred objects to an eldest son. Even when inheritance was not along the maternal line it usually was to an immediate family member.

Recent Historic Changes

THE RESERVATION   Effective Federal control over the Crow began with the second Treaty of Laramie in 1868. In this treaty a clearly defined reservation was established, and the first Crow agency was built at Mission Creek near the modern town of Livingston, Montana. It was moved to Absaroka in 1875 and then to Crow Agency in 1884. From the beginning of the reservation period the Federal goal was to destroy the traditional basis for Crow life. Christian church services were to replace heathen ceremonies, the people were to wear "civilized" clothing and live in log cabins, the men were to become farmers, and children were forced to attend school. Furthermore, Indian agents were always powerful, and they often were corrupt.

Diverse circumstances combined to the detriment of Crow prosperity. Foremost was the abrupt decline of bison in the Yellowstone Valley. From 1879 to 1882 some 250,000 bison hides were obtained there; in 1882–1883 the harvest was 45,000 skins, but after 1883 bison had virtually disappeared. Most animals were killed by white hunters, who took the hides, tongues, and only a little meat. For many whites the slaughter was worthwhile to make way for cattle. Thus the economic basis for Crow life diappeared almost overnight. The most immediate result was to make the people highly dependent on Indian agents to obtain food and goods promised by treaty and badly needed for survival. But these agents often cheated the people and most adequately provided food to Indians willing to accept Federal policies, which was in direct defiance of treaty arrangements. Frequent Sioux raids contributed to Crow desperation until 1876 when these conflicts had nearly ceased. Whiskey traders operated just outside the reservation border and were a further cause of trial and trauma. The impact of the Homestead Act of 1862 began to be felt in the 1870s as whites surged into Montana Territory. These newcomers re-

The Crow: Plains Warriors and Bison Hunters

Plate 8–7 School boys and girls. From left to right: ?, ?, Russell White Bear, Henry Shin Bone, Annie Wesley, Addie Bear in the Middle, Fanny Butterfly, Kitty Deer Nose. (Courtesy of The Montana Historical Society)

sented the fact that eight million acres of land was for the Crow and pressured the Federal Government to reduce the size of the reservation; they were successful in 1882, 1891, and again in 1904. Efforts from 1910 to 1919 to have Congress withdraw even more Crow land from the reservation failed. Whites insisted that the Indians did not utilize the land effectively—a dominant theme in frontier history—and Congress responded by liberalizing the lease laws. With grants of land to railroads and for a dam the Crow holdings declined to about two million acres by 1968.

DISAPPEARANCE OF BISON   After the disappearance of bison in the early 1880s, life lost much of its meaning for the Crow. Perhaps the greatest trauma was psychological. With the reason for moving about gone and enemies as no longer a major threat, the people had very little to occupy their time; boredom and idleness dominated reservation life. Farming was proposed as a new economic base, but the first politically appointed agents usually knew little about either Indians or farming. The monetary rewards offered people to farm went begging, and during the early reservation years only agency employees planted crops. The most appealing work for men was to serve as scouts for the U.S. Army. In time, however, some Indians turned to agriculture, and one of the first to do so was the great chief Plenty Coups. His example encouraged others because he faced the white world in a painfully realistic manner. Indian agents made great efforts to have the Crow abandon their tepees and live in log cabins. Even when houses were built for them many people preferred to camp in nearby tepees. The cultural geographer John W. Stafford (1972, 132) summarized the prevailing white attitudes in terms of

Plate 8–8 A Crow camp. (Courtesy, Field Museum of Natural History, Chicago)

"good" and "bad" Indians. "The idea of a good Indian was nurtured. To the 'good' Indian who cooperated by cutting his hair, sent his children to school, and took up farming were given special monetary rewards, wagons, and cattle. Other 'good' Indians were given jobs in the agency. Leaders who cooperated were flattered with trips to Washington. On the other hand 'bad' Indians were threatened with loss of rations."

For the Crow as well as other Indians the Dawes Act of 1887 attempted to make them farmers and to destroy tribal life by treating each family individually. The head of a Crow household was forced to accept a 160 acre land allotment, but most people still did not recognize farming as a legitimate occupation. As soon as they could, many persons leased or sold their allotments to whites. A revised Allotment Act of 1920 increased the size of the Crow holdings to about 1000 acres per person, of which 320 acres could not be alienated for twenty-five years. Crow declared "competent" could sell their remaining 680 acres, and many did so as soon as it was legally possible. As a result white and Indian lands form a checkerboard on the reservation. Over the years even those Crow who attempted to keep their land were faced with one problem above all others. As land was inherited the plots were divided time and again.

Modern Life

Surprisingly little has been published by anthropologists about the Crow of recent decades. The impression gained is that significant aspects of traditional life have continued to flourish. Sacred bundles continued to be regarded as sources of power, but a traditional Sun Dance had not been held since about 1875, and sweatbaths were more often taken for pleasure than for purity. The military societies apparently had disappeared and men could not

The Crow: Plains Warriors and Bison Hunters

recall the names of some sodalities. The Tobacco Society and its daughter chapters continued to function; plots of sacred tobacco were planted with accompanying ceremonies and new members were adopted.

SUN DANCE   Fred Voget provides excellent documentation for tradition, change, and reintegration for the early 1940s in an account about the introduction of the Wind River Shoshoni Sun Dance to the Crow. A biographical sketch of one of the principals, William Big-Day, born in 1891, is revealing. He lived in the Pryor area, the most isolated sector of the Crow Reservation with the most conservative population. As a youth he frequently was ill and seldom attended school or had meaningful contacts with whites. He was baptized a Roman Catholic but was forced to leave the church as he began participating in peyote rituals when he was about thirty-five. Like many other Crow he felt that Christianity imposed unreasonable restrictions on a person's life. When he was about nineteen, he began to dream that he should fast and seek a vision in the mountains to gain success and wealth. He did not do so until he was about forty when he sought power to cure illness in himself and others. His first attempt failed, and the second time, some four years later, he was only partially successful. Big-Day subsequently dreamed of hearing songs that made people happy. A short time later he attended a Shoshoni

Plate 8–9 A chief at the Fourth of July celebrations in 1894.
(Courtesy of The Montana Historical Society)

Plate 8–10 Drummers at a ceremonial dance on July 3, 1925.
(Courtesy of The Montana Historical Society)

Sun Dance where he heard the songs of his dreams and was flabbergasted.
The next year he participated in the dance and was also cured of a chest pain
by John Truhujo, the man of Shoshoni and Mexican ancestry who led the
dance. This convinced Big-Day of the power of the Shoshoni Sun Dance.
When his adopted son was desperately ill during the winter of 1939, Big-Day
held the boy up to the Sun and pledged to participate in a Sun Dance if the
child recovered. When this came to pass he kept his pledge. The next year his
brother's child was ill, and Big-Day vowed to hold a Sun Dance among the
Crow if the child recovered. When this child was well a dance was held in
1941 with the assistance of John Truhujo. In 1943 another Crow held a Sun
Dance to help insure the safe return of his warrior sons fighting in World War
II, and still others held additional dances.

William Big-Day and others who were key personalities in the introduction of this form of Sun Dance among the Crow shared a number of critical
characteristics. Each had either rejected or abandoned the economic life of
whites and subsisted on income from land leases and odd jobs. In the modified
and yet traditional economic system the only way to increase one's wealth was
through shamanism, but the practitioners of old had all died. Big-Day and
another Sun Dance leader had little faith in Western medicine, which was no
small consideration, and they were discriminated against by whites, which
made it very difficult to succeed in white terms. Then too these leaders had
been expelled from Christian churches. Each rejected the white American

The Crow: Plains Warriors and Bison Hunters

value system, and Big-Day sought to develop a new religion that would "bring a new life to the Indian" (Voget, 1948, 646). Thus this was an embryonic nativistic movement.

LAND PROBLEMS   Much of the information about the early reservation era was drawn from a study by the geographer John W. Stafford. His work is also an important source for what happened from 1934 to the early 1970s. Perhaps the most striking recent trend noted by Stafford has been the rapid growth in Crow population. An all-time low of about 1625 was reached in the early 1930s, but with increased health care beginning around this time their number increased rapidly and soon was doubling each generation. By 1942 the reservation population was about 2100, and in 1969 the figure was 3500, a 66 percent increase. This growth rate of 2 percent a year is nearly double that of the United States in general. Furthermore, in 1942 about 250 people worked and lived off of the reservation, and this number increased to about 1500 by 1968. Some of these Crow are well established elsewhere, but others came and went with the job opportunities. Thus the expectation is that in difficult economic times the reservation population expands significantly, leading to increased stress in finding local employment.

Equally notable has been the recent decrease in the reservation land base. Since 1953 the amount of allotted trust land has been reduced to about 380,000 acres, a decline of about 22 percent. By 1961 nearly a third of all reservation land had been sold to whites, and much of the remaining land had little water for grazing stock or for farming. The Federal Government recently initiated the policy of prohibiting the sale of reservation land to whites, and between 1961 and 1968 the Crow tribe bought about 55,000 acres that previously would have been purchased by whites.

The lease of reservation lands to whites for grazing cattle and later for farming has been a significant source of income as well as a serious problem. The first lease was to the U.S. Army in 1882 for grazing cattle, and to increase food production during World War I thousands of acres were leased to whites for raising wheat. The Crow Allotment Act of 1920 permitted "competent" Indians to lease or sell their lands. Those who leased often were persuaded by whites to sign leases at very low rates, and some of these whites became wealthy. Revisions in the leasing laws consistently have favored whites, and the only condition beneficial to the Indians is that most leases are short-term. Few Crow were ever willing to become farmers, and since they did not usually have the resources to raise stock on a large scale, lease arrangements were appealing. By 1962 most land allotments, about 90 percent, were leased to whites for grazing cattle or for farming. The Crow know full well that leases are profitable to whites at Indian expense, but there is little that they can do about the situation. For example, when a white owns land along a stream and a Crow owns adjacent land without water, the Indian's holdings are of little value because there is no access to water. However, for the white with water leasing Indian land at a very low rate can be very profitable. The same applies to small, scattered parcels of Indian-owned land. They cannot be utilized effectively by the Indians and again may be leased at very low rates. A significant reason for continuing leases as a major source of income is that the pattern is well established.

The allotment process was a gross intrusion on the integrity of the Crow tribe—as it was meant to be—but the problems it created for later generations were and are nearly overwhelming. A serious difficulty stems from the failure of the Federal Government to make reasonable allowance for births, deaths, and population growth. No land was set aside, as in some Canadian treaties, for future generations. An extreme case will illustrate the magnitude of the problem. One 160 acre allotment made in 1887 passed to 245 heirs before 1967 when it was consolidated into 86 claims. Of these the largest was for about 11 acres, and the smallest was for 0.0014 acre! The land was not physically divided, but all the heirs held an interest in it and shared any income derived from it. Most land with many owners was leased by the B.I.A., and annual payments were made to the heirs. The yearly profit for the person owning the 0.0014 acre mentioned above would be less than a cent if the rent rate was $.50 per acre. The same conditions prevail for leasing dry farm land or the small amounts of irrigated land.

It might seem as though cattle ranching could serve as a sound economic base for many Crow, but this is not the case. Over the years diverse efforts were made to encourage ranching, but in 1968 only 9 percent of the reservation families raised cattle and the herds usually were quite small. A successful rancher required not only a block of grazing land but also a large capital investment and knowledge about raising and marketing cattle. Again farming had little potential because in 1968 only about 13 percent of the trust land was suitable for dry farming and less than 2 percent could be irrigated. This is one good reason why the Crow have been reluctant to become farmers. The sale of land to whites, Crow biases against farming, and their acceptance of leasing arrangements or wage labor employment are additional factors. It appears that since 1953 fewer than fifty Crow have farmed or ranched. Stafford compared Crow land use with that on the nearby Blackfoot, Cheyenne, and Sioux-Assiniboin reservations and found that these tribes were more successful farmers. He concluded that the major difference was the far less rigid control by the B.I.A. of Crow leases than for those of the other tribes.

Most local opportunities for wage labor were in farming or ranching for whites. The B.I.A. and the U.S. Public Health Service employed about 130 people in 1969, and about 100 persons found seasonal work in commercial sugar beet operations. Local jobs in construction were also important, but the seasonal unemployment rate was as much as 45 percent or more. In 1966 an industrial park was built at Crow Agency with Federal funds and money received in land settlements with the Federal Government. Among the firms established there was a carpet mill that employed seventy-five people in 1967,

The Crow: Plains Warriors and Bison Hunters

all but five of whom were Crow. Other small factories were not very stable nor did they employ many people.

Recently, money received from land claims against the Federal Government has become an important source of development capital. The Crow began their first suit in 1904, and in 1961 they were finally awarded a settlement of 10.2 million dollars. About 4.3 million dollars went into the Family Plan Program. Each single person or family head submitted a plan describing how he would spend $1000. Plans were approved if the money was to go for capital improvements, such as for housing, wells, and pumps, or special needs such as education. Most other money from the settlement went to industrial development, land purchase, and a loan program.

The Crow now are engaged in yet another struggle for survival, this time over coal. The reservation contains about 17 billion tons of low sulfur coal, about a fourth of which can profitably be strip mined under prevailing economic conditions. The B.I.A. and Department of the Interior approved leases and prospecting permits for about 235,000 acres of Crow land. Tribal Council approval was not granted although the six-man Oil and Gas Committee did approve. The royalty rate was 17½ cents per ton and $1. per acre for several years. When questions began to be asked about these leases it turned out that, among other things, an environmental impact study had not been made. The B.I.A. maintained that it was not necessary on Indian lands and did not begin to make a study until forced to do so by the courts. Furthermore, many leases were for larger areas than permitted by the Code of Federal Regulations, the Crow land owners were not consulted, corporate papers were not filed, and many other legal obligations were ignored by the Department of the Interior and especially by the B.I.A. The Crow Tribal Council adopted a resolution in 1974 that declared all coal permits and leases null and void. The Department

Plate 8–11 Participants at a Crow feast in 1940. (Courtesy of Fred W. Voget)

Plate 8-12 Crow women chatting while working on hides in 1941. The woman on the left is Woman-on-Top-the-Ground and the one on the right is Well-Known-Writing. (Courtesy of Fred W. Voget)

of the Interior ignored this action, and the Crow Tribe brought suit against the Secretary of the Interior in 1975. The case was dismissed on a technicality and refiled in 1976. The Crow have firmly and overwhelmingly opposed any leases for an indefinite period. The strategy of the large fuel companies involved has shifted to dealing directly with the Indians. One company offered 45 cents per ton and a $200 bonus for each member of the tribe. The strategy to divide and conquer the Indian goes on and on and on.

CROW IDENTITY   A traveler through the reservation in the early 1970s would find that Crow homes had the same general appearance as those of whites living in their midst. The most obvious signs of a Crow home were a distinctively Indian name on a mailbox and tepee poles, used for tepees at the annual Crow Fair or on other special occasions, leaned against a house or tree. The younger Crow usually followed contemporary clothing styles, but most older women still wore long braids, moccasins, and leggings. Most men wore modern clothing although a few old men still wore braids and high hats. Thus the outward appearance of most persons was not distinctive. Since numerous marriages to whites have taken place, some people were not obviously Indian in appearance. Yet aspects of the Crow cultural tradition have persisted. Most people speak Crow as well as English, and more important, 90 percent of the

The Crow: Plains Warriors and Bison Hunters

Plate 8–13 Men at Crow Agency in 1976. (Courtesy of William M. Oswalt)

children speak Crow because it is the language most often used in homes. As recently as 1969 at least a few men fasted in the mountains during vision quests. Sun Dances continued to be held at lodges built in a traditional manner. One dance in 1969 was held to celebrate the safe return of a Crow soldier from Vietnam. Likewise the Tobacco Society has continued to induct new members, but the meaning of both ritual complexes was unknown to most younger persons. Most people apparently considered themselves Christian, but many did not attend church or realistically subscribe to Christian tenets.

In 1941 and 1946 Voget distinguished four groups of Crow on a cultural

Plate 8–14 Children at Crow Agency in 1976. (Courtesy of William M. Oswalt)

and social basis, and these clusters were equally apparent to Stafford in the late 1960s. A small number of older people still clung to Crow attitudes and values, but their number was ever decreasing. At the opposite extreme were those who sought assimilation into the dominant society and identified with non-Indians. Some of these Crow lived on the reservation, but ever-increasing numbers had left to establish themselves where opportunities for employment existed. The majority of the people, however, sought accommodation with whites while at the same time retaining their identity as Crow, and they preferred to live on the reservation. Then there were those who integrated into the greater society and secondarily identified themselves as Crow. They stressed education for their children and were the most intense participants in Christian churches. Yet they too found satisfaction in retaining select aspects of their Indian heritage.

Comparisons

As intensive hunters Crow subsistence pursuits invite comparison with those of the Chipewyan and Caribou Eskimos. All three depended primarily on large herd animals for food and hunted these animals both seasonally and cooperatively. Obvious differences prevailed that can be explained by environmental contrasts, but what specific traits could be considered as a direct result of their common economic foci and what sociopolitical correlates can be isolated?

Four peoples with clan organizations now have been described. The Cahuilla and Fox had patriclans while the Pawnee and Crow had matriclans. In each instance people felt a primary allegiance to the clan of their birth. What are the traits common to the clans of all four peoples, and what are those found among tribes with either matriclans or patriclans? One might also seek to identify examples where the prevailing clan system seems incompatible with the life-style and explain why this is so.

Voluntary associations or sodalities existed among most of the peoples described, and we may seek to identify their common attributes. We also may compare their aboriginal forms on the basis of purpose, recruitment or durability, and then note changes in historic times. The next step would be to explain why some sodalities endured and others became extinct.

Sacred bundles were a central focus for religious behavior among the Cahuilla, Fox, Pawnee, and Crow. Comparisons might be made on the basis of their acquisition, purpose, integration into ceremonies, warfare, and social life. If we assume that personal association with sacred bundles was a basic configuration, may we also identify the logical steps by which they might emerge as clan or tribal symbols of unity?

Enough different tribes have been described at this point to identify distinct stages in Indian-white contacts. Most peoples received Euro-American

The Crow: Plains Warriors and Bison Hunters

trade goods before they met explorers. What were the contact stages that followed, why did they vary, and what general processes may be identified?

Additional Readings

Robert H. Lowie's book *The Crow Indians* is the standard general source. This work, and Lowie's technical monographs about the Crow, cited in the references to this chapter, contain more of the information about these people for the late 1800s. One of the best accounts by a fur trapper is the book by Zenas Leonard, and Edwin T. Denig's report is the best record by a fur trader. The autobiography of the Crow chief Plenty Coups collected by Frank B. Linderman is a sensitive and highly informative report of Crow life spanning from the hunting and fighting days to the reservation period. The account of James P. Beckwourth, a black man, about his life among the Crow is a colorful and usually reliable report for the early fur trade era. The unpublished doctoral dissertation by John W. Stafford contains a wealth of information about the reservation era down to 1971.

The massacre of Lieutenant-Colonel George Custer and his command at Little Big Horn in 1876 is of some interest in Crow history because Custer's scouts were Crow. A great deal has been written about the Battle of Little Big Horn; the events leading up to the massacre are well described in the journal of Lieutenant James H. Bradley edited by Edgar I. Stewart as *The March of the Montana Column* (Norman, 1961).

The best regional overview is *Indians of the Plains* (New York, 1954, 1956) by Lowie. The best regional ethnohistory is *Indian Life on the Upper Missouri* (Norman, 1968) by John C. Ewers; everything that Ewers has edited or written about Plains Indians is worthwhile. The best ethnohistorical study dealing exclusively with the Crow is the doctoral dissertation by Charles A. Heidenreich.

References

Akwesasne Notes (American Indian Newspaper). Rooseveltown, New York. 1976.

Beckwourth, James P. *See* Thomas D. Bonner.

Bonner, Thomas D. *The Life and Adventures of James P. Beckwourth*. Delmont R. Oswald, ed. Lincoln. 1972.

Catlin, George. *North American Indians*. 2 v. London. 1841 (later editions in 1880, 1903, 1913, and 1926).

Daniels, Robert E. "Cultural Identities among the Oglala Sioux," in *The Modern Sioux*, Ethel Nurge, ed., 198–245. Lincoln. 1970.

*Denig, Edwin T. *Five Indian Tribes of the Upper Missouri*. John C. Ewers, ed. Norman. 1961. From 1833 to 1854 Denig was a fur trader in the upper Missouri country. His description of the Crow is outstanding for its breadth and clarity.

DeSmet, Pierre-Jean. *Life, Letters and Travels of Father Pierre-Jean DeSmet. S. J. 1801–1873*. Hiram M. Chittenden and Alfred T. Richardson, eds. v. 1, New York. 1905.

Donaldson, Thomas. "The George Catlin Indian Gallery in the U.S. National Museum," *Annual Report of the Board of Regents of the Smithsonian Institution, 1885*. pt. 2 Appendix. 1886.

Ewers, John C. "The Emergence of the Plains Indians as the Symbol of the North American Indian," *Smithsonian Report for 1964*. 531–544. 1965.

Hanson, Marshall R. Plains Indians and Urbanization. Ph.D. dissertation, Stanford University. 1960.

*Heidenreich, Charles A. Ethno-documentary of the Crow Indians of Montana, 1824–1862. Ph.D. dissertation, University of Oregon. 1971. Verbal and pictorial accounts of the Crow by fur traders and travelers are examined for insight into the changes in Crow life produced by the fur trade.

Hilger, M. Inez. "Notes on Crow Culture," *Baessler-Archiv*, n.s. v. 18, 253–294. 1970.

Kurz, Rudolph F. "Journal of Rudolph Friederich Kurz," *Bureau of American Ethnology, Bulletin* 115, J. N. B. Hewitt, ed. 1937.

Larocque, François A. "Journal of Larocque," *Publications of the Canadian Archives*, no. 3, L. J. Burpee, ed. 1910.

*Leonard, Zenas. *Adventures of Zenas Leonard, Fur Trader*, John C. Ewers, ed. Norman. 1959. Leonard was a Mountain Man who was among the Crow in the 1830s. His is one of the rare accounts about the Rocky Mountain fur trade by a participant. The information provided about the Crow is superior.

Linderman, Frank B. *Plenty-Coups*. London. 1930.

Lowie, Robert H. "Social Life of the Crow Indians," *APAMNH*, † v. 9, pt. 2. 1912.

Lowie, Robert H. "Notes on the Social Organization and Customs of the Mandan, Hidatsa, and Crow Indians," *APAMNH*, v. 21, pt. 1. 1917.

† *Anthropological Papers of the American Museum of Natural History*

The Crow: Plains Warriors and Bison Hunters

Lowie, Robert H. "Myths and Traditions of the Crow Indians," *APAMNH*, v. 25, pt. 1. 1918.

Lowie, Robert H. "The Tobacco Society of the Crow Indians," *APAMNH*, v. 21, pt. 2. 1919.

Lowie, Robert H. "The Religion of the Crow Indians," *APAMNH*, v. 25, pt. 2. 1922.

Lowie, Robert H. "The Material Culture of the Crow Indians," *APAMNH*, v. 21, pt. 3. 1922.

Lowie, Robert H. "Crow Indian Art," *APAMNH*, v. 21, pt. 4. 1922.

Lowie, Robert H. "Minor Ceremonies of the Crow Indians," *APAMNH*, v. 21, pt. 5. 1924.

*Lowie, Robert H. *The Crow Indians.* New York. 1935 (revised, 1956). The major work about the Crow under one cover. For details about diverse topics see Lowie's monographs cited above.

Maximilian, Alexander P. *Travels in the Interior of North America.* In *Early Western Travels, 1748–1846.* Reuben G. Thwaites, ed. v. 22–24. Cleveland. 1906.

Russell, Osborne. *Journal of a Trapper.* Aubrey L. Haines, ed. Portland. 1955.

*Stafford, John W. Crow Culture Change. Ph.D. dissertation, Michigan State University. 1972. Stafford is a cultural geographer and the only person to systematically analyze contemporary Crow life in detail. In addition to abundant information about modern Crow economic life he provides a great deal of background information about the development of the Crow Reservation in historic terms.

Thwaites, Reuben G., ed. *Original Journals of the Lewis and Clark Expedition, 1804–1806.* v. 5. New York. 1905.

*Voget, Fred. "Individual Motivation in the Diffusion of the Wind River Shoshone Sundance to the Crow Indians," *American Anthropologist*, n.s., v. 50, 634–646. 1948. An excellent study of cultural change and its stimulus among the Crow.

Voget, Fred. "Crow Socio-cultural Groups," in *Acculturation in the Americas*, Sol Tax, ed., 88–93. Chicago. 1952.

Wassaja, A National Newspaper of American Indians. San Francisco, California. 1974–1976 articles.

Wildschut, William. "Crow Indian Medicine Bundles," *Contributions from the Museum of the American Indian, Heye Foundation*, v. 17. 1960.

The Yurok: Salmon Fishermen of California | 9

Geographic Myth

For the aboriginal Yurok in northwestern California the center of the world was near the Klamath and Trinity river junction, and from there the earth was thought to extend in a seventy-five mile radius. Surrounding this mountain and forest country was an ocean of water and then a sea of pitch. Westward beyond the water lived a culture hero, The Widower across the Ocean, and north of his home lived the salmon, then dentalium shells, and finally another supernatural to the northwest. At the edge of the land to the south was the country of geese, and on their migration north they flew through a hole in the sky and disappeared. Thus was the world conceived by these stay-at-home Indians.

People, Population, and Language

The name "Yurok" means "downstream" in the language of the Karok, their neighbors to the interior. The aboriginal Yurok may have numbered about 3000 persons who lived on some 700 square miles of land dominated by Douglas fir and redwood forests. By 1910 they numbered 700, and their land

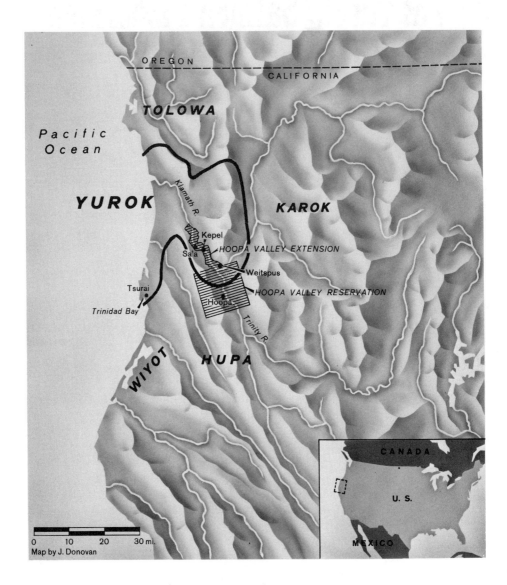

Map by J. Donovan

298

base had been reduced drastically. In 1975 they numbered about 3300, but most of them did not live on reservation lands, and many had been marrying whites for generations. In early historic times most Yurok lived along the Klamath River, and these are the ones stressed in the pages to follow, although Yurok settlements also were maintained along the adjacent coast. Comparatively little contact was maintained between the coastal and riverine Yurok during the late aboriginal period, and this produced dialectic and cultural differences. Their language was most closely related to that of the Wiyot to the south. The Yurok and Wiyot are members of the Macro-Algonkian linguistic phylum but are a long distance from their linguistic relatives in the eastern United States such as the Fox.

Reasons for This Selection

Indians along the Northwest Coast had far more abundant and dependable sources of food than did other peoples north of Mexico who hunted, fished, and collected. Salmon contributed the most to their plenitude, but other fishes and sea mammals frequently were important edibles. The region as a whole is best known for its massive totem poles and giveaway feasts or potlatches, yet a great deal of local variability prevailed and requires recognition. Near the northern range of the Pacific salmon lived the previously described group of Eskimos, the Kuskowagamiut, who depended heavily on salmon for food but did not develop a highly complex life-style because of other constraints. The Yurok, who lived near the southern limit of salmon, represent an amalgamation of Northwest Coast Indian emphasis on wealth and prestige with a simpler material culture typical of northern California Indians. The comparatively unelaborate nature of Yurok technology and social norms attracts attention. Perhaps the most interesting facet of Yurok life was the great stress placed on personal wealth. The individualistic nature of Yurok society also was reflected in the absence of any village-wide or tribal power structure.

Prehistory and Early History

Excavations at coastal sites, especially at Tsurai along Trinidad Bay, suggest that from about A.D. 1000 to the recent past was an era of very little change, and presumably the Yurok lived there throughout this period. Chipped stone arrowpoints, ground stone net sinkers, pipes, pestles and mortars, and antler harpoon heads typify the finds. The Yurok diet, as reflected in these remains, consisted largely of sea and land mammals and shellfish. The conservative nature of the occupants was reflected in their gradual adoption of Western material culture.

The Portuguese explorer Sebastian Cermeno probably discovered Trinidad Bay in 1595. The area was revisited in 1775 by Spanish explorers and by the English navigator George Vancouver in 1793. From 1800 to 1817 the Yurok were involved in the fur trade. Like most other Indians along the north Pacific coast they hunted sea otter and exchanged their pelts for trade goods. Between 1818 and 1848 there was little known contact with whites, but in 1849 the mining of placer gold on the Trinity River made Trinidad Bay the most important transshipment point for goods and equipment destined for the mines. For the Yurok as a whole there was little contact with outsiders prior to 1849, but from that time forward exotic influences expanded greatly, both in scope and intensity.

Aboriginal Life

ORIGIN MYTH   The Widower across the Ocean made soil that he kept in a deerskin container, and by spilling it he created the firm earth of the world. Since he could not see his creation, he caused the sun to give light in the daytime and made the moon to give light at night. The earth was without life, and to replace the desolation he created the varied landscape, with streams flowing to rivers and these emptying into the ocean. He made the forest and the animals. The first animal created was a white deer, and then a red eagle was made to command the skies. After the creation of other animals and plants the first real man was formed of soil, and then a woman was created to keep him company. This couple wandered from their home in the north and finally came to settle in the Klamath River valley.

GEOGRAPHY   The Yurok view of the world was exact: the land was a flat, circular expanse that rested on water and was surrounded by it. As breakers rolled in from the sea, people observed the gentle rise and fall of the land. Regional designations were unusual; instead they concentrated on naming particular localities or spots on the landscape. Thus the Klamath River was not named but was conceived in terms of particular locations along it or on adjacent streams. It required twelve days to traverse the land by canoe from one side to the other, a distance of approximately 150 miles according to the Yurok. As would be expected, the Yurok were not great travelers; they had contact with their neighbors but apparently did not journey deep into the territory of other peoples. Not only did they refuse to go abroad, but strangers were regarded as a threat. It was thought that normal people stayed close to home with relatives and friends. Directions were not conceived as cardinal points on a compass but in terms of water flow. Thus, there were an upstream and a downstream, and it did not matter if a river meandered in different directions. Calculating direction in terms of water flow was applied to the coast also, north being regarded as downstream. People usually traveled by boat,

300

The Yurok: Salmon Fishermen of California

Plate 9–1 A young man drawn by Seth Eastman from a sketch by George Gibbs in 1851. The sword-like object in his right hand probably is an obsidian blade. (Courtesy of the Smithsonian Institution National Anthropological Archives, Neg. No. 2854-F-27)

but they also maintained overland paths. These trails were thought of "like people" and had designated rest stops along them; to pause at a spot that was not a traditional resting place invited ill fortune.

APPEARANCE AND CLOTHING   Women wore basketry hats over their braided hair adorned with flowers. As children they were tattooed with three parallel bands from the lower lip to the chin; their tattoos were said to have been made so that older women would not look like men. Women pierced their ears for wearing ornaments and had necklaces of bone, shell, or small

pieces of fruit. They wore a short apron of skin with shells, nuts, or pieces of obsidian attached to the fringe. A longer skin apron was placed over the first and partly obscured the inner garment. Little girls wore aprons after they were about two years of age, but boys went without clothing, except for furs worn during the winter, until they reached puberty.

Men wore their hair long and loose over the shoulders or else tied it in a knot on top of the head; in his hair a man might wear a garland of flowers or feathers. Facial hair was plucked with hinged mussel shell tweezers. A man's earlobes were pierced to hold ornamental pins of bone or shell. Men painted their faces with line and circle designs; white pigment signified mourning, red was for joy, and black for war. Several lines were tattooed on a man's arm to serve as gauges for measuring lengths of dentalium shells that were used as "money." Most young men folded skins around their hips, but older males as well as some younger ones wore no clothing. When traveling overland a man wore skin moccasins, and when hunting in deep snow he wore knee-length

The Yurok: Salmon Fishermen of California

leggings and used snowshoes. During cold weather both men and women wore skin capes.

SETTLEMENTS   Villages were built along the banks of the Klamath River, on the borders of coastal lagoons, or at places where streams and rivers flowed into the sea. Most settlements were composed of three to seven houses, sweathouses, and menstrual huts. Each dwelling was named and identified with a specific male line (patrilineage). Villages appear to have been abandoned rather often as the result of floods, disease, family quarrels, or simply from boredom with the setting.

The rectangular houses, about twenty feet across, were built in deep excavations. The thick adzed planks, set vertically to form the walls, were as much as ten feet in height at the center of the house front and back. At the peaks were ridge plates, and at right angles to these, overlapping roof boards extended from the ridge to beyond the sidewalls; poles were tied over the roof to hold the boards in place. A rectangular opening was left near the center of the roof to permit smoke from the interior fire to escape and sunlight to enter. A house was entered through a round hole in a front wall plank, and the area in front of the doorway was paved with flat stones. Inside a house, some four feet from the door was a partition; the room was piled with driftwood, trash, and assorted equipment such as large, cone-shaped carrying baskets, seed beaters, and trays for collecting seeds. A large door in the center of the partition opened onto the main living area. Dominating the room was a central pit up to five feet deep and ten feet square, reached by climbing down a notched log. Earth at the sides was retained by a series of logs, and in the center of the pit was a small stone-lined fire pit. Overhead a pole framework was suspended from the ceiling, and from it fish were hung to dry. All the members of a family ate around the fireplace; women and children usually slept there. Scattered about were wooden serving trays for meat, twined cooking baskets for preparing acorn meal, and similar but smaller baskets in which food was served. Spoons were made from antler, a mussel shell, or the top of a deer skull. Wooden bowls nearby were used for washing one's fingers after eating, and small redwood stools served as seats for men. At the side of a house sometimes was a lean-to of planks, which served as a menstrual hut; in other cases, the menstrual hut was a separate structure built a short distance from a dwelling.

A bathhouse served from one to three dwellings, and it was here that adult males lounged and men and boys bathed as well as slept. No prohibition existed to prevent women from being in bathhouses, and they sometimes slept there on cold nights. However men did not relish having women in a bathhouse, saying that they had too many fleas. The women in turn maintained that the men talked too much in the bathhouses and they would just as soon not be there. A bathhouse was built in a pit that measured about ten by fourteen feet. The vertical sidewall planks, about four feet in length, reached just to ground level, while the vertical end wall planks were cut to form a gabled

Plate 9–3 A group of houses. (Courtesy of the Lowie Museum of Anthropology, University of California, Berkeley)

roof, which was spanned with a ridgepole and roof planks. On the top of the gable an old canoe was placed facing downward to prevent water from seeping in along the ridge. The area around the entrance in a sidewall was paved with stones. The floor of a bathhouse was paved with stones or planked and was reached by descending a notched log; a stone-lined fire pit was near the center of the room. In one of the end wall planks was a small, round exit hole. The only furnishings were pillows made from blocks of redwood. The wood for a bath was collected by men, and as they returned to the bathhouse, they sang songs to bring good fortune. A fire was built, and the wood was allowed to burn down to a bed of coals, after which the men undressed and entered. They placed covers over the entrance and exit and sat in the intense heat for about half an hour. After crawling out the exit, they lounged on the stone paving in front of the entrance and repeated the songs they had sung while gathering the firewood. Once they had cooled off, they swam in a stream or river and returned home to their evening meal.

CONVEYANCES The craft item requiring the most time to produce was the dugout canoe, made from a driftwood log of redwood. The log was split in half by pounding antler wedges into it with stone mauls, and a fire was built along the center of one section of the split log. The charred wood was cut

The Yurok: Salmon Fishermen of California

Plate 9–4 Bathhouse in the foreground and dwellings in the background. (From Thompson, 1916)

away with a shell- or stone-bladed adz and the process repeated until the vessel was hollowed out. A typical canoe was eighteen feet long and fifteen inches wide, with a rounded bottom and sides some forty-five inches high. At the front of the canoe on the inside, a small knob of wood was left, and in its center was a shallow hole. This was the "heart" of the canoe, and without it a vessel was "dead." Pitch from conifers was used to caulk cracks in the wood, while crosspieces fore and aft prevented the sides from warping. These vessels were propelled by poles or long-bladed paddles used by men standing in the front; a shorter paddle was used as a rudder by a man seated in the stern. Neither paddle form included a crutch handle. These canoes were designed for river travel and drew as much as six inches of water when fully loaded. Given the rounded bottoms of these boats, a man sitting in the stern could quickly change course to avoid obstructions in the rushing water. When they traveled in the ocean, men sang songs and recited formulas to prevent their boat from capsizing and to keep the water smooth. Considering how ill-adapted such a vessel was to ocean travel, these precautions seem quite reasonable.

The only other manufactured form for travel was the snowshoe. Used by men hunting in deep snow, snowshoes were small with grapevine outer frames and wooden crosspieces.

SUBSISTENCE ACTIVITIES   The most important food was salmon, termed "that which is eaten" (Waterman, 1920, 185), followed by acorns and then by the far less important game and plant products. Success in getting food depended to a large extent on access to sites with exploitative potential. These usually were owned by an individual, family, or community and included fishing spots along the river, oak groves, seed collecting areas, places for snares along game trails, and stretches of riverbank extending about a mile inland. The most important riverine localities were sites where salmon could be dip-netted easily. Pools with an eddy where salmon rested while ascending the river to spawn were particularly important spots to own. A platform was erected over the pool, and it was fished with a long-handled dip net lowered into the water. As soon as a fish was caught, the net was jerked from the water and the salmon clubbed over the head. In a single night a fisherman might take as many as a hundred salmon this way. The right to use an eddy was owned by an individual or a group of individuals and could be sold for money, inherited, or bartered away. Its worth was determined by the number of fish that could be taken. As many as ten men might jointly own an excellent dip net site, but these pools were not everlasting, for a shift in the river channel could change the productivity of an eddy. Gill nets were used, and these as well as the netting for dip nets were made from iris leaf fibers. The nets were weighted with stones, and floats most likely were made from short sections of wood. Salmon also were taken with seines and with toggle-headed harpoons. The harpoon shafts were as much as twenty feet in length, and at the forward end were two slightly diverging foreshafts. To each foreshaft was attached a toggle harpoon head with a line leading from the head to the shaft. When a salmon was struck, the harpoon head detached, and it was drawn in with the hand line. Salmon were split with a flint-bladed knife, dried, smoked on a rack over the fireplace in a house, and then packed in baskets.

Kroeber (1925, 87) wrote with economy and precision, "Acorns were gathered, dried, stored, cracked, pulverized, sifted, leached, and usually boiled with hot stones in a basket." Unshelled acorns were stored in large baskets inside the house and were later processed by removing the nuts from their shells and pounding the meal on a stone slab with a pestle. The bitter acid was leached by placing the ground meal in a sand basin and pouring hot water over it. Acorn meal was cooked by placing hot stones in a basket containing the meal and water. The mixture was stirred with a spatula to prevent the stones from burning the woven container.

Land animals were hunted with a bow and arrows, but the practice does not appear to have been important. The hunting bow was strung with a sinew cord and backed with strips of sinew (sinew-backed bow). A feather-vaned arrow had a separate wooden foreshaft with a stone arrowpoint attached. Arrows were carried in a quiver made by turning the skin of a small animal, such as a fox, inside out. Deer and elk were chased with dogs but probably were more often taken in snares. Dogs were never eaten since their meat, like that of reptiles, was considered poisonous.

A fish or mammal killed for food was not, in Yurok thinking, really destroyed. The spirit continued to exist, leaving only its physical form behind for the hunter or fisherman. A number of restrictions on the taking of salmon will be cited later, but here it is appropriate to mention some of the observances surrounding deer. This animal was thought to have many likes and dislikes that had to be accommodated to kill it successfully. Deer did not like a house that seemed unoccupied; they were attracted to hunters from dwellings where there was smoke. The reason for washing one's hands in flowing water after eating deer meat was to avoid drowning the deer. Deer meat was eaten from wooden platters, and care was taken during a meal so that none of the meat dropped to the floor. Only by observing these and other taboos could deer be taken successfully.

The Yurok were not farmers, but they planted tobacco. The plants were cultivated and the crop harvested for use by the grower or for sale to others. The mature leaves were dried in the sun or by a fire, pulverized, and placed in baskets. The cultivated species apparently was the same as the local wild tobacco, but the latter was not smoked for fear that it might have grown on a grave. Tobacco was smoked in tubular pipes that most often were made from wood, and the smoke was inhaled. Most men smoked just before bedtime, but some old men were addicted to tobacco and smoked more often. Old female shamans appear to have been the heaviest smokers; other women did not smoke.

MONEY   In the broadest sense, money is a divisible and portable class of objects having a standardized value and acceptable in exchange for goods or services. In terms of this definition, money clearly was important among the Yurok, and dentalium shells were the most widely circulated form. These small mollusks had tusk-shaped shells that ranged up to about three inches in length. They were most abundant in the coastal waters off British Columbia and were collected there with a comb-like device that was thrust into the sandy ocean bottom to stab as many dentalia as possible. In western North America the shells were traded from the subarctic to southern California. Among the Yurok, as with most Indians, the shells were graded according to size, with the largest shells having the greatest value. The six named sizes of dentalia ranged in length from 2½ to 1⅞ inches. An eleven-shell string, with each shell 2½ inches long, was valued at about $50 during the early American period; a string of the same length with fifteen 1⅞ inch shells was worth only about $2.50. Other monetary units included redheaded woodpecker scalps ranging in value from 10¢ to $1.50 each. Ordinary deerskins, after being prepared for ceremonial use, were worth from $50 to $100; skins of albino deer were valued at from $250 to $500, although they were never sold. Blades flaked from black obsidian were worth $1.00 for every inch in length until they reached a foot; blades longer than this were worth a great deal more.

Many, if not most, items of material culture were scaled in value against dentalium shells. Around the turn of the present century, a small dugout canoe was worth a thirteen-shell string or three large redheaded woodpecker scalps; a house was valued at from three to five strings of shells; an oak grove from one to five strings; a fishing spot from one to three strings; a shaman's fee from one to two strings; a slave one string, and a woman's basketry cap filled with tobacco was one small shell. A few items were so valuable that they normally could not be exchanged but were passed along a patrilineage. These

Plate 9–5 A woman dressed in her finest garments. (Courtesy of the Lowie Museum of Anthropology, University of California, Berkeley)

were most important as exhibits during ceremonial occasions. Included were fine albino deerskins with transparent hoofs and huge obsidian blades which were nearly a yard in length.

LEGAL SYSTEM   Yurok customary law was based on the idea that wrongs were committed against individuals, and claims were calculated in terms of material goods rather than physical punishment. All claims were settled with the exchange of specific forms of material property. Marital arrangements, which led to the exchange of money, will be considered later, but it is fitting to mention other legal situations in which wealth changed hands. Any deviation from a behavioral norm necessitated a compensatory settlement, and extenuating circumstances rarely were considered. The age, sex, and previous behavior of an offender were unimportant, but his or her wealth was relevant. Finally, once a dispute had been settled, no further recourse was possible. The major grounds for claims were murder, seduction, adultery, saying the name of a deceased person, trespassing, or a shaman's refusal to treat a person who was ill. Failure to ferry someone, even an enemy, across a river led to a claim. If someone injured himself while on the land of another, the owner was responsible for compensation. This was true even of a trespasser, but the landowner would likely press a counter claim for trespassing. If a shaman refused to accept the responsibility for treating a patient and the person died, the shaman was liable. To pass before a village by boat when a family in the village was mourning a death from natural causes was grounds for a claim. If it happened that a person became hopelessly in debt because of some drastically antisocial act, he could, in lieu of payment, become the slave of the one he had offended. For example, if a poor person used the name of a deceased individual of wealth or struck the son of a rich man, he could settle his debt through "debt-slavery" of himself or one of his female relatives. "Slaves" were never killed or abused but performed the more difficult subsistence tasks. A slave owner was free to integrate the individual into his household or to maintain his status as a slave. A slave could not escape because no one would receive him. Foreigners or prisoners from raids were never made slaves. The former always were killed if they arrived unannounced, and prisoners were held for ransom.

DESCENT, KINSHIP, AND MARRIAGE   In this social system the most important ties were those along a line of males. It is tempting to regard the descent system as strictly patrilineal, and unquestionably a man was most concerned with his relatives along a male line. Still, there was recognition of a wife and her relatives in calculating social ties. Perhaps it would be best to characterize these people as patrilineal with a distinct and recognized tendency to consider relatives on both sides of a family as important (bilateral or nonunilineal descent).

In the kinship terminology, a man referred to his father by one term; for his father's brother and his mother's brother, he used another term. For the mother's side of the family, the terminology was comparable to that on the father's side (lineal terms). Thus the Yurok employed terms for the parental generation that are of the same type as those used in the United States today. On Ego's generation, the term for sister was extended to all female first cousins, and the word for brother extended to all male first cousins (Hawaiian cousin terms). It would seem that if one were to call cousins "brother" or "sister," the parents of these individuals would be referred to as "mother" and "father," but such was not the case.

The only bar to marriage was the prohibition against taking a spouse from among near relatives. An individual in a small settlement was obligated to seek

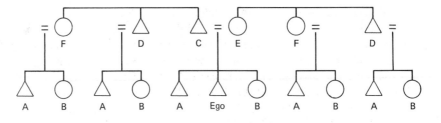

a mate from elsewhere since all the occupants were near relatives, but a partner could be found easily in another village or another tribe. At the same time the tendency in large settlements was to find a mate in one's home community (village endogamy). It has been reported also that men tended to seek their wives from downstream settlements. Ideally the couple lived in the settlement and house of the groom (patrilocal residence), but alternative arrangements were not unusual. Were a man's wife to die before she bore three or four offspring, the woman's family was obliged to offer one of her sisters or female relatives to replace her (sororate). Conversely, when a married man died, his brother was expected to marry the widow (levirate).

SOCIAL DIMENSIONS   Personal ambition and extreme individualism dominated in social life. The core members of each community were persons who traced their descent along the male line to a known common ancestor (patrilineage); within this unit there were lines of familial authority, with a wealthy old man most likely to have jurisdiction over other members of the unit. A hamlet contained one or more patrilineages, each structured as the other, but no organized system of village-wide authority existed. An individual also was bound in a network of kinship ties with persons in other settlements through bonds of blood and marriage. There were also riverine and coastal dialect groups, but this dichotomy did not have known political ramifications. Then there were the adjacent Karok, Hupa, and Wiyot, from whom one might acquire a wife. Relations with these people were structured as with in-laws. Finally, there were strangers, equated with enemies. Thus, any alliances not based on kinship or marriage seem to have been absent.

Within a patrilineage and beyond it, worth was based on ownership of material property, and families were rich, well-to-do, or poor. It was difficult to move up in social standing since everyone coveted wealth and was reluctant to part with it, but the possibility of a poor boy acquiring riches through persistence and supernatural aid did exist. The Yurok believed that constant thoughts about money led to its acquisition. Meditating about wealth when preparing for, taking, or resting after a bath was thought to be most propitious. An ambitious young man was urged to fast and work hard for ten days while concentrating on dentalium shells. When he gathered wood for the bathhouse, he collected it from the upper branches of trees where he visualized the dentalia to be hanging. As he bathed, he thought of shells, and when peering intensively into the river, he imagined that he saw huge dentalium shells. Such a person would say to himself, "I want to be rich," and he would make a tearful invocation for wealth but not to any particular spirit or supernatural power. The primary earthly force that counteracted the quest for money was women. A young man seeking wealth was warned not to have anything to do with women, while an adult man should not copulate with his wife in the house where his wealth was kept.

The nature and texture of life varied widely from one Yurok family to another. An almost insurmountable social barrier separated very rich, aristocratic families from the poor, and poverty was thought to have a genetic basis. A man was poor, lazy, and ill—except for instances of sorcery—because these conditions prevailed in his family line. The economic distinction was apparent in various dimensions of life. The speech of aristocrats was different from that of commoners, and the rich were wary and guarded in what they said. Rich people were "high" class and lived "clean" lives. An aristocrat knew the "law" and adhered carefully to its letter, while poor persons were far less familiar with it and also were careless, unclean, and lacked social graces. To prevent an ambitious commoner from reaching a position of power, sorcery was practiced that would dissipate his wealth or lead to deaths in his family. Thus social distinctions ran deep throughout a Yurok's life, and to improve one's condition was quite difficult.

As would be expected, formal warfare could not exist in this society where political ties were absent. Conflicts that did erupt were between families, and they might develop into small or great feuds, depending on the size of the families involved, their wealth, and how quickly a settlement could be arranged. Fighting was with bows and arrows except for using short stone clubs in hand-to-hand combat. Protective armor was made either from elk hide or vertical wooden rods bound together, and it seems to have been worn only during prearranged battles. Serious feuds apparently were caused by murders committed either in the heat of anger or by witchcraft. In either instance the near relatives of the dead person sought revenge. They might approach their enemy's village secretly and attack before the defenders could rally, or they might ambush the offending family on the trail. Following a successful raid or ambush the contending parties might negotiate a meeting to settle their differences. The two sides armed themselves, painted their faces, and formed lines separated by the distance an arrow could be shot. Songs were sung and a dance of settlement performed; at this point fighting might resume if the arrangements broke down. Otherwise negotiations continued uninterrupted. The contesting parties carried with them the full amount of property necessary for a settlement. The side that had killed the most people and destroyed or seized the greatest amount of property was the "winner" but was at the same time required to relinquish the most property. The items to be distributed were placed in baskets and held over a fire as songs were sung and a dance performed. This ritual was to cast away any feelings of hostility and to make any lasting feelings of vengeance the responsibility of the other party. If all went well, the settlement was made, and neither side could make further claims nor hold a grudge.

RELIGION   The only time that diverse families cooperated fully was in fulfilling ceremonial obligations. Collective rituals were held to renew and perpetuate the natural world with its resources as an orderly system. The principal ceremonies were performed to prevent disease, famine, and cataclysms such as earthquakes and floods. The ceremonial procedures were based on precedents set by immortals before the present race of people occupied the country, and the formulas recited concerned these immortals. Ceremonies were fixed calendrically and usually were held at the spots where they reportedly had been enacted for the first time. During certain ceremonies men displayed their wealth and greatest treasures, and Deerskin and Jumping Dances might be held.

An abbreviated account of the most elaborate ceremonial performance, the Kepel fishweir ceremony, illustrates the integration of subsistence activities and religious rituals. The community of Kepel was on the south side of the Klamath River, and at the nearby village of Sa'a were the sacred house and bathhouse associated with the Kepel ceremonies. At Kepel the river is wide but shallow, and it was easy to drive stakes into the gravel bottom to support a weir. Before the weir at Kepel could be built, a ceremony was performed at the Klamath River mouth to remove the prohibition against eating salmon caught that year. A ritual formulist dominated the Kepel rituals, assisted by a man and a woman. The formulist or weir chief achieved his position by memorizing all the recitations required to build the weir; this knowledge was passed from a father to one of his sons. The rituals began in the late summer when persons in a village near Kepel presented to the weir chief a deerskin robe that he wore throughout the ceremonies. During the next ten days one or more of these principals became deeply involved in ritual duties. These included visiting sacred spots, burning incense, fasting, dancing, singing, bathing in a special manner, and reciting formulas. After a ritual visit to the places where the weir poles were to be cut and where the weir was to be anchored, the male assistant went to adjacent communities to announce the date for beginning construction of the weir. On that day each man who responded was assigned to a work crew, probably ten in number; each crew of ten men was responsible for a named section of the weir.

The following morning and for the next five days the crews cut and limbed small pine trees, peeled the bark off, and split the poles lengthwise. They also collected hazel shoots for binding the poles into mats that were carried to the weir site. On the fifth day the weir chief cut a pole for each end and the center of the weir. After he split the center pole, the workers split other poles and then joked for the remainder of the day. At this time no offense could be taken against jokes at one's expense, no matter how abusive they might be. Actual construction of the weir was begun the next day, with the first pole driven by the weir chief, who used a special maul weighing about fifty pounds. As he drove the pole into the river bottom, he prayed for salmon. Others drove the remaining poles into the gravel at different angles so that they would not dislodge with the current. The formulist and his male assistant arranged the first stringer along the tops of the poles, and after the other stringers were arranged, all were bound into place. On the downstream side of the weir the workers constructed ten traps, each about twelve feet long and fourteen feet wide, with movable openings at each end; the woven mats were placed in the pole frames to complete the weir-trap. Near the south bank an opening was left in the stringers so that boats could pass through and some salmon could escape.

At noon on the tenth day boys made ribbons of bark, imitations of pipes, and other carvings that they attached to a pole raised near one end of the weir. The female assistant ran from Sa'a to the site with a basket of acorn dough and placed it on a pile of sand. Girls began dancing and later stopped to cover the female assistant with their bodies as a boy threw a basket of water high in the air, attempting to shower the girls. As he did this, other boys climbed on the pile to protect the female assistant from the spray and from the poles the workers let fall simultaneously on the throng. Afterwards, the people in the pile rapidly dispersed on all fours. The three principals then returned to the weir, and the male assistant removed the first salmon caught. Part of it was taken by the female assistant for her evening meal, but no one else could eat salmon until the following day. The nearby dance ground was cleared for the Deerskin Dance. One was held here and another at a spot ten miles downstream. The ordinary participants attended one dance or the other and then returned home, but the weir chief and his male assistant remained at the site until the weir was destroyed two to three months later.

A Deerskin Dance was a colorful event, with each male dancer wearing the skin of a civet cat or deer around his waist. The dancers were not clothed above the waist, but around each man's neck hung massive strings of dentalium shells. His head was adorned with a browband of wolf fur and a stick on which eagle or condor feathers were arranged to appear as one very long feather. Each dancer carried a pole with a stuffed deer head at the top and the deerskin hanging loose to sway back and forth as the pole was moved. In the center of a line of dancers were a singer and two assistants dressed similarly to the others. The line of dancers stamped one foot and then the other, the standard dance step. While they performed, as many as four other men paraded before the dancers, blowing whistles and holding obsidian blades encased in deerskins. These men wore a double layer of deerskins wrapped around their bodies, wolf-fur browbands, and another band of leather around their heads with the canine teeth of sea lions attached. From their heads hung netting painted with designs and fringed with feathers. During the Deerskin Dance, as at ceremonies in general, members of the host community danced and were followed by performers from each represented village. Morning and evening

Plate 9–6 Deerskin dancers ready to perform, ca. 1900. Note the obsidian blades held by the men in the foreground. (Courtesy of Ericson Collection, Humboldt State University Library)

dances were given by each group for a twelve-day period. On the final day men danced with their finest white deerskins, and others displayed their most beautiful obsidian blades.

Formal ceremonies at the Kepel fishweir ended with the performance of a two-day Jumping Dance held a few miles above Kepel. Dancing males wore a double layer of deerskin about their hips and many necklaces of dentalium shells. Each man wore a deerskin headband covered with woodpecker scalps and trimmed with a white band of deerskin; a white plume extended above his head on a stick. From the sides of his headpiece hung long skin flaps that swung rapidly as he performed. In one hand a dancer carried a cylindrical basket with an opening along one side. Two steps were performed in the Jumping Dance; both involved hopping or jumping as the baskets were lowered.

The Yurok: Salmon Fishermen of California

After the Kepel weir was readied for use, three traps were reserved for the principal participants in the ceremony, and the others were designated for particular individuals and their relatives. Salmon were removed from traps with dip nets in the mornings; afterwards the weir chief opened the upper ends of the traps for great numbers of salmon to escape upriver. Many of the fish caught were processed for future consumption. The people fished for two to three months, always with the weir chief and his assistants nearby. The weir finally was destroyed by the rushing water, and the ceremonialists as well as the fishermen returned to their homes.

While the Kepel fishweir ceremonies were the most elaborate, portions of the Yurok population participated in other ceremonies as well. At the junction of the Trinity and Klamath rivers in a community called Weitspus a ceremony was held to renew the world each September. It was designed specifically to avert natural disasters and disease. At two coastal villages, a village at the Klamath River mouth and another a little less than halfway between the Trinity junction and the sea, four other world-renewal ceremonies were held. Yurok participation in these and other ceremonies produced a form of integration along sacred, not secular, lines.

Another popular celebration, called the Brush Dance by Anglo-

Plate 9–7 Jumping Dance performers, ca. 1900. (Courtesy of Ericson Collection, Humboldt State University Library)

Americans, was held to treat an ill child, but it also served as entertainment for most participants. The event was held in a dwelling from which the roof and part of the sidewalls had been removed. On the first night a formula was recited for the ill child, and men danced about the fire holding boughs. Nothing took place the second night, but on the third and fourth nights the Brush Dance continued until dawn. On each night a series of three dances were performed by competing sets of dancers. The sick child was integrated into the performances with the recitation of formulas and the waving of torches above him.

Formulas were very important in the Brush Dance as well as in calendrical ceremonies, and they also served individual needs under other circumstances. Some formulas involved the recitation of a list of sacred spots which someone long ago had visited to accomplish a particular purpose. Others were recitations or prayers, including the spirit responses. Offerings of tobacco and the use of plant products were associated with the formulas.

CURING   Women were the healers, and they usually acquired their power in a dream, either unanticipated or sought-after, about a dead shaman. From this deceased curing specialist the potential shaman obtained a "pain." It was considered a tangible object that entered her body and became the nexus of her power. Once power had been acquired the next step was to bring it under control by fasting and dancing in a bathhouse for ten days under the supervision of other shamans. The goal was for the tyro to be able to vomit forth her pain and to swallow it again. As a further step the aspirant and a male relative visited a supernatural spot on a mountain for one night during the summer. On the mountain the woman recited a formula, smoked, and danced near a fire. Another ten days in the bathhouse, performing as before, was followed by a dance around a large hot fire to bring the pain fully under the woman's control. This dance was the final step in becoming a shaman.

When a woman was asked to heal a patient, negotiations were made by the relatives of the sick person, and the amount of payment was settled before a cure was attempted. A female curer's equipment consisted of a pipe, two strings of feathers in her hair, and an ankle-length skirt. A cure was effected by chanting over the patient, smoking, and dancing for as much as six hours. A long session sometimes was necessary to see into the body of the patient and to locate the pains that caused the disease. The pain, or pains, were then removed by sucking. If the shaman was unable to remove the pains, she referred the patient to another curer. If a patient died, the shaman's fee was returned.

In a second category of curers were males who probably did not acquire their power from supernatural sources but intensified it by supernatural means. They visited mountain tops, recited formulas, bathed ritually, and smoked in order to reinforce their power. These men relied on a pharmacopoeia consisting of plant and mineral products. This knowledge and the position was passed from father to son or to another close male relative. Like a

The Yurok: Salmon Fishermen of California

female shaman, the male was paid before he attempted a cure and returned the payment if he was unsuccessful. Among the illnesses treated were wounds, snakebites, and "chronic diseases," as well as other forms of unidentified sickness. One source states that male curers served as a check on the ambitions of female shamans. Apparently the duties of female and male shamans were distinct, females handling cases of psychological ailments with supernatural cures and males treating physical disabilities from natural causes.

SORCERY   Some female shamans had the reputation of using their powers for antisocial purposes, the motivation being material profit. A person was made ill and then a fee collected to cure him. Another technique was to leave one of multiple pains in the body of a person who was treated in order to be called back when this pain became troublesome. Other persons were more truly witches; they acquired a malignant object by purchase or special knowledge and used it to kill individuals. If the possessor of such a power went out at night, the power appeared as sparks or as a bluish light. It could be placed on the end of a miniature arrow and shot from a small bow at the home of the victim. The victim would die if not treated by a shaman. A person also could be harmed by a poison made of crushed meat from a dog, frog, rattlesnake, or salamander. After the poison was added to a victim's food, the individual remained healthy for a year, but he then became ill and died if not cared for by a very powerful shaman.

When a person's rights were violated and just compensation could not be obtained by legal means, the only alternative was to turn to a sorcerer. These usually were men, and they customarily charged as much as a bride price, which meant that their services could be commanded only by aristocrats. A sorcerer was either of high social standing or was attempting to achieve higher status. He owned two to twelve "poisons" that ranged in effectiveness from very mild to lethal; each strength was represented by a different miniature arrow. The mildest form produced a headache or cold, and the middle level caused chest pains that led to the victim's confinement. From the eighth level upward, all were lethal and were associated with behavior while sleeping. Once the fee and the degree of illness to be induced were agreed on, the sorcerer went outside the victim's house disguised as a dog. He shot the mildest arrow from a miniature bow and returned at specified intervals until he reached the level of illness desired. When the victim showed symptoms of illness, a shaman was hired to extract the "pains," but very few shamans had the power to remove lethal arrows. If a shaman could suck the pain from a victim, she spit it out of her mouth, and the arrow rose into the air and flew back to its maker, with only the shaman seeing the return. It was essential for a sorcerer to handle the objects of his power with great care. When not in use, they were buried in a cache of stones, but it was necessary for the owner to use the force of the poison at least once a month. If he did not, the power would harm his children, or himself if he was childless. This form of sorcery possibly de-

veloped during the early historic period when the economic position of aristocratic families was threatened by white intrusions.

Life Cycle

The first time a woman conceived, her offspring was born after ten
months, according to tradition, but later births required only nine-month
pregnancies. Births were most likely to occur in the spring, but not because
there was a mating season as once was suggested. The reason was that a man
stored his material wealth in his wife's house, and riches were diametrically
opposed to sexual activity. To have sexual intercourse in the house was to invite poverty. Therefore, a couple was most likely to copulate in the summer
when they slept out-of-doors. The people feared the birth of twins of the opposite sex because they thought such twins would have an incestuous relationship when grown; one, usually the female, was smothered or starved to
death. Identical twins, however, were raised. A pregnant woman worked
hard, ate little, and was concerned with the physical actions of the fetus. The
fetus was thought to be influenced by the woman's activities; a large neonate
was born if the mother ate too much and slept excessively. A pregnant woman
bent forward when working so that the fetus would not "rest against her
spine," and as it developed she rubbed her abdomen in the afternoon to prevent the fetus from sleeping at this time of day, which was to invite evil. It
was thought that a male fetus was more active than a female one. In giving
birth a woman rested on her back with her feet braced against a midwife, and
her arms were bound with leather straps suspended from the ceiling. During
labor she was told by the midwife when to lift herself with the thongs, and she
was cautioned to keep her mouth closed in order to ease the birth. The newborn was steamed over wild ginger, and a preparation from ground land snail
was applied to the navel. The severed cord was put inside a pine tree branch
that had been split to receive it. The Yurok regarded the colostrum from the
mother's breast as harmful to the infant's jaws; as a consequence, a baby was
fed hazelnut soup for the first ten days and then nursed. After twenty days of
life, a grandmother, probably most often the paternal grandmother, began to
massage the infant's leg muscles to encourage it to crawl while still very
young. Between the time of birth and the healing of the navel, parents observed food taboos, and they were prohibited from having sexual intercourse
until the baby crawled. Cradleboards were made in such a manner that the infant sat, with its legs hanging free. The baby could move its legs at any time,
which was in keeping with the desire to have it crawl at a tender age. Many, if
not most, aspects of rearing an offspring were designed to encourage self-
reliance. This attitude clearly is reflected by the practice of weaning at one
year, which is earlier than among most American Indians.

Two developmental stages of childhood were identified: an early one when a child could not be taught in an orderly manner and a later stage when systematic training was possible. A child's readiness to learn was judged on the basis of its ability to remember, not on its chronological age. It probably was named when it showed this capability, at about eight or nine years of age. The names for male children were selected by their father, and female children were named by their mother. Each family seems to have had its own set of male or female personal names. Nicknames of girls often contained some reference to marriage, for example, Married a Rabbit and Married into Snail's House. Personal names were used in referring to or addressing individuals, but they were dropped at the time of an individual's marriage.

When a child could remember instructions, formal education began. Children were taught to eat slowly, to chew thoroughly, to think of money as they ate, not to seize food greedily, and not to snack. At mealtimes girls sat near their mothers and boys near their fathers, with the respective parent responsible for instructing them. If a child did not obey mealtime restrictions, the parent removed his food basket, and the offender was expected to leave the house. A child was shown rock figures and told that they formerly were persons who did not follow societal norms. One rock in particular was pointed out as once having been an errant child. Animals and birds too were the subjects of stories stressing social norms. One particularly vivid tale concerned the greedy buzzard who put his entire head in his soup while it was still hot. He scalded the top of his head and henceforth ate only old, rotten food. Another

Plate 9–8 A man on a fishing platform raising a dip net. (Courtesy of the Lowie Museum of Anthropology, University of California, Berkeley)

dominant concern of parents was to insure that a child learn not to offend the dead. Any direct statement about the dead or reference to items associated with death was a form of swearing. A rude gesture accompanying swearing was to hold out one's hands with the fingers outstretched and the thumbs together, since this was how the dead swore. The probable reason for disapproving of such behavior was that it led to claims by the relatives of a deceased person. To discourage such words or gestures a mentor placed nettles on a child's lips or hands, a very effective punishment.

Small girls played house using mud dolls, cradles, food, clothing, and equipment, as well as imitation money. The toys of boys included canoes, but they were used in small bodies of water rather than in the streams or rivers. As children grew older, they were instructed formally by a mature man who taught a group of from five to seven children the norms of adult behavior and technical skills. During this instruction the teacher received no compensation, but students were expected later to provide their former teachers with food. Not all children accepted formal lessons, and those who did not respond positively were not considered at fault. Their misbehavior resulted from seeing bad spirits of a special kind, and such a child was sent home. More serious childhood misbehavior was thought to have been caused by "wise people." These were spirits about the size of children and were nonsexual; they matured at six months and were immortal. A Yurok child might behave in an incorrect manner because it had seen wise people. A grandmother of such a child went to the spot and sang her particular song to counteract the spirits. If this did not succeed, a neighboring grandmother tried, and if she too failed, a female shaman was called in. She treated the patient in the usual manner and went on to probe the affairs of the household. The shaman was likely to establish the fact that in the afflicted child's home an older woman was attempting witchcraft against another, or that a man who prayed for money also had been having sexual intercourse. The accused confessed freely, which normalized the household setting and no doubt led to a more harmonious environment for the child and a cessation of his symptoms. A shaman knew her patients well and from a standard list of transgressions would be likely to predict the faults of family members. The psychoanalyst who recorded these facts, Erik H. Erikson, seemed able to establish rapport easily with an old female shaman, which is not surprising since they had methodological concepts in common.

The most important skill to be acquired by a young girl was basket weaving since a great deal of prestige accrued from making excellent baskets. Usually a girl was about six years old when she attempted to weave her first basket. She tried a simple form, and often after the first few rows were completed, her mother added others to straighten the weave. If the girl's interest was sustained, a skilled basket weaver trained her informally. Only one set of techniques prevailed for weaving, and therefore all baskets were similar, differing only in quality and less importantly in their design elements.

When a girl first menstruated, she spent most of ten days sitting silently in a corner of the house, facing away from the fire. Whenever she needed to scratch, she used a special stick, and she wore a skirt of inner bark like that of a female shaman. The girl moved about as little as possible but brought in a load of firewood each day. For at least the first four days she ate no food, under the assumption that the longer she fasted the more wealth she would accumulate later in life. When she did eat, it was at the bank of a roaring river where she would hear no sound but the water. Each night she bathed the number of times equal to the days of her confinement, except that on the ninth night she bathed ten times. At dusk of the tenth day each small child living nearby washed her back. Finally, her mother or another woman told her she would have ten boys and ten girls. For a boy there were no comparable restrictions at the time of puberty.

A maturing girl of good breeding was watched carefully by her parents to make certain that she did not fornicate. The prohibition was not so much a matter of morality as to prevent the girl from becoming pregnant and thereby decreasing the amount of bridewealth she would bring. A girl who conceived before marriage attempted to abort by placing heated stones on her abdomen; if successful, she threw the fetus in the river. A young man was exhorted to work hard at adult skills, to carry wood for the bathhouse frequently, and to concentrate on money.

Property exchanges at marriage were critical because a person's social standing depended on the amount of bridewealth offered at the time of his mother's marriage. At the bottom of the scale was a nonlegitimate offspring who had no formal standing. Next was a poor person, whose father had offered little for his wife; he in turn could provide his son with very little bridewealth. A third level of prestige was achieved by men who offered substantial wealth. Finally, some rich men provided far more wealth than was necessary to consummate a marriage. Marital arrangements were not a simple offering of a given amount of wealth to the bride's family; instead there often were manipulations and compromises. According to the ideal, a man with wealth suggested a suitable amount of material goods to the girl's relatives, had it accepted, and took the girl to reside in his settlement (patrilocal residence). Such was a "full-marriage." Any particular groom was unlikely to possess enough wealth of his own to satisfy the girl's relatives, but his father or father's brothers ideally gave the young man the necessary balance. The bride of a wealthy man brought with her a considerable amount of property, which partially offset the outlay of the groom and his relatives. A girl of high social standing might bring ten baskets of dentalia, otter skins, a canoe, deerskins, and other small assorted valuables. It was possible also for a man with a small daughter to be deeply in debt to a man with a young son and to offer the girl in marriage when she was quite young. The girl grew up in the household of her prospective in-laws and married the boy after puberty. Sometimes a father was so covetous of his wealth that he refused to give his son a sufficient

321

Life Cycle

amount for a full-marriage. If the son worked hard, sweat often in the bath-house, cried for wealth, and fasted, after about four years the girl's relatives might feel sorry for him and permit a full-marriage.

Another form of marriage was "half-marriage," which meant usually that the groom could not accumulate the necessary wealth to make a full-marriage payment and was forced to be content with lower social standing. He offered his potential father-in-law all the wealth he possessed and went to live in the girl's village, either in the same house or in a nearby house (matrilocal residence). In a typical marriage of this sort, the children of the couple were affiliated with the wife's family, and the bridewealth given at the marriage of their daughter went to the wife's kinsmen. Furthermore, the woman in a half-marriage could correct her husband openly and supervise his subsistence activities, while the children were under her direct control even concerning their marital arrangements. A half-marriage sometimes was negotiated quickly if a girl was pregnant in order to prevent the social stigma of bearing a bastard. Finally, a greedy father of a girl who was a successful shaman might force a half-marriage upon her to continue his claim on her earnings. In a record of 356 marriages, 25 percent were half-marriages, indicating that either the number of persons with little wealth was small or that extenuating circumstances often were involved in a marriage. At the same time full-marriages were not all equal, for very rich men would offer far more than the minimum amount of wealth necessary in order to acquire increased prestige for themselves and their children.

Possibly the most common grounds for divorce was failure of the wife to conceive, and if she could not be replaced by a kinswoman, the bridewealth was refunded. If a man abused his wife in a full-marriage so much that she returned home, the husband was obligated to pay the woman's family an additional amount before he could receive her back. If he did not do so, the girl's family probably would return part of the bridewealth, and the couple was considered divorced. If a husband being divorced refused to accept a refund of the bridewealth, he retained the children, and the daughter's bridewealth went to him.

Following a death, the corpse was washed, but it was touched as little as possible. The deceased was painted, clothed, wrapped in a skin, and placed on a plank for twenty-four hours. Mourners wailed before the body, and then it was removed from the house through an opening made in a wall. After additional rituals the body was carried to a cemetery maintained in the midst of the settlement to prevent wild animals from disturbing the dead. A grave was excavated and lined with planks; the plank on which the corpse had rested in state served as the coffin lid. During burial the mourners wept, sang appropriate songs, and said good-bye as they stated their relationship to the deceased. One stone marked the head of a grave and another the foot; a wide plank was placed across the grave and staked in place. A fence was built around the grave, with posts at the head and the foot; on the posts were fastened cross-

The Yurok: Salmon Fishermen of California

pieces from which hung deerskins, with the heads and bodies stuffed with grass. Items such as baskets and plates were placed on top of the grave.

The spirit of a good person traveled a narrow, winding trail north until it climbed a ladder into the sky to a peaceful afterlife. The soul of an unworthy individual traveled a broad trail to a river where an old woman and a dog live. Sometimes the dog drove the soul back into the dead person's body, and he came to life again. This was rare, and if it did happen, the person was not happy and would meet a sudden death. When the old woman had control of the soul, she sent it across the river in a waiting canoe of the Yurok type but without a "heart" near the bow. A young man propelled the canoe and landed the soul in a damp, depressing land where food, although plentiful, was unpalatable. As described, the fate of souls sounds as if it might be of Christian derivation.

Recent History

GOLD MINERS   When gold miners moved into the Trinity River country in 1849, the most dramatic effect on the Yurok was the realization that foreigners, equated with enemies, were permanently in their midst. Their primary contacts were with traders, who offered not only useful material goods but intoxicants as well. These Indians not infrequently fought whites when either or both were intoxicated. Another serious problem was that of compensation in Indian terms. In one instance a trader hired Indians to transport supplies for his store from the coast, and when the canoemen drowned, the trader was held responsible. Since he would not compensate the relatives of the deceased, they laid siege to his store. He summoned U. S. Army soldiers as protection, and finally the Indians retaliated by killing a white who had nothing to do with the affair. Problems such as these during the early period of intensive contact appear to have been relatively common.

GHOST DANCE   Within a generation of the first intensive contacts with whites, the Yurok were exposed to a Ghost Dance. It was originated in 1869 by Wodziwob, a Paviotso Indian (Northern Paiute) who was said to have died about three years after having his most important visions. He and a disciple were said to have returned from the place of the dead with the report that the dead would come back to earth, and they carried messages from the dead to the living. The Ghost Dance was performed at Paviotso meetings, but they did not consider it important. As the doctrine spread in Oregon and California, it was changed from its original form. Yurok reaction to the basic tenets is revealing. The dogma introduced included an end of the present world when nonbelievers, including whites, would turn to stone; believers would survive and be joined by the dead. Some Yurok, however, thought that all people would die, and others that everyone would survive the world's end. Individual wealth was to be exposed during the Ghost Dance performances or else it would be worthless in the new world. To facilitate the return of the dead, fences were removed from graves in some localities. The message appears to have won support for a short time, with the strongest adherents being the young and the poor, but the Ghost Dance of 1870 made no lasting imprint on Yurok life, possibly because the doctrine had no precedent in the mythology and was without the traditional formulas that formed the core of Yurok supernaturalism.

THE RESERVATION   In 1864 the Hoopa Valley Reservation was established by the U. S. Congress in an area occupied aboriginally by the Hupa (Hoopa) and Yurok. The Hoopa Extension was created by an Executive Order of the president in 1876 in an area that was exclusively Yurok. These reservations joined one another, and the separate rights of the Hupa and Yurok were not explicitly defined. By 1898 most of the 30,000 acres of the Hoopa Extension had been allotted to individual Indians, and the balance of the land was sold to whites with the money earmarked for Indian welfare. Those persons with allotments were encouraged to sell their valuable timberland to whites, and by 1971 only about 3400 acres remained in the hands of individual Yurok. By contrast most of the Hoopa Reservation land was not allotted. Thus the Yurok, who are identified primarily with the extension rather than the Hoopa Reservation, now are virtually landless. This has led to a great deal of bitterness with the Hupa, who emerged as exclusively identified with the Hoopa Reservation, where most of the land is still held by the tribe and is quite valuable.

Modern Life

Published anthropological information about the present status of the Yurok is nearly nonexistent. Fortunately, however, two anthropology students at the University of California, Los Angeles, Cynthia Burski and Dorothy Hosler Runge, visited the Yurok in 1965 and graciously made their field notes available to me. Most of the information that follows is from their work.

In 1926 the Indian Shaker Church had gained converts among the Yurok, and by the 1930s it had enough adherents to become influential in local life. One result was that sorcery by professionals had almost disappeared although knowledge about it remained widespread. It apparently was not uncommon for a person from an "enemy" family to whistle near one's house at night as a means of frightening the occupants, but this "deviling" was more often mischievous than harmful. Among the Yurok in the late 1960s persons still were suspected of practicing sorcery if they had threatened someone who became ill months or even years later. Individuals also were suspect if they behaved in a suspicious manner, for example, if they wandered alone late at night. Sus-

324
The Yurok: Salmon Fishermen of California

pected sorcerers, who most often were old, poor, and lived alone, were avoided.

During December of 1964 there was a severe flood along the Klamath River. The region was designated as a National Disaster Area, and the amount of Yurok property swept away or damaged by the flood was great. Some thirty-five Yurok houses along the Klamath were completely destroyed. The people were appalled by their material losses but were able to receive temporary supplies and clothing through the disaster program. Some Yurok had predicted that disaster would follow the cutting of a road through a sacred mountain by the Division of Highways two years before. Other Yurok offered a host of possible causes for the disaster. They noted, for example, that a Deerskin Dance held at Hoopa did not last the traditional number of days. Furthermore, in the fires built during a recent Deerskin Dance driftwood, not the traditional timber from the mountainsides, was burned. Another mistake connected with this dance was that water was sprinkled on the dance area by a truck before the event. Then, too, one man refused to display his wealth at the dance, which again invited disaster. The people were distressed also because cemeteries had been washed away and the bones of the dead had been exposed. The tradition-oriented Yurok explained the continuing rains of January, 1965, as being caused by the exposure of bones of the dead; they thought the rains would continue until the bones once again were covered.

The views of many local whites about these Indians are stereotypic and fall into an expectable pattern. The Indians were considered drunkards with little or no respect for the law; dirty, irresponsible employees, and generally

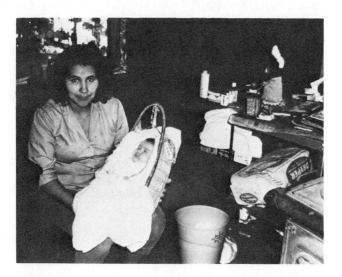

Plate 9–9 A mother with her infant in a cradleboard in 1965. (Courtesy of Dorothy Hosler Runge)

unreliable. Unquestionably, there was a certain amount of truth in the opinion of the whites, for the consumption of intoxicants did seem to be important to many individuals, and the attitudes of many Yurok toward wage labor were not shared by whites. The Yurok considered whites to be greedy and felt that they looked down upon Indians. More important to the Yurok were their specific complaints against the Hupa who, they felt, were unjustly favored by the Bureau of Indian Affairs, and against B.I.A. officials for both real and imagined injustices.

Modern Yurok social life still was built on the nuclear family residence unit, but a striking population characteristic was the tendency for Yurok of both sexes to marry whites and for young Indian boys to court white girls. Yurok Indian clothing did not differ from the garments of whites in the area since both men and women wore store-bought clothing exclusively. The Yurok homes were large, rectangular frame dwellings with four or more rooms. One characteristic of households was their cluttered appearance, the result of a great accumulation of material goods. Household furnishings included expected items such as refrigerators, stoves, tables and chairs, plus many seemingly useless items. The clutter apparently was compatible with older housekeeping norms. Houses contained collections of baskets, an overt sign of their Indian heritage. Production of baskets was limited since few women retained the skill to make them, and they were sold primarily to Yurok. The bathhouses, which once were so extremely important, had ceased to function. Stools, which were one of the few items of aboriginal furniture, were occasionally seen in the dwellings, but they were regarded more as heirlooms than as furnishings. The traditional forms of Yurok wealth, such as elaborate ceremonial costumes, dentalium shells, and white deerskins existed as treasures.

Subsistence fishing for salmon was relatively unimportant although certain family fishing spots were owned and trespassers prosecuted. The timber industry was the primary source of employment, followed by road construction. During the summer months, numerous men served as hunting and fishing guides for tourists. Loggers earned $3.50 an hour, and in a nine-month season they accumulated as much as seven thousand dollars. This was the most lucrative type of employment, especially when wages were supplemented by unemployment insurance payments for the balance of the year.

Attendance at Christian church services seemed to be the most important form of organized religious activity. The world-renewal ceremonies had died out long ago, but the Deerskin Dance still was held sporadically. One was given in 1955, and the next was held during seven days of August in 1964. Reportedly in 1955 most of the boats were lost in a flood, and their destruction made traveling to a dance difficult. The same year much of the ceremonial equipment was destroyed by fire; this caused the long delay between Deerskin Dances. The secular Brush Dance continues to be held on the Fourth of July and lasts for three days.

The Yurok: Salmon Fishermen of California

Plate 9–10 The heirlooms of a Yurok man in 1965. (Courtesy of Dorothy Hosler Runge)

LAND CLAIMS   Many Yurok difficulties have been building over the years and are without ready solutions. The sale of most allotments on the Hoopa Extension effectively destroyed their traditional land base. Their distinct tendency to marry whites attenuates their identity as Indians, and alcoholic consumption has for some persons reached alarming proportions. Furthermore, they have been unable to organize a tribal council, making collective action difficult. But there is a brighter side.

By the late 1940s the timber on the Hoopa Reservation had increased so much in value that lumber companies sought permission to harvest it. In leading the negotiations the B.I.A. compiled a roll of persons eligible to make the decision and to reap the profits. The roll was limited to Hupa on the reservation, and they voted to approve the exploitation of their timber by lumber companies. By 1972–1973 each of the nearly 1400 Hupa had received about $3000 as their share of the forestry operation, a record high payment. They also used timber money to build a community and shopping center complex and improve reservation housing. However, lawyers representing about 3300 Yurok went to court seeking a retroactive share and future shares to Hoopa Reservation resources in what came to be known as the Jessie Short case. The Yurok contended that the Hoopa Reservation and the Hoopa Extension were a single unit conceived to benefit all of the Indians involved. The U.S. Court of Claims ruled in favor of the Yurok, and the U.S. Supreme Court refused to review the case. With their far greater number it appears that the Yurok may soon dominate the Hoopa Reservation. The Hupa are understandably bitter and are contesting the roll of Yurok who will benefit. It might be added that many tribes around the nation filed "friend of the court" statements with the U.S. Supreme Court. They deplored the decision in favor of the Yurok, contending that it threatened to cloud the title of any reservation lands where there was no clear statement of the tribe or persons for whom it had been created.

Salmon fishing, the clear basis for riverine Yurok welfare in aboriginal times, has continued to be important. However, since most of the land along the Hoopa Extension now belongs to whites, the State of California claimed jurisdiction over fishing rights. The dispute peaked in 1969 when a Yurok was cited by the California Fish and Game Department for gill netting along the lower river. By 1975 the courts had ruled in favor of the Yurok, upholding their aboriginal rights. As a result of the court decisions, the Yurok set up a Fishing Committee to consider their course of action. Some favor the creation of a department to regulate and license non-Indian fishing, others favor subsistence fishing for Indians only, and still others seek to organize a commercial salmon fishing operation under Indian control. One major problem remains, however; since the Yurok still do not have a legally constituted tribal organization, they have a difficult time dealing with Federal and State agencies, with each other, and with other Indians. Nonetheless with the prospects of timber money and control over salmon fishing on the lower Klamath, the outlook is for the Yurok far better than it has been for many years.

Comparisons

Yurok values invite comparison with the contemporary American ethos as influenced by capitalism and the Protestant ethic. Walter Goldschmidt has presented a systematic comparison of the values of northwest California tribes, drawn primarily from Yurok sources, with the "protestant ethic." Goldschmidt (1951, 513) summarized the Indian pattern as "a system in which the individual was placed chiefly by personal acquisition of wealth which in theory was freely attainable by all, with both status and power resting upon the ownership of property." There was a basic value put on hard work, obtaining wealth, self-denial, and the full responsibility of the individual for his own behavior, which was consistently aggressive.

The ways in which people coordinate and combine their diverse activities as a harmonious unit may be termed *sociocultural integration*. To explore the aspects of integration it is helpful to identify three primary networks: the interactions of people in social and political terms, human relations with the supernatural, and the relations of people with the environment. Integration is broadly expressed in the articulations of these three dimensions, according to Mischa Titiev in *The Science of Man* (1963, 598–599). Note, for example, how loosely integrated Chipewyan caribou hunting was with supernaturalism but the comparatively high degree of integration between Yurok rituals and construction of the Kepel fishweir. Further comparisons between peoples presented in this book serve to point up differences in integrative networks among them and with our own life-style.

Additional Readings

The best discussion of Yurok material culture is by Kroeber, and the best account of their personality is by Erikson. O'Neale has written a very insightful analysis of Yurok basket-making in terms of individual weavers. The best ethnographic accounts are by Kroeber and his collaborator Spott. The book by Lucy Thompson, a Yurok woman, is a fine account of an Indian about her own people. Unfortunately no one has conducted recent studies among these people.

References

Burski, Cynthia, and Dorothy H. Runge. Field notes, January, 1965.

Cooke, Sherburne F. *The Aboriginal Population of the North Coast of California.* Anthropological Records, v. 16, no. 3, 1956.

DuBois, Cora. *The 1870 Ghost Dance.* Anthropological Records, v. 3, no. 1. 1939.

Elsasser, Albert B., and Robert F. Heizer. "Excavation of Two Northwestern California Coastal Sites," *Reports of the University of California Archaeological Survey*, no. 67. 1966.

*Erikson, Erik H. *Observations on the Yurok: Childhood and World Image.* UC-PAEE,† v. 35, no. 10. 1943. Erikson, a psychoanalyst, visited the Yurok in the 1930s and collected information primarily about children. His field observations and the ethnographic data collected by others are interpreted in terms of psychoanalytic theory to provide a rare dimension in the analysis of ethnographic sources.

Gifford, Edward W. *California Kinship Terminologies.* UCPAEE, v. 18. 1922.

Goldschmidt, Walter. "Ethics and the Structure of Society: An Ethnological Contribution to the Sociology of Knowledge," *American Anthropologist*, v. 53, 506–524. 1951.

Heizer, Robert F. "A Prehistoric Yurok Ceremonial Site (HUM-174)," *Reports of the University of California Archaeological Survey*, no. 11, 1–4. 1951.

*Heizer, Robert F., and John E. Mills. *The Four Ages of Tsurai.* Berkeley and Los Angeles. 1952. The only systematic Yurok archaeology is reported in this history of one coastal settlement. The travelers' accounts presented are an invaluable source on Yurok history.

Hoopa Area News, v. 9, no. 3 (mimeographed). 1964.

Klamath River Indian People. *A Final, Desperate Appeal for Justice to the President and the Congress of the United States by the Klamath River Indian People of the Hoopa Valley Indian Reservation, Humboldt County, California.* (mimeographed) no date.

*Kroeber, Alfred L. *Handbook of the Indians of California.* Berkeley, 1953. The first ninety-seven pages of this volume contain a well-balanced ethnographic description of the Yurok.

Kroeber, Alfred L., and Edward W. Gifford. *World Renewal, A Cult System of Native Northwest California.* Anthropological Records, v. 13, no. 1. 1949.

McDonell, Terry. "Bury My Heart in the Hoopa Valley," *San Francisco*, May 1975.

Moratto, Michael J. "Tsahpekʷ: An Archaeological Record of Nineteenth Century Acculturation among the Yurok," *Archives of California Archaeology*, no. 7. 1970.

O'Neale, Lila M. *Yurok-Karok Basket Weavers.* UCPAAE, v. 32, no. 1. 1932.

Progress Report to the Legislature by the Senate Interim Committee on California Indian Affairs. Senate Resolution No. 115. State of California. Sacramento. 1955.

*Spott, Robert, and Alfred L. Kroeber. Yurok Narratives. UCPAAE, v. 35, no. 9. 1942. Robert Spott was an old and well-informed Yurok who

† University of California Publications in American Archaeology and Ethnology.

related to the recorder, Kroeber, historical accounts, tales of the more distant past, and myths. The historical accounts are particularly enlightening since they provide insight into the functioning of the sociocultural system.

Stearns, Robert E. "A Study of Primitive Money," *Report of the U.S. National Museum, 1887.* 297–334. Washington, D.C. 1889.

*Thompson, Lucy. *To the American Indian.* Eureka. 1916. Written by a Yurok woman, this book is one of the key ethnographic sources and ranks with the studies by Alfred L. Kroeber.

Transmitting Report by Subcommittee on Indian Affairs. Senate Committee on Rules Resolution No. 8. State of California. Sacramento. 1961.

Valory, Dale K. Yurok Doctors and Devils. Ph.D. dissertation, University of California, Berkeley. 1970.

Wassaja. American Indian Historical Society newspaper, 1974–1976 issues.

*Waterman, Thomas T. *Yurok Geography.* UCPAAE, v. 16, no. 5. 1920. This monograph is one of the most fascinating specialized studies about the Yurok. The detailed analysis of Yurok geographical concepts and the ways in which the Yurok conceived of the world offer a dimension of culture rarely considered systematically.

Waterman, Thomas T. "All is Trouble Along the Klamath," in *American Indian Life*, Elsie C. Parsons, ed., 289–296. New York. 1922.

Waterman, Thomas T. *The Kepel Fish Dam.* UCPAAE, v. 35, no. 6. 1938.

Waterman, Thomas T., and Alfred L. Kroeber. *Yurok Marriages.* UCPAAE, v. 35, no. 1. 1934.

10

The Tlingit: Salmon Fishermen of the Northwest

Legend about European Contact

One day during the summer of 1786 a Tlingit hunter looked seaward from Lituya Bay on the Gulf of Alaska and was startled by what he thought he saw. Imitating the call of a wolf to signal important news, he ran to a nearby village. As people gathered, he called, "Raven is coming." He told them that Raven was white and could be seen on the horizon to the west. Everyone knew that Raven had been white before he was turned black, and thus his reappearance as white was not surprising. This was a great moment because Raven, their creator and culture hero, had said he would return to reward people who obeyed his teaching and turn the others into stone. Some persons looking seaward peered at the white object through hollow stalks of kelp so that they would not be blinded by Raven's brightness. As Raven came into the bay, he folded his wings. Those individuals who expected to be turned into stone stood erect and cut their chests with stone knives; others who felt no guilt began painting their faces to receive this great and honored visitor. One wise old man decided to go out to Raven and ask to be turned into stone so that others might be spared. He paddled a canoe to Raven and was lifted, canoe and all, from the water onto Raven's body. Here the old Tlingit saw men with white faces, brown hair, and blue eyes; their clothing was

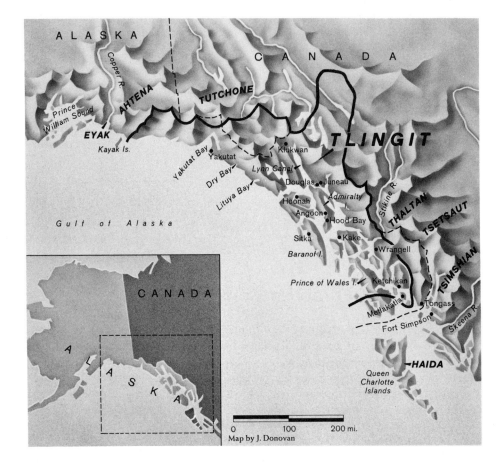

ALASKA

Copper R.

Prince William Sound

AHTENA

TUTCHONE

CANADA

EYAK

Kayak Is.

TLINGIT

Yakutat Bay

Yakutat

Dry Bay

Klukwan

Lynn Canal

Lituya Bay

Douglas • Juneau

Hoonah

Admiralty I.

Angoon

Hood Bay

Stikina R.

THALTAN

TSETSAUT

Gulf of Alaska

Sitka

Kake

Baranof I.

Wrangell

Prince of Wales I.

Ketchikan

TSIMSHIAN

Metlakatla

Tongass

Fort Simpson

Skeena R.

HAIDA

Queen Charlotte Islands

CANADA

A L A S K A

0   100   200 mi.

Map by J. Donovan

334

strange to him. The old man began to wonder whether he truly was in Raven's midst. A man far better clothed than the others appeared, and he was assumed to be Raven. The old man asked for mercy, but the man in fine clothing sent for food. One of the foods seemed to be a section of a human skull, and something else looked like maggots. Finally he was offered a red liquid that looked like blood; he declined to eat any of these things. The well-dressed man then crossed his hands in the air twice, and the old Indian knew that this was not Raven after all since the sign he made was the one used for trading. The old man exchanged his hat and garments of sea otter skin for a piece of iron and a small bell. Then, without clothing he got into his canoe, was lowered into the water, and paddled back to the village. He carried his prizes ashore and told the people of his great experience. This account by the northern Tlingit recalls the visit to Lituya Bay by Captain Jean de La Perouse of the *Astrolabe* and Paul-Antoine de Langle on the *Boussole*, the first Europeans to visit the locality.

People, Population, and Language

Tlingit, which means "people," is the term by which these Indians call themselves. Their language belongs to the Na-Dene phylum and is a single language at the family level. They possibly numbered 10,000 at the time of historic contact, but by 1975 about 15,000 Indians in southeastern Alaska identified themselves as Tlingit.

Reasons for This Selection

Although their prehistory is still largely unknown, we probably have more information about the Tlingit from early historic to modern times than for any other Northwest Coast salmon fishermen. Characteristics of Northwest Coast Indians include totem poles and potlatches, and these prevailed among the Tlingit. Their complex social networks and ceremonial life invite comparison with other salmon fishermen, the Kuskowagamiut and Yurok, represented in this book. The Tlingit serve as an excellent example of a people who lived in a land where food resources usually were abundant. They stressed wealth as well as social achievements within family lines. They had not organized politically at the tribal level; instead, narrowly defined bonds of kinship focused their economic, political, and social lives. Totem poles usually are assumed to have been an aboriginal characteristic of Northwest Coast Indians, but it will be shown that they are a relatively recent development, quite possibly stimulated by the fur trade. In addition long-term Tlingit success in coping with Western society is outstanding and contrasts with that of peoples described previously.

335
Reasons for This Selection

Prehistory

The dense vegetation and unstable coastline in the Tlingit region make it difficult to find early historic sites, and prehistoric remains are even more elusive. Sites that had been coastal 5000 years ago are now located a mile or more inland and are covered with trees. When de Laguna excavated in the Yakutat Bay area, she was unable to locate remains dating earlier than A.D. 1000; from these finds to historic Tlingit culture a continuity was clear. In the Glacier Bay region, Robert E. Ackerman found stone chopping tools that bear similarities with finds elsewhere that date as early as 7000 B.C., suggesting an early occupation for this area. The best overall evidence about Northwest Coast prehistory results from the excavations and interpretive studies by Charles E. Borden at sites along coastal British Columbia. He has established that a group of people lived along the coast just north of Vancouver Island before 7000 B.C. They fished for salmon and depended heavily on sea mammals for food. The implications are that they had a maritime economy that included seagoing boats and specialized equipment for taking the species involved. Borden suggests that these remains belonged to people who originally had lived inland and then moved to the coast to exploit its more plentiful resources. Much the same process was occurring farther south, but there molluscs, not sea mammals, were important. He interprets the cultural elaborations of historic Northwest Coast Indians as the result of an amalgamation of these two coastal traditions. Although this hypothesis does not reveal anything directly about Tlingit prehistory, it does suggest that north Pacific maritime adaptations are much older than previously had been thought possible.

Early History

As early as 1582 a Spanish explorer sailed along the Tlingit coast, but he apparently made no contact with the people. A Kamchatkan expedition led by Vitus Bering sailed in 1741 to determine whether the Asian and North American landmasses were continuous. The ship that Bering commanded anchored off Kayak Island, at the northern fringe of Tlingit country, and although no people were seen, the sailors found a camp with a burning fire. The commander of the other vessel, Alexei Chirikov, anchored off the southern shores of Tlingit country. He sent two boats to investigate the coast, but neither boat returned. Indians later paddled two canoes toward Chirikov's ship but withdrew before making contact. On the return voyage Bering and his crew were forced to winter on what came to be known as Bering Island off the coast of Kamchatka. Here Bering died, but his men returned to Kamchatka the next year with valuable pelts of sea mammals. Russian adventurers hastily formed trading and hunting expeditions and sailed to the Aleutian Islands in a quest for furs, especially for sea otter pelts because of their extremely high value in

The Tlingit: Salmon Fishermen of the Northwest

China. Before many years passed, Russian fur hunters and traders had reached the Alaska mainland. In the late 1700s as competition from European and American trading vessels seeking sea otters increased, Russian merchants moved to gain firm control over the north Pacific trade. In 1799 the Russian-American Company was granted a monopoly by Czar Paul I.

The Russian-American Company was dominated by one man above all others, Alexander Baranov, who had established a permanent base on Kodiak Island in 1791. Baranov's first contacts with the Tlingit were in Prince William Sound, where he and his party were mistaken by Yakutat Tlingit for Chugach Eskimos and attacked in the middle of the night. The Russians and the Aleuts who were with them fought off the Indians, but each side suffered casualties. This encounter with the Tlingit, like all earlier contacts by traders and explorers, was hostile. Early European explorers and traders often described these Indians as haughty, aggressive, thieving, and bellicose, especially when they outnumbered intruders. A fort and trading post was established at Sitka in 1799, and as long as Baranov was there the Indians did not attack, since they respected his bravery. After he left in 1801, the Indians destroyed the fort and killed the members of the small garrison. In 1804 Baranov, hoping to establish a fortress on a steep hill formerly occupied by the Indians, returned with almost 900 men. The Tlingit withdrew to a nearby fort, and the Russians founded their hilltop settlement, New Archangel (Sitka). Anchored before Sitka was the *Neva*, which under the command of Urey Lisiansky was the first vessel to sail to Russian-America from European Russia. The Indians were determined to drive the Russians away if possible, but they could not withstand the bombardment from the *Neva* and withdrew from the fort.

After the retirement of Baranov in 1818 a succession of administrators controlled the fortunes of the Russian-American Company, and relations with the Tlingit fluctuated with the abilities of the chief administrator. Throughout the latter part of the Russian period, Sitka was the primary trading center for the Tlingit, but American trading vessels and traders of the Hudson's Bay Company competed successfully for Tlingit pelts. The destructive Indian and Russian hunting techniques led to a rapid decline in the fur trade. When the Russian flag at Sitka was lowered on October 18, 1867, and the flag of the United States was raised, one era came to an end as another began.

Aboriginal Life

ORIGIN MYTH   According to the Tlingit the first people simply existed, and no explanation was sought for their ultimate origin. From these people, according to one tale, arose a woman whose sons were killed by her brother. She decided to commit suicide, but an old man told her to swallow a heated beach pebble. The woman followed his instructions and became pregnant. She bore an offspring, who was Raven in human form. When Raven was older, he visited his uncle in spite of his mother's warnings that his uncle had killed his ten older brothers. The uncle attempted to kill Raven, but because of his supernatural powers Raven saved himself. Finally, Raven caused a flood, and all the people perished except for Raven and his mother, who donned bird skins and flew into the air. Raven stuck his beak in the sky and hung there for ten days. After the water subsided, he fell to earth and landed on a heap of seaweed. Raven went to the house of Petrel, a man who had always existed. In a small locked box, on which he sat, Petrel kept water, and when Raven was thirsty, he was given only a little. Raven tricked Petrel into thinking that he, Petrel, had excreted in his bed. While Petrel was outside cleaning his blanket, Raven drank more than his fill of water and then flew to a tree with pitch in it. Petrel built a fire beneath the tree, and the smoke turned Raven from white to black. Later the trickery of Raven released the stars, the moon, and finally the sun into the sky. Raven was a creator or releaser of forces in the world, a culture hero, and above all else an inordinate trickster.

APPEARANCE AND CLOTHING   These people were lean, medium to tall in stature, and had skins no darker than those of many persons in southern Europe. Women wore their hair loose and had striking adornments. From their pierced earlobes hung ornaments of shell, stone, or teeth, and a woman's nasal septum was pierced to receive a bone pin. Each woman also wore a large medial labret inserted through a hole beneath the lower lip. The initial opening was made about the time of puberty and was fitted with increasingly larger labrets until the hole was as much as four inches across; as one observer noted,

Plate 10–1 A girl in the Yakutat area with earrings, a nose pin, and labret sketched by Don Tomás de Suría in 1791. (Courtesy of Yale University Library)

The Tlingit: Salmon Fishermen of the Northwest

these women could not kiss. Men wore their hair loose and rubbed it with grease; while their whiskers were not numerous, they were nonetheless plucked. When a male was young, his nasal septum was pierced, and through the opening a small ring was suspended. Men wore ear ornaments like those of the women, and a man of great achievements might have bits of wool or small feathers stuck in several small holes around the outer edge of his ear. Facial paints were worn by men and women on special occasions and as protection from temperature extremes and insects.

Adults of both sexes dressed in long-sleeved shirts of dehaired skin, over which they wore sea otter skin capes with the fur facing outward. The processed skin undergarments of women reached from the neck to the ankles. During severe weather they wore moccasins made by interior Indians or styled after their footwear. Tlingit hats, worn for hunting and ceremonies, were woven from roots or grass and were shaped like a truncated cone with a flat top. Their clothing hardly seems adequate to an outsider, but these people conditioned themselves to accept temperature extremes. They not only bathed in cold or icy waters but lived in scorching houses.

SETTLEMENTS   Tlingit country is a mass of mountains that reach a sea marked by islands, deep bays, and glaciers. This verdant land with its tranquil and turbulent waters had rich exploitative potential. Along the northern third impressive mountains abruptly meet the sea, and sheltering bays are rare. In the balance of their country innumerable large and small islands front a fractured coastline. The mild temperatures and heavy precipitation produce a lush and varied vegetation, including stands of red cedar and Sitka spruce. Considering the geographical configuration, it is understandable that travel by boat was far more important than walking, although paths to the interior existed along certain rivers and over low divides and were negotiated for trading or raiding ventures.

Winter villages were built along bays, inlets, or the lower courses of rivers where good fishing grounds were nearby and where canoes could be landed safely. The square, plank-covered houses had gabled roofs. At small villages houses were built in a line facing the water, but the houses in larger settlements were arranged in rows. In house construction a massive post was sunk in the ground at each corner and extended ten feet above the ground surface. On the tops of these and mid-wall support posts rested plates. Near the center of the front and back walls were higher posts supporting beams extending the length of a house. Above secondary roof beams were overlapping horizontal planks held in place with poles or stones; the sidewalls were likewise plank covered. Toward the middle of the roof an opening to let light in or smoke out was covered with a plank in foul weather. Before the round doorway were steps or a platform, and a mat covered the opening. The plank-covered floor of a small dwelling was at ground level, but the central area of larger houses was dug down about three feet. Along the sides at ground level were board or mat enclosed compartments to be used for sleeping, bathing, or storage. Around the fire pit were stones to be heated in the fire and placed in containers for cooking food. Overhead along the beams were stored hunting and fishing devices, and fish might be hung from the roof beams to dry. Among the northern Tlingit, in particular, the house of a leading lineage was likely to have decorated wall partitions or panels called heraldic screens. It appears that behind these screens were the apartments of the house chief. Around the entry to a house, or even around an entire village, were palisades to protect the occupants. A bough-covered structure might be leaned against the outer wall of a house or built close to it for women to use during menstrual periods or childbirth. Scattered about a settlement were pole racks for drying fish, and a short distance away, either toward the forest or sea, were clusters of graves. At summer camps, where the winter supply of fish was obtained, families lived in flimsy plank structures, some of which were walled only on the windward side.

The people were divided into named geographical groups called *kons*, and each had a principal village. From north to south the first kon was Yakutat, with its most important settlement along Yakutat Bay. The most powerful kon was that of the Chilkat, with four major villages along the shores of the upper Lynn Canal. One of these, Klukwan, had sixty-five houses and about 600 residents. The only interior group, the "Inland Tlingit," lived around a series of lakes and occupied the largest area. The other kons, each of which had at least one large village, were the Auk, Taku, Huna, Killisnoo, Sitka, Kake, Kuju, Stikine, Henya, Tongass, and Sanya. Tlingit tradition relates that the kons arrived in their present area from the south, somewhere around the Skeena River, except for the Kake, who came from the interior.

Within a village the land was owned by groups of persons who traced their descent to a presumed common female ancestor (matriclan), and land was subdivided among house groups. Plots of ground near houses were owned by the adjacent households, but village paths were common property. Trails were cleared by community members as a group, and the beach was open to use by everyone. Each kon had its geographical boundaries, and each village controlled the sector it exploited. Within the domain of a village, each represented clan had particular localities defined as its own. Unclaimed sectors could be exploited by anyone. A clan, or portion thereof, owned fishing streams, land of a stream's drainage used for hunting, sealing islands, mountains inhabited by mountain goats, ocean banks, berry patches, and house sites. They conceived of ownership in terms of specific spots utilized rather than as geographical areas exploited.

Tlingit craft skills rank high among tribal peoples anywhere in the world. Their manufactures in bone, stone, and wood are justly famous. In a typical aboriginal household were a wide variety of wooden containers. One style was made from a thin plank of cedar that was steamed and bent into a rectangular form, then overlapped and sewn with root. A wooden bottom was fitted into

The Tlingit: Salmon Fishermen of the Northwest

Plate 10–2 Potlatch bowl from Sitka with abalone and bone insets. (Photograph courtesy of the Alaska State Museum, Juneau, Alaska, Catalog No. II-B-802)

place and a top sometimes added. Some of these boxes had bulging sides that were painted or carved. The largest and most elaborately decorated boxes were used for the storage of valuables, and others were for cooking or food storage. Another common wooden form was made from a single piece of wood and ranged from round, to oval, to rectangular in outline. To these basic forms were adapted various animal shapes, such as a beaver lying on its back, with its head at one end, legs on the sides, and tail opposite the head. Other household items included dishes, spoons, and ladles of mountain sheep or goat horn. Oval lamps of pecked and polished stone furnished light as fish oil burned on a moss wick.

Family members gathered around the fire pit to rest, eat, or work during the day. At the fireplace meals were prepared at irregular times of the day for as many as thirty house occupants. Boiled foods were cooked in wooden or woven containers. Water was placed in them, and hot stones were dropped in to simmer the meat or fish before the lid was put on. Fish were boiled, roasted, or dried and served as the principal foods, supplemented by flesh from land and sea mammals. Also eaten were shellfish, vegetable products, and fruit, particularly a wide variety of berries, but these foods were relatively unimportant; however, shellfish were important in times of food stresses. Boiled foods were dipped from their cooking containers into large spoons, which served as plates, and large quantities of water were consumed at every meal.

ART   Northwest Coast Indian art has attracted a great deal of lasting attention, and as Franz Boas pointed out, two basic styles prevailed. The first was created by men; it was largely symbolic and was manifest in sculpture, carving, and painting. The second, or women's style, was largely formal, with little or no attending meaning and was manifest primarily in basketry designs. Although the Chilkat robes contained symbolic designs, the women who wove them reproduced symbolic paintings made on boards by a male designer. The

Plate 10–3 Chilkat woman weaving a dance robe. (From Krause, 1885, v. 1)

carving skills of men were expressed primarily in wood; red cedar was the favorite medium. The men likewise carved horn and ivory, pounded and incised copper, and used shell, hair, and skin for decorative elements. The women in their artistic crafts used animal wool and spruce or cedar root fibers. Their basketry designs usually were geometric, and the specific motifs were named. The baskets had nearly straight sides and were flat-bottomed. The sides were decorated, but rims usually were plain.

The crest of a clan was carved on any object by a member of the opposite moiety who held a rank equal to that of the individual requesting the carving. By preference this would be a wife's brother; if such an individual was not a capable carver, he could hire someone else of either moiety to make the object. The man who was first asked to do the work paid the craftsman and in turn was paid by his brother-in-law. Carvings produced in this manner fulfilled ritual obligations, and the labor involved was ceremonial.

Among the common elements in symbolic art were symmetrical, stylized figures. Animals most often were the subject matter, but human figures also appeared. Sometimes these seem to have been portraits of individuals. Tlingit art was not as complex as that of those Indians to the south; neither was it so

342

monumental, possibly because of the scarcity or absence of great cedar trees in most of the Tlingit area. The Tlingit did excel in producing a wide variety of imaginative masks used by performing shamans. The human faces might be supplemented with animal figures, which were the familiars of shamans. The carvings on utilitarian objects served to enhance their beauty and bring prestige to their owners. Distortion was an important consideration in their creations, since traditional forms were adapted to diverse surfaces. Carving a bear on a totem pole was very different from fitting the bear motif on a rectangular vessel, the handle of a horn spoon, or a flat screen painting. Another characteristic of the artistic symbolism was to emphasize features of an animal as a key to its identification. The beaver was characterized by its incisor teeth and tail, while the killer whale was keyed to its prominent dorsal fin. So it was with other totemic representations. Prominent and recurring characteristics included the skeletal motif, the use of joint markers, and the prominence of stylized eyes. Tlingit craftsmen employing these motifs produced outstanding works of art.

CONVEYANCES   The most important manufacture for subsistence activities was the canoe, normally built in the winter when unhurried production led to attractive and sound vessels. The best wood was from a straight-grained red cedar blown over by the wind or felled by building a fire at the base. With a stone-bladed adz the log was hewn and scraped. To spread the sides of the hollowed log the cavity was filled with water, and hot stones were dropped into it. As the log expanded, pieces of wood were wedged across the gunwales to give the sides the desired degree of flare. The outer sides might be painted with designs and the bow carved. A small canoe carried two or three persons, whereas larger ones held sixty persons and were forty-five feet in length. Canoes were propelled with paddles, and an extra-long paddle was used for steering. When not in use, a canoe was covered with mats or blankets to protect it from the sun, and water was sprinkled over the sides. A small canoe made from a cottonwood log was used for fishing and river travel.

Snowshoes were essential for overland mobility during the winter, especially among the Chilkat who went inland to trade at this time of year. The light maple or birch snowshoe frames were heated over a fire and shaped; the netting was made from rawhide thongs. The shoes were about four feet in length and ten inches wide at their broadest point, with rounded toes that turned up at the front and pointed heels.

SUBSISTENCE ACTIVITIES   Terrestrial fauna included both black and grizzly bears, fox, wolves, wolverine, lynx, and deer on some islands. Scattered caribou herds occupied mainland plateaus, and mountain goats as well as mountain sheep frequented the coastal ranges. Smaller species included hare, squirrel, ermine, porcupine, muskrat, and a few beaver. Among the marine mammals were whales, hair and fur seals, sea lions, and sea otter. Of all the fish

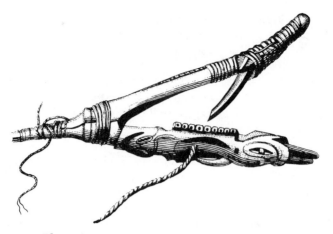

Plate 10–4 Halibut hook. (From Lisianskii, 1814)

the most important were the salmon and candlefish (eulachon); halibut, haddock, trout, and herring also were caught. Along the edges of the sea were edible algae, crabs, sea urchins, mussels, and cockles. The avifauna included the bald eagle, raven, owl, and migratory waterfowl that summered in the area.

The subsistence cycle ebbed during the winter, and even March did not offer reliable weather for fishing. Nonetheless, it was during March that the subsistence year began anew. Canoes were repaired, fishing gear was readied, and men waited anxiously. In calm weather they fished for halibut along the coast fronting the Pacific Ocean. Two men fished from a canoe, maintaining about fifteen lines with baited V-shaped hooks and a wooden floater for each. When a fish was hooked, they paddled to the bobbing float, raised the line, and clubbed the fish to death as it was boated. Trout fishing with baited hooks also was important at this time. Following the ice breakup in March women fished for trout with gill nets of rawhide with inflated bladder floats and stone sinkers. One woman usually paddled a canoe as a second handled the drifting net. Clams and mussels were collected in large quantities and were either dried and smoked for future use or were steamed in a pit by pouring water over hot stones and a leaf covering. The pelts of fur animals were prime in March; fox, mink, wolf, and river (land) and sea otter all were sought. Some of these animals were trapped in deadfalls, but sea otter were hunted with harpoon darts.

Candlefish were a rich source of the oil that was drunk during feasts but more commonly served as a dip for dried salmon. These small fish were taken in traps or dip nets in the spring as they ascended rivers. Their processing began by placing the fish and water in a canoe half-buried in the sand. Heated stones repeatedly were dropped into the mass, and as the oil from the cooked fish came to the surface it was ladled into wooden containers. In mid-April herring spawned in shallow bays and were so numerous that they could be impaled on sharp tines set in the side of a pole. The tine-studded pole was drawn back and forth in the water, and the pierced herring were shaken off into the canoe. They either were eaten soon after being caught or were strung on ropes and dried.

Chilkat men traveled inland trading fish oil to Athapaskan Indians in exchange for caribou skins, moccasins, sinew, and lichens to be used for a particular form of dye. During the summer great canoes were paddled south to Haida and Tsimshian country, and in early historic times trading canoes even ventured as far as Puget Sound. They carried copper from the Copper River and other local products that were exchanged for dentalia, haliotis, shark teeth, and slaves.

Sea mammals usually were hunted with harpoon darts that had a line running from the detachable dart head to the shaft. When an animal was struck, the barbed dart head held beneath its skin, and the shaft was dragged through the water as the animal sounded. When it surfaced, the captive was harpooned again or killed with a spear or club. The most important species hunted were dolphin, seals, sea lions, and especially sea otter in early historic times. Only the Yakutat Tlingit hunted great whales, and they seem to have done so under stimulus from their Eskimo neighbors. From the ethnographic accounts it would seem that sea mammal hunting was not very important; neither does it appear that inland hunting was important at most settlements. If bears or mountain goats were pursued, they were cornered with the aid of dogs and killed with bone-pointed spears.

In the late summer berries were collected and stored with candlefish oil in airtight boxes. Salmon eggs, oil, and berries were similarly mixed and preserved. If large land mammals were killed, their flesh usually was cut into strips and sun-dried or else boiled and stored in oil. Some foods were stored for winter at this time of the year, but it was not until September that the winter food supply became a major concern. Diverse species of salmon were taken during the summer, but no great effort was made to catch and dry quantities of them until September. The species available included dog (chum), humpback (pink), king (chinook), silver (coho), and sockeye (red), and these were taken from July through December. The principal salmon-fishing device was a funnel-shaped trap set with the mouth opening downstream. The stream was blocked with a weir, which opened only at the trap. Fish caught in September were cleaned and hung on racks to dry or were smoke-cured in the house. After being dried or smoked, they were bundled and stored. As soon as a house group obtained enough salmon for the winter, the members left their fishing camp and settled down in their village until April. Very little food was gathered during the winter months, for this was the season of feasting, storytelling, and leisure.

DESCENT, KINSHIP, AND MARRIAGE   The people of each kon were divided into two groups (moieties) that were represented in each of the geographical areas. The moieties were named Raven and Wolf, with the Wolf moiety called Eagle in the north; these were in turn divided into named descent groups traced through females (matriclans). The Tlingit considered that certain personality characteristics were associated with the moieties. Raven people were expected to be wise and cautious, but the Wolves were quick-tempered and warlike. According to Aurel Krause the clans of the Raven moiety included the Frog, Goose, Owl, Raven, Salmon, and Sea Lion. Clans of the Wolf moiety included the Auk, Bear, Eagle, Shark, Whale, and Wolf. These lists, although far from complete, identify the important clans in early historic times. Someone who was not a member of any clan was thought of as a stranger and was addressed as uncle or son-in-law, reflecting his in-marrying status. At Klukwan the most important clans were the Wolf and Eagle; these were divided into named subgroups that probably were lineages. Within each clan the lineage with the greatest amount of wealth was most influential. Ideally the leadership of a lineage was passed from a man to his sister's son, but apparently this practice could be bypassed by appointing a new chief while the old one was still alive. Each settlement with a number of clans represented had more than one chief, but one dominated because of his wealth and personality. A person in one moiety was obligated to seek as a mate someone in the opposite moiety (moiety exogamy); further ramifications of marital arrangements are presented in the section about the life cycle.

Each clan recognized a particular settlement as the place of its ultimate origin. Although a clan was identified initially with a specific site, by the time of historic contact a number of different clans usually were represented in most villages. If a clan was large in a particular settlement, it was divided into lineages represented by house groups. In theory, the clans of each moiety possessed distinctive titles and associated design motifs which only members could use. These might be lent temporarily or even usurped by a more powerful clan. Again in theory, only members of the Raven moiety had the right to the raven design and those of the Wolf moiety, the wolf design. House names usually were derived from a clan myth, from the clan's name, or by assuming the name of another clan's house for legendary or historical reasons. What we see are moieties, each divided into a number of matriclans that in turn were divided into house groups composed of nuclear families, again related through females.

Nuclear family unity did not exist because the parents were of different clans and moieties. Since various clans were represented in most areas, geographical groupings acted as a unit only in those rare instances when a feud affected all sections of the clan. A clan had no common leader or unified territory, and even crests often were identified with localized lineages rather than with the clan as a whole. Finally, each clan included persons ranked as nobles, commoners, or slaves, depending on the social standing of particular lineages.

In the kinship system we find that a single term embraced all the people of the grandparent generation. To these persons Ego was attentive and re-

The Tlingit: Salmon Fishermen of the Northwest

spectful. The ties between a mother and her son were close even though the son might leave home to live with his mother's elder brother, who was for him the most powerful individual in Tlingit society and his authority figure. Fathers were considered too lenient to discipline their sons effectively, and of course a father did not belong to his son's clan or moiety. Parents especially were concerned about the welfare of a daughter, who would command a large bride-price only if she was well-mannered and a maiden; thus she always was watched by someone. A mother's sister was called by a term for diminutive mother and was treated as one's mother. The "little mother" term was extended to all the other women of her moiety in her generation. A mother was aided and advised in raising children by her sister. A father's sister was termed differently from mother and mother's sister, with the father's sister word extended to all women of her moiety in both her generation and the next descending generation. The father term was unique, but a diminutive word for father was employed for father's brother and extended to the other men of his moiety of his generation as well as the next lower one. A man treated his father's brother with respect, and a girl on rare occasion married her father's brother. A man ideally married his father's sister, and because she was a potential mate, their relationship was always warm. At one's generational level a man distinguished between older and younger brothers, and these terms were extended to the other men of one's generation and moiety. Older and younger male sibling distinctions were highly important because an older brother had the first rights of inheritance, greater authority, and more ceremonial responsibilities. A woman made the same distinction among sisters. There also was a particular term for a man's sister and one for a woman's brother; these were extended to all the members of that sex of Ego's generation and moiety. Brothers were socially and physically close since they were of the same clan and lived in the same house; with a sister a man must be distant and withdrawn, although he was concerned for her welfare. A mother's sister's children were termed as brother and sister, and the boys were raised in the same household as Ego. The terminology for the first ascending generation was essentially bifurcate merging, and the cousin terminology was of the Crow type. One overriding principle governed the kinship terminology of the Tlingit: to

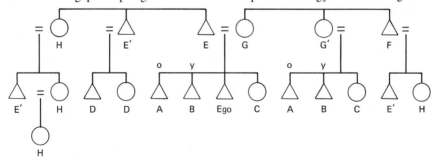

Aboriginal Tlingit kin terms

separate blood relatives in one's own moiety from those in the opposite moiety. The average adult avoided using relationship terms in direct address in everyday conversation for fear of offending someone since there was a great deal of emphasis on an exact ranking of individuals. Thus nicknames and given names were in common use. Relationship terms were employed primarily on ceremonial occasions.

SOCIAL DIMENSIONS   The most important social and economic unit was the household, and it had a significant place in the ceremonial life of the clan and moiety. A house group ideally was composed of Ego and his brothers, as well as his mother's sister's sons who were classificatory brothers, and the sons of the sisters of these individuals, plus the sons of the daughters of these sisters. All were members of one matrilineage, and there were additionally the in-marrying spouses. It was a household of this nature that functioned as an economic unit, with members working for their common welfare. In particular it was brothers, led by the eldest, the Keeper of the House, who aided one another in feuds, potlatches, and other matters of house group concern. The importance of the Keeper of the House in directing house group life cannot be overestimated. He directed the economic activities of household members and was deferred to by the other men in his residence unit. The house group leader allotted items obtained in trade, was given choice foods, and was freed from any humble form of household labor. It was this man, the eldest brother, who represented the household in ceremonial activities as well as in clan councils. Furthermore, when he died the rights to his position fell to the next oldest person called "brother." In addition to the position of Keeper of the House the wealthiest of the local household heads in any clan, and thus the ranking Keeper of the House, was designated Rich Man. These men more than any others were responsible for the fortunes of their clan units.

TOTEM POLES   Of all the fascinating subjects connected with the Northwest Coast Indians none has received more attention than totem poles. Their size and romantic appeal have long attracted description and comparison. The first account of a Tlingit totem pole was the report of Alexandro Malaspina in 1791 about a Yakutat area mortuary pole. The most detailed discussion of Tlingit totem poles is by Edward L. Keithahn, who reports that carved posts in house interiors and mortuary posts existed among the Tlingit in prehistoric times. He also observed that it was not until between 1840 and 1880 that the pole standing apart from a house became common along the northwest coast. Even during this era totem poles were not widespread among the Tlingit, and Keithahn questions whether any great totem poles could have been carved before the general availability of iron-bladed tools; however, it appears that a well-developed woodworking technology predates the use of iron tools on the Northwest Coast. The erection of great totem poles became a means for house groups who became wealthy through the fur trade to record

348

The Tlingit: Salmon Fishermen of the Northwest

Plate 10–5 The earliest illustration of a Tlingit mortuary pole and graves, 1791, for the Yakutat area. (From Malaspina and de Bustamante y Guerra, 1885)

their increased prestige. Some aspiring persons did not have the right to carve the heraldic crests, and so they originated new symbols such as the bull and ship, basing their right to use these forms on the claim that they were the first to see them. When the Krause brothers were among the Tlingit in 1881–1882, it was noted by Aurel that one totem pole was found among the Chilkat, none were among the Sitka and Killisnoo groups, but many existed at the Stikine settlement near Wrangell.

Tlingit totem poles were erected to serve diverse purposes. The four main posts inside houses normally were not carved, but they were faced with carved pillars or panels, some of which still stood inside modern Tlingit houses at Klukwan in the early 1960s. The pillar faces were carved with clan crests. Often included were abalone shell inlays, and sometimes human hair or ermine fur was attached. A second form was the mortuary pole with a box at the top for the burnt bones and ashes of the dead. In historic times a crest figure was placed on the top of this form, and the ashes were placed in a recess at the back of the pole. A later style of mortuary pole had story figures carved on it. A third type was the memorial pole, which most often was raised by a maternal nephew or a younger brother in memory of a house group leader who had died. These poles were erected within a year of the commemorated person's death and were not habitually raised at the site of interment. Memorial poles not only honored the dead but validated the succession of the new house group leader. Modern forms of memorial and mortuary poles are tombstones made of granite or marble, with crests carved on them by the monument companies. The heraldic pole, the fourth form, was erected at the front and center

Plate 10–6 Chief's house with painted front and totem poles in 1899. (Courtesy of Smithsonian Institution National Anthropological Archives, neg. no. 43, 548-H)

of a house, and an oval opening near the base served as the house entrance. Carved and painted on a pole of this form was a tale associated with the house group. The fifth type, the potlatch pole, is the most recent form to develop. These were raised to enhance the prestige of the family group who had accumulated and distributed wealth earned by trading furs or working directly for whites. Such poles recorded the holding of an elaborate potlatch. The sixth and final form was the ridicule pole, which usually was raised to force a house group to recognize and compensate for a debt. For example, one ridicule pole is said to have been carved and erected to shame a white trader for not repaying a potlatch given in his honor.

For the Tlingit the erection of a totem pole was an end in itself. A pole carved and raised for a particular purpose was unimportant afterwards as a physical object. As a pole tilted with age or threatened to fall, it was not supported in any manner. Restoration necessitated an outlay of wealth and ceremonial involvements equal to that expended when the original pole was raised, and therefore it was more sensible to erect another pole and bring even greater

The Tlingit: Salmon Fishermen of the Northwest

honor to the house group. Since poles deteriorated rapidly in this damp area and comparatively few new poles were raised after the turn of the present century, most have rotted away.

The totemic symbols exhibited on poles were associated with one or the other of the moieties, with clans, or with house groups. All of the Raven moiety members employed the Raven design as their primary symbol. The Wolf moiety had the Wolf as its chief totem in the south and the Eagle in the north. Not only the actual crests but the names of animals associated with a clan were important, and their uses were validated through the potlatch system. These honorific names often drawn from the clan or moiety totems tended to pass from great-grandfather to great-grandson. The animals associated with a moiety could be killed and eaten by moiety members, however, and the uniform eating habits of all the tribe indicate no taboo on eating one's totemic species.

Plate 10–7 The totem pole erected at the town of Kake in 1971 is 136 feet high, reportedly the tallest pole ever raised. (Courtesy of Alaska Division of Tourism)

Aboriginal Life

ENTERTAINMENT   An important pastime among adult males was gambling, and some men were so addicted that they sometimes lost prized possessions and even a wife. The most important form of gambling was a hand game in which one man guessed which hand of an opponent held a uniquely marked stick. The game was played by teams, but only one man of each team handled the sticks at any one time. Other adult diversions included dice games and a ball game in which the purpose was to drive a ball along the tidal flats to the opponent's goal. Boys played a game that involved throwing a stick at a rolling wad of grass. They also wrestled, hunted, and swam for entertainment. A favorite diversion among little girls was to arrange beach pebbles in the form of figures.

POLITICAL LIFE   Conflicts between moieties were common, and modern Tlingit liken their disputes to relations between European nations. For real or imagined injuries either material goods were exchanged or a life was taken. The nature of a settlement depended on the ability of the guilty to pay and the power of the offended to collect. Minor conflicts eventually were settled at feasts that included property settlements. When a person was grievously offended, the only acceptable retribution was the offender's murder, but this was bound to lead to a retaliatory killing. When the persons murdered were of unequal rank, there was the further problem of establishing a value for each death. Sometimes when an individual felt badly wronged and had no means to retaliate, he committed suicide, and his relatives then pressed for compensation. On occasion clan disputes were settled by a duel between warriors who represented each group. Murders were from ambush as were raids against other clans or tribes. The only crimes occurring within a clan were incest and witchcraft, each punishable by death. It should be stressed that overall political unity did not exist within a moiety, and some of the bloodiest feuds were between clans of the same moiety.

Raids were conducted to avenge a death and to obtain slaves. Preparations for impending conflict involved abstaining from all contact with women and fasting. In addition a warrior conditioned himself for combat by bathing in the sea, even at the coldest time of the year, and by being whipped by an older man. As a raiding party traveled, it seized property from camps along the way irrespective of whether the residents were friendly or not. A shaman always accompanied the party and predicted events of the near future. Plans for an attack on an enemy community were kept secret, and the foray was launched at dawn. Rod or skin armor protected a man's body; his face was covered with a mask, and his head with a wooden helmet. All the enemy men who did not escape were killed with daggers; women and children were taken as prisoners. A reprisal attack would be expected to avenge the murders. A copper-bladed dagger, spear, and a war club appear to have been the most important weapons. Scalps were taken at times, and the scalped person's head sometimes was impaled on a stick and exhibited. The men in a war party sang of victory as they returned to their village, and the paddle of each warrior killed was stuck up at the spot he had occupied in the boat. To bind peace hostages might be exchanged and kept for a year or longer. Peacemaking followed a pattern of ceremonialism, which climaxed with the exchange of hostages, termed "deer," since they were to behave as timidly as these animals.

Most slaves were captured in raids or purchased from peoples to the north or south. Others were the children of indebted men who could find no way out of their dilemma except to offer themselves and as many of their children as necessary to cancel the debt. These slaves, unlike the captives, might be redeemed. Slaves usually were well cared for by their masters since they were a valuable form of property. Yet there are reports that picture the lot of slaves as extremely difficult since they performed all odious tasks and might at any time be killed at their owner's fancy. Sometimes slaves were killed to emphasize the importance of their owner, for instance when he built a new house. To gain prestige one man might kill a number of slaves; his rival would be obligated to kill a greater number, and so it went until one contestant had no more slaves. The ownership of slaves apparently provided prestige more than economic gain. The proportion of slaves to free persons is not known, but ten slaves in a house was a large number.

SHAMANISM   Knowledge about the natural world was crystallized and integrated into a loosely ordered system. The world was thought of as a flat expanse with the sky as a dome above the earth. In all this space everything that existed was alive: spirits lived on the sun and moon; stars were the lights of distant towns or houses; clusters of stars sometimes were named, and Venus was identified. A rainbow was the path of dead souls to the upper

Plate 10–8 Shaman's mask of painted wood. (Courtesy, Field Museum of Natural History, Chicago)

world, and the northern lights were human spirits playing. Everything on earth was possessed by a spirit quality, which had subordinates or helpers; each trait, every fire, and everything that one did had its main spirit and helpers.

Tlingit shamans reputedly were the most powerful on the north Pacific coast, and their effectiveness came from the spirits they controlled. The usual manner in which a clan acquired a new shaman was for the spirit of the clan's shaman to leave his body at death and enter the body of an upstanding clan youth. Nephews who aspired to the position went into trances around the dead man's body, and the one who remained in a trance the longest was most likely named the successor. After this supernatural visitation the novice and certain near relatives went into the forest, ate little, and searched for a sign. The most propitious was to see a bird or an animal drop dead; the spirit of this creature henceforth aided the tyro. After the young man demonstrated that he had his uncle's power, he inherited the ceremonial equipment.

Shamans controlled the spirits represented on their masks, and while most spirits served specific clans, some could be controlled by any shaman. The latter category included a spirit associated with the souls of persons who were lost at sea or died alone in the forest. The primary protecting spirit was represented as the main figure on a mask, and helping spirits also might appear. A secondary spirit might be posed around the eyes of a mask, thereby increasing the vision of the primary spirit. A shaman neither cut nor combed his hair, and about his neck he wore a bone necklace and a small whetstone, the latter used for scratching his head. A shaman owned rattles that had spirit associations and were used in his performances. The split tongues of animals, especially the river otter, and the claws of eagles were sources of power; both appear to have been placed in bundles of cedar bark, grass, and devil's club. After a shaman bathed, he rubbed himself with the bundle, and he used it in all his rituals. Among the spirit helpers were those of the sun, the sea, and the crest animals of the shaman's clan. After summoning his spirit helpers, a shaman cured an afflicted individual by blowing, sucking, or passing an object over the locus of the disease, which drew out the cause. Other services of a shaman included locating food sources and predicting the future. A shaman and his family usually lived in a separate residence, and in the forest near the house was his shrine. From time to time shamans retreated for extended periods to intensify their spirit relationships.

A number of charms appear to have been employed by ordinary persons. Made from parts of plants, they were used in such diverse activities as foreseeing the future, attracting a woman, making one wealthy, or improving hunting abilities. A few additional items seem to have served as secular cures, but these were rare and apparently unimportant. In general, it would appear that curing and supernaturalism were shamanistic matters. It is interesting that salmon, which were the all-important subsistence item, were not dealt with in a sacred manner. They simply were accepted as present and were

Plate 10–9 Ivory carving that was possibly a shaman's charm. (Courtesy of the Museum of Primitive Art, New York, photograph by Lisa Little)

caught and eaten. Even in the mythology salmon play a relatively unimportant role; they seem to have been regarded as a constant part of the environment.

Witchcraft most often was performed by obtaining an item intimately associated with the victim and using it in a representation of the victim in the form desired. If a person became ill, the cause was attributed to sorcery, and the offender was named by the curing shaman. Persons accused of being witches usually were women, children, or slaves. They were tortured to extract a confession or even killed if a confession was not forthcoming. An accused witch was bound by members of his clan and refused food and water for eight days or even longer. If he did not confess, it was expected that he would die; when a witch did confess, the bewitching substance was scattered in the sea.

RECIPROCITY   The complex ceremonial network centered on critical moments in the lives of individuals and on events that were important in a clan or community. Thus, birth and death, successful raids, the completion of a new house, property redistribution, or the settlement of disputes required ceremonial acknowledgment. The duration of a ceremony indicated its importance; it might last for one night, several days, or longer if the host could continue providing food. Ceremonies usually included feasts, songs, dances, and the presentation of gifts to honored guests. The most elaborate ceremonies were held in association with the death of an important individual. First there was the cremation ceremony shortly after death; later there might be an anniversary feast to honor the deceased and establish the social position of his successor. The key to Tlingit ceremonial involvement was the emphasis on reciprocity. Whenever a child's lip or ears were pierced, a person was initiated into a secret society (a recent Tlingit ritual complex), or the dead buried, someone of the opposite moiety was responsible for carrying out the proper procedures. A house group accumulated food and resources for a year or longer to host a ceremony. At the ceremony guests were fed and presented gifts for their labor. Songs and dances were performed by hosts and guests alike, each alert to any affront in the words of the other participants or to any mistake in the performance. Any error in a dance or song was grounds for a property claim, and if breaches of etiquette were flagrant, fights took place.

The institutionalized redistribution of goods played an important part in the economic lives of the Tlingit. Exchanges or gifts linked the various interdependent units of the society in diverse ways. The Tlingit distinguished numerous forms of exchanges, beginning with barter, then gift exchange, food gifts, feasts, the ceremonial exchange of labor, and finally, ceremonial gifts or potlatches. Through barter or gift exchanges one might acquire a needed item or one that he could not personally make very well. Such exchanges were made by individuals even within the same house group. The protocol was to work through an intermediary, having him present a gift to the craftsman and make the request. When a large item such as a canoe was desired, a number of gifts were offered to the craftsman at intervals. If the gifts offered did not measure up to the product sought, the craftsman produced an inferior object. Gifts of food, particularly to members of other house groups in the same clan, were offered when a particular house group had a product in abundance. There was no great concern to equalize such gifts, although in time they should balance one another. Feasts were given by a house group when success in hunting, fishing, or trading had been inordinate. Near relatives were invited, and the food not consumed was taken home by the guests. As mentioned elsewhere, the exchange of labor between moieties was socially integrating and economically significant. With the exchange of labor went feasting and reciprocal gifts of property. The most important potlatch goods were slaves, who were killed or more often freed. Second, plates of native copper pounded into shield-like forms, a means of concentrating wealth, were exchanged intact, cut into sections as mementos to guests, or thrown into the sea as an ultimate proof of one's wealth. Finally, blankets, which were not really blankets at all but ceremonial robes, were given as gifts or torn into sections and distributed to guests to commemorate a potlatch. Items offered in a potlatch were borrowed by the house group within its clan, manufactured by the house group, and sometimes borrowed from other clans in the same moiety. There was the

356

The Tlingit: Salmon Fishermen of the Northwest

constant effort to give greater potlatches than one's rivals, and as a result emphasis was placed on the production and accumulation of these goods.

A POTLATCH   John R. Swanton's account of a potlatch is summarized here because such descriptions of Tlingit ceremonies are rare. The purposes of this potlatch, performed around the turn of the present century, were to commemorate the erection of a new house, honor a deceased chief, and rebury his remains. In this instance a Raven house builder at Klukwan and a second host sent the former's wife and her friends to Sitka to extend the invitation. When they arrived, the builder's wife distributed leaf tobacco, fed the people, and told of her mission. The invited guests danced and displayed their crests to demonstrate their respect for those extending the invitation. These activities were repeated the following day. The next morning the wife of the Klukwan Raven threw a piece of charcoal outside as a sign that her people, the Wolves, should give property to her. The reason for the request was that the Wolves at Klukwan had helped build her husband's house but that the Sitka Wolves had not. She was given property totalling more than $2000 in value. After the Wolves of Sitka had prepared all their ceremonial equipment, they set off in boats for Klukwan, followed by the woman and her friends. When they camped, the four dance leaders of the guest party practiced their dances, abstained from women, fasted, and made medicine. As they moved north they plundered towns for provisions, and because they were so powerful no one dared stop them.

When the guests arrived at Klukwan, one of the hosts met them with his bow and arrows in hand. He pretended to release an arrow, showing how brave he was to be in the pending distribution of great wealth. The second host received the guests, and everyone crowded in one house to dance. The Sitka Wolves danced and then the Klukwan Eagles. Somewhat later the guests were feasted, the main dish being roasted salmon, a favorite dish of the deceased chief in whose honor the potlatch was being held. Another dance was held, followed by a greater feast, and still another dance was given by the guests, competitive with that of the hosts. Food was brought, and a huge platter was set before two male guests. They were expected to eat it all, but when they could not quite finish the meal, the Klukwan people mocked them. Then all of the guests ate, using horn spoons belonging to the dead chief of the Klukwan Ravens, and after they finished, the hosts ate.

The following morning the Sitka people discussed with those from Klukwan the reburial of the chief's remains. This was the real reason they had been summoned. The guests reburied the bones and erected a carved monument. The following morning the guests were served the best of foods, and the house builder whose wife had extended the invitation doubled the amount of property she had received and presented it to his guests. As the property was being brought out, the guests were paid to dance and sing, with the most important persons receiving as much as $200 for dancing. It required four

Plate 10–10 Dance rattle. (From Lisianskii, 1814)

days to give out all of the blankets. The house builder wore a hat that had been used by his uncles and grandmothers; by wearing it, along with distributing so much property, he established his social position as the Raven chief at Klukwan. The two hosts alone distributed about $11,000 worth of property. After a final feast the guests "left a dance" as a gesture of respect for their hosts. There was a song contest at the end of the potlatch to see who knew the most songs, and after all was over, the overloaded canoes of the Sitka Wolves departed for home.

The pageantry of Tlingit ritual performances brought drama into their ceremonies. The drums, either box or tambourine, provided background music, along with wooden rattles on certain occasions. The ritual dramatizations were derived from the mythology and accompanied by chants as well as songs. The performances took place around the central fireplace of a house. The actors were dressed in their finest apparel, and their typical step was to a two-four beat of the drums. The steps of the dancers were repetitive, with the greatest variations in tense movements of the shoulders, trunk, legs, and arms.

LIFE CYCLE   Childbearing was prohibited within the mother's home because it would have brought ill fortune to the men of the house. Thus a birth took place in a shelter never visited by men. During the birth slaves and a midwife, always a member of the opposite moiety and preferably the woman's husband's sister, aided the woman. Inside the structure a pit was dug and lined with moss, and a stake was driven into the center of the hole. While giving birth, the woman squatted in the pit, holding the stake. After the birth the umbilical cord was cut and placed in a bag hung around a neonate's neck for eight days; the umbilical cord of a boy later was placed under a tree where an eagle had nested to make the boy a brave adult. To prevent a baby from crying repeatedly, the first cry was caught in a container and apparently buried where many people walked so that it was smothered as the baby grew. The baby was wrapped in skins, with moss for a diaper, and was tied to a board. The mother carried the cradleboard with her or hung it from a roof beam when she was in the house. A mother placed woodworm burrowings on

358

her nipples so that as the baby nursed it would swallow the burrowings and would be neat in later life. A child was nursed for three or four years and was given its first solids after about a year. An infant born to a woman without a husband normally was suffocated. A baby was named after a maternal ancestor; the name itself was taken from an animal associated with the clan. Later in life a child could acquire a name from its father's clan if a potlatch was held for the event. A man who gave his son a second name soon after its birth obligated the offspring to give great potlatches. With the birth of a son the parents referred to themselves by the son's name, as the father or the mother of the son (teknonymy). A family with great wealth could enhance the social standing of all their children by freeing a slave for each child and building a new house. Property was distributed to all those who aided in the construction, and the ceremonial climax occurred when the children had their earlobes pierced by a woman who would receive many gifts. Such children were termed " of the nobility," and their descendants were referred to similarly.

Children were encouraged to behave in a manner appropriate to adults of the same sex. They were taught to restrain any sign of emotion, to be dignified and aloof. Physical punishment of children occurred only if they refused to bathe in cold water during the winter; they were expected to take cold baths daily from the time they learned to walk. When boys moved to the household of their mother's brother, they were switched by this man after bathing and were forced to run up and down the beach. After this physical exertion, they were instructed by older men in the customs and history of the clan and learned certain skills by watching the men perform routine tasks. As a boy grew, he came increasingly under the influence of his maternal uncle and performed tasks for this older man rather than for his father. A boy tended to gravitate toward a particular uncle whom he wished to emulate in his exceptional skills relating to carving, hunting, or the supernatural. The uncle gave honorific names to his young charges and taught them clan lore, but there were no secret initiations. The most important nephew was the oldest, for he would inherit from his maternal uncle not only material property and wives but titles as well. Even while young, boys were free to use a maternal uncle's tools with permission. If a mother died, the father was obliged to place the offspring in the custody of the mother's siblings.

When a girl first menstruated, she was confined to a brush-covered shelter or to a separate compartment in the house behind the heraldic screen. Her face was covered with charcoal, and she was attended by female relatives and a slave if her parents were wealthy. A high-born girl was isolated for a year, and one of lower birth was confined for at least three months. She drank water through a bird-bone tube and went outside only at night, even then wearing a broad-brimmed hat so that she would not taint the stars with her gaze. During isolation her mother instructed her about proper female behavior and taught her clan myths and songs. At the beginning of her confinement her lip, nasal septum, and possibly her earlobes were pierced by a woman of the opposite moiety. When she came out of seclusion, she wore new clothing, and her slave attendant, if she had one, was freed. The girl would marry soon, and to insure that she remained chaste she slept on a shelf above her parents' bed. The rank of a person was reckoned through both sides of the family and depended largely on the amount of bride-price paid by one's father for one's mother; thus parents attempted to provide a daughter with all the advantages of careful rearing and wealth.

Moiety exogamy was strictly observed, and a match was initiated by the suitor, who used a go-between to approach the girl and her family. If favorably received, he sent presents to his future father-in-law. The most desirable marriage partners, in decreasing order, were a father's sister, brother's daughter, father's sister's daughter, and finally mother's brother's daughter. In the ideal form of marriage with father's sister, the groom assumed the role of his mother's brother. However, the most common marriage was with a father's sister's daughter, and this was preferred by a young man. Marriage to near relatives served two important functions: to keep wealth concentrated and to provide spouses of nearly equal rank.

A wedding ceremony was held in the bride's house. Here relatives of the groom assembled as he sat in the middle of the floor wearing his most elaborate ceremonial garb. The bride was concealed in a corner of the house and was lured to sit beside the groom by the singing and dancing of the assembled group. The guests were feasted, but this was not a formal potlatch event. A month after the ceremony the couple was considered married. Marriage residence was with the family of either spouse (bilocal), depending on the wealth and standing of the principals. If the couple moved into the man's household, the bride's relatives presented him with property equal to or exceeding the value of that presented by his relatives. A man of wealth might have multiple wives (polygyny), with the first wife holding a rank superior to that of any subsequent spouses; five wives appear to have been the maximum. A woman sometimes had more than one husband (polyandry) but only if the second husband was a brother (fraternal polyandry) or near relative of the first. A widow customarily married her late husband's brother (levirate), and if the deceased husband did not have a brother, his sister's son married the widow. If neither category of individual was available, a widow could marry any man of her former husband's clan. If his mother's brother died, a man was obligated to marry the widow even though he might already have a wife, and he inherited his uncle's wealth. In spite of the ideal that a man live in the house of his mother's brother, inherit his wealth, and marry his daughter or another person in this line, his father's clan attempted to lure him into its domain. This especially seems to have been true for a boy who had married into the community. When a married woman was seduced, blood revenge might be exacted by her husband, or the seducer might make a property settlement. If the seduction was by a near relative of the husband, the offender was expected to become the woman's second husband.

360

To outsiders the Tlingit were not likable. Physicians for the Russian-American Company at Sitka in 1843–1844 described the people as follows (Romanowsky and Frankenhauser, 1962, 35): "The Kolosches are proud, egoistic, revengeful, spiteful, false, intriguing, avaricious, love above all independence and do not submit to force, except the ruling of their elders." Still adults were patient and persistent; they never seem to have hurried; and they angered only with provocation. During the fishing season they worked long hours, but winter was a time for leisure. During the winter women made their famous robes and baskets; in general, women appear to have had less free time than the men. The social position and respect that a woman commanded depended on her personality and standing within her clan; a woman with abilities was listened to by the men. Women had well-defined rights and relatives who were willing to come to their defense in case of any injustice from the husband's side of the family. An individual, whether male or female, was expected to behave in accord to his rank. Persons were of higher rank if their clan was large, wealthy, and powerful. Still, not all such persons were noble in their behavior, in which case they were treated as though they belonged to a lesser clan. Were a person from a high-ranking clan to behave coarsely as judged by his fellow clan members, he might be killed by them.

As soon as someone died, relatives began to wail, and the body was arranged at the back of the house in the place of honor, where it remained for four days or longer. Along the rear wall the greatest treasures of the household were displayed. Each night songs were sung, and guests of the opposite moiety were feasted. Near relatives of the deceased singed their hair and blackened their faces during these ceremonies. As the rituals drew to a close,

Plate 10–11 A man lying in state amidst his wealth, ca. 1890.
(From Porter, 1893)

the body was dressed in fine clothing and taken from the house through a hole made by removing a plank from one wall. A dog was thrown through the opening first to drive evil away from the house. The body was carried to a funeral pyre behind the house and was placed in the midst of heavy logs. Slaves might be killed and placed on the pyre of a wealthy man. A eulogy was delivered, oil was poured over the logs, and the fire was lit, but the mourners left before the body was burned completely. Women returned later and retrieved some of the bones from the ashes, wrapped them, and placed them in a small box. This mortuary box was placed on top of a post that sometimes was adorned with carved figures or paintings. An alternative was to place the ashes in a grave house resting on the ground. After the cremation a death potlatch was held and gifts distributed to those persons of the opposite moiety who had participated in the ceremonies. All of the major duties connected with the interment were performed by persons of the opposite moiety, including preparation of the body, ritual wailing, and carving a mortuary or memorial pole.

When a shaman died, his body was placed in a different corner of the house each night of the funeral ceremonies, and the house members fasted. For the burial on the fifth day, the shaman was clothed in his best garments. Through his nose was placed a sacred bone that he had used, and another was stuck in his hair. A large basket covered his head, and he was buried in a coffin placed on four posts at a point overlooking the sea. The body of a slave was thrown into the sea without ceremony.

The period of mourning for an ordinary person was one year, and the property of the deceased went to a sister's son. If such an individual did not exist, it was passed to a younger brother; this kept the wealth in the clan of the deceased. If the person's death was not from violence or drowning, his soul traveled along a rainbow to the upper world of the stars, moon, or sun. There existence was a state of happiness. A world above this upper world was inhabited by the souls of persons killed by violence, but one could enter this realm only if his death had been avenged. A world beneath the earth held the souls of drowned persons.

Historic Changes

From the time the Russians reestablished themselves at Sitka in 1804 until 1867, Sitka was virtually the only Russian center in southeastern Alaska. During the early period of contact the trade item most desired by the Tlingit was iron. They were keen traders always ready to accumulate material wealth at the expense of someone else. Russians and shipborne European or American traders found them cunning and dangerous hagglers. Traders who ventured to deal with the Tlingit were most eager to obtain sea otter pelts. As trading intensified the Indians were increasingly selective. They wanted woolen blankets because they traded away their animal pelt clothing; they also desired

The Tlingit: Salmon Fishermen of the Northwest

firearms and obtained them from non-Russian sources. Standard early trade items included tobacco; vessels of tin, iron, or copper; axes; glassware; and clothing, especially gaudy uniforms. During the span of Russian contact there never was any effective political control over the Tlingit. The Indians governed themselves, and the Russians did their best to keep violence to a minimum in the vicinity of Sitka.

Russian efforts to Christianize the Tlingit never were very successful because of the strong aboriginal religious system dominated by shamans, the restricted area of Russian penetration, and the scarcity of clergy. A Russian priest made an unsuccessful attempt to vaccinate the people at Sitka against smallpox in 1834. Then in 1835 a smallpox epidemic struck. No Russian died, but half of the Tlingit are estimated to have perished. When the Indians realized their shamans could not cure the disease, they lost faith in these curers and turned to the Russian medical doctor for vaccinations. Europeans introduced syphilis to the area, but according to reports in 1843, it was relatively uncommon.

In 1867 the formal transfer of Alaska from Russian to American ownership took place at Sitka. The Tlingit were not permitted in Sitka for the ceremonies, but they watched from canoes in the harbor. With American occupancy fortune seekers of almost every variety arrived, and to the Indians this influx must have been shocking. Russian inhabitants had the option of returning to Russia within three years or becoming United States citizens; nearly all of them left within a few weeks of the transfer. For ten years civil government did not exist, and the U.S. military garrisons stationed at Sitka, Tongass, and Wrangell were a primary source of trouble rather than a means to establish order. The Tlingit clashed repeatedly with the military over Indian deaths that went uncompensated, which led to murders and the destruction or threatened destruction of Tlingit settlements. The most serious difficulties were the failure of the military to understand Indian mores, the wholesale smuggling of intoxicants, and the prevalence of stills among the Indians. After the troops departed, only the U.S. Revenue-Cutter Service vessels and the collector of customs represented legal authority. In 1878 the customs officer at Wrangell stated that within a month he had a thousand complaints from Indians but had no way to deal with them. The difficulty became acute with the influx of miners who wintered that year at Wrangell. In 1880 gold was discovered near the present city of Juneau, which brought more miners and confusion; still it was not until 1884 that a civil government began to function in the more populous areas of Alaska.

The Presbyterian Sheldon Jackson was successful in establishing a mission at Sitka in 1878, and a lasting school was founded in 1880. The missionaries found that Tlingit women were more amenable than the men to the strictures of Christianity. Since women were influential in this matrifocal society, working through them became an important avenue of culture change. Girls also attended school more regularly than boys and became interpreters more often than men, which gave them increased standing and influence. Certain Biblical messages the missionaries considered important could be accepted readily by the Tlingit. For example, the sacrifice of Jesus Christ for the sins of mankind was fully comprehensible in terms of compensation. A Tlingit also considered it much better to give than to receive, which again was a Christian ideal but with a different meaning. The people then came to expect gifts as rewards for becoming Christians. When asked to attend church, an old Tlingit was likely to respond, "How much you pay me?" Compensation also was expected by parents when they permitted their children to attend school. The schools were the most important institution for the introduction of systematic change among the Tlingit, and it was through the schools that the missionaries were most successful in winning converts.

One of the diverse problems of concern to the missionaries was the condition of Tlingit slaves. Except in rare instances slaves were not freed when Alaska was purchased by the United States, because there was no effective governmental representative to force emancipation. The missionaries also took a firm stand against cremation, shamans, the potlatch system, polygyny, and intoxicants.

By the early 1880s most changes were material ones. Women had stopped wearing the labrets that began going out of fashion fifty years before. Bracelets and finger rings made from silver coins were popular. Skin garments were replaced by cloth clothing, and woolen blankets were worn as capes. The people raised vegetables, especially potatoes, introduced by the Russians, and women were the gardeners. Intoxicants were unknown in aboriginal times but had become an important trade item. A discharged American soldier taught the people how to distill their own alcohol, and this drink, called hoochinoo, became extremely popular.

Apparently settlements had begun to consolidate in late prehistoric times, and this pattern became intensified. Early in the twentieth century the forces leading to population concentrations included the following: decline in number due to wars and diseases; depletion of fish and game in some areas by whites; the availability of better boats, which provided mobility from a consolidated settlement; the efforts of traders, missionaries, and Federal officials to have fewer and larger settlements for more efficient trade, Christianization, and administration; the desire of the Indians to live in larger communities; and the economic advantages of settling near white communities. During the same era frame dwellings built to house nuclear families became more popular, but at some villages, such as Hoonah, clan houses were occupied until quite recently. In 1944 almost all of Hoonah was destroyed by fire, and only after this time were nuclear family residence units constructed.

As mentioned earlier the house group was the most functionally integrated social unit in aboriginal Tlingit society. It was likewise the most important economic and ceremonial unit within a clan. In aboriginal times, how-

Plate 10–12 Heirlooms in front of the Shark House at Yakutat in about 1912. From left to right are two spruce root hats, a killerwhale box drum with its fin on top, a cane, a killerwhale fin dance paddle behind the girl wearing a Chilkat blanket, and a post from the old Shark House in a protective cover behind the boy wearing a Chilkat blanket. (Photograph by Fhoki Kayomori, Courtesy of the Alaska Historical Library)

ever, each man in a house group supplied pelts for his own nuclear family. In historic times when trapping became a primary means of livelihood, individual trappers built cabins on clan lands and claimed local areas for their exclusive exploitation. The economic focus shifted from the house group to the individual, and the cohesion of the house group began to decline. This was one factor leading to the construction of nuclear family dwellings.

The economy continued to center on fishing and the sea, but new skills associated with fishing were beginning to emerge. The halibut hooks of old were replaced by modern metal hooks. Individuals of both sexes began to work in canneries, and some men were attracted to jobs in the gold mines. A few men hunted sea otter until 1911 when laws were introduced to protect these animals clearly headed for extinction. The skills of the men as woodcarvers and metalworkers led them to manufacture craft items for the tourist trade, and women wove robes and baskets for the same market. Knowing the

Plate 10–13 A funeral picture at Yakutat before the Thunderbird House screen of the Wolf clan. The house was built in about 1919, and the screen was sold to the Alaska Historical Museum about 1950. (Photograph by Fhoki Kayomori, Courtesy of the Alaska Historical Library)

independent nature of the Tlingit, it is understandable that they were not reliable employees. To be ordered about was to be insulted, and as domestic servants or laborers they usually did not satisfy their white employers.

The potlatch system continued to function, and it retained much of the pageantry and drama known in aboriginal times. The predilection for borrowing and imitating the songs, dances, and costumes of foreigners continued. For example, some shipwrecked Japanese arrived at Dry Bay in 1908; in performances in 1909 a memorable imitation of Japanese clothing and hairstyles was presented by the women. Changes also took place in the form of potlatch gifts. Blankets from traders came to be more important than Chilkat robes; silver dollars were a favorite gift item, followed closely by store-bought food.

ALASKA NATIVE BROTHERHOOD (A.N.B.)   Perhaps the best means of tracing Tlingit entry into the modern world is with a discussion of the A.N.B., which was intensively studied by Philip Drucker. The Brotherhood was founded in 1912 by ten men, nine Tlingit and one Tsimshian. They all were established Presbyterian leaders strongly committed to integration into white society. An important concept of the A.N.B. was its regional focus. Chapters, or camps as they are termed, were organized initially at Sitka, Juneau, and Douglas. By the 1920s chapters had been established in most southeastern Alaskan Indian villages. Within a few years of its organization, a parallel group, the Alaska Native Sisterhood, was formed for women and was made up mostly of local women's church groups. These organizations held a joint annual convention attended by three delegates of each local chapter in addition to the officers and past presidents of the central organization. Decisions were made at other times by an executive committee.

The Brotherhood colors were red for salmon and yellow for gold; these were displayed on ceremonial sashes. The official song was "Onward, Christian Soldiers." The primary goal of the organization was stated clearly in the first article of the constitution: "The purpose of this organization shall be to assist and encourage the Native in his advancement from his native state to his place among the cultivated races of the world, to oppose, discourage, and overcome the narrow injustice of race prejudice, and to aid in the development of the Territory of Alaska, and in making it worthy of a place among the States of North America" (Drucker, 1958, 165). The aim of the Brotherhood clearly was the rapid assimilation of the Tlingit into white society in southeastern Alaska. The Indian's ties with the past had to be broken, and this was attempted in two different ways. First, speaking English was considered to be very important; in fact, eligibility for membership was restricted in Article II to "English speaking members of the Native residents of the Territory of Alaska," and the constitution was printed in English. A second target was to destroy the potlatch system that represented the aboriginal past in the minds of both the missionaries and the Indians.

Brotherhood policy concentrated on gaining rights for Indians equal to those of whites. In the Russo-American treaty of sale it was stated that the uncivilized tribes, which included most Tlingit and other aboriginal Alaskans, were to be subject to such laws as the United States might pass. With the purchase there was no attempt to negotiate treaties nor to establish Indian reservations, and therefore the citizenship status of aboriginal Alaskans remained unclear. They were not "wards of the government" in the sense of reservation or treaty Indians. They came to consider themselves as citizens, but the whites in Alaska usually regarded them in the same light as Indians in the United States. Until they were declared citizens, the Tlingit could not file on mining claims, and this was a cause of resentment. Under the terms of the Dawes Act of 1887 or a Territorial Act of 1915 they could become citizens by demonstrating that they were following a civilized way of life, but few persons sought citizenship under these laws. The issue of citizenship was forced in 1922 by a Tlingit lawyer, William L. Paul, who was extremely active in Brotherhood affairs. The case in question involved a Tlingit who had voted previously but whose vote was challenged in a primary. Through court action by Paul he was cleared of illegal voting. As a result of Paul's efforts Alaskan Indians, in theory, had full voting rights before the Federal Government passed the Citizenship Act of 1924 granting full citizenship to all Indians who were not previously citizens. In 1924 William Paul was the first Indian elected to the Territorial Legislature.

Through the years the A.N.B. actively fought for Indian rights. By 1929 the segregated white-Indian school system in Alaska was successfully challenged in the courts. About 1929 Indians openly objected to "For Natives Only" signs in the balconies of motion-picture houses, and an effective boycott brought an end to the practice. Not until 1946 did the Territorial Legislature pass an antidiscrimination law however. In 1939 the Brotherhood organized fishermen's unions under the Wagner Act and soon became affiliated with the American Federation of Labor, although the Brotherhood retained its power as the bargaining agent. The A.N.B. attempted to recruit Athapaskan and Eskimo members beginning about 1962, but the Alaska Federation of Natives formed in 1966 became the most active cover organization working for the causes of Alaskan Aleuts, Eskimos, and Indians.

The original Brotherhood goal of doing away with aboriginal customs was only partly successful by mid-century. The principal target for attack, the potlatch, was regarded as heathen and most deplored; however, as Drucker points out, it actually was primarily social, not religious. Certain potlatch customs became incorporated into the Brotherhood structure; these included addressing persons of the opposite moiety in a ceremonial fashion; fining individuals for infractions; making gifts to the organization; and gift giving by the family of a deceased person for burial services provided by the opposite moiety through the Brotherhood. In one sense the A.N.B. served as a new institution through which the moieties reciprocated. Furthermore, although the ideal of speaking English continued, the business meetings of local chapters were sometimes conducted in Tlingit, particularly since the most active members normally were older and were not likely to speak English with ease.

Modern Life

In a brief but revealing study of Hoonah in 1961 the anthropologist Seymour Parker recorded a continuing emphasis on rank. "High class people" were persons prominent as fishing boat captains or as businessmen. The former also were likely to have prominent positions in their clans. Individuals in this general category were expected to finance potlatches and aid the community in funding various projects. The "common" or "average" people usually were members of fishing boat crews, and while they accepted Federal or State relief, they did so with feelings of shame. The lower class was described as "living from day to day." They felt little reluctance in accepting relief funds and had the reputation for heavy drinking of intoxicants. Parker

The Tlingit: Salmon Fishermen of the Northwest

emphasized the strong sense of individualism that pervaded the value system of the modern Tlingit. Familial, clan, and community ties certainly existed and were on occasion important, but the individual achieved largely on the basis of his own abilities. Previously a man was largely bound to the destiny of his matrilineage, although wealth and prestige were desired by all. With a disintegration of the old clan and moiety system but a continuing emphasis on material wealth and prestige, the modern Tlingit has strong incentive to compete with other persons in southeastern Alaska.

LAND CLAIMS   With land and property rights paramount in aboriginal Tlingit life it is not surprising that the seizure of their lands by whites without compensation has been a lasting source of contention. Until recently the settlement of whites in southeastern Alaska had been more widespread and intensive than elsewhere in the state, and it seldom had clear legal justification. In 1935, under pressure from the A.N.B., the U.S. Congress passed legislation permitting the Tlingit and Alaska Haida to sue the United States for land losses. Nearly all of southeastern Alaska had been set aside as the Tongass National Forest, Glacier Bay National Monument, and a reservation on Annette Island for Tsimshian Indians immigrating from Canada. The Tlingit and Alaska Haida sued for 80 million dollars, but the Court of Claims decided that they were entitled to 7.5 million dollars as compensation for the 16 million acres of land involved.

The Alaska Native Claims Settlement Act of 1971, described at the close of Chapter 4, included Tlingit claims not settled by earlier court decisions. Under the terms of the settlement act, the Tlingit and Alaska Haida formed one of the original twelve regional corporations, the Sealaska Corporation. As the largest of the regional corporations, with nearly 16,500 stockholders, it had received 45 million dollars from the Alaska Native Fund by 1974. The total assets of the Sealaska Corporation in 1975 were about 200 million dollars, and they have been invested broadly. A large new 3.5 million dollar office building was constructed in Juneau; the corporation owns a large building supply products company in Anchorage, with assets of about 15 million dollars in 1975, and is promoting the development of local industries to create jobs for stockholders.

By the 1970s the original Alaska Native Brotherhood goal of Tlingit assimilation was realized in many ways. The regional corporation was well financed and under effective leadership; although the administration was dominated by whites, Tlingit were being trained for managerial positions as rapidly as possible. Yet the pride in their cultural heritage has never died. While it probably is not correct to write of a Tlingit "renaissance," there clearly is a revival in traditional nineteenth century Tlingit life, clearly distinct from aboriginal life. In some conservative villages moiety exogamy still prevails, potlatch dances are being taught to the younger generation, and for the first time school districts are integrating units about traditional Tlingit life in their instructional programs. But what of the symbol of Tlingit culture, the totem pole? No new totem poles appear to have been erected with the essential potlatch celebration from 1904 until 1971. In the fall of 1971 the community of Kake raised a new totem pole with the proper ritual observances in a three-day ceremony. In keeping with Tlingit values this pole is the tallest one ever raised; it is 136 feet high.

Comparisons

The Tlingit and Yurok placed far more stress on secular wealth than did any of the other peoples discussed. They shared a sharp social distinction between rich and poor persons, and they carefully defined the contexts in which wealth changed hands. Salmon fishing was the basis for the livelihoods of both groups, and neither were subjected to starvations. How do we explain their different attitudes toward wealth in ecological, different social, and political contexts?

The Pawnee, Crow, and Tlingit shared matrilineal descent systems, which invites comparison. Special attention should be given to the rights and duties in the matrilineages and matriclans. At the same time none of these people were strictly matrilineal in all aspects of their social lives, which leads to further comparisons. One may also strive to explain why the Tlingit, as opposed to the others, had not organized at the supra-clan or tribal levels.

Note that the Cahuilla, Fox, and Tlingit each had moieties and the Crow had phratries. What were the similarities and differences in moiety or phratry structure or form and in their function or purpose?

This is an appropriate point at which to examine the culture area concept with special reference to three peoples described. The Kuskowagamiut are in the Eskimo culture area, while the Tlingit and Yurok are in the Northwest Coast culture area. Yet all three populations depended heavily on salmon for food, a parallel suggesting that other aspects of their lives might be significantly similar. It is profitable to compare the Kuskowagamiut with the Yurok, and more especially with the Tlingit, and ask whether the Kuskokwim Eskimo life-style might not fit in the Northwest Coast culture area. What important economic, social, political, and religious characteristics do these Eskimos share with both the Tlingit and Yurok, and what do they share only with the Tlingit? After these comparisons are made, the reader will be more fully aware of the limitations and the problems inherent in the culture area concept.

Additional Readings

An overview of Tlingit ethnography for the late historic period is only available in the account published in German by Aurel Krause (1885), translated into English by Erna Gunther (1956). The only comprehensive ethnographic reconstruction for one geographical segment of the Tlingit population is the three-party study of Yakutat area people by Frederica de Laguna. Tlingit social life, as it existed at Klukwan, is brilliantly described in a book by Kalervo Oberg. The best study of totem poles that has special reference to the Tlingit is by Edward Keithahn, and the best general work to date is the two-volume monograph titled *Totem Poles* by Marius Barbeau (National Museums of Canada, 1950; reprinted in 1964). *Northwest Coast Indian Art* (Seattle, 1965) by Bill Holm is the most insightful booklength discussion of the subject. The best comparative study of Northwest Coast Indians is *Cultures of the North Pacific Coast* (San Francisco, 1965) by Philip Drucker.

References

Ackerman, Robert E. *The Archeology of the Glacier Bay Region, Southeastern Alaska.* Washington State University Laboratory of Anthropology, Report of Investigations no. 44. 1968.

Bancroft, Hubert H. *History of Alaska, 1730–1885. The Works of Hubert Howe Bancroft*, v. 33. San Francisco. 1886.

Boas, Franz. *Primitive Art.* Dover (republication). 1955.

Borden, Charles E. *Origins and Development of Early Northwest Coast Culture to about 3000 B.C.* National Museum of Man, Mercury Series. Ottawa. 1975.

Drucker, Philip. *Culture Element Distributions: XXVI. Northwest Coast.* Anthropological Records, v. 9, no. 3. 1950.

*Drucker, Philip. *The Native Brotherhoods.* Bureau of American Ethnology, Bulletin 168. Washington, D. C. 1958. The Alaska Native Brotherhood, which has been a Tlingit-dominated organization since its founding in 1912, is the subject matter for half of this study. The second half of the volume is devoted to a similar organization in British Columbia. Drucker's largely historical study is a highly significant contribution since it is devoted to one of the organized efforts by the Tlingit to promote assimilation into white Alaskan society.

Drucker, Philip. "Sources of Northwest Coast Culture," in *New Interpretations of Aboriginal American Culture History*. Clifford Evans and Betty Meggers, eds., 59–81. Anthropological Society of Washington, D. C. 1955.

Federal Field Committee for Development Planning in Alaska. *Alaska Natives & the Land*. Washington, D. C. 1968.

Fraser, Douglas. *Primitive Art*. Garden City. 1962.

"From Ketchikan to Barrow." *Alaska*, December, 1971.

Goldschmidt, Walter R., and Theodore H. Haas. *Possessory Rights of the Natives of Southeastern Alaska*. A Report to the Commissioner of Indian Affairs (mimeographed). 1946.

Jackson, Sheldon. *Alaska*. New York. 1880.

Jones, Livingston F. *A Study of the Thlingets of Alaska*. New York. 1914.

Kashavaroff, Andrew P. "How the White Men Came to Lituya and what Happened to Yeahlth-kan who Visited Them," *Alaska Magazine*, v. 1, 151–153. 1927.

*Keithahn, Edward L. *Monuments in Cedar*. Seattle. 1963 (revised edition). This study is particularly useful in any attempt to trace the origins, antiquity, and development of various forms of totem poles.

*Krause, Aurel. *The Tlingit Indians*. 2 v. Jena, 1885; translated edition, Erna Gunther, tr., American Ethnological Society. 1956. The 1881–1882 field study by Aurel and Arthur Krause, written by the former, is the standard Tlingit source. The breadth and balance of the study make it the first to be consulted in any serious study of the Tlingit.

de Laguna, Frederica. "Some Dynamic Forces in Tlingit Society," *Southwestern Journal of Anthropology*, v. 8, 1–12, 1952.

*de Laguna, Frederica. *The Story of a Tlingit Community*. Bureau of American Ethnology, Bulletin 172. Washington, D. C. 1960. Based on archaeological and ethnographic fieldwork in 1949 and 1950, this report concentrates on the Angoon area and its people. The archaeological data are supplemented by historical records and ethnographic field information.

de Laguna, Frederica, et al. *Archeology of the Yakutat Bay Area, Alaska*. Bureau of American Ethnology, Bulletin 192. Washington, D.C. 1964.

*de Laguna, Frederica. "Under Mount Saint Elias," *Smithsonian Contributions to Anthropology*, v. 7. 1972. This three-part ethnohistory and ethnographic reconstruction, based on fieldwork in the early 1950s, is the most thorough presentation for any segment of the Tlingit population. It is especially strong where Krause is weak, in dealing with the individual in a cultural context.

The Tlingit: Salmon Fishermen of the Northwest

Lisianskii, Urey F. *A Voyage Round the World*. London. 1814.

McClellan, Catharine. "The Interrelations of Social Structure with Northern Tlingit Ceremonialism," *Southwestern Journal of Anthropology*, v. 10, 75–96. 1954.

Malaspina, D. Alejandro, and Don Jose de Bustamante y Guerra. *Political-Scientific Trip around the World* (translated title). Madrid. 1885.

Morgan, Lael. "Tlingit-Haida Renaissance," *Alaska Magazine*, June, 33–39, 78. 1975.

Niblack, Albert P. "The Coast Indians of Southern Alaska and Northern British Columbia," *Annual Report of the Smithsonian Institution, 1887–88*, 225–386. Washington, D.C. 1890.

*Oberg, Kalervo. *The Social Economy of the Tlingit Indians*. Seattle. 1973. This book is based on fieldwork at Klukwan in 1931–1932 and stands beside the studies of Krause and de Laguna in terms of merit. Oberg's discussions of the social system and economy are outstanding for their clarity and breadth.

Parker, Seymour. See Ray, Charles K., et al.

Porter, Robert P. *Report on Population and Resources of Alaska at the Eleventh Census: 1890*. Washington, D.C. 1893.

*Ray, Charles K., et al. *Alaskan Native Secondary School Dropouts*. University of Alaska. 1962. The report in this volume by Seymour Parker on the Tlingit at Hoonah is brief but very good. Parker spent only about a month at Hoonah in 1961, and although his emphasis was on values, considerable additional information is included.

Romanowsky, S., and Frankenhauser. "Five Years of Medical Observations in the Colonies of the Russian-American Company," *Medical Newspaper of Russia*, v. 6, 153–161. St. Petersburg. 1849 (translated from German and reprinted in *Alaska Medicine*, v. 4, 33–37; 62–64. 1962).

*Swanton, John R. "Social Condition, Beliefs, and Linguistic Relationship of the Tlingit Indians," *Bureau of American Ethnology, Twenty-sixth Annual Report*, 391–512. Washington, D.C. 1908. This study based on fieldwork in 1904 at Sitka and Wrangell is not a balanced ethnography, nor does it purport to be, but it does serve as a good supplement to the works of Krause and Oberg.

Wardwell, Allen, compiler. *Yakutat South*. Chicago. 1964.

Willard, (Mrs.) Eugene S. *Life in Alaska*. Philadelphia. 1884.

Young, Samuel H. *Hall Young of Alaska*. Chicago and New York, 1927.

The Hopi: Farmers of the Desert

11

Reasons for This Selection

For some people Plains Indian warriors have the most romantic appeal of all Indians, but they shone only briefly in their bellicose glory. Indians who farmed in the Southwest and lived in pueblos probably better typify American Indian life, or at least have been more lasting than most Indian groups and are more justly a stereotype of Indians. Massive pueblos, painted pottery, colorful ceremonies, and katcina dolls characterize these people to most outsiders. While Plains warriors have faded into memory, pueblo peoples, such as the Hopi of northeastern Arizona, continue to live in their desert setting, and some of them have clung tenaciously to their identity as Indians. Their culture does not survive in all its past vitality, but it is remarkable that they have endured as a people at all given the centuries of forces bent on their destruction. As an example of the persistence of their ways, Christian missionaries began working among the Hopi in 1629, but by the 1950s fewer than 2 percent of the Hopi were practicing Christians. Additional reasons have led to singling out the Hopi for attention. They, more than any other pueblo people, display an appealing continuity with the past. Their ancestors settled in northern Arizona at least 1000 years ago, and the Hopi village of Oraibi is one of the oldest continuously occupied settlements north of Mexico. Nowhere else are

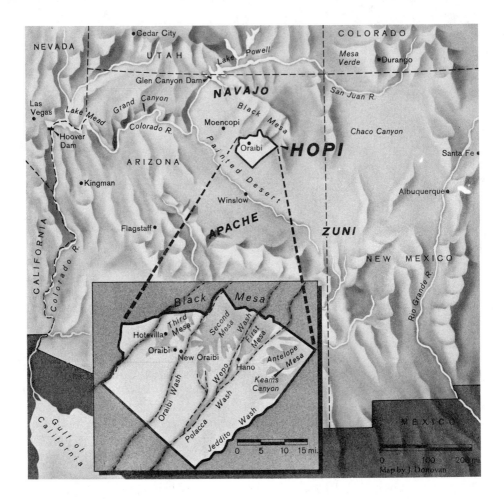

Map by J. Donovan

376

Indians so intimately associated with one locality. Nowhere else among Indians do the past and present blend into such a consistent whole. Furthermore, a wealth of information exists about the Hopi. They long have attracted the attention of ethnographers, resulting in detailed studies of their lifeways. In the author's opinion the very best American Indian ethnography is the Hopi study *Old Oraibi* by Mischa Titiev.

People, Population, Language, and Habitat

"Hopi" is the term that these people applied to themselves. It means good, or peaceful, the ideal for all individuals in this society. In linguistic terms the Hopi language is of the Aztec-Tanoan phylum and the Uto-Aztecan family. Their aboriginal population was approximately 2800. After dropping to 2000 in 1907, it has now reached about 5000. Their Arizona homeland is one of deserts and plateaus with sporadic and unpredictable rainfall. The only reason the Hopi and their ancestors have been able to farm in this arid area is that there are seepages. Rainwater from the upland sandstone region seeps down to a layer of shale and emerges at the ends of mesas in moist areas and springs. At higher elevations on the mesas, juniper and scattered pinyon grow. This flora is replaced by grassland nearer the valley floors, and in the lower sections desert vegetation, including saltbrush, greasewood, and sagebrush, dominates. In damp localities or along irregularly flowing streams cottonwoods and willows grow.

Prehistory

The culture of Indians in the Southwest around the time of Christ is termed "Basketmaker." They occupied dry caves or rock shelters, especially in the San Juan River drainage. Their houses were round with walls made from poles and sticks bonded with mud. In these substantial structures were food storage pits and food grinding equipment, manos and metates. On the adjacent flood plains maize and squash were cultivated with digging sticks. The people hunted deer and mountain sheep with spears and throwing-boards, called atlatls in the Southwest. Nets and snares were used to take small game. The only domestic animal was the dog; there were two varieties, one similar to a shorthaired terrier and the other like a collie. Coiled baskets in many shapes were common, but pottery was just being introduced, probably from the south. Clothing included sandals woven from yucca fiber and blankets woven from strips of rabbit skin with the hair intact. Burials at cave sites usually were in former storage pits, and multiple burials were the rule, usually without any sign of violent death. The bodies were flexed and wrapped in rabbit-skin blankets, a large basket often was placed over the head, and the body was accompanied by diverse grave goods. These people obviously were well-established farmers and hunters with a comparatively stable and sedentary way of life.

Around A.D. 500 there were changes of sufficient magnitude to distinguish a new culture termed Modified-Basketmaker. The people lived in villages of round, then oval, and finally rectangular houses by the end of the era in A.D. 700. Houses were built in pits at first and had attached anterooms and entrance passages. Later, the passages became ventilating shafts, and the dwellings were entered through the roof. In the hard clay floor of a house was a fire pit, and a hole in the floor probably was a *sipapu*, an entryway for spirits, known from modern pueblo ceremonial structures. New varieties of maize as well as beans were added to the diet, and weapons now included the bow and arrow. Pottery was coiled, scraped smooth before it hardened, and fired. The earliest vessels were decorated with black designs, often modeled after those on baskets. The most important observation to make about these artifacts is that many changes occurred relatively rapidly within a 200 year span.

In the same general area between A.D. 700 and 1400 Pueblo Indian culture emerged, and three periods have been distinguished: Developmental, Great, and Regressive Pueblo. Emerging from a Basketmaker background, with new ideas from within and from afar, the Pueblo periods represent a climax in American Indian cultural developments. The early Pueblo peoples artificially flattened the backs of infants' skulls against cradleboards to produce an altered head shape. The garb of the people changed when domestic cotton was introduced as a cultivated plant. The women may have worn cotton blankets, the men kilts and breechclouts. Developmental Pueblo housing represented continuity with the past. Dwellings evolved into aboveground masonry structures with contiguous units. In the pit house tradition were the round, subterranean ceremonial structures or kivas walled with coarse stone. The interior arrangements included an encircling bench, a fireplace, and a sipapu. The roofs were cribbed, with an opening for entry. The economy remained as before, with cotton as the only new crop and a flaked-stone hoe that often was unhafted as a new farming tool. The only new domestic animal was the turkey, most likely raised for its feathers rather than its meat. Pottery was made with a fine paste, and a thin clay slip often was added before the vessel was fired. Designs were applied to pots in two color combinations, black-on-white and red-on-orange; the motifs most often were geometric.

Southwest Indian culture climaxed with the Great Pueblo period beginning around 1050. This was an era of great stonemasonry, with hundreds of residence and storage rooms built into a multistory pueblo. Mesa Verde was occupied at this time as was Chaco Canyon. The productivity of the cultivated flood plains was great, and irrigated acreage was added. With dependable food surpluses some persons were freed from tilling the soil, and craft specializations developed. Potters became artists producing individualistic painted vessels, and the leisure time available may have fostered the elaborate ceremonial

378
The Hopi: Farmers of the Desert

life. Quite suddenly, by 1300, the area was almost abandoned. The exodus may have been triggered by an extended drought between 1276 and 1299. Arroyo cutting left the flood plains dry and irrigation ditches waterless. Raids by the nomadic Apache and Navajo may have contributed to the downfall of most pueblo peoples. Their way of life endured but at very few settlements.

The Hopi mesas were one locality in which the Regressive Pueblo period survived despite what must have been drastic population displacements. Here rows of masonry houses were constructed around plazas, and small rectangular kivas, or ceremonial structures, were the focus of religious activities. The striking cultural achievement was in pottery, with bichrome and polychrome vessels considered among the most pleasing Indian pottery made in North America. The ware was usually black-on-yellow or else red-and-black-on-yellow. Not only were fine-lined geometric designs executed, but representations from life also appeared. This era ended about 1700, after the first Spanish contacts.

Early History

The last year of Hopi prehistory was 1539; in July of the following year the first Spanish were seen. A small group under Pedro de Tovar came from the pueblo of Zuni where Francisco Coronado, the expedition leader, rested. When de Tovar arrived at one of the eastern Hopi settlements, he was met with hostility; he attacked the village and defeated the Indians. De Tovar then peacefully visited the six other Hopi communities, and later a party of the same expedition traveling to the Grand Canyon passed through Hopi country without meeting any resistance. The Spanish search for gold led Antonio de Espejo to enter the region in 1583, and he was welcomed by the people in the five villages. More lasting contact was made by Juan de Onate in 1598 when the Hopi peacefully submitted to the authority of the Spanish king. The Spanish hoped to make these people Christians, but Franciscan missionaries did not settle among them until 1629. Churches were built at three settlements, and two more missionaries joined the first three. The Franciscans reported great progress, but the poisoning of one of the priests in 1633 suggests that all Hopi were not contented charges. Vigorous Franciscan efforts to destroy the old Hopi religion led to cruel punishments for backsliding Indians. In 1655 a missionary caught a Hopi performing an "act of idolatry." The man was beaten severely in public and again beaten inside the church; turpentine was applied to his body and ignited, and he died. The missionary was relieved of his post, but no punitive action was taken against him.

In 1650 the Hopi refused to join the other pueblo peoples in a revolt against the Spanish, but they supported fully the Pueblo Revolt in 1680. Their major contribution was to kill the four missionaries stationed among them. The Hopi indirectly aided the insurrection by permitting Indian refugees from the Rio Grande pueblos to live among them when the Spanish struck back; two communities were constructed for these friendly allies. The Hopi feared Spanish reprisals, and three villages were relocated on mesa tops that could be better defended than their valley bottom settings. The Spanish returned in 1692, and when the Indians willingly swore to support the Spanish king, peace was established. By 1699 the Spanish were in firm control of the Rio Grande pueblos, and this led a Hopi faction that favored Catholicism to request missionaries from the authorities at Santa Fe. A missionary visited, but after he left, the community was summarily destroyed by the anti-Catholic Hopi faction. The men who resisted were killed; their wives and children were scattered among the remaining settlements. The pagan Hopi under the leadership of a man from Oraibi went to Santa Fe and told the Spanish governor that the Hopi would make peace if they were permitted to continue their old religion. This, however, was unacceptable to the Spanish. In retaliation for the murder of Christian Hopi the Spanish in 1701 attempted to defeat the Hopi in battle, but the smallness of the Spanish force and the adequate defensive positions of the Hopi led the attackers to withdraw. The Hopi retained their freedom not so much by their military skill and determination as by the distance that separated them from Santa Fe and the difficulties the Spanish were having with other Indians. Throughout the 1740s and early 1750s the Hopi thwarted all Spanish efforts to bring them under effective control.

Beginning in 1755 the course of Hopi history gravitated increasingly toward accepting the Spanish. When a sequence of dry years exhausted their reserve of food, they were faced with hunger. By 1779 many of them had abandoned their homeland and moved among the Zuni to survive. The next year most Hopi were so scattered that the local population was reduced to about 800 persons. In the midst of this struggle came the smallpox epidemic in 1781. In this same year, however, rain was plentiful, and the bountiful crops made it possible for the population to reconsolidate. Pressures by marauding Navajos forced the Hopi to request aid from the Spanish in 1818, but the Spanish, who were faced with their own survival problems, were unable to help. The most striking characteristic of Hopi historical contacts with the Spanish was the ability of these Indians to withstand Spanish pressures toward acculturation, particularly in the religious sphere. It is evident that Hopi resistance against the Spanish was not unanimous, but the pro-Spanish faction seems to have been of minor importance.

The next serious problem faced by the Hopi was how to deal with another group of non-Indians who began to enter their country as early as 1826. Were these the legendary Bahana who were to come from the east and aid the Hopi? It was thought that the Anglo-Americans might well be the Bahana since their men were successfully preventing the Navajo from seizing Hopi land.

380
The Hopi: Farmers of the Desert

Aboriginal Life

ORIGIN MYTH   In primeval times, according to a myth recorded at Oraibi, there was no light or living thing on earth, only a being called Death. Three caves beneath the earth's surface likewise were engulfed in darkness. In the lowest cave people existed in crowded and filthy conditions. Two brothers, The Two, lamented the plight of men and pierced the cave roof; they grew one plant after another trying to reach the second world. After a particular type of cane grew tall enough, the people and animals climbed it to the second cave world. This level finally was filled with people, and they ascended to the third cave. Some climbers fell back to the second world, as had also happened in the ascent from the first cave. In the third cave the darkness was dispelled by fire found by the brothers. The people built houses and kivas and traveled from one place to another. Great turmoil developed here when women neglected their duties as wives and mothers, preferring instead to dance in the kivas. Finally the people, along with Coyote, Locust, Spider, Swallow, and Vulture, emerged at the fourth level, which was the earth. They wandered about with only torches to light their way. Together the men and the creatures with them attempted to create light. Spider spun a white cotton blanket that gave off some light. The people then processed a white deerskin and painted it turquoise. This skin was so bright that it lighted the entire world. The painted deerskin became the sun, and the blanket was the moon. Stars were released from a jar by Coyote.

Once the earth was lighted it was realized that the land area was limited by surrounding water. The Vulture fanned the water with its wings, and as the waters flowed away mountains appeared. The Two made channels for the waters through the mountains, and canyons and valleys were formed. The people saw the tracks of Death, Masau'u, and followed them to the east. They caught up with Masau'u, and a girl conspired with him to cause the death of a girl she envied. This was the first death among people, the conspirator was the first witch, and her descendants became the witches of the world. The dead girl was seen living in the cave world below the earth, which had become an idyllic place. The witch caused conflicts with people who had emerged on earth before the Hopi, particularly the Navajo and Mexicans. Another deity helped people by making their maize and other seeds ripen in a single day. Of the two brothers who led the people from the underworld, the younger brother was the ancestor of the Oraibi people. The older brother went east but promised to return when the Hopi needed him. After many generations and in accord with this promise the older brother's descendants, the Bahana, were to return when the Hopi were poor and in need. The Bahana would be rich and would bring food and clothing for the Hopi. The Hopi would reject the Bahana, but the Bahana would treat them kindly.

APPEARANCE AND CLOTHING   A girl wore her hair long until she passed through a puberty ceremony; it then was put up in two disk-shaped bundles, one over each ear. After she married, her hair was parted in the middle and worn long again. A woman's clothing consisted of a wraparound cotton blanket that passed under her left arm and was fastened together over the right shoulder. This garment extended a short distance below her knees, and she wore leggings as well as moccasins. Men wore headbands to control their hair, which might be relatively short or long and knotted behind the neck. Everyday male clothing included a breechclout of deerskin or cotton cloth and a cotton cloth kilt, belted at the waist. A man also might wear deerskin leggings and moccasins or sandals.

SETTLEMENTS   At the south end of Black Mesa are three tongues of land, and on the westernmost, called Third Mesa, the village of Oraibi is located. This is the community where Titiev worked, and whenever possible the descriptions will focus there. The pueblo is laid out in a series of eight nearly parallel streets with scattered kivas and a plaza between two streets. In aboriginal times the square houses were made from stones dressed and set in place for the floor and walls by the men. The roof beams were placed on the uppermost course of stones, and the women for whom a house was being built prepared and applied a mud plaster to the inner walls. A woman and her friends completed the roof by adding brushwood, grass, and finally mud. The dwellings were owned by women, and a new one usually was built next to the

Plate 11–1 The village of Oraibi with melons and peaches drying on the roof in the foreground. (Courtesy of the Southwest Museum)

The Hopi: Farmers of the Desert

residence of the woman's mother or another close female relative. Houses were windowless, and no doors opened on the street. They often were multistory with access through an opening in the ceiling, beneath which was placed a notched log ladder. On one side of a room were bin metates or milling stones of different degrees of coarseness for grinding maize, and fireplaces completed the furnishings. The rooms without an outside opening often were used for storing food and material goods. A kiva or ceremonial structure was a rectangular subterranean room entered by descending a ladder from an opening in the roof. The section of the floor where observers sat was slightly raised, and the remaining portion included a fire pit and sipapu. Along most walls were stone compartments that held sacred objects. At Oraibi there were about fifteen kivas, each owned by a matriclan.

The most elaborate manufactures of the Hopi were textiles, usually woven by men. They carded and spun cotton into thread and then wove textiles on looms in their homes or in kivas. The fiber often was dyed black, green, orange, red, or yellow. On a vertical loom suspended between the ceiling and the floor they made square and rectangular cloth for blankets. Belts were made on a waist loom attached to a beam at one end and to the weaver's waist at the other, being held taut with his body. Women wove only rabbit-skin blankets on vertical looms. The most important textiles woven by men for women were for wedding robes, belts, dresses, and shawls. For themselves they wove kilts and sashes for ceremonies and blankets, kilts and shirts for daily use.

The pottery made by women was either undecorated ware for cooking and storage or polished and decorated forms for other uses. Clay was collected from nearby deposits, soaked, and kneaded into a paste, with ground sandstone added to the paste of utility wares. Long coils were added to the flat clay bottom, and each seam was pinched to join the preceding piece and then obliterated by hand-smoothing. The completed containers were dried, and utility ware was fired without further processing. A pot to be decorated was smoothed and thinned with a piece of sandstone after it had dried. The vessel then was moistened and polished with a stone, later to be slipped and painted. Pottery was painted black, orange, red, white, and yellow, and the prevalent designs were quite similar to those used in early historic times. This is not an example of long-term stability in design styles but a revival of old designs. In 1895 an archaeologist excavated an abandoned Hopi pueblo, and one of his Indian workmen was the husband of Nampeyo, widely recognized as one of the best pueblo potters. She found the beautifully executed, painted pottery unearthed at the site fascinating and studied the sherds to become familiar with the patterns. She developed a style based on these originals, and it became very popular.

SUBSISTENCE ACTIVITIES   The economic year began when crops were planted. The time to sow was established by a Sun Watcher, who based his determination on the occurrence of the sunrise at a particular spot on the

Plate 11–2 A woman grinding grain in a bin metate. (Courtesy of the Southwest Museum)

horizon. At the stipulated time the men of a matriclan planted as a group, and this work unit continued through the harvest. A married man planted the clan land allotted to his wife and her immediate family. Men owned crops until the harvest was taken into a wife's house; afterwards it was her property. Farmland at the foot of Black Mesa was watered by ground seepage or from stream overflow (floodwater farming). A plot was prepared by trampling the weeds or cutting them with a broad-bladed implement and breaking up the soil with a pointed stick. Maize, the most important crop by far, was planted in holes made with a digging stick. Ten to twenty seeds were dropped into a single foot-deep hole, and if a planting did not sprout in about ten days, it might be reseeded. As plants grew they were weeded, and the soil was loosened about the roots. Fields, which were about one acre in extent, were not rotated nor was the maize hilled. Beans sometimes were planted among the maize stalks but more often were raised in separate plots. Squash and cotton too appear to have been raised in separate acreage. During planting and harvesting a Masau'u impersonator was usually present, but there were no specific planting and harvest rituals. Most other Hopi subsistence activities also were group endeavors, organized by individuals or societies to embrace some

The Hopi: Farmers of the Desert

or all community members. One cooperative, communal task was to clear sand and debris from village springs that were owned by the Village Chief but used by everyone.

About forty types of plants were cultivated in the 1930s. Of this number only five species were aboriginal (kidney and tepary beans, maize, cotton, and squash); four others may have existed prior to Spanish times but more likely were postcontact domestics (Aztec and lima beans, gourds, and sunflowers). Five species were introduced during the Spanish period (chili peppers, onions, peaches, watermelons, and wheat); all others were introduced by Mormon farmers or other Anglo-Americans. Ten species of wild plants were cared for by the Hopi, but the seeds apparently were not sown regularly. Seeds from two different species of wild tobacco were sown when necessary to provide sufficient leaves for ceremonial uses. Likewise, wild dock root was used for dye, and the seeds sometimes were planted. Fifty-four different wild plants were eaten, fifty were used to make or decorate artifacts, sixty-five were used medicinally, and forty had ceremonial or magical purposes. Although there is some overlap in these listings, the Hopi obviously used a wide variety of plant species. About 200 wild flowering plants grew locally, of which half commonly were utilized.

The primary staple, maize, was the symbol of life to the Hopi, and they grew three varieties. In early historic times the flint variety was important since the hull of each grain was hard and not easily destroyed by weevils in storage. The flint variety was so difficult to grind, however, that it had declined in importance. The most popular variety of maize in recent times has been the flour type, which is grown by every farmer. Sweet corn was raised in small quantities, with only two different named strains.

A wide variety of dishes was prepared from maize. The harvested product usually was stored on the cob and shelled as needed. Ground maize was made into gruel, dumplings, soups, and bread. Hominy was prepared by soaking shelled maize in a mixture of juniper wood ash and water, then boiling the grains and washing them to remove the hulls. Maize also was roasted on the ear, parched, or baked in pits. One very important food made of maize, *piki*, was used as bread. It was made from a finely ground cornmeal mixed with water, using ashes as leavening, and was cooked on a special stone slab over a fire. The stone was heated and greased, and the bluish-gray liquid was poured onto it. After cooking, the piki was folded or rolled into "loaves" for later consumption. It often was eaten by dipping one end into liquid food and biting off the moistened portion.

Compared with the farming rituals, the ceremonial preparations for a hunt were elaborate. The most important species hunted were antelope, cottontails, and jackrabbits. Rabbits often were hunted in the late summer, when crops did not require attention. A man organizing a hunt could be from any clan so long as he made prayer offerings to the God of the Hunt. Details of the time for the hunt were announced by a crier, and the next day the organizer performed further rituals. In the hunt, men formed a surround and moved in until they could kill the encircled animals with throwing sticks (boomerangs, rabbit-killing sticks) or with hurled clubs. The surround was formed repeatedly, and the game continued to be taken until the leader called an end to the hunt. When they returned to the village, each man gave his kill to his mother, sister, wife, or father's sister. The recipient made a ritual offering to the dead animal to restore the game to the God of the Hunt.

Before hunting antelope, deer, and mountain sheep, the organizer as well as all the others in the party made prayer offerings, and there was ritual smoking. The surround method was used to capture these animals in aboriginal times. The pattern seems to have been to run down and suffocate an antelope. A deer apparently was shot with arrows or clubbed to death but not stabbed. Once again there was a ritual propitiation of the deceased animal. Coyote hunts were conducted by kiva members collectively, and as usual the surround technique was employed. After a hunt each coyote was taken to the kiva and given a lighted corn husk cigarette and spoken to as a child before the owner took the animal home.

DESCENT, KINSHIP, AND MARRIAGE   As already indicated, the Hopi traced descent through females (matrilineal), and grooms always joined the households of their brides (matrilocal). Matrilineages were very important in social terms, and matriclans were overwhelmingly important ceremonial units.

From the point of view of a male Ego, the terminology for designating blood relatives often was coextensive with his natal household. Ego termed his mother the same as his mother's sister and would not distinguish between them in normal conversation. Father and father's brother were termed alike, but mother's brother was termed differently. The designations for females in the first ascending generation paralleled those for males, because father's sister was distinguished from mother and mother's sister (bifurcate merging terminology). This usage is reasonable since mother and mother's sister were of the same clan, and father was in the same clan as father's brother. In the cousin terminology parallel cousins were termed as siblings, whereas mother's brother's children were termed as one's own children, and a father's sister's daughter was called the same as father's sister. Finally a father's sister's son was termed father (Crow type cousins). The most distinguishing characteristic

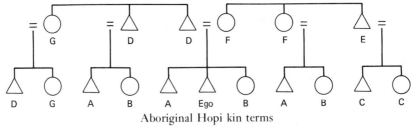

Aboriginal Hopi kin terms

386

The Hopi: Farmers of the Desert

of the cousin term is the ignoring of certain generational distinctions. The kinship terminology provided the framework for lifelong responsibilities, with particular forms of behavior expected in each set of relationships. One of the most bitter overt displays of anger against a relative was to renounce kinship ties.

SOCIAL DIMENSIONS   The Hopi knew of no term for household, yet this social unit dominated and guided the life of each individual. A child was born into this unit and retained a strong emotional identity with it throughout life. The household consisted of a core of women—grandmother, daughters, and daughters' daughters—plus unmarried sons and in-marrying husbands. All except the husbands belonged to the same matriclan; also members of the lineage were those males born into the unit but now married and living in the houses of their wives. When the members of a household outgrew its space, a room was added on to accommodate the newer members. This adjacent household retained its ties with the parent matrilineage, held farmland in common, and worshipped a common fetish. The lineage fetish (sacred bundle) was in the custody of the oldest female lineage head, and the associated ceremonies were conducted largely by the old woman's brother or son. These ritual obligations were passed down the most direct maternal line. Common lineage problems were discussed at the original lineage residence, and it remained the heart of the matrilineage, sometimes even after it was abandoned as a residence. From a leading matrilineage, with the greatest rights and duties, subordinate (daughter) lineages developed. As a daughter lineage grew, it might become socially removed from the original group and lose the underlying ties. The distant lineages would become separate entities if they created new bundles and acquired distinct names. Members of a named group who traced their ties through the same bundle formed a matriclan even though they could not trace connecting genealogical ties.

By 1906 there were about thirty named matriclans at Oraibi, a number which represented splits as well as the possible settlement there of new clans. The names, including Bear, Bow, Butterfly, and Lizard, were linked with happenings in mythological times or referred to clan ancestors. These ancestors were termed *wuya* and might or might not be tangibly represented by a clan bundle. A bundle sometimes included more than one wuya; this led to alternative names for the clan and probably represented the consolidation of two clans. Clans formed nine larger groups (phratries) that were associated with the mythological past but not named; possibly clans of the same phratry stemmed ultimately from the same lineage base. Members of the same phratry shared common ceremonial and land-holding interests, and they could not marry within the group (phratry exogamy).

POLITICAL LIFE   Overall village control was in the hands of two persons, the Village Chief and the War Chief. The Village Chief was from the

Bear clan, and a sacred stone in his possession verified his authority. The stone reportedly was brought from the underworld by the legendary village founder. Covering the stone were engraved motifs, including human figures, and their interpretation was the basis for a division of lands among the clans. The stone was inspected as a part of each Soyal Ceremony that the Village Chief headed. The Village Chief had not only the greatest sacred responsibilities at Oraibi but important secular duties as well. He settled land disputes, the most important differences between villagers. His sacred duties, in addition to those dealing with the Soyal Ceremony, included offering prayers for village welfare. It was the Village Chief who remained up late each night smoking and musing about pueblo conditions after most people had gone to sleep. For any critical community matter, his advice was sought, although he could not compel the actions of others. The office of the Village Chief was passed to a brother or to a sister's son after a long period of training. The Village Chief wore no badge of office, but he had a distinctive style of body painting for certain ceremonies and a sacred stick or cane of authority.

The only person at Oraibi with permanent power and authority was the War Chief, who attained his position by being the most outstanding warrior. He had the right to inflict either verbal or physical punishment for nonconformity. On occasion, when parties of men were organized for a community project, certain katcinas assembled the workmen and directed their activities. A lazy man might be reprimanded or even in extreme instances beaten by a katcina. The authority and power of the overt leaders never extended beyond the village. There was no means for uniting the Hopi as a tribe; in fact, the only time they clearly joined in a common cause was during the Pueblo Revolt of 1680.

The Hopi prided themselves on being peaceful people who disliked shedding the blood even of animals, and yet they were organized for armed conflict. They fought to defend their pueblo, and the role of a warrior was recognized as dangerous, important, and necessary. Im primeval times, when the Hopi emerged from the underworld, the Kokop and Spider clans introduced a warrior society. Every man was a member, but not all were of the same rank. Membership was divided into ordinary warriors and stick-swallowers. Boys were trained for warfare with a rigorous program of cold baths, races, archery practice, and rising early. The Warrior Society held a ceremony each year during the late fall, using the sacred equipment held by the Spider and Kokop clans. The two days of rituals involved making prayer objects, ritual smoking, offering prayers, and building altars. A war medicine was prepared and drunk, after which there were exhibitions of stick-swallowing by one branch of the membership. For the real warriors, those who acknowledged killing and scalping an enemy, there was a special initiation which involved fasting and secret rituals.

Warfare was said always to have been defensive. Men went into battle clad in ordinary clothing but with the addition of caps made from mountain

The Hopi: Farmers of the Desert

lion skin to which eagle feathers were attached. A warrior fought with a bow and arrows, stone club, spear, and throwing stick. Before a battle the men prayed to the Masau'u and to long-dead warriors, and they also sang songs to make themselves brave. Armed only with a stone club, the War Chief led them into conflict. A slain enemy was scalped to the accompaniment of a scalping song, and scalps were carried into the pueblo on poles. A Navajo scalp was worthless, but one from an Apache or Ute was valued. The permanent resting place for a scalp was in the home of its taker. A scalp was washed with yucca suds and intermittently "fed" by its owner.

THE KATCINA CULT   Katcina "dolls" have attracted widespread attention from whites and have been collected avidly for many years. They are small, painted and adorned wooden images usually made by men prior to katcina performances. The figures were presented to children by katcinas and were considered by them as gifts from the gods. These katcina images were hung from the rafters of the homes to familiarize the children with the many different forms. Katcina figures frequently are called dolls, but this is a misnomer. They were not toys but served mainly to instruct uninitiated children about one aspect of the religious system. Over 240 different forms were made by the Hopi; they fit into six groups, including chief katcinas, clowns, and runners. A figure was carved from cottonwood tree roots, shaped, and then smoothed before appendages such as ears or horns were pegged in place. A thin layer of white clay was applied, and the clay was painted in vivid colors, the same ones used for the body paintings of real katcinas. Finally feather adornments often were added to complete the figure.

Katcina carvings are stylized renditions of the disguises worn by the men who portrayed katcinas when they supposedly were on earth during the summer. Participation as a katcina was open to all village men under the general sanction of the Village Chief, and the activities of katcinas were under the control of the Badger and Katcina clans. The head of a katcina impersonator was covered with a basketry or leather mask, and he peered through small slits or holes that had no relationship to the eyes on the mask. Noses were highly stylized protuberances, and mouths might be tubular, beak-shaped, or painted in various ways onto the flat mask. The top of a mask often was adorned with a wooden tablet, feathers, hair, or wool. A fox-skin boa encircled the neck where the mask met the body. A wide variety of costumes prevailed, with a white cotton shirt, cotton kilt, sash, and green moccasins common for chief katcinas. Vivid paints applied to the bodies of the impersonators made them even more striking. Colors symbolized the direction from which the katcina came: yellow stood for north; blue-green, west; red, south; white, east; while red, yellow, white and blue-green in combination indicated the zenith, and black the nadir. The mask, body, and legs were often painted with representations of heavenly phenomena, animal tracks, and phallic or vegetable symbols. These vivid colors of the gods were a striking contrast to the drab desert

Plate 11–3 Katcina figures. (Courtesy of the UCLA Museum of Cultural History)

setting and the bland colors found in the village environment.

Once long ago, according to Tawaqwaptiwa, the late Village Chief of Oraibi, after the Hopi had departed from the uppermost level of the underworld they wandered on earth with their gods the katcinas. They were attacked by "Mexicans," and all the gods were killed. The dead returned to the underworld, and the Hopi divided their ceremonial paraphernalia in order to impersonate them. Impersonations of katcinas formed the core of Hopi rituals. When a man wore the sacred costume of a katcina, he became a god, and his mask was the most sacred item of his costume. As masks wore out, became soiled, or broke, they were replaced or repaired, but this did not detract from their sacredness. The chief katcina masks were the only ones not replaced or duplicated. It was possible also to vary a new katcina mask from the original without impairing its supernatural associations. Katcinas were present at Oraibi from the winter solstice until the summer solstice, and then they were in the underworld except for Masau'u Katcina, representing the God of Death, who was about the earth the year long. A Hopi adult did not believe that an impersonator was a god but rather considered his role as a friend of the gods. Small children by contrast were told that these were the actual gods.

The nature of the katcina cult as a whole is expressed well by Titiev (1944, 129). He writes:

> *The complexities of their Katcina worship are of little moment to the Hopi. They make no effort to systematize or to classify their beliefs, but are content to regard the Katcinas as a host of*

390

The Hopi: Farmers of the Desert

benevolent spirits who have the best interests of the Hopi ever at heart. To impersonate them is a pleasure, to observe them a delight. Quite apart from its more formal features, the operation of the Katcina cycle brings more warmth and color into the lives of the Hopi than any other aspect of their culture.

INTEGRATING CONCEPTS   The relationship of people with the gods formed an orderly system built around the concept of continuity between life and death. An integrated relationship was maintained between the living and the dead, with the spirits of the dead becoming clouds that brought rain to the living. The activities of katcinas on earth and in the underworld benefited the living. To the Hopi there was a duality in being human. People possessed a physical body and a "breath-body," spirit or soul. When an individual died, preparations for burial were in many ways the same as for the newborn, since the corpse was sprinkled with cornmeal, bathed, and given a new name. The breath-body journeyed to the underworld, where its existence was like that of the Hopi on earth, except that when the dead consumed food they took only of its essence. Because of their weightlessness the dead could rise into the sky and become clouds. By bringing rain, the deceased aided the living in a very meaningful manner. The God of Death, Masau'u, logically was a god of fertility since the rain led to fertility and growth. The sun, also a god of fertility, had an intimate association with the dead. The sun spent half of its time in the underworld, the land of the dead, and half of its time on earth. It was

Plate 11–4 Sand mosaic in an Antelope kiva. (Courtesy of the Field Museum of Natural History, Chicago)

Plate 11–5 Summer altar for the Marau ceremony. (Courtesy of the Field Museum of Natural History, Chicago)

by prayers and offerings to the dead and to the sun that blessings were realized on earth.

Dual concepts integrated Hopi society still further. An individual was born to this earth; in death he was born to the underworld, only again to "die" in the underworld and become reborn on earth. Even in death, the breath-bodies were capable of returning to earth. As there was an earthly life cycle for an individual, there was a daily and yearly cycle for the sun. Each morning the sun left its eastern home and at sunset entered its western home; thus it furnished light equally to the earth and the underworld. On a yearly basis, winter began with the summer solstice and ended with the winter solstice, while summer began about mid-December and lasted until about mid-June. The winter solstice on earth was a summer solstice in the underworld, and the reverse also was true. When a major ceremony was being held on earth, a minor one was celebrated in the underworld by the katcinas. As would be expected, death in theory held no fears, for the living and the dead were one.

CEREMONIES The religious system required a series of annual and bi-annual ceremonies to be held by particular religious associations or societies. Each important ceremony was controlled by a particular organization that was linked to a different matriclan. A male elder of the leading lineage in each clan usually headed the religious association of his clan. In the possession of the clan was a bundle called the "mother" or "heart" of the clan, which consisted of an ear of maize, feathers, and coverings as well as other sacred objects. The equipment was owned by the leading lineage, and there was an associated kiva where services usually were held. Rituals were conducted at times established by phases of the moon, the location of the sun when it rose, or the number of days since another ritual ended. The patterning for all major ceremonies was

The Hopi: Farmers of the Desert

similar. The rituals spanned nine days, and when kiva members were so occupied, a flag was attached to the kiva ladder to warn off nonmembers. During the rituals there was a prohibition against eating fatty foods, meat, and salt. Sexual activities were restricted before as well as during the time of these celebrations. The first day was a perfunctory beginning; the next eight days were divided into two four-day segments, with the final day usually devoted to a public ritual. The specifics of the ceremonies included the use of altars and associated wooden, stone, or clay tablets. On the tablets were painted motifs symbolic of animals, clouds, maize, and rain. Prayer offerings were left at the proper shrines. Sand paintings and certain fluids with a water base likewise were important. Each secret society was associated with curing a particular disease, and to be taken ill with a disease controlled by a society was one means for induction. Initiation rituals usually took place around the midpoint of the ceremony and involved among other things having one's head washed with yucca suds as well as being given a new name by a ritual sponsor who was already a member of the society.

To benefit by all the advantages of being a Hopi in this and the underworld it was essential to participate actively in the affairs of one or more secret societies. At about nine years of age boys and girls were initiated into either the Katcina Society or the Powamu Society, the latter being more restricted in membership. Within the next few years a girl was expected to join the Lakon, Marau, or Oaqol society; boys joined the Antelope, Blue Flute, Gray Flute, or Snake society. Occasionally a woman joined a man's society and vice versa to fulfill a particular role, but by and large the ceremonial socie-

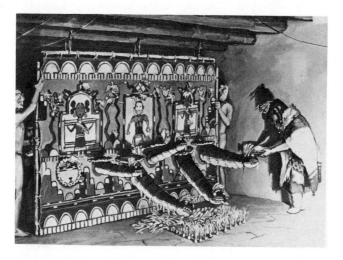

Plate 11–6 A 1900 illustration of Water Serpents in a kiva being manipulated behind a screen in a symbolic harvest of small maize plants. (Courtesy of Smithsonian Institution National Anthropological Archives, neg. no. 1813-B)

ties were divided along sexual lines. When a boy reached adolescence, he was expected to undergo the Tribal Initiation; only then was he free to participate in the most sacred of all ceremonies, the Soyal.

The ritual calendar may arbitrarily be considered to begin with the winter solstice or Soyal Ceremony. The Soyal was conceived around that mysterious moment each year when, in Hopi thinking, the sun rises at the same place for four days, and the days are shortest. The Soyal Ceremony was conducted by men who had completed the Tribal Initiation. At Oraibi the Wuwutcim Society conducted the most sacred of the Soyal rituals, and it was far more popular than the others. This society was composed of Bear clan members and directed by the village chief. The principal purpose of the ceremony was to compel the sun to begin the trip back to its summer home so that it would bring warmth enough for the crops to be planted. The climax of the rituals came when the "Star Priest," called Sun Priest at other times, performed a dance representing the cycle of the sun. The ceremony had the complementary purposes of inducing fertility in both women and plants, and participation was village-wide. The katcinas and particular men and women dancers performed. The typical smoking and prayers were accompanied by the manufacture of a large number of diverse prayer offerings of corn husks, feathers, and prayer sticks.

The Powamu Ceremony began when the February new moon first was seen, and it climaxed in the forced growth of beans in the kiva of the Powamu Society. Fifty to one hundred bean plants also were raised by each man in his own kiva. The beans were well watered, and the kiva fires burned hot day and night to force the sprouting. The sprouted beans were cut and bundled to be presented by katcinas to the grower's uninitiated offspring, his ceremonial children, and favored relatives. If a child was to be initiated into the Powamu Society, he saw the sacred rituals for the first time on the fifth day. This new knowledge was not to be revealed, under threat of punishment by the katcinas. By undergoing the initiation, participants became members of the Powamu Society and were permitted to impersonate katcinas, to participate in katcina rituals, and to become katcina fathers or ceremonial sponsors. Not all children were inducted into the Powamu Society; the remaining children were inducted into the Katcina Society on the sixth day of the Powamu ceremony.

In August another high point in the ceremonial round was reached with the performances of the Antelope-Snake or Blue and Gray Flute society ceremonies on alternate years. The Antelope and Snake societies were separate organizations, but they combined for their major ceremony. The two societies manufactured prayer offerings jointly, then went to their respective kivas, where they performed secret rituals. At this time the Snake Society members collected snakes in each of the four directions on four different days. At the proper time a Snake man received a snake that he held by his lips or teeth just behind the snake's head. He danced around the plaza several times as a partner

The Hopi: Farmers of the Desert

brushed his shoulders with a "snake whip," a short stick with eagle feathers attached. Each snake was danced with and then released on the ground at the plaza. The snakes then were gathered together in a circle and sprinkled with cornmeal by females of the Snake clan. Finally, younger men of the Snake Society picked up as many snakes as they could handle and took them to shrines in each of the four cardinal directions.

The public performances of Snake Society members have attracted more popular interest among whites than any other American Indian ritual. The reason, of course, is that the snake dancers carried prairie rattlers in their mouths as often as they carried harmless species such as the bull snake. Snake Society members handled poisonous and harmless snakes with equal ease, and yet prairie rattler bites occasionally are fatal. Illness or death from snakebite among the dancers is unreported, and various explanations have been offered concerning the Indians' ability to handle poisonous snakes. No evidence suggests that the members had an immunity to snake venom or that the snakes were charmed or drugged. Furthermore the Hopi did not have an effective antidote for venom, which was proven by laboratory tests of their snake medicine. Historically, there appear to have been two different answers to Hopi success in handling rattlesnakes. In 1883 a herpetologist visited a kiva where

Plate 11–7 A Snake Dance at Old Oraibi. (Courtesy of the Southwest Museum)

rattlesnakes were being kept for a dance; he inspected the fangs of one rattler and found them intact. After the dance he sent two of the rattlesnakes which had been used to the U.S. National Museum, and the venom glands were found to contain poison. Thus it would seem almost certain that the fangs were milked before the public ceremony. The next snake captured after a snake dance was taken in 1932; another herpetologist recovered a rattler from a shrine following a snake dance. The snake's fangs had been cut away rather skillfully. Similar evidence that the fangs were cut out in recent times was obtained in 1951 when another rattlesnake recovered after a ceremony was found to have had its fangs removed. Thus, the limited evidence indicates that the Hopi in aboriginal times and into historic times milked the poison from the fangs of rattlesnakes but that between 1883 and 1932 they shifted to cutting away the fangs. The logical conclusion is that as the Hopi came to understand white attitudes toward rattlesnake bites, they eliminated the risk by an operation on the dangerous snakes.

The final ceremony of major importance was the Tribal Initiation. Controlled by the Agaves Society, it was held only when this society had at least one candidate for initiation. During this ceremony adolescent males were initiated into one of four secret societies, the Agaves, Horns, Singers, or Wuwutcim. It should be recalled that a male could not be a fully participating adult in Hopi society until he had passed through this initiation. The Tribal Initiation was the most complex of the ceremonies and a cornerstone of Hopi religion. It took place in November at a time established by the Sun Watcher. A new fire was made in the Agave kiva by the kiva chief, and some embers were carried to the other participating kivas. An idol called Dawn Woman was brought from her shrine and exhibited on top of the kivas until the fifth day of the ceremony, when she was returned to her shrine after "delivering" her offspring. All candidates slept in their kivas, and the dances performed on the third and fifth days were clearly associated with fertility, with phallic symbols and simulated pregnancies presented. These events, and many others, symbolized the ritual rebirth of male children into manhood and reaffirmed the integration between the living and the dead.

Participation in secret societies was not restricted to men. Women controlled three voluntary religious associations, the Lakon, Marau, and Oaqol. Just as the secret societies of men included a few women, so the religious associations of the women included a few males. The organization of women's societies was similar to that of males: they were controlled by a lineage in a particular clan, possessed bundles, carried out secret rituals in a kiva, and performed certain ceremonies in public.

RELIGION   Hopi religious dogma was precise, the ceremonial round was exacting, and the katcinas played a vital ceremonial role. To maintain the balance in nature and to sustain man's relationship with the gods each individual was obligated to contribute to the best of his ability. An individual's contribution was manifest in being *hopi* or good. The anticipated behavior for an individual was spelled out in detail since being hopi involved more than goodness alone. A Hopi ideally was cooperative, self-effacing, and nonaggressive. He had moral as well as physical strength and health. He accepted collective responsibilities and concentrated on good thoughts. Conversely, an evil or bad person was kahope, with personality traits opposite those of the ideals.

Contemplation of the Hopi religious system reveals that it was a finely tuned totality. The katcinas always fulfilled their obligations in the underworld, and if the Hopi on earth did the same, there was no privation or unhappiness. It was the responsibility of each person to fulfill his or her social and ceremonial obligations by being hopi. Community-wide prosperity indicated that each individual had contributed his or her utmost, and the ideals of the Hopi Way thus were achieved. But what about failures? Why was it that during some years rain did not fall, winds dried the ground and blew seeds away, and the streams did not flow with water? Obviously, it was essential to be able to explain why it sometimes came to pass that nature did not respond to the complex ceremonies. The burden of failure was said to rest with individuals, persons who were kahopi, thinking evil and doing evil; these persons were witches.

SORCERY   The origin of witchcraft was traced to Spider Woman, who caused the first human death. Hopi have reported that they believed a typical village included more witches than ordinary people. Witches might be male or female and from any clan; no one was considered to be incapable of witchcraft. A Village Chief or ceremonial leader might be suspect simply because he held an important office. Any self-assertive person was open to the accusation of being a witch because such behavior was not hopi. It was possible to become a witch either by voluntarily practicing sorcery or by unknowingly being inducted into a society of witches as a child. In the latter instance, existing witches reportedly carried off a related child while it slept and inducted it into a secret society that followed the patterning of other Hopi secret societies. The initiate was taught the witches' art of assuming the shape of an animal to pursue their nefarious craft by night. The power of a witch was derived from association with an animal familiar, such as a coyote, owl, wolf, or small black ant, from whom the greatest forces of evil emanated; quite logically, sorcerers possessed "two hearts," their own and that of their animal familiar. Sorcerers worked evil by sending pestilence to the fields, by causing land erosion, or by driving off rain clouds and replacing them with a conjured windstorm. A witch was not content with destroying crops but killed people as well. Murder probably was the most important activity of a sorcerer because he extended his own life by killing one relative each year. A relative was killed or his illness caused by shooting stiff deer hairs, ants, a bit of bone, or some other object into his body without breaking the skin.

Ordinary people could best protect themselves against a witch, who was most likely a near relative, by wearing arrowpoints of stone, regarded as the ends of lightning flashes associated with the clouds. The Hopi did not attempt to interfere with the activities of witches because they believed that they would die prematurely or encounter misfortune. A witch's spirit thirsted and hungered for the underworld and approached it by one step a year. The sanctions against a witch were not in this world but in the underworld; when his or her spirit arrived there, it was burned in an oven and became a beetle.

SHAMANS   Some persons harmed and killed people by supernatural means, but others, shamans, cured people through their special abilities. A society of curers existed in early historic times, but it became extinct before being reported adequately. In any event, in the more recent past there were curing specialists who relied on pharmacopoeia and massaging techniques. Some shamans were secular healers; they set broken bones and prepared herbs for patients. Their rather complex body of knowledge required specialized training, and a secular shaman was likely to pass his information on to a sister's son. In another category were the shamans who performed supernatural cures. These "two hearted" individuals were supposed to employ their powers only for curing illness caused by witches. Obviously such a person would be suspect in a sorcery case and a dangerous individual in any event. He chewed jimsonweed root or some other plant to induce a vision that aided in diagnosing the source of a malady.

LIFE CYCLE   As might be anticipated the Hopi stress on fertility led to certain forms of behavior thought conducive to pregnancy. A woman should pray to the sun at each dawn, and she was most likely to conceive if she had sexual intercourse while menstruating. Pregnancy was recognized by failure to menstruate, and if a woman suspected that she was carrying twins, a shaman's aid was sought to make the twins one. To bear twins was considered difficult, and it was thought that if both lived one parent would die. A pregnant woman prayed to the sun and sprinkled cornmeal while she prayed to ease the labor of childbirth. She was active during her pregnancy, and she as well as her husband observed diverse taboos.

A woman bore her offspring in the house of her mother, often the same dwelling in which she had been born. She was unaided and gave birth while squatting over a layer of sand. The blood, afterbirth, and sand were covered with cornmeal and hidden in a special crevice. If a young person had contact with the blood and afterbirth, he would become ill. Immediately after delivery, the grandmother entered the room, severed the umbilical cord, and took charge. In a short time the father's closest female relative, his mother or sister, arrived to wash the head of the neonate and to direct the activities of the next twenty days, which culminated in a naming ceremony and a feast. Later in life the child developed warm social ties with his father's close female relatives. The father was nowhere to be seen during the birth, and usually for forty days thereafter he withdrew to his kiva away from the bustle and confusion in the house of his wife.

An infant was nursed whenever it cried and was not weaned for two to four years or even longer. To quiet an unhappy child a mentor might rub its sexual organ, and a small child might masturbate without reproof. When a child was able to walk, he was encouraged to urinate and defecate outside the house; if he should defecate inside, he might be scolded or slapped on the head. Matters pertaining to sex were accepted among the Hopi with casual regard. Since a child slept in the same small room with his parents, their sexual activities easily were observable. Children were not instructed about sexual matters but came to understand them through observation. It was not unusual for males and sometimes women to urinate before persons of the opposite sex. Furthermore jokes that we would consider obscene were taught to small boys to be used when they performed as ceremonial clowns. Yet shyness was characteristic of young girls, and a licentious person sometimes was called crazy.

When katcinas were abroad, children were warned that when they misbehaved something out of the ordinary would happen; girls were told to prepare ground cornmeal and boys to trap small mammals for the giants who were coming, or else the giants would take them away. A few days later awesome giant katcinas arrived, wearing frightening masks and carrying weapons and a basket in which to take away children. Having been previously instructed by parents, the katcinas cited particular transgressions of children and threatened to seize them. Parents defended them, and girls offered the katcinas baked cornmeal, which was accepted, although the small animals proffered by the boys were rejected. Finally, the katcinas left, but only after they had received gifts of meat from the parents.

The onset of puberty was not given ceremonial recognition for either boys or girls, but it was customary for boys in their early teens to begin sleeping in a kiva rather than at home. A girl was, however, expected to pass through a ceremony before she married. Each year girls between the ages of sixteen and twenty assembled at the house of a paternal aunt of one girl. The event usually was directed by a female who recently had passed through the rituals, and she was aided by two boys. For most of four days the girls ground maize in a darkened room; they observed food taboos and drank liquids only at midday. The boys organized a rabbit hunt on the third day, and the girls spent most of their time baking piki. Afterwards, the girls appeared for the first time with new coiffures termed "butterfly wings" or "squash blossoms." A girl continued to wear her hair in this manner until she married. She was most likely to marry someone from within the community (village endogamy) soon after passing through this ceremony.

Fornication between teenagers was expected and was formalized in the *dumaiya*. As a boy began sleeping in a kiva, he was free to roam the pueblo at night and did so wrapped in a blanket so that he could not be easily identified. As the members of his amourette's household slept, he crept in carefully to the

399

side of the girl, who in a whisper asked who it was. The boy answered, "It is I," and from the sound of his voice, the girl identified her caller. If she were willing, which usually was the case since the boy went only where he thought he would be received, he passed the night with the girl, leaving just before daylight. A dumaiya supposedly was secret, but it could not remain so in a small community like Oraibi. The girl's parents did not interfere if they regarded the boy as an acceptable husband for their daughter. A girl was not likely to have only a single lover, and before long she might become pregnant. If this happened, the girl named the boy she liked best as the father, and the formalities of arranging a marriage were begun. It also was possible for a girl to propose directly to a boy during certain festive or ceremonial occasions. A couple did not court unless they stood in a proper social relationship with one another. A person could not marry another in the same clan or phratry and should not marry someone from his father's clan or phratry, but the latter rule was not observed with care.

After the relatives of a couple approved a match, the girl ground maize for three days at the groom's house to demonstrate her abilities as a home-maker. There was no comparable trial for the groom. While the girl was in the boy's home, his paternal aunts attacked the boy's mother and her sisters with mud and water for permitting the girl to "steal" their "sweetheart." The fight was in an atmosphere of jovial hostility. On the fourth morning the couples' hair was washed in one container by their respective mothers and female relatives. A mingling of their hair symbolized the marital union. Once again the paternal aunts of the boy attempted halfheartedly to disrupt the ritual. After their hair had dried, the couple stood at the mesa edge to pray to the sun and later returned to the groom's home for a wedding breakfast. They were now man and wife, but they continued to live in the groom's house until the bride's wedding costume was completed by his male relatives and any other men who offered to help. The men prepared the cotton and wove two sets of wedding garments, a small robe, and a white-fringed belt; in addition they prepared skins and sewed white moccasins and leggings. During the manufacture of these items the groom's family feasted the workers. After a month or more, the garments were completed; wearing one set and carrying the second in a reed container, the bride returned home. Her husband informally and unobtrusively took up residence in her household. The wedding garments were very important because they were required for entering the underworld after death.

All Hopi women appear to have married, but such was not the case for men. Indirect pressure was put on a girl by her brothers and her mother's brothers to bring another male into their economic unit. A boy's parents did not encourage him to marry because they then lost him as a productive family member. Any form of plural marriage was prohibited, but many unions were transient. It appears that over 35 percent of the people had from one to eight divorces. The most common grounds for divorce was adultery, followed by

The Hopi: Farmers of the Desert

what probably would be termed incompatibility in our society. Divorce was a simple matter since it was only necessary for a man to rejoin his natal household or for a woman to order her husband from her household. The primary pressures against a divorce came from a girl's family since they did not relish losing an economically productive male. The mother and her small children continued to reside in their old abode; an older offspring might join either parent.

The social core of a household consisted of a line of females. Within this setting the closest bonds were between a mother and her daughters. Daughters were destined to spend their lives in their mother's home or in an adjacent residence, and eventually they assumed their mother's role. From her mother a girl learned domestic skills and the norms of proper behavior. A mother guided the most important decisions in the ceremonial life of a girl and was likely to have a voice in the selection of her mate. As a girl's menarche arrived, she was instructed by her mother about caring for herself. The girl was not isolated at this time, nor at any other menstrual period; neither was she restricted from participating in ceremonies while menstruating. Were a mother to die the mother's sister, who was called mother, replaced the biological mother in the girl's affection. Between a mother and her son the social bonds were not as close. A mother indulged an offspring of either sex, but a son in his early teens soon found his identity with a kiva group. A man's natal home remained the residence with which he felt most identified, however. He returned there if divorced and was a frequent caller in his mother's house. Like a girl, a man identified closely with his mother's sister, especially if the mother had died. A father was not overtly important in the upbringing of his children. He was, however, interested in having his daughter find a good husband, who by his farming activities could lighten the father's economic labors. A father took comparatively little active interest in a son until the latter's Tribal Initiation. Then the father selected the boy's ceremonial sponsor, which was an important decision. As a boy grew older, his father assumed a major role as his teacher. He imparted farming and ceremonial skills as well as advice about being hopi.

The maternal uncle of a young boy was the only male of his parents' generation who was of the same lineage and clan as himself. If such an uncle were a ceremonial leader, a boy might follow him in office, which called for systematic training of the youth. A mother's brother was likely to be the most important figure of authority associated with the boy's home, and he did not hesitate to apply discipline. A mother's brother was not all sternness toward his sister's children, however. He often told them myths or tales about their clan and occasionally presented them with gifts. One very warm relationship was between a man's sister and his son. As a small child, a boy soon learned that he was always a welcome guest in this woman's home. Here he received favored foods and frequent demonstrations of love and affection. As he grew older, he took game to his paternal aunt and exhibited his warm feeling toward her.

Sexual relations with this aunt and her daughter were possible, and Titiev suspects that in the recent past a youth may have been expected to marry a father's sister's daughter.

As death approached it was said that a person's body became swollen. Youths as well as most adults left the house because they feared being present at the time of a death. The body and hair of a deceased person were washed, and then he was reclothed. After a man was wrapped in a deerskin or a woman in her wedding blankets, the corpse was flexed into a sitting position. Prayer offerings were fashioned by the father of the deceased or another male in his clan. A prayer feather was placed beneath each foot and in each hand, as well as over the navel, the location of a person's spirit. The face was covered with cotton, symbolic of the time the dead become clouds, while food and water were placed with the body as sustenance on the journey to the underworld. The body was carried to the cemetery by men from the house of the deceased; here a hole had been dug just large enough to receive the bundled corpse. It was faced west, and soil was spread hastily on top. Men who attended the dead purified themselves afterwards by washing in a boiled juniper preparation, and there was a ritual in the household of the deceased to protect members against spirits. The next day the man who had manufactured the prayer offerings took cornmeal and five prayer sticks to the grave. The prayer sticks would help the person on his travels to the land of the dead, and the food was to feed the spirit. A prayer was offered, and the spirit was told not to return for anyone else in the community. Later, each household resident washed his hair and smoked himself over hot coals on which pinyon gum had been placed. All possessions of the deceased were thrown away. A separate cemetery was provided for the stillborn, infants, and children. The spirit of an infant did not travel to the underworld but lingered above the house, to be reborn again as a person of the opposite sex. The death of an adult was surrounded with misgivings and fear in spite of the fact that most dead were to be reborn into a peaceful world which was an intimate part of the Hopi Way.

Recent History

Among the earliest Hopi and Anglo-American contacts was a conflict that took place in 1834; white trappers raided Hopi gardens and killed about fifteen people. In 1850 the Hopi asked Anglo-American authorities in Santa Fe for help in controlling Navajo depredations, but no action was taken until later. Most Hopi took a cautious approach toward whites. Everyone knew the origin myth in which an elder brother of the Hopi, a Bahana, departed and promised to return when the Hopi were in need. They reasoned that perhaps Anglo-Americans were the Bahanas, or White Gods, but no one knew for certain how to identify them. Continuing Navajo intrusions on their grazing lands, a severe drought, and a smallpox epidemic were traumas in the 1860s. The

The Hopi: Farmers of the Desert

Hopi were recognized by the Federal Government in 1870 when the Moqui Pueblo Agency was established, and a school supervised by missionaries was founded in 1874. The Moqui Pueblo Reservation (later changed to Hopi Indian Reservation) was created by an Executive Order in 1882, but the land set aside was for Indian, not exclusive Hopi, use. Passage of the Dawes Act in 1887 resulted in Federal pressures on the Hopi to shift from family and community landholdings to individual allotments. The Bureau attempted to force the allotment program in 1907 but did not succeed. Conflicts with the Navajo over grazing lands intensified since there had been no boundary survey when the Hopi Reservation was established, and Navajo encroachment on Hopi lands has continued. Through a series of executive orders the Navajo Reservation came to surround the Hopi, and about 1937 the Bureau of Indian Affairs reduced the area officially designated as Hopi land to about one-fourth its original size, or 1000 square miles.

By the beginning of the present century, the Hopi subsistence cycle had undergone major changes. The primary reliance on maize, beans, and squash remained, but new crops and animals became increasingly important. Probably the most important new animal was the sheep, and virtually every man had at least a small flock by 1900. Each animal was owned by an individual, but they were herded cooperatively by men. Most often a man tended a combined flock for a few days, and then his brother, with whom he was a herding partner, took charge. Sheep were held as wealth and were butchered only for ceremonial feasts. Any unconsumed meat was dried as jerky or dried, pounded, and mixed with fat as pemmican. Cattle were less popular because of their initial cost and because the pattern of allowing them to graze freely led to the destruction of crops, with ensuing disputes over crop damage. The difficulty in maintaining horses, which were broken to the saddle, was the nuisance of rounding them up each day for pasturing, usually at a considerable distance from the community. Like the sheep, they were individually owned but often were tended jointly by men.

Modern Life

Mythology and history have had a profound effect on contemporary Hopi life, especially in the village of Oraibi. To understand what has happened there and why, we must go back to the late nineteenth century.

In the earliest contacts with Anglo-Americans it appears that the chiefs at Oraibi were unfriendly. In 1871 the Moqui Pueblo Special Agent was well received everywhere except at Oraibi, and the Oraibi people were angry when neighboring villagers accepted whites. For a number of years the Oraibi chief had been a man serving only until one of his two eligible sons was old enough to assume the position. The younger son, Lololoma, became the Village Chief some time prior to 1880, and he continued his father's anti-American policies.

Soon after assuming office, Lololoma traveled to Washington, D.C., with a party of Hopi to appeal to the Federal Government to contain Navajo encroachments on their land. After the trip, Lololoma reversed his attitude toward Anglo-Americans and became the leader of the progressive, friendly, or pro-Anglo faction. The anti-Anglo faction, called conservatives or hostiles, was led by a male called "Uncle Joe" by Anglos but actually named Lomahongyoma. He was a leader in the Soyal Society, head of the Blue Flute kiva, and from the same phratry as Lololoma; this made his challenge to the latter's leadership legitimate. The progressives and conservatives grouped behind their able leaders, and the great drama at Oraibi began.

Because a critical issue in the dispute was the precise identity of the Anglo-Americans, each faction drew on sacred myths to validate its stand. Were these Anglos the Bahanas? The hostile faction said no, for a real Bahana would be able to speak the Hopi language and could produce a stone matching the one held by the Village Chief at Oraibi. Obviously these Anglos were not Bahanas, and if the progressives accepted them as gods, they were likely to arouse the anger of a supernatural who would send a flood to end the world. The progressives traced Hopi difficulties not to Anglo-Americans but to the underworld and witchcraft. The sides chosen by particular individuals were influenced by a number of factors, among which were their clan and phratry ties as well as the nature of their close kin ties with the outstanding personalities in the conflict.

The attitude of the conservatives was reflected in their categorical rejection of American ways. When they refused to send their children to school at Keams Canyon in 1887, Lololoma identified them to government officials and some were arrested. The remaining hostiles then confined Lololoma to a kiva, from which he was rescued by U.S. Army soldiers. When in 1891 an attempt was made by Federal representatives to survey Oraibi land, the hostiles disrupted the efforts. A small group of soldiers came to unseat the leader, but they were surrounded. A ceremonial declaration of war was issued with great drama, and the soldiers prudently withdrew. A larger U.S. military force sent to Oraibi shortly afterwards arrested the hostile leaders as well as some of the progressive leaders.

By 1891 the friendly and hostile factions were at such bitter odds that they could not be reconciled. Since the hostiles were more numerous, their leader, Lomahongyoma, declared that he was the Village Chief. The fracture became a fissure when attention turned to ceremonial issues. Neither side would cooperate with the other in presenting the sacred ceremonies; nor would either permit the use of its ceremonial equipment by the opposite faction. In 1897 the Soyal Society members were forced to align themselves with one of the two leaders, depending on whether they supported the hostile or the friendly faction. In spite of the bitterness between them, each faction held its own Soyal ceremony without interference from the other.

What happened at Oraibi affected the entire tribe because the village con-

The Hopi: Farmers of the Desert

Plate 11–8 The original caption on this picture reads: Mosqui Indians Chief Lo-Ma-Hung-Yo-Ma, arrested at Oraibi, November 25th and 26th 1894, for seditious conduct and confined at Alcatraz Island, California, since January 3rd 1895. (Courtesy of the Southwest Museum)

tained 1200 of the 2200 Hopi listed on the official census of 1890. Laura Thompson points out that behind the rupture at Oraibi was the problem of land. Not only were there Navajo encroachments, but disputes also had arisen between clans over the lands of an abandoned pueblo. Successful farming in the past was based on community recognition of clan holdings and clan cooperation in farming, but Federal pressures were great to have the Indians accept individual family land allotments between 1892 and 1911.

About 1901 there was a change in the leadership of the progressives. Lololoma died, and a younger sister's son replaced him. This young, aggressive man, Tawaqwaptiwa, was selected over his older brother because of his more forceful qualities. In September of 1906 open conflict developed. After some scuffling the conservative leader drew a line on the ground, and a push-of-war was held. Before the pushing began it was decided that the losers would leave the pueblo. The hostile leader was the object to be pushed, with people pushing him from behind or in front. The hostiles or conservatives lost the struggle, and that same evening about 300 of them took their belongings and abandoned the settlement. They founded the new village of Hotevilla, about seven miles to the north of Oraibi. The nature of the split clearly illus-

Plate 11–9 Flute dance at Oraibi in 1901. (Courtesy of the Field Museum of Natural History, Chicago)

trates that the sociopolitical structure of the community could not resolve conflicts of this nature.

The Bureau of Indian Affairs authorities came on the scene soon after the rupture. They sent the conservative leaders to jail and relieved Tawaqwaptiwa temporarily as chief. He was sent to the Indian school at Riverside, California, to learn to speak English and practice American ways. When he returned to Oraibi in 1910, he was extremely anti-American; Titiev (1944, 94) records accounts which describe him as "quarrelsome, stubborn, vindictive, and unusually licentious." Over the next twenty years Tawaqwaptiwa managed to alienate most of the remaining residents of Oraibi. He forced Mennonite converts and sympathizers, in addition to those who accepted only some American customs, away from the settlement with his constant antagonism. By 1933 only 109 Hopi remained in Oraibi. Some had moved to New Oraibi, on the valley floor beneath Oraibi, and others settled some forty miles to the northwest at Moencopi on the Navajo Reservation. As Thompson has pointed out, the disintegration of Oraibi relieved the local pressures for land, but social cohesion did not develop in the offshoot communities. The most conservative community by the 1940s was Hotevilla. The people had a nearly complete ceremonial cycle when they left Oraibi that September night in 1906. Through the years their resistance against whites became almost an end in itself, and the reasons behind it were logical. After the split, most of the Hotevilla men were impounded by the Federal Government, and it was very difficult for the women and children to survive until their return. Then too, children were forced by soldiers to attend school, and the people were forcefully dunked in sheep-dip during a 1912 epidemic. These people scorned outside interference and wanted to be left alone.

After 1906 a complete ceremonial round could no longer be held at Oraibi because some clans were no longer represented, but Chief Tawaqwaptiwa faced the situation calmly as he aged. He maintained that the time would soon

406

come when everyone would abandon him, and he alone would carry on the Soyal. Then there would be a great famine, and following it, all of the old ceremonies would be reinstituted at Oraibi. Again the village would thrive in all of its colorful glory. Tawaqwaptiwa waited and waited and died still waiting.

Many details of the changing Hopi lifeway in the comparatively recent past were reported by Thompson following her admirable fieldwork from 1942–1944. She obtained a vast amount of diverse information, of which the following is especially pertinent here. In the 1940s about 4000 Hopi were located in fourteen different settlements, including Moencopi, on land which had been set aside for Hopi occupancy adjacent to the Colorado River. The critical problems facing the people were a population increase on a smaller land base and the increasing erosion of the land. The land depletion apparently resulted from a dry climatic phase as well as overgrazing by livestock. Government efforts to remedy the situation were aimed first at a reduction in livestock. The people of the Third Mesa area were required to reduce their holdings by nearly 45 percent, while on the other two mesas reductions were about 20 percent. Thus, the Oraibi area residents were hardest hit by the program. The Federal Government had for many years encouraged herding, and sheep had become a very important item in the Hopi economy. Third Mesa people resisted the reduction with vigor but finally succumbed to Federal pressures. Along with stock reduction a program was instituted to encourage better stock management practices, and cooperatives were organized. The farming practices of old remained although the plow was replacing the digging

Plate 11–10 Women cleaning corn. (Courtesy of the Field Museum of Natural History, Chicago)

stick. Most of the fields were watered from stream flooding or else were dry land plots. An effort to irrigate Hopi lands was not overly successful and even at best could have included only 400 acres. The typical farmer, which meant almost every man, raised a wide variety of crops, but the essentially meatless diet consisted mainly of maize, white flour, beans, potatoes, sugar, and coffee. The nutritive value of the diet was below normal standards for children and just barely sufficient for adults.

All aspects of life at Oraibi had undergone tremendous readjustments following the 1906 rupture. When the full ceremonial cycle no longer could be held, the kiva-centered life of a male was destroyed, and the significance of the nuclear family unit increased proportionally. Tests administered by Thompson and her associates demonstrated that Oraibi children looked to their mothers as the dominant family member, while to children from First Mesa the father and mother both were important. Furthermore, boys from First Mesa were outgoing in their responses, while those of Oraibi were "definitely constricted and are troubled by a vague anxiety," according to Thompson (1950, 97). At the same time the Oraibi children were judged to reflect greater sensitivity than the others tested. In all social units males had suffered more from disorganizing influences than had females; if anything, the position of women had been strengthened. The net result was a fostering of previously unheard-of male individualism. Seemingly, about the only course of action remaining for men was to seek to better their position. Since the Oraibi land base was not adaptable to the accumulation of farmlands or even male control of such lands, there was a move toward wage labor by the ambitious males. Another avenue open to individual males was political leadership, but in this role an individual encountered more of the pervasive Hopi feeling against personal achievements.

No modern ethnographer has devoted more attention to the Hopi than Mischa Titiev. In addition to his fieldwork in 1932–1934 that led to the publication of *Old Oraibi*, he spent ten summers at Oraibi between 1937 and 1966. Thus it is fitting to turn to his report of changes at Oraibi in recent years.

Titiev felt that abandonment of traditional Hopi life had intensified in the recent past as a result of many factors, one of the most far-reaching being the construction of paved highways linking Black Mesa with cities and towns. An end to their physical isolation turned the Hopi outward toward the white-oriented world. Many people bought automobiles or trucks, ending travel by wagon or on the backs of burros and horses. Men often worked in nearby towns and commuted daily to jobs or else worked in more distant cities, returning to the village on weekends. Some men worked as farmers only on the weekends. Crop surpluses could be transported over highways to distant markets, and in times of local food scarcity a staple, such as maize, could be imported. Good roads also brought large numbers of tourists, especially during ceremonies such as the Snake-Antelope dance.

The physical settlement had undergone less profound but equally far-reaching changes. The number of occupied houses was about the same as in the early 1930s, but larger houses were being built. Cinder block and cement were replacing local stone and adobe as building materials. As in the past, women performed lighter house-building tasks such as plastering. Outhouses became common, and most people owned store-bought furniture and appliances. The matrilocal marriage residence pattern and clan ownership of houses continued, but in recent years no woman shared a household with her mother. When a woman married, she wanted an official American civil or religious ceremony to document the event. Experience had taught Hopi women that documents were required in any legal dealings with whites. Each bride, even if she married elsewhere, still received traditional wedding garments from relatives.

The population of Oraibi was 112 in 1933 and had increased to about 130 in the mid-1960s. The emigration of young adults was more than counteracted by a decline in infant mortality attributable to Western medical practices. The young who remained at Oraibi were indifferent to the orthodoxy of the Hopi Way beyond participating in an occasional katcina dance. Gods of old had come to be displaced by technological forms; to obtain water had become a secular, not a sacred, process.

Not so very long ago the consumption of alcohol was shunned by the Hopi. Some veterans returning from World War II were heavy drinkers, and intoxicants became increasingly popular, with accompanying drunkenness. Social life changed in yet another respect because numerous clans died out and some others were represented only by males. They too will become extinct unless outsiders who are members marry into Oraibi. Political life assumed an unprecedented turn when a woman became the Village Chief because the people could not agree on a male successor. Hopi religion has disintegrated, and the Soyal ceremony is no longer performed. By 1955 at Oraibi the only remnant of this ceremonial event was that two men stayed up all night making prayer sticks for the sun.

LAND PROBLEMS   A recent Hopi-white problem has posed an added threat to the Indians. To meet the ever-increasing demands for electrical power in southern California, the Las Vegas area of Nevada, and sectors of Arizona, the Western Energy Supply and Transmission Associates (W.E.S.T.) was formed by municipal, state, and federal power companies. The Mohave plant in eastern Nevada began operations in 1970 and is powered by coal that is strip-mined at Black Mesa in Hopi and Navajo country about 270 miles to the east. Pulverized coal and water are pumped as slurry through a pipeline to the Mohave powerplant. The transport system requires up to 4,500 gallons of water a minute, which are drawn from wells some 2,000 feet in depth; during peak operations it is expected that three million gallons of water a day will be pumped from wells on Black Mesa. Aside from serious air pollution, there is the danger that if the deep well casings become cracked or broken, the water of shallow wells and springs of the Hopi would flow deep

Plate 11–11 Coal mining on Black Mesa in 1971. (Courtesy of Daniel B. Gridley)

into the ground, and they could no longer live in the area. An additional danger is posed by the runoff from the ridges of overburden (spoil banks) left by the strip-mining operation. Some of these cut across wash drainages, and if water from them enters cultivated fields the sulfur concentrates probably will ruin the land.

Hopi political structure was not seriously disrupted by outside pressures until passage of the Indian Reorganization Act of 1934. Under the terms of this law a Hopi Tribal Council was organized, but the traditionalists or conservatives among them never recognized the legitimacy of this organization and have refused to elect representatives to it. They reason that to acknowledge the existence of authority that supersedes their religious and political institutions would be to break their covenant with the gods. In 1964–1966 through the Department of the Interior, the Peabody Coal Company as a subsidiary of the Kennecott Copper Corporation negotiated the lease to mine coal on Black Mesa with the Hopi and Navajo tribal councils. The Hopi Tribal Council, representing the progressives, approved the lease, but the manner in which it was "negotiated" and the legality of the lease are subject to grave doubts.

A great deal of secrecy surrounded the negotiations leading to the entire W.E.S.T. development. No announcements were made before contracts were signed, no public hearings were held, nor was there any open discussion of what was happening. It is abundantly clear that the Department of the Interior, through the Bureau of Indian Affairs, worked very closely and quietly with representatives of W.E.S.T. for the benefit of industry at the expense of Indians. In the lease contracts with the Hopi approved by the Bureau of Indian Affairs there were no guarantees about water, reclaiming areas stripmined, or regulating spoil bank runoff. Furthermore the Peabody Coal Com-

The Hopi: Farmers of the Desert

pany lease was approved in part by noncertified representatives to the Hopi Tribal Council. Thus, it would appear that the lease is not valid. The Hopi do derive direct and indirect monetary benefits from the mining operation, but they had no idea what would happen to their lands, nor had they been made aware of the possible spoilage by the Bureau of Indian Affairs.

Another long-festering Hopi problem has been with the Navajo over land rights. When the Hopi Reservation was created by Executive Order in 1882, the land was not designated for exclusive Hopi use. The Navajo population grew rapidly and came to occupy much of the land on the Hopi Reservation that traditionally had belonged to the Hopi. In 1934 about 1.8 million acres of Hopi land, from a total of 2.5 million acres, were made a part of the Navajo Reservation. In 1962 the Supreme Court ruled that the land detached from the Hopi had in fact been set aside for both tribes; however, the Navajo retained effective control. In an effort to resolve the matter the U. S. Congress passed and the president signed a bill to divide the disputed land between the two tribes; the bill stipulated that if they could not reach an agreement on the partition, the U. S. District Court was empowered to make the division. Just after this legislation was adopted, the Hopi sued the Navajo for over three-quarters of the Navajo Reservation land, maintaining that a large part of the Navajo Reservation had not been set aside exclusively for the Navajo and that much of the area had belonged to the aboriginal Hopi. Clear resolution of Hopi land claims is not yet in sight.

A Hopi prophecy states that Indian lands will be seized or spoiled and that those of the Hopi will be the last to go. It also is prophesied that when this happens, if the Hopi and their friends cannot prevent these disasters, the world will end by turning over.

Comparisons

The peoples described up to this point have either focused their food-getting energies on hunting and fishing or farming and hunting. Differences in subsistence patterns invite comparison in terms of supernatural involvements. We may seek to establish whether the key edibles were or were not enmeshed in rituals and ceremonies. The mythological origins of foods do not seem nearly as important as ongoing supernatural associations represented in ceremonies designed to perpetuate species, rituals related to preharvest and harvest activities, or supernatural involvements in handling foods after they were obtained. Great differences separate the peoples in these respects. Comparisons might well take into consideration species characteristics, the settings in which the edibles mature, and whether one or more persons harvest a particular food.

The Hopi appear to have had more permanent settlements than any of the other peoples, although the Yurok and Tlingit have occupied the same sites for generations. The relative degree of sedentation for the members of one society as opposed to another has important cultural implications. For example, fully sedentary people can build substantial houses and accumulate far greater amounts of material goods than those who move about often. Further comparisons based on differences in settlement stability invite the identification of potential social, political, and religious correlates.

Additional Readings

The monograph by Ernest and Pearl Beaglehole provides a good introduction to the Hopi, as does the Hopi section in a book by Cyril D. Forde. The best works about a particular village are Titiev's studies at Old Oraibi. Alexander M. Stephen's diary offers a wealth of information about most aspects of Hopi life, but it is difficult to use. The best biography of a Hopi was edited by Leo W. Simmons, and the best ethnohistory is included in a book by Edward H. Spicer. Laura Thompson is a superior source for the emergence of the Hopi into modern times.

References

Beaglehole, Ernest and Pearl. *Hopi of the Second Mesa.* American Anthropological Association, Memoir no. 44. 1935.

Blundell, William E. "Ecological Shootout at Black Mesa," *Wall Street Journal,* April 18, 1971.

*Bunzel, Ruth L. *The Pueblo Potter.* New York. 1929. The discussion of Hopi and other pueblo Indian pottery is one of the finest studies of aboriginal ceramics. The text is particularly noteworthy when dealing with the ways in which designs were conceived and executed.

Colton, Harold S. *Hopi Kachina Dolls.* Albuquerque. 1949.

Colton, Mary-Russel F. "The Arts and Crafts of the Hopi Indians," *Museum Notes, Museum of Northern Arizona,* v. 11, 3–24. 1938.

Cushing, Frank H. "Origin Myth from Oraibi," *Journal of American Folklore,* v. 36, 163–170. 1923.

Forde, Cyril D. *Habitat, Economy and Society.* London. 1934.

Hurbert, Virgil. "An Introduction to Hopi Pottery Design," *Museum Notes, Museum of Northern Arizona,* v. 10, 1–4. 1937.

The Hopi: Farmers of the Desert

Josephy, Alvin M. "The Murder of the Southwest," *Audubon*, July, 52–67. 1971.

Jones, Volney H. "The Establishment of the Hopi Reservation, and some later Developments Concerning Hopi Lands," *Plateau*, v. 23, 17–25. 1950.

Oliver, James A. *Snakes in Fact and Fiction.* New York. 1958.

*Simmons, Leo W., ed. *Sun Chief.* New Haven. 1942. This Hopi autobiography is an extremely valuable document, for it offers great insight into the life of one individual.

Spicer, Edward H. *Cycles of Conquest.* Tucson. 1962.

Stephen, Alexander M. "Hopi Journal," *Columbia University Contributions to Anthropology*, v. 23, 2 pts. 1936.

Thompson, Laura, and Alice Joseph. *The Hopi Way.* Chicago. 1944.

*Thompson, Laura. *Culture in Crisis.* New York. 1950. The ethnographic background to Hopi life is provided in summary form, with the addition of the 1942–1944 findings of Thompson, her co-workers and assistants. The volume is devoted in part to Hopi administration by the Bureau of Indian Affairs, but also provides diverse information about Hopi acculturation.

Titiev, Mischa. "Notes on Hopi Witchcraft," *Papers of the Michigan Academy of Science, Arts, and Letters*, v. 28, 549–557. 1943.

*Titiev, Mischa. *Old Oraibi.* Papers of the Peabody Museum of American Archaeology and Ethnology, v. 22, No. 1. 1944. The classic study of a Hopi community through time—a key source.

Titiev, Mischa. *The Hopi Indians of Old Oraibi.* Ann Arbor. 1972.

Whiting, Alfred F. *Ethnobotany of the Hopi.* Museum of Northern Arizona, Bulletin 15. 1950.

Wormington, Marie M. *Prehistoric Indians of the Southwest.* Denver Museum of Natural History. 1951.

The Iroquois: Warriors and Farmers of the Eastern Woodlands

12

Reasons for This Selection

Anthropologists long have had a special fondness for the Iroquois and not without good reason. The first essentially modern account of an aboriginal people was written about them by the Jesuit missionary Father Joseph F. Lafitau and published in 1724. This work appeared in French, however, and did not make an immediate impact on Americans or Europeans. Then in 1851 Lewis Henry Morgan published a book about the Iroquois that became a model for ethnographers in America and many other countries. Furthermore the Iroquois played a decisive role in shaping the North American colonial empires of the British and French and continued in importance during the American Revolution. From colonial times to the present the names of outstanding Iroquois leaders have been known to many Americans. During the colonial period Hendrick was an outstanding warrior and military leader, Joseph Brant was a warrior and politician, while Red Jacket was a great orator. Kateri Tegaquitha, born about 1656, is being considered for canonization as a saint by the Roman Catholic Church. General Ely S. Parker, as secretary to General Ulysses S. Grant, drafted the terms of peace at Appomattox to end the Civil War. Finally there is the Iroquois Jay Silverheels, better known as Tonto, of *Lone Ranger* fame. The Iroquois, famous in war and politics, have re-

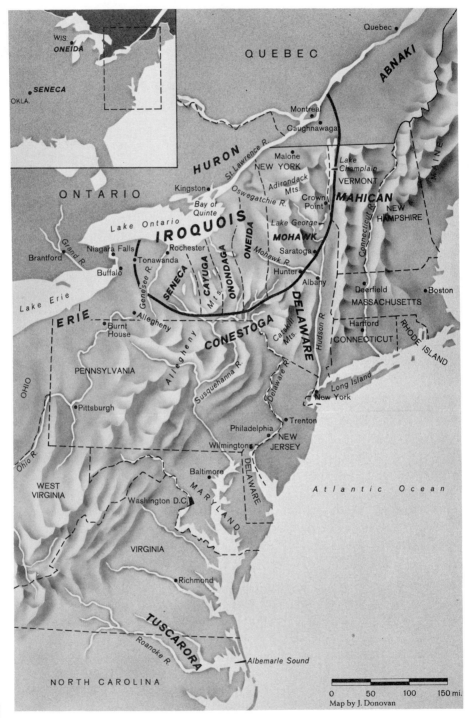

416

tained their identity with a rare resilience, but now their battles most often are fought in courtrooms.

People, Population, and Language

The original Five Nations or Iroquois League consisted of the Cayuga, Mohawk, Oneida, Onondaga, and Seneca tribes. The word Iroquois is based on an Algonkian word translated "real adder" with a French suffix. The aboriginal Iroquois lived from Lake Champlain and Lake George in the east to the Genesee River drainage and Lake Ontario in the west. The northern boundary was the St. Lawrence River, and Iroquois domain extended south to the upper Susquehanna River. Each nation occupied an oblong strip of country, and it is estimated that collectively at the time of early historic contact they numbered 10,000. By 1904 the Six Nations (adding the Tuscarora) numbered at least 16,000, and the modern Iroquois population is estimated to be about 20,000.

The Iroquois spoke a language of the Macro-Siouan phylum and the Iroquoian family. The dialects of the Iroquois include Cayuga, Mohawk, Oneida, Onondaga, and Seneca. Cherokee, which is of the same family as Iroquois, separated from Iroquois about 100 B.C. Separations of the member dialects within Iroquois took place about A.D. 700. All of these estimates are based on the results of glottochronology.

At some unknown time in prehistory the Tuscarora split from what was later to become the League and settled along the Roanoke and nearby rivers in North Carolina and Virginia. Hostilities with white settlers erupted in the Tuscarora wars of 1711 and 1712–1713. The second war ended with some Tuscarora moving north to join the League members. They were adopted formally by the Oneida in 1722 as members of the League, and the Iroquois then became the Six Nations.

Prehistory

The first people in the northeastern United States apparently were big game hunters, and they are known only from scattered lithic finds. They arrived around 9000 B.C. and have left spearpoints, knives, and scrapers behind. Following this relatively unknown era populations usually termed Archaic arose and became more sedentary, possibly representing a settling-down of the big game hunters. The earliest Archaic peoples are not much better known than their predecessors, but shortly before 2000 B.C., with the Late Archaic, the picture becomes somewhat clearer. The technology came to include ground stone tools; adz blades, gouges, grooved stones, and slate points are examples. Soon after 2000 B.C. pottery was first made, and such items as bannerstones and semilunar knives were new manufactures. This cultural complex was the base from which Early Woodland developed around 1000 B.C., and it seems to have been a localized development. Cremations became more important, as did the use of red ocher in burials, and there was an increase in the quantity of grave goods. The climax development was the Adena culture found in the Ohio River area before 200 B.C. There were burial mounds and, later in the same culture complex, earthworks, some farming, and a great diversity of artifacts. The middle period of Woodland is associated mainly with the Hopewell culture that emerged about A.D. 1 from an Adena base influenced by outside contacts. As James B. Griffin (1964, 241) has written, "There is a growing tendency to view Ohio Hopewell as a uniform cultural complex dominated by an elite class that marshaled its manpower for conquest and the establishment of outlying subject groups." He doubts that Hopewell sociopolitical organization was as advanced as that of the historic Iroquois. Associated with Hopewell are complex earthworks, settled communities, farming, and a highly varied material culture. This cultural period did not dominate the eastern area; instead we find the Point Peninsula cultural remains, which were left in the east by central-based hunters and collectors who perhaps cultivated a few plants. Their technology included chipped as well as polished stone weapon points, knives, and ornaments. The general tradition seems to have developed from an Archaic subsistence pattern based on hunting and fishing. Direct continuity exists into the Lake Woodland culture reflected in the Owasco and associated developments in New York State and adjacent areas. The population was more sedentary than that previously noted for the area, the villages were fortified, and the people depended on crops they raised more than on gathering activities. Their pipe forms and dwellings were of the Iroquois type, and these Indians have been identified as Iroquoian. Tribes related to the historic Mohawk and Onondaga were in the Montreal region in the early 1500s and moved to New York State about 100 years later. Two conclusions were reached by Griffin concerning the archaeological remains of the Iroquois. Their way of life developed in the northeastern area, and their material culture does not seem out of the ordinary in its complexity for the area in general.

Early History

The French entered the St. Lawrence River system in 1534 with the explorations of Jacques Cartier, and they soon established contact with the Algonkian, Huron, and Montagnais. By the time the imaginative and aggressive French explorer Samuel de Champlain turned his attention to the south he had allied himself with the Algonkians against their enemies, the League tribes. Little did Champlain realize what a powerful adversary he was to confront. As Francis Parkman (1901, v. 1, 9) wrote, the League was "foremost

The Iroquois: Warriors and Farmers of the Eastern Woodlands

Plate 12–1 Defeat of the Iroquois by Samuel Champlain and Algonkians at Lake Champlain in 1609. (By permission of the Champlain Society)

in war, foremost in eloquence, [and] foremost in their savage arts of policy . . ." In 1609 Champlain, with a group of Algonkians, canoed to the lake that bears his name and met a party of Iroquois. The Iroquois attacked with confidence only to be thunderstruck and defeated by the white men in strange garb who used exotic weapons. The Iroquois never forgave the French or the Algonkian for the defeat; they soon recovered to raid and terrorize the French and Indian settlements along the St. Lawrence River.

Colonial Europeans began dealing with one League tribe after the next, and within the League members deliberated whether to ally themselves with the Dutch, French, British, or to remain neutral. These decisions usually were followed by raids against enemies and counter raids by the Europeans and their Indian allies. During Queen Anne's War between the English and French, beginning in 1702, the Iroquois as a whole remained neutral. However in 1704 those Mohawk who had been induced by the French to settle at St. Louis or Caughnawaga, near Montreal, accompanied a French-led party to Deerfield, Massachusetts, where there were about 300 persons at the time. In a predawn attack about 110 persons were taken prisoner and about 50 others killed. During the rapid return to Canada, most of the prisoners who could not keep up with the fast-moving party were killed; only somewhat more than half of them were restored eventually to the English.

When Queen Anne's War ended and the Treaty of Utrecht was signed in 1713, English control over much of eastern America was consolidated, and members of the League were recognized as British subjects. In 1711 Queen's Fort (later Fort Hunter) was founded, and a Church of England missionary began working with the Indians there but with little success. Children soon wearied of attending school, and the general conditions among adults were not what the missionary desired. One of his principal complaints was the traffic in intoxicants from Dutch traders to the Indians. The Iroquois passion for alcohol is well documented, and the missionary unsuccessfully attempted to stem its flow. In 1719 the mission was abandoned. Incidentally it was in 1712 that Lafitau arrived in New France and began his six-year stay at Caughnawaga, working among the Mohawk there.

The War of the Austrian Succession, erupting in 1740, again pitted the French against the English in Europe and North America. The French sought Iroquois support, and together they raided and burned outlying settlements, bringing turmoil to the Albany area. In reprisal, the English sent raiding parties into French territory under the Mohawk Hendrick in 1747. After peace was concluded the following year, an English missionary went to Albany and Fort Hunter and found cause for both joy and anxiety. The Mohawk received him in friendly fashion and obviously had retained at least some of what they had been taught by his predecessors. One Indian had even taken it on himself to spend most of his time preaching and instructing others. The distressing aspects of the scene were that intoxicants had become popular and highly disruptive in Indian domestic life and that the Roman Catholic priests at Fort Frontenac (Kingston, Ontario) had been successful in inducing more Mohawk to move to Canada.

About 1750 the French sought to dominate the Lake Erie and Lake Ontario regions as well as to establish closer contacts with the Cayuga, Onondaga, and Seneca by building a mission at the junction of the Oswegatchie and St. Lawrence rivers. A major in the militia, George Washington, unsuccessfully attempted to induce the French to abandon one post they had seized. He later fought the French to dislodge them from the upper Ohio River area but was defeated; this greatly strengthened the position of the French with local Indians. In 1756 a formal war, the French and Indian War, was declared between England and France. The English were defeated soundly until they took Fort Frontenac, which soon forced the French to withdraw from Fort Duquesne, later called Fort Pitt and then Pittsburgh. In 1759 the English began a two-pronged attack against the French that led to an end of French colonial power in Canada. At the famous battle for Quebec on the Plains of Abraham the English line met the charging French and did not fire until the advancing army was thirty-five paces away. The French force was nearly destroyed, and a French effort to retake Quebec ended in failure. In the spring of 1760 the English formulated a plan to take Montreal with converging armies. The plan succeeded, and by the end of the year the French had been forced to surrender their principal holdings in North America.

Action was taken by the British Government in 1763 to license traders to

420

Indians and to prohibit the alienation of Indian lands except with the approval of the Governor-in-Council. These were two extremely important precedents in guiding Indian policies in Canada and the United States.

THE AMERICAN REVOLUTION AND JOSEPH BRANT   The final drama in which the Iroquois were to play a significant role in American history began in 1775. The Iroquois were as a whole loyal to the British, and at best the colonial rebels could hope only to neutralize them. The loyal subjects of the Crown in turn did their utmost to induce the Iroquois to support the British cause actively. At the second Continental Congress an Indian Department was created with Northern, Middle, and Southern divisions, and the commissioner of each was charged with rendering the Indians neutral. At a meeting of the Northern Commissioner with the Iroquois, a systematic effort was made to insure their neutrality. Joseph Brant, who was loyal to the British, visited England in 1775 to clarify the position of the Iroquois whom he represented. While there he was made a captain in His Majesty's Army and pledged Iroquois support. On his return Brant led a force of Mohawk against the American rebels. With the Declaration of Independence in 1776 the political break between rebel colonists and the British was complete, and war began. The policy of unanimity among the League tribes broke down as a result of the conflict. The Mohawk and Onondaga were divided internally, some supporting each side; the Cayuga and Seneca supported the loyalists; the Oneida and Tuscarora were in theory neutral but in fact gave the rebels aid.

After the successful attack of forces under Joseph Brant and Walter Butler to the south of the Mohawk River, the Americans organized an army against these Iroquois. In 1779 the troops of General John Sullivan succeeded in destroying Iroquois communities, crops, and grain caches. Iroquois effectiveness was ended, and many fled to Canada, abandoning their traditional lands forever. In Canada the Mohawk settled temporarily near Montreal, where they were given lands. When the treaty of peace was signed in 1783, there was no mention of the Indians and their future status. In recognition of Mohawk aid, the British granted these Indians land along the northern shore of Lake Ontario and along Grand River, which flows into Lake Erie. About 1600 Iroquois began moving to the Grand River drainage in 1784. A separate treaty was made between the Six Nations and the United States, in which the Oneida and Tuscarora, who had remained neutral in the conflict, were permitted to retain most of their land, but the other League nations, who had fought for the British, were forced to relinquish claim to most of their land.

THE WAR OF 1812   The last time the Six Nations asserted political power in an international dispute was in the War of 1812. The Americans were quick to assure the Six Nations members that invading forces would not disturb their interests, but the Iroquois were unimpressed. Yet they were unwilling to commit themselves wholeheartedly to the British cause for good historical reasons; an initial call to arms for the British brought forth fewer than fifty Iroquois. Later victories by the Canadians induced some 500 Six Nations warriors to fight with distinction, but before the end of the war any effective Iroquois cooperation had ceased.

Early Historic Life

One difficulty in assembling Iroquois sources is to separate information about the Iroquois in general from that pertaining to a single member nation. The problem cannot be resolved successfully because we do not have parallel information for all the League nations. The descriptions to follow represent a composite view stressing the Mohawk and Seneca. A second difficulty is in obtaining comprehensive accounts of early historic conditions; thus the sketch to follow represents a reconstruction of Iroquois life from diverse historic sources.

ORIGIN MYTH   In the beginning there were six men who were carried about by the winds since there was no land. They learned of a woman in the heavens and decided that one of them should go there since they felt that they would perish without women. The man chosen was named Wolf, and he was carried high on the backs of birds to a tree near a spring where the woman went for water. When she appeared they talked, and Wolf gave her bear fat to eat. He soon seduced her, and the master of the heavens cast her out for this act. She fell onto the back of a turtle in a sea of water where otter and fish were digging up clay from the bottom to form land. The land grew little by little to its present configuration. All people are descended from this woman who gave rise to people identified with the wolf, turtle, and other species.

CLOTHING   Garments were made principally from deerskins sewn with deer-bone awls and sinew threads. Women wore underskirts that hung from the waist to just above the ankles, with designs in porcupine quills along the lower border. Over this garment was a long dress with fringed sleeves and fringe along the bottom. From their knees to their moccasins were short leggings, and in cold weather a skin cape was worn about the shoulders. Men wore kilts that reached their knees and were belted at the waist. Kilts were fringed at the bottom and decorated with dyed quills sewn on to form designs. Men also wore fringed shirts and long, fringed leggings; on their feet they wore quill-decorated moccasins.

SETTLEMENTS   It was customary to build villages on hilltops, and a particular community usually was occupied for about ten years. After this period accessible farmland was relatively unproductive, firewood scarce, and dwellings decaying. About twelve villages, each with 300 to 600 residents, are

The Iroquois: Warriors and Farmers of the Eastern Woodlands

Plate 12–2 Model of a village with a longhouse under construction. (From the collections of the Rochester Museum and Science Center, Rochester, New York)

reported before the turn of the eighteenth century. The Mohawk had three communities, and a series of major and minor trails connected these with the other settlements of the League. Villages were not dispersed widely but clustered along an east-west line. Specially trained runners could carry messages throughout the League in about three days.

A typical village was surrounded by a ditch and up to three rows of wooden palisades. Beyond the enclosure were many acres of cultivated fields. Dwellings, which were of the well-known longhouse type, were from 50 to 130 feet long and about sixteen feet wide. A house was built of seasoned posts, poles, and bark. Bark was stripped from trees in sheets, and these were piled on top of each other to flatten as they dried. Four stout posts with forked tops, one at each corner, formed the outline of the structure. Smaller forked poles were spaced between the main posts, and in the crotches of the forks poles were strung; other poles were placed at right angles to form the rafters. The arched roof was made with bent poles, and an entire frame was covered with overlapping sections of bark lashed into place and held firm with retaining poles.

A house interior was partitioned into two main sections, each about twelve feet long; between the sections were compartments for storing maize and other provisions. Along the center of a longhouse were fireplaces, with each family occupying an apartment opposite a fire. Smoke from the fires drifted through an oblong roof opening that also admitted light. In windy or rainy weather bark slabs covered this opening. Each family had an apartment

Plate 12–3 Model of one portion of a Seneca longhouse.
(From the collections of the Rochester Museum and Science
Center, Rochester, New York)

with two platforms, and there might be as many as twenty apartments in a
house. An upper platform, some five feet above the ground and six feet from
front to back, was covered with bark, reed mats, and with skins. The lower
platform was of similar dimensions and was about a foot above the ground.
On these platforms family members lounged or napped during the day and
slept at night. At each end of a longhouse was a doorway leading into the
storage rooms that opened to the outside. The outer doors were of bark and
were hinged at the top. In the winter a skin covering was added to the door.

For a small family or as a temporary residence, a less permanent dwelling
was built. It was triangular in outline, with poles at each corner converging at
the top, and was covered with overlapping bark slabs. An opening in one side
served as the doorway, and one at the top was for smoke from the interior
fireplace. Maize was stored in houses as well as in underground caches. These
excavated pits were bark lined, and the grain was placed inside. Bark slabs
were added as waterproof roofing, and the cache was covered with soil. Similar underground caches were lined with deerskins to hold dry meat.

The relatively permanent nature of their settlements made it possible for
the Iroquois to accumulate a wide range of material objects. Surprisingly
enough few manufactures were of stone although it was widely available as a
raw material. Arrowpoints and ax blades were fashioned from chipped stone,

The Iroquois: Warriors and Farmers of the Eastern Woodlands

while mortars and adz blades were produced by grinding and polishing. Bark was an important raw material from which diverse forms were made. Among these were barrel-shaped storage containers, trays for mixing cornmeal, deep folded trough-like receptacles for maple sap, and ladles. Deep-bowled wooden ladles were used to eat soup or hominy. Grit-tempered pottery vessels of up to six-quart capacity were used for cooking and storage. Basketry was limited, but containers made from animal skins commonly were used to store household items. A skin bag hung from the waist of a hunter or warrior contained most of the artifacts he required while traveling.

CONVEYANCES   Summer travelers used overland trails, waterways, or a combination of the two. To carry a load, a tumpline was passed over the forehead and attached to a basket, cradleboard, or pack frame. A pack frame, made from sections of hickory, was fitted to the back and might be supported by a chest strap, a tumpline, or both. A canoe was covered with the bark of red elm or hickory since both trees were small in this area and the bark could be pried off in one piece. Canoes were from twelve to forty feet long. The rounded ribs and the gunwales were made from ash, and both ends had a slight upturn. They were propelled with single-bladed paddles. For winter travel snowshoes were made of hickory frames laced with babiche. They were relatively short and broad and well adapted to walking through timbered areas. Reportedly a person could travel as many as fifty miles a day on snowshoes.

SUBSISTENCE ACTIVITIES   Most food was cultivated, and the right to use farmland belonged to the persons who cleared and planted it. Farming was a primary activity of women, who appear to have cleared the land, sowed the seeds, cut the weeds, and harvested the crops. The most important plant raised was maize, and at least fifteen varieties were identified. The women also planted varieties of beans and squash. The most important farming tools were the digging stick and a hoe made with a scapula blade. Tobacco was also raised for smoking in elbow pipes made from fired clay. Once planted, tobacco seeded itself and from year to year required only thinning. The leaves were picked in the fall after a frost and were dried before use. Tobacco was used only in pipes and often was kept in a weasel skin pouch attached to a man's belt. Women collected wild plant foods, including over thirty different wild fruits and about fifty plant products ranging from roots to leaves. These were added to the maize-bean-squash diet and were important if crops failed.

Beyond the farmlands of a settlement were hunting, fishing, and collecting areas belonging to the community. From harvest time until midwinter people abandoned their villages and scattered to hunt; again in the early spring they left their villages to collect maple sap, fish, and hunt pigeons. Deer were hunted communally by driving them between converging lines of brush with bowmen concealed at the end. The most effective means for taking a single deer was to set a spring-pole snare in the animal's trail. When the snare peg was tripped, the spring pole righted itself, and the deer was lifted into the air by its hind legs. Snares were set for bears on their trails, and as an animal became entangled, a heavy pole fell on its back to pin it down. Bears also were chased for long distances until they tired and could be shot with arrows. When a large animal was killed in the winter near the home of a hunter, he brought it in on a toboggan improvised from bark. At other times the prey was butchered at the kill site; the meat was removed from the bones, dried before a fire, and placed in bark containers for transport.

In the late spring as women planted crops near the villages men fished and harvested birds. A common fishing technique was to use cone-shaped traps about three feet in length made from converging splints of black ash bound together with fiber cords. Such a trap was placed beneath the water facing a rapid or ripples, and the fisherman used a stick to guide fish downstream into it. Birds were snared with elm bark nooses, and some species, especially quail and pigeons, were taken in nets made from shredded bark. After their spring subsistence activities were completed, men spent most of the summer engaged in ceremonies, council meetings, and war.

The only scheduled meal was in the morning, and at this time men ate before the women and children. At other times people ate when they were hungry, but a woman always offered food to all visitors and to her husband when he returned from working. Foods prepared from maize dominated, with hominy, cornmeal "bread," succotash, roasted corn, and boiled corn probably eaten most often. Of these the most important food was hominy gruel called sagamite, which is an Algonkian term. To prepare bread the kernels were taken from the ear, boiled in water with wood ashes to remove the hulls, ground in a tree trunk mortar with a wooden pestle, passed through a sieve, and shaped into loaves that were boiled in water. For roasting, the ears were placed in a line next to a fire. After roasting, some ears were shelled and the grains dried further in the sun and stored. To store maize on the cob the husks were stripped back and braided into bundles of twenty ears each. To the maize diet meats and soups might be added as well as wild vegetable products.

DESCENT, KINSHIP, AND MARRIAGE   A longhouse was occupied by women of a matrilineage, their in-marrying husbands, and their children (matrilineal and matrilocal). The matrilineages were joined into fifteen named matriclans; among these were the Bear, Beaver, Deer, Hawk, Turtle, and Wolf clans. The clans of the Cayuga, Onondaga, Seneca, and Tuscarora were divided into moieties, but the Mohawk and Oneida had no moiety divisions and had only the Bear, Turtle, and Wolf clans. The matriclans cut across national lines so that members of the Wolf clan, for example, were found in each nation, in different villages within a nation, and in one or more households within a settlement. Where the moiety division existed, it once was said to have formed the exogamous unit; any combination of marriages between per-

The Iroquois: Warriors and Farmers of the Eastern Woodlands

sons of opposite moieties was permitted. By Morgan's time only clan exogamy and matrilineal descent prevailed. Inheritance was from a man to his brothers, his sister's children, or some other person in his matriclan. The importance of the clan cannot be overestimated in Iroquois society; not only was it the property-holding unit, but it was empowered to invest, and renew if necessary, political leaders. Members cooperated in economic and political life and judged disputes with other clans. Furthermore each clan had a common burial ground, held religious ceremonies, and could adopt outsiders.

In the kinship terminology a person referred to his father and father's brother by the same word, and mother was termed the same as mother's sister. There were separate and different words for father's sister and mother's brother (bifurcate merging terms). The words for parallel cousins (i.e., father's brother's or mother's sister's children) were the same as for biological brothers and sisters, but cross-cousins (i.e., father's sister's or mother's brother's children) were "cousins." This then is an "Iroquois" type of cousin terminology. By extension all individuals of one's matriclan, irrespective of their tribal affiliations, were drawn into the system as blood relatives. The basis of Iroquois political life was an extension of household and community kinship ties at the national and League levels.

SOCIAL DIMENSIONS   The Iroquois often have been characterized, especially in older writings, as one of the best examples of a matriarchy, but this is an unfortunate label. It does not appear that any aboriginal society was overtly dominated by women as the term implies. Because the Iroquois were matrilineal and matrilocal and because women were a very powerful political force, it certainly is appropriate to label the Iroquois as a matricentered or matrifocal society. The position of Iroquois women in the early seventeenth century, and probably for many earlier years, was well summarized by Lafitau (1974, 69): "In them [women] resides all the real authority: the lands, fields and all their harvest belong to them; they are the soul of the councils, the arbiters of peace and war; they hold the taxes and the public treasure; it is to them that the slaves are entrusted; they arrange the marriages; the children are under their authority; and the order of succession is founded on their blood." Lafitau leaves no doubts about the power of women, yet formal, overt leadership was in the hands of males no matter how much they may have been manipulated by women.

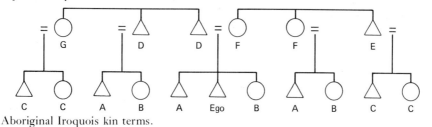

Aboriginal Iroquois kin terms.

The Iroquois clearly distinguished between the activities of men and women, and no close bonds other than family ties joined members of the opposite sex. Men sought the company of men, and women preferred to associate with other women. The primary duties of women were to care for children; to plant, cultivate, and harvest crops; to collect wild food products, and to prepare meals. Men never farmed but devoted their energies to hunting, politics, and warfare. The behavioral ideals for each sex were set forth in their oral traditions, and children were taught these values by their parents. Each person was identified with the totemic group of his mother but also had a personal totem, or perhaps more aptly, a guardian spirit comparable to the Algonkian manitou. A guardian spirit, or *oki*, was acquired in a dream or vision; represented by an object in a personal medicine bundle, its purpose was to aid the possessor.

When a woman died, her farmland, along with her material property of a domestic nature, was usually inherited by her children, although she might will them to other persons. A man's property normally was passed to his matrilineage, whose members disposed of his separate dwelling or apartment in a longhouse as well as his other material goods. The members might keep some items by which to remember the deceased. A man too could will his property to his wife or children if he made his desires known before a witness.

An analysis of historical references to Tuscarora personality characteristics by Anthony F. C. Wallace provides what possibly are general traits of aboriginal Iroquois. Their "demandingness," which Wallace thought masked their extreme dependency, was best exhibited in personal expectations from others; they never ceased, it seems, to expect goods and services. The same attitude was reflected in their use of intoxicants; their desire apparently knew no limits in early historic times. They blamed the difficulties resulting from intoxication on the white traders or on the rum itself but not on the person drinking it. Another striking characteristic of the Tuscarora and apparently of other Iroquois was the absence of fear of heights. It was observed that they walked over creeks on small poles without hesitancy and could stride along the peak of a gabled roof casually and without any fear.

DREAMS   Wallace has studied early historic records about Iroquois dreams and found that the meanings they attached to dreams were in some respects similar to ideas developed by Sigmund Freud. The Iroquois in general believed that dreams expressed inner and symbolic unconscious desires which if frustrated could cause psychosomatic illness. An individual could not always interpret his dream properly, in which case he consulted a shaman versed in such matters. The dreamers most often mentioned in the literature were adolescent boys who embarked on vision quests, warriors who feared torture, and the ill who feared death. The young boys had dreams of the visitation form, according to the twofold Iroquois dream classification of Wallace. In these the supernatural communicated with the dreamer, bestowing power such as good

The Iroquois: Warriors and Farmers of the Eastern Woodlands

fortune in hunting or war or some other inordinate ability. One of the most important powers given was a capacity to predict the future. Symptomatic dreams told one of the desires of his soul. Wallace (1958, 244) writes, "that the only way of forestalling realization of an evil-fated wish was to fulfill it symbolically. Others were curative of existing disorders, and prophylactic only in the sense of preventing ultimate death if the wish were too long frustrated. The acting out patterns can also be classified according to whether the action required is mundane or sacred and ceremonial." It was under the compulsion of fulfilling a symptomatic dream that men were tortured by their friends, some material object sought even if it meant great hardships, traditional but special ceremonies held, or a new ritual introduced. In summary Wallace's (1948, 247) concluding paragraph is best quoted. "The culture of dreams may be regarded as a useful escape-valve in Iroquois life. In their daily affairs, Iroquois men were brave, active, self-reliant, and autonomous; they cringed to no one and begged for nothing. But no man can balance forever on such a pinnacle of masculinity, where asking and being given are unknown. Iroquois men dreamt; and, without shame, they received the fruits of their dreams and their souls were satisfied."

ENTERTAINMENT   Diversion in the form of games of chance and skill played an important part in Iroquois religious and social life. The contests were between individuals or teams organized within a community or beyond it, even including different tribes. The teams generally seem to have been divided along clan lines. These people were avid gamblers, and betting on the outcome of a game was intense. A man might even gamble all of his property on the outcome of a game. The favorite game was lacrosse, played on a field about 450 yards long. Each of the six to eight players on a team carried a crook that had netting strung from the curved end to about halfway up the stick; the ball could be moved only with this racket. The object was to drive a deerskin ball from midfield through the opposing team's goal, which consisted of two poles near each other at one end of the field. The rules allowed a variation from five to seven in the number of goals necessary to win a game. Another game was to throw a javelin through a rolling hoop or to throw it farther than an opponent could.

The snow snake game was played mainly by children. The snow snake was a thin, smoothed hickory shaft some six feet in length, with the forward end increased in diameter and slightly upturned. There were up to six players, with three to a side, and each hurled his snow snake across a snow surface. The game was scored according to the distance achieved until the specified number of points had been reached by one side. The snow boat game was based on the snow snake principle. A snow boat, constructed from a solid piece of beech wood, looked like a round-bottomed vessel with an upturned bow. The boat had small feathers at the top of the stern and an oblong central opening in which was placed an arched piece of wood hung with rattles. On a hillside each player trampled a runway in the snow, iced the depression, and propelled two or three boats down the chute and as far as possible across the snow below.

THE LEAGUE OF THE IROQUOIS   The League of Hodenosaunee or Iroquois was originated to bring peace among warring Iroquois tribes. The League was structured to handle civil affairs only; most military activities were pursued outside its framework. The date of the League's founding is open to dispute. Some authorities place it as early as A.D. 1400 and others as late as 1600; the latter date seems more likely.

The original League included fifty permanent offices that were filled with persons from each of the five member nations. The Onondaga contributed fourteen; Cayuga, ten; Mohawk and Oneida, nine each; and the Seneca, eight. These representatives have been called sachems in the literature. This title is derived from a word used by diverse Algonkian language speakers in the eastern United States to refer to the holders of hereditary offices. Among the Iroquois a sachem was called a "Counselor of the People." Sachems were drawn from the matriclans of the nations; for example, three Mohawk sachems were chosen from each of the three matriclans. The sachems collectively formed the Council of the League, which had legislative, executive, and judicial authority over the combined nations. Historically, the first annual League meetings were held at Onondaga to invest new sachems. In theory, and seemingly in fact, each member tribe had an equal voice. The unequal distribution of sachemships among the nations was not a key to power because decisions made in the name of the League were unanimous. When the Tuscarora were adopted by the Oneida in 1722, they too became members of the League.

The stated purpose of the League was to avoid the constant wars that occurred before its foundation. League meetings were called to deal with internal and external affairs, to invest new sachems as well as mourn the ones replaced, or to carry out religious obligations. The influence of any particular sachem depended on his abilities as a speaker. Occasionally there was conflict between different members of the same clan in different nations. An individual's allegiance was strongest toward his own household, less important toward the clan in general, and least important beyond his nation. Feuds sometimes erupted between clans of different League nations, but no doubt these quickly were brought before the League Council for settlement.

Sachems did not seek nor gain distinction as individuals but acted collectively, and their achievements were reflected only in group judgments. At a League Council sachems could not decide an issue according to their personal feelings, but were obligated to reflect their constituency. The frequency of interaction among member tribes and the close kinship bonds created a feeling of League unity even when the organization was not in session. Member tribes frequently joined to hunt, fight, and participate in religious ceremonies. If a group of individuals, such as a band of warriors, chiefs, or women, thought a

430

particular matter was important, they met to discuss the issue and appointed an orator to convey their views to a sachem. If the subject was considered significant it would be introduced by a sachem at the next meeting. If an alien tribe desired to submit a question to the League, the foreign ambassador first went to the Seneca, who decided whether a question of foreign origin was important enough for a League meeting. If so, they sent runners to the Cayuga with a wampum belt in which had been "read" the time, place, and purpose of the meeting. Each member nation in turn notified the one to the east. When the topic for consideration was of widespread interest, people came from all over the League territory. A meeting opened with prayers, and the matter at hand was put forth by the envoy, who then withdrew from the meeting. Discussions were held, and orators spoke about the issue. When the time to reach a decision arrived, groups of sachems debated among themselves until they agreed. The next step was for one from each group to act as a spokesman in consultations with other sachems who were similarly selected. Finally, the varying conclusions were offered. If unanimity could not be reached, the matter was set aside. When a unanimous decision was reached, an orator summarized the proceedings and gave the decision to the envoy. Only once, it appears, was the principle of unanimity set aside; this was when the Oneida sachems refused to agree with the others to side against the colonists during the American Revolution. The conclusion then was to permit each member nation to determine its own position.

In the original League were the sachems Daganoweda and Hiawatha, the legendary founders of the League. Their offices were not filled on their deaths. Although in theory each sachem had the same power as any other, certain sachemships were more honored than others. The most notable example was the Onondaga sachem position titled Tododaho; this man had two other sachems as his assistants. The Seneca sachem Donehogaweh was the Keeper of the Door in the council house, and the Onondaga sachem Honowenato was the Keeper of the Wampum for the League. Certain obligations were attached permanently to a particular nation of the League. The Onondaga, since they were centrally located in the League, were in charge of the council hearth and wampum. In ordinary session the Council of the League met each fall among the Onondaga. Special sessions, however, might be convened among any member nation. The Seneca were the Keepers of the Door because they faced the hostile tribes to the west. The Mohawk, the easternmost Iroquois, were given the right to receive tribute, suggesting that the Indians to the east were subject peoples.

Any important decision was recorded through the medium of wampum. In treaties with whites as well as with other Indians wampum belts were exchanged to bind the contract. The decision or agreement was "talked into" the beads, and the Keeper of the Wampum taught the texts to his successor. The wampum beads were spiral-shaped, freshwater shells strung together or made into belts. The word wampum is derived from Algonkian and means "a string of white beads." In general, the Iroquois used white beads in a religious context and purple ones as a mnemonic device to recall the details of political decisions.

At the death, or removal from office, of a sachem, his successor was "raised-up" at a council meeting. His former name, the one acquired as an infant, was dropped, and his new name designated the office he was to hold. The meeting was held at the council headquarters or capital of the nation involved in the replacement, and the tribe of the sachem to be elevated served as hosts to the League. There were prayers, a mourning rite for the sachem to be replaced, recitations of ancient traditions by reading the wampums, and finally the investiture of the new sachem. The religious ceremonies were punctuated with feasting, games, and social dances that relieved the solemnity of the occasion. Sachemships were passed along matrilineal lines with an office normally passing to a brother or to a sister's son. The ability of logical successors was considered, and the person thought most fitted for the office was invested. If no such individual existed within a matrilineage, which was rare, the selection was made from another closely related matrilineage. The most influential person in selecting a sachem was the oldest woman in the matrilineage through which the clan title passed. In the event that it was necessary to displace a sachem before his death, this action could be taken only by the clan council of the nation to which the sachem belonged.

Each nation handled its own domestic problems through its sachems. Thus the nine Mohawk sachems were the final authorities on Mohawk internal affairs, and they functioned in the same manner as did the League Council as a whole. Furthermore if a sachem from one tribe visited another in the League, he was accorded the same status that he enjoyed at home.

After the League had been functioning for an unknown length of time, a nonhereditary office, that of chief, was created. Such a person was called Pine Tree Chief, An Elevated Name, or Brace in the Long House. Chiefs were elected by the clans of a nation for the lifetime of the individual. There was no set number of chiefs, and they were selected on the basis of such qualifications as oratorical skills or deeds in warfare. The chiefs first served as local leaders and as advisers to the sachems. Later they sat in the League Council and rivaled the sachems in authority; at this time they were invested by the sachems. According to tradition the creation of the office of chief was the only innovation in League structure after it was founded. In general the League was bound to follow as closely as possible the organization and purposes established at its founding.

WARFARE   The League was structured to handle only civil affairs, and most military activity was pursued outside its framework. If a sachem planned to participate in warfare, he first was obligated to resign his office temporarily. When the League as a whole declared war against an enemy tribe, hostilities were coordinated by the sachem war chiefs, although these men did not neces-

The Iroquois: Warriors and Farmers of the Eastern Woodlands

sarily play a part in the direct conflict.

The principal weapon was a wood stave or self bow with a slight outward curve at the ends; a bow was so rigid that it could be strung only with practice. The arrows were feather vaned and tipped with antler or flint arrowpoints. About fifteen arrows were carried in a skin quiver that hung on a man's back. One club used in close combat was made from a two-foot length of ironwood with a large knot at the end. Another form of club had a slightly curved wooden handle, and set into the convex surface was a sharp, curved antler point. The famous tomahawk apparently was not an aboriginal Iroquois weapon, but it was known among the eastern Algonkians, from whom the word was derived. The blade was hafted in the manner of a modern hatchet; tomahawks soon were manufactured from metal in Europe for the Indian trade and sometimes had a pipe bowl at the head.

Near the center of each settlement was a war post, and a chief who sought to organize a fighting party whooped about the village, stuck a red tomahawk adorned with red feathers into the war post, and danced around it. Any man willing to join the party participated in the dance. After a band of warriors had been organized, women began preparing food for the venture. The standard fare was very dry, pulverized maize mixed with maple sugar and placed in a bearskin bag. A Pine Tree Chief customarily led a raiding party,

Plate 12–4 An aquatint of a warrior in 1787. (Courtesy of the Library of Congress)

and each was organized as a small contingent that might join one or more similar units. The units had no overall commander; each party leader was responsible for his group. Participants were free to act according to their personal feelings, and proper behavior could not be dictated. Just before they left, they peeled the bark from a large tree and with red paint depicted the number of raiders. An animal symbol was painted on the bow of the canoes to represent the enemy they were setting out to conquer. At their camps each night the attackers marked trees with symbols indicating the size of their party and its destination. When the party returned, they painted the marked tree, or one nearby, with a pictorial account of the venture. In the painting the canoe paddlers faced the settlement, scalps were symbolized in black paint, and the number of prisoners was indicated by bindings used to fetter captives. When a party returned from a raid or war, the authority of the temporary leader ended. Since warfare focused the lives of men and brought them glory and prestige, the organizer of a war party could recruit a following easily. The Iroquois considered themselves at war with all Indians with whom they had no alliance; thus there always were potential victims.

When a returning war party passed through a League village, its captives were forced to run the gauntlet naked, and according to Cadwallader Colden (1755, v. 1, 9), "The Women are much more cruel than the Men." As the party approached their home village, they sounded a war whoop and danced as they led their captives. At the war post they were welcomed and praised by an elder. In reply warriors narrated their exploits and performed the War Dance. Captives were repatriated only under very extenuating circumstances. A man either was adopted into the tribe or was tortured to death. The one exception was to free an extremely brave enemy warrior. If the warriors had lost one of their number to an enemy, the Iroquois widow could adopt any male prisoner to take the place of her husband. First, however, he was obliged to run a gauntlet to his new home. The women and children lined up with whips, and the potential adoptee ran between the lines. If he stumbled and fell, he was considered an unworthy person and was killed; if he ran the lines successfully, he became a member of the tribe.

The fact that widows had first choice concerning the fate of captives has been cited as evidence that women were important in decision making. In addition there are records of women inducing men to go on war parties or restraining them under certain circumstances. Evidence such as this has led to the generalization that Iroquois society was dominated by women. In a review of ethnohistorical writings about the status of Iroquois women, Cara B. Richards concludes that they gained dominance in relatively recent times. She notes that early reports state that the fate of captives was determined by the captor and the council. If a woman disagreed with their decision, she could not take effective counteraction until after the captor and council released the prisoner. Later in time the release of a prisoner by the council was an unimportant formality, indicating increased female authority. One factor leading to

The Iroquois: Warriors and Farmers of the Eastern Woodlands

the expanding importance of women in decision making may have been the instability in village life after the introduction of firearms and the subsequent increase in mortality among warriors.

The general League pattern was to assimilate distantly related defeated tribes. Thus after the Erie, Huron, and Neutral were conquered, they were brought into the League, but not with a voice equal to that of the original Five Nations.

The League nations are famous not only for their complex political structure and its successful implementation, but for their treatment of prisoners. The tortures conceived were diverse and diabolical. A summary of their methods prepared by Nathanial Knowles (1940, 188) gives a good idea of the variations. Among the techniques "were: applying brands, embers, and hot metal to various parts of body; putting hot sand and embers on scalped head; hanging hot hatchets about neck; tearing out hair and beard; firing cords bound around body; mutilating ears, nose, lips, eyes, tongue, and various parts of the body; searing mutilated parts of the body, biting or tearing out nails; twisting fingers off; driving skewers in finger stumps; pulling sinews out of arms; etc." The usual practice, except for a person slated for possible adoption, was to begin abusing a captive soon after he was taken. Only the Onondaga tortured young and old, male and female; the other nations reserved their tortures for men. The general pattern was to begin the systematic torture of a victim when he arrived in the settlement of the captor. The prisoner was forced to run around inside a longhouse as young men burned him, primarily on the legs, until he fainted. As he was slowly being tortured, he was expected to sing about his lack of fear. After a captive fainted, he was revived and the tortures repeated. Care was taken to see that he did not die from the tortures because he was to mount a platform at dawn. Here he was bound so that he could move about and was tortured more before the entire community. When the captive was very near the point of dying, he was stabbed to death or his head was smashed. Normally the body of a tortured person was cooked and eaten.

RELIGION   The Iroquois world was occupied by a host of invisible spirits. The most powerful deity was the Great Spirit, who created people, other animals, plants, and forces for good in nature. The Great Spirit indirectly guided human affairs but could not be appealed to directly. He was capable of countering the Evil Spirit by applying his energies, and people passed through life between these competing fraternal deities. Among the lesser supernatural controlling forces for good was the Thunderer, who was capable of bringing rain or exacting vengeance, especially against witches. Associations of the Thunderer with productivity are reflected in prayers offered to him when crops were planted and the thanks expressed after a harvest. The Spirit of the Winds commanded the winds and therefore could be helpful or harm people. The Three Sisters, the spirits of Maize, Beans, and Squash, were conceived as lovely women and collectively called Our Life. Everything that aided people, including particular plants, fire, and water, had its spiritual associations. Some spirits assumed human form and were assigned specific obligations, and all bore the general name, the Invisible Aids. It was possible to communicate with the lesser spirits for good by burning tobacco, since it was thought that through this medium prayers and special needs could be made known to the gods. Gratitude was expressed in thanksgiving statements.

The Evil Spirit controlled a host of lesser spirit beings who brought pestilence to people and to crops, but few of these forces were systematized in the thinking of the Iroquois. One organized group of evil supernaturals was the False Faces, who were able to send death and destruction. They existed as contorted and evil-appearing faces and lived in out-of-the-way places; anyone who chanced to see them became paralyzed.

The most dreaded antisocial actions were performed by witches in league with the Evil Spirit. Anyone could conceivably assume the form of an animal, bird, or reptile in his desire to do evil. Witches were difficult to detect because they transformed themselves into inanimate objects at will. Witches were thought to have had a society with regular initiations; to become a member an initiate had to kill his closest friend by supernatural means. Anyone who saw a witch practicing was free to kill him, and the normal punishment for unconfessed witches was death. It was possible to establish at a council meeting whether someone was a witch; if the accused confessed and promised to reform, he was freed.

Religious specialists, or Keepers of the Faith, were chosen by female and male elders of the matriclans and were expected to serve when requested. Both sexes were represented in nearly equal numbers, and all members held equal rank. Each was invested by being given a new name announced at the next general meeting of the nation. Their primary duty was to arrange and conduct the main religious ceremonies; sachems and chiefs were ex officio Keepers of the Faith. Among their other duties was the censuring of antisocial behavior; the strongest form of censure was to report serious transgressions to the tribal council. A person could choose to relinquish the obligations of Keeper of the Faith by assuming his or her old name.

Six major religious ceremonies were held; in sequence of occurrence they were the Maple, Planting, Strawberry, Green Maize, Harvest, and New Year's (Midwinter) ceremonies. The first five were similar in many respects, as in sharing the common feature of public confessions prior to group observances. During these confessions a string of white wampum was held as a symbol of sincerity. The audience did not pass judgment on transgressions, but it was expected that future behavior would reflect renewed purpose and intent. On the day of any ceremony sacred rituals were held in the morning. The religious aspects included speeches by the Keepers of the Faith about the precedent and purpose of the ceremony, offerings of burnt tobacco, prayers, and thanksgiving speeches. In the afternoon and evening social festivities included dances and feasting. One of the most popular dances was the Feather Dance,

436

which included not only a dance but accompanying songs of thanksgiving.

The seven-day New Year's Ceremony usually was held in early February. Before the rituals began, people who had dreamed went from house to house asking the residents to guess the nature of their dreams. Dreams were regarded as important supernatural signs and were treated seriously. When someone suggested a reasonable text and meaning for a dream, the dreamer ceased his quest for an interpretation. If the accepted text and its meaning included statements about the future behavior of the dreamer, he was obligated to behave as directed. Jesuit missionaries who witnessed the dream procedure in 1656 record it as a violent affair, with the threatened and actual destruction of a great deal of household property by the dreamer until he was satisfied with an interpretation.

The New Year's events were initiated by two Keepers of the Faith disguised in skin robes and cornhusks that hung from their heads, over their bodies, and from their wrists and ankles. Their skins were painted, and they carried pestles for pounding maize as they visited every household during the morning. In each dwelling they made a formal statement concerning the ceremony and sang a song of thanksgiving. In the afternoon they returned to recite a second speech and sing another song. The day's activities included strangling one or two white dogs that symbolized purity. The body of a sacrificed dog was spotted with red paint and adorned with feathers; white wampum was hung from its neck, and it was suspended from a branch of a pole erected for this purpose. On the following day in the morning, again at noon, and in the evening the Keepers of the Faith returned to the houses. Dressed as warriors, they stirred the ashes in the fireplace with a shovel, sprinkled ashes over the hearth, and offered a prayer, followed by a thanksgiving song. The people dressed in their best clothing and visited each house twice during the day. The next two days, the third and fourth, were allotted to dancing and additional visits. At this time, too, groups of boys, accompanied by an old woman carrying a large basket, visited each house. The boys danced for the family, and if they were given presents, they went to the next dwelling. If they received nothing, they attempted to steal whatever they could before they moved on; if caught in the theft, they gave the item back without hesitation. After they had visited the houses, they feasted on their take. On the fifth day the white dog or dogs were taken from the poles and placed on a platform in the council house. A speech was made by a Keeper of the Faith about the meaning of the sacrifice and expressing thanks to the Great Spirit. A song was sung, and the dog's body was carried out to be burned in a fire built by the Keepers of the Faith. This ritual was to purge any evil and transfer it to the sacrificed animal, who carried the message of contrition to the Great Spirit. The offering also reflected the thanks of the people for the year's rewards. As the dog burned, a Keeper of the Faith recited an invocation three times to gain the attention of the Great Spirit. The most important event of the sixth day was the Thanksgiving Dance, and the final day was devoted to gambling. Some evidence

Plate 12–5 Seneca False Face Society mask. (Courtesy of UCLA Museum of Cultural History)

suggests that the white dog sacrifice was not associated with the New Year's Ceremony in aboriginal times.

FALSE FACE SOCIETY   A group organized to counteract the Evil Spirit and his emissaries was the famous False Face Society. A male became a participant by dreaming that he was a member, and one left the society by dreaming that he was no longer active. The only woman member was the Keeper of the False Faces, who not only kept the ceremonial paraphernalia but was supposed to be the only one who knew the identity of all the members. A False Face Society probably was represented in each village; its duties included curing illness and keeping evil spirits at bay. If someone was ill from a disease often treated by the society, and if he dreamed of false faces, it was a sign that

438

The Iroquois: Warriors and Farmers of the Eastern Woodlands

he could be cured by the False Face Society. The society was most noted for its ability to cure eye inflammations, nosebleeds, swellings, and toothaches. The Keeper of the False Faces was notified when someone hoped to be cured, and she assembled the members, each of whom covered himself with a face mask and blanket and carried a turtle shell rattle. The patient was sprinkled with hot ashes, the members performed a dance, and then they withdrew. William Fenton records that another function of the False Face Society was to clear disease from a village at regular intervals.

The false face masks were inspired by mythological beings and creatures seen during dreams. A mask was carved from a living basswood tree and portrayed one of about a dozen facial types. As the most distinguishing feature some had crooked mouths, others a smile, some a protruding tongue, and so on. They might be painted black, brown, red, or white. Another type of mask was made from braided and sewn corn husks. These represented important farming and hunting deities. Corn husk masks also could be differentiated according to facial features.

Historic Changes

The earlier chapters about specific peoples all include sections about the life cycle, but comparable information is largely unavailable for the Iroquois. Thus attention shifts to change, especially in the belief system since it is so well documented.

THE NEW RELIGION   As mentioned earlier the League began to disintegrate when member nations could not agree on a unanimous course of action at the outbreak of the American Revolution. The Seneca were torn in two directions. Some favored neutrality, but most supported the British cause. Among the Seneca leaders was Cornplanter, who received a British commission as a "captain." To persuade other Iroquois to remain neutral, the Americans laid waste to their villages and farmlands in 1779, and about 1780 Cornplanter and his followers moved to the upper Allegheny River drainage.

Shortly afterward the Americans were searching for an Indian group to counteract the influence of Joseph Brant and his pro-British Mohawk, and they selected Cornplanter and his people. He accepted the responsibility and actively sought supporters for the Americans. In the course of his official travels he went to Philadelphia on a number of occasions and became acquainted with the Quakers. In 1795 the Commonwealth of Pennsylvania granted Cornplanter a fee patent title to three separate plots of land, each about a mile square, very near the New York State line on the Allegheny River. One plot was called Burnt House, and here Cornplanter had soon gathered about him some 400 persons in thirty dwellings. One of the persons living in the home of Cornplanter was his half-brother, Handsome Lake or

Plate 12–6 Cornplanter, the Seneca chief and half-brother of Handsome Lake. (From McKenney and Hall, 1933)

Ganiodayo. Quaker missionaries went to Burnt House in 1798, and one of them, Henry Simmons, stayed at the settlement. In his study of what happened at Burnt House at this time, Merle H. Deardorff includes information from the Simmons diary, an ethnographic gem, and other Quaker writings. We learn that Simmons was asked by Cornplanter about his beliefs and that answers were offered cautiously. As Deardorff (1951, 90) writes:

> *Questions about theology and morals had been referred to Simmons, and answered in the Quaker way: Look inside. You have a Light in there that will show you what is good and what is bad. When you know you have done wrong, repent and resolve to do better. Outward forms and books and guides are good; but they are made by men. The Great Spirit himself puts the Inner Light in every man. Look to it. Learn to read and write so that you may discover for yourself whether or not the white man's Book is true. Learn to distinguish good from*

The Iroquois: Warriors and Farmers of the Eastern Woodlands

*evil so that you may avoid the pricks of conscience in this world
and prosper; and that you may avoid punishment in the next.*

The missionary, however, did note many forms of behavior that were not compatible with his beliefs. He particularly was annoyed at the preparations for a "Dancing Frolick," and the council decided to stop them, in part as a result of Simmons' objections. Furthermore the men returned from Pittsburgh with intoxicants that they had received in trade for furs, and consumption of these led to a community binge of several weeks' duration. This brought reproval from the Quaker, and the contrite Indians resolved that two chiefs would be appointed to curb drinking. The killing of a witch and dances held for the dead were other distressing events that Simmons witnessed.

At the house of Cornplanter his half-brother Handsome Lake appeared to be near death in June 1799. On the fifteenth of the month Handsome Lake had a vision, the details of which were recorded by Simmons. In summary, Handsome Lake saw three men carrying different types of bushes with berries attached. The men asked him to eat some of the berries, for by doing so he would live to see berries ripen in the summer. The men told him that the Great Spirit was unhappy about the drunkenness of the people, and said that if Handsome Lake recovered he was not to drink intoxicants. The three men said further that a fourth man would visit him later. When Handsome Lake regained consciousness, he asked Cornplanter to assemble the council, repeat what had occurred in the vision, and have each person eat a dried berry; these instructions were followed. Handsome Lake still was very ill, and within a short time he had a vision in which the fourth man, assumed to be the Great Spirit, came to take him because he pitied him in his suffering. When Handsome Lake awoke, he sent for Cornplanter and after talking with him fell into a trance for seven hours. Simmons (Deardorff, 1951, 91) wrote, "his legs and arms were cold, his body warm but breathless." Handsome Lake revealed later that he was led by a guide who was clothed in a "clear sky colour" and carried a bow and a single arrow. Soon he met his dead son and Cornplanter's daughter who recently had died. The girl told of her unhappiness because her father and her brother argued, while the son of Handsome Lake revealed that he was sorry that he did not care for his father better. The guide then stated that sons should treat their fathers well, that Handsome Lake must not drink intoxicants and that he must give up all dances save the Green Maize Ceremony. The guide pointed toward a river where canoes were loaded with barrels of whiskey. There was an evil man in charge of the cargo who was (Deardorff, 1951, 91), "going about very busy doing and making all the noise and mischief he could amongst the people." Furthermore, Handsome Lake was told that if all the people agreed, it would be proper to accept whites as teachers. Finally, the guide said that Handsome Lake was to return among the living and he would see no more of these things until he died; in death he would return to this setting if he behaved properly.

When Handsome Lake recovered, he began preaching his doctrine, which came to include the rejection of schools and a return to a subsistence-based economy. In 1802 his cause received American support when Handsome Lake went to Washington, D.C., with other Iroquois and President Thomas Jefferson condoned his teachings. Partly because of this official sanction Handsome Lake became an acknowledged prophet. From the time of his recovery until his death, Handsome Lake visited Seneca communities to influence the behavior of others. By 1807 his fame as a prophet had spread widely among the Iroquois and to other eastern tribes as well. When the War of 1812 began, the Iroquois had learned their lesson, and most of them did not participate. Handsome Lake in particular preached neutrality because of his continuing close ties with the Quakers. In 1815 the prophet moved to Onondaga, and it was here that he died the same year.

As Deardorff has noted, the Handsome Lake revelations, or Gaiwiio (Good Message), came to include not only the revelations but biographical material, prophecy, law, parable, and anecdote. Its members called the entire system the New Religion, but the Good Message was not the only basis for the New Religion. Some of the more important changes proposed in the revelation had been initiated before Handsome Lake's trances. If only the text of the revelations had survived, it might have been assumed that Handsome Lake was a great innovator, but from the diaries of the Quaker missionaries it is obvious that the revelations were in step with what were recognized and pressing problems at Burnt House. Like all prophets, Handsome Lake is remembered because he was the right man at the right moment in history. Most important, and unlike many other Indian prophets, he was willing to adapt his basic ideas to accommodate Quaker beliefs and even certain material aspects of white culture such as agricultural methods. This flexibility contributed to the improvement of Iroquois life in his time and unquestionably aided in the long-range survival of the Good Message. Soon after Handsome Lake's death, other Christian missionaries proselytized among the Seneca, and the Indians labored in council to establish a uniform approach to religion. The time-honored pattern of unanimity, however, could not be reached, and by 1820 the New Religion was separate from other Iroquois religious patterns. The Good Message was not recorded systematically until 1845, and no single text has become standard. By 1949 the New Religion was taught in ten ceremonial structures, each termed a longhouse, on the meeting circuit of the Six Nations. Most of the preachers required four days to relate the Good Message. The Tonawanda Longhouse was the Central Fire, and here were kept the most sacred strings of wampum that had belonged to Handsome Lake.

The New Religion includes the following tenets: the prohibition of intoxicants; obedience of children toward their parents and care of aged parents; faithfulness of married couples; reproval of gossiping or boasting; killing of witches; awareness of a hell for sinners and heaven for persons who have lived good lives or repent having lived evil lives; and the acceptance of the ways of

whites save for schools. As was noted by Edmund Wilson (1960, 87) the New Religion "has a scope and a coherence which have made it endure as has the teaching of no other Indian prophet, and it is accepted at the present time by at least half the Iroquois world as a source of moral guidance and religious inspiration."

Modern Life

THE SIX NATIONS RESERVE   A surviving stronghold of Iroquois culture exists among the descendants of the people who followed Joseph Brant to Canada. In 1956 the Six Nations Reserve population consisted of 6500 Iroquois living on 72 square miles of land. The reserve was far from homogeneous in its members' approach to life; in fact diversity was the norm, and there was no clear sense of tribal identity. The study of the Six Nations Reserve by Annemarie A. Shimony ranks with the work of Morgan. No attempt is made to summarize her wealth of detailed information; instead the focus will be largely on political life and the New Religion. It should be noted that Shimony concentrated her fieldwork among the more conservative segment of the population, those who adopted some white ways but rejected rapid assimilation.

People lived at scattered homesteads on reserve land that belonged to the band, not to clans, and individual holdings were inherited by members. The stress placed by Canadian authorities on patrilineal inheritance confused the traditional matrilineal system of the Indians. If a man owned land, it passed to his wife and children unless he made a will to the contrary, and when there were no heirs the land reverted to the band. Individual rights to band membership, like inheritance rights, were calculated in a patrilineal line according to the Canadian authorities but matrilineally by the Iroquois. The Canadian Government normally did not interfere with the decisions of the elected council in determining band membership and was sympathetic to the old system. The nuclear family as an important social unit was comparatively new to these people, and Canadian emphasis on it robbed the clans of important functions. A newly married couple on the reserve lived with either the husband's or wife's relatives initially, depending on which side of the family could best accommodate them. Such residence was temporary, and the couple established their own household (neolocal residence) as soon as they were economically able to do so. The combined matrilineal and matrilocal family no longer existed; for some women the family meant the nuclear family and for others, the matrilineage. The matrilineages were important in selecting sachems and chiefs of the clan, and disputes arose over which were the leading lineages with the vested rights. Members of the leading lineages of a clan were most likely to be familiar with their clan ties and were able to establish their political and religious authority. A real difficulty, however, stemmed from the fact that even some conservative families no longer knew their clan affiliations. As would be anticipated, many of the earlier functions of the clans were dropped. At the time of Shimony's studies, 1953–1960, the clans invested sachems and chiefs and could remove them from office. The exogamous nature of the matriclans continued to be observed by some people, but others felt it was satisfactory to marry anyone to whom close genealogical ties could not be established.

The New Religion had four local congregations, each symbolized by a "fire" and centered at a different longhouse. The "head fire" was at the Tonawanda Longhouse in New York State, and there each preacher on the longhouse circuit was invested. Each longhouse had wampum to validate its legitimacy, but the head fire had no jurisdiction over the "home" fires. The rituals of the four longhouses were essentially the same. The particular longhouse to which a person belonged was determined by matrilineage ties and by its proximity, although all four were within eight miles of each other. Active members wanted to live near their longhouse in order to hear of each event.

Longhouses were rectangular wooden buildings, usually with doors at each end and with wood-burning stoves near the ends serving as the fires for moieties. Benches were along the walls, and the central area of the room was left open. Moieties reciprocated in filling ceremonial and social obligations as well as in maintaining the building. Reciprocity was a basic characteristic of the longhouse organization. The moiety alignments were not the same as reported in early historic times, and while three of the longhouses were named for tribes, there was no clear indication that they represented these nations.

Longhouse leaders were Keepers of the Faith or deacons, as they more

The Iroquois: Warriors and Farmers of the Eastern Woodlands

commonly were called. Each longhouse had a leading male and female Keeper of the Faith, chosen on the basis of merit. They guided all longhouse functions, their advice was sought on ceremonial as well as secular matters, and they tended to represent the longhouse at political functions. With a breakdown of the clan structure, the group of Keepers of the Faith had an increased voice in community affairs. Some of these people inherited the office through the matrilineal line; others were selected by deacons because of their abilities or ties with a sachem. Nonaggression was a personality trait expected of all these persons in dealings with each other and the congregation. The most capable longhouse leaders successfully and without obvious pressures induced members to participate in the longhouse as fully as possible. A second longhouse functionary was the Keeper of the Fire, who was the guardian of the longhouse wampum. His moiety and clan affinities were unimportant, but he had to be a staunch believer in the New Religion. The wampum was highly symbolic of the longhouse traditions, and the people believed that Canadian officials would like to destroy the wampum and thereby eliminate the longhouses. The final category of longhouse leaders was the Speaker, who presented traditional and extemporaneous speeches to the congregation. Such persons were not invested in any formal office, nor were they usually preachers on the longhouse circuit. A speaker was required to have a talent for public speaking and a knowledge of traditional speeches.

A longhouse served many functions in the members' efforts to resist becoming like other Canadians. The organization fulfilled social, medical, economic, and political needs. Social gatherings included softball or lacrosse games, raffles, and dances. Organized social activities sponsored outside the longhouse usually were closed to longhouse members by their own dogma. The longhouse ceremonial round was rich in detail; it was based on the Handsome Lake revelations plus the aboriginal planting and harvest ceremonies, and the old and new means for curing. An important aspect of almost any longhouse function was the recitation of a formal address of thanks to the Great Spirit for the continued life of the persons attending and thanks to the participants for attending. In all longhouse activities the ritual and social language was Iroquois; speaking English was disapproved in any context. To the members, participation in longhouse events gave real purpose to life and at the same time offered a systematic philosophy for living. People were encouraged to remember the teachings of Handsome Lake and to live good lives. At times the younger members were told not to imitate such fashion extremes of whites as high-heeled shoes and low-cut dresses for girls. Neither should one listen to the radio, watch television, or drink intoxicants, for such behavior was not in keeping with the New Religion. Behind it all was the real fear that the longhouse members would become carbon copies of their white Canadian neighbors. The conflict of values seems often to have led to trauma at the time of death for those individuals who had at some time followed forbidden white ways.

For members of the New Religion and other Iroquois as well there was a deeply rooted focus on death. Death could be caused by failure to accept a time-honored view about the spirit world, by showing a lack of respect for plants or animals, or by failing to hold rituals as directed. Furthermore the dead had great power over the living, and to neglect them was an invitation to disease and death. In general, it was thought that souls resided in a pleasant upperworld or else suffered punishment. Souls bent on evil could assume animal forms, but ordinarily they were nonmaterial or a light vapor. All of this concern with death and the dead necessitated the proper performance of obligations to the dead. To avert death and illness for the community or the individual the Ceremony for the Dead was held at least once and preferably twice each year.

The sachems, who were now either Christians or members of the New Religion, represented traditional authority and functioned as the officially recognized political body until 1924. The longhouse sachems considered that their Christian counterparts could not legitimately hold political office, however, unless invested at a longhouse ceremony, which was comparable to raising up a sachem in the old League. The sachems divided also over whether or not they favored closer rapport with Canadian officials. In 1924 a group of World War I veterans and other more acculturated persons, collectively termed "warriors," sought governmental recognition of an elected council. In the ensuing investigation of Six Nations Reserve affairs the sachems would not present their case to the governmental representatives; thus the government heard only the acculturated faction, which supported elected chiefs. The Canadian Government itself favored elected leaders since it received little cooperation from the sachems. An elected council was installed during 1924; the New Religion sachems were locked out of the council house, and Royal Canadian Mounted Police officers enforced the government's decision. The sachems were bitter toward the Canadians as well as against their factional opposites. Continuing opposition on the part of the sachems and their supporters was demonstrated by their refusal to accept some forms of Canadian aid such as Family Allowance and Old Age Assistance payments. The elected council clearly did not have widespread support. This was indicated by voter participation; although there were burning issues, from a total population of 7000 only about 600 ballots were cast in typical elections. This reflected the idea of conservatives that to vote constituted recognition of the elected council and the Canadian government's right to validate it. By not voting they expressed their continued opposition.

WORK IN HIGH STEEL   It will be recalled that some of the Mohawk were attracted to Canada by Jesuit missionaries in the late seventeenth century. They were known as the Praying Indians and came to occupy their present reservation after three short moves before 1719. The land they occupied was a mission holding until 1830, but in that year it became a reservation. Land was alloted to families, and other ground was held for future gener-

The Iroquois: Warriors and Farmers of the Eastern Woodlands

ations. The holdings might be leased to anyone but were sold or given only to other members of the reservation. The Caughnawaga Reservation extends about eight miles along the St. Lawrence River and is up to four miles wide. In the 1940s the reservation population was nearly 3000 persons. Some 2700 were Roman Catholics, 250 were Protestants, and fewer than 100 belonged to the New Religion. The Roman Catholics have been losing ground since the 1920s. Some persons have become Protestants, and since World War I small numbers have been attracted to the doctrines of Handsome Lake.

Following the move to Caughnawaga in the early 1700s, the economy of the migrants underwent a series of major adjustments. At first the Jesuit priests attempted to teach the men to farm, but because this was regarded as woman's work men continued to hunt or fight enemies at every opportunity. Before long increasing numbers of men were attracted to the fur trade and worked as canoemen or voyageurs for French trading parties, sometimes fighting as they moved through hostile country. After the British controlled the area, the Mohawk continued working in the fur trade until its decline about 1800. Following this stage some of the men were employed by the logging industry to raft timber through rapids and along fast water; this work was as dangerous as being a canoeman or warrior. At about this time some men finally turned to farming, and others became the first medicine show Indians, traveling about New England by horse and buggy selling Indian medicinal preparations. Others seem to have performed with circuses during summer months and returned to the reservation for the winter. Another group became obsessed by alcohol; although they found temporary employment in Montreal, much of their time was spent drinking excessively.

In 1886 the Dominion Bridge Company began construction of a cantilever bridge across the St. Lawrence River, using reservation land for a bridge abutment. In obtaining permission to use the land the company agreed to hire reservation Indians, but only for unskilled labor jobs. The Mohawk were unhappy with this arrangement and could not be kept off the bridge as the span was being built. Soon it became apparent that they not only were unafraid of heights but were pleased with the new experience. The din of riveting did not faze them in the least. After pestering the crew foreman, a few men finally were hired, and they turned out to be excellent workers. It appears that three crews were trained on this bridge. In the erection of a bridge of this type precut and drilled beams and girders are hoisted into place with a crane or derrick, temporarily bolted and plumbed, then riveted. The Iroquois were to become members of riveting crews, the most dangerous as well as the most lucrative work.

The Caughnawaga Mohawk continued to work on bridges and systematically trained riveting crews. By 1907 there were over seventy skilled workers, about half of whom were employed on the Quebec Bridge, which spans the St. Lawrence River near Quebec City. On August 29, 1907, "the disaster" occurred; the span fell, and ninety-six men, including thirty-five Caughnawaga, were killed. Bridgework now took on a new meaning; obviously dangerous, it became a more attractive form of employment than either timber rafting or performing in circuses. The reservation women had a somewhat different attitude; one of their first moves was to force the gangs to work on many different projects so that a similar disaster could not affect so many families. Since there were relatively few bridge jobs in Canada, some men found employment on other high steel projects. The women also demonstrated that their Christian faith had not been shaken by purchasing a large crucifix of St. Francis Xavier for the church.

About 1926 three or four high steel crews from the reservation went to New York City to work, and three more gangs arrived in 1928. With the construction of Rockefeller Center in the 1930s, more gangs arrived in the city. They became members of the Brooklyn local of the International Association of Bridge, Structural, and Ornamental Iron Workers and roomed nearby in the North Gowanus area. By the late 1940s, the North Gowanus locality was occupied by about 125 steel workers and their families. While their families lived in Brooklyn, the men traveled across the country, working on various jobs. The reason offered for moving about was the overtime pay at distant jobs, but this simply was a rationalization of their desire to wander. They would hear of a new job, and they soon would leave for it with little or no warning.

North Gowanus consisted mainly of tenements and some factories. The Mohawk lived within ten blocks of each other in the best houses. Households were composed of related females and their families who occupied one or adjacent apartment buildings. The residences were furnished in the manner typical for local whites with the addition of Mohawk artifacts on a wall or mantel. In these homes, where the men frequently were away, many women spent their free time making what have come to be regarded as typically Indian craft items. These were sold at fairs in the New York State area by the most Indian-looking men of the group. Other members of a household were single girls from the reservation. They worked in nearby factories, not infrequently married non-Indians, and were lost to the Iroquois community. The boys raised in these households adjusted well to school life, but they dropped out after fulfilling the minimum state requirements to become workers in high steel. Since very little training was necessary, it was not long before a boy could work as an adult in one of the gangs and earn about $150 a week (ca. 1955).

Social life of the Brooklyn Mohawk centered at a particular bar in the North Gowanus neighborhood. The high steel men dropped by at the end of the work day; on weekends and in the evening they brought their wives. On the walls of the bar were a reproduction of "Custer's Last Stand," drawings of Iroquois warriors, and steel workers' helmets. According to Morris Freilich (1958, 479), "Periodically, the Indians tear the place apart; they feel it their right, since it is their home. If outsiders give any sign of attempting to make it

448

The Iroquois: Warriors and Farmers of the Eastern Woodlands

their clubroom too, blood flows fast and furious." The combative nature of the individual Mohawk existed still, and examples of bloody fights were not uncommon. They nurtured the element of daring in their jobs and in dealings with others, and their continued use of intoxicants led to other forms of recklessness. Again to quote from Freilich (1958, 478). "Some examples from my field work include driving 90 miles per hour on a winding road at night in the mountains of New York State in an old car while inebriated; accepting a dare to go faster than the speedometer could register and two men having sexual intercourse with a girl while her fiance was asleep beside her."

Ties with Caughnawaga were maintained by the Brooklyn residents. Reservation members came to work in Brooklyn, and relatives arrived to visit, especially in any time of crisis. A man might take his family to the reservation for the summer, but he remained with them for only a short time. When a steel worker retired, he was likely to return to the reservation, but his adjustment to the uneventful and sedentary life was difficult. One response was to return to Indian ways to the point of not speaking English and to become deeply involved in reservation politics and social life.

In a search for the reasons behind the striking success of the Mohawk in high steel work, Freilich has made some noteworthy observations. First, he felt that they were behaving in the pattern of warriors, exhibiting no fear of heights as a warrior would in theory not fear the enemy or death. From listening to a conversation about heights among moderately intoxicated Mohawk, he learned that they did in fact fear heights. They concealed their fear to prove their courage and to maintain their reputation as being unafraid. Surprisingly, work in high steel was highly compatible with many essential features of the old Mohawk way of life. The men left home to work for extended periods as they left to hunt and fight in aboriginal times. There was danger and possible death in what they did as there was danger of old. When a man returned, he could boast of the tall buildings on which he had worked, just as he once boasted of his skills in combat. The modern steel worker was subject to little authority, and if he was displeased he could quit his job just as he formerly could drop out of a war party. These and other parallels lent support to the traditional status of the male in a nontraditional setting.

THE CAUGHNAWAGA RESERVATION   After studying conservative persons on the Caughnawaga Reservation, Fred Voget described their way of life in the 1940s. The "native-modified" population, as Voget termed them, felt that they had been forced by the French to become Roman Catholics, and that they had been losing their physical strength and stature, as well as their lands, since they abandoned their old religion, which was conceived in terms of the Good Message of Handsome Lake and his followers. To regain their physical strength and political powers of old they felt they had to return to an Indian religion. They considered themselves chosen people and advocated retention of their identity as a means for consolidating and achieving their pur-

Plate 12–8 View of the Chief Poking Fire tourist attraction at Caughnawaga in 1950. (Courtesy of Fred W. Voget)

poses. Voget (1951, 223) also stressed, "the important historic role of the Iroquois has awakened a national consciousness based on their original autonomy and structured according to the traditional organization of the League of the Five (or Six) Nations." The efforts of these Caughnawaga led to a modern nativistic movement striving for the freedoms of old. This movement was centered in the councils at the Grand River Reserve in Ontario and the Onondaga Reservation in New York State.

IROQUOIS PERSONALITY   The personality characteristics of the modern Tuscarora, as presented by Wallace, may be extended cautiously to the Iroquois in general. The people retained their strong desire for alcohol, but its consumption now was channeled more than in early historic times. When the study of the New York State Tuscarora was made in 1948–1949, the Indians still were legally prohibited from consuming intoxicants, but this restriction had not been successful in the past nor was it at the time. The Indians frequented bars known to sell intoxicants to Indians. By drinking mainly in bars they were subject to the authority of the bartender, and there was always the possibility of police intervention if there were disturbances. Furthermore since they drank away from home, at least one man in a group remained sober to drive the others home. Thus there were regularized controls over the behavior of drunken persons. A counterforce also had developed in the Indians' attitudes toward intoxicants. Some persons rejected alcohol because of traumatic childhood experiences with drunks, and some were reformed middle-aged drinkers. A nearby Baptist Church to which most of the Tuscarora belonged rejected drinking, and there was also a local Temperance Society. These were possible ways out of drinking problems for individuals, and in addition gossip about problem drinkers had become an important means of curbing drinking.

The Iroquois: Warriors and Farmers of the Eastern Woodlands

ATTITUDES: IROQUOIS AND WHITE   Iroquois and white American attitudes were in so many ways fundamentally different that it is little wonder one group failed to understand the other. Whites were in general thrifty, coveting wealth to accumulate more wealth; the Iroquois were generous and wasteful with money and material things. Whites were orderly in keeping house, and their dwellings, which were built by contractors, followed standard plans. Indian houses were untidy, jerrybuilt, and often left unfinished. Whites were time-oriented and considered promptness a great virtue, but "Indian time" meant being late or not appearing at all. The old Tuscarora demandingness ran wild in their dealings with the State of New York. The State supplied schools, school buses, welfare, road maintenance, and other services. The Indians not only accepted these but expected more. Their dependency, to their thinking, was based on obligations of the Federal and State authorities stemming from old injustices that were both real and imagined.

IROQUOIS NATIONALISM   In recent years the Iroquois have attempted to assert their nationalism by means of diverse protests. For example, most of the United States Iroquois have refused to vote, although they all have had the right to do so since the Citizenship Act of 1924. By not voting they indicated that they did not recognize United States political domination over them and in the process reinforced their own identity. During World War I they separately declared war on Germany. In World War II when subject to selective service as a result of the Citizenship Act, some went to jail or in other ways evaded the draft. The Iroquois in New York State have resisted strongly all efforts by state officials to intervene in their affairs. Justification for the Indian position was that treaties with the Federal Government implied equality in national standing between the Six Nations and the United States. Predictably, the Iroquois have resisted both State and Federal income taxes and have fought efforts to use reserved lands for the St. Lawrence Seaway, needs of the Power Authority of New York State, and the relocation of highways. These disputes usually were complicated by the fact that elected chiefs cooperated with the whites, but the hereditary chiefs did not.

In 1958 the very dynamic nationalistic Iroquois leader Mad Bear accepted an invitation to visit Cuba, where he met with Fidel Castro. Mad Bear and his followers hoped that they could be admitted to the United Nations under Cuban sponsorship. The current emergence of highly nationalistic governments in various parts of the world has given the Iroquois hope, strengthened their position, and contributed to the consolidation of their own nationalism. They want the day to come when the League of the Iroquois or Hodenosaunee again will guide the destiny of its people.

In recent years the St. Lawrence Seaway and the Power Authority of New York State nibbled away at Iroquois lands, but a more bitter dispute involved the Federal Government and the Seneca. To control flooding of the Ohio River, a series of dams was to be built on the Allegheny River. The

451
Modern Life

Seneca opposed the one that was to be at Kinzua, Pennsylvania, because the reservoir would flood 10,000 acres of their best land in the Allegheny Reservation in New York State and would require the relocation of 130 families. The Seneca involved sought to have an alternate plan accepted that would not involve their lands, but the U.S. Army Corps of Engineers objected because of its greater cost. The Indians attempted to block the project through the courts, but each of the 1957–1959 decisions supported the right of the Federal Government to condemn the land involved. The Seneca persistently maintained that a Six Nations treaty assured their lasting right to the land and that the Federal Government had no right to abrogate it. The treaty was signed in 1794 and stated the following about these and other Iroquois lands, "Now the United States acknowledges all the land within the aforementioned boundaries to be the property of the Seneka nation; and the United States will never claim the same, nor disturb the Seneka nation . . ." "Never" is a time past, since the Kinzua Dam was built.

Yet times are changing! In 1976 the Seneca of the Allegheny Reservation signed an agreement with the State of New York as equals. This is the first time since the early 1800s that the state has recognized the sovereign or national status of the Seneca. To build a highway through the reservation the State attempted to exercise its power of eminent domain, but the courts, including the U.S. Supreme Court, held that the State had no right to condemn reservation lands for the highway. As a result the State negotiated with the Seneca and received an easement, but not title to, 795 acres of land. In return the State agreed to pay 2 million dollars, give the Indians *title* to 795 acres of land from the adjoining Allegheny State Park, and provide other benefits.

Comparisons

The unique structure of the League and its effectiveness in dealing with other Indians and colonial Europeans invite "what if" questions. What if the Hopi had achieved a political institution comparable to the League; what internal changes in their political life might have produced a League structure, or was the possibility unrealistic? What if the Iroquois had been patrilineal and patrilocal; what forms of kinship terminology could have emerged? What if aboriginal Iroquois men had been farmers; what accompanying differences would be anticipated in sociocultural terms? Exercises such as these lead to speculations about what peoples were in historical, functional, and ecological terms, and potentially this offers greater insight into that which actually was.

The bellicose quality of the Iroquois invites comparison with other peoples described, especially the Pawnee and Crow. What common characteristics did they share in terms of recruitment, organization, methods, and constraints placed on warriors? It also is worthwhile to identify childrearing practices that were compatible with a stress on warfare and other clear adjustments that were made to support the war complex.

The Iroquois: Warriors and Farmers of the Eastern Woodlands

Additional Readings

The book by Morgan remains the standard Iroquois source, and the most thorough study of these people in recent times is by Shimony. The leading authority on ethnohistorical aspects of Iroquois life is Fenton. The writings by each of these authors are cited in the references that follow.

References

Beauchamp, William M. "The Principal Founders of the Iroquois League and its Probable Date," *Proceedings of the New York State Historical Association*, v. 24, 27–36. 1926.

Biggar, H. P., ed. *The Works of Samuel de Champlain*, v. 2. Toronto. 1925.

Colden, Cadwallader. *The History of the Five Indian Nations of Canada*. 2 v. London. 1755.

Cory, David M. *Within Two Worlds*. New York. 1956.

Deardorff, Merle H. "The Religion of Handsome Lake: Its Origin and Development," *SI, BAE,* † *Bulletin* 149, 79–107. 1951.

Faber, Harold. "Senecas and State of New York Strike Historic Pact as Equals," *The New York Times*, July 11, 1976.

*Fenton, William N. "Problems Arising from the Historic Northeastern Position of the Iroquois," *Essays in Historical Anthropology of North America*. Smithsonian Miscellaneous Collections, v. 100, 159–251. 1940. An excellent study of the Iroquoian tribes from the time of early historic contact until the modern period.

*Fenton, William N. "Tonawanda Longhouse Ceremonies: Ninety Years after Lewis Henry Morgan," *SI, BAE, Bulletin* 128, 140–166. 1941. Included is a detailed summary outline of the Tonawanda Seneca ceremonial calendar which provides comparable detail for each event.

Fenton, William N. "Locality as a Basic Factor in the Development of Iroquois Social Structure," *SI, BAE, Bulletin* 149, 35–54. 1951.

Fenton, William N. "The Concept of Locality and the Program of Iroquois Research," *SI, BAE, Bulletin* 149, 1–12. 1951.

Fenton, William N. "Iroquois Studies at the Mid-Century," *Proceedings of the American Philosophical Society*, v. 95, 296–310. 1951.

† *Smithsonian Institution, Bureau of American Ethnology*

Fenton, William N. "Long-Term Trends of Change among the Iroquois," *Cultural Stability and Cultural Change*, 30–35. American Ethnological Society. 1957.

Freilich, Morris. "Cultural Persistence among the Modern Iroquois," *Anthropos*, v. 53, 473–483. 1958.

Gridley, Marion E., ed. *Indians of Today*. 3rd ed. Chicago. 1960.

Griffin, James B. "The Iroquois in American Prehistory," *Papers of the Michigan Academy of Science Arts and Letters*, v. 29, 357–374. 1944.

Griffin, James B. "The Northeast Woodlands Area," in *Prehistoric Man in the New World*, Jesse D. Jennings and Edward Norbeck, eds., 223–258. Chicago. 1964.

Hewitt, John N. "Legend of the Founding of the Iroquois League," *American Anthropologist*, v. 5, 131–148. 1892.

"Indians Debating use of $5-million," *The New York Times*, March 17, 1974.

Indians of Quebec and the Maritime Provinces. Department of Citizenship and Immigration, Indian Affairs Branch. Ottawa. n.d.

Johnston, Charles M. *The Valley of the Six Nations*. Toronto. 1964.

Kinzua Dam (Seneca Indian Relocation). Hearings before the Subcommittee on Indian Affairs of the Committee on Interior and Insular Affairs, House of Representatives, 88th Congress, 1st session. Washington, D.C. 1964.

Knowles, Nathaniel. "The Torture of Captives by the Indians of Eastern North America," *Proceedings of the American Philosophical Society*, v. 82, 151–225. 1940.

*Lafitau, Joseph François. *Customs of the American Indians Compared with the Customs of Primitive Times*, William N. Fenton and Elizabeth L. Moore, eds. and trans. v. 1. Toronto. 1974 (v. 2 Toronto. 1977). This was the first systematic study of the Iroquois and often is stated to be a classic in ethnographic writings.

Lounsbury, Floyd G. "Iroquois-Cherokee Linguistic Relations," *SI, BAE, Bulletin* 180,9–17. 1961.

Lydekker, John W. *The Faithful Mohawks*. Cambridge. 1938.

McKenney, Thomas L., and James Hall. *The Indian Tribes of North America* v. 1. Edinburgh. 1933.

Martin, Paul S., et al. *Indians Before Columbus*. Chicago. 1947.

*Morgan, Lewis H. *League of the Ho-De-No-Sau-Nee or Iroquois*. 2 v. 1851. (The 1901 and 1904 editions were edited and footnoted by Herbert M. Lloyd and were reproduced in 1954 by the Human Relations Area Files.) The

The Iroquois: Warriors and Farmers of the Eastern Woodlands

standard Iroquois ethnography and a key Iroquois source; more precisely, a detailed description of one group of Seneca living between 1841 and 1850 and capable of recalling the past.

Mitchell, Joseph. (*see* Wilson, Edmund.)

Parkman, Francis. *A Half-Century of Conflict*. 2 v. Boston. 1892.

Parkman, Francis. *The Conspiracy of Pontiac and The Indian War after the Conquest of Canada*. 2 v. Boston. v. 1, 1901; v. 2, 1902.

Richards, Cara B. "Matriarchy or Mistake: The Role of Iroquois Women through Time," *Cultural Stability and Cultural Change*, 36–45. American Ethnological Society. 1957.

Schoolcraft, Henry R. *Notes on the Iroquois*. New York. 1846.

*Shimony, Annemarie A. *Conservatism among the Iroquois at the Six Nations Reserve*. Yale University Publications in Anthropology, no. 65. 1961. The best comprehensive study of the Iroquois since Morgan's ethnography, the second key Iroquois source, and one of the finest studies of North American Indians.

Speck, Frank G. *The Iroquois*. Cranbrook Institute of Science, Bulletin no. 23. 1955.

Stone, William L. *Life of Joseph Brant-Thayendanegea*. 2 v. New York. 1838.

Thwaites, Reuben G. *Travels and Explorations of the Jesuit Missionaries in New France*. v. 13. 1898.

Voget, Fred. "Acculturation at Caughnawaga: A Note on the Native-Modified Group," *American Anthropologist*, v. 53, 220–231. 1951.

Wallace, Anthony F. C. "Some Psychological Determinants of Culture Change in an Iroquoian Community," *SI, BAE, Bulletin* 149, 55–76. 1951.

Wallace, Anthony F. C. "Dreams and the Wishes of the Soul: A Type of Psychoanalytic Theory among the Seventeenth Century Iroquois," *American Anthropologist*, v. 60, 234–248. 1958.

*Wilson, Edmund. *Apologies to the Iroquois*. (Includes a reprinting of "The Mohawks in High Steel," by Joseph Mitchell.) New York. 1960. The study by Mitchell is the most complete discussion of the history of Iroquois work in high steel and should be consulted in conjunction with the study of the same subject by Morris Freilich. The balance of Wilson's book is a sensitive analysis of the modern scene in New York State and in Ontario, Canada.

Wintemberg, William J. "Distinguishing Characteristics of Algonkian and Iroquoian Cultures," *Annual Report, 1929, National Museum of Canada*, 65–125. 1931.

The Eastern Cherokee: Farmers of the Southeast

13

Reasons for This Selection

In the early history of the Southeast, four tribes were larger and more influential than any others; these were the Cherokee, Chickasaw, Choctaw, and Creek. Along with the Seminole, who arose as a distinct entity in historic times, they have been called the Five Civilized Tribes. The largest aboriginal nation in the southeastern United States was the Cherokee; the one with the greatest political influence early in its history was the Creek. The Choctaw soon were divided internally, which dissipated their political effectiveness, while Chickasaw strength declined early in the historic period. Each nation owned land that white settlers coveted, and with the Federal "Removal Policy" of 1830 these Indians were moved west of the Mississippi River. They often were driven from their homes and their property seized illegally; thousands died from calculated cruelties and gross negligence of white oppressors. Some Cherokee, who lived in the southern Appalachian Mountains, refused to leave. They hid in the mountains, and when it was safe, they reestablished themselves in North Carolina, where they have continued to live. These people are described because they successfully resisted removal and because they are the largest aboriginal tribe remaining in the Southeast. Furthermore they exhibit a vitality that is refreshing, and the numerous scholarly studies

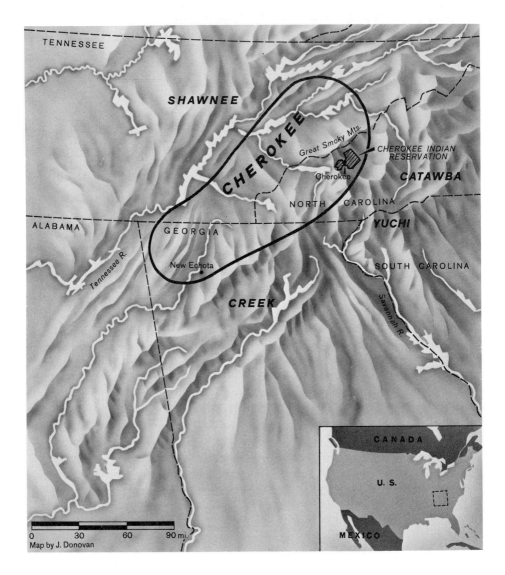

458

about them make it possible to plot the changes in their way of life with considerable precision.

People, Population, and Language

Many theories, most of them fanciful, have been offered to account for the presence of the Cherokee in the Southeast. The archaeological record is sufficient for Joffre L. Coe to suggest that ancestors of the Cherokee occupied the southeastern area for thousands of years. At the time of historic contact their number was estimated at 22,000, but this may be an exaggerated figure. "Cherokee" is a corruption of the "Tsalagi," the term they used for themselves. Their language belongs to the Iroquoian family and to the Macro-Siouan phylum; thus their closest linguistic relatives are the Iroquois. When first encountered they lived in what is now eastern Tennessee and western North Carolina and spread into Kentucky on the north and Georgia to the south. They occupied the Great Smoky Mountains, and in part because of the rugged nature of the terrain, they lived in four regional groups that had a certain degree of mutual isolation reflected in dialectic differences. The people discussed in this chapter are designated as the Eastern Cherokee to distinguish them from the Cherokee of Oklahoma. The Eastern Cherokee own about 57,000 acres in western North Carolina, and in 1970 they numbered about 3500.

Prehistory

As is true for North America in general, no one really knows when people first arrived in the southeastern United States. A survey by Don W. Dragoo calls attention to the pebble tools found throughout the Southeast and elsewhere. These seem very old and were possibly derived from eastern Asia, suggesting that people lived in the eastern states at least 30,000 years ago. Vagueness about this era is followed by evidence that by 8000 B.C. people occupying the Southeast made fluted spearpoints in the Llano (Clovis) stone-working tradition and probably hunted big game. By the Archaic, about 5000 B.C., regional adaptations had emerged, and by 1000 B.C. these Indians had become settled and numerous, living as successful hunters and collectors who maintained extensive networks of trade. Pottery was made in the Southeast by 2500 B.C., possibly having diffused there from South America. The transition from Archaic was gradual, with the burial ceremonialism of the Archaic becoming even more important in Early Woodland times. The Early Woodland people depended increasingly on local wild plants, such as goosefoot and sunflowers, for food and eventually began raising them. The first exotic domestic plants to arrive were pumpkins and squash from Mesoamerica, and maize was introduced by about 300 B.C. As the exploitation of cultigens intensified, populations expanded, and social distinctions became more pronounced. These developments, which were Hopewellian, began giving way to the Mississippian tradition about A.D. 700. The change apparently was stimulated by a breakdown in the patterning of Hopewell and by the introduction of a new variety of maize as well as beans from the Southwest.

The archaeology of the historic Cherokee homeland has been most carefully detailed by Bennie C. Keel. He considers Cherokee culture as developing from a local base in the Pisgah phase, which dates from A.D. 1000 to 1500. Some of these farming people lived in villages surrounded by log palisades. Their rectangular houses had clay hearths, and public buildings were built on earthen mounds. Most people occupied scattered homesteads, and this pattern continued through the next phase. Pisgah pottery vessels were stamped with complicated rectilinear designs and were found in conjunction with animal head effigies, beads, and clay pipes. Stonework included chipped arrowpoints, gravers, and perforators as well as ground stone celts and pipes. Pisgah was followed by the Qualla phase that introduced the Cherokee to history. The patterning of their settlements was much the same as before, with small ceremonial centers and scattered homesteads. Their pottery was stamped and incised with complicated patterns probably derived from the ceramics of the previous phase, and their work in stone and shell was essentially unchanged. As European contacts were sustained, shellwork expanded to include gorgets, ear pins, and beads. In the early 1700s the Cherokee began receiving trade goods and were living in the manner recounted in this chapter.

Early History

The expedition led by Hernando de Soto possibly passed through a Cherokee community in 1540, but not until the late 1600s were white intrusions relatively common. Firearms and other trade goods became available about 1700, and shortly thereafter traders settled among them. It was not long before the Cherokee were embroiled in hostilities with white colonists from the eastern seaboard, and old rivalries with other Indians became intensified. In a series of conflicts with English colonists in 1759–1761 many settlements were destroyed, and the Cherokee were defeated. Soon thereafter intrusions by white settlers became increasingly common, and the Cherokee were forced to give up large sectors of land. In the American Revolution, they understandably fought on the side of the British, an alliance that led to the repeated destruction of their settlements. Peace was made in 1794, and some Cherokee decided to settle west of the Mississippi River because they felt that whites would never be satisfied in their desire for more land. Most Cherokee remained, however, and became prosperous farmers, even organizing a government modeled after that of the United States. Yet pressures by whites for land

The Eastern Cherokee: Farmers of the Southeast

never ceased, and by 1839 all the Cherokee had been forced from their homes. About 1000 escaped to live in the mountains as fugitives; the descendants of these persons are the Eastern Cherokee who now live in the North Carolina mountains.

Early Historic Life

SETTLEMENTS   The Cherokee were not described in reasonable detail until the mid-1700s, and since their ties with traders and other whites were well-established by then, an aboriginal baseline ethnography was never assembled. In reasonably early historic times they lived in scattered settlements because relatively level plots of ground suitable for cultivation were scarce. Communities were built near streams and rivers to have access to fish and the game attracted to water and also for religious reasons. A large settlement might encompass 450 acres, but a typical community covered a much smaller area. A large village or a number of smaller ones formed a political aggregate, or band, of from 350 to 600 persons. As a group approached the larger number, the tendency was for a portion to separate and organize as a new unit. In the early 1700s some sixty settlements were represented by about thirty-five bands.

People lived in rectangular houses built by setting poles vertically, weaving twigs between them, and coating the walls inside and out with a mixture of moist clay and grass. These gable-roofed houses sometimes had two stories and often were divided into rooms. In one room was a fireplace, and above it a hole in the roof let the smoke out. The most prominent furnishings were raised beds made of poles with wooden crosspieces covered with mats and skins. A cone-shaped building, termed a "hot house," appears to have been used as a bathhouse for purification or as sleeping quarters on cold nights. The most imposing structure was the council house, used for religious or social functions as well as political ones; some of these buildings accommodated 500 people. A council house was seven-sided, framed with logs, and had a roof supported by concentric circles of interior posts. The entire structure was covered with earth except for a narrow doorway and a smokehole at the center of the roof. Inside were benches and a central fireplace.

Among their domestic artifacts were a wide variety of well-made large and small baskets woven from split canes. These probably served as dishes, storage containers, carrying baskets, sifters, and winnowing trays. The Cherokee also made superior pottery containers for use in cooking food and for storage. Also outstanding were their pipes made with long wooden stems and platform bowls of stone with sculpted figures of animals or persons.

CLOTHING AND APPEARANCE   As was true for other Indians in the Southeast, most clothing was made of deerskins sewn with sinew thread. A

The Three Cherokees, came over from the head of the River Savanna to London. 1762
& their Interpreter that was Poisoned.

Plate 13–1 Three Cherokee men during a visit to England in
1762. (Courtesy of The British Museum)

man's basic garment was a breechclout, and women wore knee-length skirts.
Their moccasins were deerskin, and they wore bison skin robes during cold
weather. Summer capes were made of feathers attached to a fiber base. Buckskin shirts and cloth boots were added in early historic times. The most distinctive personal adornment was the ear decoration of males. A section of the
outer border of each ear was cut free, stretched, and wound with wire to hold
it in an expanded arc. This aboriginal practice declined in popularity when
silver jewelry became popular in the late 1700s. Wealthy persons wore collar-
like bands of clamshell beads around their necks. Youthful warriors were tattooed by pricking the skin with a needle and rubbing bluish coloring in the
openings. Designs of animals, flowers, and geometric forms were tattooed on
the chest or muscular parts of the body. All the hair was plucked from a man's
head except for a scalp lock at the back; it was decorated with beads or
feathers. The hair of women appears to have been drawn back into a very long
bundle held with ribbons.

SUBSISTENCE ACTIVITIES The most important crops in aboriginal
times appear to have been maize, beans, pumpkins, and tobacco, but the
Cherokee began to raise cultigens of European origins even before whites ap-

462

The Eastern Cherokee: Farmers of the Southeast

peared in their area. In early historic times, and presumably before, the maize harvest was critical for economic welfare. Gardens were planted, tended, and harvested by women, who were helped by men. When the maize crop failed, families dispersed to hunt and collect plant products. Even in ordinary times wild plants were important in the diet; included were berries, grapes, persimmons, plums, nuts, and wild roots.

The most important meat animals were bison, deer, and game birds. Large game and birds were killed with self bows strung with bear sinew. The reed arrows were headed with points made from bone, fish scales, or metal. Small game was taken with darts shot from blowguns; a nine-foot blowgun fashioned from a reed had an effective range of sixty feet. Fish were harvested with hooks, leisters, or traps, and any discovered in shallow water were driven into baskets. Dogs were the only aboriginal domestic animal, but in later times hogs, horses, and other species of European derivation were raised.

The only important conveyance was the dugout canoe. Made from a log up to forty feet long, the canoe was hollowed by building a fire along one side and chipping out the charred wood. A vessel was about two feet wide, straight-sided, flat-bottomed, and capable of carrying twenty persons. Canoes made of wood frames covered with bark were known but were not important.

DESCENT, KINSHIP, AND MARRIAGE   Descent was traced through females (matrilineal), and a person was prohibited from marrying a member of his or her own matriclan (clan exogamy) or father's clan. A man's preferred mate was from his father's father's or mother's father's clan. After a man married and moved to another settlement, he still was regarded as a member of the clan of his birth. The members of a localized clan segment made certain that a spouse was mourned properly and that men fulfilled familial obligations. Violations led to public whippings by the women of the clan involved. A widow was expected to marry her deceased husband's brother (levirate), and a widower was supposed to take his deceased wife's sister as a spouse (sororate).

The aboriginal Cherokee kinship terminology reportedly was the "Crow

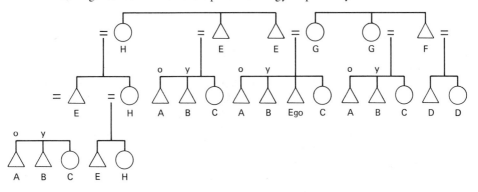

Aboriginal Cherokee kin terms.

system," meaning that the cousin terms were of the Crow type and descent was matrilineal. In this cousin terminology a father's sister's daughter and mother's brother's daughter were termed differently from each other and from sisters or parallel cousins (mother's sister's and father's brother's daughters). However, a father's sister's daughter was classed with father's sister. The kinship terminology made it possible to distinguish precisely the four matrilineages that were most important to an individual; these were the matrilineages of mother, father, mother's father, and father's father.

SOCIAL DIMENSIONS   Eighteenth century Cherokee households usually consisted of a number of nuclear families related through females (matrilineal extended family). Ideally the household included an elderly couple, their daughters, the daughters' husbands (matrilocal residence), unmarried males born into the household, and the daughters' daughters. The mutual obligations of household members and their relationship with the members of other such units were defined with precision. A father taught his son to hunt, but a mother's brother, who lived in another household, was a child's disciplinarian. An in-marrying male was respectful toward his in-laws but was expected to joke with his wife's brothers and brothers-in-law; through the jokes of others, one became aware of his erring ways. In-marrying males retained close ties with their natal households and the clans of their birth, yet a household's members formed the most closely cooperating economic unit in the society.

In social and political terms matrilineages were less important than matriclans. Members of the same clan in a band acted collectively. Apparently seven named clans were represented in each village, and members of a clan cooperated closely at the village level. The seven clans in a settlement allotted farmlands to member households and regulated marriage. Another important obligation of a clan was to settle disputes with the members of another clan. The most serious crime was murder. If someone killed a person in another clan, all local members of the murderer's clan were held responsible, and all males of the dead man's clan were obligated to seek revenge. Preferably the offender himself was killed in revenge, although one of his clan mates might be substituted.

Eighteenth century Cherokee ideals about adult behavior emerge with clarity from an analysis of myths and ethnographic accounts. A good man interacted congenially with others to maintain harmonious interpersonal relations. As Fred Gearing (1962, 31) noted, a guiding principle behind behavior was embodied in the statement "thou shalt not create disharmony." In their ethos a man studiously avoided face-to-face conflict, he was cautious in his dealings with others, and if overt conflict did arise he withdrew emotionally and physically if at all possible. Conflict was expressed at a distance through gossip and backbiting or more seriously in the use of magic to cast a spell over an adversary. An important means for eliminating personal animosities was a yearly ceremony to expose and purge ill-feelings against other villagers.

The activities of women tended to be much the same throughout the year. They cooked and prepared foods for storage, cared for children and the ill, and fashioned artifacts for domestic use. Farming activities introduced the greatest change from this routine. As Gearing has described the tempo of eighteenth century Cherokee life, the routine of the males varied seasonally. In the summer after helping women plant the crops, young men played stickball (lacrosse), sometimes hunted, and constructed or repaired buildings. In the late summer they helped harvest the crops and then devoted three weeks to a series of ceremonies. In the fall and winter the young men hunted, fought, and held their ceremonies.

POLITICAL LIFE: EARLY   In the fall, between the harvest ceremony and the rekindling of a sacred fire, a white flag often was raised above the council house as a summons for the people to assemble. A small number of el-

Plate 13–2 Watercolor of a Cherokee man by Baroness Hyde de Neuville, ca. 1820. (Courtesy of The New-York Historical Society, New York City)

derly men sat near the center of the building, and other men and women sat on benches in separate clusters by clan. Older men spoke at length, younger males made their opinions known, but women seldom expressed themselves at these times. A village council considered relations with other Indians or Europeans, decided questions of war or peace, and determined trading arrangements. The general council of elderly men, called "beloved men," was led by a chief priest, three other priests, and a secular officer, all of whom lived near the council house. An inner council consisted of seven beloved men, one from each clan. Questions before the council were stated repeatedly until there was a consensus of support or opposition. Deliberations might span days or even weeks until unanimous decisions were reached. The priests could not coerce or compel others to act in a particular manner; instead, they were arbitrators who reconciled differences. It appears that the members of each clan discussed particular problems among themselves before a council meeting and attempted to reach a unified position. The seven clan representatives met with the priests, expressed their feelings, and reported back to their constituents to discuss the matter; they then reassembled as a body to deliberate. If a clan had maneuvered as much as possible and still could not support an emerging consensus, it withdrew from the deliberations to avoid an open conflict.

A village council served one large settlement or a cluster of smaller communities, but no larger political structure united the bands or the nation. Each village was an independent political entity that sought to live in harmonious relations with other such units. Gearing (1962, 83) reasoned that prior to 1730 the Cherokee comprised a "jural community," meaning that they were united by cultural and social ties. The members of one village might cooperate with those in another, and they appear never to have fought against each other, although they often were at war with adjacent tribes. Some villages were more important than others because of their strategic location, the learning of their priests, or the importance of a secular leader, but no village appears to have been dominant for very long. Conflict between Cherokee villages most likely developed if a man killed someone from another village. This was a matter to be resolved by the members of the clans involved, and since each clan was represented by fictive brothers in any other village, these ties, and the ideals of proper behavior in times of disputes, were enough to avert open conflict.

POLITICAL LIFE: BRITISH INFLUENCES In 1730 the village council still functioned at the local level as it had in the past, but British colonial administrators began viewing the Cherokee as a single political unit rather than as an aggregate of independent villages. Thus, when a raiding party attacked a frontier settlement or interfered with the activities of a white trader, all of the Cherokee were held responsible. To avoid unexpected reprisals, a tribal political network began to develop among the Cherokee. The first person to emerge with political authority beyond the village level was Moytoy, a man from the Tennessee River drainage group (Overhill Cherokee) who presumably was a

The Eastern Cherokee: Farmers of the Southeast

war chief. He was crowned "Emperor" of the Cherokee in 1730 by the British representative Alexander Cuming, who was largely responsible for originating the office. The Overhill settlements long had been influential, and they became more important as the military effectiveness of the Chickasaw declined. This placed the Overhill communities on the French frontier and led to their strategic importance to the British and Cherokee alike. The influence of Moytoy was not acknowledged among all Cherokee, but his political office was widely recognized as legitimate. A smallpox epidemic in 1738–1739 appears to have killed about half of the people, and as a result the curers, who probably were the war party doctors, lost their position of respect, so much so that they destroyed their ritual equipment. This resulted in even more power shifting to political leaders. With the death of Moytoy in 1741 his son Amouskosite became the leader. Presumably it was he who threatened to destroy a Cherokee village and kill all the inhabitants if they did not kill a man who had murdered a trader. The pressure to take action against the murderer had come originally from the Governor of South Carolina, who threatened to cut off trade to the Cherokee. Without arms and ammunition they would have been unable to defend themselves against the French and their Indian allies. Thus the actions of any one village began to be subordinated to tribal interests. In this and other episodes particular individuals emerged as spokesmen for the Cherokee but only in dealing with alien powers. By 1753 a priest state was beginning to emerge, roughly paralleling the village level organization. The capital settle-

Plate 13–3 Pencil drawings by George Catlin of Cherokee men. (Courtesy of The New-York Historical Society, New York City)

ment was the residence of the most notable leader and the chief priest. Other leaders from representative villages met there to deliberate. The major problem was how to prevent warriors from launching raids. The tribal council could punish raiders after the fact but had no institutionalized network to prevent raids. The inability of Amouskositte's successor to prevent raids against frontier settlements led to a war with the English that lasted from 1759 to 1761. The destruction of numerous villages forced the Cherokee to sue for peace. Raids continued to be a problem, however, and as white settlers boldly began farming Cherokee land, retaliatory raids increased.

POLITICAL LIFE: INFLUENCE OF WARRIORS   By 1768 it was decided to include outstanding warriors among the decision makers at the tribal council meetings. Heretofore warriors played an integral part in council decisions only during preparations for conflict and when actually at war. Although the tribal council in theory remained opposed to reprisal raids, integrating the warriors into the tribal political organization meant that any activities they undertook would be legitimate. The American Revolution and the opening of Kentucky to white settlers split the Cherokee into two factions. Most young warriors sided with the British and were armed by them; the old men only sought peace. Raids by warriors led American military forces to destroy nearly all Cherokee settlements, but the people were not destroyed. When their villages were burned, they fled to the mountains, and after the conflict they returned to reestablish farming communities. Although they repeatedly were forced to give up land, in 1800 they still held title to about 43,000 square miles, about half of it in Tennessee and the remainder in adjacent sectors of Alabama, Georgia, and North Carolina. In the 1800s the Cherokee set out to establish a new way of life based on a reformulation of their old ways and selected white customs.

WARFARE   In the 1700s much of Cherokee energy was focused on raids and war as a direct and indirect result of white contact. When a council decided to make war, a red flag was raised over the council house, and the war organization began preparations. Rituals by priests, fasting and dances by warriors, narrations of heroic deeds, and ritual bathing all were involved. An oration by the war speaker preceded the formal departure of a war party. When venturing forth, the warriors were elaborately painted red and black. The war club, with a projection at one end, was either hand-held or thrown. They also used bows and arrows and spears when fighting. In early historic times the metal tomahawk of European manufacture was popular, but these and earlier weapons were replaced by imported firearms and knives as they became available.

In enemy country a war party erected a small post bearing carved symbols that indicated their past exploits; such a post appears to have been a declaration of war. If the raiders succeeded in an attack, they might carve symbols on a nearby tree to record their victory. Two classes of men, warriors and chiefs, appear to have fought, and some women were famous for their abilities in battle. The leader of a war party had only nominal control over his following, and apparently a warrior could leave at any time except during actual combat. They attacked stealthily, attempting to kill and scalp as many persons as they could before withdrawing with captives if at all possible. Before returning home, the raiders painted the scalps red and tied them to a pole that was carried ahead of the line of warriors as they entered their village. Captives might be adopted, but more often they were tortured to death slowly by males and females, young and old. Women whose relatives had been killed by members of the victim's tribe were the most persistent torturers.

RELIGION   Many activities in the 1700s were linked to a round of religious observances. In the fall the first of three important ritual sets was the harvest ceremony. Held in late September after the maize crop matured, this celebration included processions in which green boughs were carried and also four days of dancing. Religious dances were held in the council house, and there were social dances in which women participated. Soon after these festivities and when the moon was new, the council house became the center for ritual offerings to a sacred fire. Later a priest led the villagers to a river, where each person bathed seven times, and then they all feasted. About ten days after the completion of this ceremony, rituals were held to negate any ill-feelings that a person might harbor against others. The purpose was for each individual to become ritually pure. Then the sacred fire in the council house was extinguished and rekindled. The members of each household lit new fires in their homes from embers of the new sacred fire. The people bathed in a river, permitted their old clothing to drift away, and put on new garments when they emerged. During the time between these ceremonies the most important political conferences of the year were held.

Later Historic Changes

ADAPTATIONS   The Cherokee Nation founded in 1820 was modeled after the government of the United States with executive, judicial, and legislative branches. A capital with Euro-American architectural style buildings was constructed at New Echota, Georgia, in 1825. Soon after the nation was founded, Sequoya (George Gist), who was of Cherokee and white ancestry, presented to the leaders a proposal for writing their language. In 1809 Sequoya had become impressed with the importance of writing, and he finally originated a system whereby symbols represented syllables in the Cherokee language. Within a few months after the syllabary was adopted in 1821, thousands of Cherokee had learned to read and write their own language. A print shop was established at New Echota, and the first issue of a newspaper, the

Plate 13–4 Sequoya (ca. 1760–1843) originated the Cherokee syllabary adopted by the Cherokee Nation in 1821. (From McKenney and Hall, 1933)

Cherokee Phoenix, appeared in 1828. By this time the Cherokee were numbered among the "Civilized Tribes." Their population was about 13,500 in addition to nearly 150 white men who had married Cherokee women and about 75 white women who had Cherokee husbands. At this time too they owned nearly 1300 Negro slaves, which indicates that some members of the nation were succeeding in the southern economic system.

REMOVAL   The rich farmlands of the more southern Cherokee, their ever-increasing affluence, and the discovery of gold in northern Georgia were too much for covetous whites. With the Federal policy to remove all eastern Indians to land west of the Mississippi River, the new Cherokee Nation was doomed. Some persons signed an agreement with Federal agents to move to Oklahoma and give up their land for 5 million dollars. In spite of the fact that the agreement was not made by the leaders of the nation, the Federal Govern-

The Eastern Cherokee: Farmers of the Southeast

ment considered it binding on all Cherokee. In 1838 a military force began dislodging people from their lands and making certain that they migrated west. The most inaccessible and conservative groups in the north, those with less desirable lands, were not pressured as much, and many were able to hide in the mountains. The most southern groups, those who had most successfully adapted to the southern farming economy and to white governmental procedures, were the ones forced to migrate to Indian Territory.

LAND CLAIMS   About 1000 conservative Cherokee escaped to the mountains of North Carolina to hide until 1842. As an indication of their traditional nature it was recorded a few years later that only a few mixed-blooded and no full-blooded Indians spoke English. William H. Thomas, a white trader and the adopted son of a chief, emerged as influential with this group. He spoke Cherokee, became the Indian agent, and eventually established the right of the Cherokee to remain in the locality. With the money paid to compensate for the illegal seizure of their property, Thomas and other sympathetic whites began buying parcels of land for the Indians, because Indians could not legally own land under the state constitution. The plots were held by Thomas in his name; when he became ill and in debt following the Civil War, his creditors claimed all this land. However, Congress sued the creditors to preserve the land for these Indians, and the matter was settled in favor of the Cherokee in 1874. To protect them in the future, the Commissioner of Indian Affairs was made their trustee, and a deed for their holdings was obtained in 1876. The Cherokee refugees who had reestablished themselves in North Carolina became relatively prosperous farmers. Yet they still spoke Cherokee, their clan organization was maintained, and many traditions of old remained intact. During the Civil War those who fought did so for the Confederacy, although a few later joined the Union Army. Unfortunately a returning Union soldier carried smallpox, and more than 100 of the 2000 Indians died of the disease. By and large the Cherokee lived throughout this period as self-sufficient farmers on scattered homesteads where they grew maize as their most important crop and raised livestock.

During the time that their right to the land was in question, the Cherokee drafted a Constitution providing for a chief and one representative for each settlement. In 1870 this body began to function as the Eastern Band of Cherokee, but it was not incorporated formally until 1889. The 1887 passage of the Dawes Act and separate efforts to allot Oklahoma Indian lands led to rumors that Eastern Cherokee land was to be allotted. A long-standing complaint, and one that would recur, was that some whites used devious means to become tribal members in the hope of obtaining land. Some whites reportedly became "Five Dollar Indians" by paying this amount as a bribe to be entered on the roll. These whites, in addition to the children of white-Indian marriages, have, over the years, led to a significant number of "white Indians."

Plate 13–5 A North Carolina home in 1888. (Courtesy of the Smithsonian Institution National Anthropological Archives, neg. no. 1000-b)

SCHOOLS   Schools were opened in 1881 by the Society of Friends on a contractual basis with the Federal Government, an arrangement that lasted until 1892. The Quakers succeeded in upsetting the pattern of Indian life, but not nearly as much as did their educational successors in the Bureau of Indian Affairs. The pattern of formal education under the bureau was for a child to attend a day school through the fourth grade and then attend a local boarding school through the ninth grade; his education was completed at a distant boarding school such as the one for Indians in Carlisle, Pennsylvania. The goal of compulsory education was to destroy Indian life; children were punished for speaking Cherokee, chained to their beds if they repeatedly ran away, and forced to learn white ways.

POLITICAL, SOCIAL, AND ECONOMIC UNITS   When William H. Gilbert studied the Eastern Cherokee in 1932, the political units created after removal were continuing to function. The six towns had locally elected officers, and there was an elected Band Council that regulated land usage. The State of North Carolina controlled taxation and the law, and the Federal Government had jurisdiction over education and welfare. The towns were not only political units but also served important economic and social functions. The *gadugi* or Free Labor Companies were not as important as in the past but provided significant services for their members. A typical Free Labor Company had about a dozen members who annually elected officers from the mem-

The Eastern Cherokee: Farmers of the Southeast

bership. Participants contracted their labor as a unit and helped each other in farming and other activities; a member could borrow money from the collective treasury as well. The gadugi was an important cooperative enterprise in the historic past and apparently had an aboriginal base. Around 1900 as the Free Labor Companies began to hire themselves out to whites with increasing frequency, they were judged taxable by the State of North Carolina, which led to their decline.

The aboriginal Cherokee had performed a wide variety of dances, and by the early 1930s most of these were remembered. Of the large number still performed, one of the best known was the Booger Dance. The word "booger" had the same root as the English word "bogey" meaning goblin, but in its Cherokee context it closely approximated the idea of a ghost. Masks worn during the dance were designed as caricatures of aliens. Originally the dance may have been performed to induce warriors to join war parties and to dilute the harmful effects of the spirits of foreigners. By the 1930s, however, the dance was almost free from religious associations. The masks at that time portrayed Indian enemies: Negroes; Chinese, who were identified with an old Cherokee myth, and whites. The dances were performed by a small number of men and sometimes by a few women, all of whom were disguised. The performers danced in a circle, frightened children, and joked with adults who stood in a proper joking relationship to them.

The gadugi, the dances, the importance of clans in regulating marriage, and much of the additional substance of traditional life were waning in importance by the late 1950s. Furthermore, earlier decisions about the qualifications

Plate 13–6 Booger Dance masks. (Courtesy of the UCLA Museum of Cultural History)

of an Indian contributed to a reformation of what it meant to be an Eastern Cherokee.

Modern Life

ECONOMIC BASE   The Eastern Cherokee lands consist of nearly 57,000 acres in western North Carolina adjacent to the Great Smoky Mountains National Park. The Qualla Boundary area with some 44,000 acres is the largest reservation. Eighty percent of it consists of mountain slopes, and the balance is bottomland, although not the rich bottomland of nearby areas. Until the turn of the century these holdings were adequate for their subsistence-based agriculture. They also raised cattle and hogs, but stock-fencing laws and then the chestnut blight, which depleted the prime source of food for hogs, ended these enterprises by the late 1920s. By this time too the population had increased, and all possible land had been brought under cultivation. This combination of factors brought a crisis in the economy. Eastern Cherokee isolation was broken by an ever-expanding network of roads, and the Indians were drawn into a cash economy. Most persons maintained gardens for produce, but they also needed wage employment. Since there were comparatively few jobs, the standard of living became increasingly depressed. The tourist trade began to emerge around the turn of the present century, but it was not sizeable until after World War II. Tourists then began to arrive in greater and greater numbers, and by the late 1950s over 2,000,000 automobiles passed through the town of Cherokee, North Carolina, each summer.

At the community of Cherokee two major north-south and east-west highways intersect, and in the late 1950s much of the automobile traffic was bound for the Great Smoky Mountains National Park and to see the Cherokee. Many stores sold souvenirs, and each had an official greeter wearing a feather headdress and other items of Indian clothing. These men could be photographed next to a totem pole or tepee for a fee. The number of motels, restaurants, and gas stations was growing rapidly, and all were likely to have Cherokee employees. The largest tourist-oriented enterprise was the Cherokee Historical Association. It sponsored the drama "Unto These Hills," which was performed nearly every day during the summer, and maintained a museum as well as a reconstructed aboriginal village. The Bureau of Indian Affairs had an agency center and schools here as well as at other localities. There was a U.S. Public Health Service hospital and a nursing facility. This was no ordinary "reservation" however, because the Eastern Band of Cherokee Indians, a legal, corporate entity, owned the land. Some Cherokee family lines had occupied a particular acreage for generations, but they did not own land as individuals. The Tribal Council dealt with land allotments and reallocations as well as leases of land to non-Indians; these were controlled with particular care and on a short-term basis. Leases to business establishments provided

474

about 80 percent of the money received by the council. One function of the council was to settle disputes over land; these were made more difficult by the fact that some boundaries were ill-defined.

During the late 1950s a majority of the approximately 700 households depended on subsistence farming for most of their food, and intermittent wage labor in the summer was the major source of cash. Some families relied on welfare payments during at least part of the winter; this also was characteristic of non-Indian farmers in the region. Very few individuals had full-time jobs that provided their sole income, and conservative families had the most difficulty in making the transition from subsistence farming to a cash economy. In spite of the depressed standard of living for most persons, very few Eastern Cherokee were willing to move away permanently. Most experience outside the area had occurred after World War II and included residence at boarding schools, time spent in the armed service, or temporary jobs elsewhere.

EDUCATION   The New Deal for Indians, as for the rest of the country, which began in 1934, was a concerted effort to accept the diversity in cultural and historical background of the different tribes under Federal control. It was a humanistic endeavor to respect the integrity of Indian cultural traditions and to encourage their on-going vitality. An effort was made to teach the Cherokee syllabary in Federal schools, but the program was abandoned because of a lack of local interest. Some local programs did succeed, however. Attempts to do away with boarding schools were not successful until 1954 because of the distance separating some homes and school facilities. The study by Sharlotte Neely Williams of Eastern Cherokee education, which is the key source for information about schooling, indicates that in 1954 some high school students began attending county schools. With reference to the previous pattern Williams (1971, 44) wrote, "the students were boarded at schools so that their association with Anglo-American cultural phenomena would outweigh their exposure to Cherokee culture in their homes." Further changes included the consolidation of four grade schools as the Cherokee Elementary School in 1962 and the end of the last Indian day school in 1965.

In the 1950s the educational stress continued to be on vocational training with an emphasis on farming skills; academic courses were similar to those in other sectors of rural North Carolina. Since wage labor employment was difficult to obtain and the farms were declining in value, it was hard for high school students trained in this way to succeed locally. As the tourist business increased and some industries began to move into the area, the employment opportunities expanded, but because the Indians tended to be noncompetitive in terms of white values, they were at a distinct disadvantage in the job market.

In the early 1970s a new direction to Eastern Cherokee education seemed to be emerging through the Headstart and Follow Through programs. The small classes, well-trained staff of teachers, predominantly Cherokee teacher aids, and community-wide interest suggested an intensity of concern over education that was far greater than in the recent past. Over 90 percent of the children spoke English at home, and thus they did not have to learn a "school" language. Furthermore, there were physical reminders of their Cherokee heritage such as paintings of Indians along the halls and Indian as well as white dolls with which to play. Classroom instruction included Cherokee culture when appropriate, and instruction in the aboriginal language was initiated in the Follow Through Program.

VOLUNTARY ASSOCIATIONS The Free Labor Companies, although smaller in number, were a source of pride for the Eastern Cherokee in general. Such an organization was most often made up of conservative Indians. One person directed the company, composed of a group of workers, and certain women cooked for them. Mutual aid was extended in crises, and the members cooperated in farming activities. Unlike the situation in early historic times a Free Labor Company did not embrace all persons in a settlement unit. In its more recent form a company had elected officers and about twenty male members who helped one another plant and harvest maize, chop wood, and repair or build houses. Money for a treasury, from which members might draw funds, accrued from food sales.

Stickball, from which the game of lacrosse is derived, was a popular sport, and each township fielded a stickball team until they were done away with in the 1930s at the insistence of the Bureau of Indian Affairs. Two reasons appear to have accounted for the repression. One was that the games were played as battles, which resulted in many injuries, and the other was that spectators were so unruly that serious disturbances sometimes resulted. Softball games replaced the stickball contests but did not serve as a direct substitute. The teams were organized by township, and attendance was good, but the rivalry and spectator participation was subdued.

Since 1914 the Cherokee Indian Fair had been held on an annual basis in the fall and attracted all the people. In recent years rides and games of chance were provided by a traveling carnival company. The most important dimension of the fair, however, was that fostered by the Fair Association, whose president was the tribal chief. The association's goal was to show progress in terms of farming and business enterprises, and diverse exhibits for which there were competitive prizes figured as important. The fair also featured a stickball game, with twelve players, apparently drawn from the conservative population, on a team. Every player carried a stick that had a small loop and a wire-mesh pocket attached at the end. The object of the game was to carry a small ball across the goal of the opposite team. The ball could be carried in one hand, in the mouth, or in the mesh pocket of the stick. Any means, including the use of the stick, could be employed to obtain the ball; injuries, both purposeful and unintended, were difficult to prevent. In aboriginal times the game was preceded by an elaborate ritual, and at least some teams still

The Eastern Cherokee: Farmers of the Southeast

observed rituals before a game. In 1959 the Chamber of Commerce began sponsoring weekly games played by teams representing all the townships. The frequency of the encounters led to increased competitiveness, which resulted in some serious injuries to players, and spectator involvement recalled the problems of the 1930s.

LANGUAGE   All of these people spoke English in the late 1950s, but some older persons rarely conversed in it. Although their aboriginal culture had long since disappeared, a large percentage of the population, especially those identified as conservative, spoke Cherokee. In one sector all members of about 40 percent of the households spoke it by preference. Households in which the aboriginal language was used most often were composed of persons who were considered as being full-blooded Indians or having only a quarter of non-Indian blood. John Gulick reasons that the prevalence of spoken Cherokee among them has been, and will continue to be, sustained as long as such persons marry one another. The persons who retained their language of old appeared to have done so because it symbolized their Indian identity. The syllabary developed by Sequoyah still was in use, and the Bible printed in it continued to be available. Some of the Free Labor Companies recorded their minutes in the syllabary, but its most important use appears to have been to record the formulas of shamans.

KINSHIP AND FAMILIES   The kinship terminology of old was known only to some of the most elderly Eastern Cherokee in the late 1950s. The majority of persons familiar with the Cherokee terms employed them in such a way that the words were comparable in usage to those employed by English speakers. In other words, the terminology that had made it possible to distinguish relatives according to lineage and clan lines had been modified for bilateral usage.

It appears that these people preferred household units to be comprised of a nuclear family, and most houses were so occupied. A significant number of additional households contained a number of related nuclear families, that is, small extended families. These households often were the nuclear families of siblings, or a nuclear family plus grandchildren. The larger living units tended to occur more often among conservative families, and one reason might have been because they placed a high value on hospitality. These people also tended to be poor and lived together out of necessity. Then too daughters with nonlegitimate children often lived in their parents' households. Yet no clear evidence suggests that large households represented continuity with former residence patterns.

The matriclans that regulated marriage in aboriginal and early historic times had declined. In the early 1950s older people still were familiar with the clan system, and about 80 percent of the marriages were in accord with it. By the mid-1950s the percentage had dropped to 20, and it was not certain that all of these marriages had in fact taken clan regulations into conscious consideration. "Common law" marriages seemingly were typical, and nonlegitimate offspring were not stigmatized. It is noteworthy that those young adults with a minimum percent of Indian blood tended to marry persons with a greater proportion in order to insure the rights of Eastern Cherokee for their children.

KINDS OF INDIANS In the 1950s when persons identified as Eastern Cherokee considered their Indianness in abstract terms they expressed a clear dichotomy between "Full Bloods" and "White Indians." A Full Blood was genetically Indian or nearly so, spoke Cherokee, belonged to a Free Labor Company, and subscribed to the traditional Cherokee value system. White Indians had the attitudes and values of whites, spoke English, and had comparatively little Indian blood. This dichotomy was neat, but it did not always appear valid even to the Cherokee themselves. A person might be judged an Indian in one context and white in another; clearly there were gradations and contexts to being Indian. This led Robert K. Thomas to define four value systems among these people. The conservatives, who possibly numbered about one-fourth of the population, were "true Indians" in blood, language, and behavior. A "Generalized Indian" thought of himself as an Indian, but unlike a conservative he attempted to accommodate the white world. He accepted important values of conservatives and whites alike and thus was not a White Indian. A "rural-White Indian" did not look like an Indian, he had a minimal degree of Indian inheritance, and his general attitudes were those of whites in the rural south. Such persons seldom were active in purely Cherokee institutions but were likely to be members of such white organizations as the 4-H

Plate 13–7 Tourist-related enterprises are a major source of income for the Eastern Cherokee; note the totem poles and tepee. (Courtesy of Sharlotte Neely Williams)

The Eastern Cherokee: Farmers of the Southeast

Plate 13–8 The Cherokee Horse Dance being performed in 1973 by traditional dancers at the annual Fall Festival held on the Qualla Boundary. (Courtesy of Sharlotte Neely Williams)

Club. These individuals might interact with Generalized Indians but did not usually function well with conservatives. Finally there were the "Middle Class Indians," the smallest group in numerical terms, who were involved in non-farming businesses or were office workers. They tended to socialize with non-Indians holding similar jobs.

HARMONY ETHIC   An insightful contribution by John Gulick and his associates concerns the values of the conservative segment. The analysis demonstrated that this behavioral system was not an odd assortment of "survivals," but an integrated configuration termed the "Harmony Ethic." A critical component was the minimization of overt and direct aggression in face-to-face situations; the aggression that did occur was expressed indirectly as gossip and sorcery. A high positive value was placed on being generous with other people in terms of rendering personal services and providing food. Conservatives did not assert themselves; they withdrew in the face of potential conflict and made a point of "minding their own business." Given these attitudes there were no well-defined leaders even in situations where they might be expected. For example, the officers in a Free Labor Company worked together as a group rather than in a hierarchical decision-making structure and tended to render decisions that reflected common consent. Because the concept of disagreement ran contrary to this value system, conservatives tended to cast an affirmative vote or did not vote at all.

LAND CLAIMS   In 1972 the Eastern Cherokee met in a general council for the first time since 1838. They gathered to decide whether they should accept nearly 2 million dollars from the Federal Government for 25 million acres of land lost to whites. They agreed to receive the settlement and divide the money; each person received less than $300.00. An old grievance finally was resolved, and other factors were beginning to favor them as well. The tourist industry continued to expand broadly, and two-thirds of the nearly 175 enterprises, although not the most lucrative, were Cherokee owned. Light industries were being introduced, there was a surge in construction jobs, and tribal assets had increased significantly. However, as a group their average income was still only 60 percent of the national average.

OUTLOOK: ACCOMMODATIONS   One of the most overworked and least satisfying words used by anthropologists with reference to historic changes in Indian life is "acculturation." It often is employed with the presumption that total assimilation is the logical end product, yet there is no justification for this assumption in the definition of the word. In general, acculturation is used to indicate the ways in which Indians are becoming more like white Americans; it might be more correct to use the word "accommodation." With this notation in mind we may consider the Eastern Cherokee further as they have been described by Kupferer, Thomas, and Williams.

The aboriginal Cherokee first accommodated white traders and soon became dependent on them in economic terms. This in part led to their political involvements with the eighteenth century colonists. Both before and after removal, marriages with whites not only introduced white "blood" but also affected Eastern Cherokee accommodations because the outsiders moved into their homes. Before 1880 the general pattern was for persons of mixed blood to identify with the Cherokee, not with whites. When the missionary-teachers and later teachers alone entered the scene, they emphasized Anglo-American rather than Cherokee ways in an effort to absorb these Indians into the dominant cultural system. Kupferer reasons that the conservative-modern dichotomy became crystallized as a result of the emphasis formal education gave to white ways and its competition with the Cherokee lifeway. The Harmony Ethic emerged in competition with the Protestant Ethic.

In the decade following 1934 the Federal Government's efforts to revitalize Eastern Cherokee culture failed, possibly because absorption had come to be accepted as the only possible goal by most persons. The great influx of tourists after World War II brought an increasing awareness of what it was to be an Indian; in practical terms, one of the immediate effects was a market for craft items. Williams feels that these people have an expanding interest in reestablishing their clear identity as Indians and that this is best reflected in the Follow Through Program and aided by instruction in the Cherokee language. Similarly there is a growing pride in those business enterprises that focus on Indian productions. If efforts to revitalize Cherokee culture continue to ex-

The Eastern Cherokee: Farmers of the Southeast

Plate 13–9 The Ed and Ella Jackson family and friends in their new house at the Snowbird community in 1975. (Courtesy of Walter L. Williams)

pand, the differences between conservative and "modern" Eastern Cherokee should decline, and their lasting identity as a people will become more assured.

Comparisons

The value system or ethos of a people is essentially the total of their behavioral principles, and we find that these were well defined for peoples described in recent chapters. The "Protestant Ethic" of the Yurok, the Hopi Way, the New Religion of the Iroquois, and the Harmony Ethic of the Eastern Cherokee are examples. After identifying each, comparisons are worthwhile in terms of how people actually behaved in terms of their ethical systems, the historic pressures to change them, their responses, and what they do and did to counter nonconformity.

Eastern Cherokee and Fox comparisons are especially pertinent. In neither case is a baseline ethnography available, which makes clear background data unavailable. However, we do know that both peoples were battered by colonial powers seeking farmland and yet retained their identity even though surrounded by whites. They were not put under the same form of Federal control as most Indians. Further comparisons might focus on their changing political and economic lives to generalize about the process, not the specific traits, in their sociocultural change and adaptations. If we assume that the continuity of Indianness is a desirable and attainable goal, what might be done within each society by its members to achieve this end most effectively?

Additional Readings

The best general background information about the Cherokee is in the 1900 report by James Mooney. The historical section of this publication was republished as *Historical Sketch of the Cherokee* (Chicago, 1975). Fred Gearing's study of historic Cherokee political development is worthy of careful study as is the analysis of the early historic legal system titled *A Law of Blood* (New York, 1970) by John P. Reid. The most insightful studies of culture change are by John Gulick (1960) and Harriet J. Kupferer (1966). The *Appalachian Journal* (v. 2, no. 4, 1975) devoted an issue to recent Cherokee studies; these include information about Eastern and Oklahoma Cherokee. The book *Southeastern Indians Since the Removal Era* (in press), edited by Walter L. Williams, provides a further update, as does the Epilogue by Sharlotte Neely Williams in the 1973 edition of *Cherokees at the Crossroads* by John Gulick (1960).

References

Bloom, Leonard. "The Acculturation of the Eastern Cherokee: Historical Aspects," *The North Carolina Historical Review*, v. 19, 323–358. 1942.

Coe, Joffre L. "Cherokee Archeology," *SI, BAE†, Bulletin* 180, no. 7. 1961.

Cotterill, R. S. *The Southern Indians*. Norman. 1954.

Dragoo, Don W. "Some Aspects of Eastern North American Prehistory: A Review 1975," *American Antiquity*, v. 41, 3–27. 1976.

Fogelson, Raymond D., and Paul Kutsche. "Cherokee Economic Cooperatives: The Gadugi," *SI, BAE, Bulletin* 180, no. 11. 1961.

*Gearing, Fred. *Priests and Warriors*, American Anthropological Association, Memoir 93. 1962. This is the major ethnohistorical study about eighteenth century Cherokee political organization. Gearing carefully plots the major changes in political structure and explains why shifts occurred.

*Gilbert, William H. "The Eastern Cherokee," *SI, BAE, Bulletin* 133, 169–413. 1943. In 1932 Gilbert made a field study among these people which focused on an analysis of the kinship terminology, but he also considered diverse aspects of life at that time and presented a brief review of ethnohistorical sources which is very useful.

Gilbert, William H. "Eastern Cherokee Social Organization," in *Social Anthropology of North American Tribes*, Fred Eggan, ed., 283–338. Chicago. 1965.

*Gulick, John. *Cherokees at the Crossroads.* Chapel Hill. 1960. Based on 1956–58 field studies by Gulick and his students, this is the most comprehensive and thoughtful presentation of changing Cherokee life in recent times.

Keel, Bennie C. *Cherokee Archaeology.* Knoxville. 1976.

*Kupferer, Harriet J. "The 'Principal People,' 1960," *SI, BAE, Bulletin* 196, no. 78. 1966. In 1959–1960 the author studied the Eastern Cherokee and focused especially on degrees of acculturation as reflected in educational attitudes and health concepts.

Kupferer, Harriet J. "The Isolated Eastern Cherokee," in *The American Indian Today*, Stuart Levine and Nancy O. Lurie, eds., 143–159. 1968.

McKenney, Thomas L., and James Hall. *The Indian Tribes of North America*, v. 1. Edinburgh. 1933.

Mooney, James. "Myths of the Cherokee," *SI, BAE, 19th Annual Report*, pt. 1, 1900.

Speck, Frank G., and Leonard Broom. *Cherokee Dance and Drama.* Berkeley and Los Angeles. 1951.

Swanton, John R. *The Indians of the Southeastern United States. SI, BAE, Bulletin* 137. 1946.

Thomas, Robert K. *See* Gulick, John.

Williams, Sharlotte Neely. "The Quaker Era of Cherokee Indian Education," in *Appalachian Journal*, v. 2, 314–322. 1975.

Williams, Sharlotte Neely. (edited by Walter L. Williams) "Acculturation and Persistence among North Carolina's Eastern Band of Cherokee Indians," in *Southeastern Indians Since the Removal Era.* In press.

The Natchez: Sophisticated Farmers of the Deep South

Reasons for This Selection

Along the eastern bank of the lower Mississippi River emerged the most elaborate American Indian cultures reported north of Mexico. Nowhere else were similar heights of complexity reached, and the group that best represents this climax of achievements was the Natchez. The word Natchez apparently is derived from a French interpretation of the name of their settlement called Naches, but these people called themselves the Theloel. They maintained a highly developed class system, possessed luxuries of rare elaboration, and paid homage to a god-king. The Natchez were selected because of their sophistication and because they were better described early in their history than any other southeasterners at a similar level of achievement. Also, in their relationship with the French they passed through stages that were rather well-defined and often paralleled the developments between Europeans and other North American Indians.

Language and Population

The language of the Natchez is classed in the Macro-Algonkian phylum and the Algonkian family, but it is distinct and has no close ties to any other.

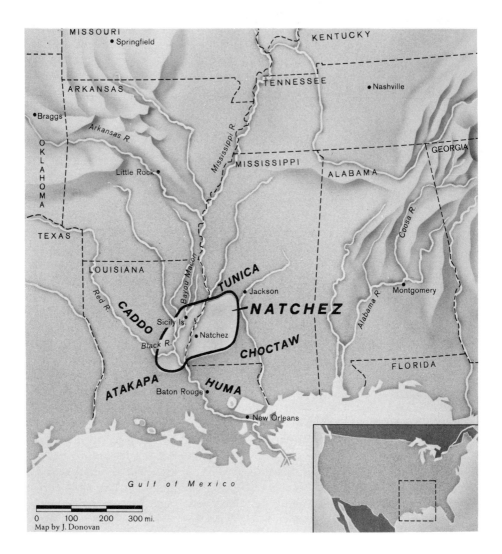

Map by J. Donovan

486

It is interesting to note that while the women spoke the same language as the men, women were said (Le Page du Pratz, 1774, 312) to "soften and smooth their words, whereas the speech of the men is more grave and serious." Since the French learned the language from women, their pronunciation was feminine and was ridiculed by both Natchez men and women. At the end of the seventeenth century the Natchez numbered about 3500, and in 1720 they could assemble 1200 warriors, including refugees they had absorbed and the Tiou, who were a dependent people. By 1731 only 300 warriors could be mustered, and a few years later they were a remnant people, although a few survived into the present century.

Prehistory

The rapid historic disappearance of Natchez culture was preceded by two or more millennia of prehistory coursing toward a complex way of life. The beginnings of human occupancy along the lower Mississippi River are mysterious, even for those who have studied the problem most. Apparently the present alluvial valley surface dates from about 3000 B.C. It is reasoned that if people lived there then or earlier, the evidence would now be deeply buried or washed away. One of the oldest excavated sites along the lower Mississippi River drainage is Poverty Point in northeastern Louisiana. The remains from this settlement reflect an already well-developed way of life. The site was occupied about 700 B.C., and it includes an artificial mound that is almost seventy feet high and has a base measuring some 640 by 710 feet. To the east a series of slightly rounded ridges, about five feet high, form half an octagon measuring some three-quarters of a mile across. It may be that the octagon originally was more nearly complete, but the Bayou Macon has cut into the area of the other possible half. About a mile and a half from the octagon is another mound essentially the same shape as the one at Poverty Point, and it has been suggested that both mounds originally were intended to represent birds. Beneath the ridges at Poverty Point is a thin layer of cultural debris, indicating that the area had been occupied for at least a brief period before the construction of the ridges. No evidence of structures was found on the ridges because the surface had eroded, but it is probable that the ridges were bases for houses. Hundreds of tons of small irregularly shaped lumps of fired clay were found at the site. These clay objects probably were heated in fires and dropped in vessels to cook food; cooking stones are common in parts of North America, but stone is rare in this area. A few crude clay figurines were found along with pottery, but very few sherds were recovered, suggesting that the pottery was not of local manufacture. Steatite vessels, or at least the raw material, were imported from the southern Appalachian region, apparently in large quantities since many fragments were found. Other nonlocal raw materials included red sandstone from northern Mississippi, galena and gray-white chert from the Ozark Mountains, and even copper from the Lake Superior area. All of this implies established routes of trade, but the reuse of flaked stone, the repair of steatite vessels, and other patchings suggest that raw materials or artifacts from afar were not abundant. A wide variety of chipped stone projectile points, knife blades, and other tools were made. Furthermore stone was ground and polished to produce blades and ornaments. The general configuration resembles Archaic developments, but farming was added and very likely was the economic base. The excavators of the site, James A. Ford and Clarence H. Webb, felt that the people represented two different groups, a lower class from an Archaic background and a ruling class of Hopewellian origin.

Joseph R. Caldwell has proposed that we recognize a Gulf Tradition along the northern part of the Gulf of Mexico, with the Natchez of Mississippi and the Timucua of Florida as the best examples reported for early historic times. The tradition was derived from an Archaic base and received from the north Mississippian influences that were strong or weak, depending on the locality affected. The Gulf Tradition includes class-stratified societies with retainer sacrifice, elaborate burials, temple mounds and plazas, pottery effigy vessels, and painted clay vessels. Caldwell suggests that these characteristics had their origins in Mesoamerica and spread northward in a west-to-east direction. The rise of the later Mississippian Tradition is viewed as an integration of the Gulf Tradition with local cultures in the heart of the Southeast. The Mississippian Tradition was based on intensive maize cultivation in the rich bottomlands and gave rise to towns, temple mounds, extended burials, and elaborate ceramic forms. About A.D. 1300 the Southern Cult (Southern Death Cult) climaxed from a local base influenced by Mesoamerica. Elaborate grave goods made at this time included representations of the sun, death, and winged serpents. The late prehistoric cultural manifestations of this cult apparently were on a decline in the Southeast by the time the French arrived, but their essence still existed among the Natchez. What we see in the lower Mississippi River area are long-established traditions of a cultural complexity based on rather intensive farming. The Natchez and closely related peoples with similar cultural foci controlled both sides of the Mississippi River between the junctions of the Arkansas and the Red rivers at the time of historic contact.

History

The Natchez attacked the Spanish expedition under the original command of Hernando de Soto as it descended the Mississippi River in 1543. The next known contact was with the French explorer Sieur de La Salle in 1682. In an important study of the course of French and Natchez relationships, Andrew C. Albrecht labeled this as a first phase, one of visiting explorers.

The Natchez: Sophisticated Farmers of the Deep South

The Natchez were gracious hosts to the La Salle party. They provided the French with food and smoked the peace calumet with them, but these Indians were not overawed by the Europeans. La Salle was respectful toward them since he was well aware that they were the most powerful tribe in the region. Friendly relations were disrupted temporarily when two Frenchmen were killed in 1690, but in 1698 four missionaries sent from French Canada to the lower Mississippi remained briefly among the Natchez. In 1700 one baptized 185 children. In the same year Pierre de Iberville established friendly relations between the Natchez and the French who were penetrating from the lower Mississippi River. De Iberville attempted to wrest political control from the French in Canada to establish an independent colony. With the arrival of missionaries and fur traders from Canada a new phase of contact began, but neither the traders nor the Roman Catholic missionaries were very successful. As will be understood later, the religious system of the Natchez was so highly integrated with social and political life that the task of making Christians of these people was nearly impossible. In addition, the great distance between the lower Mississippi River and eastern Canada made these trading and mission ties tenuous. The French administration independent of Canada, which was established by de Iberville, became the most influential force in the lives of the Natchez. During the early 1700s English traders operating from the Carolinas were successful in winning the support of a leading Natchez called Bearded Chief, who apparently dominated the communities of White Apple, Hickory, and Grigras. The settlements of Grand Village, the home of the Great Sun who was the reigning ruler, and Flour were loyal to the French.

The third phase of Natchez relations emerged in 1713 with the establishment of a French trading post in their midst. Antoine Crozat was granted a monopoly on all the trade in Louisiana, with the stipulation that he was to bring slaves from Africa and settlers from France. The post built by Crozat possibly was at Grand Village, but it did not succeed. Intrigue by English traders and Bearded Chief apparently led to its being plundered in 1715. The French now found themselves in a tenuous position; the obvious solution was to subjugate the Natchez and establish military control over the area. The fourth phase, military control, began in 1716 when Jean de Bienville with a force of no more than fifty men tricked the Indians so that he was able to seize and kill those who had plundered the trading post and had killed some Frenchmen. The Natchez agreed to peace with the French and aided in the construction of the stockaded Fort Rosalie, which was built to the west of their villages and overlooked the Mississippi River. For the moment relations temporarily became stabilized, with the Natchez controlling their settlements and the small French garrison representing the outpost of an empire. In 1717 Crozat terminated his monopoly, and soon afterward the Western Company of John Law assumed the responsibility for trading and colonizing. It obtained the right to grant lands to private individuals and proceeded to do so. The company attempted to settle the country with a French landed nobility who would bring with them tenants, skilled craftsmen, and slaves. In 1718 the fifth phase began when concession holders began arriving, and two years later French immigrants were well established. The French farmers prepared the land for raising tobacco, and Indian-French relationships were quite congenial. In 1718 the colonist to whom we are most indebted for our knowledge of the Natchez settled in the area. He was Antoine S. Le Page du Pratz, a Dutchman by birth, who remained in Louisiana until 1734. The French were provided land and food by the Indians, who in turn were offered guns, powder, lead, intoxicants, and cloth; this was highly satisfactory to both parties. Then in 1723 at Fort Rosalie an old Natchez warrior was killed needlessly by a soldier, and his murderer went unpunished by the French commander of the fort. In retaliation the Natchez killed some French settlers. Peace was reestablished within a few days, but a course toward further hostilities had been set. After the peace the French attacked White Apple, demanding and receiving the head of a leader who had been hostile to them. The Natchez could not understand this deception by the French and subsequently avoided contacts with them.

At this crucial period in Natchez-French relations two deaths occurred among the Natchez that quite possibly led to temporary Indian disorganization. In 1725 the younger brother of the Great Sun, Tattooed Serpent, died, and three years later the Great Sun himself died. Thus in 1728 a young and inexperienced Great Sun was in power. In the next year, 1729, a new commander of the Fort Rosalie garrison decided quite arbitrarily that he required the land of White Apple for settlement. When he told the Natchez leader of the community to forfeit the village, the noble refused, and the commander became furious. The Natchez parleyed to decide what course of action should be taken. It was decided that because the French were becoming more numerous, were corrupting the Natchez youth, and were breaking their promises, the French should be destroyed. Thus began the sixth and final phase, the Natchez revolt. The Great Sun agreed, and the Natchez sought the aid of neighboring tribes. In spite of an attempt by the leaders to keep their decision from the women, one noblewoman, Tattooed Arm, the mother of the Great Sun, prodded her son into revealing the general plan. She warned the French, but the commander would not take this and other warnings seriously. Finally the Natchez fell upon the French and killed more than 200 persons who were at or near the fort. As an aside it is perhaps noteworthy that the Natchez warriors had such great contempt for the French commander that he was not killed until late in the massacre and then was beaten to death by a commoner with a wooden war club. The Yazoos, allies and neighbors of the Natchez to the north, killed the small number of French among them but not until after the massacre by the Natchez. Apparently Tattooed Arm, the woman who had warned the French, altered the time of the attack and made the Natchez uprising premature, which angered their allies. The Choctaw were to have aided the Natchez but could not do so because of the time change. They were angry too because the Natchez did not share the spoils with them, and so the Choctaw subsequently aided the French against the Natchez. In late January 1730 a French and Choctaw force, estimated between 700 and 1600, attacked the Natchez at two forts they had constructed. A larger French force arrived in mid-February and bombarded the Natchez with cannon fire. Before long, however, the French began to run low on ammunition, and their Choctaw allies talked of withdrawing. By mutual agreement the Natchez released the captives they still held, and the French withdrew to the Mississippi River. Then the Natchez with their loot slipped across the Mississippi River and escaped. They ascended the Red River to the Black River and built a fort at Sicily Island. In 1731 another French and Indian force was sent against the Natchez, and about 400, including the Great Sun, were forced to surrender. John R. Swanton, whose study of Natchez sources is monumental, stressed that these people were not destroyed by the two French campaigns against them; in fact, the French efforts were quite clumsy. What did destroy the Natchez was frequent skirmishing with other Indians and the illness and death caused by physical exposure in the swamps where they took refuge. Those who escaped or were not at the fort, some 180 warriors, eventually joined the Chickasaw, against whom the French turned for having received these refugees. Some of the Natchez did not remain with or join the Chickasaw after their defeat, but lived with the Creek. This group probably included the largest number of survivors. They came to occupy a town near the Coosa River in Alabama, and in 1764 they had about 150 warriors. In 1832 the Natchez and the Creek were displaced to Indian Territory as a result of the Federal removal policy. To complicate the matter further some of the Natchez who joined the Catawba after their wars with the French later left them and lived with the Cherokee. In 1907 Swanton located some Natchez near Braggs, Oklahoma, in the southwestern part of the Cherokee nation; five of the individuals he found still knew some of the language. In 1934 when Mary R. Haas worked among the Natchez living near Braggs, she found that only two Natchez speakers had survived.

Aboriginal Life

ORIGIN MYTH   The mythological beginnings of the Natchez offer special insight into the form of sociopolitical structure that they developed. According to tradition a man and his wife entered an already established community to the southwest of historic Natchez county. The newcomers were so bright in appearance that they seemed to have come from the sun. The man said he had noted that the people did not have effective means for governing themselves and that he had come from the sky in order to instruct them. He told the people about the Great Spirit and what they must do to please it. Among the rules of behavior were a series of prohibitions: do not kill except in one's own defense; do not have sexual intercourse with a woman not one's own; do not steal, nor lie, nor become intoxicated. Finally, he said that the people should give freely of what they had to those in need. After hearing these rules of conduct, the people agreed to their wisdom and asked the man to be their leader. He said he would do so only under certain conditions. Among these were that the people must obey him but no other and they must move to another country to which he would lead them; finally, he set forth the rules for selecting his successor. He said too that they should build a temple in which the leaders could communicate with the Great Spirit. In the temple would be an eternal fire that he would bring from the sun. The people agreed to these and other conditions, and the sacred fire was brought from the sun. This man then became the first Great Sun.

SETTLEMENTS   The main area of settlement was along the eastern bank of the Mississippi River near the present city of Natchez, but the Natchez also seem to have controlled adjacent land on the west bank of the river. During the French period the main settlement area was a rolling plain of black soil covered with grasses, hickory forests, cane thickets in the draws, and pine or hardwood forests nearby. Nine communities may have existed in the early historic period, but five usually are mentioned by later sources. Grand Village, the principal settlement and the one that may have been termed Naches, was the residence of the Great Sun, and the other villages were nearby. These included Grigras, a community of refugees among the Natchez; Hickory, sometimes termed Walnut; Flour, and White Apple, which has also apparently been called White Earth. It is by no means certain that there were five distinct villages; the designations simply may have been references to neighborhoods

Plate 14–1 The plan of a fort and torture methods. (From Le Page du Pratz, 1758, v. 2)

492

The Natchez: Sophisticated Farmers of the Deep South

around Grand Village. The only site identified with reasonable certainty is Grand Village, which has been partially excavated. It is difficult to reconstruct the configuration of a typical settlement, and the text to follow is a composite of reported characteristics.

In the center of Grand Village was an open plaza measuring 250 by 300 paces with a flat-topped mound at each end. On top of one mound was a temple, and on the other was the home of the Great Sun. The temple mound was about eight feet high, relatively steep on three sides, and sloped gently to form a ramp on the side toward the open plaza. The temple on top probably was about thirty feet long and somewhat narrower. This structure was built of thick logs ten feet in height and plastered on the outside with mud. The roof was ridged, and three large wooden figures of birds adorned the peak. Entered through a rectangular doorway, the temple was divided into two rooms. In the larger outer room was a perpetual fire, and on a nearby platform was a cane coffin containing the bones of the most recently deceased Great Sun. In the inner room were two special boards with unidentified items attached. The wooden box that contained the stone statue of the first Great Sun probably was kept here. Reportedly he turned himself into stone because he feared that his remains would be tainted if placed in the ground. The bones of other persons probably were stored in this room.

The home of the Great Sun was on an earthen mound some eight feet high, and the house itself was twenty-five feet wide and forty-five feet long. All other houses were at ground level, but the eight homes nearby were larger than the other houses. At the death of a Great Sun his house was burned, and the same mound probably was increased in size and used as a foundation for the home of his successor. The houses in general appear to have been square, rectangular, or, less often, round. Their straight walls were not less than fifteen feet high, and they had rectangular doorways but no windows. Hickory trees were embedded in the ground at the four corners; they were bent over at the tops and tied to form a dome. Along the sidewalls similar poles were embedded in the earth, bent, and tied to the primary dome branches. Poles forming the inner walls were tied in place, and the inner as well as outer walls were spread with a clay and moss plaster and covered with split cane mats. The roof was covered with a mixture of sod and grass and topped with cane mats. Houses were occupied for about twenty years. In the winter a fire was built for warmth, and the smoke filtered out the entrance. It appears that the houses may have been scattered widely. Somewhere near a village were raised platforms on which the bodies of deceased persons were placed. Covering a body was a woven mat smeared with mud; the head of the individual was left uncovered so that food offerings might be placed beside it. After the flesh had decayed, the bones were moved to the temple.

A number of household artifacts were reported among the Natchez, and others were excavated from a historic site. Within the cane-walled dwellings were household goods not usually reported north of Mexico. The most prominent furnishings were beds made from poles and cane with bearskins over the frame, a bison skin cover, and log pillow. When relaxing during the day, the people sat either on the beds or on short-legged wooden stools. In common usage were pottery vessels, including some with shallow bowls decorated with incised scrolls or meanders. Some large pots for bear oil held up to forty pints. A wide variety of cane basketry included sieves of various grades for sifting maize, containers for small items of adornment, and hampers for maize. Their knives were made from split sections of hard cane, and stone-bladed axes served for heavy wood work.

APPEARANCE AND CLOTHING   The Natchez were striking in appearance according to the French. They had a proud air and noble bearing that became the American Indian stereotype among Europeans. Du Pratz described them as five and a half feet or more in height, lean, sinewy, with rectangular features, coarse black hair, and black eyes. To him they were "naturals," but to other French observers they were "savages." As infants their foreheads were flattened by the straps that held them in cradleboards. Women wore short bangs in front and bound their long hair in a mulberry thread net with tassels at the ends. A woman's ears were pierced, and from each large hole hung an elongated shell ornament. Around her neck she might wear strings of small stones or perforated shell disks. Around a man's head was a band of short hair. A few hairs were allowed to grow long at the crown, and white feathers were worn in these scalp locks. Often the young Natchez dandies painted themselves red and wore bracelets made of steamed deer ribs bent in circles and then polished to a high luster. They might even carry fans of turkey tail feathers, and they wore necklaces of stone beads like those of the women. The people plucked their axillary hair, and the men plucked their whiskers. The tattoos of these people were impressive in their diversity and complexity. Youthful males and females were tattooed with lines on the face. Persons of the nobility and warriors were elaborately tattooed on the body, head, and limbs. The patterns were of serpents, suns, and other undescribed forms. Warriors who had slain an enemy were permitted to tattoo themselves as evidence of their kills, and for a brave deed a man had the right to tattoo a war club on his shoulder with a sign beneath symbolizing the people involved in his conquest. The tattooing method was to prick the skin until blood flowed freely and then rub charcoal, red pigment, or blue pigment into the openings. Warriors pierced their earlobes and expanded the holes until they would hold decorative plugs about an inch in diameter.

Males younger than twelve years and girls younger than nine went without clothing. An older girl's primary garment consisted of a short, fringed skirt made from the threads of mulberry inner bark. An adult woman wore a deerskin that was fitted about the waist and reached the knees. Some upper-class women wore cloaks of netting made on a loom from mulberry inner bark. The netting was covered with overlapping rows of bird feathers. In cold

The Natchez: Sophisticated Farmers of the Deep South

weather a woman wore a cape, probably of skins, that passed under her right armpit and fastened over the left shoulder. Ordinary men wore skin breechclouts that were belted and colored white; breechclouts of nobles were black. The leggings of men reached from their thighs to their ankles, but they wore skin moccasins only when traveling. In cold weather a man wore a poncho-like shirt of deerskin that was sleeved and reached below the knees. In severe weather a bison-skin robe with the hair intact and facing inward was worn. Deerskin garments were sewn with sinew after an awl was used to pierce the skins. Class distinctions in dress and adornment included elaborate tattoos for the nobility, feather-covered mantles of the noblewomen, and black breechclouts of the chiefs or nobles. Infants of the nobility wore two or three pearls about their necks. These ornaments were taken from the temple and were returned when a child was about ten years old.

SUBSISTENCE ACTIVITIES   Cultivated crops were the most important source of food; hunting and fishing clearly were secondary. A plot to be farmed was cleared of cane, which was dried and burned, and the ground was broken up with an L-shaped mattock of hickory. Maize was planted by making holes in the ground with a digging stick and dropping a few grains of corn in each hole. They probably cultivated their crops with a hoe made by hafting a bison scapula blade at right angles to a wooden handle. The principal cultigen was maize, and from two varieties some forty named dishes were prepared in the Natchez area. Maize was mixed with beans, smoke-dried, ground into meal, prepared as hominy, or parched. Ground meal was made into cakes that were roasted in ashes, baked, or boiled in water. Additional crops included pumpkins and beans, while two species of wild grass were cultivated along riverbanks. The Natchez made bread from walnuts and consumed chestnuts as well as acorns, but these were not important dietary items. There were no set mealtimes except for feasts. When an ordinary meal was served, the males, including those who were very young, ate before the females.

One of the primary reasons the French established plantations in the Natchez region was for the cultivation of tobacco. The Indians had raised tobacco in aboriginal times, and the people were described as avid smokers. They smoked pipes of unknown form and inhaled the smoke. Smoking was not merely a pleasant activity; pipes and smoking played an important part in events surrounding war and peace.

Hunting was most important in the fall, and deer sometimes were pursued by about 100 men at a time as a sport. Once a deer was located and surrounded, men forced the animal to run back and forth until it was exhausted. It was taken alive to the Great Sun or his representative, who killed it and divided the meat among the leaders of the hunt. In ordinary hunting a man wore a deer disguise when animals were cautious, and the deer's call was imitated to attract an animal closer. Hunters used self bows of locust wood strung with plant fiber or twisted sinew. Arrows of cane or wood had feather vanes and heads made from splinters of bone, garfish scales, stone, or a fire-hardened shaft tip. Cane-shafted spears were tipped with flint points and used when hunting large game such as bear, bison, or deer. Bison were taken in winter on grasslands away from the river. They were approached by wearing a disguise or else stalked against the wind. When a kill was made near a settlement, the hunter returned with the choice parts and sent his wife to retrieve the remainder of the animal. Meat was either cooked or smoke-dried for future use. Bear meat was eaten only if lean, but bears were killed when they were fat to obtain the oil. These animals were smoked out of their holes in trees, and if a cub was found, it was sometimes taken alive to the village and tamed. The only domestic animal of the Natchez was the dog. It was used to tree turkeys so that they could be killed with arrows. Fishing was a less important means of obtaining food than either farming or hunting. Among the fishing devices were gill nets made from organic fibers and fish arrows that had pointed bone tips and wooden floats attached by a cord to the shaft. Hooks likewise were used, and the species most often taken were suckers and catfish.

For water transportation both rafts and canoes were reported. Rafts were used to carry relatively light loads and were made from bundles of cane lashed together. For transporting heavy loads large canoes were made from hollowed-out cypress or poplar logs. The interior of the log was removed by controlled burning, followed by chipping away the charred wood. These dugout canoes were some forty feet in length, had three-foot beams, and could carry up to twelve tons.

SOCIAL DIMENSIONS   Social life was structured primarily around the people's relationship to the Great Sun. This leader held absolute control over his subjects and was served by the tribe as a whole but especially by personal retainers and slaves. He was spoken to at a distance of four steps; he was thanked and bowed to no matter what he said, and when leaving his presence a person walked backward. He was saluted whenever seen by ordinary persons, and he could have a person killed by saying to a retainer, "Go and rid me of that dog." The administrative offices delegated by the Great Sun included two war chiefs, two leading priests at the temple, two men who dealt with the external affairs of war and peace, one in charge of public works, and four who arranged public feasts. The decisions of the Great Sun were tempered by the amount of influence brought to bear upon him by near relatives, particularly his brother and mother. He also consulted a council of elders, the leaders of the various villages, and outstanding old warriors.

More printer's ink has been spilled over the Natchez social system than over that of any other people. Studies of their marriage and descent patterns suggested that it was unique and difficult, if not impossible, to explain in terms of existing sources. A thoughtful reevaluation of the original sources by Carol Mason appears to have resolved what sometimes has been termed the Natchez "riddle" or "paradox," and conclusions similar to Mason's were

The Natchez: Sophisticated Farmers of the Deep South

Plate 14–2 The Great Sun being carried on a litter. (From Le Page du Pratz, 1758, v. 2)

reached by Elisabeth Tooker. Since the previous debate now seems to have had a spurious basis, no purpose is served by presenting it. As Mason reconstructed the system, the Great Sun was at the apex of the social hierarchy, and nearly as important were his siblings, his mother, and other near relatives through females (matrilineage) who, like himself, were members of the Sun matrilineage. All such persons were required to marry persons from other lineages (matrilineage exogamy). Children of a Sun man belonged to their mother's lineage because of the matrilineal descent system, but since they were indirect issue of the Sun lineage, they were accorded the title of "noble"; they were "honored persons" if their relationship was more distant. The titles of noble and honored person were ascribed for these persons, but they also could be achieved by commoners. An ordinary person could become titled by performing heroic deeds in warfare or by sacrificing his infant at the death of a Sun. Summarily, the Sun matrilineage was the ranking social group and was exogamous.

POLITICAL LIFE AND WARFARE   From early French attitudes toward the Natchez, it is apparent that they were considered successful warriors under able leaders. Although the Great Sun headed the nation, the Great War Chief was appointed by him. At one period this position was held by Tattooed Serpent, the brother of the Great Sun and a very powerful individual in his own right. There were lesser war chiefs, probably leaders of different villages, and warriors of three grades: apprentice, ordinary, and true warriors. Most, if not all, men belonged to one of these three categories or were numbered among the old warriors. When hostilities were contemplated, a pole was raised at the entrance of the house where a decisive meeting was to be held. Attached to the pole was the war calumet, a pipe adorned with red feathers, tufted and tasseled in black, with the black skin from the neck of a buzzard surrounding the pipe itself. The meeting was attended by old warriors, the Great War Chief, lesser war chiefs, and the Great Sun. The grievance against the potential enemy was presented vividly by the Great War Chief. The rationale for aggressive action was real or fabricated; it might be that another people had hunted on Natchez lands, for example. The offense was discussed, but the opinions of the old warriors were decisive. A delegation of warriors led by an old warrior went to the offenders carrying a peace calumet but without gifts so that they could not be considered appeasers. Arriving under these circumstances, they generally were received well and were sent home with gifts as an admission of the wrong done to them. Open conflict seldom erupted if this approach to an offense was taken.

When an attack was anticipated, they usually decided in council to defend themselves rather than appease the aggressors. They warned outlying families to join the main group and posted guards to watch the approaches to their settlements. Another defensive move was to build palisaded fortifications. Forts were rather complex structures built around a tall tree that served as a watchtower. The trunks of trees were stripped of branches and were set in the ground to reach a height of about ten feet. The palisades were arranged in a roughly circular form with an overlap at the ends. Inside were structures to protect the women and children from arrows. The entrance was protected by towers, and in the passage to the outside were placed brambles and thorns. When an attack was imminent, emissaries carrying a peace calumet were sent to enlist the aid of friendly peoples. In the meantime the Great War Chief cited in council the reasons for defending themselves. He sought the support of older warriors by reminding them of their honor and pointing out the vengeance they could obtain, and for youths there was the hope of glory.

If it was decided to fight another people, the warriors hunted and returned with their kills to the home of the Great War Chief. For the three-day celebration that followed the warriors painted their bodies different colors and wore only breechclouts held in place by belts decorated with rattles. A war club was stuck in a man's belt, and he carried a round bison skin shield in one hand and his bow in the other. At a clearing a pole that represented the enemy was erected; it was carved to look like a man, painted red, and had a war calumet attached to it. At the base of the pole was placed a large dog roasted for the occasion, and different foods were nearby. One dish contained coarse cornmeal cooked in fat; the coarseness of the meal was a reminder that warriors did not require dainty foods. They also were served deer meat to make them swift as a deer. Before the meal the oldest warrior, who was no longer active, recounted his deeds of bravery and instructed the party how to begin a battle and to fight. The old man then lit the war calumet, and the Great War Chief smoked it first. The others smoked in rank order, and the old warrior drew on the pipe last before returning it to the pole. The Great War Chief ate a piece of dog meat, and the others followed in succession. By partaking of the dog a warrior demonstrated his willingness to participate in the pending hostil-

The Natchez: Sophisticated Farmers of the Deep South

ities. Later the war drink, a powerful emetic, was brought forth, and each person who drank it vomited violently. The retching could be heard at a great distance according to one observer. Each man ran up to the war pole, uttered a death cry as he struck it, and told of his past deeds of valor. After seasoned warriors had recounted their achievements, each apprentice warrior told what he hoped to accomplish, and then a war dance was performed. During the three days of ceremony, dances were held before the temple, along with recitations of personal accomplishments and the singing of death songs. The women prepared food for the men to take on their expedition, and old men refurbished war clubs and incised graphic symbols on a bark tablet. A symbol of the sun, representing the Natchez, was set above the figure of a naked man with a war club. An arrow was shown as though about to strike a fleeing woman, near whom was the sign of the enemy nation. Another set of symbols recorded the forthcoming month and the day when an attack would take place in force if this was included in the planning.

A raiding party of 20 to 300 warriors traveled only at night as they neared an enemy and sent scouts to reconnoiter. The party's long pole with fetishes attached was leaned toward the enemy each time the warriors camped. If any sign was interpreted as an ill omen for the venture, the men returned to their villages in spite of their elaborate preparations. Likewise when raiding parties encountered each other unexpectedly they withdrew. An attack was made at daybreak, and the persons to be killed were dispatched as quickly as possible. Women and children were taken alive, as was at least one man if at all possible. The raiders withdrew as quietly as they had arrived, taking their prisoners and leaving behind the inscribed bark, two red-painted arrows crossed and stuck in the ground, and the scalped dead. If the raid had been anticipated and the enemy had prepared themselves in a palisaded fortification, the Natchez searched for hunting parties to kill. If one of the raiders was killed, his comrades attempted to scalp him, to prevent the enemy from obtaining a Natchez scalp; on their return the Great War Chief would compensate the dead man's family for its loss. The party returned home in honor if they had captured a living enemy man.

Back in their own village they planted two poles in the ground if a male captive had been taken; on them a crosspiece was lashed near the ground and another somewhat higher than a man's head. The captive was stunned with a blow at the base of the skull and was scalped by his captor. The victim's naked body was tied in spread-eagle fashion on the pole frame. The young persons in the assembled throng gathered canes and lighted them; the first flaming cane was applied to the captive by his captor. The torturer was free to apply the cane anywhere he chose, and it was most likely to be on the arm with which the victim had best defended himself. The victim was then burned by the others as he sang his song of death. Some sacrificial victims were reported to have sung for seventy-two hours without pause before dying. However not all captive males were dealt with in this manner; if a young woman whose husband had been killed claimed the captive, he was given to her as a husband. Captive women and children had their hair cut short and became the servants of their captors.

Warriors who had distinguished themselves were given new names by the Great War Chief. These denoted particular levels of achievement in warfare. For example, the name Great Man Slayer could be claimed by a warrior after he had taken twenty scalps or ten prisoners. A warrior also might tattoo his body to commemorate an achievement or might be elevated in social class.

RELIGIOUS SYSTEM   The Natchez religious system was a formalized network of beliefs, ceremonies, and dogma maintained by specialists who devoted all their time to supernatural matters. These persons, who were priests in a generic sense, served as guardians of the major temple. One of these men explained Natchez religion to du Pratz. He recorded that they believed in an all-powerful Great Spirit who created all things good and was surrounded by lesser spirits that did his bidding. A particularly malignant spirit led the spirits of evil, but because he was tied up forever by the Great Spirit, he could do no great harm. The Great Spirit molded the first man from clay, and the figure grew to the proportions of a normal man. Woman probably was created in the same manner, but since man was created first, he was stronger and more courageous. The Great Spirit apparently sent the first Great Sun among the people to establish the line of Suns. Of the Great Sun's eldest daughter's children, the eldest son became the next ruling Great Sun, while her eldest daughter became the mother of the next Great Sun. Thus, the spiritual leadership passed along a matrilineage to the oldest son.

The reigning Great Sun, the highest authority on earth, combined the qualities of a god and a king. His power and authority over things religious were paramount, and his decisions were very important in secular matters. In this theocratic state, all religious, social, and political control was, in theory, in the hands of this individual. The Great Sun was surrounded by warriors and retainers wherever he went. When he traveled about, he was carried on a litter by eight warriors; in his dwelling he sat on a small wooden throne. The Great Sun was distinguished in his dress from others; for example, his normal headdress was a net covered with black feathers and bordered in red decorated with white seeds; hanging from the top of the headdress were long white feathers in front and shorter ones behind. Lesser Suns appear to have worn similar headpieces.

The core of religious life was a sacred temple fire tended by eight elders; two of them cared for the fire continually and were killed if they permitted the fire to go out. When an ordinary person walked in front of a temple, he put down any load that he might be carrying and extended his arms toward the temple as he wailed loudly. The same type of behavior was followed when he passed before the Great Sun. The great Sun visited the temple daily to make certain that the fire still burned, and each morning at sunrise he faced the east,

The Natchez: Sophisticated Farmers of the Deep South

bowed to the ground, and wailed three times. With a special calumet he blew smoke first toward the rising sun and then in each of the other cardinal directions. Thus, the Great Sun venerated the sun and was in turn venerated by all other persons in the tribe. What we see is a direct line of continuity into the past functionally linked to the Great Spirit, the Great Suns, and an eternal fire.

RELIGION: CEREMONIES   The heads of families took their first harvest of any food to the temple; the guardians received it and conveyed it to the Great Sun, who could distribute it as he chose. Seeds to be sown were blessed at the temple before they were planted. The thirteen months of the calendar were named for the most important food of the prior month, and the beginning of each month was celebrated by a feast where either the Great Sun or a lesser Sun presided. The feast of the first month, corresponding roughly to March, was called Deer, and marked the beginning of a new year. Each year during the month of Deer a celebration was held to commemorate the liberation of a former Great Sun who had been captured by enemies. After ceremonies and ritual acts gifts were presented to the Great Sun as he sat on his throne.

The seventh or Great Corn month was ushered in by the most important yearly ceremony, one that celebrated the first harvest of maize. The corn used in the ceremony was from virgin ground and had been sown and tended by warriors. When the crop was harvested and stored in a granary of cane, the Great Sun was notified. All the villages assembled at the cache to receive the Great Sun, who arrived on his litter with a canopy of flowers. After a fire was

Plate 14–3 A dance scene. (From Le Page du Pratz, 1947)

kindled by rubbing sticks together, maize was presented to the female Suns and then to all other women. The maize was cooked and eaten during a feast that was followed by speeches and dancing throughout the night to the accompaniment of a drum and gourd rattles. When dancing the women moved in one direction and the men in the opposite direction, and as a person tired he or she was replaced by someone from the audience. The next day a ball game was held. The warriors were divided into two teams, one led by the Great Sun and the other by the Great War Chief. In the hair of the Great Sun's men were white feathers, and the other team wore red feathers. The object of the game was to force a ball to one end of the plaza. The winning team was presented with gifts by the captain of the losing team, and the winners were permitted to wear their feather headdresses until the game was played again. After the ball game, a war dance was performed by the warriors. The festivities were not over until all of the harvested maize had been consumed. The celebrations just described were at the capital settlement, but similar festivities were led by local Suns at other settlements.

Religion embraced more than the temple cult, for there were a host of spirits that probably were lesser agents of the Great Spirit. Power existed in the honey locust tree, and under one such tree near the temple the wood was kept for the sacred fire. Any tree struck by lightning was burned completely by the Indians, and snakes were regarded with terror. The Great Sun and people of all classes fasted to bring rain. When commoners fasted on certain days, they smeared black paint on their faces and did not eat until the sun had set.

RELIGION: SHAMANS   The position of shamans is obscure, but they appear to have functioned outside the sun-centered theocracy. An individual aspiring to become a shaman went into isolation for nine days and consumed nothing but water until a spirit appeared. During this time he reportedly learned certain skills such as how to change the weather or cure illness. Spirit aids were kept in a small basket and included such tangible objects as owl heads, animal teeth, small stones, and hair from a deer. A shaman had very real obligations to those he served. Were a patient to die the shaman might be killed, but success brought material gain. Among the techniques for curing and weather changes were fasting, smoking, singing, and dancing. A shaman could, after rubbing himself with a particular form of root, handle poisonous snakes without fear. One cure included making an incision at the locus of an illness and sucking blood from the wound. When the shaman spit the blood into a container, not only blood was seen but also a foreign object such as a piece of wood, straw, or leather; the illness was attributed to this item.

LIFE CYCLE   Soon after a baby was born, it was tied to a cradleboard, and strips of deerskin were bound over its forehead to flatten it. The cradleboard was placed in a bed beside the baby's mother. Infants were smeared

The Natchez: Sophisticated Farmers of the Deep South

with bear oil to keep flies from biting them and to make them supple. When nearly a year old an infant was encouraged to walk, but it was nursed until it weaned itself or until the mother again became pregnant. As children grew they came under the influence of an elder male in their extended family; this man counselled all the nuclear families within his group. A child termed this man "father," but he might be a great-grandfather or even a great-great-grand-father. Children were discouraged from fighting with the threat that they would be sent away from the Natchez. Boys were encouraged to exercise and gradually acquire adult skills from about the age of twelve, and the sexual division of labor was instilled at this time. Hunting, fishing, fighting, some farming, and the manufacturing of most artifacts were male activities. Carry-ing home game or fish, most of the farming, preparing food, and manufac-turing clothing, baskets, or pottery were female responsibilities, along with the raising of children.

Following puberty youths were free to have sexual intercourse, and girls apparently did not bestow sexual favors without material gain. A potential husband was proud of the amount of property his bride-to-be might ac-cumulate in this manner. Males did not marry until they were about twenty-five, but a girl appears to have been somewhat younger. Once the couple decided to marry, the man went before the heads of their respective families to be questioned. If no close blood ties existed and if the pair loved each other, the elders sanctioned the marriage. On the wedding day the girl was led by the elder of her family, and followed by the remainder of her family, to the home of the man. Here they were greeted and invited into the house where, after a pause, the elders of both families asked the couple whether they loved each other and were willing to be man and wife. The ideals of domestic har-mony were set forth, there was an exchange of vows by the couple, and a gift was made to the bride's father. The bride's mother handed her a laurel branch to hold in one hand and an ear of corn to hold in the other hand. She gave the corn to her husband, and he said, "I am your husband," to which she an-swered, "I am your wife." Finally the husband told his wife, "There is our bed, keep it tight," which was an injunction against committing adultery. After a special meal the couple and their guests danced from early evening through the night. In this description of a marriage by du Pratz it is not speci-fied whether or not these customs were observed by everyone. The need for such clarification is evident since other descriptions of Natchez marriages dif-fer from this form.

Plural marriages were known, with sororal polygyny being the most com-mon form, although nonsororal polygyny was also practiced. Plural marriages were more common among the nobility than among commoners. A noble with many wives retained only one or two in his house; the others lived at their natal homes where they were visited by him. In the polygynous households the wife who bore the first offspring supervised the other wives. Divorce was ex-tremely rare for most persons, but an upper-class woman married to a common man was free to take other husbands. Furthermore such a woman could have her husband put to death if he committed adultery. This is an unusual form of the double standard of morality. Berdaches (transvestites) were reported, but their position in the society is not clear.

The writings of du Pratz and a few others convey the essence of the ideals that guided adult life. Tribal unity did not prevail during the brief historical era, and there is good evidence of a power struggle among leading upper-class persons that influenced intervillage affairs. Some communities were friendly to the French while others were hostile, suggesting that the Great Sun could not, or did not, effectively control all the members of his lineage. Yet is appears that village-wide harmony existed and the upper class did not abuse its power. The people in general were honorable in their dealings with each other and with the French. It will be recalled that in the myth about the acceptance of the first Great Sun certain specific rules of behavior were stated; they were maintained insofar as possible by the priests and the upper class in general.

One of the most vivid descriptions by du Pratz was of the funeral for the Great War Chief, Tattooed Serpent, who was the brother of the Great Sun and nearly as powerful. When he died everyone was greatly distressed because each brother had vowed to kill himself at the death of the other. The temple guardians urged du Pratz, who was influential among the Natchez and a friend of the Great Sun, to avert the leader's potential suicide. Du Pratz and other whites went to the home of the Great Sun and talked with him. The Great Sun was grieved deeply over the death but was successfully restrained from committing suicide.

At the house of Tattooed Serpent his corpse lay on the bed he had occupied while alive. His face was painted red, and he was clothed in his finest garments, including a feather headdress. Beside the bed were his weapons and the peace calumets he had received during his life. From a pole stuck into the ground hung forty-six linked sections of red-painted cane representing the number of enemies he had killed. Gathered around the body were his "chancellor," physician, chief domestic, pipe bearer, two wives, some old women, and a volunteer from among the noblewomen, all of whom were to be killed as a part of the funeral ceremony. The next day included a "Dance of Death" and two rehearsals for the deaths of persons to be killed. At about this time the commoner parents of a child strangled their offspring out of respect for Tattooed Serpent; by doing so they were raised to noble standing and would not be killed when the Great Sun died. Some warriors also had apprehended a common man who had been married to a Sun woman but had fled at her death to avoid being killed. His capture once again slated him for death, but three old women related to him offered themselves to be killed in his place. The man in turn was elevated to the upper class by the women's sacrifice.

On the day of the funeral the "master of ceremonies" was painted red above the waist and wore a garment about his waist with a red and white feather fringe. On his head was a crown of red feathers, and he carried a red

The Natchez: Sophisticated Farmers of the Deep South

staff with black feathers hanging from the upper part and a crosspiece near the top. When this impressively arrayed individual approached the house of the deceased, he was greeted with "hoo" and by wailing indicating death. A procession formed behind the master of ceremonies; he was followed by the oldest warrior carrying the staff from which hung the red cane rings and a war pipe that reflected the honor of the dead man. These men were in turn followed by six temple guardians who carried the body on a litter; then came those who were to be killed, each accompanied by eight relatives who served as executioners. Each of these relatives was subsequently freed from the probability of being killed at the death of the Great Sun and seemingly was raised to the class of noble. The procession circled the house of the deceased three times, and then the litter bearers walked in intersecting circles to the temple. The dead child was thrown repeatedly in the path of the bearers and retrieved by its parents. After the body of Tattooed Serpent was placed in the temple, the sacrificial victims, their hair covered with red paint, were drugged with tobacco and strangled. Within the temple the two wives of Tattooed Serpent and two men were buried in the grave with him. The other victims were buried elsewhere, and the funeral ended by burning the home of Tattooed Serpent.

   With a great man's death pomp, pageantry, and human sacrifice unrolled;

Mort et Convoy du Serpent piqué

Temple.

Plate 14–4 The burial of Tattooed Serpent, the brother of the Great Sun. (From Le Page du Pratz, 1947)

the death of a Sun was a tragic highlight to life. The number of persons killed at the funeral of Tattooed Serpent unquestionably was fewer than would have been considered fitting before the French arrived. For other people to die was of lesser moment, and yet any death was surrounded with further deaths. When an outstanding female Sun died, her husband, a commoner, was strangled by their eldest son. Then the eldest surviving daughter ordered twelve small children killed and placed around the bodies of the deceased couple. In the plaza fourteen platforms were erected, and on each was a man who was to die during the funeral. These men danced before the house of the deceased every fifteen minutes and then returned to their platforms. It was said that after four days the "March of the Bodies" ritual took place. The dead children previously had been placed outside the dead woman's home, and with them were the live victims. The woman was carried out on a litter, and the small bodies were dropped repeatedly before the procession so that by the time the litter reached the temple the corpses of the children were in pieces. After the woman's body was inside the temple, the fourteen victims were strangled, but not before they had received water and wads of tobacco that drugged them into unconsciousness. The living mourned for an important deceased person by weeping for four days. In general, mourners cut their hair but did not paint their faces, and they avoided public gatherings. The temporary grave was on a raised platform. A shelter of branches formed a vault over the body, and there was an opening at the end near the head where food was placed. The mourners grieved at the grave each day at dawn and at sunset for a month. After the flesh had decayed, the bones were placed in a basket in a temple.

The custom of executing persons at the death of the Suns and other upper-class individuals may seem barbaric and senseless, but it had very real advantages to the individuals involved. In their belief system one's spirit under such circumstances would accompany the deceased upper-class person to the world of the dead and serve him or her there in perennial happiness. The same future awaited all others who observed the rules of the society during their lifetime. It was thought that a person who had broken the rules of the people would go to a place covered with water; naked, he would be bitten by mosquitoes and have only undesirable foods to eat.

AN ORATION   Only a few short years following the dramatic burial ceremonies for Tattooed Serpent, the Natchez nearly were extinct. It seems fitting to record a speech that Tattooed Serpent made to du Pratz (1774, 40–41) after a war with the French and shortly before the Natchez were destroyed.

> *I did not approve, as you know, the war our people made*
> *upon the French to avenge the death of their relation, seeing I*
> *made them carry the pipe of peace to the French. This you well*
> *know, as you first smoked in the pipe yourself. Have the French*

The Natchez: Sophisticated Farmers of the Deep South

two hearts, a good one to-day, and to-morrow a bad one? As for my brother and me, we have but one heart and one word. Tell me then, if thou art, as thou sayest, my true friend, what thou thinkest of all this, and shut thy mouth to everything else. We know not what to think of the French, who, after having begun the war, granted a peace, and offered it of themselves; and then at the time we were quiet, believing ourselves to be at peace, people come to kill us, without saying a word.

Why . . . did the French come into our country? We did not go to seek them: they asked for land of us, because their country was too little for all the men that were in it. We told them they might take land where they pleased, there was enough for them and for us; that it was good the same sun should enlighten us both, and that we would walk as friends in the same path; and that we would give them of our provisions, assist them to build, and to labour in their fields. We have done so; is not this true? What occasion then had we for Frenchmen? Before they came, did we not live better than we do, seeing we deprive ourselves of a part of our corn, our game, and fish, to give a part to them? In what respect, then, had we occasion for them? Was it for their guns? The bows and arrows which we used, were sufficient to make us live well. Was it for their white, blue, and red blankets? We can do well enough with buffalo skins which are warmer; our women wrought feather-blankets for the winter, and mulberry-mantles for the summer; which indeed were not so beautiful; but our women were more laborious and less vain than they are now. In fine, before the arrival of the French, we lived like men who can be satisfied with what they have; whereas at this day we are like slaves, who are not suffered to do as they please.

Comparisons

The scope of available information about the Natchez makes most comparisons difficult except in terms of social and political life. Natchez political structure was far more developed than that reported for the other peoples. One might seek to identify its most salient structural characteristics and compare these with the historic "priest state" of the Cherokee and with the League of the Iroquois. Special attention should be given to ascribed as opposed to achieved status differences among leaders, contrasts in clothing and adornments between ordinary people and their leaders, the recruitment of leaders, their extraordinary rights and duties, and their number of retainers. Broader comparisons with the political networks of peoples presented throughout the book are invited. Note how unorganized, largely individualistic responses to external stress among the Chipewyan give way to more unified but still largely unstructured responses by the Kuskokwim Eskimos compared with the far more developed organization of the Fox, and so on.

Natchez social structure placed inordinate stress on birth order and sex within a leading lineage. How does this compare with the Iroquois and Hopi? What key traits are shared by all, and how may we explain the similarities and differences?

Additional Readings

The most worthwhile source is by Le Page du Pratz; this was the primary source for the preceding descriptions. For additional details and a comparative view of the Natchez and other Indians in the Southeast the best source is the 1946 publication by John R. Swanton.

References

Albrecht, Andrew C. "The Location of the Historic Natchez Villages," *Journal of Mississippi History*, v. 6, 67–88. 1944.

Albrecht, Andrew C. "Indian-French Relations at Natchez," *American Anthropologist*, v. 48, 321–354. 1946.

Albrecht, Andrew C. "Ethical Precepts among the Natchez Indians," *Louisiana Historical Quarterly*, v. 31, 569–597. 1948.

Caldwell, Joseph R. *Trend and Tradition in the Prehistory of the Eastern United States*. American Anthropological Association, Memoir 88. 1958.

Ford, James A., and Clarence H. Webb. *Poverty Point, A Late Archaic Site in Louisiana*. Anthropological Papers of the American Museum of Natural History, v. 46, pt. 1. 1956.

Griffin, James B., ed. *Archaeology of Eastern United States*. Chicago. 1952.

Haag, William G. "The Archaic of the Lower Mississippi Valley," *American Antiquity*, v. 26, 317–323. 1961.

Mason, Carol. "Natchez Class Structure," *Ethnohistory*, v. 2, 120–133. 1964.

*Le Page du Pratz, Antoine S. *The History of Louisiana*. Paris. 1758: London. 1774 (reprinted at New Orleans in 1947). Between the years 1718 and 1734 the author lived most of the time near the Natchez, where he owned a plantation. The observations by du Pratz concerning these Indians are

The Natchez: Sophisticated Farmers of the Deep South

the most systematic of all the firsthand accounts. The book is very enjoyable to read and is at the same time highly informative.

Quimby, George I., Jr. "The Natchezan Culture Type," *American Antiquity,* v. 7, 255–275. 1942.

Swanton, John R. *Indian Tribes of Lower Mississippi Valley and Adjacent Coast of the Gulf of Mexico.* Bureau of American Ethnology, Bulletin 43. 1911.

Swanton, John R. *Social Organization and Social Usages of the Indians of the Creek Confederacy.* Bureau of American Ethnology, Annual Report 42. 1928.

*Swanton, John R. *The Indians of the Southeastern United States.* Bureau of American Ethnology, Bulletin 137. 1946. Virtually all that is known about Natchez ethnography is in this volume. It is a monumental regional culture history and a key secondary source on the Natchez.

Swanton, John R. *The Indian Tribes of North America.* Bureau of American Ethnology, Bulletin 145. 1953.

Tooker, Elisabeth. "Natchez Social Organization: Fact or Anthropological Fancy?" *Ethnohistory,* v. 10, 358–372. 1963.

Red Man–White Man

15

Soon after the discovery of the New World, a great debate raged in Spain about the humanness of Indians. Regardless of the manner in which the conquistadores were received, they argued that Indians were irrational, heretical, and tainted with mortal sin. This attitude served to justify the inhumane treatment of Indians and the seizure of their land or property. Francisco Vitoria, a professor at Salamanca and the founder of international law, argued against this thesis. He noted that in Europe even heretics were privileged to own property and could not be punished for sins without a trial. Implicit in Vitoria's argument was the acceptance of Indians as human beings. When the exploiters of Indians maintained that the Pope of the Roman Catholic Church had granted title to all newly discovered lands to the kings of Spain and Portugal, Vitoria countered that the Pope had no power over the aborigines and their land, and that title by discovery could apply only to unoccupied lands. In a papal bull of 1537 Pope Paul III proclaimed "that the Indians are truly men and that they are not only capable of understanding the Catholic faith, but according to our information, they desire exceedingly to receive it" (Cohen, 1960, 290). Considering Indians as human beings gave the church new millions of immortal souls to be saved. Regardless of the Pope's motives, however, the acknowledgment of Indian humanness and Indian ownership of land served as a guide for colonial governments in all of the Americas. In the

511

section to follow most of the information has been drawn from the scholarly studies of Roy H. Pearce (1965), Lewis O. Saum (1965), and Edward H. Spicer (1969).

White Attitudes and Policies

Early European maritime explorers found the Indians fascinating because they illustrated what people could be like when stripped of Christian and civilized behavior. They were considered savages who lived more like animals than men; although human in form, they were barely human in their customs. A word often used to describe them was "beasts," and while their land might be attractive, many settlers felt that the Indians were its blight. A brief review of early contacts in diverse areas conveys an overview of Indian-white relations that leads to a greater understanding of the subsequent course of history.

The Virginia charter of 1606 provided for bringing God to the savages since adopting Christian ways was equated with being civilized. Land was purchased from the Indians, and settlers were certain that they could live in harmony with these infidels who soon would be Christianized. Before many years had passed about fifty missionaries were sent to the colony to work with Indian children because it was felt that they would learn more readily than adults. The colonists were convinced that their efforts were succeeding since there were no serious hostilities. Actually the most powerful Indian leader, Powhatan, was waiting and hoping that the colony would fail, but the English grew more firmly entrenched and confident with each year. In 1622 Powhatan's successor finally decided he had waited long enough, and the colonists were attacked. Nearly 350 whites were killed, and the only reason the colony was not destroyed completely was that a Christian Indian had warned the English at the last moment. To the colonists the massacre was clear evidence of inborn Indian treachery, and the settlers now felt justified in destroying these savages whom they no longer wanted to understand. The Indians in Virginia were viewed as an impediment to the march of civilization, and within the next fifty years they were systematically destroyed or displaced.

The "Indian experience" of no two colonies was the same because of the settlers' backgrounds and the nature of the Indians encountered. The Anglicans and Roman Catholics who established Maryland in 1634 protected the local Indians against the far more powerful tribes living nearby. Here the Indian lands always were obtained by purchase, the aboriginal population was well treated, and Jesuit missionaries worked to Christianize them. It might be anticipated that the Quaker settlers of Pennsylvania would be the most successful in making Indians into Christians given their commitment to nonviolence and humanistic tolerance of others. The Quakers stressed the common denominators that unite all men and did not seek to identify differences between themselves and Indians. They offered Indians love and peace, but they

Plate 15–1 This 1493 woodcut accompanied the Italian printing of the first letter by Christopher Columbus about his New World discoveries. In the background is one of the earliest representations of aboriginal Americans. (From Winsor, 1889, v. 2)

won few converts. To the Indian, religion meant comparatively little without ritual and ceremony, and the Quaker approach to God was largely devoid of both. The Quakers remained neutral when non-Quakers in and beyond Pennsylvania intrigued and fought with Indians in their midst and at their frontiers.

The Pilgrims and Puritans of New England believed that God would guide their affairs with Indians, who were to them descendants of Noah through the Tartars. They had entered the New World from Asia as fallen people in the grip of Satan. When many Indians died in a "wonderful plague" of smallpox, it was God's way of furthering the goals of the settlers. The Puritans knew that Indian lands were intended for Christian English use, and they were purchased only to keep peace. These colonists did not hesitate to raid and war against Indians or to foster dissension for Puritan purposes. Yet it was recognized that the savages should be civilized. Missionaries like John Eliot concerned themselves with Indians, but the number of conversions was few and successes transient. As savages they stood in opposition to civilized persons, and while they might manifest natural virtues, they seldom were noble. Efforts by these colonists to integrate Indians into transported Western European culture failed for obvious reasons.

The Spanish who first entered the Southwest in 1540 expected to find barbarians or savages and felt a strong obligation to civilize them. Church and civil authorities alike accepted this as their primary goal after it was realized that the area was not going to yield great riches. The gross patterning of Spanish life was to be introduced to Indians, but not as an attempt to replace Indian customs since they were thought to be without real meaning. The Spanish would decide what was best for the Indians, and the advance agents of their culture usually were Roman Catholic missionaries. They built churches and quarters near established pueblos, instructed certain individuals in Catholic doctrines, and soon recruited others as catechists and helpers. The missionaries usually were responsible for introducing the structure of civil government, new crops, and novel crafts; their goal was to create self-sufficient Roman Catholic communities. The missionaries in New Mexico usually were accompanied by soldiers who reinforced Spanish authority; in general, the priests here treated Indian transgressions far more harshly than did their counterparts farther south. Soon the Eastern Pueblos were paying tribute to the king of Spain, a good indication of the program's effectiveness.

Apart from the mission environment, Spanish frontiersmen impinged on the Indians of New Mexico through the policy of giving land grants to soldiers for services rendered. The great encomienda grants in New Mexico did not include any of the large pueblos, but the people who lived in the small communities in the midst of such grants were forced to work these lands for the Spanish, usually with little or no compensation. Before long Spanish employees of encomenderos married Indians and came to acquire their lands. Abuses in the encomienda system engendered a great deal of hostility in some pueblos and eventually led to its abandonment. Smaller land allotments or "village" grants were made for unoccupied lands, or at times for land near an Indian settlement, and once again intermarriage began to bind the settlers and Indians into a single social matrix. Spanish towns, with Santa Fe as the prime example, formed another culture contact setting, but since Indians were drawn to them only for services, their impact was relatively minor.

When the Mexican War for Independence ended in 1821, Indians in the Southwest were granted the full rights of Mexican citizens. All persons born in Mexico became citizens, irrespective of their culture or race, and efforts were made to incorporate Indians into national life. This goal was not achieved in New Mexico, however. Americans began to penetrate New Mexico in the 1840s, and their attitudes contrasted rather strikingly with those that previously had prevailed. The mission settlement had no place in their plans. They regarded the pueblo-dwellers as moderately "civilized," but most of the less sedentary Indians were considered "wild." The Anglo-American policy was to push Indians aside, either peacefully or by force, to facilitate their westward expansion.

Effective Spanish intrusion into California, beginning in 1769, was guided by the same policies that they had brought to the Southwest, but the Indians were quite different. In the Southwest the Pueblo peoples were sedentary farmers, and the wandering tribes, such as the Apache, were warlike. Most California Indians, except for the farming peoples along the lower Colorado River, were wanderers, moving often in their search for nuts and seeds, but they were far from bellicose. A primary purpose of the Spanish colony in California was to Christianize Indians and have them settle at self-sufficient missions; thus Indians were very much a part of their economic order. Yet most of the people who were drawn to the missions, either voluntarily or by force, were unlikely to adapt to a sedentary life in crowded conditions with a rigid work routine. The experiment rather clearly failed by the time the missions were secularized, beginning in 1834. Souls had been saved, but the cost in human life was great.

It has been seen that Indians in the northeastern states were confronted by white settlers in search of lands to occupy. Indians hindered progress and were displaced by gentle, callous, or cruel means; they had no place in the colonial order except as converts of the missionaries. In the Southwest the primary Spanish goal was to civilize Indians, and the development of Spanish farming and ranching establishments was largely a by-product of this effort. The Spanish penetration of California was a political move to prevent Russian intrusions from the north. Missions were founded in California to save Indian souls, and the pattern of contact parallels that in the Southwest. In the northern portions of the continent, the English, French, and Russian ventures were of a different order. Here the fur trader, not the settler or missionary, usually was the most important advance agent of Western culture. Irrespective of their national origins and time of contact, fur traders viewed Indians very differently than most other white intruders did. Indians and traders were joined by economic ties that profited them both. The areas where the fur trade dominated longest were those unsuitable for large settlements of whites, and thus the Indians' way of life was not disrupted by large groups of intruders. Furthermore the fur trader and the Indian could maintain their relationship only as long as the Indian trapped and retained the essence of his aboriginal way of life.

Frequently it has been maintained that French traders dealt with Indians more effectively than did their English counterparts. English traders often have been characterized as intolerant of Indian customs as well as haughty and aloof in business or personal contacts. The French have been depicted as sympathetic and understanding, with an ability to establish good rapport quickly with Indians; in a word the Indians could be friendly with the French but not the English. Saum studied primary sources by writers of both nationalities and challenges these stereotypes. The truth appears to be that all parties involved were guided by self-interest that at times made them devious. The French and English vilified each other, and men of both nations were at times difficult. Regardless of nationality, they could be intolerant or tolerant, cruel or kind, depending on their personalities and experiences with Indians. Another dichotomy often noted between traders does stand as valid; free traders often were unscrupulous compared to licensed traders and those representing large trading companies.

Unlike the white settler on his farm or the land-hungry pioneer pushing westward, whether into Ohio, Manitoba, or California, the trader lived among Indians and became a part of their way of life. A trader was necessarily tolerant of his clientele, if only to further his enterprise; at times his very survival depended on aid from Indians. These were practical men of action, not philosophers; they had the hearts and heads of merchants. In their judgment some Indians and tribes were good while others were bad—it was that simple. They were parsimonious with their praise and often characterized Indians as "scoundrels" and "rascals," on occasion even as "monsters" or "inhuman." Yet an active and productive Indian was an essential ingredient to a successful trading enterprise, and the Indians as well as the traders appreciated the fact. These generalizations about traders apply to those of English and French origins who were important over most of the continent. A brief summary of the relationship between the Eskimos of Greenland and the Danes was presented in the opening chapter. It remains to discuss the Russian fur trade in brief, expanding on the information in Chapters 4 and 10.

When the men who accompanied Vitus Bering on the Russian expedition of 1741 returned to Kamchatka the following year, they brought with them the pelts of sea otter. To obtain more of these valued pelts, a host of small-scale expeditions soon reached the Aleutian Islands, and the Alaskan mainland along the northern Pacific Ocean was discovered. The men who launched these ventures were *promishleniki*, the Russian counterpart to the French *coureurs des bois;* the Russians, however, were bold and cruel. The atrocities which the promishleniki committed against the Aleuts and Pacific Eskimos were numerous. Not until the founding of the Russian-American Company in 1799 were the most gross transgressions against aboriginal Americans curbed with a certain degree of effectiveness. Members of the company founded their first station or redoubt along a Bering Sea drainage in 1818, and they built only two other such establishments in this area before the purchase of Alaska by the United States. During the latter part of the Russian era the administrators were naval officers, but it apparently was common for ordinary employees to be criminals from Russia who chose to work for the company in Alaska rather than go to jail in Russia. A number of men who held high posts in the company were "creoles," or persons of mixed Russian and aboriginal Siberian or American ancestry; these men appear to have been much more even-handed in dealing with the fur trade clientele than were their Russian counterparts. One indication of the administration's view of the aboriginal people is to consider the words that the commanders-in-chief used in their official correspondence when referring to them. In the Russian-American Company records for the years centering about 1830 the chief colonial administrator referred to southwestern Alaskans as "savages" more often than by any other

Red Man–White Man

Plate 15–2 The earliest known illustration of Eskimos, printed in Germany probably in 1567. (From Sixel, 1966)

term, although the terms "people" or "natives" also were used. By and large during the latter part of their period of control the Russians assumed a stern but essentially paternalistic attitude toward the native peoples. They always were anxious to expand the fur trade but not at the expense of drastically altering the economic foundations of the Eskimos and Indians with whom they dealt.

Peoples Destroyed and Displaced

It would be difficult to prove, but it seems likely that after initial historic contact far more Indians were killed by diseases introduced by whites than by bullets. It also appears that more Indians were killed by other Indians than by whites although many such murders unquestionably were abetted by whites. It is probable that every tribe was subjected to at least one severe epidemic, and there were very few Indians whose way of life was not altered dramatically, or even destroyed outright, soon after contact.

In the preceding chapters the impact of disease was documented for specific peoples, and its disruptive force cannot be underestimated. Certain diseases that had been prevalent among Europeans so long that they were less virulent could nonetheless be deadly to a virgin population; measles and whooping cough are two examples. Other diseases might rage through Indian and white populations alike, as did malaria. Tuberculosis was a dreaded killer of Indians but was somewhat less lethal for whites.

Records of tribes destroyed by diseases are not difficult to locate; two depressing examples will illustrate the speed of the demise. The Massachuset, whose population was estimated at 3000 in 1600, numbered only 500 by 1631 as a result of a terrible epidemic, possibly smallpox, and soon thereafter smallpox reduced them even more. By 1663, when John Eliot published a Bible in their language, they were practically extinct. The Mandan of North Dakota possibly numbered about 3600 early in their history. A population estimate for 1836 was 1600, but as the result of a smallpox epidemic during 1837 the tribe was reduced to sixty-one. The Massachuset tribe ceased to exist, but the Mandan slowly increased in number from the point of virtual extinction.

Even though disease might not destroy a tribe, an epidemic might kill so many people that they could not defend themselves against outsiders or continue their cultural traditions. For example, a malaria epidemic struck in the Central Valley of California and along the Columbia River in the early 1830s. A mortality rate of about 75 percent made it impossible for the survivors to resist subsequent white intrusions effectively or maintain their ways of old.

The extinction of a population unquestionably is tragic, but another consequence of white dominance was nearly as sad. Because of the intimate associations of Indians with their traditional homelands, their displacement to other areas was often heartrending. One example will suffice. In aboriginal times the Delaware lived in New Jersey and adjacent areas, but in the early 1700s the Iroquois dominated them politically and sanctioned their displacement by white settlers. Before long many Delaware settled in eastern Ohio but only after wandering largely homeless for some time. By 1820 some lived in Arkansas, and others had ventured on to Texas. Some fifteen years later many of them had settled on a reservation in Kansas, from which they were moved to Oklahoma in 1867. Most of them remain there today, but there are Delaware Indians scattered from eastern Canada to Montana, far from each other and from their eastern homeland.

The personal and cultural trauma wrought by purposefully displacing a tribe from its home is tragic in itself. But the Federal policy of moving all the Indian tribes from one vast area into another violates the very principles on which the United States was founded. Yet such was the case, and the drama began to unfold with clarity about 1800. One overwhelming argument was advanced to justify assuming control of Indian lands, and it *never* has changed. Indians obstructed the progress of whites who could utilize land much more effectively, and thus it was the God-given right of the settlers or real estate promotors to obtain such ground. Indian displacement became a blanket policy with the Removal Bill of 1830, and it was supported vigorously by President Andrew Jackson. New England whites could deplore this policy elsewhere because they long ago had resolved their Indian "problem." It was the residents of the southeastern states and settlers venturing into the midwest who became the wanton, immoral destroyers of Indian property rights and tribal life.

Most surviving tribes with large landholdings east of the Mississippi River were bribed and intimidated into moving westward. By 1831 the states of Alabama, Georgia, and Mississippi had forced the removal of the Choctaw, Chickasaw, and Creek. Fox and Sauk reluctance to forsake their lands led to the Black Hawk War (*see* Chapter 6), and Cherokee resistance to removal was described in part in Chapter 13. The Cherokee had adopted civilized ways and had become successful farmers, which was highly disconcerting to politicians in Georgia who yearned to bring their productive lands under state control. In 1829 the Georgia legislature passed a law incorporating much of the land of the Cherokee Nation as state holdings. Under terms of the act all previous Federal legislation and regulations were to be null and void by June of the following year. In addition Indians were prohibited from testifying in court cases involving whites, and prohibitions were established against interference with removal plans. About this time gold was discovered on Cherokee holdings, and the governor declared that all gold-bearing lands belonged to the state. The actions of the Georgia legislature led to the famous *Worcester v. Georgia* case, which reached the Supreme Court in 1832. The court judgment, under John Marshall as Chief Justice, was that the Federal Government, not the state of Georgia, was responsible for the Cherokee. This decision led Jackson to make his famous remark, "John Marshall has made his decision, now let him enforce it." Illegal seizures of land and property by whites, conflicting policies of the Indian leaders, intrigue by unscrupulous whites and Indians, and harassment by state representatives finally led to the 1835 Treaty of Echota and Cherokee removal.

Before the Cherokee treaty leading to their "legal" removal, gross injustices were perpetrated by citizens and representatives of the state of Georgia. Indians were forced from their lands at bayonet point, they were removed in chains without due legal process, they were sold intoxicants in violation of Federal regulations, and their movable property often was stolen with impunity. A state law prohibiting a Cherokee from employing a white was used as a pretext for seizing plantations; these then were disposed of to whites by lottery. The Cherokee were allowed by law to transfer land only to the state. When some families finally were forced to leave Georgia, much of the property they carried with them was seized and their money extorted. Food and shelter during the forced migration often were inadequate or nonexistent, and the weakened emigrants were struck by cholera, along with other diseases. Yet by 1838 when all of these people were supposed to be gone, only 2000 had been deported; the other 15,000 still believed that somehow they would not be driven from their homeland. Such was not the case. About 7000 soldiers under General Winfield Scott moved against the Cherokee, who previously had been disarmed. Scott ordered that within a month's time every Cherokee must be moving westward. Soldiers went from house to house, forcing people to leave at once. Often the Indians were not allowed to take anything with them, and they were impounded in stockades until they could be shipped west. Their journey to Oklahoma is known to the Cherokee as the Trail of Tears; about 4000 people died as a direct result of their forced removal. The Cherokee look back at the Trail of Tears in much the same way citizens of the United States remember the Bataan Death March. The Cherokee do not see the United States Army as heroic on the Trail of Tears.

Treaties

Most of the land in North America was used by Indians when Europeans arrived, but Indians now own and occupy only a very small portion. As is obvious from the preceding chapters most Indian lands were obtained by treaties negotiating the relinquishment of land in one area for that in another, often with monetary compensation as added inducement. The treaty arrangements with a number of tribes have been documented, yet it is worthwhile to present a brief overview of the changing status of Indian lands in historical perspective.

In northeastern North America in the 1700s the Dutch and English administrators held that Indian tribes were sovereign nations and the legitimate claimants to the lands they occupied. Land acquired from Indians was obtained on a national, not an individual, basis. The pre-Revolutionary War treaties of the British dealt primarily with the questions of boundaries and the acquisition of Indian lands. As early as 1670, during the reign of Charles II, England was concerned that those tribes desiring her protection should receive it; her treaties and agreements with New England tribes date from 1664. By 1755 a bureau was founded to deal with Indian matters, and formal recognition of Indian title to land was to guide policy in both Canada and the United States.

Between 1778 and 1871 the United States Government negotiated formal treaties with Indians in the same manner as with foreign powers. Tribes were classed as "dependent nations," and treaties were considered in the same light as other statutes of the U.S. Congress. In some instances early treaties prohibited United States citizens from trespassing on Indian lands without passports, but more often the subordinate position of Indian nations to the United States is made clear by the provisions. It may come as a surprise that in spite of the hostilities between the Federal Government and various tribes, the United States never drew up a formal declaration of war against any hostile Indians.

Many treaty obligations still are being met by the Federal Government though no new treaties have been made with Indians for about a century. Furthermore treaty arrangements have become the basis for Federal Indian law. In treaties the Federal Government reserved the right to regulate Indian affairs, and seldom was this right relinquished to a state. Once a treaty was negotiated and ratified, it could not be nullified, even if duress, fraud, or improper Indian representation prevailed during the negotiations. Treaties might be renegotiated by mutual government and Indian consent, and a treaty could be superseded by other Congressional action. Hostilities could invalidate, modify, or nullify a treaty. Yet it was a general policy of the government to interpret ambiguities in treaties in favor of Indians and to consider the circumstances under which a treaty was negotiated. The courts could not interpret a treaty in a manner not intended in the original wording, however.

Treaties with Indians were negotiated by the President of the United States and were binding when approved by the Indians and two-thirds of the U.S. Senate. It is important to note that a treaty could not provide funds for Indians; monetary commitments required separate Congressional action. The subjects dealt with in Indian treaties varied widely, and nearly 400 treaties were negotiated. The greatest number, nearly 260, were arranged between 1815 and 1860, during the great westward expansion of white settlers following the War of 1812. The majority of these treaties, 230, involved Indian lands. A block of 76 treaties called for Indian removal from their lands and resettlement on other lands. As early as 1818 a treaty reserved land for a specific tribe, but most reservations were established much later. Nearly 100 treaties dealt primarily with boundaries between Indian and white lands and affirmed the friendly relations between a tribe and the United States. Two tribes, the Potawatomi and Chippewa, negotiated 42 treaties each, which is a record number.

Most early treaties made no attempt to regulate or control the internal affairs of a tribe. As Federal power over Indians increased, this policy changed, and treaties began regulating the behavior of tribal members in their own communities. The shift occurred in 1849 in a Navajo treaty stipulating that the Federal Government could (*Federal Indian Law*, 1948, 163) "pass and execute in their territory such laws as may be deemed conducive to the prosperity and happiness of said Indians." By the 1860s the Federal Government made treaties that could be amended unilaterally by Congress. This was an anticipation of the end of treaty making. By the mid-1800s it was becoming increasingly apparent that treaties with Indian tribes were unrealistic because of the increased Indian dependence on the Federal Government. It was not until 1871, however, that the last treaty was negotiated and ratified by the U.S. Congress.

The end of treaty making resulted from a dispute between the U.S. Senate and the House of Representatives. The Senate approved treaties, but the House appropriated the money stipulated in them. The failure of the House and Senate to agree on appropriations brought an end to the treaty period.

An interesting sidelight in Federal dealings with Indians was the attempt to have Indian representation at the national level. The first treaty of the United States with Indians was with the Delaware in 1778, and it provided that at a future date this tribe might consolidate with others and form a state, with the Delaware as the leaders. The state was to have Congressional representation, but nothing ever developed from the possibility. In a treaty of 1785 and another of 1830 it was proposed that Indians send a representative to Congress, but again this possibility was never realized.

In the United States, Indians have land rights based on aboriginal possession, treaty, Congressional act, executive order, purchase, or the action of some colony, state, or foreign nation. Reservations were created by treaty arrangements before 1871, by acts of Congress after that time, and by executive orders of the President. In almost every instance the Federal Government retained the title to reservation lands. Some treaty reservations were created in recognition of aboriginal title and others in exchange for lands; other treaties arranged for one Indian group to join another on its reservation. Statutory reservations usually consisted of public domain or land purchased by the Federal Government for use by designated Indians. The legality of reservations established by executive orders was uncertain, but their validity was established in the General Allotment Act (also known as the Dawes Severalty Act or Dawes Act) of 1887. Reservations were created by executive order between 1855 and 1919. This practice met resistance from Congress, however, and was brought to an end except for the addition of some Alaskan reservations. From time to time Indians have purchased lands with their own funds for the group as a whole, and these properties have been supervised by the Federal Government. Since nearly all of the land that is now the United States was held earlier by a European-based power, the rights of Indians under British, Dutch, French, Mexican, Russian, and Spanish rule have been taken into consideration when there was a transfer of sovereignty. In each instance at least some recognition was given to aboriginal rights of occupancy by the Indians.

As Allan G. Harper has noted, the Canadian government was not particularly generous in its treaties with Indians, but the promises that were made have been kept rather faithfully. In general, treaties with Canadian Indians were arranged before the arrival of settlers in any area of Indian occupancy; thus there were no great conflicts between Indians and whites in Canada. The cornerstone of Indian policy was embodied in the "Proclamation of 1763," issued at the time British sovereignty was established. This proclamation contained the guiding principles for Indian-white relations: Indians possessed the rights to all lands not formally surrendered; Indians could not grant to whites any lands that had not been surrendered; land could be surrendered only to

Red Man–White Man

the Crown. Between 1781 and 1836, twenty-three treaties were negotiated, and all but one included remunerations to the Indians involved. It was only in the Crown Colony of British Columbia that the governor had control over Indians, and this special condition ceased to exist after Confederation in 1867. In a treaty of 1850 the stipulations of all later treaties were set forth. The major points were that the Crown alone had the right to receive Indian land; reserves were established for Indian use; payment was made for the surrender of land, with perpetual annuities to the Indians involved; and Indian rights to hunt and fish on ceded lands were recognized. Between 1871 and 1921 the final eleven treaties were negotiated.

In Canada the earliest significant grant of lands to Indians was made in 1680 by Louis XIV to a band of Iroquois in Quebec. This land still is occupied by the Iroquois. The next large grant of land was to the Six Nations, who were Iroquois, in 1784. They received nearly 700,000 acres for their loyalty to the British during the American Revolution. By 1821 the Six Nations had alienated nearly half of the original grant by selling land to whites before the practice was prohibited. In the early 1940s some 5,500,000 acres of land were held in trust for Indians by the Dominion Government. Under the Canadian Act of 1870 reserved lands may be held by a particular Indian under an allotment system. This means that the allottees have exclusive rights of use and occupancy. They may pass the land on to heirs or sell it to another Indian of their group, but they do not receive clear title to the holding. Indians with more land than is necessary for their welfare may surrender some and use the money derived from the sale for the benefit of the group. Under certain rare conditions an individual Indian obtained clear title to the land; for example, if he or she requested Canadian citizenship or enfranchisement and it was granted, he or she could obtain title to the land by receiving the consent of his or her group and the Dominion Government and then paying the band for the land.

As a closing observation about treaties with Indians it must be noted that they seldom were "negotiated" in any meaningful sense. Representatives of a particular tribe or tribes were assembled, and a treaty was offered for their approval. The signers seldom had any realistic opportunity to modify the terms. Then too, treaties often were made through "chiefs" who were sympathetic to the whites, and in certain areas of the United States it was not uncommon for intoxicants to be distributed freely at treaty-making sessions. In addition the interpreters often could not or did not set forth the details of an agreement in true detail or spell out the implications of what the Indians were losing and what they gained. A most important final observation along these lines is that most Indians had no concept of the permanent alienation of land. Since they had never bought and sold land, their concept was that they were granting whites the rights to its use. Thus, many such agreements were not "treaties" in a strict sense of the word.

Administration

In 1775 the Continental Congress of the United States created three agencies, on a geographical basis, to deal with Indians. The commissioners in charge of the northern, middle, and southern areas were instructed to make treaties, to establish friendly relations with Indians, and to prevent them from aiding the British. The general structure of Indian administration was the same as that existing under British control. The persons in charge of the middle area included Benjamin Franklin and Patrick Henry, and their appointment indicates the importance attached to Indians. In 1786 Indian administration was placed under the Secretary of War, with north and south departments whose administrators were empowered to grant licenses to trade and live among Indians. With the adoption of the Constitution of the United States, the War Department maintained jurisdiction over Indians. The first Congress of 1789 appropriated funds for negotiating treaties and placed the governors of territories in charge of local Indian affairs. The next year Congress, in an important step toward Federal control, began licensing traders among Indians. The Bureau of Indian Affairs was created in 1824 within the War Department. Its framework was clarified by a Congressional act in 1834, and the only significant alteration occurred in 1849 when the overall control of the Bureau passed from military control into the hands of the newly created Home Department of the Interior. The flagrant corruption and mismanagement in the Bureau led to the creation of a Board of Indian Commissioners that functioned from 1869 to 1933. It was composed of ten outstanding citizens who were appointed to serve without compensation by the President, and they reported to him. The Board oversaw the expenditure of funds for Indians and advised the Bureau of Indian Affairs.

In Canada, Indian affairs were delegated to the Commander of the Forces in the British North American Provinces in 1816. In 1830, their management in Upper Canada passed into civil control, but in Lower Canada it remained under military jurisdiction. By the Act of Union in 1841, the administration was consolidated into a single Department of Indian Affairs. With the Confederation of Canada in 1867, Indian administration passed into the hands of the Dominion of Canada. A separate Department of Indian Affairs was founded in 1880 with a minister who was the Superintendent General of Indian Affairs. The portfolio of this minister was always held by someone with another ministerial post, usually the Minister of the Interior. In 1936 the Department of Indian Affairs was changed into a branch and placed under the Department of Mines and Resources. In 1950 it was shifted to the Department of Citizenship and Immigration and then to the Department of Indian Affairs and Northern Development.

The Dominion Parliament alone is responsible for legislating for Indians. The general structure for rights and services was framed in the Indian Act of

1876. The administration was to control the management of Indian lands—both the reserves and other lands set aside for use only by Indians—as well as the Indian Trust Fund, an accumulation of money derived mainly from the sale of natural resources on Indian lands. The Indian Act of 1876 also recognized that the Dominion Government was responsible for relief, education, health services, and Indian-based agriculture and industry. Finally, the Parliament was made responsible for the enfranchisement of Indians to full Canadian citizenship.

Canadian Indians with white blood deserve special comment because of their somewhat different treatment from full-blooded Indians. In general mixed bloods, or Metis, were given all the rights of Indians, and those Metis who lived as Indians had the right to be treated as Indians. Efforts by the Metis to protect their land rights largely were responsible for the Red River Rebellion of Manitoba in 1869. As a result of this uprising the rights of the Metis were more fully acknowledged in Manitoba, but they were not implemented in the intent of subsequent legislation. The Metis could obtain either money or land to extinguish their claim, but it appears that some ineligible persons received claims and some allotments may have been duplicated. The success of the Metis in Manitoba led those in the Northwest Territories to press their claims. Yet it took the threat of rebellion in 1885 before the government finally made a settlement offer. In 1899 for northern Manitoba and 1906 for northern Saskatchewan the claims of Metis were recognized in terms of land or money settlements. Those who received money or land had their aboriginal rights extinguished, and any further claims must be in terms of inequitable settlements.

The next major revision of Indian policy in Canada, the Indian Act of 1951, is, with its subsequent revisions, the legal basis for current policy. The Act sets forth in exact terms the authority and power of the Governor in Council, the Minister, and the Minister's field representatives, the superintendents. Robert W. Dunning, in discussing the effects of the act on the Indians, stresses the power of the superintendent on a reserve and his flexibility in formulating and administering local policy. A reserve superintendent determines who may become members of a band, screens enfranchisement applicants, and administers welfare, relief, and education on the reserve. He furthermore may accept or veto the nomination of an Indian to a band council.

Treaties and laws referring to both Canadian and United States Indians often made reference to the consumption of intoxicants. In Canada Indians who were not enfranchised could not buy liquor legally for ordinary consumption until 1951. The Indian Act of 1951 permitted the provinces or territories, with the approval of the Governor in Council, to allow Indians to consume intoxicants in public places. This condition existed over most of Canada until 1958. Between 1958 and 1963 the restriction was lessened in most provinces and territories to permit Indians to buy alcoholic beverages in the same manner as Canadian citizens in general, that is, either in a public place or from a package store. A band has the option of prohibiting intoxicants on its reserve lands. In the United States the first Federal regulation of intoxicants among Indians occurred in 1802. The law was modified periodically to ease enforcement and to cover loopholes. The Federal Government did not repeal this law until 1953. Prohibition still was possible on any reservation under local option. Before Indians could consume intoxicants in some states, state laws against the sale of liquor to Indians had to be changed.

At the time of their discovery, cultural diversity among Indians to the north of Mexico was great. They spoke many very different languages, often gained sustenance by contrasting means, and varied in political structure from unelaborate to highly organized forms. In comparative terms the European intruders were homogeneous in cultural background, their linguistic diversity was comparatively minor, and their political organization and religious convictions differed only in narrow dimensions. In comparison with the European migrants the Indians living in the New World were fractured and fragmented along many dimensions, and the agents of Western civilization often exploited these differences to divide them further still.

Indian tribes were relatively free and independent nations until the War of 1812 ended. Soon thereafter they became "domestic, dependent nations" and lost any realistic control over their destiny. The Removal Act of 1830 was a clear indication of the change in white-Indian relations. The end of treaty making in the United States in 1871 was another important plateau, but it was the Dawes Act of 1887 that had the strongest effect in changing Indians into white Americans. Under its terms the President was authorized to allot the lands of most reservations to individual Indians. The Indians were to select their acreage, and the Federal Government was to hold a trust title for twenty-five years or longer, during which time the land could not be encumbered. Surplus reservation lands then were sold and the funds derived were held in trust for the tribe, subject to use for education and civilizing the tribe when Congress approved this use. Over the next ten years the Dawes Act was modified in some of its aspects to permit the leasing of allotted lands and to validate claims of descendants from marriages that were in keeping with tribal customs. Indian education came to be stressed with particular enactments from 1892 to 1897. These provided for schools and virtually forced the attendance of Indian children, while Federal support of church schools was withdrawn. An important supplement was made to the Dawes Act in 1906; it permitted the President to extend the trust period for allotted lands. Again in 1910 the act was revised to resolve problems arising from inheriting allotments, leasing timber lands, and replacing trust patents for reservation lands with others of comparable value. The aim of the Dawes Act and its amendments was to bypass tribal organizations and make land allotments to individual Indians. The act was designed to destroy the tribes by doing away with the land base held in collectivity and at the same time to integrate Indians into the dominant society. Many whites who truly were concerned with Indian welfare felt that the sterile and depressing quality of reservation life should be destroyed and that the means to accomplish this end was to make individual Indians property holders and farmers.

Pan-Indianism

Indian efforts to halt white intrusions and to reject all Euro-American ideas were doomed to failure. Yet from the tribal resistance to assimilation has arisen the Pan-Indian movement, and in it Indianism and Indianness have crystallized. Many whites have long felt that their pervasive control of Indians eventually would lead to total Indian assimilation. However, past experience and present trends indicate a great deal more vitality in Indian culture than was recognized by those predicting its doom. By now Indian resistance to white dominance, as manifested primarily in political and religious movements, has become a part of their heritage.

PROPHETS   Religious prophets emerged repeatedly and advocated what Indians must do to free themselves of white control, but we know comparatively little about most of these men. One such person was Neolin, better known as the Delaware Prophet. By the 1760s, when he came into prominence, the Delaware and other Algonkians had been displaced from the East by whites and were living in Ohio. They expected a surge of whites into their adopted homeland and were uncertain how to respond. Neolin, like other contemporary Delaware prophets, urged his people to abandon European customs and return to their aboriginal ways. God had revealed to him that if Indians once again lived a simple life, recited certain prayers, and dispelled whites, then game would return and the purity of Indian ways would prevail. Neolin made a map which charted the way to heaven and the obstacles placed along the way by whites. His message was appealing to many Indians, and he won converts not only among his own people but among other tribes in the Ohio valley. His words had special appeal to the Ottawa chief Pontiac, because this religious revelation served as partial justification for aggressive action. He planned a sudden attack against British outposts and a general uprising. A number of forts were taken and their garrisons massacred, but the attempt to take Detroit by siege failed. Indian dominance was of brief duration since the confederation was organized so loosely that the British soon divided the Indians and were able to reconsolidate their position.

SCHOOLS   Much of the background for Pan-Indianism may be traced to the efforts of men such as Pontiac and Handsome Lake, but there were essential non-Indian elements as well. The most important of these was the formal education process imposed on Indians. In government and mission schools on reservations instruction was in English, and it became the language for communication between members of diverse tribes. It was the boarding schools, however, that had the most profound influence. None was more famous than the Carlisle School in Pennsylvania. It was founded in 1879 by Richard H. Pratt, who was a lieutenant in the army at the time, and was attended by members of far-flung tribes. Pratt's philosophy was remarkably clear. He viewed the boarding school environment as the most useful waystation between the reservation and assimilation. His slogan was, "Kill the Indian and save the man!" Carlisle often is thought of as a college because its football team played many university teams, but it was largely a secondary school that stressed vocational training and the fundamentals of English. Indians who attended Carlisle and other boarding schools often had a difficult time readjusting to reservation life. Although some went "back to the blanket," meaning that they reverted to Indian ways, others were assimilated into the white world, and many worked for the Indian Service.

CHRISTIANITY   Christianity also was an important influence on Indians at this time. Missions maintained many schools, and diverse white organizations with Christian backing were concerned with Indian welfare. These included the Women's National Indian Association (founded in 1879), the Indian Rights Association (1882), and the Lake Monhonk conferences (1883), all of which lobbied for Indian justice. At the same time members of these organizations sought to assimilate Indians, and most members had little tolerance of Indian customs. These white activists in Indian affairs supported the principles of the Dawes Act but deplored the injustices of its administration. As Hazel W. Hertzberg (1971, 22) noted in the best study of this era, "All unwittingly the reformers—the Indians' chief friends in court in the white world—thus helped to break down Indian self-respect and Indian attempts at self-help." Many Indian leaders were Christian, but at the same time they often were unwilling to abandon their Indian heritage. They sought accommodation with white customs, and their general approach has endured among many Indians seeking to retain their identity. For many others assimilation into white society was desired and realized.

PEYOTE CULT   Indians of many tribes with different historical backgrounds were drawn into the Pan-Indian movement through the peyote cult. The peyote plant, which grows in central Mexico, is a spineless cactus with "buttons" containing alkaloids that are stimulants or sedatives in varying proportions. When consumed, buttons produce a wide range of reactions. A common response to taking peyote is exhilaration and an inability to sleep for about twelve hours; depression and hallucinations, sometimes including color visions, follow. This nonhabit-forming drug was consumed in Mexico in aboriginal times but was not widely used in the United States until more recently. It became popular among Indians of the southern Plains between

1850 and 1900 and spread to other western tribes. Early use in the Plains appears to have been associated with warfare, and it was taken only by men. People began using peyote more widely when they were suffering in the dismal aftermath of military defeat, physical displacement, and confinement to reservations. The Bureau of Indian Affairs, Christian missionaries, and white reformers all were actively opposed to the peyote cult, and its adherents were harassed. In spite of the oppression by whites and some Indians there were about 12,000 members in 1918. Efforts were made in 1916 and again in 1917 to pass a Federal law against the use of peyote, but these bills failed. In 1918 as a response to white opposition a group of participants incorporated as a formal religious institution, the Native American Church. Although a number of states soon passed laws against the use of peyote (e.g., Kansas, 1920; Arizona, 1923), seven states had chartered Native American Churches by 1925. As members of a formal religious organization, they were afforded far greater protection from persecution than previously.

A typical peyote service among Plains tribes was held in a tepee and lasted all night. Participants sat around a central fire, and peyote buttons were passed for each person to take as many as he chose. A special gourd rattle and a drum were used to produce distinctive music. One person after another chanted his sacred song either in English or in his tribal language. Bibles and crosses might be part of the ceremonial equipment. The goals of the ceremony were to achieve physical and spiritual well-being and to promote harmonious relations with others. Brotherly love, self-reliance, and a disapproval of alcohol all were important values held by participants. The psychedelic experience gained through the use of peyote was never an end in itself.

According to Hertzberg the peyote religion had appeal because old tribal religions had lost their meaning and Christian teachings seemed remote from reality. Furthermore this was an Indian religion that united members of different tribes in a common sense of brotherhood. Peyote often was considered a powerful medicine for the diseased, and also the rituals provided an opportunity for social gatherings. Some Indians, such as the Pueblo peoples, Five Civilized Tribes in Oklahoma, and Iroquois, were relatively untouched by the peyote religion, but it became *the* religion for many Indians by 1934.

THE PLAINS INDIAN IMAGE   The Plains Indian has come to symbolize Indians to whites, and to members of the Pan-Indian movement in particular. How is it that Indians in one sector of the country now represent all Indians?

Indians of the Great Plains were seen first by Spanish and then by French and English explorers, yet they were nearly unknown until after the Louisiana Purchase of 1803. In 1821 members of Plains tribes visited Washington, D.C., and none was more popular than Petalesharo, the Pawnee who rescued a Comanche girl from being sacrificed to the Morning Star. In three paintings of him by different artists he wore a flowing feather headdress, and according to John C. Ewers this probably was the first pictorial record of the feather "war

Plate 15–3 The first illustration of a Plains Indian tepee to be published, appearing in 1823. (From Ewers, 1965)

bonnet." Many other Indians in the same party had their portraits painted, and their exhibit long was a popular attraction in Washington. The earliest picture of a Plains tepee appeared in 1823, and the first illustration of a Plains Indian on horseback was printed in 1829. This beginning possibly never would have led to the emergence of the Plains tribes in popular fancy were it not for the efforts of Karl Bodmer and George Catlin, who painted Plains Indians in the 1830s. Catlin especially was important, for he not only painted many pictures of Indians but exhibited his Indian Gallery widely in the United States and then in London and Paris. His book *Manners, Customs and Condition of the North American Indians*, first published in 1841, had a wide distribution, and this two-volume work with over 300 engravings was reprinted again and again. To Catlin the noblest Indians clearly were those of the Plains. His paintings and those of Bodmer were copied or modified and also served to inspire other artists to venture west to paint Indians.

The Plains Indian symbol crystallized in Buffalo Bill's Wild West Show that opened in 1883. It was seen by millions of people in Canada, the United States, and Europe during its run of more than thirty years. William F. Cody or "Buffalo Bill" was a colorful frontier figure who became the hero of innumerable dime novels. The show, a reenactment of episodes in Plains life, was highlighted by an Indian attack on a stagecoach and its dramatic rescue by cowboys led by Buffalo Bill. Other Wild West shows that imitated the original and Indian medicine shows intensified and spread the Plains Indian image. By the turn of the present century Indians all over the country were beginning to dress as Plains Indians for special occasions.

James H. Howard (1955) made one of the first studies of the modern Pan-Indian movement and identified its roots as being in Oklahoma, especially among the small tribes originally from the East. Howard felt that racial discrimination against Indians was an important factor fostering solidarity among them. Coupled with poverty, apartheid tended to bind Indians of diverse background together. Other contributing elements were the peyote religion, intermarriage between members of different tribes, the use of English as the common language, and the schools. Pan-Indianism was identified best with particular traits associated with powwows. The "war dance," which possibly began among the Pawnee, originally had religious associations with a men's war society but became a social dance. Men danced as a group, yet each man performed in his own style to the accompaniment of singers and a drum. Thus no rehearsals were necessary, which made the dance ideal for persons from diverse tribes performing together. A modified Plains Indian scalp dance, the buffalo dance, and stomp dance were likely to be performed; the latter was once a religious dance among tribes in the East. The feather roach headdress,

Plate 15–4 Probably the first published illustration of a Plains Indian warrior on horseback, appearing in 1829. (From Ewers, 1965)

feather shoulder bustle and back bustle of feathers, a choker neckband, and hard-soled Plains type moccasins prevailed among the performers. Indians and whites alike found that the Plains Indian dances were the most exciting and the costuming from this area the most visually appealing.

Indian Reorganization Act

The most basic change in Federal Indian policy after the Dawes Act of 1887 was the Indian Reorganization Act (I.R.A.) of 1934. Earlier legislation was designed to force individual Indians to become self-sufficient farmers as full citizens and to break away from tribalism and the stagnation of reservation life, but Indians received their own special New Deal in 1934. The Indian Reorganization Act was intended to end the alienation of Indian lands through the allotment process. In fifty years of allotments Indians had lost nearly 90 of their 138 million acres of land, and about half of the remaining land was desert. The most effective means to permit retention of the land base was to extend the period of trust holding. Furthermore additional land was acquired for Indians, declared exempt from taxation, and placed under Federal control.

The Commissioner of Indian Affairs from 1934 to 1944 was John Collier, who was deeply committed to the reformulation of American society in a less competitive mold with greater social justice. He hoped in fact that restoring vitality to Indian societies could make them a model for community living for other Americans. Two guiding principles of the I.R.A. were self-government with democratic ideals and parliamentary procedures and communal enterprises as the best avenue to bettered economic conditions. Tribes were encouraged to form chartered corporations and operate essentially as local governments; revolving credit funds helped those choosing to incorporate. One important condition of the original law was that it would apply only to those tribes that by majority vote decided to come under its provisions. Initially 181 tribes accepted, and seventy-seven rejected the I.R.A. Fourteen groups came under it because they did not vote, and the Act was extended in 1936 to include Alaskan and Oklahoman peoples without their vote of approval. Since Indians in general had come to distrust the Federal Government, the Indian response to this enlightened legislation was not as positive as had been hoped for by its creators. Some tribes favored allotments and were able to obtain clear title to their land in spite of the I.R.A. Other tribes, such as those that stressed individual wealth, did not even agree with the principles behind the I.R.A. World War II disrupted the program, and soon after the trend reverted to a policy of rapid Indian assimilation.

Termination

The policy changes conceived in the late 1930s were hampered by the economic depression and then by World War II. After the war the Federal Government began to divest itself of diverse obligations to Indians much more systematically than ever before. In spite of claims to the contrary the Federal Government clearly is "getting out of the Indian business." Documentation is in order.

1. Indian Claims Commission Act 1946. This legislation was designed to settle claims, by any "identifiable group" of Indians, against the United States, arising from various inequities, including when "fraud, duress, unconscionable consideration, mutual or unilateral mistake" were involved. By 1976 a total of about 560 million dollars had been awarded in claims to tribes, and many claims denied by the commission have been appealed to the Court of Claims.

2. Relocation program, 1950. In the 1930s efforts were made to encourage Indians to seek employment in urban centers, but the economic conditions were not propitious. In 1952 the B.I.A. began its intensive program to resettle reservation Indians in urban areas. The offices for relocation that have continued to function include those in Chicago, Cleveland, Dallas, Denver, Los Angeles, Oakland, San Francisco, and San Jose. It is estimated that about 100,000 persons, including dependents, were relocated by 1971; this figure re-counts persons who were relocated more than once. The cost of the program in 1967 was about 4 million dollars. From 1953 to 1957 three out of ten relocated Indians returned home during their first year in a city. Return and repeat rates are not obtainable after 1959 because these statistics had proven too useful to opponents of the program!

3. House Concurrent Resolution 108, 1953. This was a strong expression of congressional sentiment that Federal control over Indians should be ended as soon as possible. The advocates of termination argued, just as the supporters of the Dawes Act had reasoned, that the reservation system has denied Indians their self-reliance and freedom. It also was felt that the Federal Government could save considerable amounts of money by "buying off" treaty and other obligations. Specific tribes were earmarked for termination in the near future, and subsequent legislation ended Federal responsibilities to the Klamath of Oregon, the Menominee of Wisconsin, the Paiutes and Utes of Utah, and small groups in Oregon and Texas. The results have by and large been disastrous because the people involved were unprepared to assume the responsibilities thrust on them. In 1971 the U.S. Senate passed a resolution disavowing the termination policy of 1953.

4. The transfer of Bureau of Indian Affairs health services to the Department of Health, Education, and Welfare, 1955. Before this change Indian health care had been underfunded and often was deplorable. Money for Indian health care tripled from 1955 to 1966; mortality and morbidity rates have declined dramatically. The status of Indian health is now vastly improved, which very well may be used as an argument for termination in the future.

5. Alaskan Native Claims Settlement Act, 1971. Very few reservations were created for aboriginal Alaskans, but encroachment on their lands has increased steadily. Before the State of Alaska could gain control over large portions of land still held by the Federal Government, it was mandatory that native claims be settled. As a result of the 1971 settlement some 76,500 Aleuts, Eskimos, and Indians will receive title to some 40 million acres of land and some $960 million from Federal appropriations and mineral royalties.

With termination of the Indian Claims Commission in 1977 and implementation of the Alaska Native Claims Settlement Act the Federal Government will have discharged its last important responsibilities involving land. With its efforts to raise the standard of Indian health to a satisfactory level and to resettle large numbers of Indians in urban areas, the Federal Government is reducing its involvement in Indian affairs.

In 1969 the Minister of Indian Affairs and Northern Development issued a White Paper that set forth a new direction for Indian policy in Canada. In essence the report was a framework to terminate Federal responsibilities to Indians on reserves. The proposal met with firm, united opposition from Canadian Indians. They feared that if implemented the proposal would lead to a disaster like that resulting from the termination policy in the United States in the 1950s. Canadian Indians felt strongly that since treaty obligations were "forever" the government had no legal or moral justification for termination. The Prime Minister shelved the White Paper and promised a reevaluation of the question.

Jorgensen's Thesis

Since the 1930s the concept of "acculturation" has been dear to the hearts of many anthropologists. It has come to mean the steps by which Indians are gradually absorbed into the dominant sociocultural pattern. With assimilation acculturation is complete. Yet few anthropologists are satisfied with the concept because it fails to define the stages leading to assimilation or to explain the persistence of Indianness in the face of hundreds of years of pressures to negate it. Quite clearly the idea of acculturation does not allow for the lasting quality of Indian identity. By far the most bold and innovative approach to the general problem has been conceived and articulated by Joseph G. Jorgensen.

The central idea of Jorgensen's thesis is that tribes were in fact integrated into national economic and political life as soon as they came to be controlled by the United States. He attributes the deplorable conditions under which most Indians live to the economic order imposed on them. Efforts to gauge relative degrees of acculturation fail to recognize that Indians are enmeshed in a political system which essentially is colonial. He identifies the "metropolis" as the center where economic and political power are concentrated; the manipulators of it are able to promote legislation to sustain their goals and insure their growth. Thus the politically weak rural areas are exploited by the metropolis for its growth, and this applies to the rural areas in which Indians live as well as any others. Indians are subject to the same laws that apply to everyone else in addition to those imposed by Federal control through the B.I.A.

In developing his approach, Jorgensen notes that most reservations are located in arid and semiarid areas, and it is not possible for the Indians to develop successful large-scale farming enterprises because their small and often scattered plots of ground cannot be cultivated efficiently. Even if all land were farmed at its maximum productivity, the harvest would seldom be sufficient to provide a reasonable standard of living. Since reservations usually are remote from major markets or industrial developments, comparatively few nonfarming jobs are available. The economies of rural areas near reservations have declined as farms in other areas have grown larger and more technologically sophisticated under the management of large corporations. Of great importance in terms of metropolis control, the large-scale farming enterprises have received far more government aid than have the small farmers. For example, in 1967 65 percent of the Federal subsidies to farmers went to the top 10 percent of the producers. It is not surprising that as the economic base for the small rural white farmer has declined disastrously, the position of the Indian farmer has grown desperate. The B.I.A. has attempted to promote industrial development on or near reservations. Between 1962 and 1968 some 10,000 jobs were created, but about half of these have been held by non-Indians. " 'Industrial development' has been mostly talk; development has accrued to industry and not to Indians or Indian-owned and controlled industry" (Jorgensen, 1971, 83). Understandably with economic conditions so bad on and near reservations, Indians have moved to cities in ever-increasing numbers.

In essence Indians are enveloped in a culture of poverty, and the move from a reservation to a city is to substitute an urban ghetto for a rural one. Since Indian migrants to cities have few skills, little confidence, and a foreign cultural tradition, they are not likely to succeed. Often they make a little money and then return to their reservation. If they remain in urban centers, they usually have the poorest paying jobs and very little job security. The growing body of studies about urban Indian life is very depressing. The unemployment rates among them, the arrest rate for drunkenness, the suicide rate, and so on are incredible.

Urban Indians

By the mid-1970s about half of all the Indians in the United States lived in urban areas, but urban Indians usually were ignored by anthropologists until the 1960s. Two reasons above all others may account for this neglect. Reservations were the traditional study sites for anthropologists, and equally important, fieldwork in urban areas was the purview of sociologists. Pioneering articles about urban Indians were written in the 1960s by Joan Ablon (1964), Wesley R. Hurt (1961–1962), and John R. Price (1968). When "urban anthropology" emerged as a topic of expanding interest in the 1960s, numerous studies were made of Indians in towns or cities, but most of these works are unpublished doctoral dissertations. Published articles about Indians in particular cities are becoming more numerous, yet few persons have attempted to formulate a model that will explain why there are urban populations of Indians. In this context I find the approach offered by Karen Tranberg Hansen as the most insightful.

The essence of Hansen's thesis is that the migration of Indians to urban areas is best analyzed in the context of Federal legislation. Hansen points out that while it is difficult to document in detail, the move of Indians to cities and towns is an old and well-established pattern. It appears to have developed as an aftereffect of the Dawes Act in 1887 when Indians began receiving individual land allotments and "surplus" land was sold to whites. Land set aside for reservations initially was, in most instances, far less desirable than other land that a tribe had occupied. Then too many Indians never accepted farming as a legitimate economic base for men, and they were ill-prepared for the sudden shift from tribal life to individual responsibility. Furthermore, subsequent legislation did not effectively compensate Indians for their land losses. As a result of this Federal policy significant numbers of Indians began leaving their reservations. The existence of urban Indians first was clearly recognized in a study of the B.I.A. in the 1920s by the Brookings Institution (1928). This analysis noted that the trend toward urban living could be expected to continue and recommended that efforts be made to ease the adjustments for the persons involved; no broadscale or effective steps were taken in this direction. As noted earlier the Indian Reorganization Act of 1934 attempted to restore economic vitality to reservations and to increase the land base, but with the beginning of World War II these efforts were discontinued. Off-reservation job opportunities in cities during this war attracted about 90,000 Indians in 1943 and 1944. Then too about 24,000 others entered the armed forces. When the war ended, most Indians were laid off from their jobs, and large numbers returned to the reservations along with many veterans. How many remained in urban areas is not known, but the number appears to have been great.

With the Indian Claims Commission Act of 1946 the Federal Government made a move to "get out of the Indian business" by settling old claims. Then in the early 1950s two Federal policies had a more profound and immediate influence on American Indian life. One was House Concurrent Resolution 108 in 1953. It was designed to end Federal responsibilities to Indians on an established timetable. Menominee and Klamath terminations were an immediate result, and, for some Indians, such Federal services as schools, welfare, and law enforcement were placed under state jurisdiction. This was accompanied by the Relocation Program that encouraged Indians to move to urban areas. It began in 1950 and was soon followed by a vocational training program to teach Indians job skills that were more useful in nonreservation contexts. By the early 1970s about 10,000 Indians left their reservations each year to live in cities either on a temporary or permanent basis. Thus the purpose of the most important legislation since 1946 has been to force Indian assimilation.

Some Indians, no one knows how many, clearly have assimilated into the greater society, but often the quality of their life is dreadful, especially in urban settings. The high rate of alcoholism, high suicide rate, high percentage of unemployment, and generally low economic status commonly are noted. The B.I.A. maintained that the Relocation Program was voluntary, which simply is untrue; people were encouraged to leave the reservations and quotas for relocated Indians once existed. Typically Indians are scattered about poorer areas in cities, and they often return to their reservations because they cannot find jobs or to visit. Yet despite all the pressures for assimilation, most Indians have resisted successfully, and have retained their identity. They usually associate with other Indians during their leisure time, and some are active in athletic, church, or social groups that are Indian-centered. They have not disappeared into the urban mass nor have they typically settled in ghettos or enclaves. Thus the model of Indian acculturation leading to their assimilation seems discredited. Most Indians have learned to live in two cultures, an adaptation called biculturation that has become a highly successful life-style for urban and reservation Indians alike.

Statistical Information

In 1970 the reported Indian population of the United States was 763,594 or four-tenths of 1 percent of the total. The three largest tribes were the Navajo, 96,743; Cherokee, 66,150; and Chippewa, 41,946. Ten percent of all Indians in the United States lived in urban areas in 1930, but by 1970 about 45 percent, or 340,000, lived in urban areas. This increase is proportionally greater than for any other ethnic group. The most dramatic ten-year increase in urban Indian population was in Los Angeles County, California. In 1960 Los Angeles County had 8109 Indians, and the official figure rose to 24,509 in 1970. The accuracy of the 1970 census of Indians in the Los Angeles area has been questioned; some observers have estimated that the number was as high as 60,000 in the early 1970s.

Eighteen states east of the Mississippi had small Indian populations in 1970, but most of these people had no ties with the Federal Government. For example, Alabama, Georgia, and Tennessee each had about 2500 Indians; there were about 6600 in Ohio and 200 in Pennsylvania. The largest group without Federal recognition as Indians are the 44,000 Lumbee concentrated in Robeson County, North Carolina. These people claim descent from Indians who married whites from the lost colony of Croatoan established in 1587 by Sir Walter Raleigh on Roanoke Island, Virginia.

In 1970 the state with the largest Indian population was Oklahoma, with 97,731; it was followed by Arizona, 95,812; California, 91,018; New Mexico, 72,788; and Alaska, 51,528. In the same year 17 percent of the total Alaskan population was Aleut, Indian, or Eskimo, while the Indian proportion of the population in New Mexico was 7.1 and 5.4 in Arizona. The B.I.A. estimated in 1970 that it provided services to about 477,000 Indians of the total 763,000.

It should be noted that many persons who consider themselves Indians in at least some contexts were not identified in the 1970 Federal census. Alaska provides an example. In March 1973 when the original enrollment for benefits under the Alaska Native Claims Settlement Act was closed, 77,000 eligible Aleuts, Eskimos, and Indians had enrolled; of this number about 11,000 lived outside Alaska. This would mean that the 51,000 Aleut, Eskimo, and Indian total recorded for Alaska in 1970 did not include at least 5000 who actually lived there.

Indian life expectancy in 1970 was 47 years compared with the national average of 70.8. In the early 1970s reservation Indians had the lowest income for a family of four ($1500) of any minority group. A conservative estimate of unemployment rates on some reservations was from 30 to 40 percent. Only 5 percent of Indians entering the first grade complete college compared with a national rate of 20 percent. The Indian suicide rate is twice the national average and peaks between the ages of twenty-four and thirty-four, compared with a national average that peaks in the seventy-year-old group.

Canadian Indians registered with the Federal Government in late 1971 numbered 257,619, and about 65,000 others were not registered. Registered Indians comprised 560 bands living on 2200 reserves that covered about 6.3 million acres of land. The Province of Ontario had the most Indians, 56,553 in 1971, followed by British Columbia, 49,194, and Saskatchewan, 37,565. Of the nearly 18,000 Canadian Eskimos in 1971, about 12,400 lived in the Northwest Territories, 3800 in northern Quebec, 1000 in Labrador, and 800 in northern Ontario. In 1976 about 40,500 persons in Greenland were regarded as Eskimo and about 1000 others of Greenlandic Eskimo descent lived in Denmark.

Recent Developments

IROQUOIS WAMPUM   An example of the new assertiveness by Indians is the controversy over wampum originally belonging to the Iroquois. The Onondaga requested that twenty-six wampum belts purchased by or given to the State of New York in 1898 be returned to the Onondaga. The stated reason for the request was that the sacred belts were necessary in their religious rituals. In 1970 the Assembly of the State of New York approved a bill for the return, but it was killed in a Senate committee. Before the end of the session the Committee on Anthropological Research in Museums of the American Anthropological Association urged the governor of New York to oppose the return of this wampum. The committee reasoned that since the League of the Iroquois had ceased to function as a political body with the end of the American Revolution, the traditions associated with "reading" the wampum had been forgotten, and the importance of the wampum in their religion was only partially valid. They wanted the state to retain custody because they felt that the return of this wampum would set precedent for the descendants of other once aboriginal peoples to make similar requests. An editorial in *The Indian Historian* (1970 v. 3, no. 1) expressed the opinion that a majority of interested scholars disagreed with the five signers of the memorial, representing the Committee on Anthropological Research in Museums. In 1971 the legislators passed a bill providing for the return of five wampum belts on the condition that they be appropriately protected in a museum. However, the Iroquois Indian Confederacy was not satisfied with this condition, and in 1975 they began preparing a suit against the State of New York for the unrestricted return of the wampum. One wampum in particular, the Hiawatha belt, has great symbolic value since it reportedly is the official record of the creation of the League of the Iroquois.

MENOMINEE TERMINATION   In 1953 when termination of Federal responsibilities to Indians in the United States became the official policy, two tribes with comparatively large landholdings were singled out as ready for termination; they were the Klamath of Oregon and the Menominee of Wisconsin. Thanks to Nancy O. Lurie, early events in the Menominee case were carefully documented. The Menominee Reservation land was considered relatively undesirable when the reservation was created in 1854, but the Indians accepted it rather than move from Wisconsin. The land was not divided into individual holdings, and since they already had organized to govern themselves they were not covered by the I.R.A. The Menominee filed suit in 1934 against the Federal Government for the mismanagement of their timber lands, and finally in 1951 the U.S. Court of Claims awarded them nearly 8 million dollars. Yet the money was held by the Federal Government and required congressional approval before any disbursement. As unbelievable as it may seem, these people were forced to accept termination before they could obtain the money awarded them by the courts. When a vote was taken, 169 persons favored the "principle of termination," and five opposed it. This vote represented only 10 percent of the eligible voters. Some who voted had been led to believe that they were voting for the release of the money due them. Others thought they were voting for the "principle" of termination, which would give them bargaining power against unilateral Federal action. Many persons appear to have abstained from voting to express their negative feelings toward the proposal. In any event a law to terminate them was passed in 1954. Per capita payments were to be made from the money owed as settlement of the timber suit, and the tribal roll was closed after a ninety-day period. Thus, a Menominee born after that time was not an "Indian" in terms of Federal responsibilities.

Following termination, tribal assets were consolidated in Menominee Enterprises Incorporated. Jurisdiction over the land was transferred from the Federal Government to the State of Wisconsin, and Menominee County was created from the old reservation. The people owned shares in Menominee Enterprises, but they were only "certificates of ownership." A Common Stock and Voting Trust comprised of seven persons, including three whites, voted the shares for most adults and elected the corporation directors. An Assistance Trust held and voted certificates for minors and "incompetents." Thus parents had no control over the rights of their children, and incompetency was established by the B.I.A., not the courts. The organizational maze could not function, the county soon was deeply in debt, the lumber mill was turned over to the corporation in such poor condition that it was forced to lay off workers, welfare aid to these unemployed contributed to the impossible strain on county finances, and persons who bought their land—as they had been encouraged to do—could not pay their taxes. The corporation was forced to go into partnership with a land developer to sell lots to whites just to expand the tax base on a short-term basis.

By 1960 the population was about 2500, and over 90 percent of the families had an income of less than $1000 per year. Economic conditions deteriorated badly in the 1960s in spite of State and Federal aid and efforts to develop recreational facilities for whites on Menominee land. In 1961 termination was final, although some people fought hard for a return to Federal control. They succeeded in 1973 with the Menominee Restoration Act by Congress. This was a landmark decision in modern Indian policy because it set precedent for restoring to Indians Federal rights that were ended by questionable means.

INDIANS AND ALCOHOL   Probably the most serious problem of reservation Indians who move to an urban setting is arrest for intoxication. Some anthropologists write about this situation *ad nauseam*, but when Fred W. Gabourie discusses the subject, his insights as a lawyer and an Indian are refreshing. Between 1802 and 1953 Federal laws prohibited Indians from legally purchasing intoxicants. After the latter date, and after the revocation of state

540

Red Man–White Man

laws dealing with the matter, Indians could drink just as anyone else, although some reservations were "dry" by local option. To Indians the right to drink had great symbolic meaning, and often it was interpreted quite literally. When this right was abused on the reservation, the intoxicated person most often was put to bed by a local policeman or jailed overnight and released. Gabourie points out that when reservation and rural Indians visit local towns for relaxation, they usually frequent a "skid row" because only there are Indians welcomed in bars. When these Indians move to distant urban centers, they are attracted to skid rows for the same reason. Even many successful urban Indians visit such sectors of a city to socialize with other Indians. In a city an intoxicated Indian is booked and jailed like any other skid row drunkard. The likelihood is that he cannot post bail or does not have enough assets to be a satisfactory risk for a bondsman. Since he often cannot pay a fine and probation does not suffice, a jail sentence is the result. A pilot program in Los Angeles to provide information about the law and legal services has been conducted by a private law firm and has succeeded in greatly reducing the difficulties of urban Indians and also is lowering the arrest rate.

For hundreds of years the general opinion prevailing among whites is that Indians have a tolerance of alcohol lower than that of whites. Indians have maintained that this is untrue. Some white administrators used the stereotype of the drunken Indian as a rationalization for not taking more constructive steps to resolve depressive social and economic conditions among Indians. A comparatively recent Canadian study tended to support the differential abilities of whites and Indians to tolerate alcohol, but in it healthy whites were compared with hospitalized Indians. Lynn J. Bennion and Ting-Kai Li (1976) compared the rate of alcohol metabolism in thirty whites and thirty full-blooded Indians who had had some prior exposure to alcohol. They wrote, "Since our study showed no significant difference between American Indians and whites in rates of alcohol metabolism, the conclusion cannot be drawn that racial variations in proclivity to alcohol abuse can be accounted for by racial variations in alcohol metabolic rates" (Bennion and Li, 1976, 12).

CANADIAN INDIAN LAND CLAIMS   During the next decade a rapid increase in the exploitation of natural gas and oil in the Canadian arctic seems probable, and plans are being made for long-distance pipelines. Before route selection and construction begin, Eskimos, Indians, and Metis are attempting to unite and gain a settlement of old and new claims. The Dene Alliance of 1972 represents about 7000 treaty Indians and 10,000 Metis, and their claim is to 450,000 square miles of the Mackenzie River valley. Northern Canadian Eskimos organized as Inuit Tapirisat seek 3 percent of the revenues from the exploitation of gas, oil, and minerals recovered from about 750,000 square miles in the Canadian arctic, and they also are attempting to gain political control of the area they would like to call Nunavut (Our Land) Territory.

RED POWER   In essence Red Power is a form of Pan-Indianism committed to radical political action. The first broad-based and enduring Indian organization with political change as its purpose was founded soon after World War II. About 25,000 Indians had served in the armed services and on returning to civilian life were unwilling to accept the Indian stereotype. They were largely instrumental in founding the National Congress of American Indians (N.C.A.I.) in 1944, an organization designed to speak for Indians. The philosophy of the group is that individuals should be able to choose between retaining their identity as Indians or assimilating, but should not be pushed in either direction. They also consider Federal obligations to Indians that resulted from treaties and agreements as permanently binding and strongly oppose any efforts to end these responsibilities. The activities of the organization include aiding local groups in taking effective stands, pooling useful information, and lobbying for Indian causes. In 1976 the N.C.A.I opposed Federal aid to Indian tribes not generally recognized by the Federal Government; that stand appeared to alienate a significant number of Indians.

As Murray L. Wax and Robert W. Buchanan (1975, 190) have pointed out, the N.C.A.I. represented tribal governments above all else, but as increasing numbers of Indians moved to urban areas, tribal interests became more remote. As a result a more radical organization called the National Indian Youth Council was founded in 1961 by college-educated Indians. They were highly critical of the N.C.A.I., whose members they regarded as representing wealthy acculturated persons with an Indian identity more in terms of blood than culture. The newer organization purported to represent the "real Indian," meaning those who were more traditionally oriented. They adamantly opposed the B.I.A. and wanted it replaced by agencies that would advise and guide Indians, but not control them. They resented the fact that large sums of money designed for Indians were consumed in the bureaucratic structure of the Federal Government. Members joined the poverty march on Washington, D.C., and rallied supporters in the name of "Red Power."

The most radical organization is the American Indian Movement (A.I.M.) founded in Minneapolis, Minnesota, in 1968 to seek greater equality for Indians in terms of their civil rights. They made two dramatic moves that gained them national attention. First, in 1972 several hundred Indians seized the B.I.A. offices in Washington, D.C., in what was called the "Trail of Broken Treaties." They were protesting government failure to live up to treaty arrangements or to seek meaningful solutions to Indian problems. Under A.I.M. leadership, too, the small town of Wounded Knee on the Pine Ridge Reservation in South Dakota was seized in 1973, and a prolonged confrontation resulted.

At Wounded Knee Creek about 300 Sioux men, women, and children were massacred by U.S. Army troops in 1890, and the site has since been a significant symbol of white injustice. The small Oglala Sioux settlement of Wounded Knee is near the massacre site on the Pine Ridge Reservation. Here living conditions have been depressed for a long time. For example, in the early 1970s the average life expectancy of these people was 44.5 years, the unemployment rate was about 50 percent, infant mortality was about 30 percent, and the suicide rate was ten times the national average. The B.I.A. has been accused of being unresponsive to severe local problems, but of even greater importance, many persons were opposed to the leadership of Richard Wilson, the chairman of the Oglala Sioux Tribe, and unsuccessfully attempted to impeach him in late 1972. Wilson was a staunch foe of the A.I.M., and it appears that two goals dominated when A.I.M. members and their sympathizers occupied the town of Wounded Knee on February 27, 1973. One aim was to call national attention to the plight of Indians, and the second was to force a confrontation with the Oglala tribal chairman and the B.I.A. representatives.

Under A.I.M. leadership eleven people at Wounded Knee were seized as "hostages," the Roman Catholic Church was seized, and both the store and trading post were looted. Reportedly more than 80 percent of the people initially involved were Oglala. The B.I.A. officials called in Federal marshals and the Federal Bureau of Investigation (F.B.I.) to protect B.I.A. property. Heavily armed law enforcement agents ringed the community. It was reported that 150 marshals, 40 B.I.A. policemen, and 125 F.B.I. agents were involved in the siege; about 250 Indians occupied Wounded Knee. The insurgents sought redress of Oglala grievances and amnesty for all participants. When four men drove from the occupied area, they were arrested and charged with burglary, larceny, and assault. Wilson as tribal chairman spoke out in favor of vigorous prosecution of the arrested men. His attitude reflected his feelings about the A.I.M. and its effect on the Sioux. Because of his opposition to the A.I.M., Wilson refused to permit their meeting on the reservation, even though one A.I.M. leader, Russell Means, was an Oglala Sioux.

The activist Indian newspaper *Wassaja*, published in San Francisco, California, serves as a primary source for the previous account and most of what follows. It offers a thoughtful analysis, but it is apparent that a great deal of conflicting information prevails about the Siege of Wounded Knee. The siege lasted for seventy-one days, and from 225 to 400 Indians participated. Seven indictments were handed down by a Federal grand jury, and about 600 people were arrested as a result of their activities relevant to the siege. Russell Means and a second major leader, Dennis Banks, were jailed. Two Indians reportedly were killed as a direct result of the confrontation, and one F.B.I. agent was wounded. A referendum vote was demanded to seek removal of Richard Wilson as Oglala tribal chairman.

A change of venue was obtained for the main defendants, Means and Banks, and after the case went to the jury, the charges against them were dismissed by the judge. Indians charged that the trials were politically motivated and that the F.B.I. committed crimes in cover-up activities during the trial and persuaded witnesses to perjure themselves. By early 1975 the Means-

Banks case was under appeal by the government; sixty to eighty cases remained to be tried, forty to fifty dismissals or acquittals had resulted, and there were six convictions and two guilty pleas.

In the first tribal election following the Siege of Wounded Knee, Russell Means lost to Richard Wilson, but irregularities in voting were charged. In a second election, under Federal supervision, Wilson ran against Albert Trimble, who was a native of the reservation and the first Sioux superintendent of the B.I.A. there. He ran as a "peace candidate" and defeated Wilson.

American Indian Studies

Traditional ethnographies, as described in the Introduction, began changing character by the early 1930s, but it was not until much later that most anthropologists realized what had happened. The long-term ideal of reconstructing aboriginal baseline accounts rarely could be realized after about 1940. The first person to focus a field study on contemporary Indian lifeways was Margaret Mead. In 1930 she worked among the Omaha Indians and subsequently published *The Changing Culture of an Indian Tribe* (1932). This was a watershed in North American Indian studies and anticipated hundreds of broadly similar works about Indian acculturation. By 1940 even the most remote Indians had had substantial contacts with Euro-Americans for at least forty years, and indirect contacts had introduced Anglo-American trade goods and exotic diseases long before. It appears that historic changes loomed large in many ethnographic accounts that attempted to reconstruct aboriginal conditions; thus they were inaccurate as aboriginal baseline studies. Yet the training of ethnographers continued to stress interviews with informed persons, observant-participation, genealogical techniques, reasonable efforts to learn the language of the people studied, and the usually superficial analysis of pertinent historical writings. Because original fieldwork was nearly essential to gain professional status, it remained a dominant training device but with a shift to acculturative field studies of tribes or communities as the aboriginal ideal was replaced by acculturative realities. As ethnographers became methodologically more sophisticated, the emphasis shifted even further. Problem-focused studies began to dominate, with one or more aspects of Indian life singled out for detailed attention. Sociological methods became increasingly important as greater emphasis was placed on sampling techniques and as larger aggregates of people were studied. Some ethnographers preferred to stress "behavioral science" rather than anthropology, and some justly could be called sociologists. At least one trend is toward more intensive studies of Indians in urban environments. This is an attractive field setting for some anthropologists because of their training and because Federal research funds are more readily available for studying this highly visible "problem."

Clearly the data base of old has disappeared, and the study of urban Indians or certain aspects of modern reservation life, such as health or land tenure, has been one response. An approach favored by persons more interested in traditional Indian life has been the study of pertinent historical documents, often with accompanying field studies for additional information. The study of historical records long has been the purview of historians, and some of them, such as William T. Hagan, Roy H. Pearce, Lewis O. Saum, and Wilcomb E. Washburn, have a keen understanding of the Indian in American history. For American anthropologists concentrating on Indians north of Mexico an appreciation of historical developments has been rather recent. One of the earliest studies was that carried out in 1928–1930 by Felix M. Keesing (1939) concerning the Menominee of Wisconsin. The next major work was by Oscar Lewis (1942) and dealt with Blackfoot culture change. Thus "ethnohistory" as an anthropological focus is a comparatively new development, and *Ethnohistory*, a journal devoted to the subject, did not originate until 1954.

Ethnohistory has yet to emerge as a significant focus among anthropologists, and possibly it never will. In addition to archival and library research field studies often are recognized as valuable; some Indians clearly remember certain historical events that have never found their way into written records. The study of historical records has led to major revisions in our understanding about some tribes early in their history. Chipewyan ethnography provides an excellent example. Before the ethnohistorical studies, summarized in Chapter 2, by Beryl C. Gillespie, David M. Smith, and James G. E. Smith, we were not sure which Indians were Chipewyan, where they lived in early historic times, nor how much of an effect the early fur trade had on some bands. All of this new information has appeared since 1970. The doctoral dissertation by Charles A. Heidenreich in 1971 about Crow ethnohistory is a fine example of how much new information could be derived from words and illustrations previously recorded about these people. We also are gaining an insightful perspective on modern developments among the Eastern Cherokee with the work of Sharlotte Neely Williams. Yet we still search in vain for an ethnohistory of such groups as the Cahuilla, Iroquois, or Yurok. The information about the Iroquois in particular is rich but never has been integrated. It probably is true that every tribal ethnography for aboriginal or early historic times could be made far more accurate after a careful study of existing archival and published records. Thus superior accounts for many tribes are yet to be written.

Indians and Anthropologists

American anthropologists have had a deep and abiding interest in American Indians for obvious professional and less obvious personal reasons. Since Indians in the United States and Canada were quite accessible and usually considerate hosts, they have served as the subjects for thousands of ethnographic studies. A well-established tradition in cultural and social anthropology is the study of people in at least one other society as a part of professional training. In this manner the observer not only gains meaningful cross-cultural experience, but assembles a body of information that contributes to a broader understanding of humanity in general. The personal dimension is important because ethnographers often, if not typically, come to feel a great affinity for the people whom they study and empathize with Indians in a way other whites do not. The field study of an ethnographer has two primary goals: to record the activities of others and to employ this information for the solution of theoretical or practical problems. In recent years a growing number of Indians have become resentful of anthropologists, and it is well to ask: What do anthropologists do that displeases Indians?

It would appear that describing Indian life would be a relatively neutral activity. This is the main business of ethnographers and is important if only because they describe customs that otherwise would go unrecorded and be lost to history. To record soon-to-be-forgotten information has been a very real concern of many investigators, especially those who were convinced that they were witnessing the rapid disappearance of aboriginal ways of life. Some ethnographers, especially those around the turn of the century, became secular crusaders who devoted their lives to recording cultural ways before they were gone forever. Surely this is a worthwhile, if not noble, goal.

With aboriginal customs as their focal point, many ethnographers recorded forms of behavior that lived only in the memories of Indians. Counting coup, scalping an enemy, bison hunts, and feather headdresses were given emphasis in descriptive accounts, conveying the impression that these forms and norms typified Indian life in the recent past. Modern Indians sometimes cry "foul" because in their lifetimes, or even during the lives of their grandparents, these customs did not prevail. Such ethnographies misrepresented Indians because they froze them in time, and this was true of most pre-1930 studies. The false impression conveyed of Indian life became at least an implicit rationalization for administrators and politicians not to make any serious effort to improve the deteriorating quality of Indian life. In retrospect anthropologists did not lack compassion, but, unfortunately, they did produce a distorted picture of past practices lasting into modern times.

Directly contributing to this atmosphere of misunderstanding is the fact that aboriginal Indian life often was described in terms of the "ethnographic present." This means that even though an ethnographer was describing extinct customs, the information was reported in the present tense as a literary technique to impart vitality to the behavior described. Indian life of fifty or twenty years ago no longer exists, but many ethnographers continue to describe it in the ethnographic present, which is highly misleading. Criticisms of this technique clearly are valid, especially because so much has happened to Indians historically and in the recent past. It clearly distorts contemporary realities and contributes further to unreal views of Indians.

D'Arcy McNickle suggests that the use of the ethnographic present, and the failure by ethnographers to present the adaptive changes in Indian life-ways, has led to another unfortunate result, that of abetting the advocates of Indian assimilation. Acculturation studies have been important to ethnographic fieldwork since the early 1930s, and most of them have stressed the negative aspects of reservation life. This hardly is a criticism of the Indians involved, however, nor was it intended as a prop for assimilation programs. Instead it often was an expression of dismay about Federal programs as they were administered at the time.

Older Indians often are quite sympathetic when an eager ethnographer arrives to collect information about the past, but younger ones often have neutral or hostile attitudes toward these efforts. The older people see what they regard as the essence of Indian life disappearing, and they are well aware that their children or grandchildren usually have little or no interest in their cultural heritage as Indians. Thus an old man or woman finds it very satisfying to talk about the past to an ethnographer and have the conversations recorded with care. The attitude of many younger Indians about such information is one of disinterest or of shame about old customs. If or when these younger people decide to learn about their past as Indians, it is probable that they will have to rely on the writings of the very ethnographers that they now resent.

In a discussion of anthropologists and Indians it should be noted that a number of Indians have emerged as outstanding anthropologists with ethnography as their specialization. In fact, white anthropologists long have encouraged—and continue to encourage—Indians to join their ranks. White anthropologists are more keenly aware than anyone else that a perceptive insider is likely to be a far better reporter and interpreter of Indian life than an outsider, even a knowledgeable, understanding one. The names of a number of Indian anthropologists come to mind. Francis La Fleshe (1857–1932), an Omaha, first collaborated with Alice Fletcher and then worked for eighteen years as an ethnographer for the Bureau of American Ethnology. William Jones (1871–1909), of Fox and white ancestry, earned a Ph.D. degree at Columbia in 1904 and is notable for his research among Algonkian Indians. He was killed by the Ilongots on a field trip in the Philippine Islands. J. N. B. Hewitt (1859–1937), of Tuscarora and white ancestry, was an authority on the Iroquois. Edward P. Dozier (1916–1971), raised in the pueblo of Santa Clara, New Mexico, was noted for his writings on Pueblo Indians. Established anthropologists today who are American Indians include Edward Castillo, Cahuilla; Pasqual D. Chavers, Lumbee; David Draper, Choctaw; Lathel F. Duffield, Cherokee; Frederick J. Dockstader, Oneida and Navajo; Marcia Herndon, Cherokee; D'Arcy McNickle, Flathead; Kenneth R. Martin, Sioux; Mary E. Fleming Mathur, Abnaki and Mohawk; Beatrice Medicine, Standing Rock Sioux; Alfonso Ortiz, Tewa, and Robert K. Thomas, Cherokee.

Possibly a more important question than why Indians object to being studied by anthropologists is: If anthropologists know so much about Indians, why have they not played a greater role as "experts" in guiding culture change? The basic reason is quite straightforward. The guiding principle behind Federal Indian policy in the United States has been assimilation, and the sooner the better. This view runs contrary to the values held by many anthropologists. By training and inclination they find the death of any culture sad and regrettable. At the time the Indian Reorganization Act went into effect, because it was designed to bring vitality back into reservation life, a number of outstanding anthropologists worked for the B.I.A. to further provisions of the act. However, World War II diverted national attention from this program, and the early 1950s ushered in the termination policy, which found little sympathy among anthropologists. In theory the B.I.A. always has been committed to a policy of Indian assimilation, but as most bureaucratic organizations it has in fact devoted a great deal of energy to its own expansion. From 1955 to 1968 the number of B.I.A. employees rose from 9500 to 16,000. Furthermore, bureau personnel often regard anthropologists as "Indian lovers" and neither seek nor welcome their advice. Anthropologists in turn have little sympathy with bureau policies in general and have preferred not to become involved in their programs.

Anthropologists clearly have served Indians in diverse useful and positive ways. The Fox Project is the example most completely discussed in the text. Anthropologists have worked for the Department of Health, Education, and Welfare to improve the effectiveness of health programs; they have given evidence before the Indian Claims Commission in order to validate claims; they have testified in vigorous support of the Native American Church; they often have served as advisors to Indians in economic development programs. Furthermore, anthropologists have played an important role in interpreting Indian behavior to interested whites, both in the classroom and outside of it.

One chapter of *Custer Died for Your Sins* by Vine Deloria, titled "Anthropologists and Other Friends," is an Indian attack on anthropologists. The text is very clever and often most perceptive. Deloria objects to the use of anthropological data about Indians to build theoretical models. He feels that the models distort what Indians really are. However, models are designed to distill an essence of behavior, not to convey details about reality, and while they may not be beneficial to Indians, neither are they dangerous. Furthermore, he blames anthropologists for many of the ills which beset Indians. The implication is that anthropologists have had a profound influence in plotting the course of Federal policies concerning Indians, which is quite doubtful. He also stresses that anthropologists have produced a vast archive of information that is useless to many persons. Yet these writings exist and are valuable sources for many persons, although they are totally ignored by others. Deloria also writes, "Why should we continue to be the private zoos for anthropologists?" The answer is clear. Indians need not accept anthropologists if they are disinclined to do so. If the purpose of a study seems questionable or offensive, the

Red Man–White Man

Indians involved have the clear right to refuse their cooperation.

Numerous anthropologists, myself included, are distressed by some of the prevailing criticisms, such as those offered by Deloria. I always have considered anthropologists to be the group of non-Indians most interested in Indian customs and most supportive of Indians. At one time some, or possibly many, anthropologists hoped that old Indian ways would be preserved, but just as Indians have changed so have anthropologists.

Indians often have been called the "first Americans," indicating the priority of their residence in North America. Because they were the established occupants when whites arrived, Europeans at first attempted to deal with Indians as if they were nations in the European sense. As whites came to dominate Indians in political and economic terms, they reassessed their position and considered Indians as dependent nations and then simply as tribes.

The administrative paternalism that evolved recognized the unique status of Indians among American minorities. Indians themselves are increasingly aware that their cultural identity is important to them, no matter how different it may be from life when whites first arrived. Many feel that they are *special Americans* to whom national governments have lasting, extraordinary obligations. Many Indians seek not just tolerance of their ways but meaningful financial and moral support in order that their identity may endure so long as the waters shall flow and the sun shall shine. This is their clear right and our abiding obligation because this land indeed was theirs.

Additional Readings

Numerous books and many articles that interpret North American Indian developments from many different perspectives have appeared recently. As a reference guide book-length studies are arranged by topic, and comments are added if appropriate. (The reader is reminded that the best ethnographic bibliography on a tribal and regional basis is the *Ethnographic Bibliography of North America* [New Haven, 1975] by George P. Murdock and Timothy J. O'Leary.)

HISTORIES   One brief but effective history is *American Indians* (Chicago, 1961) by William T. Hagan, and another, which includes pertinent documents, is *A Short History of the Indians of the United States* (New York, 1969) by Edward H. Spicer. For Canada *The Canadian Indian* (Don Mills, Ontario, 1972) by E. Palmer Patterson II should be studied. *The Indian in America's Past* (Englewood Cliffs, New Jersey, 1964) edited by Jack D. Forbes is conceived around quotations by contemporary observers at different stages in Indian history. It provides a good overview in comparatively few pages. *The Indian and the White Man* (Garden City, New York, 1964) edited by Wilcomb E. Washburn traces the past through documentary sources.

ADMINISTRATIVE POLICIES   For the United States important works are *American Indian Policy in the Formative Years* (Lincoln, 1970) by Francis P. Prucha and *The Indian, America's Unfinished Business* (Norman, 1966) compiled by William A. Brophy et al. The best study of the General Allotment or Dawes Act is *The Assault on Indian Tribalism* (Philadelphia, 1975) by Wilcomb E. Washburn. *The Reformers and the American Indian* (Columbia, Missouri, 1971) by Robert W. Mardock presents the post–Civil War years with insight. A valuable book about research resources pertaining to Indians in the United States is *The Office of Indian Affairs, 1824–1880: Historical Sketches* (New York, 1974) by Edward E. Hill.

For Eskimos the key sources are all by Diamond Jenness; the *Arctic Institute of North America Technical Paper* Number 10 (1962) is devoted to Alaska; Number 14 (1964) to Canada; Number 16 (1965) to Labrador, and Number 19 (1967) to Greenland. Jenness also published an overview as Number 21 (1968).

For Canada *Native Rights in Canada* (Toronto, 1972) edited by Peter A. Cumming and Neil H. Mickenberg is outstanding. *Indian Claims in Canada* (Ottawa, 1975) was released by the Research Resource Centre, Indian Claims Commission and is primarily a bibliography, but it includes a very good introductory essay about recent developments.

MODERN DEVELOPMENTS   The emergence of the Pan-Indian movement is detailed best in *The Search for American Indian Identity* (Syracuse, 1971) by Hazel W. Hertzberg. D'Arcy McNickle in *Native American Tribalism* (New York, 1973) provides the background to modern conditions and discusses contemporary trends as well. Superior sources about governmental relations with Indians are *American Indians and Federal Aid* (Washington, D.C., 1971) by Alan L. Sorkin and *The States and Their Indian Citizens* (Washington, D.C., 1972) by Theodore W. Taylor. *Solving "The Indian Problem"* (New York, 1975) is a series of reprinted articles with editorial commentaries by Murray L. Wax and Robert W. Buchanan. The articles are timely and the interpretive comments insightful. *The American Indian Today* (Baltimore, 1968) edited by Stuart Levine and Nancy O. Lurie contains a series of articles about diverse topics of contemporary importance. *Indian Americans* (Englewood Cliffs, New Jersey, 1971) by Murray L. Wax provides a background to modern conditions and also examines contemporary trends, including those in cities.

URBAN INDIANS   The standard text, *The American Indian in Urban Society* (Boston, 1971), is edited by Jack O. Waddell and O. Michael Watson. The best general survey is *Reservation to City* (Chicago, 1971) by Elaine M. Neils. For Canadian Indians, Mark Nagler's book about Toronto, *Indians in the City* (Ottawa, 1970), is a worthwhile source. *Eskimo Townsmen* (Ottawa, 1965) by John J. and Irma Honigmann is the most important source about Eskimo "urbanities"; it is about the settlement of Frobisher Bay in northern Canada. Jeanne Guillemin's book *Urban Renegades* (New York, 1973), about the Micmac

Indians in New England and the Canadian Maritime Provinces, is refreshing in approach, topic, and style.

ADDITIONAL TEXTBOOKS   For a distributional analysis of American Indian traits *Indians of North America* (Chicago, 1969) by Harold E. Driver is excellent. The compilation of diverse and notable articles edited by Roger C. Owen et al., *The North American Indians, A Sourcebook* (New York, 1967), provides a good overview. Essentially the same is true of *North American Indians in Historical Perspective* (New York, 1971) edited by Eleanor B. Leacock and Nancy O. Lurie, as well as *The Emergent Native Americans* (Boston, 1972) compiled by Deward E. Walker. Regional developments, stressing archaeological background and aboriginal conditions, are best set forth in *The Native Americans* (New York, 1977) by Robert F. Spencer et al.

References

Ablon, Joan. "Relocated American Indians in the San Francisco Bay Area," *Human Organization*, v. 23, 296–304. 1964.

Agreement-in-Principle as to the Settlement of Inuit Land Claims in the Northwest Territories and the Yukon Territory. Unpublished. 1976.

Bennion, Lynn, and Ting-Kai Li. "Alcohol Metabolism in American Indians and Whites," *The New England Journal of Medicine*, v. 294, 9–13. 1976.

Brookings Institution, Washington, D.C. Institute for Government Research. *The Problem of Indian Administration.* Baltimore. 1928.

Canada Year Book, 1973. Ottawa. 1973.

Cohen, Felix S. *The Legal Conscience.* Lucy K. Cohen, ed., New Haven. 1960.

Cook, S. F. *The Epidemic of 1830–1833 in California and Oregon,* University of California Publications in American Archaeology and Ethnology, v. 43, no. 3. 1955.

Cumming, Peter A., and Neil H. Mickenberg, eds. *Native Rights in Canada.* Toronto. 1972.

Deloria, Vine. *Custer Died for Your Sins.* New York. 1969.

Donaldson, Thomas. "The George Catlin Indian Gallery in the U.S. National Museum," *Annual Report of the Board of Regents of the Smithsonian Institution, 1885.* pt. 2 Appendix. 1886.

Duran, James A. "Canadian Indian Policy: A Year of Debate," *The Indian Historian*, v. 4, no. 3, 34–36. 1971.

Ewers, John C. "The Emergence of the Plains Indian as the Symbol of the North American Indian," *Smithsonian Report for 1964.* 531–544, 1965.

Foreman, Grant. *Indian Removal.* Norman. 1932.

Gabourie, Fred W. *Justice and the Urban American Indian* (pamphlet). Sherman Oaks, California, nd.

Hagan, William T. *American Indians.* Chicago. 1961.

Hansen, Karen Tranberg. Coping with Change: Urban Migration. Paper presented at the Northwest Coast Studies Conference, Simon Fraser University, 1976.

Harper, Allan G. "Canada's Indian Administration: The Treaty System," *American Indigena,* v. 7, 129–148. 1947.

Hertzberg, Hazel W. *The Search for American Indian Identity.* Syracuse. 1971.

Howard, James H. "Pan-Indian Culture of Oklahoma," *Scientific Monthly,* v. 81, no. 5, 215–220. 1955.

Hurt, Wesley R. "The Urbanization of the Yankton Indians," *Human Organization,* v. 20, 226–231. 1961–2.

Indian Record. Winnipeg, Manitoba. 1975–1976 articles.

"The Iroquois Wampum Controversy," *The Indian Historian,* v. 3, no. 2, 4. 1970.

Jorgensen, Joseph G. "Indians and the Metropolis," in *The American Indian in Urban Society,* Jack O. Waddell and O. Michael Watson, eds., 66–113. Boston. 1971.

Keesing, Felix M. "The Menomini Indians of Wisconsin," *Memoirs of the American Philosophical Society,* v. 10. 1939.

La Barre, Weston. "Twenty Years of Peyote Studies," *Current Anthropology,* v. 1, 45–60. 1960.

Lewis, Oscar. *Effects of White Contact upon Blackfoot Culture.* Locust Valley, N.Y. 1942.

Lurie, Nancy O. "Menominee Termination," *The Indian Historian,* v. 4, no. 4, 33–43, 1971.

Lurie, Nancy O. "The Contemporary American Indian Scene," in *North American Indians in Historical Perspective,* Eleanor S. Leacock and Nancy O. Lurie, eds., 418–480. New York. 1971.

McNickle, D'Arcy. "American Indians Who Never Were," *The Indian Historian,* v. 3, no. 3, 4–7. 1970.

Officer, James E. "The American Indian and Federal Policy," in *The American Indian in Urban Society*, Jack O. Waddell and O. Michael Watson, eds. 8–65. Boston. 1971.

Pearce, Roy H. *The Savages of America*. Baltimore. 1965.

Population Census, 1970. v. 2. 1973. Washington, D.C. 1973.

Price, John A. "The Migration and Adaptation of American Indians to Los Angeles," *Human Organization*, v. 27, 168–175. 1968.

Rogers, George W. "Goodbye, Great White Father-Figure," *Anthropologica*, n.s., nos. 1–2, 279–306. 1971.

Saum, Lewis O. *The Fur Trader and the Indian*. Seattle. 1965.

Sixel, Friedrich Wilhelm. "Die deutsche Vorstellung vom Indianer in der ersten Hälfte des 16, Jahrhunderts," *Annali del Pontificio Museo Missionario Etnologico già Lateranensi*, v. 30, 9–230. 1967.

Sorkin, Alan L. *American Indians and Federal Aid*. Washington, D.C. 1971.

Spicer, Edward H. *Cycles of Conquest*. Tucson. 1962.

Taylor, Theodore W. *The States and their Indian Citizens*. Washington, D.C. 1972.

Thomas, Robert K. "Pan-Indianism," in *The American Indian Today*, Stuart Levine and Nancy O. Lurie, eds., 128–140. Baltimore. 1970.

Waddell, Jack O., and O. Michael Watson., eds. *The American Indian in Urban Society*. Boston. 1971.

Wallace, Anthony F. C. "New Religions among the Delaware Indians, 1600–1900," *Southwestern Journal of Anthropology*, v. 12, 1–21. 1956.

Wassaja, A National Newspaper of American Indians. San Francisco, California. 1972–1976 articles.

Wax, Murray L. *Indian Americans*. Englewood Cliffs, New Jersey. 1971.

Winsor, Justin. *Narrative and Critical History of America*, v. 2. Boston. 1889.

Name Index

555

General Index

563
General Index

207, 410, 532, 536, 539
Indian Rights Association, 528
Indian Service, *see* Bureau of Indian Affairs
Indian Shaker Church, 324
Infanticide, 39, 84, 119, 243, 359, 504, 506
Influenza, 124, 260–261
Initiations, *see* Puberty ceremonies
Intoxicants, 55, 57–58, 135, 136, 139, 150,
    199, 207, 282, 323, 363, 364, 368, 409,
    420, 428, 441, 445, 449, 450, 525–526,
    540–541
Inuit Tapirisat, 541
Inupiat Paitot, 140
Iowa Indians, 222
Iowa-Oto Indians, 259
Iroquois Indians, 15, 183, 518, 523, 539

Jesuit missionaries, 183, 446–447, 512. *See
    also* Roman Catholic missionaries
Jimsonweed, 162
Jumping Dance (Yurok), 312, 314

Kamia Indians, 158
Karok Indians, 297, 310
Kashgee, 110, 115, 120–121, 123, 134
Katcina, 388, 389–391, 394, 399, 409
    Society, 393, 394
Kayak, 76, 111–112, 128
Keeper of the House (Tlingit), 348
Keepers of the Faith (Iroquois), 436–437,
    444–445
Kepel fishweir (Yurok), 312–315
Kickapoo Indians, 181
Kindred, 41, 112, 204
Kinzua Dam, Pa., 452
Kiowa Indians, 200
Kiva, 378, 382, 383, 386, 393
Klamath Indians, 533, 537
Klukwan, Alaska, 357–358
Kolmakov Redoubt, Alaska 106, 123–124,
    125, 126, 127
Kon (Tlingit groupings), 340, 345–346
Kuskokwim Community College, 141

Labrets, 107, 338–339

Lacrosse, 429
Lake Ile a la Crosse, 34, 88
Lake Monhonk conferences, 528
Lamanites, 3
Language family, Algonkian, 19, 181, 485
    Athapaskan, 31
    Caddoan, 221
    Chukchi-Kamchatkan, 13, 69, 105
    Eskimo-Aleut, 13, 69
    Iroquoian, 417, 459
    Siouan, 259
    Uto-Aztecan, 148, 377
Language phylum, American
    Arctic-Paleosiberian, 13, 69, 105
    Aztec-Tanoan, 148, 377
    Macro-Algonkian, 181, 299, 485
    Macro-Siouan, 221, 259, 417, 459
    Na-Dene, 31–32, 335
L'Anse aux Meadows, Newfoundland
    (site), 12
League of the Iroquois, 417, 418, 419, 421,
    427, 430–432, 435, 439, 446, 451, 539
Levirate, 83, 163, 246, 280, 310, 360, 463
Lewisville, Texas (site), 11, 12
Livingston, Montana, 282
Longhouse, 423, 428, 444–445
Lost Tribes of Israel, 7, 8
Luiseno Indians, 150
Lumbee Indians, 538, 547
Lumpwood (Crow society), 268–269
Lutheran missionaries, 6

Maize (corn), 2, 4, 149, 189, 222, 228, 377,
    378, 384, 385, 403, 425, 426, 459–460,
    462–463, 495, 501–502
Mammoth, 11, 221
Mandan Indians, 259, 260, 261, 518
Manitou, 48, 188, 193–195, 428
Mano and metate, 153, 377, 383
March of the Bodies (Natchez), 506
Marriage residence, bilocal, 53, 360
    matrilocal, 40, 112, 228, 245, 246, 267,
    322, 386, 426, 443–444, 464
    neolocal, 53, 83, 133
    patrilocal, 83, 133, 156, 163, 310, 321
Masau'u (Hopi deity), 381, 384, 389, 390,
    391

569
General Index

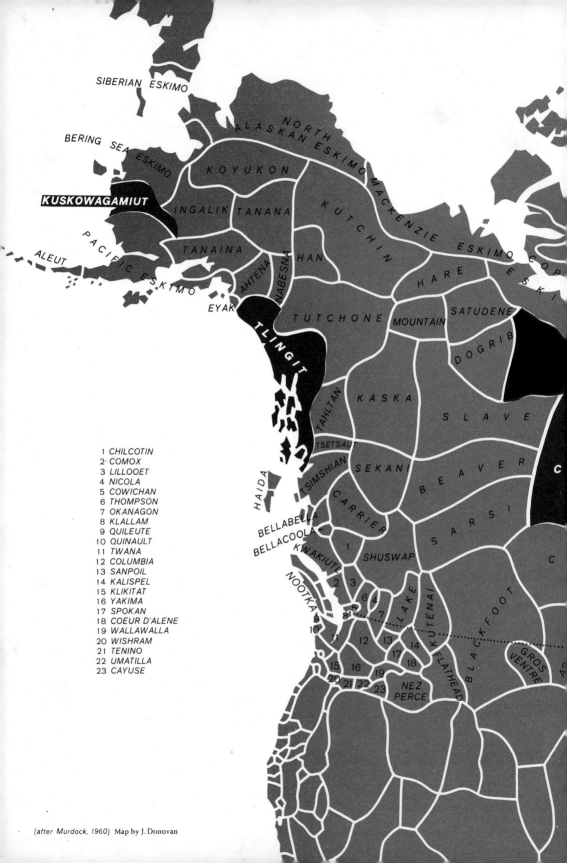

SIBERIAN ESKIMO

BERING SEA ESKIMO

KUSKOWAGAMIUT

ALEUT

PACIFIC ESKIMO

NORTH ALASKAN ESKIMO

KOYUKON

INGALIK TANANA

TANAINA

AHTENA

NABESNA

HAN

EYAK

TLINGIT

MACKENZIE ESKIMO

KUTCHIN

HARE

COPPER ESKI

TUTCHONE

MOUNTAIN

SATUDENE

DOGRIB

SLAVE

TAHLTAN

KASKA

BEAVER

TSETSAUT

SEKANI

SARSI

C

HAIDA

TSIMSHIAN

CARRIER

BELLABELLA

BELLACOOLA

KWAKIUTL

1

SHUSWAP

C

NOOTKA

2

3

6 4

LAKE

KUTENAI

BLACKFOOT

GROS VENTRE

9

8

5

7

10

11

12

13

14

17

18

FLATHEAD

15

16

19

20 21 22 23

NEZ PERCE

1 CHILCOTIN
2 COMOX
3 LILLOOET
4 NICOLA
5 COWICHAN
6 THOMPSON
7 OKANAGON
8 KLALLAM
9 QUILEUTE
10 QUINAULT
11 TWANA
12 COLUMBIA
13 SANPOIL
14 KALISPEL
15 KLIKITAT
16 YAKIMA
17 SPOKAN
18 COEUR D'ALENE
19 WALLAWALLA
20 WISHRAM
21 TENINO
22 UMATILLA
23 CAYUSE

(after Murdock, 1960) Map by J. Donovan